Second Edition

SEX-RELATED HOMICIDE *and* DEATH INVESTIGATION

Practical and Clinical Perspectives

CRC SERIES IN
**PRACTICAL ASPECTS OF CRIMINAL
AND FORENSIC INVESTIGATIONS**

VERNON J. GEBERTH, BBA, MPS, FBINA *Series Editor*

Investigating Computer Crime
Franklin Clark and Ken Diliberto

Practical Homicide Investigation Checklist and Field Guide
Vernon J. Geberth

Practical Aspects of Munchausen by Proxy and Munchausen Syndrome Investigation
Kathryn Artingstall

Quantitative-Qualitative Friction Ridge Analysis: An Introduction to Basic and Advanced Ridgeology
David R. Ashbaugh

Practical Criminal Investigations in Correctional Facilities
William R. Bell

Officer-Involved Shootings and Use of Force: Practical Investigative Techniques, Second Edition
David E. Hatch

Sex-Related Homicide and Death Investigation: Practical and Clinical Perspectives, Second Edition
Vernon J. Geberth

Global Drug Enforcement: Practical Investigative Techniques
Gregory D. Lee

Practical Investigation of Sex Crimes: A Strategic and Operational Approach
Thomas P. Carney

Principles of Bloodstain Pattern Analysis: Theory and Practice
Stuart James, Paul Kish, and T. Paulette Sutton

Cold Case Homicides: Practical Investigative Techniques
Richard H. Walton

Practical Crime Scene Processing and Investigation
Ross M. Gardner

Practical Bomb Scene Investigation
James T. Thurman

Practical Analysis and Reconstruction of Shooting Incidents
Edward E. Hueske

Tire Tread and Tire Track Evidence: Recovery and Forensic Examination
William J. Bodziak

Bloodstain Pattern Analysis: With an Introduction to Crime Scene Reconstruction, Third Edition
Tom Bevel and Ross M. Gardner

Serial Violence: Analysis of Modus Operandi and Signature Characteristics of Killers
Robert D. Keppel and William J. Birnes

Practical Crime Scene Analysis and Reconstruction
Ross M. Gardner

Second Edition

SEX-RELATED HOMICIDE *and* DEATH INVESTIGATION

Practical and Clinical Perspectives

Vernon J. Geberth

CRC Press
Taylor & Francis Group
Boca Raton   London   New York

CRC Press is an imprint of the
Taylor & Francis Group, an **informa** business

CRC Press
Taylor & Francis Group
6000 Broken Sound Parkway NW, Suite 300
Boca Raton, FL 33487-2742

© 2010 by Taylor and Francis Group, LLC
CRC Press is an imprint of Taylor & Francis Group, an Informa business

No claim to original U.S. Government works

Printed in the United States of America on acid-free paper
10 9 8 7 6 5 4 3 2 1

International Standard Book Number: 978-1-4398-2655-3 (Hardback)

Library of Congress Cataloging-in-Publication Data

Geberth, Vernon J.
  Sex-related homicide and death investigation : practical and clinical perspectives / Vernon J. Geberth. -- 2nd ed.
    p. cm. -- (CRC series in practical aspects of criminal and forensic investigations)
  Includes bibliographical references and index.
  ISBN 978-1-4398-2655-3 (hardcover : alk. paper)
  1. Homicide investigation--Handbooks, manuals, etc. 2. Sex crimes--Investigation--Handbooks, manuals, etc. I. Title. II. Series.

HV8079.H6G44 2010
363.25'9523--dc22   2010012608

Visit the Taylor & Francis Web site at
http://www.taylorandfrancis.com

and the CRC Press Web site at
http://www.crcpress.com

Dedication

This book, like Practical Homicide Investigation, *is dedicated to the men and women entrusted with the profound duty and responsibility of investigating sudden and violent death.*

In memory of those innocent victims of homicide and their surviving families who must find the strength to go on without their loved ones.

May justice prevail.

The Lord God said. . .

Thou Shalt Not Kill

THE FIFTH COMMANDMENT   Book of Exodus, 20 of THE HOLY BIBLE

THE OATH OF
PRACTICAL HOMICIDE INVESTIGATION

HOMICIDE INVESTIGATION IS A PROFOUND DUTY. AS AN OFFICER ENTRUSTED WITH SUCH A DUTY, IT IS INCUMBENT UPON YOU TO DEVELOP AN UNDERSTANDING OF THE DYNAMICS AND PRINCIPLES OF PROFESSIONAL HOMICIDE INVESTIGATION.

PRACTICAL HOMICIDE INVESTIGATION SUGGESTS THAT "THINGS BE DONE RIGHT THE FIRST TIME", AND "KNOWLEDGE IS POWER". KNOWLEDGE WHICH HAS BEEN ENHANCED WITH EXPERIENCE, FLEXIBILITY AND COMMON SENSE.

PRACTITIONERS MUST BE PREPARED TO USE TACTICS, PROCEDURES, AND FORENSIC TECHNIQUES IN THEIR PURSUIT OF THE TRUTH: AND THEN FOLLOW THE COURSE OF EVENTS AND THE FACTS AS THEY ARE DEVELOPED TO THEIR ULTIMATE CONCLUSION.

DEATH INVESTIGATION CONSTITUTES A HEAVY RESPONSIBILITY, AND AS SUCH, LET NO PERSON DETER YOU FROM THE TRUTH AND YOUR OWN PERSONAL COMMITMENT TO SEE THAT JUSTICE IS DONE. NOT ONLY FOR THE DECEASED, BUT FOR THE SURVIVING FAMILY AS WELL.
      AND REMEMBER; *We work for God®*

Lt. Cmdr. (Ret.) VERNON J. GEBERTH
NEW YORK CITY POLICE DEPARTMENT
FORMER COMMANDING OFFICER
BRONX HOMICIDE TASK FORCE

©Vernon J. Geberth 1988

Editor's Note

This textbook is part of a series entitled "Practical Aspects of Criminal and Forensic Investigations." This series was created by Vernon J. Geberth, a retired New York City Police Department Lieutenant Commander, who is an author, educator, and consultant on homicide and forensic investigations.

This series has been designed to provide contemporary, comprehensive, and pragmatic information to the practitioner involved in criminal and forensic investigations by authors who are nationally recognized experts in the respective fields.

Table of Contents

6 Collection and Preservation of Physical Evidence in Sex-Related Death Investigations   235

13   The BTK Investigation   599

14 Investigative Analysis: Criminal Personality Profiling and the Signature Aspect 639

15   Psychopathic Sexual Sadism: A Clinical Study   703

Preface

Sex-Related Homicide and Death Investigation: Practical and Clinical Perspectives, First Edition, has become the definitive tome on violent sexual assault investigations. As Michigan Assistant Attorney General Donna Pendergast stated, "This comprehensive volume is an incredible compilation that exhausts the subject. Vern's remarkable experience and unmatched expertise have given him unparalleled insight into the investigation of sexually deviant crimes and the psyche of those who perpetrate violent sex-related crimes."

The first edition, which was written to address the increase of sex-related homicides and deaths that law enforcement encountered in the new millennium, continues to be a tremendous asset to investigators and prosecutors of sexual predators. According to the reviews of my peers, *Sex-Related Homicide and Death Investigation: Practical and Clinical Perspectives* has become the framework of reference on sex-related homicide and death for investigators who actually conduct investigations as opposed to those who simply do research.

As the legendary criminal profiler Robert K. Ressler wrote, "*Sex-Related Homicide and Death Investigation* is truly a chronicle of practical and clinical case studies, combined with invaluable investigative guidelines that takes the reader to another level of knowledge in this unique field. It represents an accomplishment that no other author has yet achieved."

The second edition of *Sex-Related Homicide and Death Investigation: Practical and Clinical Perspectives* has been completely revised with full-color photos and expanded with an additional chapter (13) and a number of new case studies, as well as current advances in forensic techniques, to provide the reader with a practical reference.

I was fortunate to have the expertise of Brian Wilson, Medical Legal Art, who produced all of the medical forensic illustrations, and of Chicago homicide detective Mark Czworniak who provided many exquisite crime scene photographs as well as crime scene investigation (CSI) photos to illustrate documentation and collection procedures.

The book is based on my over 40 years of law enforcement experience. Formerly a New York City detective, detective supervisor, homicide commander, and now a nationwide homicide and forensic consultant, I have integrated this knowledge with my association with experts in the sphere of forensic science and criminal investigation. I include personal interviews with other homicide authorities and present an extensive search of forensic literature offering as many actual case histories as possible. My goal is to provide a comprehensive and practical resource text that will serve as an investigation guide and clinical reference to those involved in sex-related homicide and death investigations.

This second edition of *Sex-Related Homicide and Death Investigation* is intended to be used as a companion text to my *Practical Homicide Investigation: Tactics, Procedures, and Forensic Techniques, Fourth Edition,* textbook. The basic criminal investigative techniques stressed in my "Practical Homicide Investigation®" protocols are essential for effective inquiry into sudden and violent death.

Sex-Related Homicide and Death Investigation: Practical and Clinical Perspectives, Second Edition, has been designed to provide the most practical and conventional information from many various disciplines to make a complete resource and reference book for investigators responsible for conducting intelligent investigations into violent sex-related homicides and sudden death. The text will also address specific types of sex-related homicides.

As Judge Phillip Schnelwar, former chief of the Bronx District Attorney's Homicide Bureau stated, "The new second edition explains every aspect of a sex-related homicide investigation with an easily understood, how-to approach, complete with do's and don'ts from someone who has been there. This treatise covers the basics, as well as the cutting edge forensic techniques available, along with case studies and practical examples of the psychopathology involved and clinical considerations needed to understand the significance of the behaviors of the sexual offender."

I have provided additional case histories and practical examples of the psychopathology involved as well as some very important clinical considerations in making determinations and understanding the significance of the behaviors of the sexual offender.

As Detective Sergeant Eric Schroeder, criminal profiler for the Michigan State Police stated, "*Sex-Related Homicide and Death Investigation* clearly demonstrates Geberth's talent for translating the most horrific crimes imaginable into an accurately documented and easily understood resource for those involved in the investigation of violent crimes. If I can't have Geberth himself standing next to me at a crime scene, at least I know that his works will never be more than an arm's reach away."

Dr. Ronald Turco, a forensic psychiatrist and reserve police officer wrote, "This book took courage to write and the author does not mince words or principles! This volume is a must for every homicide detective and should be studied daily. *Sex-Related Homicide and Death Investigation* is the most comprehensive and up-to-date text regarding sexual death investigation that I have come across in the forensic and psychiatric literature. This book is a gift to the law enforcement community and a contribution of historical importance."

The Increase of Sex-Related Homicides: A Personal Perspective

One could propose that the etiology of an increase in sex-related homicides could be traced back to the mid-1960s era. The "free-thinking" professors and groups of radical student activists were acting out on campus, along with some misguided PhDs, on the academic level, who targeted and attacked the "establishment," government, religion, the military, and any other issue they could think of during the Vietnam era and the turbulent 1960s decade. There was an underlying sexual theme to some of these protests—"Make love not war"—many of which included "in-your-face" nudity and other manifestations of sexuality along with the proliferation of the experimentation and recreational use of drugs.

The insidious devaluation of religious beliefs, the philosophical question of whether or not there is a God, or a concept of good and evil, set the stage for further outrageous expression. I personally recall a professor asking a student, "Do you mean to say that you go to an empty building and pray to an invisible man?" The question was meant to be an obvious satire of a person who went to church or temple, prayed to God, and practiced a formal religion.

In any event, this breakdown of moral authority coupled with the mentality of "do your own thing" and "if it feels good do it," continued into the 1970s and 1980s and certainly had an effect on the moral fabric of society. This was an era when people were encouraged to experiment with their sexuality, without reference to their responsibilities and or the consequences of their actions. Sexual relationships were being depicted as recreational sport.

If one were formally married, divorce was considered a "no-fault" experience. Parental responsibility was replaced with excuses, such as: "We were young once," "The kids will be fine," "Leave them alone," "Let them learn from experience." The mantra of the 1970s and 1980s was sexual freedom without consequences.

This philosophy continued to spiral through the 1990s and into the new millennium. Society is constantly bombarded by Hollywood's most controversial, provocative, and sexually violent movies. Teen sex, according to a most recent study, has been on the rise. A report by researchers at Child Trends indicated that, by the time students are in the 9th grade, 34% have had sexual intercourse. That rises to 60% by the 12th grade. Fifty-six percent of the respondents indicated that they had had sex in the family home or at the home of the partner's family. Clearly, this research indicated that parents could have a significant impact on children's decisions about sex. More importantly, from an investigative standpoint, this phenomenon suggests that the level of victimization could very well increase. Teenagers, who are beginning to experience their sexuality, may be at greater risk to predators. Their reported inclination toward sexual intercourse and the allure of sexual activities among their peers, coupled with the Internet, raise serious concerns.

The advent of the Internet, which certainly represented technological progress, provides an abundance of information and contacts that can be effectively utilized to make our lives more comfortable. Today, computers and Internet access are affordable and available to almost everyone. The commercial possibilities of the Internet are extraordinary. Many people nearly have personal e-mail, shop online, and use the Internet in their day-to-day activities.

The downside to the Internet is that it also provides contacts, materials, and information that might not be so beneficial. "Hacking," computer crime, stealing personal identities, and access to information, such as bomb making, are just a few of the examples of the problems presented by the Internet. However, one of the most potential evils of this technological development is the proliferation of pornography and the easy access to this material on the "net." Even unsolicited pornography permeates the e-mail of many people online.

In fact, the Internet has proved to be a new sexual threat as predators use the Internet as a tool to seek out victims, stalk their prey, and sneak into your home through the telephone lines. The number of pedophile and sex-related events associated with the Internet that law enforcement has encountered is undeterminable. However, the author can state unequivocally that there has been a definite increase in sex-related events since the explosion of the Internet.

It is interesting to note that society has always had sexual perversions. In fact, in *Psychopathia Sexualis*, written by Richard von Krafft-Ebing in 1886, the reader is informed that someone somewhere practiced just about every sexual perversion one can think of at any given time in history. Today, many of these perversions are clinically referred to as paraphilias, which are recognized as diagnosable sexual disorders.

Prior to mass communication and distribution of sexually explicit materials, the individual who suffered from some paraphilia was considered weird or perverted and generally was ostracized by society. This effectively neutralized sexual offenders. However, today they can go online and look for materials related to their specific sexual interest. The sexual perverts can go into chat rooms and meet other perverts just like themselves. Sexual offenders, therefore, are able to validate their perversions by discovering that there are others "just like themselves" and what they do is [quote/unquote] perfectly normal and acceptable behavior.

Interestingly, within the mainstream, we have reality TV; sexually explicit programming involving nudity, vulgarity, drugs, and violence; and "shock jocks" advocating sexual escapades that further add to the desensitization of our society to sexual issues. In fact, there are studies that indicate that within every hour of TV programming there are at least five acts of violence. Obviously, if a child is exposed to violence, then it is only logical to assume that the child will respond with violence. If the violence is sexual, then there will be sexual violence. The consequence is that we in law enforcement have experienced an overwhelming increase in sex-related assaults and homicides.

Furthermore, I would suggest that although progress is good and beneficial and understanding our sexuality is healthy, there is a downside to a free and unrestrained expression of our most primal instincts. We, as a people, need the very essential primary, secondary, and tertiary restraints, such as religion, family, and societal responsibility to maintain a moral, civilized, and decent life. Respect for one another is taught through example. It is known as modeling and is nurtured through conditioning and reinforced by behavior. When a society's moral compass is sharp and clear with recognized boundaries of acceptable behavior, mores, and values, then sexual deviance is recognized for its evil.

I would suggest that as a nation we might have raised a generation of psychopaths through a very liberal and irresponsible atmosphere. This atmosphere encourages the types of behavior we have sadly come to accept through a new definition of tolerance. Many deviant behaviors have been "normalized" in recent years as evidenced in the American Psychiatric Association's revised *Diagnostic and Statistical Manual IV-TR*. Decades of political pressure by advocacy groups and ideologues have left society with the inability to recognize sexual deviance when it is seen and, more importantly, have desensitized society to a point that the unacceptable is now acceptable.

This has ultimately contributed to the current situation. We now have an increase in sexual predators, sexual deviance, and serial killers.

Are There More Serial Killers Today?

One of the questions I am constantly asked is: "Are there more serial killers today than before, or is it just that serial killers are more researched?" It is an interesting question and a legitimate insinuation regarding the research on serial killers.

In my opinion, as a society, we have inadvertently elevated the most reprehensible elements of the human race to celebrity status through the many books, TV shows, movies, and even games that have been designed around the serial killer. If an inadequate individual perceives that being a serial killer will provide him with recognition and notoriety, he has an abundance of study materials and literature to provide him with a frame of reference to achieve his goal.

In fact, many serial murderers were "students" of serial killings and had read about the activities of other serial murderers in the many popular books detailing these cases. I have had cases in which serial killers have replicated the activities of other serial killers in an attempt to enhance and expand on their own psychosexual needs.

The United States has the dubious distinction of having the most serial killers of any civilized country in the world. I would suggest that the upsurge of serial killers through the 1970s to the present once again might be traced to a sequence of events in our society beginning in mid-1960.

Many persons who were serial rapists have escalated to serial killings. They kill their victims rather than risk identification and jail. Permeating our society is the whole attitude and mindset that: "It's someone else's fault and I'm not responsible." The truth of the matter is that the sex-related cases that I am encountering today are more frequent, vicious, and despicable than what I ever experienced as a professional homicide cop in a major city police department.

The sexual stimulation of inadequate personalities is partly to blame for the upsurge in sexual crimes involving both assault and murder. Psychopathy accounts for the balance. Therefore, the answer is, Yes. There are more serial killers today and it has nothing to do with research or the available data. In my opinion as an expert in homicide investigations, without a doubt we have had a proliferation in serial murder events as well as sex-related homicides.

The Investigative Response

Homicide investigation is a profound duty with awesome responsibilities. It requires the professional homicide detective to develop an understanding of the dynamics of human behavior as well as the essential details of professional investigation.

The world of the homicide detective is permeated with human tragedies, which involve a variety of sudden and violent death scenarios. Many of these events, which are seemingly beyond the comprehension of the average person, reveal motivations and patterns of repetition, which are recognized by the experienced homicide detective. Professional homicide investigators become keenly aware of the reality of death and the impact it has on both society and the surviving family.

Within this text, the author will present a variety of the most horrific sex-related murder cases imaginable. It is of vital importance that the investigator be prepared to confront the reality of this evil so that he or she can conduct a professional investigation.

This textbook stresses the basics, indicates the practicalities of certain investigative techniques, and provides the reader with patterns upon which to build a solid foundation for a prosecutable case. There is deliberate repetition throughout the text. I have strategically placed these cues throughout because certain investigative principles can never be stressed enough.

Sex-Related Homicide and Death Investigation: Practical and Clinical Perspectives, Second Edition, begins with a completely rewritten Chapter 1 co-authored with Dr. Judith Reisman, an internationally recognized author, scientist, educator, and expert witness on matters concerning human sexuality and human behavior.

This comprehensive discussion of "Human Sexuality and Sexual Deviance," subtitled "Research and Reality," debunks much of the junk science of notorious "sexperts" like Alfred Kinsey and John Money, and contains current research with clinical references and case examples. This is followed by Chapter 2, which provides excellent examples of the significance of fantasy in sex-related events and references cases throughout the book with illustration and case histories.

In Chapter 3, the only chapter that has not been revised, the author provides a case history involving a serial rapist who kept a journal in which he described his day-to-day life as well as his sexual thoughts and fantasies. In this "Journal of Depravity," the offender's chilling personal accounts provided authorities with a graphic description of each of his sexual assaults. It also presents an unprecedented and comprehensive assessment of the thinking process of a serial rapist's mind, which validates much of the research on sexual predators.

The book then focuses on specific types of sex-related deaths in chapter format to include a completely updated and revised chapter on sexual asphyxia; followed by revised chapters on rape- and sodomy-oriented murder; domestic violence homicides; lust murder and deviant-oriented assault; serial murder, and child murder and child abduction homicides, along with many new case histories and photos to provide a frame of reference to the reader.

In Chapter 5 the author then presents crucial dynamics involved in the search of the crime scene and the collection of evidence in sex-related events. The crime scene search is the most important phase of the investigation conducted at the scene. The second edition of *Sex-Related Homicide and Death Investigation* includes a discussion of legal considerations in the crime scene search process. Major decisions of the courts restricting admissibility of testimonial evidence have significantly increased the value of physical evidence in homicide investigations.

The author presents various types of physical evidence encountered in sex-related homicides as well as trace evidence, the concept of linkage, and the importance of the "primary crime scene." Within Chapter 5, there is a discussion of the preliminary steps to be taken at the scene as well as an in-depth presentation on the crime scene search, the search of the body, and the crime scene photographs to be taken. The chapter concludes with a series of checklists including a Sex-Related Crime Scene Checklist.

Chapter 6 discusses collection and preservation of evidence in sex-related death investigations, which is of paramount importance to the overall investigation. This includes types and classifications of evidence as well as direct and indirect transfer. There are guidelines on how to collect and preserve specific types and pieces of evidence as well as field-testing and related topics, along with reference to explicit case histories. The chapter focuses on the most common types and pieces of evidence recovered in sex-related investigations. The author presents an up-to-date section on DNA (deoxyribonucleic acid) analysis, which provides the reader with the most current and practical application of this DNA technology.

The author includes an updated and revised Chapter 12 on the Sex Slave Torture and Serial Murder Case, which involved a serial killer who designed his own torture chamber and was responsible for the death of over 30 young women whom he tortured and killed in a most perverse manner. My friend and colleague, Prosecutor Jim Yontz, stated, "As the prosecutor in the David Parker Ray case, which is featured in Chapter 12, I wish I had had this book as a reference before that case broke. ... Had I been so fortunate, we, prosecutors and investigators, would have saved ourselves hundreds of man-hours in research, evaluation, and investigative time. Our investigation and prosecution would have been more focused and directed. ... We could have followed the roadmap Vernon provided."

I present this case history for its relationship to Chapter 2—"The Investigative Significance of Fantasy in Sex-Related Incidents." This case history will include the actual taped transcripts of the offender's instructions to his sex slaves. The transcripts go into graphic detail as the offender describes the various sexual acts and perversions that the victim will endure.

I have added a new chapter (13) on the BTK (bind, torture, kill) serial murder investigation, which involved a 30-year murder investigation, finally ending in 2005 with the arrest of Dennis Rader, whose activities and behaviors illustrate the psychopathology of the sexual offender. The information in Chapters 12 and 13 exemplifies the reality of psychopathic sexual sadism and provides a frame of reference for criminal profiling and investigative analysis.

The text then continues with an updated and expanded Chapter 14 on criminal profiling entitled "Investigative Analysis: Criminal Personality Profiling and the Signature Aspect." Topics discussed are the typology of offenders, organized and disorganized; the investigative approach to profiling; clinical considerations and descriptions of behavior; crime scene and profile characteristics of organized and disorganized murderers; criminal personality profiling, the signature aspect in criminal investigation; and linkage blindness, including the author's research on the frequency and characteristics of sexual posing in homicides as well as the high percentage of strangulation in sexual posing cases and its investigative significance.

Sex-Related Homicide and Death Investigation: Practical and Clinical Perspectives concludes with an in-depth clinical study of psychopathic sexual sadism. Chapter 15 examines serial murderers, who violated their victims sexually, as reported within the journalistic, academic, and law enforcement literature. It is based on the author's experience and case studies that he has personally been involved in, as well as a clinical study reported in *Journal of Forensic Science*.

As Dr. Robert Hare noted in his review, "Unlike many investigators, Geberth has paid close attention to the scientific literature on the PCL-R conception of psychopathy and, by integrating it with his own extensive experience and clinical insights, has produced an outstanding chapter on practical applications to criminal investigation. His discussions of the differences among several apparently related concepts—psychopathy, sociopathy, and antisocial personality disorder—are right on the mark, as is his appreciation of the behavior of psychopaths during the investigative process."

The author's intention and goal in this final chapter is to suggest that the dual diagnosis of psychopathic sexual sadism best describes offenders who obtain intense sexual arousal while violating their victims and engage in sexually sadistic activities including torture, mutilation, and/or killing to achieve sexual gratification. In the author's opinion, psychopathy coupled with sexual sadism and evidence of deviant sexual arousal clearly indicates dangerousness and the potential for recidivism.

A Psychology of Evil

In Chapter 15, the author will fully discuss the concept of a "psychology of evil." However, in this preface, I would like to reiterate that there is "good and evil" in the world. I believe that the outrageous atrocity visited upon the World Trade Center in New York City, the Pentagon in Washington, D.C., and citizens of the United States by an Islamic evil orchestrated by Osama bin Laden was a heinous attack on humankind. This was an evil act of genocide perpetrated by fanatics, who shrouded themselves in a religious cause by bastardizing the legitimate religion of Islam. There are many manifestations of evil: political, religious, educational, business, etc.

However, in this text we will focus on sexual evil. There is a developmental process involved in evil. In my opinion, people are not born evil. We do have free will and can choose to do good or bad. An evil person exercises his free will and chooses to do evil and characteristically is hedonistic and feels superior to other human beings.

There are people who are sexual psychopaths and serial murderers who "kill" because they "like to kill." These killers have conscious and detailed plans to murder. They certainly know right from wrong; they just don't give a damn. Their fundamental mechanism of conscience, responsibility, and feeling for fellow human beings is totally lacking. Their will to do evil takes precedence over humanity. Evil people take and destroy lives without the least bit of hesitation or remorse because they are evil. Many of the cases within this text are representative of that evil.

Our Mission

Homicide investigators have a *mission*. Our mission is to bring justice to the deceased and their surviving family. We do this by conducting a professional and intelligent investigation, which results in the identification and apprehension of the killer and the successful prosecution of the case. In order to conduct an efficient and effective investigation, the detective concentrates first on the mechanical aspects of the death, that is, motives and methods, wound structures, crime scene reconstruction, and the cause, manner, and time of death as well as other factors that provide clues to the dynamics of the event.

The professional homicide investigator must learn to deal with death in a clinical manner. Detectives should afford themselves with an emotional insulation by not projecting a personality into the body. (Personally speaking, if you begin to look upon that body as your wife, daughter, son, mother, or father, you are going to lose that professional objectivity that is so necessary in the murder inquiry.) My way of dealing with the reality of sudden and violent death is a strong belief in God and a belief in a higher order of things in our existence. My theology informs me that there is an afterlife and I believe that the soul of the murder victim has left the body.

In real life, you get only one shot at the homicide crime scene and a limited opportunity to question the suspect. Therefore, I recommend that the reader follow the investigative checklists and basic principles in this text and then follow the principles that I have espoused from my first edition of *Practical Homicide,* published in 1983, to the present. Remember: "Things are not always as they appear to be" and "Do it right the first time, you only get one chance."

Death investigation constitutes a heavy responsibility and, as such, no person, system, or circumstance should deter you from the truth and your own personal commitment to see that justice is done, not only for the deceased, but for the surviving family as well. That is why my personal philosophy as a murder cop is: Remember: *We Work for God*®.

To the Reader

The author is involved in a number of professional consultations on cases that are either actively in prosecution or on appeal. Due to legal restrictions they are not included in the textbook. However, as these cases are resolved and/or the author can provide further investigative research you are invited to access his Web site at www.practicalhomicide.com to obtain information on research materials or current events.

Vernon J. Geberth

Foreword to the Second Edition

Sex-Related Homicide and Death Investigation: Practical and Clinical Perspectives

Vernon Geberth has been my friend and professional colleague for more than 25 years. He has shared with me more than his friendship through those years. He has shared his expertise, experience, education, energy, and enthusiasm on more than a few occasions.

Prior to my retirement in 2007 as director of the Kansas Bureau of Investigation (KBI), the various editions of Vernon Geberth's *Practical Homicide Investigation: Tactics, Procedures, and Forensic Techniques,* as well as the companion *Practical Homicide Investigation: Checklist and Field Guide,* were on a bookshelf next to my desk. My office walls were adorned with the popular *We Work for God*® cards and the famous *Thou Shalt Not Kill* certificates, personally obtained from more than one of Vern's "Practical Homicide Investigation®" training seminars and lectures.

In the KBI, as throughout the American law enforcement community, we considered *Practical Homicide Investigation* the bible for homicide investigators. The special agents of our KBI Cold Case Squad carried Geberth's homicide textbook (the bible) and his field guide in their crime scene kits.

In 2003, with the same graphic clarity with which he defined both the act of murder and its various solutions in *Practical Homicide Investigation,* our author gave us *Sex-Related Homicide and Death Investigation: Practical and Clinical Perspectives.*

Therein, he vividly described the evil of the sexual criminal and outlined the investigative path to that criminal's identification, apprehension, and prosecution. That effort, as did Geberth's books on homicide, successfully combined theory and practice in a refreshing format. There was a minimum of theoretical deliberation and a maximum of common sense.

He brought to that important publication the usual Geberth common sense, practicality, and graphic simplicity that characterized all the editions of *Practical Homicide Investigation.*

Following my retirement, the four editions of *Practical Homicide Investigation,* the wall adornments of souvenirs of Geberth's seminars and lectures, and the first edition of *Sex-Related Homicide and Death Investigation,* for which I was honored to write the foreword, all found their way to my den in our home in Lawrence, Kansas.

Now, the retired commander of the famous Bronx Homicide Task Force, who has personally investigated, supervised, assessed, researched, and consulted on over 8,000 death investigations in his experience, revisits *Sex-Related Homicide and Death Investigation,* the Bible for sex-related homicide investigators, and adds a New Testament (revisions and updates) to that Bible in this second edition.

As with all four of the editions of *Practical Homicide Investigation* and the original edition of *Sex-Related Homicide and Death Investigation,* the fainthearted should proceed with caution. Again, in typical Vernon Geberth style, we do not merely read of the sexual murder.

The crime is not simply described to us. We are not just told about the sexual violation and homicide. We are thrust into the horror. We are transported to the crime scene. We live it, we smell it, we hear it, we see it, we experience it, we feel it, and we understand it. We also detest it and know we must solve it. We must identify the criminal, capture him, and prosecute him. We pursue justice and, God forgive us, revenge, for victim, family, and friends.

As always, the author simplifies complex forensics in general and DNA in particular. He simplifies sexual-criminal motive and sexual-criminal modus operandi. He, above all, simplifies the investigative strategy for sex-related homicides.

In this second edition, Vern has revised, updated, or tweaked every chapter except Chapter 3 (Journal of a Serial Rapist) which, of course, defies change.

I appreciate his substitution of Dr. Judith Reisman's material on human sexuality for that of Alfred Kinsey in the first chapter (Human Sexuality and Sexual Deviance).

I'm especially grateful for the inclusion in this edition of a chapter (13) on BTK, Kansas' most famous serial killer, given the KBI's significant investigative and forensic participation with the Wichita Police Department and the FBI in the BTK Task Force, in 2004 and 2005, in the investigation, identification, arrest, and prosecution of Dennis Rader, who murdered 10 citizens of Wichita, Kansas, between 1974 and 1991.

New photographs, case studies, and/or research have been added to 14 of the 15 chapters, and, once again, as in the first edition of *Sex-Related Homicide and Death Investigation*, the author dares to discuss everything from human sexuality, the initial crime scene, auto-erotic fatalities, and sex-related child homicides to sex slave torture, gang rape–murder, and sexual sadism. There is no aspect of sexual criminality he avoids, regardless of how troubling or controversial.

This edition retains all the merits of the first, and more, and remains the best and most thorough text on the subject of sex-related homicide I have seen. It demonstrates again why *We Work for God®*.

Larry Welch, Director (Ret.)
Kansas Bureau of Investigation
Lawrence, Kansas

Special Acknowledgment

To my wife and family, I wish to extend a very special acknowledgment.
   To my children:

- Vernon Anthony, BA, Verizon security specialist OPS Northeast Region; Retired Detective in the Joint Terrorist Task Force in the New York City Police Department
- Robert Joseph, BA, MPA, trooper–investigator with the New York State Police
- Christopher James, a CPA, vice president finance executive
- Laura Marie, BSW, my very special daughter, who is also a mystery romance writer

   And, most affectionately, my wife Laura, MSW, CSW, chief operating officer of a social services organization, who always assists me with her support and encouragement as my life partner.

The Author

Vernon J. Geberth, M.S., M.P.S., B.B.A., FBINA, is a retired Lieutenant-Commander of the New York City Police Department with over 40 years of law enforcement experience. He retired as the commanding officer of the Bronx Homicide Task Force, which handled over 400 murder investigations a year. During his career, he was a detective, a precinct detective squad commander, temporary commander of the 7th Homicide Zone in the South Bronx, and commander of Bronx Homicide. He has personally investigated, supervised, assessed, researched, and consulted on over 8,000 death investigations. In addition, Commander Geberth has been the recipient of more than 60 awards for bravery and exceptional police work and is a member of the Honor Legion of the City of New York Police Department.

Commander Geberth has a master's in professional studies (MPS) from C.W. Post College, Long Island University, and an MS in psychology, California Coast University, Santa Ana. He earned his Bachelor of Business Administration (BBA) at Iona College in New Rochelle, New York, and he is also a graduate of the FBI National Academy in Quantico, Virginia, 119th Session, (1979). Commander Geberth is a Fellow in the American Academy of Forensic Sciences (AAFS).

Geberth is a charter member of the International Homicide Investigator's Association and serves as a certification board member for the United States Association of Professional Investigators, Washington, D.C. He has served on the New York State Governor's Commission on Domestic Violence Fatalities and is a charter member of the Pennsylvania Homicide Investigator's Association, a charter member of the Washington Violent Crimes Investigator's Association, and a Life Member of the Indiana Homicide and Violent Crime Investigator's Association.

Commander Geberth was awarded the prestigious International Homicide Investigator's Associations (IHIA) Award of Excellence in 2006 for his contributions to training of homicide investigators throughout the world at the IHIA 13th Annual Symposium in New Orleans, Louisiana.

He has served as an adjunct professor of criminal justice at Mercy College, Dobbs Ferry, New York, and John Jay College of Criminal Justice in New York City. He was affiliated with the University of Delaware's Continuing Education Program as an associate professor, and was a member of the faculty of Northwestern University Traffic Institute as a homicide instructor. Commander Geberth continues to serve as a homicide instructor for the New York City Police Department's Homicide Investigator's Course, which is sponsored through the Chief of Detective's office.

Commander Geberth has provided consultation and homicide instruction to many major police departments across the United States including the Texas Rangers; Las Vegas Metropolitan Police Department; Miami, Miami Beach, and Escambia County, Florida; Chicago Homicide Division; Westchester County, Suffolk County, Nassau County, and Yonkers, New York; Philadelphia; Honolulu; the Kansas Bureau of Investigation, Lawrence; Buffalo; Denver; Warwick, Rhode Island; and Boston.

Commander Geberth served as an instructor for the Missouri Highway Patrol National Homicide Seminar. He has instructed at the New Jersey State Police Homicide School, the New York State Police Colonel Henry F. William's Homicide Seminar, and the Delaware State Police Homicide Conference. He has also been an instructor for the Arizona Department of Public Safety (DPS), and the Illinois, Maine, Massachusetts, New Hampshire, Connecticut, New Mexico, Illinois, Indiana, Maryland, West Virginia, Kentucky, Mississippi, Alabama, Kentucky, and Pennsylvania State Police, as well as The Police Training Division of the New York Office of the FBI.

In addition, Commander Geberth has appeared in numerous television productions on the subject of homicide and death investigation and has been referenced as a media consultant on myriad national major cases across the United States.

Retired Lieutenant-Commander Geberth is the author of *Practical Homicide Investigation: Tactics, Procedures, and Forensic Techniques, Fourth Edition*, which is recognized in the law enforcement field as "the Bible of homicide investigation," and the *Practical Homicide Investigation Checklist and Field Guide,* which is considered by professionals as an essential prerequisite in conducting proficient death inquiries. Commander Geberth is also the author of this newly revised *Sex-Related Homicide and Death Investigation: Practical and Clinical Perspectives, Second Edition*, which will continue to be considered the benchmark textbook on sex-related homicide and death investigations and has established a framework of reference in the field sex-related murder.

Commander Geberth has published extensively on topics relating to criminal investigation and forensic techniques and applied criminal psychology. He was a contributing author for *The Encyclopedia of Law Enforcement, The Criminal and Civil Investigations Handbook* and the *Encyclopedia of Police Science*. He has been and continues to be a contributing author for *Law and Order Magazine.* His comprehensive study of serial killers in the United States, which he co-authored with a forensic psychiatrist, was published in the *Journal of Forensic Sciences* in January 1997, and his published works are cited in numerous professional publications throughout the United States, Canada, and Europe. In addition, he created and serves as the series editor of *Practical Aspects of Criminal and Forensic Investigations* for Taylor & Francis Group/CRC Press in Boca Raton, Florida, and has proposed and edited over 47 titles within this series.

Commander Geberth is president of P.H.I. Investigative Consultants, Inc., a New York–based corporation, which provides state-of-the-art instruction as well as consultation in homicide and forensic case investigations for a number of law enforcement agencies throughout the United States and Canada. Over 62,000 members from over 7,500 law enforcement agencies have attended Geberth's "Practical Homicide Investigation®" seminars, which marked its 30th anniversary in 2010.

Geberth is a nationally renowned lecturer, author, educator, consultant, and expert witness on the subject of death investigations.

Acknowledgments

A special word of thanks is extended to Larry Welch, Esq., former director of the Kansas Bureau of Investigation (KBI), an honorable representative of professional law enforcement, and also a good friend and colleague who cordially provided the Foreword, as well as the Honorable Jeanine Pirro, former District Attorney, Westchester County District Attorney's Office, White Plains, New York, a nationally recognized authority on the prosecution of sex-related incidents, specifically domestic violence, who is currently the host of the *Judge Jeanine Pirro Show,* and a friend and colleague who graciously provided the Introduction. Also thanks go to the staff at Taylor & Francis Group/CRC Press: project editor Mimi Williams, who painstakingly assured that every possible editorial detail was accomplished; production coordinator Pat Robertson and cover designer Shayna Murray; senior editor Becky Masterman, who encouraged me and made significant editorial and design contributions.

AAFS
American Academy of Forensic Science

Marc Abdilla
Detective
Township of Van Buren, Michigan, Department of
    Public Safety

Ray Adornetto
Detective
South Euclid, Ohio, Police Department

Steve Alexander
Lieutenant
Salt Lake County, Utah, Sheriff's Office

Ronald Antonucci
Detective
Wayne Township, New Jersey, Police Department

Arkansas
Arkansas State Police

Michael Baden, M.D.
Former Chief Medical Examiner, Forensic
    Pathologist
New York City Medical Examiner's Office

Frank Baldwin
Captain
Union County, South Carolina, Sheriff's Office

Keith Batchelor
Detective
Pontiac, Michigan, Police Department

Kenneth Bilodeau
Detective Corporal
East Providence, Rhode Island, Police Department

Ray Biondi
Detective Lieutenant (Ret.)
Sacramento County, California Sheriff's
    Department

Robert Bittle
Detective Sergeant (Ret.)
Judicial Inv. 12th District North Carolina

Doug Bluthardt
Detective (Retired)
Topeka, Kansas, Police Department

William J. Bodziak
Supervisory Special Agent (Ret.)
FBI Laboratory Division, Washington, D.C.

Frank Bolz
Detective Captain (Ret.)
New York City Police Department

K.W. Bonsal
Detective Sergeant
Pasadena, Texas, Police Department

Andy Bradley
Detective Lieutenant
Indian River County, Florida, Sheriff's Department

Dale Brady
Detective Lieutenant
University Heights, Ohio, Police Department

LaVern Brann
Detective Killed in the L.O.D.
Battle Creek, Michigan, Police Department

John Briscoe
Agent–Case Manager
New Mexico State Police

Pierce Brooks
Captain (Ret.) (now deceased)
Los Angeles, California, Police Department

Katherine Brown, Ph.D.
Assistant Professor, Criminal Justice
Criminal Justice & Forensic Science University of
    New Haven
Connecticut

Ann W. Burgess, DNSc.
Professor of Psychiatric Nursing
Boston College Connell School of Nursing
Massachusetts

John Burney
Detective Corporal
East Providence, Rhode Island, Police Department

Chris Callabrese
Detective Lieutenant
Westchester County, New York, Police Department

Michael Carona
Sheriff
Orange County, California, Sheriff's Department

Ronald Carpenter
Detective
Pontiac, Michigan, Police Department

Bruce L. Castor, Jr.
First Assistant District Attorney
Montgomery County, Pennsylvania, District
    Attorney's Office

Joey Catalanotto
Detecitve Sergeant
New Orleans, Louisiana, Police Department

James Cioti
Special Agent
Ohio Bureau of Investigation

Arthur Clark
Detective Corporal
East Providence, Rhode Island, Police Department

Dennis Clay
Detective
Grand Prairie, Texas, Police Department

Rusty Clevenger
Coroner
Spartanburg County, South Carolina, Coroner's
    Office

Phil Cline
Chief of Detectives (Retired)
Chicago, Illinois, Police Department

Matthew Cody
Detective
Chambersburg, Pennsylvania, Police Department

Bill Coffey
Sheriff
Spartanburg County, South Carolina, Sheriff's
    Office

Karl Compton
Captain
Howland Township, Ohio, Police Department

Thomas A. Condon
Attorney
Birbrower, Montalbano Condon & Frank, P.C.

Rheta Conley
Crime Scene Detective (Retired)
Gastonia, North Carolina, Police Department

Connecticut
Connecticut State Police

Barbara Corey-Boulet
Prosecutor
Pierce County, Washington, Prosecutor's Office

Terry M. Cousino
Detective
Toledo, Ohio, Police Department

Jonathon Cox
Detective
Larimer County, Colorado, Sheriff's Department

Matthew Coyne
Certified Public Accountant
Financial advisor and personal friend

Tom Cronin
Commander (Retired)
Chicago, Illinois, Police Department

Linda Crumb
Detective
Dallas, Texas, Police Department

Mark Czworniak
Detective (Area #3)
Chicago, Illinois, Police Department

Edward Dahlman
Detective
Columbus, Ohio, Police Department

John D'Alessandro
Detective Sergeant
Yonkers, New York, Police Department

Edward Davies
Detective
Montgomery Township, Pennsylvania, Police
    Department

Mike Dawson
Arkansas State Police

Charles De Angelo
Attorney and personal friend
Jamestown, New York

John Dean
Chief of Police
Waterford Township, Michigan, Police Department

David Deerwester
Detective
McClean County, Illinois, Police Department

Frank Del Prete
Lieutenant (Retired)
Bergen County, New Jersey, Prosecutor's Office

Delaware
Delaware State Police

Gary A. Dias
Captain, Scientific Department
Honolulu, Hawaii, Police Department

Dominick J. DiMaio, M.D.
Former Chief Medical Examiner (deceased)
New York City Medical Examiner's Office

Vincent J.M. DiMaio, M.D.
Chief Medical Examiner Retired
Bexar County, Texas, Medical Examiner's Office

Dee Ann Dionne
Mother of Joely Arnold
Secondary victim of homicide

Sondra Doolittle
Meetings and Expositions Manager
American Academy of Forensic Sciences

Thomas Dolye
Detective Lieutenant
East Lake, Ohio, Police Department

John Dotson
Chief of Police (Retired)
Sparks, Nevada, Police Department

Roy L. Douglas
Homicide Detective (Retired)
St. Louis, Missouri, Police Department

Chris Dukas
Producer
Inside Edition

Barbara Egenhauser
Second Deputy District Attorney
Westchester County, New York, District Attorney's
    Office

Alan Ellingsworth
Colonel (Retired)
Delaware State Police

Rod Englert
Forensic Expert
R.E. Forensics, Oregon

Ken Espinoza
Detective
Pueblo, Colorado, Police Department

Mike Essig
Detective
McClean County, Illinois, Police Department

Thomas Fahey
Assistant Chief–Manhattan Detectives (Retired)
New York City Police Department

Terry M. Fail
Postal Inspector
U.S. Postal Inspections Service

Tyler Fall
Laboratory Specialist
Kalamazoo, Michigan, Department of Public Safety

John Fallon
Lieutenant
Montgomery County Detectives, Pennsylvania

Pete Farmer
Detective Sergeant (Retired)
Hobbs, New Mexico, Police Department

Steve Fermon
Captain
Illinois State Police

James Ferrier
Captain (Retired)
Milwaukee, Wisconsin, Police Department

Mike Fetrow
Detective-Sergeant
Denver, Colorado, Police Department

Hal Fillinger, M.D.
Forensic Pathologist (deceased)
Mongomery County, Pennsylvania, Medical
    Examiner

Dale Foote
Detective (Retired)
Bellevue, Washington, Police Department

Former 7th Homicide Zone
South Bronx
New York City Police Department

Nola Tedesco
Foulston District Attorney
Wichita 18th Judicial District
Sedgwick County, Kansas

Robert W. Fox
Chief of Police (Retired)
Sieverville, Tennessee, Police Department

Director of Safety & Security
Dollywood Corporation, Tennessee

William Frank
Attorney and my Counsel
Birbrower, Montalbano, Condon & Frank, P.C.

William "Bill" Franks
Chief of Police (Retired)
Stony Point, New York, Police Department

Wiliam Frisby, Jr.
Detective
Chambersburg, Pennsylvania, Police Department

Mark Fritts
Detective Lieutenant (Retired)
Hobbs, New Mexico, Police Department

Pete Gagliardi
DEA Manager of IBIS (Retired)
Forensic Technology, Inc.

James Gannon
Detective Captain
Morris County, New Jersey, Prosecutor's Office

John Geis
Detective
Yonkers, New York, Police Department

Dan Gilliam
Evidence Specialist
Larimer County, Colorado, Sheriff's Department

Thomas P. Gordon
Colonel–Chief Department Public Safety
New Castle County, Delaware

Dana Gouge
Detective
Wichita, Kansas, Police Department Homicide
    Section

Nathan Graham
Crime Analyst
FBI VICAP Highway Serial Killer Initiative

Edward Grant
Lieutenant — Criminal Profiler
New York State Police

Fredric Green
Chief, Sex Crime Bureau Assistant District
    Attorney
Westchester County, New York, District Attorney's
    Office

Frank Griffin
Captain
Connecticut State Police

John Grimmich
Detective Sergeant
Indian River County, Florida, Sheriff's Department

Steve Gurka
Detective Sergeant
Dearborn Height, Michigan, Police Department

James J. Hackett
Lieutenant-Colonel Chief of Detectives
St. Louis, Missouri, Police Department

George O. Haggerty
Detective Captain (Retired)
New Castle County, Delaware, Department of
Public Safety

William "Bill" Hagmaier
Supervisory Special Agent (Retired)
Behavioral Science Unit FBI
Quantico, Virginia

Oscar Hale
Senior Police Administrative Aide (Retired)
Bronx Detective Area, New York City Police
    Department

Larry Hallmark
Detective Sergeant
Grapevine, Texas, Police Department

Michael Harrigan
Supervisory Special Agent FBI
Highway Serial Killer Initiative

Jim Harper
Detective (Retired)
Topeka, Kansas, Police Department

Kurt Harrelson
Detective Sergeant Killed in the L.O.D.
Thibodaux, Louisiana, Police Department

Steve Harsha
Lieutenant Colonel
Topeka, Kansas, Police Department

William Harvey
Detective Sergeant
Oakland County, Michigan, Police Department

Robert R. Hazelwood
Supervisory Special Agent (Retired)
FBI Behavioral Science Unit
Quantico, Virginia

Harry Hegger
Detective Captain
St. Louis, Missouri, Police Department

Jack Henander
Detective (Retired)
Larimer County, Colorado, Sheriff's Department

Gary Henderson
Texas Ranger

James Hendricks
Detective
New Castle County, Delaware, Department of
    Public Safety

Tara Henry
Forensic Nurse
Anchorage, Alaska

Keith Hiller
Chief of Police
Waseca, Minnesota, Police Department

Mark A. Hilts
Unit Chief
FBI Behavioral Analysis Unit
Quantico, Virginia

Larry Hobson
Assistant Chief Investigator (Retired)
San Luis Obispo, California, District Attorney's
    Office

Frank Horvath, Ph D.
Emeritus Professor
Michigan State University

Larry Houpt
Special Agent
FBI

Bill Huffmeir
Detective
Topeka, Kansas, Police Department

Illinois
Illinois State Police

Robert Italiano
Lieutenant (Retired)
New Orleans, Louisiana, Police Department

Ken Jako
Detective-Sergeant
Kalamazoo County, Michigan, Sheriff's Department

Lynde Johnson
Captain Major Case Unit
Rochester, New York, Police Department

Mark Johnson
Detective
Thibodaux, Louisiana, Police Department

Cheryl Johnson
Detective
Ft. Worth, Texas, Police Department

Linda Jones
Sales Department
Taylor & Francis Group
Boca Raton, Florida

Tom Jordan
District Court Judge, Magistrate Court
Centre Hall, Pennsylvania

Mark A. Joseph
Detective
Whatcom County, Washington, Sheriff's Office

Andy Josey
Sergeant
Larimer County, Colorado, Sheriff's Department

Edward Kallal
Crime Scene Technician
Illinois State Police

Kansas
Kansas Bureau of Investigation

Kansas
Lawrence, Kansas, Police Department

Nick Kaylor
Postal Inspector
U.S. Postal Inspections Service

Dianne Kelso
Detective Sergeant
Chambersburg, Pennsylvania, Police Department

Michael Kelty
Detective First Grade (Retired)
New York City Police Department

Kentucky
Kentucky State Police

Rod Kicklighter
Special Agent (Retired)
FBI

Gregory Knack
Detective
Willoughby, Ohio, Police Department

Darrell Knutson
Detective
Rock County, Wisconsin, Sheriff's Office

Raymond Krolak
Detective Lieutenant (Retired)
Colonie, New York, Police Department

Kevin Krugman
Police Officer
Avon, Ohio, Police Department

Aaron Kusterman
Crime Analyst
Illinois State Police

Wes LaCuesta
Agent
New Mexico State Police

Kenneth F. Landwehr
Detective Commander
Wichita, Kansas, Police Department Homicide
    Section

Christina Lane, Ph.D.
Department of Criminal Justice
St. Rose College
Albany, New York

Renee Lano
Sergeant
New Castle County, Delaware, Department of
    Public Safety

Manfred Lassig
Detective Sergeant
Salt Lake County, Utah, Sheriff's Office

Wendy Lavezzi, M.D.
Forensic Pathologist, Assistant Medical Examiner
District 5 State of Florida,
Leesburg, Florida

Henry Lee, Ph.D.
Director Emeritus
Connecticut State Forensic Laboratory

Lowell J. Levine, DDS
Forensic Odontologist
Medicolegal Investigation Unit , New York State
    Police

Rich Libicer
Agent–Intelligence Officer
New Mexico State Police

Steven Little
Sergeant
Columbus, Ohio, Police Department

Lowell J. Lowenstein
Detective
Westchester County, New York, Police
    Department

Andrew Lugo
Detective First Grade (Retired)
New York City Police Department

Leslie Lukash, M.D.
Former Chief Medical Examiner (deceased)
Nassau County, New York, Medical Examiner's
    Office

Raymond Lundin
Senior Special Agent
Kansas Bureau of Investigation

John Lynch
Detective Lieutenant
East Providence, Rhode Island Police Department

Steve Mack
Detective (Retired)
Huntington Beach, California

Anthony Magnetto
Captain
Troy, New York, Police Department

Mike Malchick
Trooper-Investigator (Retired)
Connecticut State Police

Roz Malloy
Finest & Bravest Equipment
New York City

Mark Marotta
Vice-President Financial Advisor
Merrill Lynch

Michael Martin
Captain
Thibodaux, Louisiana Police Department

John Marzulli
Investigative Reporter
New York Daily News,
New York, New York

Robert Matuszny
Detective
Cleveland, Ohio, Police Department

Anthony Maxwell
Special Agent
FBI

James A. McCarty
Deputy Division Chief
Westchester County, New York, District Attorney's
    Office

Becky McEldowney
Senior Editor
Taylor & Francis Group
Boca Raton, Florida

Thomas McKay
Chief Investigator
Dearborn, Ohio, County Prosecutor's Office

Chris McMurrary
Special Agent
FBI

Edward McNelley
Detective Captain (Retired)
Boston, Massachusetts, Police Department

Mark Meyers
Detective
Las Cruces, New Mexico, Police Department

Tom Meloni
Deputy Chief
Wheaton, Illinois, Police Department

Jocelyn Mercier
Detective
St. Louis, Missouri, Police Department

Michigan
Michigan State Police

Bill Miller
Senior Investigator
San Luis Obispo, California, District Attorney's
    Office

John Miller
Lieutenant
Delaware State Police

Melaine Minch
Account Manager
Taylor & Francis Group
Boca Raton, Florida

Missouri
Missouri State Highway Patrol

Tom Monahan
Lieutenant-Commander Detectives
Las Vegas, Nevada, Metropolitan Police Department

Chris Morgan
Lieutenant (Retired) Criminal Investigations
Raleigh, North Carolina, Police Department

Pamela Morrell
Typesetter Supervisor
Taylor & Francis Group
Boca Raton, Florida

Robert J. Morton
Supervisory Special Agent FBI
Behavioral Analysis Unit

Scott Mummert
Detective
Chambersburg, Pennsylvania, Police Department

Christopher D. Munger
FBI (Retired) Training Coordinator
New York Office of the FBI

Patricia Murphy
Chief, Superior Court Trail Division 2nd
    Deputy D.A.
Westchester Count, New York, District Attorney's
    Office

Mitch Murray
District Attorney, Eighth Judicial District
Larimer County, Colorado

Shayna Murry
Book Cover Designer
Taylor & Francis Group
Boca Raton, Florida

Cathy NaHirny
Administrative Manager
National Center for Missing and Exploited Children

Courtney Nelson
Detective
Salt Lake County, Utah, Sheriff's Office

Nevada
Las Vegas, Nevada, Metropolitan Police Department

New Jersey
New Jersey State Police

New Mexico
New Mexico State Police

New York
New York State Police Department
New York City Police Detective Bureau
New York, New York

Thomas Nye
Major (Retired)
Warwick, Rhode Island, Police Department

Oakland County
Sheriff's Department
Oakland County, Michigan

John O'Malley
Detective
Cleveland, Ohio, Police Department

Kelly Otis
Detective
Wichita, Kansas, Police Department Homicide
    Section

Richard Ovens, Psy.D.
Psychologist
New York State Police (Retired)

Pat Postiglione
Detective Sergeant
Nashville, Tennessee, Homicide

Todd Park
Detective
Salt Lake County, Utah, Sheriff's Office

Alan Patton
Detective Sergeant
Grand Prairie, Texas, Police Department

Richard Peffall
Detective
Montgomery County Detectives, Pennsylvania

Donna Pendergast
Assistant Prosecutor
Michigan State Attorney's Office

Sam Pennica
Lieutenant
Cumberland County, North Carolina, Sheriff's
     Office

Pennsylvania
Pennsylvania State Police

Pennsylvania
Pennsylvania Homicide Investigators Association

Larry Petersen
Detective
King County, Washington, Sheriff's Office

J.L Phillips
Senior Trooper-Investigator
Martinsburg, West Virginia, State Police

Raymond Pierce
Criminal Profiler–Consultant
New York City Police Department (Retired)

Joseph Pietropaolo
Detective Sergeant
Yonkers, New York, Police Department

Jeanine Pirro
Former Westchester District Attorney, Judge
Judge Jeanine Pirro Show, Warner Brothers

Pontiac Police
Police Department
Pontiac, Michigan

P.O.M.C.
Parents of Murdered Children

Thomas E. Pope
Solicitor
16th Judicial District South Carolina

Pottawatomie Sheriff's Department
Westmoreland, Kansas

Mark Prach
Lieutenant
Morris County, New Jersey Prosecutor's Office

Phil Redstone
Captain (Retired)
Indian River County, Florida, Sheriff's Department

Marsha Reed
Detective (Retired)
Ft. Collins, Colorado, Police Department

Lynn Reed
Coroner
Illinois Coroner and Medical Examiner Assoc.

Victor Regaldo
Detective
Tulsa, Oklahoma, Police Department

David G. Reichert
Sheriff
King County, Washington, Sheriff's Office

Judith Reisman, Ph.D.
Institute for Media Education in Arizona
California Protective Parents Association,
     California

Robert K. Ressler
Criminal Profiler (Retired)
FBI Behavioral Science Unit
Quantico, Virginia

Jack Reyes
Detective
New Castle County, Delaware, Department of
     Public Safety

Mark Reynolds
Homicide Detective
Harris County, Texas, Sheriff's Department

Norman Rhoads
Special Agent
New Mexico State Police

Greg Riat
Sheriff
Pottawatomie Sheriff's Department

Jim Ripley
Lieutenant
Missouri State Highway Patrol

Pat Roberson
Project Coordinator for textbook
Taylor & Francis Group
Boca Raton, Florida

Ken Roberts
Detective (Retired)
East Lake, Ohio, Police Department

K.C. Rogers
Crime Scene Commander
New Mexico State Police

Paul T. Romond
Detective Lieutenant
Avon, Ohio, Police Department

John Rumancik
Detective Sergeant
Howland Township, Ohio, Police Department

Anny Sauvageau, M.D.
Forensic Pathologist
Office of Chief Medical Examiner
Edmonton, Alberta, Canada

Bruce Saville
Detective
Upper Merion, Pennsylvania, Police Department

Gerald Schmidt
Detective
Pottawatomie Sheriff's Department

Phillip Schnelwar
Judge, Rockland County, New York
Former Homicide Bureau Chief
Bronx District Attorney's Office

Eric Schroeder
Detective-Sergeant
Michigan State Police

Reine Sears
Project Manager
Louisiana Supreme Court

Santiago Serna
Detective
Pontiac, Michigan, Police Department

Robert Shaler, Ph.D.
Director of Serology
New York City Medical Examiner's Office
Professor at State College, Pennsylvania

James Sharkey
Detective Sergeant
New Castle County, Delaware, Department of
    Public Safety

Peter Seikman
Coroner
DuPage County, Illinois, Coroner's Office

Marv Skeen
Chief Criminal Investigator
Washington State Attorney General's Office

Bryan Skordahl
Detective
Clark County, Washington, Sheriff's Office

Candice Skrapec, Ph.D.
Psychologist
California State University Fresno

Jeffrey Smith
Detective Sergeant
Pontiac, Michigan, Police Department

David Smith
Detective
Baton Rouge, Louisiana, Sheriff's Department

South Bronx
Homicide Squad Former 7th Homicide Zone
    Detectives
New York City Police Department

Richard T. Spooner
Major (Retired)
U.S. Marine Corps, Quantico, Virginia

Howard Springer
Detective
McClean County, Illinois, Police Department

Robert Swackhammer
Detective Sergeant (Retired)
Michigan State Police

Don Swanz
Evidence Technician
Grand Prairie, Texas, Police Department

Joseph Swiski
Detective
Delaware State Police

Texas
Texas Rangers

Larry Thomas
Assistant Director (Retired)
Kansas Bureau of Investigation

Laren Thorsen
Former Michigan State Police
PHI Coordinator, Michigan ICT Training

Jerry Townsend
Detective Sergeant
Salt Lake County, Utah, Sheriff's Office

John Trice
Deputy District Attorney
San Luis Obispo District Attorney's Office

Betty Tufariello
Trademark Attorney PHI
P.B. Tufariello, P.C.

Pamela Tully
Special Agent-in-Charge
North Carolina State Bureau of Investigation

Ronald M. Turco, M.D.
Forensic Psychiatrist
Portland, Oregon

Teri Turner
Crime Analyst
Oklahoma Bureau of Investigation

J.C. Tyus
Detective
Denver Police Department

Brian Van Nest
Detective
St. Louis, Missouri, Police Department

Dean Vosler
Detective
Bay City, Michigan, Police Department

Penny Vought
Captain
Waseca, Minnesota, Police Department

Robin Wagg
Chief Criminal Investigator
Douglas County, Washington, Sheriff's Office

James Walker
Special Agent
Illinois State Police

Roy & Ellen Walters
P.H.I. printing and presentation materials
Haverstraw Bay Press
Haverstraw, New York

Donald Watts
Detective
Dallas, Texas, Police Department

Larry Welch
Director (Retired)
Kansas Bureau of Investigation

Sean Welch
Trooper-Investigator
Kentucky State Police

Howard Wells
The Sheriff
Union County, South Carolina, Sheriff's Office

Arthur Westveer
Homicide Instructor (Retired Lieutenant)
FBI Academy
Quantico, Virginia

John Wiggins
Instructor-Coordinator
North Carolina Justice Academy

Bob Wilbanks
Sergeant
Grand Prairie, Texas, Police Department

Mimi Williams
Manager, Production Editing
Taylor & Francis Group
Boca Raton, Florida

Brian Wilson
Graphic artist
Medical Legal Art (MLA)
Atlanta, Georgia

John Wisniewski
Agent, Headquarter's Division
U.S. Postal Inspection Service

Barbara Wolf, M.D.
Chief Medical Examiner, Forensic Pathologist
District 5 State of Florida, Leesburg, Florida

Jim Yontz
47th District Attorney Office Potter County, Texas
Formerly of New Mexico 7th Judicial District

Tracy Yuhasz
Lieutenant
Escambia County, Florida Sheriff's Office

Angie Zimmerman
Daughter of Rita, Sister of Mandy
Secondary victim of homicide

Frederick T. Zugibe, M.D.
Chief Medical Examiner (Retired), Forensic
  Pathologist
Rockland County, New York, Medical Examiner's
  Office

Introduction

For murder, though it have no tongue, will speak with most miraculous organ.

—Hamlet, Act ii Sc. 2

Like his earlier work, *Practical Homicide Investigation: Tactics, Procedures, and Forensic Techniques, Fourth Edition,* Vernon Geberth's newly revised text of *Sex-Related Homicide and Death Investigation: Practical and Clinical Perspectives, Second Edition,* will continue to be the recognized standard on sex-related crimes and yet another bible for America's detectives. This newly revised second edition is printed in full color with new cases and a format that matches Geberth's indispensible fourth edition of *Practical Homicide Investigation.*

Law enforcement today is confronted with devious and cunning criminals who scour the Internet for their victims, use condoms to avoid leaving their DNA behind, and study the works of other serial murderers to better conceal their crimes. Writing for the practitioner in the trenches, and without the academic psychobabble, Geberth arms today's homicide detectives and those who deal with sexual predators with the ammunition they need to enter into a new millennium crowded with deviant criminal predators.

In this "no excuses" analysis of the psychology of evil, Geberth brings his extensive expertise and knowledge to dissect the thought processes that underlie these sex offenders. By detailing the case histories of specific murders, as well as the practical knowledge he has gleaned from thousands of investigations, Geberth provides critical information that can explain the inexplicable at crime scenes. Once armed with an understanding of the spectrum of behaviors of the sexual predators, a crime scene investigator is much more likely to discern the hidden clues at a scene. To track a murderer, the detective must know and anticipate his target, a feat made simpler by the candid education of what makes the sexual murderer tick.

Since my first visit to a homicide scene over 20 years ago, I have continued to learn about the nuances of murder investigations and the psychology of those who murder. Through much of the past three decades, Vernon Geberth has been a primary source of my developing knowledge. As a friend, counselor, and expert witness, he has helped me build cases and successfully prosecute murderers. For those of us in law enforcement, his published works on homicide investigations are required reading.

For many, murder is an abstraction. Employed by novelists, filmmakers, even video game developers, it is intended to fascinate, intrigue, revile, and excite. Hannibal the Cannibal is as well known in our society as Jack the Ripper. But, for those of us whose careers have included late night visits to gruesome homicide scenes, murder—and murderers—are hardly entertainment. The reality of death at another's hands is the most horrific of crimes. To sit with surviving family members, friends, and loved ones of a murder victim is a gut-wrenching experience. In short, for police officers, prosecutors, and forensic scientists, murder is no game.

Sex-Related Homicide and Death Investigation: Practical and Clinical Perspectives, Second Edition, has been completely revised and the author has added a chapter (13) on the BTK (bind, torture, kill) investigation, in which he participated as an advisor. The entire text takes the reader on a journey through the practical and complex factors involved in the investigation and prosecution of sex-related murder. From the work of addressing the crime scene, harvesting evidence, and recording crucial details on film and from interviews with witnesses to DNA analysis, profiling, the interrogation of suspects, and other homicide investigation strategies, this book becomes a "how-to" explanation for police, prosecutors, and others whose purpose is to understand the complicated and difficult work in which we are engaged.

No police academy, police department, or prosecutor's office should be without this important and informative work. If murder, as Shakespeare suggests, does speak, Geberth has provided all of us with the amplifier through which we will hear its voice.

Jeanine Pirro
Presently, host of the Judge Jeanine Pirro Show, *Warner Brothers*
Former District Attorney and County Court Judge, Westchester County, New York

Human Sexuality and Sexual Deviance
Research and Reality*

1

Human Sexuality

The roots of our human sexuality are found in the reproductive system and the preprogrammed need to procreate that is built into all living organisms. This automatic reproductive process allows for the procreation of species and the continuing life cycles that we have come to know as nature.

Anyone who watches the Discovery channel or other wild life documentaries becomes knowledgeable about the various mating habits of different animal species. Animal research indicates that smell dominates the procreative processes in most mammals. Humans, however, rely on our visual experience to gain most of our knowledge about the external world. Of all our primate sensory systems, our visual system has undergone the most differentiation or specialization (Norden, 2007).

The unique design and abilities of the human being have allowed us to create thousands of cultures, some generating more security and comfort than our ancestors could have imagined.

What Are the Goals/Objectives of the Human Brain?

Before proceeding to discuss human sexual conduct, it is important to define our terms. A. R. Luria, an acknowledged pioneer in brain studies, defined the three main goals and objectives of the healthy human brain:

1. To be alert, awake, aware of reality
2. To collect and store environmental information
3. To monitor and correct our conduct for health and well-being

It is only under optimal waking conditions that man can receive and analyze information, that the necessary selective systems of connections can be called to mind, his activity programmed, and the course of his mental processes checked, his mistakes corrected, and his activity kept to the proper course" (Luria, 1979).

The human brain is arguably hard-wired to enable us to make good decisions that will enhance our well-being and that of our progeny. The healthier the human psyche, the greater is one's grip on the real world (Goleman and Davidson, 1979). Something is very

---

* This chapter, as it relates to the title, was co-authored with Judith Reisman, PhD, president of the Institute for Media Education, who is an author, scientist, researcher, educator, lecturer, and expert witness on matters concerning human sexuality and human behavior.

badly wired in the brain/mind/memory and bodily system of those who engage in violent sex crimes. Why?* As we track the significant increases in violent sex crimes, we must ask what in our soft wiring—environment—is contributing to epidemic levels of barbaric, deviant sexual conduct?

Therefore, although this is not a neuroscience or psychology training manual, I think it is important to view human sexual behavior within the above generally accepted operational definition of the healthy human brain. By laying down that normal hard-wired definition, we can hope to better uncover what is causing the breakdown in sexual normality.

Artificial Human Estrus

What kind of sexual "reality" dominates the mentality of the sex criminal? What information about sex does he (still commonly *he*) collect and store from the "soft" environment? To answer that question, we first turn to the question of animal "estrus."

What is estrus? Reproduction in the animal world centers around periodic estrus (fertility, females "in heat"). Estrus triggers male "courting" behavior (Estes, 1992). During estrus, fertile females will often aggressively roam and solicit their chosen reproductive mate or mates. Studies of the great apes (McGrew et al., 1996) finds complex female primate conduct, hiding, displaying, and deceiving states of estrus (Smuts, 1995) apparently in order to negotiate levels of protection for the female and her progeny.

Psychologist Charles Snowdon and his colleagues address, "social odours in sexual arousal and maintaining pairbonds in biparental and cooperatively breeding primates." Smell acts as a kind of "matchmaker" in the wild, with research finding that the sniff test offers data on "species, kinship, sex, individuality, and reproductive state" (Snowden et al., 2006).

Yet, although animal studies find the sense of smell dominates procreation in animals, as noted previously, vision is the governing sense for primates (Norden, 2007). This is readily measured by men's and even women's arousal to pornography. *Vision has been identified as a major teaching vehicle for animals and humans.* Pictorial pornography increasingly stirs humans to act out autoerotically or seek a sexual partner or partners (Reisman, 2003a). As detailed below, the alpha male animal commonly mates with the fertile females in his harem (while in a few species, we find monogamous alpha male and female "couples"). For that procreative privilege, alpha males must constantly battle other males who would take over their herd (van Schaik and Janson, 2000).

Estes notes that while "courting" of fillies can be gentle (nibbling, mutual grooming), research also finds that stallions that overtake a harem "actually rape the mares, causing those less than six months pregnant to abort. They then quickly reenter estrus, enabling the new owner to implant his own genes." (Estes, 1992), a pattern one also sees in human societies.

Just as interesting "[y]oung stallions that have left their natal harem band and mature stallions that are without a harem group travel together as a bachelor band" acting as future threats to the dominance of alpha males (McDonnell, 1992).

Likewise, dogs and cats breed only when the female is in estrus, giving off a vaginal odor or pheromone that attracts the males. Menstruation is not a "heat" cycle and so human *females never enter estrus. Estrus* is defined as, "The periodic state of sexual

---

* Even the iconoclastic physicist Albert Einstein repeatedly said, "God does not play dice."

excitement in the female of most mammals, *excluding humans*, that immediately precedes ovulation and during which the female is most receptive to mating; heat" (*American Heritage*, 2008) (emphasis added). Estrus is also known as oestrus, "frenzy," "rut," and "mad impulse"(Reisman, 2003a).

Indeed, modern pornographic images openly mimic mammalian female estrus "frenzy," "rut," or "heat" signals (e.g., shinny or "wet" looking nude females with exposed, swollen labia painted "pink," rump up displays to cue rear penetration, female arching of the back, "lordosis"). Pictures of women with "legs spread … mouth open" (Estes, 1992), puffed red lips, pink cheeks, and eye pupil dilation are all pseudo-human estrus mating signals.

Concealed ovulation is part of the human female's psychosexual design (Marlowe, 2004). It is precisely that safety strategy of "concealed ovulation" that is violated by all "external signs" in female "erotic" displays. Any public display of women's intimate, private sexual parts or behavior as artificial estrus endangers her and those of her female class (Reisman, 2003a).

Although often more amorous when fertile, mentally stable human females are not in a "frenzy" that is driven "in heat" to mate with a proximate male or males (in pathology called *nymphomania*). Thus, depictions of human females as "in heat," like racist propaganda, lies by defining female humans as nonhuman.

Anthropologist Jack Weatherford (1986) writes that pornographers create artificial estrus by posing women in "the classic presenting stance of female baboons" while shaving the genitals and applying "makeup to moisten and redden the interior portions of the genitals." He adds that contrary to urban myth, most primitive cultures protect the genitals. Naked women "learn to walk, sit, and lie decorously so that their vulvas never show. Men keep the penis foreskin tied so that the head never protrudes in public," etc.

Evolutionary biologists Randy Thornhill and Craig Palmer (2000) argued that human rape is an evolutionary adaptation as it allows men to pass on their genes to multiple fertile females. However, Thornhill and Palmer's theory ignores the escalating rapes of infertile persons, such as boys, elderly women, and immature girls, as well as oral and anal rape, "sex-related homicides," bestiality, and such. Arguably, such nonprocreative sexual violence requires environmental, soft-wiring explanations (Brown Travis, 2003).

Whether one believes that the absence of human estrus is evolutionary or God-given, survival has largely dictated that a woman limits herself sexually to one mate who has an interest in caring for her and "their" progeny, hopefully for a lifetime. This naturally requires (1) male sexual self-control, (2) female concealed ovulation, (3) chastity until "married" to her selected mate, and (4) fidelity within that marriage. The arrangement assures the male that the offspring he invested in and reared are probably his "seed." Although cultures radically differ, these sexual negotiations create some civil societies that capitalize on the largely human innovations of "monogamy" and "fidelity."

Mammalian Monogamy

Nobel Prize winner David Barash (2001) observes that, unlike birds, only a few of the thousands of mammalian species, such as New World gibbons, tamarins, marmosets, and some rodents, are monogamous. More common, as noted, are mammalian harems, led by an alpha male who must continuously fight other roaming bachelor bands. Moreover, infanticide is common when a new male overtakes a harem (McGrew, 1996). Biologist, David Watts discusses infanticide as "part of evolved male reproductive strategies" in primate behavioral evolution. Watts (2000) summarizes the current studies that the hypothesis of sexual selection:

> ... for the evolution of infanticide by males enjoys widespread empirical support, and infanticide has been fundamentally important for social evolution in primates, some other mammals (notably carnivores and rodents), and birds.

Obviously having one's infants murdered to make way for the newest alpha male on the block might bias human females toward monogamy. Most ethologists tend to view human monogamy as a unique evolutionary advance that reduces such brutal mate competition and child murder, thereby furthering social stability and prosperity. When each man is permitted only one wife, most men get a chance to court, mate, and form families, contributing to democracy, inheritance, and societal well-being. It is telling then that only 19% of human societies, and these largely western, legally require monogamy (Shepher and Reisman, 1985).

Human Beings

Clearly, humans have evolved as a superior species in the hierarchy of creation. However one views evolution or creation, human beings are a unique intellectual, spiritual, and cultural species. The degree of success we exhibit as humans, however, depends, as Luria (1979) warned, on how well we remain awake and aware of reality, and how responsible we are in correcting our mistakes and keeping to the "proper course."

Humans have an exceptional capacity to respond to environmental cues that shape and even direct our imaginations, aspirations, and the course of our sexual conduct. Hence, western culture idealizes and promotes mutual cooperation, participation, and commitment of adult males and females in the highly complicated, ritualized, and beneficial practice of procreative monogamy.

Five Biological Categories or Levels in Establishing Gender

- Chromosomal sex; the chromosomes present in the male sperm and female egg
- The gonads
- The sex hormones
- Sex of the internal reproductive organs
- Sex of the external genitalia

The fetus develops within the womb and emerges at birth a wholly formed male or female. *In utero* and after birth, he or she is subject to a host of outside environmental features. One's family (married, divorced, unwed, and such); how little boys and little girls are treated; their names, clothing, toys, and play are all significant factors, the soft wiring that influences child development.

In some cases, an anomaly may occur in which a child is born with the genitalia of both a male and female. This birth defect is referred to as *hermaphroditism*. In the 1960s, Dr. John Money (deceased) of Johns Hopkins University pioneered surgical removal of an infant's too-small or damaged penis and excavation of a vagina to make little boys into little girls with the reverse procedure for little girls (*Nova*, 2001). Dr. Money did not believe in the genetic normality of male and female, arguing that gender was only a product of "socialization." In 2001, PBS's *Nova* screened "Sex: Unknown." The documentary exposed Money as having faked his data and that these genital surgeries were fatally flawed (*Nova*, 2001). Such infant and child sex change operations are still carried out at some hospitals.

Those still promoting sex change operations insist that before surgery, adults and youths go through extensive therapy and hormone treatments. However, there is no scientific confirmation that (1) such therapies have been successful or (2) that such surgeries are the proper answer to a patient's obvious emotional problems.

Doreen Kimura (2002) notes that since the 1960s it has been fashionable to use scientific discoveries to argue, as Money has, that if one removes a penis, carves a vagina, and gives a boy a girl's name and clothing, so long as his/her parents cooperate, boys can become normal, healthy girls and vice versa. Gender, say such Money-like scholars, is an environmental artifact. In fact, Money used David Reimer—his most infamous boy-to-girl subject—in incestuous child pornography. After proclaiming Money a monster who used him as a sexual guinea pig, David Reimer committed suicide (Colapinto, 2000). At this time, Boston Children's Hospital operates a sex change clinic where prepubescent children get potent hormones to delay puberty to prepare them for subsequent genital surgeries (Kennedy, 2008).

A warning: As is clear from the above, human sexuality studies have long been prone to political and sexual bias. For example, it turns out that John Money advocated adult sex with children in the pedophile magazine *Paidika, The Journal of Paedophilia* (1991), saying:

> If I were to see the case of a boy aged ten or eleven who's intensely erotically attracted toward a man in his twenties or thirties, if the relationship is totally mutual, and the bonding is genuinely totally mutual … then I would not call it pathological in any way.

Dr. Money argued in *The Journal of Paedophilia* that men who have sex with children have a surplus of parental love that is erotic and not disordered, that age of consent should be eliminated, and that if a boy and man had a sex ritual pact and one died, that might be seen as legal since, allegedly, there was consent.* In complete contradiction to hundreds of years of scientific study and cross cultural, historical empirical observation, Money argued that heterosexuality was a superficial, ideological concept.

Sexperts, such as John Money, have controlled the field of human sexuality research and education ever since Alfred C. Kinsey created the field by releasing his now fully discredited studies, *Sexual Behavior in the Human Male* (1948) and *Sexual Behavior in the Human Female* (1953). This will be discussed later but for now, take this as a red flag.

The Brain's Endogenous Reward System

It has been argued that "fantasies" are mere "mental events" produced by the cerebral cortex. Yet, science confirms what has long been obvious to most people. Fantasies must come from the external world in which we are engaged, out of the sights and sounds that

---

* See the last page of Dr. Money's interview in *Paidika: The Journal of Paedophilia*.

surround us. Fantasies or imaginings become our soft wiring. They reflect the culture of our time as well as our own past and our place in that culture. Therefore, "mental events" are a product of the experiences of our environmentally shaped brain/mind/memory and body (Goleman, 1997).

Our limbic system, our endogenous reward system (for internal, naturally produced neurochemical arousal), allows us to interact with the world, to experience the highs and lows of life. It plays an important role in imagining the world. However, the endogenous "high" from making love is easily hijacked by exogenous drugs like cocaine, alcohol, marijuana, and other commercial arousal stimuli.

Sexual stimuli are processed as a brain cocktail of endogenously produced neurochemicals, mimicked by exogenously produced street drugs, e.g., norepinephrine (adrenaline), testosterone steroids, endorphins (morphine-like chemicals), dopamine (the "pleasure" or love drug), serotonin (allegedly related to Ecstasy), oxytocin (the bonding chemical).*

Psychologist M. Douglas Reed (1990) writes of the self-medicating properties triggered by varied forms of arousal related to neurotransmitters, such as "dopamine, norepinephrine, or serotonin, all of which are chemically similar to the main psychedelic drugs, such as LSD" (p. 15). Moreover, our current high-tech visual world allows endogenous drug "highs" to be triggered even outside our conscious awareness. Neurologist Gary Lynch says,

> What we're saying here is that … an event which lasts half a second within five to ten minutes has produced a structural change that is in some ways as profound as the structural changes one sees in [brain] damage … [and] can … leave a trace that will last for years (Moyers and Restak, 1984).

In "Behavioral Addictions: Do They Exist?" *Science* reports that modern brain imaging technologies, such as the functional magnetic resonance imagery (fMRI), find evidence that our endogenous reward system produces long-term changes (neuroadaptation) in our reward circuitry.

> [A]s far as the brain is concerned, a reward's a reward, regardless of whether it comes from a chemical or an experience. And where there's a reward, there's the risk of the vulnerable brain getting trapped in a compulsion. (Holden, 2001)

Highly relevant to the excitement criminals often get from vicious behavior, psychologist Howard Shaffer, the head of Harvard's Division on Addictions says, "neuroadaptation—that is, changes in neural circuitry that help perpetuate the behavior—occurs even in the absence of drug-taking" (Holden, 2001). This is seen in the University of Pennsylvania research that finds sex and cocaine addicts lose their inhibitions and appear to have an "inhibitory circuitry" defect. Vanderbilt University psychiatrist Peter Martin's research on "normal subjects" finds the "brain activity experienced in sexual arousal" of his normal subjects "*looks like that accompanying drug consumption*" (Holden, 2001).

---

* Jefferson scientists show several serotonin-boosting drugs cause changes in some brain cells, http://www.antidepressantsfacts.com/Thomas-Jefferson-University-Hospital.htm (accessed August 20, 2008).

Left versus Right Hemispheric Dominance

Based on the "law of strength," brain researchers agree that the right hemisphere (of image, feeling, and excitation) will dominate over the left hemisphere (of text, cognition, and rationality). Sexual stimuli (by definition, a right hemisphere stimuli) are often said to "act like a drug." It is a "double-edged sword." Brain researchers (such as psychiatrist Langevin and others) are now researching and testifying in courtrooms on brain wiring and hemispheric dominance of sexual predators.*

The current bombardment on developing psyches of sexual stimuli would undermine the activation of inhibitory transmitters and flood the brain/body with excitatory transmitters. Since, "every second, 100 million messages bombard the brain carrying information from the body's senses," neurologist David Galin asks "which hemisphere will … gain control of the shared functions and dominate overt behavior" (Pinchot, 1984) to which neuropsychologist, A. R. Luria replies:

> [P]rocesses of excitation taking place in the waking cortex obey a *law of strength*, according to which every strong (or biologically significant) stimulus evokes a strong response, while every weak stimulus evokes a weak response. (Goleman and Davidson, 1979)

The following comments by UCLA psychologist, Dr. Margaret Kemeny, to commentator Bill Moyers can be applied to sexual exposure at school, at home, and elsewhere.

> Although it seems intangible, anytime we feel anything, anytime we think anything, anytime we imagine anything, there is activity in the brain that is taking place in the body at that time. That activity can then lead to a cascade of changes in the body that have an impact on health … on the immune system. (Reisman, 2003b)

Scientists Claiming Children Are Sexual from Birth

Such a cascade of changes can be seen to flood our children almost from their first breath. After birth, the programming of the child's brain is largely based upon the neonate's parenting. The baby's hypothalamus records its feeding, cleaning, holding, singing, the pleasure center, and nucleus of the child's reality, while the hippocampus records these events, tied to their emotional sensations, as memory. As infants develop, they become aware of the sensations from vocalization as well as the sensations in their fingers, nose, toes, tongue, ears, and later, genitals.

Dr. Money and other sexologists have long cited fetal "erection" to claim that infants are "sexual in the womb" (Reisman, 2003b). However, not only would urine cause such fetal penile erections, so too could the pressure of embryonic fluid on the infant penis. Instead, anthropologist Weatherford (1986) documents how fear and anger cause erection in little boys, and men, citing tumescence and ejaculation as common to the final death agony of a male hanging victim. Similarly, slanted claims for infant sexual arousal are argued for nocturnal vulvae congestion in girls (Fisher et al., 1983).

---

* See, for example, R. Langevin. "Heterosexual and homosexual pedophiles showed verbal deficits and apparent left hemispheric brain dysfunction, whereas bisexual pedophiles did not, but rather showed right hemispheric visual-spatial deficits," in "Studies of brain damage and dysfunction in sex offenders," *Sexual Abuse: A Journal of Research and Treatment*, 2 (2), 103–114, June 1989.

A Pedophile/Pederast Research Bias?

The developmental science of John Money (recall of *The Journal of Paedophilia* fame) stands on the fraudulent child sexuality data created by Alfred C. Kinsey for his *Male* and *Female* sex books in 1948 and 1953. Kinsey's data allegedly proved that infants and toddlers desired and benefited from sex with adults (Reisman, 2003b). This same claim is often echoed by child sexual predators (Reisman, 2003b).

Even Freud did not approve of adult sex with children, assigning children a "latency period." However, Freud's theory of a "latency period" was built on his claim that small children desire sex with their opposite sex parent until about age seven when they become disinterested in sex until roughly adolescence (Masson, 1984). This, too, is ludicrous. While curious about all of the events and objects around them, healthy children commonly remain asexual until the emergence of sexual hormones during adolescence.

Of course, our eroticized environment more and more intrudes on the child's innocence, increasingly triggering premature and gravely harmful sexual conduct among too many children.

We noted earlier in the chapter that vision is our dominant procreative sense. Children face a constant bombardment of sexual imagery and themes played out on television, movies, and kid shows including cartoons in which male and female characters interact in a boy-meets-girl scenario. Moreover, if the children have older siblings, they have real life models to emulate and imitate in their developmental patterns.

MTV presentations provide visual stimulation, which oftentimes has underlying sexual messages. Computers provide additional avenues of information and stimulation as well as other opportunities to "explore" the world of sexual interactions and could very well provide misinformation and/or unwanted communication from perverts who use chat rooms to engage unwitting and curious children in inappropriate dialogue or actions.

Major psychosexual trauma during this period may very well disrupt the normal development and consolidation of the child's sexual health. At puberty, the body normally begins to release sex hormones. The hypothalamus controls biological functions such as hunger, thirst, body temperature, fight-or-flight reactions, fear, anger, and sexual arousal, and synthesizes oxytocin, the "bonding chemical." Depending on the child's early experiences, his or her brain/mind/body remembers nurturing or overly stimulating and exploitive experiences. If he or she has been sexually exploited in some manner, the child may already have experimented with self-punishing behaviors. By puberty, the child's moral and ethical family background will face even more challenges from our highly eroticized commercial, and often the educational, environment, all vying for control of the child's evolving sociosexual template dictating the child's belief and behavior.

The Sociosexual Template

Human Sex Drive

The three components of the human sex drive are biological (instinctive), physiological (functional), and emotional (mental)—all melding into one sociosexual template of sexual values and behavior. The emotional or mental component is the manifestation of the culmination of our psychosexual development. Empirical observation, confirmed by modern research, finds the psychosexual or emotional component the strongest of the three, accounting for approximately 70% of the human sex drive. With emotions controlled by the merger of brain/mind/memory, it follows, so to speak, that "the mind controls the act." Essentially, our sexual sensibilities are conditioned by both nature and nurture, our hard and soft wiring. Sexual behaviors are socially learned. The individual develops a model of who is sexually desirable, what appears sexually satisfying, and what is socially appropriate within the context of his or her environment.

By the time we reach the level of MAN and WOMAN, we see the reproductive process richly infused with elements of behavioral distinctiveness.

- If we are stable, we show selectivity in choosing our mates.
- Sexual behavior is no longer simply instinctive, but is based upon learned patterns of attraction, values, and beliefs.
- Normal human sexual conduct thus to a large extent comes under the control of "higher" neural processes.
- These gains in flexibility and adaptability to environmental triggers may also become problematic as in the emergence of sexual deviance (often called "paraphilia").
- Depending on genetic and environmental influences, individuals will act out differently sexually.

Human Sexual Arousal and Response System

Given a nurturing, asexual upbringing by companionate parents, children appear cross-culturally and historically to emerge as similarly monogamous and faithful adults and nurturing parents. However, it has long been documented that the human psyche is malleable, for good or ill. Even in antiquity, scholars described boys as trained into becoming dominant and narcissistic in all male environments and girls as becoming wholly obedient in all female environments (deMause, 2002).

Everett Rogers' *Diffusion of Innovation* (Kotler, 1967), repeatedly republished in *Marketing Management*, outlines how a controlled media can "stimulate public opinion and miseducate" it. Employed for decades in the advertising and marketing field, Phillip Kotler defined how 2.5% of alpha men and women can sway roughly 13% of eager "early adapters," those who aim to imitate the alphas. This 13% then sway another 34% of the public into trying the new beliefs and behaviors. The process continues until a national majority accept and adapt to the proffered new product, idea, or behavior. Nations have radically, and often, changed what seemed to be solid beliefs or behaviors (such as drug and alcohol use and sexual behaviors) following the "diffusion" of new ideas (Figure 1.1).

Just as marketers normalized smoking and alcohol to largely militant nonsmoking and nondrinking women in the 1920s, so too does deviant sexual conduct become normalized.

> 1927: A sensation is created when George Washington Hill blatantly aims Lucky Strike advertising campaign at women, urging them to "reach for a Lucky instead of a sweet." Smoking initiation rates among adolescent females triple between 1925 and 1935, and Lucky Strike captures 38% of the American market.*

---

* http://www.cigarettes-below-cost.com/history_of_cigarettes.html (accessed April 16, 2008).

The Mechanics of the Shift

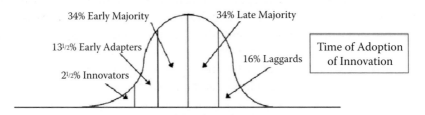

Figure 1.1 Rogers adoption of innovation curve. (From Kotler, P., *Marketing Management*, Prentice Hall, Saddle River, NJ, 1967 (1988).)

One's sociosexual template then combines one's experience, one's familial and religious values, and the values of the wider world. It is surely for this reason that all men tend to lust after whatever color and shape of the female image that the alpha males of society appear to desire. And, our sociosexual templates have been noticeably malleable by the marketing industry (Kotler, 1967). Romantic, erotic, and sexualized relationships will arise from the films and television shows one sees, the images on billboards, in magazines, and especially now, in print and Internet pornography, perhaps somewhat offset by those who have loving, monogamous couples in one's family. The active seeking of sexual partners follows that obvious protocol.

So, as humans are obviously not "sexually" complete at birth, but subject to environmental sexual marketing, the human brain can be induced to sexual deviance. Early sexual abuse of children is a direct pathway to sexual confusion, creating both biological and emotional disorders. The choice of a beloved or of many sexual partners, therefore, is impacted by biology and environment directing people into normal or abnormal relationships. One's sociosexual life is being shaped from childhood to early adulthood based on what one experiences in society.

Since Kinsey's "scale" identified most people as bisexual, sexologists have commonly argued for the normality of bisexuality, homosexuality, and variations thereof, labeling all of these practices one's "Love Map" (Money and Ehrhardt, 1972, Chapter 7; Kotler, 1967). Again, depending on one's environmental experiences, one develops a sociosexual template, a preference for the physiognomy, build, race, age, health, color, temperament, religion, politics, accent, etc., of the ideal mate. A boy and girl who share a sufficiently similar sociosexual template will often fall in love and marry.

As an example, I often ask my class, "If someone crawled into your bed in the middle of the night and proceeded to make love to your spouse, your spouse should know it's not you, right?" It not only gets a laugh, but also brings home the point that I am trying to convey about the uniqueness of our sociosexual template.

Sex in America: A Definitive Study (Michael et al., 1994), which is considered the most extensive research on human sexuality to date, provided a comprehensive and revealing report on sexual behaviors. The findings showed that "sexual behavior is shaped by our social surroundings. We behave the way we do, we even desire what we do, under the strong influence of the particular social groups we belong to. We usually have sex with people who are remarkably like ourselves in age, race or ethnicity, and education."

Alfred Kinsey, whose data had been considered the standard on human sexuality, shocked the nation with his controversial findings and conclusions. In her book, *Kinsey,*

Sex and Fraud, three years before *Sex in America: A Definitive Study* debunked Kinsey's findings, Judith Reisman (1991) exposed Kinsey's frauds and slander of American children, women, and men. "Kinsey's data on homosexuality reported that one man in three had a sexual experience with another man at some time in his life" (Michael et al., 1994). However, Reisman documented that roughly 87% of Kinsey's male population were hand-picked (see the next section). Kinsey's bogus data was the basis for the international belief that "one person in 10 in the United States is gay" (Michael et al., 1994).

Sex in America's nationwide sample of adults found that only 2.8% of men and 1.4% of women identified themselves as gay or bisexual, far below the 1 out of 10 number popularized by the Kinsey Report study (Michael et al., 1994).

Father of the Human Sexuality "Field"

If Trofim Lysenko (1898–1976) ruined Russian genetics for over a century, Alfred Kinsey (1894–1956) ruined Western sexuality for 60 years and still counting. In December 1990, on his popular TV program, talk show host Phil Donahue said:

> Kinsey was to sexuality what Freud was to psychiatry, what Madame Curie was to radiation, what Einstein was to physics. Comes along this woman [Dr. Reisman] saying, Holy cow! E doesn't equal mc[2]. We've based an entire generation of education of sexologists on Kinsey, and Kinsey was a dirty old man. But he wasn't, he wasn't!*

Representing the Kinsey Institute and the Academe, Kinsey's teammate, Clarence Tripp, reassured Donahue, saying:

> [Reisman is] talking about data that came from pedophiles, that [Kinsey] would listen only to pedophiles who were very careful, used stopwatches, knew how to record their thing, did careful surveys. ... they were trained observers.*

The North American Man/Boy Love Association agreed. Of Kinsey's *Sexual Behavior in the Human Male* (1948) and *Female* (1953), the pedophile organization said:

> Gay liberationists in general, and boy-lovers in particular, should know Kinsey's work and hold it dear. ... (I)mplicit in Kinsey is the struggle we fight today.†

So, too, did actress Laura Linney who played Mrs. Kinsey in the Fox Searchlight feature film *Kinsey*.

> Any sort of sexual education that anybody has had in the past 50 years came right from the [Kinsey] Institute. ... So his impact is enormous. ... When Kinsey published that information, he changed our culture [from] preKinsey [to] postKinsey, now (ABC News, 2004).

---

* Phil Donahue transcript #3092, National feed, December 5, 1990.
† D. Tsang, Ed., *The Age Taboo*, 1981, etc.

Decades of teachers embraced the sexuality taught by Kinsey. Yet Kinsey was finally documented as a classical sexual psychopath. According to Dr. Judith Reisman, Kinsey was an obsessive liar, an obsessive masturbator, a pornographer, an adulterer, a bi/homosexual self-torturing sadomasochist, and a pedophile advocate. Although Kinsey's pathologies are now fully documented, his disordered sexual "data" are still taught throughout our schools and courtrooms as fact, and as healthy sexuality.

What Kinsey Said Was American Sexuality in 1948

Kinsey claimed he proved that heterosexual and bi/homosexual behavior, indiscriminate multiple partners, pornography, and oral and anal sodomy are common, normal, and harmless. Based on these and other Kinsey claims, school teachers soon began to teach children about the normality of these acts, allegedly to lower sex crimes, divorce, and venereal disease (VD) because their parents were outdated and "inhibited."

In his 1962 best-seller, *The Structure of Scientific Revolutions,* science historian Thomas Kuhn called scientific elites Orwellian tyrants who "read out of the profession" any dissenter from the dominant scientific paradigm. Kinsey's frauds were the scientific backbone for U.S. Supreme Court rulings on every aspect of sexuality post 1950s. For example, Patten in the 1998 *Santa Clara Law Review* attacked "The Defense of Marriage Act" arguing:

> According to the Kinsey Report, 37% of the male population has had some homosexual experience, 13.7% has had more homosexual than heterosexual experience, and 4% were exclusively homosexual. The numbers were similar, but lower for women. For purposes of this comment, and for ease of calculation, the author uses the common belief that 10% of the population is homosexual.

Father of the Sexual and Bi/Homosexual Revolutions

The *Santa Clara Law Review* typifies over 1,000 law review articles and bad judicial decisions based on Kinsey's lies about "the greatest generation." Kinsey's charts, graphs, and statistics *proved* that mom and dad were sexual hypocrites, *pretending* to be chaste before marriage, monogamous, faithful, and heterosexual. Kinsey's data "proved" the World War II generation *was a culture* of closeted sexual wantons, more than enough to justify the 1960s youthful rebellion called the sexual revolution (Reisman, 2003b).

But it was Kinsey who lied. Kinsey said his "data" reflected roughly 20,000 average Americans (Figure 1.2). Of these, 100% of children were potentially orgasmic, 95% of males violated sex laws (so were legally sex offenders), 65% of men and 50% of women had sex before marriage (fornication), 50% of men and 26% of women were adulterous, 10% to 37% of males were homosexual at some time, 25% of wives and 90% of single pregnant girls aborted. But abortion was criminal and contraception difficult to obtain for singles. So, where were the data showing widespread epidemics of VD, divorce, homicide, suicide, and all the unwanted and the dead babies that always follow in the wake of sexual license?

Our naïve scientists and citizenry never dreamed this allegedly happily married Indiana University zoology professor would spawn a sex science cult to normalize his own sexual perversions. For with all able-bodied men in uniform during most of his study, roughly 87% of Kinsey's "average" guys were military rejects: largely prisoners, bi/homosexuals,

What Did Kinsey Say He "Found"?

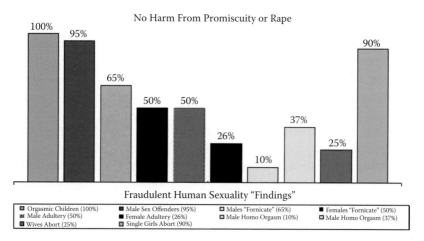

Figure 1.2 The Kinsey Chart. (Courtesy of Judith A. Reisman.)

and pedophiles. So few normal women would talk to Kinsey that he labeled any woman who lived with a man for more than a year, "a wife."

No one even disputed Kinsey's finding that of 4,441 females he said he interviewed there was "only one ... serious injury" from rape or child molestation. But don't believe me or Reisman. Read Kinsey's *Male* volume, Chapter 5, Tables 30 to 34. You judge the father of sex education's record of infant and child "orgasms" (pp. 160–161, Kinsey et al., 1948).

Human Sociosexual Arousal and Response System

The human sociosexual arousal and response system is affected by

- Hormones
- Brain's recall of pleasurable often merged with fearful/hostile arousal
- Fantasies
- Emotions
- Various sensory processes
- Level of intimacy between two people

Sex Is a Sensory Act

Sex is also a sensory act, involving the five senses of touch, sight, sound, taste, and smell. Each of the five senses is employed to a greater or lesser degree to enhance our sexuality.

SIGHT: Men tend to be more aroused by sight than women.
TOUCH: Women tend to be more attuned to touch "magic buttons" primary erogenous zones.
SOUND: Sounds during sexual sharing; sighs, moans groans, pillow talk. Highly variable.

TASTE: Relatively minor role. Some people are able to detect and appreciate tastes.
SMELL: Pheromones, colognes, odors linked to prior sexual situations, especially
during childhood, etc.

For example, according to research, men are more likely to be sexually stimulated
through sight. Sexually explicit, artificial estrus pictures, videotapes, Internet sites, and
movies are designed as arousal for men. Thus, the sight of a scantily clothed attractive
woman would commonly serve as an arousal factor for a normal man. One man thought
he was gay because he felt genitally aroused when he worked in a gym and some men
handed him their sweaty towels to clean. However, at age 16, he had been molested by a
man he trusted—in a sweaty gym.

In a recent study published in the journal *Neuron*, researchers reported that "seeing a
beautiful woman triggers a response in the man's brain similar to what a hungry person
gets from eating or an addict gets from a fix" (*New York Post*, 2001).

According to the article, researchers discovered that feminine beauty affects the man's
brain at a very primal level, and not on some higher, more intellectual plane.

Researchers showed a group of heterosexual men in their mid-twenties pictures of men
and women of varying attractiveness, while measuring the brain's responses through computer imaging. "The beautiful women were found to activate the same 'reward circuits' as
food and cocaine do. The men had a negative reaction to pictures of good looking males,
suggesting they were threatened by them" (*New York Post*, 2001). Hans Brieter, the author
of this study, stated that this research provided evidence that beauty stimulates these primal brain circuits and counters arguments that beauty is nothing more than the product of
society's values. This, of course, can be a bit more nuanced. Some societies, having survived
famine, viewed very fat women as more beautiful than fashionably thin women. Also, neg-
ativity toward various racial and ethnic groups can taint the view of beauty. Moreover,
although "health" is a large determinant of beauty, some eccentric cults have shown a
preference for ghoulish charms. Nonetheless, Brieter provides clear evidence that men are
sexually stimulated through sight or visual input.

Women tend to be more attuned to touch. The sense of touch as it relates to a ten-
der caress might be the stimulus that serves as an arousal factor for a woman. However,
as pornography has become ingrained in society, more and more women appear to be
responding with arousal to such visual stimuli. Moreover, the brain research finds that
excitatory transmitters must be controlled by inhibitory transmitters if one is to create the
"healthy brain," allowing for delayed rewards, which is the basis of Western civilization.
When excitatory transmitters dominate, the individual is likely to develop deviant, harmful forms of sexual acting out. For example, under certain circumstances, male arousal to
scantily clad women devolves into deviant, compulsive acts of voyeurism.

Sexual Deviance

Before Kinsey, sexual behaviors were classified as healthy or unhealthy, normal or abnormal,
moral or immoral, thus good or bad. With the success of the sexology field, we see sexual
behavior often defined only as *acceptable* or *unacceptable*, *appropriate* or *inappropriate*. This
determination is based on statistical, cultural, religious, and subjective considerations.

One's experience of sexuality is often in conflict with one's own values and those of society. Depending on the way the individual relates to his or her environment, one's "deviant" sexual interests will be repressed or released.

Coleman et al. (1984) claim that one's "sex drive is normally sufficiently powerful enough to override all but the most severe social sanctions. Thus, we see variant sexual needs frequently erupting into variant sexual behaviors." However, while it is obvious that the more sexually permissive the society, the more likely "variant sexual" behaviors will erupt, it is just as obvious that millions of people regularly control their sex drive despite the lack of sanctions.

Using the non-Kinsey language here, sexual deviations from the norm can be divided into two groupings. The distinction between the categories is based on social effect. Does the activity infringe on the public welfare? Or is the activity what is often seen as "a victimless sexual variant."

We in law enforcement are often called upon to investigate what are described as nuisance violations or sexual deviations. This can be an important consideration when analyzing *what took place* in a sex-related crime scene.

It also is the basis for an important investigative concept, which we in homicide investigation refer to as the "signature aspect" of the offender.

One's sociosexual template reflects the natural human development of the individual, influenced by biological aspects as well as the environment: nature and nurture.

Sexual deviation occurs when the normal, natural sociosexual template is derailed. Child molesters, rapists, deviant murderers, and others with peculiar erotic interests are an example of this phenomenon. The formulation of sexual deviance can usually be traced to aberrant sociosexual development, soft wiring, for example, either a strict antisexual or licentious prosexual upbringing, sexual abuse of a child by his/her caregivers or others (especially during preadolescence), exposure to sexually stimulating behaviors, and/or inappropriate and pathological family dynamics.

Media analyst Joseph Slade (2001) quotes psychiatrist Robert Stoller from *Perversion the Erotic Form of Hatred* (1986): "A fetish is a story masquerading as an object." That is, the fetish is the psychological history of the person engaging in it. Stoller has documented the "hate" and the "fear" components of most if not all forms of festishistic and deviant sexual conduct (Slade, 2001). Says Stoller (1979):

> Most of what we label sexual excitement is made up of several parts—different experiences of excitement felt simultaneously, co-terminously—only one of which is "erotic." Others are triumph, rage, revenge, fear, anxiety, risk, all condensed into one complex buzz called "sexual excitement."

In *Erotic Preference, Gender Identity, and Aggression in Men*, psychologist Ron Langevin (1985) writes that investigating "erotic preference … can appear hopelessly confusing" and immediately cites Kinsey's alleged finding that "37% of American men have had orgasmic homosexual experience at some time in their lives." Langevin, like most current sex researchers, denies any role of cognitive judgments of normality in researching sexual behavior. He defines sexual abnormality as "unusual," "atypical," or what we call "*sexually anomalous*." Speaking of deviance, he says, is pejorative and has "moral connotations that are inappropriate in scientific investigations" (Langevin, 1985).

Stoller (1979), however, seems to view such researcher resistance to the concept of normality as similarly biased and as undermining the ability to objectively evaluate their observations.

The term *deviant* is used here to identify deviation from the normal, objectively healthier sexual conduct. Sexual deviants are sharply aroused by images, fantasies, and practices that are socially forbidden, disapproved, ridiculed, or penalized. The price may be very severe and/or result in a death penalty. Again, all children are vulnerable to sexual dysfunctions should they be sexually traumatized in some way.

An example of creating sexual deviance is seen in the single mom who needs to have childcare in order to go to work. She meets and maintains a relationship with a male, who is basically unemployed, but is available to provide babysitting services for her while she is at work. His method of entertainment for the child is to watch violent pornographic videotapes. The child is constantly exposed to this visual and audio stimuli. The result is a temporal coupling of erotic stimulation and violence that the child incorporates into his sociosexual template as sexual "normality."

The seeds of sexual perversion are planted early on in the psyche of the sex offender. However, until the recent advent of the ubiquitous Internet, sexual perversions had not generally manifested themselves until the offenders reached puberty. The seed is nurtured through fantasy, masturbatory activities that reinforce and nourish the particular deviant imagery, as well, sometimes, as situational "acting out" of these perversions with a willing or a coerced partner. By the time an offender actually perpetrates a clear criminal assault, the sexual theme of that assault, as well as the activities he engages in with his victim, has been orchestrated many times over in the mind of that particular offender. The sexual event is the culmination of an offender's psychosocial and psychosexual conditioning and development, which includes environmental and biological attributes.

We, as a society, have always had perversions and perverts who engage in outrageous sexual behaviors. They were considered perverts and "weird" and generally were shunned by society. Presently, in this new "kinder and gentler" and overly tolerant society, many sexual perversions heretofore considered shameful and despicable are now looked upon as legitimate expressions of one's sexuality. According to some of the alleged "experts," there is no right or wrong anymore. Instead, we hear the words *preference* and *choice*. We don't hear about responsibility. We, as a society, subject our children and ourselves to the "unacceptable" in order to satisfy the very vocal "politically correct police," as well as the sexual deviates who have found support instead of ostracism. Of course, there are going to be more sexual deviations. Add to this dynamic the capability of the Internet and one can readily understand why we are encountering the unacceptable and the increasingly cruel on a daily basis.

From my perspective as a professional homicide expert, I see the tragic results of this tolerance in the crime scenes. Let me provide you with an example of how the unacceptable sexual deviance weaves its way into society. Suppose we have a person who has a specific deviance. It doesn't really matter what specific deviance. The individual is considered "weird" or perverted and generally is not accepted by the majority. So, he goes online and looks for subjects of his interest. He then goes into the chat rooms and meets others just like himself. So, the co-prophiliac (nice word for someone attracted to feces) is able to validate his abnormal perversion by discovering that there others "just like him" and what he does is "perfectly normal." Likewise, an offender who is a sexual sadist and into heavy duty sadomasochism (S&M) is able to access a neverending quantity of this material on the Internet. Oftentimes these materials fuel his fantasies of inflicting pain and suffering on his victim. When he does act out against a victim, he could very well have rehearsed for this event and validated his perversion through downloading and engaging in chat room talk with others sharing similar interests. There have been a number of sex-related homicide cases directly linked to the Internet.

Serial killer Maury Travis, suspected of killing at least 11 and possibly almost 20 women, reportedly downloaded information from a Web site that catered to depictions of torture and slavery of women. St. Louis police seized numerous items from the suspect's home. They seized his computer; ligatures, ropes, and belts spattered with what appeared to be blood; women's underwear and wigs; and videotapes. The videotape showed one woman being killed and six others being tortured (see Chapter 2 and Chapter 10).

According to Coleman et al. (1984), the sexual deviations are described as "acts which involve nonconsent or assault, and those acts, which can be described as problematic from the standpoint of the welfare of society." The sexual deviations include, but are not limited to

Voyeurism	Exhibitionism	Pedophilia
Sexual Sadism	Incest and Rape	Masochism

The term *paraphilia* (*para* = deviance; *philia* = attraction) is an attraction to deviance. "Any of a group of psychosexual disorders characterized by sexual fantasies, feelings, or activities involving a nonhuman object, a nonconsenting partner, such as a child, or pain or humiliation of oneself or one's partner. Also called *sexual deviation*" (*American Heritage Medical Dictionary*, 2008). The paraphilias are a group of persistent sexual arousal patterns in which unusual objects, rituals, or situations are required for full sexual satisfaction to occur.

Full sexual satisfaction (orgasm) is, however, a misnomer for most sexual deviants. Such an orgasm is by definition NOT necessarily sexual, but sadosexual, for shame, humiliation, pain, and such are commonly required by the deviant in order to attain the orgasm normal people experience when making love.

Neuroscientist Daniel Goleman (1984) explains, "… in crucial matters of the heart—and most especially in emotional emergencies," the neocortex "can be said to defer to the limbic system." Neuroscientist Jack Fincher (1984) adds that the limbic structures house "memory, pleasure, pain, and the brain's ability to balance the extremes of emotion" that obey "the law of strength" and dominate the limbic system in "sexual desire … memory, pleasure, pain … its seat of thought."

"The [c]onnections between the limbic system and the cerebrum [that] permit an interplay between reason and emotion [are] easily upset" (Fincher, 1984).

Psychologist M. Douglas Reed (1990) discussed the addictive nature of varied kinds of arousal, noting that "any activity that produces salient alterations in mood (which are always accompanied by changes in neurotransmission) can lead to compulsion, loss of control, and progressively disturbed functioning."

According to the APA's *Diagnostic and Statistical Manual*, 4th ed. (*DSM-IV-TR*), there are nine paraphilias: fetishism, frotteurism, voyeurism, exhibitionism, pedophilia, transvestic fetishism, sexual masochism, sexual sadism, and paraphilia not otherwise specified (American Psychiataric Association, 2000).

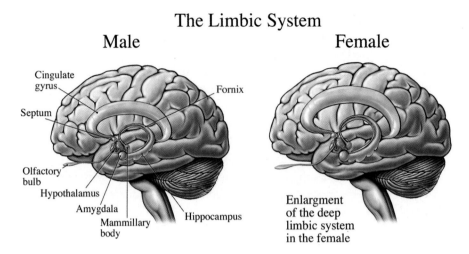

Figure 1.3 The human brain: male and female. (Courtesy of Medical Legal Art, copyright 2009. http:/www.doereport.com)

The Paraphilias

Fetishism (302.81)

Fetishism involves the use of nonliving objects (the fetish) as a source for sexual arousal. Among the more common items are women's panties or lingerie. Other objects of fetishistic lust are bras, stockings, and high heel shoes. The author has seen several cases in which an offender has committed the crime of burglary in order to secure a woman's underwear. The fetish burglar is an extremely dangerous offender and many times the fetish burglary may be the prelude to a sexual assault or a lust murder. In one such case, an offender broke into the home of a single woman and proceeded to steal all of her underwear both clean and soiled. During the time the offender was in her house, he wore one of her bathing suits and tried on some of her undergarments. He also masturbated on the victim's panties. This type of behavior in which an offender involves himself with the personal items of the victim and masturbates on these personal items is an example of symbolically violating the victim.

The woman reported the offense and was planning on selling her house and moving away. However, prior to her finding a buyer, the offender returned in the middle of the night while the victim was sleeping. He had returned to continue his fetish fantasy and be in her "presence" while he masturbated. She suddenly awoke and in a "blitz attack" the offender sexually assaulted and killed the woman. While in the woman's home, he masturbated on the undergarments, he urinated and defecated at the scene, and "played" with the woman's body.

In another brutal case, an offender appeared at the victim's beauty parlor at closing time. At gunpoint, he directed the woman to sit in one of the beauty parlor chairs and tied her up with four blue straps. What he didn't realize was that the victim had triggered a silent alarm, which alerted the police. As he tied her up, he proceeded to give her instructions as if he was following a script. He suddenly began to cut the woman's hair and shave her head. When hostage negotiators finally talked him into releasing his victim and surrendering, the hysterical woman reported what he had done to her. The police initially thought they were responding to an armed robbery. The robbery was only secondary. His motive was to

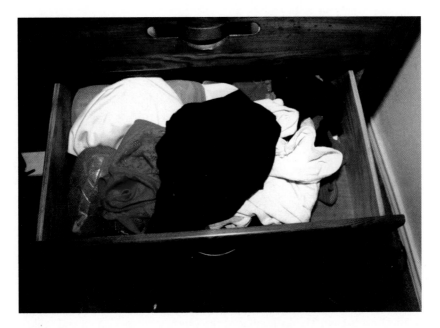

Figure 1.4 Drawers. The subject had collected a number of women's panties. Many of them were too small for him to wear and may have come from his ex-wife or girlfriends. (Photo courtesy of Retired Lieutenant Mark Fritts, Hobbs, New Mexico, Police Department.)

act out a sexual fantasy in which he would shave the head of his victim to make her submissive. After the authorities secured a search warrant, they went to his home where they recovered fantasy stories dealing with the forcible cutting and shaving of women's heads. Some pornography magazines depict women with shaved heads being raped and/or sexually abused. In addition, the subject had surveillance photographs of women with long hair and a plastic bag filled with human hair. It turned out that the suspect was a serial offender who had done this to others as a way of obtaining sexual satisfaction (Figure 1.4).

Partialism, which is an extension of the paraphilia fetishism, occurs when an individual exclusively focuses on a specific portion of the human body, a fetish for a certain portion of the human anatomy, e.g., breasts, penis, foot (Figure 1.5).

Investigatively speaking, any fetish burglary case must be treated as a very serious offense. The author cannot state that all fetish burglars will become rapists or lust murderers. However, I can emphatically state that in ALL of the lust murders that I have investigated and/or consulted on, the offender had a history of fetishistic activities.

In *Practical Homicide Investigation*®, I stress that investigators look at these types of cases as a prelude to murder and sexual assault. Any person willing to commit the felony crime of burglary to obtain a pair of panties or some other fetishistic nonliving object should certainly be considered dangerous, especially when "targeting" a specific victim.

Frotteurism (302.89)

Frotteurism involves touching and rubbing against a nonconsenting person. The frotteur obtains sexual pleasure by rubbing his genitals on the body, buttocks, or leg of an unsuspecting person or he may fondle a woman's breast or genitalia. This behavior usually occurs in crowded places, where there are opportunities to bump into someone seemingly as an accident or misstep. The usual places frequented by these types of offenders are on

Figure 1.5 Victim's Breast. The killer placed the mother's breast on an end table next to the body of her daughter whom he had killed. (Photo courtesy of Chief Criminal Deputy Robin Wagg, Douglas County, Washington, Sheriff's Department.)

public transportation facilities, at state fairs, on busy city sidewalks, on elevators, at street fairs, in crowded movie theaters, at concerts, at public events, etc., where the offender can make a quick escape.

The author remembers one specifically disgusting series of events in which an offender used the New York City subway system as his "playground." There were a series of incidents reported by female complainants to the New York City authorities. The women complained about being "bumped" or jostled by a man as the train came into the station. The man would "bump" into the women's buttocks or legs or his hand would brush their genitals. As the train stopped, the man would feign slipping during which time he would grab their breasts or touch them on the genitals. Many of the women reported that when they left the train they found ejaculate on their dresses or coats.

The suspect was caught during an undercover operation. A female decoy under the protection of a back-up team rode the subway train in the area of complaint during the times of the incidents. The suspect was arrested as he accosted the decoy. When he was arrested, he had his penis exposed. The *DSM-IV-TR* indicates that this deviance begins at adolescence and most acts occur when the person is 15 to 25 years of age. However, many of the offenders, who "work the crowds" in public places are much older than 25 and have a history of sexual offenses involving paraphiliac activities.

Voyeurism (302.82)

Voyeurism involves the repetitive looking at unsuspecting people who are either naked, in the act of disrobing, or engaging in sexual activity. The act of looking is for the purpose of achieving sexual excitement. The individual who engages in this activity is commonly referred to as a Peeping Tom. Orgasm is usually produced through masturbation. The individual who engages in this activity may have the fantasy of actually engaging in sexual activities with his victim. In some instances, the voyeur goes "high tech" and secretes a

Figure 1.6 High-tech voyeur. This individual had managed to hide a minicamera in a ladies' dressing room to "capture" them on film. He would then upload them to the Internet and compare voyeurism locations with others he met on the "net."

hidden camera in a women's dressing room to record unsuspecting young women in the process of disrobing (Figure 1.6). The author has consulted on cases in which sexual offenders had mapped out their entire neighborhood with times and locations where the best viewing would take place. In major cities where there are large apartment buildings, voyeurs place telescopes in their windows to watch their unsuspecting female neighbors as they undress, shower, or engage in sexual activities. Some voyeurs now exchange information about viewing locations on the Internet in chat rooms. Many voyeurs become rapists and lust murderers, especially voyeurs who target a specific victim for viewing. In fact, voyeurism is basically an illegal extension of legal pornography use or attendance at stripper bars, etc., in which the voyeur watches naked women, sometimes even publicly masturbating.

In one case on which the author consulted, the victim was an attractive, middle-aged, single woman who lived alone in a rural area of Washington State. The suspect, who was a fetish burglar, discovered that he could watch the victim in her house from an isolated location in the woods. He watched her for a period of time, then broke into her house to steal her panties. She chased him off and made a police report. The police made an attempt to find him. However, before they could find him, he went back to the victim's home and waited for her to return. He killed her and then acted out his most perverse fantasies with her body. The suspect cut the crotch of the victim's pants open. All of her garments were cut from her body. He removed her bra, pants, panties, and shoes from her body. The suspect made multiple 1-900 sex line phone calls throughout the day and night from the victim's residence totaling $643. He also brought pornographic magazines into the scene and a list of 1-900 numbers, which were matched to his calls from the victim's residence by detectives. He engaged in sadistic sexual activities with the victim's body, which included insertion of a saltshaker into her vagina as well as stabbing into her chest and breasts.

Sexologists had long dismissed voyeurs and all other fetishists as harmless, shy fellows who seldom if ever were dangerous. However, the fact is that, investigatively speaking, complaints about voyeurism must be treated as very serious offenses. The author cannot state that all voyeurs will become rapists or lust murderers; however, I can emphatically state that, in *all* of the lust murders that I have investigated and/or consulted on, the offender had a history of voyeurism activities.

In *Practical Homicide Investigation*, I stress that investigators look at these types of cases as preludes to murder and sexual assault. Persons who repeatedly engage in voyeurism should certainly be considered dangerous, especially when they "target" a specific victim.

Exhibitionism (302.4)

Exposing the genitals to an unsuspecting stranger for the purposes of obtaining sexual excitement is exhibitionism. The individual who exposes himself to an unsuspecting stranger sometimes masturbates while exposing the genitals. The exhibitionist might fantasize that the observer becomes aroused and may obtain satisfaction by shocking or frightening the person. According to *DSM-IV-TR*, there is generally no attempt at further sexual activity with the observer. However, the author has investigated a number of exhibition incidents, which started out with the offender exposing himself to a woman and then suddenly attacking or assaulting her. I have investigated cases where exhibitionists hang around schools in parked cars during lunch hours or at dismissal times. Sometimes an offender will request directions from a passerby and, when the person approaches the car, the offender suddenly exposes himself. By the time the victim regains composure, the offender has driven off. The police are able to obtain only a general description of the offender and his vehicle. The author has one particular case on videotape where an offender was exposing himself to the passengers on an express bus service at the scheduled bus stop. The authorities set up a surveillance camera at the bus stop and caught the perpetrator exposing himself from the window of his home.

In fact, exhibitionism, like voyeurism, is basically an illegal extension of legal pornographic displays or stripper performances, etc., in which the exhibitionist is often a naked woman, who may even publicly masturbate for observers. Again, this is a highly risky behavior for the displaying woman, and is clearly emotionally disordered behavior by both women who so display (as though in "heat," in estrus) and by their observers.

Pedophilia (302.2)

Pedophilia involves sexual activity with a prepubescent child. (generally aged 13 or younger). Although the law has determined since the mid-1950s that a pedophile must be 16 years or older and at least 5 years older than the child victim, any lust for a weak and vulnerable child, in fact, is deviant and dangerous, despite the similarity in ages. Again, although sexperts have argued that children are largely unharmed by same age sexual abuse, the data clearly indicate harm from any sexual abuse, despite the age of the offender.

Some pedophiles prefer males, others females; some are aroused by both males and females. There are more reports of pedophilia involving females than males. Individuals

1948 Kinsey to 1955 Model Penal Code Impact On Law

Laws	1948	Post 1955
Age of Consent	16, 18, 21 years old	Possible 12 to 18
Rape	Death in 18, Life in 22 States	6 months to 4 years
Statutory Rape	Death in 16 States	0 months to 2 years
Seduction	Prison and/or Fines	Legal (consent)
Adultery	Prison and/or Fines	Decriminalized
Divorce	Fault: Alimony, estate	No Fault or Alimony
Child Custody	Mother assuming a "fit" mother	Largely Financially based

Figure 1.7 Penal code impact. (Photo courtesy of Judith A. Reisman.)

may limit their activities to their own children, stepchildren, or relatives. Others may victimize children outside their families.

The definition of *pedophilia* has shifted over the years following Kinsey's claim that children are sexual from birth. Pre-Kinsey (1948) and the use of his junk science to create the American Law Institute Model Penal Code (1955), the age of consent was largely 18 with a few states at 16 and one at age 21 (Jeffrey, 2004). Even today, the dictionary definition of pedophilia ("sexual desire in an adult for a child") corresponds with the legal definition of a "child" as aged 18 or younger (Figure 1.7).

Although it was recognized that girls might marry quite young in some states, an adult having nonmarital sex with a girl under 18 tended to be viewed as perverse and often illegal ("jail bait"). However, the American Psychiatric Association (APA), following the Kinsey mold, redefined "child" for the purposes of pedophilia as "13 years or younger." In fact, in 1950, GAP (the Group for the Advancement of Psychiatry) worked with the 1955 American Law Institute Model Penal Code to urge legislators to reduce all sex crime penalties. As to pedophilia, stating that "Kinsey's data were the points by which we steered" (Allyn, 1996), GAP argued, "Full responsibility for sexuality" should begin at the age of 7 (Committee on Forensic Psychiatry, 1950).

Having relied on Kinsey's fraudulent data* for their 1976 decision to remove homosexuality as sexually deviant, by 1995, the *APA Diagnostic and Statistical Manual IV* also removed "pedophilia" from their "disordered" classification. The APA claimed that while adult sex with children is illegal, the lust and the acts are normal, unless one feels guilty.† In 2000, following public outrage, this definition was revised. The *DSM-IV-TR* (2000) now states that one is a pedophile if one has "acted on these sexual urges. ..." with a child *under age 13*. As noted above, the APA also requires that one be 16 years of age to qualify

---

* See Socarides: http://www.narth.com/docs/annals.html.
† See The Problem of Pedophilia, http://www.narth.com/docs/pedophNEW.html. (The APA did not claim sex with children was a good thing, just that it was not abnormal.)

as a sexual deviant, a pedophile. Additionally, a 19 year old who has "ongoing" sex with a 12-year-old child is not a pedophile based on the APA definition. The APA would consider this conduct "normal" unless the predator, that is, the offender, is distressed.*

This normalization of sex with children over 13 is hardly acceptable, despite the APA *DSM*. It is argued here that the APA definition of abnormality (those who engage in sexual activities with prepubescent children who are usually 13 years or younger) ignores the power and control dynamics of any elder adult engaged in sex with anyone under age 18. Moreover, also as noted above, the APA allows for a kind of "peer sex play" defense claiming a victim has to be 5 years younger than her or his teenage offender. That the cognitive, "mature" brain is undeveloped until one is in his/her twenties further implicates the salacious, sexualized mass media in sexual abuse in general and that of children in particular.

Male pedophiles who lust after boys are actually *pederasts*, homosexual child molesters. Those who lust after both boys and girls are commonly seen as pedophiles. Men who lust after girls are also called pedophiles, as are women who lust after girls. Although more males molest girls, the number of homosexual pederasts molesting boys is significantly higher within that group. Homosexual authors Jay and Young's finding of 50 to 73% of homosexual males self-reporting sex with boys (Magnuson, 1985) is much higher than the one in six or seven boys that child protection data estimate as victimized by bi/homosexual men.

Again, some predators violate only their own children, stepchildren, or relatives. Others may also victimize children outside their families. Child molester activities include showing the child pornography as a "grooming" technique, undressing and looking at a child's body, exposing themselves to children, masturbating in the presence of a child, touching and fondling the child, or photographing children in a sexual manner. Other activities involve fellatio on a little boy or cunnilingus on a little girl.

The offender might penetrate the little boy's anus and/or the little girl's vagina, mouth, or anus with his fingers, objects, or penis.

Pedophiles often place themselves in positions of trust to gain access to children. They might be priests, ministers, high school or primary grade coaches, teachers, etc. Sadly, persons whom society trusts very easily gain access to children and the harm is done before anyone even realizes what is going on. The author had a case in which a high school teacher was supposedly giving extra credit classes to his "special" students, whom he invited to his apartment after school. One of the parents who became suspicious questioned her child and found out that these extra classes were actually sex parties involving the male teacher and his male students. This pederast cultivated his victims by first showing them explicit heterosexual porno videos and then introducing alcohol to the parties. He then suggested sadistic activities ("bondage") using the elastic bands from men's underwear and introduced his "students" to homosexual magazines and group masturbation, which soon escalated to homosexual activities, such as fellatio and inserting of dildos into the anal cavities.

Other pedophiles have actually dated and married women, whose children were the focus of their desire. In homicide cases, pedophiles have abducted and murdered male and female children in their lust for this arousal. Male homosexual serial killers, such as John Wayne Gacy, who targeted teenage boys, are examples of this phenomenon. It should be mentioned, again, that following Kinsey, sexologists argued that children were largely

---

* The 1995 American Psychiatric Association (APA) *DSM IV* (*Diagnostic and Statistical Manual IV*) did not even define sex with a child as sexually deviant—the act is revised in the 2000 *DSM-IV-TR*, p. 572.

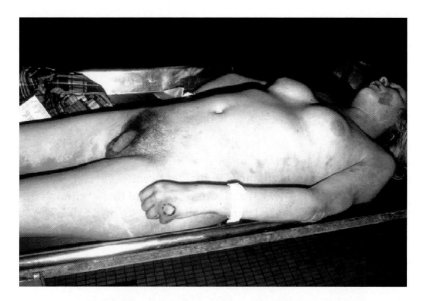

Figure 1.8 Transgendered victim. This man, who purported to be a female prostitute was killed by the "John" when he realized he was with another man.

unharmed by pederast or pedophile assaults. Judges, juries, teachers, psychologists, psychiatrists, and other professionals were trained instead to believe that children were more traumatized by the angry responses to their offender by parents, teachers, police, and other officials than by their sexual abuse.

Transvestic Fetishism (302.3)

Transvestic fetishism involves cross-dressing usually by a heterosexual male in women's attire. In many or most cases, sexual arousal is produced by the accompanying thought or image of the person as a female. Occasionally, parents initiate this behavior by cross-dressing their boy child in dainty girl's clothes because they think it is "cute" or because they wanted a little girl rather than a boy. Often the case histories of men who engage in transvestism reveal that as boys they were punished by being forced to dress in girl's clothes (Stoller, 1979). This attempt to punish by humiliation is sometimes the first step toward transvestism (Crooks and Baur, 1990).

This particular paraphilia ranges from solitary wearing of female clothing to an extensive involvement in a transvestite subculture. Some individuals may masturbate while cross-dressed and imagine themselves as both the male subject and the female object of his sexual fantasy. Other individuals dress up as females and then interact with the general population. Transvestite hookers are an example of this phenomenon. Male prostitutes, dressed as women, who actively solicit other men for prostitution can quickly become victims of homicide when and if a male customer realizes that he is with a man and not a woman (Figure 1.8 and Figure 1.9).

An extension of this paraphilia is *gender dysphoria* or *transexualism*, which is a persistent wish to be rid of one's own genitals and live as the opposite sex.

Sexual Masochism (302.83)

This paraphiliac focus involves the act of obtaining sexual pleasure from being humiliated, beaten, or otherwise made to suffer. These acts may involve physical as well as psychological suffering. The use of physical restraint, blindfolding, spanking, whipping, electrical

Figure 1.9 Transvestite hooker. Note the mesh penis restraint.

shocks, verbal and sexual humiliation are employed by some individuals to obtain sexual arousal (Figure 1.10).

Some masochists enjoy being urinated or defecated on, or being forced to cross-dress for its humiliating associations. The author has one case in file in which a homosexual male was dressed as a woman and was bound and beaten by his male partner. Other masochists engage in self-mutilation during which they bind themselves, stick themselves with pins, or shock themselves with electricity. Another dangerous form of sexual masochism,

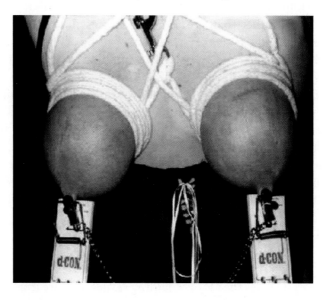

Figure 1.10 Female masochist. Note the ropes and bondage coupled with the clamps on the nipples to cause pain.

oftentimes referred to as autoeroticism or sexual asphyxia, involves sexual arousal by oxygen deprivation obtained by means of chest compression, noose, ligature, plastic bag, mask, or chemicals substances to displace oxygen to the brain. Oxygen-depriving activities, along with atypical masochistic practices, are extremely dangerous. Equipment malfunction, errors in the placement of the noose or ligature, or other mistakes, usually involving misjudgment, result in accidental deaths (see Chapter 4, "Sexual Asphyxia").

Female masochists may enjoy being subjugated and engage in masochistic fantasies that usually involve being raped while being held or bound by others so that there is no possibility of escape. The author has cases in file in which females engage in sadomasochistic activities with other women and men during which time they are nude and bound or are being whipped, along with genital manipulation, breast binding, and/or nipple piercing. Other examples of masochism are being forced to crawl nude with a dog collar and being beaten on the buttocks with a paddle. Or, in a masochistic lesbian scenario, one woman seemingly "forces" another woman to perform cunnilingus on her as she manipulates the victim's genitalia and places clamps on the victim's nipples. All of these scenes are found modeled in both "soft" and "hard" pornography.

It is always important to ascertain whether the female in these cases is behaving in this abnormal manner voluntarily and that she is not a victim of rape or sexual assault. Additionally, an investigative consideration should be given to whether the victim may have been drugged or otherwise rendered compliant through victimization (Figure 1.11 and Figure 1.12).

The author has another case in file in which a male masochist is videotaped during a "discipline" session involving a female dominatrix and her lesbian partner named Rapture. The dominatrix, who calls her herself Mistress Michelle, refers to the subject as Slave Joe. The subject, who is wearing a diaper, is instructed to lick the boots of the "mistress" and lick the feet of her lesbian partner. He then is instructed to behave like a horse and the "mistress" then rides him after whipping him on the buttocks as he neighs and performs as a horse.

Figure 1.11 Male masochist. This individual would gain sexual satisfaction through inflicting injuries to his penis. Note the nails through the foreskin and the incision through the urethra.

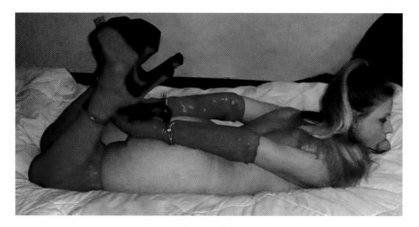

Figure 1.12 Fantasy bondage. Note the bright red vinyl, the super high heel boots and long gloves and the ball gag. This is a fantasy scenario meant to sexually arouse.

When she talks to him, he is required to answer: "Yes, Mistress "or "No, Mistress." The subject is then instructed to remove the diaper and bend over as the dominatrix paddles his buttocks. The Mistress then states that she feels like "peeing." She instructs Slave Joe to drink her urine as she pees into his mouth. She then demands that he lick her clean including her rectum, as she demands, "Lick my ass clean." The subject is then restrained in a leather straight jacket and a leather discipline mask is placed over his head.

During this $40 an hour session, the subject is hung nude from a harness. He has a butt plug in his anal cavity and he is bound and restrained as the dominatrix pierces his nipples and places a clamp on the man's penis. The dominatrix uses a cattle prod on Slave Joe's penis and then she brands him on the buttocks with a cattle branding iron.

Throughout the session, Mistress Michelle uses degrading language to Slave Joe as part of the psychological aspects of sexual masochism.

During the session, the Mistress drips hot wax on his penis. At the conclusion of the session, the dominatrix suddenly takes alcohol and sprays the man's penis. She then takes the candle and ignites the alcohol on the penis causing it to flare up. The "slave" suddenly tries to grab his penis to extinguish the fire that has ignited his pubic hair and caused him to receive burn injuries. However, he continues to participate in these self-degrading activities despite the injuries and abuse he has received.

Sexual masochism is usually chronic, and the person tends to repeat the same masochistic act. Some individuals with sexual masochism may engage in masochistic acts for many years without increasing the potential injuriousness of their acts. Others, however, increase the severity of the masochistic acts over time or during periods of stress, which may eventually result in injury or even death.

Sexual Sadism (302.84)

Sexual sadism involves acts in which the individual derives sexual excitement from the psychological or physical suffering of another, which includes humiliation of the victim. Some individuals with this deviance are bothered by their sadistic fantasies. Others act on the sadistic sexual urges with a consenting partner who may be a sexual masochist and willingly suffers pain or humiliation. Offenders, who are sexual sadists act on their sadistic sexual urges with nonconsenting victims. It is the suffering of the victim that is sexually arousing. Sadistic fantasies or acts may involve activities that indicate the dominance of

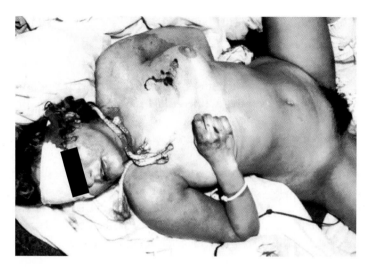

Figure 1.13 Reality versus fantasy. This 22-year-old college coed became the victim of an offender who had stalked her. He came into her apartment in the middle of the night, bound her and placed a blindfold over her eyes. He killed her by stabbing her in her breasts and chest. He did not complete the sexual assault and instead "posed" his victim's body and went back to his original voyeur location and then masturbated as he viewed his victim's body combining his fantasy with reality. (Photo courtesy of Retired Investigator Tom Jordan, State College, Pennsylvania, Police Department.)

the person over the victim, e.g., forcing the victim to crawl or keeping the victim in a cage as in the case depicted in *The Perfect Victim* (McGuire and Norton, 1988). This case involved Cameron Hooker and his wife, Janice. Cameron Hooker's fantasy was to dominate and torture nude women who were bound and helpless. His fantasies were fueled by an extensive collection of hard-core pornography, which featured bondage, leather, and handcuffs and whips. The use of sadism themes, even in early "soft" pornography has been well established in scientific studies (Reisman, 1989). The abduction and enslavement of the young woman named Colleen was the culmination of years of fantasy, experimentation, and planning. Ironically, this same book, *The Perfect Victim,* was used as a reference by David Parker Ray (see Chapter 12) to control and manipulate his sex slaves, whom he would sexually torture and eventually kill.

Cameron Hooker's depravity increased. He placed a heat lamp next to Colleen's skin as she was hanging and watched her writhe in pain as it burned. He touched her with live electrical wires. He hung her upside-down and bound in strange ways. He made her orally copulate him. He strangled her into unconsciousness and subjected her to just about anything he could imagine.

The activities of sexual sadists involve restraint, blindfolding, paddling, spanking, whipping, pinching, beating, burning, electrical shocks, rape, cutting, stabbing, strangulation, torture, mutilation, and/or killing. An example of this type of thinking is found in the following statements of a sexual sadist (Figure 1.13).

I ordered her into the bedroom, stripped her nude, blindfolded her, and taped her hands and feet. I forced her on her knees and made her suck my dick and I even fucked her mouth. She looked so incredible, nude and tied helplessly, forced to suck my dick like that. I put her in bed and touched and licked her helpless body and then I fucked her.

> A perfect ass, legs, and feet made her quite a prize. She sucked me and I played with her for an hour or so. Made her stand outside the van so I could run my hands up and down her body. Played with her some more. …

One of Kinsey's pedophile contributors described his torture of small children for Kinsey's data in a similar way, finally revealed in *Kinsey's Paedophiles,* a British documentary (Tate, 1998).

Sexual sadists may create elaborate torture chambers, such as the Sex Slave case that I reference later in the text. David Parker Ray used a gynecology chair to sexually torture his slaves in a 15′ × 25′ cargo trailer that he called the "Toy Box." This offender, whose activities are described in Chapter 12, was the ultimate psychopathic sexual sadist. He followed many of the techniques of Cameron Hooker and took them to the next level by killing at least 30 young women. He even built and designed a head box for transporting slaves based on what he had read in *The Perfect Victim.* David Ray Parker described it as a "most efficient method for silencing a noisy woman and best for transport or long-time silencing. It is claustrophobic and is good for deprivation."

He even devised an "introductory tape" for his slaves in which he explained in vivid detail what was going to happen to them. The following excerpt is an example of the instructions he provided:

> I concentrate on the sensitive parts of the body: the breasts, nipples, and sex organs. The whole area down between your legs; your thighs, vagina lips, clit, and the hole itself. Believe me, there are dozens of ways to induce pain.

Most serial killers are psychopathic sexual sadists, who enjoy the dominance and torture of their victims. Richard Cottingham, who was a sexual psychopath with an admitted attraction to sadomasochistic activities, was married and had two girlfriends. He also frequented prostitutes; some of whom he killed. He killed five victims, who had been methodically tortured and mutilated (Figure 1.14).

Jeffrey Dahmer was also a sexual sadist. He would invite his, usually young, victims to his apartment. He would drug them and then handcuff them in the event that they regained consciousness. He would then strangle them to death and engage in necrophilia with their bodies.

In these cases, as well as others the author references, there was evidence that sadistic sexual fantasies were likely to have been present in the childhood histories of these offenders. According to the *DSM-IV*, the age at onset of sadistic activities is variable, but is commonly by early adulthood. There may have been symbolic fantasy and acts of sexual sadism, such as the cutting up female undergarments, cutting up photos, placing pins in dolls, or defecating or urinating in their crime scenes.

Sexual sadism is usually a chronic condition, and practiced with nonconsenting partners it is criminal, and the activity is likely to be repeated until the person with sexual sadism is apprehended. According to the *DSM-IV-TR*, "Some individuals with sexual sadism may engage in sadistic acts for many years without a need to increase the potential for inflicting serious physical damage. Usually, however, the severity of the sadistic acts increases over time. When sexual sadism is severe, and especially when it is associated with antisocial personality disorder, individuals with sexual sadism may seriously injure or kill their victims" (APA, 2000). It is reasonable to consider all sexual sadists as having an antisocial personality disorder, although it is often, as with Kinsey, closeted.

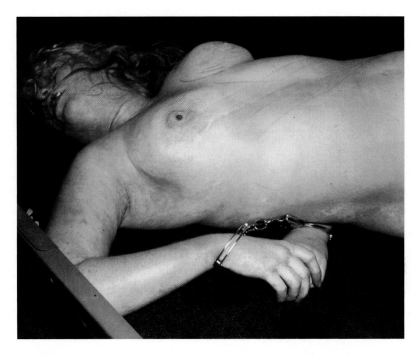

Figure 1.14 Sexual sadism. Victim of serial killer. This victim was found in a New Jersey motel. She had been sexually tortured and sexually abused. There was breast assault as well as bondage activity (handcuffs). Note the linear lines of torture on her body. (Photo courtesy of Retired Lieutenant Frank P. Del Prete, Bergen County, New Jersey, Prosecutor's Office.)

Paraphilias Not Otherwise Specified (302.9)

This category is included for coding paraphilias that do not meet the criteria for any of the specific categories. Examples include, but are not limited to, coprophilia (feces), klismaphilia (enemas), urophilia (urine), telephone scatologia (obscene phone calls), necrophilia (corpses), partialism (exclusive focus on part of body), and zoophilia (sex with animals) (APA, 2000).

Telephone Scatolgia Refers to the sexual attraction of making obscene telephone calls and encompasses lewdness in conjunction with these activities. Usually young persons, who get a charge out of the response of the person who answers the telephone, randomly make these calls. However, these calls can be sadistic when the caller "targets" a specific victim.

Necrophilia Is a sexual attraction to dead bodies and includes having intercourse with a dead human body. It is a rather bizarre and extremely rare sexual variation in which a person obtains sexual gratification by viewing or having intercourse with a corpse. This paraphilia appears to occur exclusively among males, who may be driven to remove freshly buried bodies from cemeteries or to seek employment in morgues or funeral homes where they can have access to human bodies (Figure 1.15).

There is a dual dynamic at play in this activity. The disorganized offender will engage in this activity because it sexually arouses him and basically the dead body becomes his date. However, with the organized offender, who is a sexual sadist, the necrophilia represents the total and complete domination of another person's being. Ted Bundy, Edmund Kemper, and Jeffrey Dahmer are excellent examples of this phenomenon.

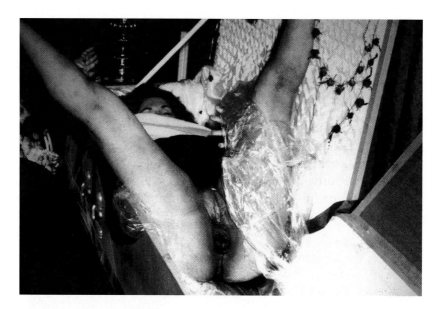

Figure 1.15 Necrophilia. In this case someone broke into the funeral home and sexually assaulted the corpse.

Partialism   An exclusive focus on a part of the human body, which is related to fetishism. The author has cases in file in which offenders have removed the breasts of their victim and kept them as their own personal sexual souvenirs. Jerome Henry Brudos, a serial killer, is an excellent example of such a circumstance. Brudos, who had a number of fetishes for both woman's panties and high heel shoes amputated the woman's foot after killing her. He preserved the foot by keeping it in the freezer in his workshop in his garage. Periodically, he would place this foot into various high heel shoes, which he had stolen from victims and kept in his workshop. He also preserved a woman's breast in an epoxy mold, which he kept on the mantel of his fireplace.

Zoophilia   This is the sexual attraction to animals, is often called *bestiality*, and involves sexual contact between humans and animals. The animals most frequently involved in sex with humans are calves, sheep, donkeys, large fowl (ducks and geese), dogs, and cats. Males are most likely to have contact with farm animals and to engage in penile–vaginal intercourse or to have their genitals orally stimulated by the animals. The frequency of such behavior among males was allegedly highest for those raised on farms.

Women are more likely to have contact with household pets involving the animals licking their genitals or masturbation of a male dog. Less commonly, some adult women have trained a dog to mount them and engage in coitus. Sexual contact with animals may or may not be a transitory experience of young people who are being sexually stimulated in the general environment and to whom a sexual partner is inaccessible or forbidden.

Most adolescent males and females who experiment with zoophilia make a transition to normal adult sexual relations with human partners. Occasionally, an adult may engage in such behavior as a "sexual adventure" or because a human partner is unavailable (Tollison and Adams, 1979; Crooks and Baur, 1990).

Investigatively speaking, most of the materials dealing with zoophilia or bestiality are produced as pornography and involve mostly women engaging in sexual activities with dogs or barnyard animals. The author has several cases in file in which zoophilia-type pornography was utilized by offenders to gain sexual arousal and/or as examples of degrading the victims. Several women have reported that, after seeing these images and stories in pornography, their husbands or boyfriends have brought home various animals and tried to force these women into sex with these creatures. According to Dr. Reisman, many abused women who fled to women's shelters with their children reported afterward that their husbands, who were involved with extensive pornography use, demanded they copulate with an animal.

Statistical information on bestiality reveals that 79% of child pornography offenders had bestiality imagery in their collections. In the study conducted by Bourke and Hernandez of 155 child porn offenders in their treatment program at a federal penitentiary in Butner, North Carolina, it was discovered that just over 30% of these offenders had engaged in sexual conduct with animals.

Coprophilia   The sexual attraction to feces. Individuals engage in such activities involving playing with and/or ingesting feces, which is referred to as coprolangia. The author has cases in file, which depict individuals acting alone or with others engaged in these activities, one of which is a videotape entitled "Brown Handkerchief Productions."

Klismaphilia   The individual becomes sexually aroused by giving or receiving enemas. It is a very unusual variant in sexual expression in which an individual obtains sexual pleasure from receiving enemas (Figure 1.16). However, the erotic arousal may be associated with giving enemas. The case histories of many individuals who express klismaphilia reveal that as infants or young children they were frequently administered enemas. This association of loving attention with the erotic pleasure of anal stimulation may eroticize the experience for some people, so that as adults they may manifest a need to receive an enema as

Figure 1.16 Klismaphilia. Sexual arousal through enemas.

a substitute for or necessary prerequisite to genital intercourse. "The Enema Bandit Case" from Champaign, Illinois, is an excellent illustration of this paraphilia. The offender, who broke into coeds' apartments at the University of Illinois, would tie up his victims and then give them enemas. Officials couldn't catch this individual until he transferred to Kansas State. When the girls in Kansas began getting enemas, it didn't take college officials long to establish who had recently transferred from Illinois.

Urophilia   The sexual attraction to urine. With this, individuals engage in such activities as "The Golden Shower" and other activities involving playing with and/or ingesting urine, which is referred to as urolangia. The author has cases on file that depict individuals acting alone or with others engaged in these activities.

Mysophilia   Refers to the individual who becomes sexually aroused by filth, i.e., smelly or dirty underwear, used menstrual pads, etc. It involves some sort of self-degradation by smelling, chewing, or otherwise utilizing sweaty or soiled clothing or articles of menstrual hygiene. Somehow, early in this person's development, a connection between filth and sexual arousal was made, which became a repeatedly preferred or exclusive method of achieving sexual excitement. This paraphilia overlaps coprophilia and urophilia (Money, 1991).

Anorectal Eroticism   Refers to an individual who becomes sexually stimulated through the insertion of objects into the anal cavity. A potpourri of items have been retrieved from the anal cavities of persons who put something where it doesn't belong. The author, who conducts seminars throughout the United States and Canada, recently was provided with an article from the American Medical Association, which listed some 282 different objects that had been removed from the anal cavities of persons who sought treatment at medical facilities across the United States. Examples would include bottles, zucchinis, balls, nightsticks, vibrators, light bulbs, snow cones, and even a cellular phone (Figure 1.17a/b).

Bondage and Discipline or Cordophilia   The individual becomes sexually aroused through engaging in bondage. This form of sadism has been relabeled *bondage and discipline* by big pornography (corporate sponsored). It is then commonly referred to as B&D or, more accurately, sadomasochism. One obtains sexual pleasure from tying up and binding one's sex partner, or gets sexual pleasure from being bound by one's sex partner. The use of blindfolds, gags, dog collars, ropes, handcuffs, belts, discipline masks, chains, locks, tape, etc., having been seen extensively in soft and hard pornography, became soft wired and, thus, very important brothel paraphernalia for this deviance. The various forms of paraphernalia to enforce obedience or enslavement are also found present in masochism, sadism, and autoerotic events. There are a number of Web sites featuring the subject of sexual torture (bondage, discipline, sadism, masochism (BDSM)) that serve to validate and justify behaviors that are dehumanizing, inherently dangerous, and, in some cases, outrageous.

The investigator should look for symmetry, balance, neatness, sophistication, similar bonds, and commercial materials in cases of sex-related homicides involving bondage. Of course, always look for the magazine or video or DVD pornography, since much of this behavior is merely mirrored by the deviant.

Many times, the offender will be acting out a fantasy based on an actual photo of sadism including the use of specific materials, which he will incorporate into the sexual crime (Figure 1.18).

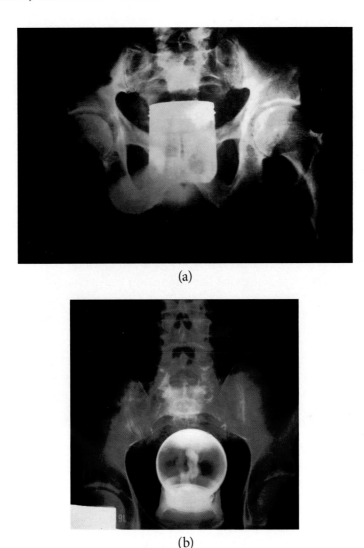

(a)

(b)

Figure 1.17 Anorectal eroticism. A paraphilia in which the individual obtains sexual arousal from the insertion of objects into the anal cavity. (a) The individual managed to get the entire jar of vaseline into his anal cavity. (b) The individual managed to insert a large artificial snowball into his anal cavity.

Hypoxyphilia   According to *DSM-IV,* a particularly dangerous form of sexual masochism that involves sexual arousal by oxygen deprivation obtained by means of chest compression, noose, ligature, plastic bag, mask, or chemicals that decrease brain oxygenation.

Miscellaneous Paraphilias

Apotemnophilia   Being sexually excited by the fantasy or reality of being an amputee. This behavior is often accompanied by obsessional scheming to convince a surgeon to perform a medically unnecessary amputation. Dr. Reisman reports an interview with a United Kingdom *Penthouse* "mother" in charge of the models who revealed one photo series she witnessed. A nude girl with an amputated leg was posed with the stump of the leg deliberately, but barely seen behind an object. Their viewers would not know she was an amputee, but something would "linger" said the photographer.

Figure 1.18 Bondage. Note the symmetry as well as the sophistication. This was collected from an offender's home during an execution of a search warrant. He was heavily into BDSM and bondage activity in which the participants would be bound in a manner to expose and accent the genitalia using the symmetry of the bindings.

Acrotomophilia   Being sexually aroused by a partner who is an amputee.

Gerontophilia   The condition in which a young adult may become sexually aroused primarily or exclusively via sexual conduct with a much older person.

Narratophilia   The need to listen to erotic narratives (stories) in order to achieve sexual arousal.

Pictophilia   Being dependent on sexy pictures for sexual response—an increasingly common deviance.

Somnophilia   Being dependent on the fantasy or actuality of intruding on and fondling a sleeping stranger in order to achieve sexual arousal.

Olfactophilia   The sexual stimulus is associated with smell and odors emanating from parts of the body, especially sexual and adjacent parts (Money, 1991).

Appendix: Quick Reference of Paraphilias

Listed here is a brief definition of paraphilias for quick reference. However, for further information, I direct the reader to *Diagnostic Manual of Mental Disorders DSM-IV-TR* (APA, 2000) and *Abnormal Psychology and Modern Life*, 7th ed. (Coleman et al., 1984).

1. **Exhibitionism** (302.4): Exposing the genitals to an unsuspecting stranger for the purposes of obtaining sexual excitement.
2. **Fetishism** (302.81): Use of nonliving objects for sexual arousal (female undergarments, panties, shoes, etc.).
3. **Frotteurism** (302.89): A sexual attraction to rubbing against the genitalia or body of another.
4. **Pedophilia** (302.2): Engaging in sexual activity with prepubescent children. However, the legal view is that any sexual abuse of someone under 18 years of age is deviant and illegal. That older teenagers may engage in sexual relations with each other may be normal, but it is still illegal. When younger children do so, this generally indicates some potentially serious problems.
5. **Sexual Masochism** (302.83): Getting pleasure from being humiliated, bound, and beaten or otherwise made to suffer for sexual arousal (considered a chronic disorder).
6. **Sexual Sadism** (302.84): The infliction of physical or psychological pain on another person in order to achieve sexual excitement (considered a chronic and progressive disorder).
7. **Transvestic Fetishism** (302.3): Cross-dressing by heterosexual male for sexual excitement (ranges from solitary wearing of female clothes to extensive involvement in a transvestite subculture).
8. **Voyeurism** (302.82): Repetitive looking at unsuspecting people who are either naked, in the act of disrobing, or engaging in sexual activity: "Peeping Tom."
9. **Paraphilia Not Otherwise Specified** (302.9): This category is included for coding paraphilias that do not meet the criteria for any of the specific categories.
   Coprophilia: A sexual attraction to feces.
   Klismaphilia: A sexual attraction to the giving or receiving of enemas.
   Mysophilia: A sexual attraction to filth.
   Necrophilia: A sexual attraction to dead bodies; having intercourse with a dead body.
   Partialism: An exclusive focus on a part of the human body; a breast, leg, penis, etc.
   Telephone Scatolgia: A sexual attraction to making obscene telephone calls; lewdness.
   Urophilia: A sexual attraction to urine.
   Zoophilia: Use of animals for sexual arousal (includes intercourse with animals as well as training the animal to lick or rub the human partner) (APA, 2000).

References

ABC News. *Primetime Live*, 2004.

Allyn, D. Private acts/public policy: Alfred Kinsey, the American Law Institute and the privatization of American sexual morality, *Journal of American Studies* 30 (3): 405–428, 1996.

American Heritage Stedman's Medical Dictionary. www.dictionary.reference.com/browse/estrus (accessed April 16, 2008).

American Psychiatric Association. *Diagnostic and Statistical Manual of Mental Disorders (DSM-IV-TR)*, 4th ed., Text revision, American Psychiatric Association, Washington, D.C., 2000.

Barash, D. *The Myth of Monogamy: Fidelity and Infidelity in Animals and People*, W. H. Freeman, New York, 2001.

Bourke, M.L. and A.E. Hernandez. The "Butner Study" redux: A report of the incidence of hands-on child victimization by child pornography offenders. *Journal of Family Violence* 24: 183–191, 2009.

Brown Travis, C. *Evolution, Gender, and Rape*, MIT Press, Cambridge, MA, 2003.

Colapinto, J. *As Nature Made Him: The Boy Who Was Raised as a Girl*, Harper Collins, New York, 2000.

Coleman, J.C., J.N. Butcher, and R.C. Carson. *Abnormal Psychology and Modern Life*, 7th ed. Scott, Foresman and Company, San Antonio, TX, 1984.

Committee on Forensic Psychiatry of the Group for the Advancement of Psychiatry. *Psychiatrically Deviated Sex Offenders, Report No. 9,* February, 1950.

Crooks, R. and K. Baur. *Our Sexuality*, 4th ed. Benjamin/Cummings Publishing Company, San Francisco, 1990.

deMause, L. *Psychohistory: The Emotional Life of Nations*, The Institute for Psychohistory, New York, 2002. See http://www.psychohistory.com/htm/eln08_childrearing.html

Estes, R. *The Behavior Guide to African Mammals*, University of California Press, Berkeley, 1992, p. 239.

Fincher, J. *The Brain: Mystery of Matter and Mind*, Torstar Books, New York, 1984.

Fisher, C., H.D. Cohen, R.C. Schavi et al. Patterns of female sexual arousal during sleep and waking: Vaginal thermo-conductance studies, *Archives of Sexual Behavior*, 12: 97–122, 1983.

Geberth, V.J. *Practical Homicide Investigation: Tactics, Procedures, and Forensic Techniques*, 4th ed. CRC Press, Boca Raton, FL, 2006.

Goleman, D. *Emotional Intelligence,* Bantam Books, New York, 1997.

Goleman, D. and R. Davidson, Eds. *Consciousness: Brain, States of Awareness, and Mysticism.* Harper & Row, New York, 1979.

Holden, C., Behavioral addictions: Do they exist? *Science*, 294 (5544): 980–982, November 2, 2001. http:// www.sciencemag.org

Jeffrey, L., *Restoring Legal Protections for Women and Children: A Historical Analysis of The States Criminal Codes*, Senator Ray Haynes (CA), ALEC (American Legislative Exchange Council), Washington, D.C., April 2004.

Kennedy, P. *Boston Sunday Globe*, March 30, 2008.

Kimura, D. *Scientific American*, May 13, 2002; also see D. Blum. *Sex on the Brain*: *The Biological Differences between Men and Women.* Viking Press, New York, 1997.

Kinsey, A.C., *Sexual Behavior in the Human Female,* W.B. Saunders Co., Philadelphia, 1953.

Kinsey, A.C., W.B. Pomeroy, C.E. Martin, and P. Gebhard, *Sexual Behavior in the Human Male*, W.B. Saunders Co., Philadelphia, 1948.

Kotler, P. *Marketing Management,* Prentice Hall, Upper Saddle River, NJ, 1967 (1988).

Kuhn, T., *The Structure of Scientific Revolutions,* University of Chicago Press, Chicago, 1962.

Langevin, R. *Erotic Preference, Gender Identity, and Aggression in Men: New Research Studies,* Lawrence Erlbaum Associates, Hillsdale, NJ, 1985.

Luria, A.R., in *Consciousness, Brain, States of Awareness, and Mysticism*, Eds. D. Goleman and R. Davidson, Harper & Row, New York, 1979.

Magnuson, R. *Are Gay Rights Right?* Straitgate Press, Minneapolis, 1985, p. 18.

Marlowe, F. Concealed ovulation, *Archives of Sexual Behavior*, 33 (5): 427–432, October 2004.

Masson, J. *The Assault on Truth: Freud's Suppression of the Seduction Theory*, Farrar, Straus and Giroux, New York, 1984; new edition 1985, Penguin Books, Harmondsworth, U.K.

McDonnell, S.M. Stallion management, *Normal and Abnormal Sexual Behavior Veterinary Clinics of North American and Equine Practice*, 8 (1): 72, April 1992.

McGrew, W.C. et al. *Great Ape Societies*, Cambridge University Press, New York, 1996.

McGuire, C. and Norton, C. *The Perfect Victim*, Dell Publ., New York, 1988.

Michael, R.T., J. Gagnon, E. Laumann, and G. Kolata. *Sex in America: A Definitive Survey*. Little Brown & Company, New York, 1994.

Money, J. *Lovemaps: Clinical Concepts of Sexual/Erotic Health and Pathology, Paraphilia, and Gender Transposition in Childhood, Adolescence, and Maturity*, Irvington Publishers, New York, 1986.

Money, J. Interview: *PAIDIKA: The Journal of Paedophilia*, 2 (3): 5, Spring 1991.

Money, J. and A. A. Ehrhardt, *Man and Woman/Boy and Girl*, Johns Hopkins University Press. Baltimore, MD, 1972.

Moyers, B. *Mind & Body*, PBS-TV, February 1993.

Moyers, B. and R. Restak, *The Brain "Learning & Memory,"* The Annenberg/ CPB, WNET/New York, 1984.

New York Post, November 10, 2001, p. 12.

Norden, J. *Understanding the Brain*, The Teaching Company, Vanderbilt University School of Medicine, Chantilly, VA, 2007.

Nova, PBS-TV/BBC, http://www.pbs.org/wgbh/nova/transcripts/2813gender.html

Patten, J.M., Comment: The Defense of Marriage Act, *Santa Clara Law Review*, 1998.

Pinchot, R., ed., *The Human Body: The Brain*. Torstar Books, New York, 1984.

Reed, M.D. The role of pornography in compulsive or addictive sexual behaviors, paper presented to the National Family Foundation Convention, November 10, 1990, Pittsburgh, PA.

Reisman, J. *Images of Children, Crime & Violence in Playboy, Penthouse and Hustler*, U.S. Department of Justice, Juvenile Justice and Delinquency Prevention, Grant No. 84-JN-AX-K007, 1989.

Reisman, J. *"Soft Porn" Plays Hard Ball*, Huntington House, Lafayette, IN, 1990.

Reisman, J. *Kinsey, Sex & Fraud*, Huntington House, Lafayette, IN, 1991.

Reisman, J. *The Psychopharmacology of Pictorial Pornography*, July 2003a; adapted from her Canadian grant report: www.drjudithreisman.com/archives/pharma.doc.

Reisman, J. *Kinsey, Crimes & Consequences*, The Institute for Media Education, Crestwood, KY, 2003b.

Reisman, J. Hazardous material: Viewing pornography for a living can be deadly. *Salvo*, (10), August 2009.

Shepher, J. and J. Reisman, Pornography: A sociobiological attempt at understanding, *Ethology & Sociobiology*, 103–114, 1985.

Slade, J.W. *Pornography and Sexual Representation: A Reference Guide*, vol. 2, Greenwood Press, Westport, CT., 2001, p. 395.

Smuts, B. Commentary: Apes of wrath, *Discover Magazine*, August 1995.

Snowden, C., et al. Social odours, sexual arousal and pairbonding in primates, *Philosophical Transactions of the Royal Society*, London, December 29, 2006.

Stoller, R. *Sexual Excitement*. Pantheon, New York, 1979.

Tate, T. (producer) *Secret History, Kinsey's Paedophiles*, Yorkshire Television, Channel 4, United Kingdom, August 1998.

Thornhill, R. and C. Palmer, *Rape: A Natural History of Biological Bases of Sexual Coercion*. MIT Press, Cambridge, MA, 2000.

Tollison, C.D. and H.E. Adams. *Sexual Disorders: Treatment, Theory, and Research*, Gardner Press, New York.

Tsang, D., Ed., *The Age Taboo*, Alyson Books, New York, 1981.

van Schaik, C.P. and C.H. Janson, *Infanticide by Males and Its Implications*, Cambridge University, Cambridge, U.K., 2000. Reviewed by David Watts, *Human Biology*, October 1, 2002.

Watts, D. Review of *Infanticide by Males and Its Implications*, *Human Biology*, October 1, 2002. Ed. C.P. van Schaik, Cambridge University Press, Cambridge, UK, 2000.

Weatherford, J. *Porn Row*, Arbor House, New York, 1986.

The Investigative Significance of Fantasy in Sex-Related Incidents

2

Human Sex Drive

The three components of the human sex drive are biological (instinctive), physiological (functional), and emotional (mental)—all melding into one sociosexual template of sexual values and behavior, which is the integration of cognitive, emotional, sensual, and behavioral experiences of the individual.

The emotional or mental component is the manifestation of the culmination of our psychosexual development. Empirical observation, confirmed by modern research, finds the psychosexual or emotional component the strongest of the three, accounting for approximately 70% of the human sex drive. With emotions controlled by the merger of brain/mind/memory, it follows, so to speak, that "the mind controls the act."

Essentially, our sexual sensibilities are conditioned by both nature and nurture, our hard and soft wiring. Sexual behaviors are socially learned. Human beings are in a constant state of development from the moment of conception until death.

Human behavior is affected by stimulation received and processed by the central nervous system (CNS). The individual develops a "model" of who is sexually desirable, what appears sexually satisfying, what is socially appropriate, and what is not sexually arousing to an individual within the context of his or her environment. The author refers to this model as the **sociosexual template**, which reflects the natural human development of the individual, influenced by biological aspects as well as the environment.

Fantasy

Fantasies, which are conjured up in the mind based on our psychosocial and psychosexual development, are a "normal" consequence of our human sexuality. All human sexual activities are initiated through fantasies, which are mental images usually involving some fulfilled or unfulfilled desire. It has been argued that fantasies are mere "mental events" produced by the cerebral cortex. However, science confirms that fantasies must come from the external world in which we are engaged, out of the sights and sounds that surround us. Fantasies or imaginings become our soft wiring. They reflect the culture of our time as well as our own past and our place in that culture.

Fantasy plays a major role in everyone's sexual behavior. It is the drive factor for sexual expression. Sexual fantasies normally consist of imaginations and/or a series of mental images that are sexually stimulating. The contrast of these normal fantasies would be the aberrant development of bizarre mental images involving grotesque unnatural distortions of sexual imagery.

For the sexual predator:

1. The underlying stimulus oftentimes is expressed through sexual aggression, domination, power, and control.
2. Sexual fantasies constructed around such themes begin to develop shortly after puberty.
3. The individual becomes aroused with thoughts and fantasies of sexual aggression.
4. Clinically speaking, the subject has developed a perverse **sociosexual template** wherein lust is attached to fantasies and practices that are socially forbidden, disapproved, ridiculed, or penalized.

The **sociosexual template** is then reinforced through repetition illustrated by the use of sadistic pornography and fantasy stories featuring sexual sadism. "Acting out" these themes with consenting partners coupled with masturbatory activities eventually formulates the subject's **sociosexual template** or what we refer to in law enforcement as the **signature** of the offender.

The individual who is aroused with thoughts and fantasies of sexual aggression oftentimes incorporates elements into his life that serve to enhance the fantasy. Pornography, fantasy drawings, and scripts merge into an insidious relationship in which fantasy and reality become integrated into one's everyday life. An engram is an example of this phenomenon. An offender can live out his sexual fantasies through fantasy drawings, which serve as a form of rehearsal before actually committing an offense.

An engram is a "mind picture" that is conjured up in the imagination and/or fantasy. Or, it may be predicated on a mental recreation of an actual event (DeRiver, 1958). Many times offenders will use pornography to enhance or to stylize the engram. Therefore, there is a greater consumption of pornography among sex offenders in contrast to nonoffenders. These offenders are constantly thinking about and fantasizing about what they are going to do. It's a 24/7 thing with sex offenders. In Chapter 3, the author presents an in-depth analysis of this 24/7 dynamic based on the journal of a serial rapist. In that journal, the offender sexualizes his personal accounts and graphic descriptions of the sexual assaults with his fantasy, which validates much of the research on sexual predators.

The author has researched numerous cases in which photographs, drawings, video tapes, books, women's lingerie, and clothing, along with anatomically correct dolls, were employed by sexual offenders and/or persons who used these materials to sexually stimulate themselves and died as a result of their autoerotic practices (Figure 2.1 and Figure 2.2).

Photographs and Magazine Pictures

Offenders and/or persons vested in a sexually arousing setting oftentimes use pictures from magazines and photographs to create or enhance fantasies. In Chapter 9, the author presents an offender who fantasized and enhanced his pornography by adding bindings to the women models. While engaged in consensual sex with a young woman, the offender couldn't perform. He proceeded to beat her about the face and head with a metal weapon. He then took a stick off the ground and rammed in into her vagina with such force that it broke off near her heart. He then posed the body at the scene with her legs spread apart and held in that position with a vine from the trees. This pose was the same as his pornography with the added bindings.

Figure 2.1 Fantasy Drawing of Sex Slave. This offender had drawn this picture of one of his sex slaves. He had hundreds of these fantasy drawings that he kept in a special folder. Take note of the detail and the location of the bindings, which are very similar to the illustration of the anatomically correct doll. (Photo courtesy of Agent Norman L. Rhoades, New Mexico State Police.)

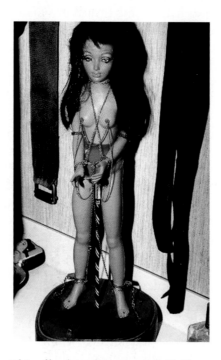

Figure 2.2 Doll in bondage. This offender, who was a serial killer, maintained a collection of anatomically correct dolls, which he placed in chains and bondage positions. The various positions and implements that he used were strikingly similar to the actual tortures he inflicted on his victims. (Photo courtesy of Deputy District Attorney Jim Yontz, New Mexico District Attorney's Office.)

The author has numerous examples of this method of acting out sadistic fantasies from criminal sexual assaults cases as well as autoerotic fatalities. Offenders use drawings and paintings, as well as pornographic magazines and regular magazines, to create specific and vivid presentations. I believe the case study on Domestic Violence Lust Murder presented later in this chapter provides an excellent example of this type of behavior. The subject had hundreds of drawings and paintings of women depicting gunshot and knife wounds. The wounds on his wife's body, as well as the knife protruding from her chest, bore an eerie resemblance to the drawings and paintings detectives located.

Alteration of Photographs or Drawings

In some cases, the subject may alter existing photographs from pornographic magazines or even regular magazines in an attempt to visualize a fantasy. The alterations might include drawing blood marks or wounds on the photograph or adding bondage devices. The subject may even cut and paste other objects or parts of bodies onto existing pictures.

Case #1: An Autoerotic Fatality

The author had the opportunity to review a death investigation involving a male who had died during an autoerotic event. I conferred with the lieutenant in charge of the investigation. The subject was a dentist who was discovered in his office by his assistant after the wife had become concerned with his absence. When the man was discovered, he was wearing female attire and undergarments including dark stockings and a girdle. Inside the girdle were various hairbrushes turned in a manner to cause the bristles of the brush to scrape against the skin. There was a plastic dildo inserted in the man's anal cavity and a noose around his neck, which was protected by some padding. The authorities had properly classified the death as accidental.

During the search of his office the authorities opened a five-drawer metal cabinet that contained hundreds of pornographic magazines, most of which dealt with bondage. The subject had cut and pasted various objects and faces on the models in the magazines. He had also created his own bondage fantasy by accenting the models' pictures with objects placed into their sexual orifices. In fact, as the reader can see in Figure 2.3, his alterations were done so meticulously that the conversion appears to be an actual photograph of a dental instrument inserted through the breast complete with shadow and blood drippings. Based on the number of magazines that were recovered and the multiple alterations the subject had made, it was quite apparent that the subject had spent an inordinate amount of time with his fantasy.

However, the most significant discovery was a black and white Polaroid photo pasted onto one of the magazine pages. It depicted two women engaged in a bondage scenario suggesting that the subject was involved with these activities with some playmates. This later proved to be of investigative significance in resolving whether or not this death was an autoerotic or group exercise event. The investigation revealed that the women were the victim's dental assistant and her lesbian lover who would sometimes participate in some sexual escapades with the dentist. Although obviously embarrassing to the other participants who played these sadomasochism (S&M) games, the actual death was an autoerotic fatality (Figure 2.4 and Figure 2.5).

Figure 2.3 Fantasy photo. The subject had taken a model from a magazine and pasted an instrument onto the model's breast. He then added blood and shadow to make it appear that the instrument had pierced into the woman's breast. (Photo courtesy of the author.)

Figure 2.4 Altered magazine photograph. The subject had five metal cabinet drawers filled with adult magazines, which he had altered for his sexual pleasure. (Photo courtesy of the author.)

Figure 2.5 A surprise find. The subject had pasted Polaroid photographs of his mistress and her lesbian friend engaging in klismaphilia. (Photo courtesy of the author.)

Case #2: An Autoerotic Fatality

In another case the author reviewed, the subject was a white male in his late forties. He had never been married and was living at home with his mother and sister.

He was discovered hanging in his basement workshop. The full case is presented in Chapter 4. The subject's fantasy is quite realistically portrayed in his many drawings, which he scripted. The significance of these drawings coupled with the writings provided an excellent insight into this man's sexual arousal and response system, which included sexual sadism and sexual masochism, as well as other paraphilias, such as urophilia, mysophilia with olfactophilia. In one of his fantasy drawings, the subject drew a sign over he toilet that stated, *"Please Keep the Comfort Station Clean,"* indicating that he most probably hung around these facilities to smell the odors, which were part of his fantasy (Figure 2.6).

Significance of Sadomasochistic Autoeroticism

In some instances, the fantasy component has been "played out" in autoerotic scenarios wherein the subject plays two parts. The subject may play the part of victim, either nude or dressed in female attire. He also acts as the choreographer in that he directs the fantasy scenario. In Chapter 4, the author provides a case in which the victim presented himself dressed as a woman hanging by the neck. He undoubtedly had planned on viewing the taped fantasy later on as a stimulus. What was of investigative interest in this scenario was the presence of drawings and sketches depicting women hanging.

The author references this autoerotic case in Chapter 4 in which the subject constructed a very ritualistic scenario depicting himself as a female hanging from a hook in the ceiling.

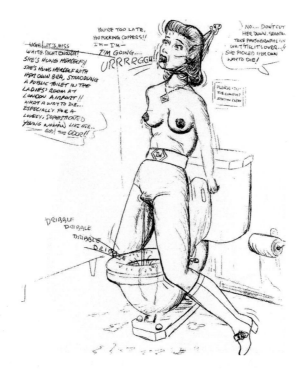

Figure 2.6 Fantasy drawing. The subject had created numerous drawings depicting S&M activities coupled with his fantasy regarding urophilia. (Photo courtesy of the author.)

The subject had covered his head with a hood and was dressed in women's lingerie. He had performed this ritual many times and always used a harness as a safety device. Obviously, convinced that he no longer needed this, he disregarded the safety mechanism and died of asphyxiation. The important point to note is that the subject, who had created this sexual fantasy, was playing two parts. He obviously had planned on viewing himself in these scenarios and using the videotapes as a sexual stimulus.

Case #3: An Autoerotic Fatality

The use of women's lingerie as a sexual stimulus was graphically portrayed in the autoerotic weight-bench case, also presented in Chapter 4. This subject had thousands of dollars worth of women's nightgowns and lingerie. He also had two very expensive women's wigs and entire ensembles of fashion designer clothing, which he purchased in his own size. His fantasies, which included bondage and autoerotic scenarios, were documented through photographs recovered at the scene and statements by his former wife who stated to police that she left him because of his "kinky sex habits." The investigative significance of this case was revealed in the evidence collected by the authorities, which revealed the subject's fantasies. The authorities collected evidence of solo sexual activity along with sexual fantasy aids (Figure 2.7 and Figure 2.8).

There had been evidence of prior dangerous autoerotic practice supported by statements by his former wife relative to his kinky sex games as well as his past autoerotic practice. There were not any apparent suicidal intentions and the investigators located photographs of the victim engaging in autoeroticism.

Figure 2.7 Autoerotic death. Cross-dressing fantasy. The subject had an extensive collection of expensive women's lingerie and would dress up for his autoerotic exploits. (Photo courtesy of Retired Lieutenant Mark Fritts, Hobbs, New Mexico, Police Department.)

Figure 2.8 Closet. An extensive collection of women's lingerie, high heel shoes, and accessories were discovered in the victim's closet. (Photo courtesy of Retired Lieutenant Mark Fritts, Hobbs, New Mexico, Police Department.)

Fantasy Drawings and Their Significance in Criminal Investigative Analysis

Fantasy plays a major role in everyone's sexual behavior. It is a driving factor for sexual expression. The individual who is aroused with thoughts and fantasies of sexual aggression oftentimes incorporates these dynamics into fantasy drawings, which serve as a form of stimulus and excitement, a rehearsal before actually committing the offense, or a mental recreation of an actual event. In that case, the fantasy drawings become actual evidence against the offender.

In the **BTK** (bind, torture, kill) serial murder case, which is presented in Chapter 13, Dennis Rader was convicted of killing 10 victims over an extended period of time. One of the issues confounding law enforcement was BTK's ability to stop killing for prolonged periods of time and then resume his killing. This dynamic just didn't fit the accepted protocol of serial killers. It was only after his arrest and subsequent confessions that authorities learned why he had these "gaps" in the murder events. Rader told the authorities that he would use his **fantasy drawings** and **pictures** of his victims to sexually stimulate himself in order to relive the murders. These fantasy drawings became significant in corroborating his statements and the evidence recovered from the execution of the numerous search warrants linking BTK to each of the murders (Figure 2.9 and Figure 2.10).

The author also has numerous cases of offenders acting out sadistic fantasies based on violent pornography as well as their own drawings and paintings depicting sexual assault. In fact, empirical studies indicate that many sex offenders reported having masturbatory

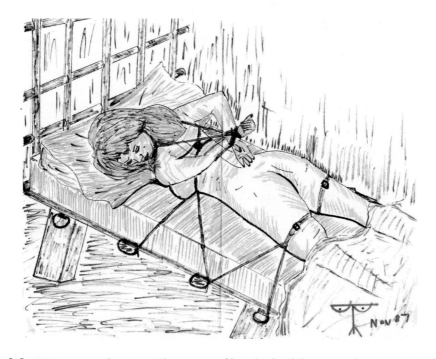

Figure 2.9 BTK Fantasy drawing. This is one of hundreds of drawings that Dennis Rader created to fulfill his fantasy of women in bondage, which explains his BTK (bind, torture, and kill) moniker. What is also significant in this drawing is the inclusion of his trademark identifier in the lower right portion of the drawing, which was his method of validation of authorship. (Photo courtesy of Retired Director Larry Welch, Kansas Bureau of Investigation (KBI).)

Figure 2.10 Polaroid™ photo of victim. BTK took a series of Polaroid photos of his victim, which he posed and propped for his psychosexual gratification. It was these photos, as well as his drawings, that provided the ability to sexually stimulate him in order to relive the murders. Take note of the similar theme as expressed in his drawing. The victim is bound face down with her buttocks exposed. (Photo courtesy of Retired Director Larry Welch, Kansas Bureau of Investigation (KBI).)

fantasies before acts of sexual aggression and that the content of the fantasy was similar to the nature of their sexual offense. McGuire, Carlisle, and Young (1965) proposed that any deviant sexual behavior is the direct product of a deviant sexual preference.

In the author's opinion, many sexual assaults and/or homicides are a direct result of an offender acting out a specific sexual fantasy fueled by sadistic pornography.

Criminal Investigative Analysis

The applications of clinical criteria and abnormal psychology to the investigative process are an integral part of criminal personality profiling and have been universally recognized and accepted as genuine and legitimate investigative techniques. Detectives and criminal investigators routinely employ these techniques in their investigation of violent crime on a case-by-case basis. From a practical standpoint, there are only so many ways to kill and only so many stories to tell as an offender attempts to explain the killings. After a while, a distinct pattern emerges that encompasses a series of clusters of behavioral information and specific typologies of offenders

Criminal investigative analysis is a process of reviewing crimes from both a behavioral and investigative perspective. It involves reviewing and assessing the facts of a criminal act, interpreting offender behavior, and interacting with the victim, as exhibited during the commission of the crime or as displayed in the crime scene.

As previously discussed, there is a behavioral distinctiveness to human sexuality. **Fantasy drawings** provide a unique insight into the mind of the offender, who is portraying pictorially and oftentimes subconsciously acting out a sexually significant behavioral pattern, which reflects the underlying personality, lifestyle, and developmental experiences of the offender. The sexual offender's love for detail and sexual expression inadvertently provides the investigator with the offenders' innermost sexual thought processes and fantasies. Not to mention evidence. When you have the innermost thoughts of an offender, written or drawn by his own hand, there are no better "data" from which to draw conclusions about a particular offender and his sexual activities.

The investigative goal is to interpret these actions and behaviors of the offender and then translate these psychodynamics into investigative reality.

Fantasy Drawings as an Investigative Roadmap

The sexual offender and other individuals who are aroused with thoughts and fantasies of sexual aggression reinforce their beliefs through repetition illustrated by the use of sadistic pornography and fantasy drawings. The accumulation of materials, including "rape and/or murder" kits that the offender used to control his victims and enhance his sexual fantasies as well as implements he used to sexually torture his victims, become an integral part of the fantasy drawings as he attempts to recreate the actual event in the fantasy drawing in order to relive the experience through fantasy. These drawings can be introduced into evidence as an example of the role of fantasy.

Fantasy drawings, pornography, writings and journals, sexual devices and toys, lingerie, bondage devices, scripted drawings, and/or photos depicting a specific fantasy are all very significant in any investigative analysis. In fact, based on my personal experience and dealings with sexual offenders and their insatiable appetite for sexual stimuli, I can guarantee that within their collection of these materials is the **specific roadmap of their offense.**

Many pedophiles have been able to circumvent the laws on child pornography through fantasy drawings and sexually explicit cartoons. There are Web sites, which feature sexually sadistic pornographic drawings of children involved with adults to satisfy pedophile fantasies (Figure 2.11).

Figure 2.11 Simulated child porn. The Web site drawings have been rendered as "simulations" to avoid child pornography laws. Their advertising states, "Only 3D toon can satisfy because CARTOONS have no Limits, no Borders, no Rules." (Courtesy of author.)

The Web site drawings have been rendered as "simulations" to avoid child pornography laws. Their advertising states, "Only 3D toon can satisfy because CARTOONS have no Limits, no Borders, no Rules." Examples include: http:/www.sin3dincest.com *and* http:/leejoy.info.

Cartoon-type drawings can sexually arouse individuals who are predisposed to the subject matter and these fantasies will tend to "linger" (see neuroadaptation in "The Brain's Endogenous Reward System" of Chapter 1). Many of these cartoon drawings are created in 3D format thereby providing a realistic impact. This would certainly be significant in a criminal investigative analysis of persons suspected in a child pornography case, who were in possession of these materials along with the fantasy drawings.

A Prototypical Case Involving Fantasy Drawings

In Chapter 12, the author presents the Sex-Slave Torture and Serial Murder Case involving an individual whom I consider to be the most evil criminal sexual sadist I have ever researched. This offender certainly illustrated the dynamics of this phenomenon in his fantasy drawings, which he used to recreate his sexual tortures and sexually stimulate himself.

In one of his drawings, he had depicted a gagged female victim who was in restraints with her arms tied behind her back and her wrists tightly bound. You could actually see the marks from a whipping. Her ankles were bound and secured to the floor and a pole. Her breasts had been wrapped and bound with straps and her nipples had been pierced and tied to a knee restraint, which secured her to a pole. There was a small dildo in her anal cavity secured by a strap, which was part of a harness attached to her hips. The drawing showed the victim being penetrated by another larger dildo with spikes attached to a pole secured into the floor. There were various sexual implements displayed within the drawing, such as handcuffs, ropes, and straps, as well as eyelets secured into the wall for victim restraint (Figure 2.12).

In addition, the offender had sketched an electric cattle prod hanging on the wall behind her and an electrical charge box with wires and electrodes plugged into the wall. The offender also drew various size dildos, which appeared on the floor, along with a bottle of petroleum jelly (Figures 2.13 through Figure 2.15).

Is This a Sexual Fantasy or Reality?

These drawings were just a few of hundreds that were recovered during a search of the offender's compound. What makes these, as well as his other drawings, so significant is that they actually portray what the offender was doing to his victims as he sexually assaulted and tortured them. The various objects drawn in the picture (dildos, electric cattle prod, electric charger box, wires, restraints, leather straps, petroleum jelly, and torture tools), in fact, were recovered by the authorities during the crime scene search. Needless to say, these fantasy drawings became an essential portion of the prosecution's case, especially when defense experts tried to portray the drawings as harmless sexual fantasies.

Fantasy Writings of Sexual Sadists

Below are some examples of actual writings of sexual sadists to illustrate how significant these fantasies become in the actual analysis of the crimes.

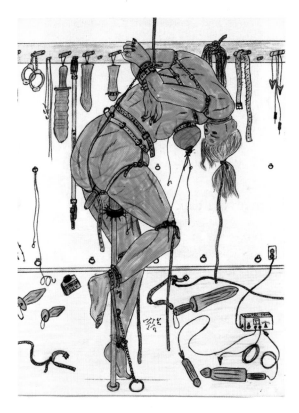

Figure 2.12 Detailed fantasy drawing. The offender depicts in this drawing what he would do to his victims. In the drawing, one can see various items that he used on his victims including the shock box, dildos, straps, and chains that come from his torture room. The victim's body also bears the stripes from being whipped. (Photo courtesy of Agent Norman L. Rhoades, New Mexico State Police.)

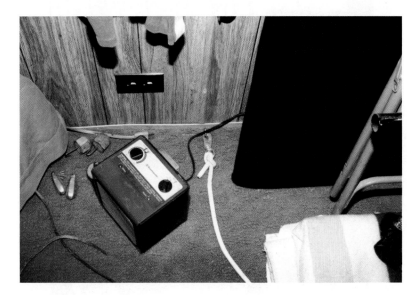

Figure 2.13 Electric shock box. Electric shock box with cables that the offender would use to torture his victim, recovered from suspect's home. (Photo courtesy of Deputy District Attorney Jim Yontz, New Mexico District Attorney's Office.)

Figure 2.14 Torture implements. This photo depicts various items used on his victims, which also appear in his fantasy drawings. (Photo courtesy of Deputy District Attorney Jim Yontz, New Mexico District Attorney's Office.)

Figure 2.15 Torture implements. This photo depicts various item used on his victims. (Photo courtesy Deputy District Attorney Jim Yontz, New Mexico District Attorney's Office.)

Case #4: Fantasy Writings

In my early teens ... my dad had this copy of a movie called Slave of the Canibal [sic] God. In one scene, the main actress was captured and tied by her hands to this pole. I guess she was to be the sacrifice to the god, but during the night one of the native men came up to her and stood in front of her and grabbed her breasts, then went behind her covering her mouth with his hand and was fingering and rubbing her pussy while she moaned and struggled to no avail. Then the other natives caught him and stopped him, but this scene excited me sexually more than I had ever been in my life. To see a beautiful woman tied and sexually taken in this way where she had no choice in the matter but to accept, it excited me to no end.

Whenever dad or mom were in another room or outside, I would repeatedly watch the few minutes of this scene over and over never getting tired of watching it and imagining that the native was me and I was the one doing that to her.

Author's Observation

The offender engaged in repetitive viewing of the portions of the film that were arousing to him, which validated and reinforced his desire for bondage and aggressive sexual conduct. When he finally acted on this criminal impulse, he incorporated his fantasy into the event, which made his writings quite revealing.

The Subject Continued

I guess the part of his hand over her mouth so she couldn't scream and the fact that she struggled and was being taken sexually and she had no choice is what excited me. Also the fact that she was bound. The bondage was the biggest part of it for me. If it haden't [sic] been for that fact and the fact that she was being raped, I would not have enjoyed it.

Reinforcement of the Fantasy

Case #4 Continued

When I got to Denver, there were a lot of sex shops. There I found bondage magazines and videos. Magazines with photos of beautiful women and young girls tied, bound and gagged in just about every way possible. I was in heaven. I bought lots of mags [sic] and videos. After a year or so of looking and watching, I wanted the real thing. I wanted a woman to [be] bound up and sexually abuse. It only changed though as the fact that I didn't want a willing partner as [NAME WITHHELD] had been. I wanted an unwilling partner. I would go out and walk the streets and visit clubs looking for the right woman or girl, but that seemed about all I could do.

Consenting Partners Used to Reinforce the Fantasy

In many cases the offenders used their girlfriends or prostitutes to "act out" their sadistic fantasies. Interestingly, from an investigative perspective, the sexual crimes committed by the offender and the activities they engaged in with their consenting partners were almost mirror-image scenarios.

Case #4 Continued

… my girlfriend [NAME WITHHELD] and me used to get into bondage. I would tie her on the bed or tie her hands above her head in a doorway and have sex with her. We had sex this way a lot. Actually, every time we had sex unless we were in the car or somewhere outside I bound her up. It got to the point where if she wasn't bound or tied up in some way I wouldn't enjoy it. To see her bound and helpless and totally under my control along with the thought that if I wanted to do something to her that she didn't, she could not stop me. She was at my mercy. She was in a sense my sex slave. I could have my way with her and untied her or I didn't have to. It was my choice… .

Serial Rapist's Diary

The offender described in his journal how he acted out a bondage fantasy, which was remarkably similar to the actual crimes he committed. It is also interesting to note that the sexual bondage and discipline magazines he had purchased were reflected in his behavior with the consenting partners as well as his victims. The difference in his mind was that he was "only playing" with the consenting partner. The reality is evident in the actual police reports of his conduct with the victims. My review of the journal entries indicated a progression of activities as the offender repeatedly acted out the scenarios depicted in the magazines and incorporated the pictures of the bound women into his fantasy system.

Case #5: Diary Excerpt

I ordered her into the bedroom, stripped her nude, blindfolded her and taped her hands and feet. I forced her on her knees and made her suck my dick and I even fucked her mouth. She looked so incredible, nude and tied helplessly, forced to suck my dick like that. I put her in bed and touched and licked her helpless body and then I fucked her.

I ordered her to strip for me and made her wiggle her cute little ass as she took off her panties. Handcuffed her, forced her on the bed, tied her handcuffed wrists to the top of the bed frame, blindfolded and gagged her, then fucked her.

I handcuffed her behind her back, blindfolded and gagged her, tied her feet and knees, hogged [sic] tied her a little, tied her elbows together and played with her.

He then writes an interesting entry. "*Got home at 11, jacked off to her helpless, bound and gagged image.*"

He had constructed an engram of his playtime bondage activities, which allowed him to vividly recall both that event as well as his crimes. This is an important investigative consideration because it revealed his "signature." In addition, we hear him state in his own words how he was actually able to fantasize himself to orgasm.

More importantly from an investigative perspective, we see the offender acting out his fantasies with a consenting partner. In cases of this nature, it is imperative that the detectives interview the significant other in an offender's life to gain insight into his actual crimes.

Interviews with Subject and His Former Cellmate

A serial killer, who had disclosed his fantasies to a cellmate, provides an excellent example of the time and effort a sexual sadist will devote to a fantasy-driven expression of sexual violence. (This case is presented in its entirety in Chapter 9, Lust Murder and Deviant-Oriented Assaults.)

Case #6: Interview of Sexual Sadist

The offender wanted to build underground caves out in the woods where he could keep his victims alive for a week or two before killing them. These caves would have "play rooms" where he could act out his fantasies with his slaves. He was also going to construct long escape tunnels in order to avoid apprehension.

According to his cellmate, the subject would fantasize about torturing and killing young women so intensely that he would experience an orgasm. The cellmate reported that there was an emotional intensity in the subject's eyes once he began talking about his fantasies.

In postconviction interviews, authorities learned that knives were a big part of his fantasy, along with cutting. The subject fantasized about mutilating his victims with his knife while they were still alive. He wanted to cut off his victim's breasts and vaginas and shove beer bottles and other instruments into their sexual orifices. This proved quite significant considering what the subject did to two of his actual victims (Figure 2.16).

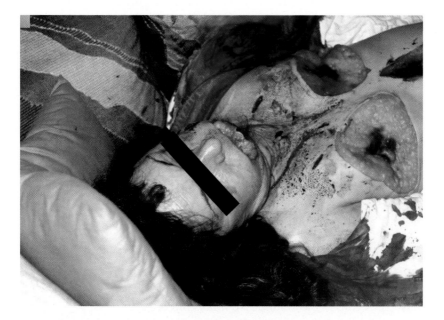

Figure 2.16 Lust murder case. The offender had fantasized about cutting off the breasts of his victims and placing objects into their sexual orifices. (Photo courtesy of Chief Criminal Deputy Robin Wagg, Douglas County, Washington, Sheriff's Department.)

Case #7: Homosexual Fantasy

In the police interview, a homosexual male admitted to having homosexual tendencies at the age of seven. His first homosexual experience was in a state hospital at age 14 when another patient forced him to have anal sex with him. He stated that it scared him, but he liked it. He stated that he had been committed to the hospital over his fantasies about killing his neighbor and had begun tape recording his fantasies.

He spent three years at the state hospital. During his stay, he reported that he constantly had these "killing fantasies." The subject and a male lover of approximately 10 years had a long history of domestic violence. The subject stated that they decided to meet each other at a motel to carry out their long-planned murder/suicide. The subject told the police that he wanted to kill his lover for all the years of bitching about his drinking. He admitted that he tried to strangle him in the past, but couldn't go through with it. They both consumed a few bottles of wine and had taken some drugs. The subject suddenly stabbed his lover and left the knife in the victim's stomach. The subject then stated that he began to think of the fantasies he had in the past of cutting up his lover and taking body parts. He would often masturbate to these fantasies and think about playing with the body parts. He started by sawing off the victim's penis and testicles and taking them to the bathroom where he washed them. He kept the penis, but flushed the testicles because he didn't like the way they looked. He then sliced off the victim's ears and put one down his throat, but then changed his mind. He wanted it back, so he cut off the victim's head and took the ear out through the neck. The subject pulled out the victim's intestines and sucked and played with them. He also sucked on the severed penis in an attempt to "make it hard." The subject took the victim's penis, ears, tongue, and armpit. First, he washed them, then he masturbated with them before pocketing them. When he was arrested, he still had the body parts in his pocket (Figure 2.17).

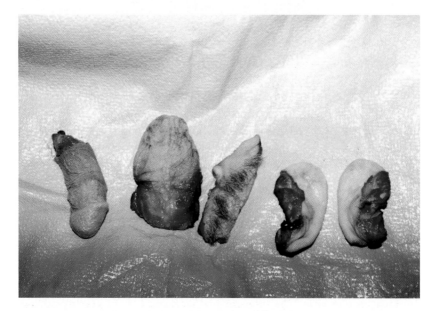

Figure 2.17 Body parts. When the man was arrested by police and searched, they found the body parts of his male lover. He was carrying them in his pocket. (Photo courtesy of Detective Sergeant Jeffrey Smith, Pontiac, Michigan, Police Department).

Figure 2.18 Posing of dead victim's body. Dahmer photographed his victim's bodies in various positions, which he found to be sexually significant to him. (Photo courtesy of Retired Captain James Ferrier, Milwaukee, Wisconsin, Police Department.)

Case #8: Jeffrey Dahmer

Jeffrey Dahmer provided an excellent example of the progression of a perverse fantasy system fueled through repetition and by recalling an after-image engram of this sensation.

He lured homosexual males to his apartment under the pretense of taking photographs of them. Once the victims were at the apartment, Dahmer offered them a drink, which contained drugs. After he drugged them, he would handcuff them in the event they regained consciousness. He would then strangle them to death and engage in necrophilia with their bodies. In some instances, Dahmer tortured his victims before killing them. He cut off the penis and body parts of his victims and preserved them in formaldehyde. He also engaged in cannibalism.

Dahmer posed his dead victims and their body parts and then photographed them with a Polaroid camera. He would masturbate to the heads and body parts as he recalled the murders and fantasized about the actual event (Figure 2.18 and Figure 2.19).

Case #9: Murder and Pornography

This subject, who was 21 years of age, worked in his mother's clothing store. He had a history of several contacts with the police in connection with sexual harassment of female joggers, indecent remarks, and other sex-related incidents.

Although he had been identified, the victims had been reluctant to press charges, so he did not have a criminal record. On the day of the incident, an attractive young mother and her 19-month old daughter went to the clothing store to make some purchases. As the young mother and her child walked toward the back of the store, the offender

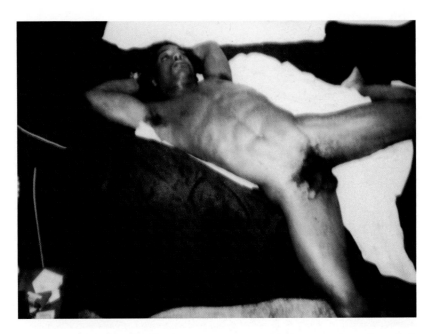

Figure 2.19 Posing of dead victim's body. Dahmer would then use the Polaroid photographs to relive the events and stimulate his obsession with sexual sadism and necrophilia. (Photo courtesy of Retired Captain James Ferrier, Milwaukee, Wisconsin, Police Department.)

quickly began ushering other customers out of the store. He then hung a "closed" sign in the window and locked the door before attacking and killing the victim and her child. He was unable to complete the rape, but he did involve himself in sexual conduct with the woman's body and masturbated on the victim and on the floor. He then disposed of the two bodies, dropping one in a National Park and the other at an abandoned commercial facility. He subsequently was identified and arrested by the police.

During the search of the clothing store, police located a number of pieces of evidence as well as a VCR and three pornographic videos in the backroom of the store. Apparently, he would entertain himself by viewing these tapes. The police also noted that the subject had made a peephole in the wall of the backroom, which allowed him to view the customers while they changed clothes in the dressing rooms (Figure 2.20 and Figure 2.21).

The police also executed a search warrant of his residence. A search of his room revealed his obsessive interest in pornography. Police also located a plastic vibrating dildo, with gels, a used rubber vagina, battery-powered testicle vibrator, and sexual magazines, cards, and photos.

Perhaps the most revealing evidence recovered during the search was a shirt that belonged to the subject. The shirt depicted a vampire ravaging a beautiful young woman with long black hair, which bore a striking resemblance to the victim. In fact, it was so compelling that the district attorney introduced this shirt at the subject's trial.

The significance of the subject's obsession with pornography, his previous behaviors, and the triggering mechanism in the form of the T-shirt are excellent examples of a fantasy-driven expression. The subject acted out on the spur of the moment with no regard for the consequences of his actions or the possibility of getting caught (Figure 2.22 and Figure 2.23).

Figure 2.20 Dressing room. This is an interior crime scene photograph of the dressing room in the suspect's mother's store. (Photo courtesy of Lt. John Fallon and Detective Richard Peffall, Montgomery County, Pennsylvania, Police Department.)

Figure 2.21 Peephole. This crime scene photo shows the hole in the wall of the dressing room. From the storage room the subject would watch the female customers as they dressed. (Photo courtesy of Lt. John Fallon and Lieutenant Richard Peffall, Montgomery County, Pennsylvania, Police Department.)

Figure 2.22 Vampire shirt. This shirt was found in the subject's room. The district attorney introduced this shirt into trial because the image on the shirt bore such a resemblance to the victim. The sexual imagery acted as a "triggering" mechanism for the subject when he saw the victim enter his mother's store. (Photo courtesy of Lt. John Fallon and Lieutenant Richard Peffall, Montgomery County, Pennsylvania, Police Department.)

Figure 2.23 The victim. (Photo courtesy of Lt. John Fallon and Lieutenant Richard Peffall, Montgomery County, Pennsylvania, Police Department.)

This case is a classic example of the disorganized offender, who was so absorbed in his perverse fantasy world that he never considered the consequences of his actions. He attacked a victim of opportunity in his mother's clothing store while he was the only clerk on duty.

Serial Killer's Fantasy

Case #10: Maury Travis—Fantasy Drawings

In Chapter 10, the author presents a serial murder case involving Maury Travis.

This offender was heavily vested in bondage fantasy and had accumulated a number of Web site references and materials that were significant to the investigation.

Detectives located a paperback book, which contained information on acts of sadism. There were various phrases or paragraphs highlighted for easy reference. Taped inside the first page of the book were newspaper articles about a young girl who had been held captive by her neighbor. The man had built a bunker (cell) in his basement to keep this young girl as a sex slave.

Investigators also located several drawings and information that Travis had gathered relative to building a concrete block cell in the basement of his residence. Travis had made reference to how the cell would be constructed and the cost of renting various pieces of equipment per hour. Travis noted, on the drawings, how his captives would be restrained, what they would be fed, and how he would make them wear "Depends" for sanitation purposes.

Interestingly, Dennis Rader (see Chapter 13) also fantasized about constructing a hidden bunker with torture rooms for his sex slaves. In fact, in one of his 11 cryptic communications to the police, he included a floor plan of his "secret lair" with a warning to authorities that it was rigged to explode if someone tried to enter. This floor plan, along with his description of the items and plans he had for each of the floors, is also an example of the significance of fantasy on the part of the offender (Figure 2.24).

Travis made references to various books and Web sites relative to bondage and torture. He had books, which referenced the Marquis De Sade, as well as other written materials relating to

- How men should enjoy every aspect of their sexuality
- How women should be used and abused
- How women should be tortured and kept in bondage, degraded, and humiliated

This offender was heavily into S&M and had videotaped some of his activities as he acted out his fantasies with his victims. The investigators located this videotape in a secret compartment in the suspect's basement. There were a number of episodes recorded on tape that eventually led to the identification of the victims.

One portion of the tape began with the camera focused on a nude, black female who appeared to be between the ages of 30 and 40. The camera recorded her performing oral sodomy on Travis. Her hands were free. She was wearing a military cold weather pile cap. Her eyes were covered with some type of cloth material, which was covered with

BOOM

If you get to close to BTK's LAIR or upon Capture and time unchecked this house will go-

Attic Area: BTK's LAIR: Second Fire escape and hidden stairway to 2ⁿᵈ Floor Master Bedroom Area. BTK's Safe Work area-desk-computer-small hobby room and file cabinets-TV Monitor for rooms below and area.	Door Bars	BTK's DTPG & BONDAGE ROOM DTPG=Death To Pretty Girl See C-9 for Hits. Barrel ___ Door Bars	Hall & Stair Elevator Heavy Locked and Alarmed Door. Door is sound proof.
2ⁿᵈ Floor: Same as 1ˢᵗ Floor. Contain Master Bedroom, other old apartment type rooms-etc. Remote Controls in Bedroom, TV Monitors. Also contains another Barrel in a locked closet. **Note: Basement and 1ˢᵗ floor Barrels fire lst.**			Heavy Fire Doors from 1ˢᵗ Floor. Elevator
1ˢᵗ Floor: Perimeter Alarm fires Primary. Count down is started. Alarm sounds for a person inside. Cut off switches hidden around the house to igniter. Secondary trigger by intrusion alarm, manual pull stations and or cellular phone call. Secondary kicks in, call to a cellular phone, for person to verify the real thing or intrusion if a person not at home-etc. Also contains another Barrel in a locked closet. **Note all closets, locks, doors, safe and explosive areas will unlock upon go Trigger Command.**			Stair and Elevator .1ˢᵗ floor lead to cover area to Garage.
Basement: Hobby Room, Dark Room, Storage, Cell for DTPG and or victim and other DTPG items including the Train Room with real tracks and Engine Wheels Simulator, that can kill or maim. Stereo Train Sounds when Simulator Running. SBT when it approaches the victim. Primary Count Down start, circuit will close when X Seconds finishes. Secondary will fire circuit on igniter at the end of count down at X Seconds if Primary and Cellular is good circuit. **Note: intrusion must be confirmed by cellular by person if away from house.** Igniter is a sparker from a gas grill. Electro-mechanic valves control gas flow. IG=Igniter Elec M ≈ Electro-Mechanic Valve M=Gas Monitor for leaks. If leak or gas smell will notify person by cellular or control box-etc. Explosive Devices-55 Gallon Sealed Drums with Propane Tanks inside. Gasoline bottles inside drums.			Stair and Elevator Sound proofing on door and closed windows
IG / Elec M V Propane Bottle from old grills Gasoline M			
Not to Scale on Simulated Layout: 3216912			

Figure 2.24 Sketch. BTK sent this sketch to the authorities with a warning that his "secret lair" would explode if the police were to enter. This sketch is definitely a fantasy drawing, which was used by the offender to excite and stimulate himself as he fantasized about his sadistic plans. (Photo courtesy of Retired Director Larry Welch, Kansas Bureau of Investigation (KBI).)

duct tape. She was on her knees on the bed facing Travis, who was apparently sitting against a pillow on the bed.

The next scene showed the victim lying face down on the bed with her hands apparently secured to the headboard of the bed in some unknown manner. Travis is engaged in anal sex with the bound victim.

The victim was heard to moan as Travis thrust himself into her. She began to cry and plead with him. She told him that it hurt. Travis told her to shut up. Travis then began to thrust harder and you could hear the victim moaning and crying out from the pain. When Travis was finished, he left the victim lying on the bed moaning. Suddenly, Travis reappeared and smacked the victim across her bare buttocks. He told her to sit still.

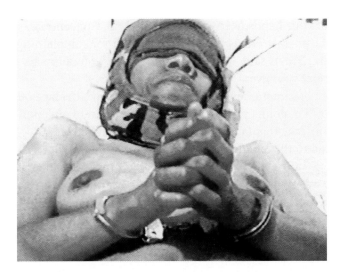

Figure 2.25 Video clip. This is a still shot from serial killer Maury Travis' video torture of one of his victims. She is nude, blindfolded, and handcuffed. The offender is videotaping her torture and she must reply, *"You are the Master, and it pleases me to service you."* (Photo courtesy of Retired Detective Roy Douglas, Homicide Section, St. Louis, Missouri, Police Department.)

Travis then focused the camera on her vagina. He fondled her vagina while holding the camera and filming closeups of his activities as he probed her. The victim continued to repeat, *"You are the master and it pleases me to serve you."* Travis said to her, "Clearer," which obviously meant to keep speaking those words. Travis then jammed his finger into her vagina and you could hear the woman cry out in pain.

Travis then replaced the camera on its tripod. He took a Corona beer bottle and inserted the neck of the bottle into the female's vagina. The victim gasped out in pain. Travis told her, "Spread your legs. Spread them wide." During this activity, the victim was constantly made to repeat the above phrase: *"You are the master, and it pleases me to serve you"* (Figure 2.25).

The next scene continued in the bedroom. The nude female is lying back on the bed with her legs spread. Her hands were cuffed together and she is heard to say, *"You are the master and it pleases me to serve you"* over and over again. Travis told her, "Say it clear. I can't hear you."

Travis then pushed the bottle up into the victim's vagina. The victim was losing her concentration as Travis pushed the bottle into her vagina and wasn't speaking clearly enough. Travis told her, "Stop. Say it. You are the master and it pleases me to serve you." The victim continued to say, "You are the master and it pleases me to serve you." Travis then told her, "Spread you legs. Put them all the way up." Travis then said, "What were you saying?"

The victim continued to say the phrase. Once Travis had her legs spread open to expose her anal cavity, he began to insert the Corona bottle into her anal cavity. You could hear the victim saying the phrase and crying out from the pain he was causing her. The victim is clearly in pain. But, Travis continued to make her utter the phrase.

He told her, "Move your hands," as she attempted to protect her self. Travis told her, "Put your hands over your head." She was crying out in pain as she uttered the phrase. Travis told her, "Shut up or I'll put this mother fucker (meaning the bottle) up your mother fucking stomach." Travis then rammed the bottle into her anal cavity and then yelled at her, "Put your hands over your head. Shut up. Concentrate." The victim continued to utter the phrase. Travis then got mad at her for complaining and he slapped her across the face. Travis said, "Sit your fat ass down, you dumb ass bitch. Lay down on the bed and close your eyes."

Apparently, out of camera range, the victim tried to take the tape off her eyes. Travis got mad and said, "I'm gonna put a plunger up your ass and I ain't pull'n it out till I see blood. Do it again. Take that tape off again and see what happens."

Travis then said to the female, "Are you sorry you jumped into a car with a mother fucker? The female said she was sorry for jumping into a car with a guy. Travis raised his voice as if he was irritated and said, "Say it like I said it: You are sorry for jumping into a car with a mother fucker." The female repeated what he told her to say. Travis then asked her if she had any children. She told him that she did. Travis asked her if she was raising her children and she said yes. Travis said, "You're not raising nothing, you are out there laying on your back, getting money for crack."

In the next scene, you observe Travis attaching a chrome-colored chain to the female's neck. During the process of attaching the chain, the female began choking. Travis said to her, "Shut up, Bitch; I'm not going to hurt you, at least not yet. I think I'm going to keep you for a couple of weeks."

The tape ended at this point. This victim was later identified as one of Maury Travis's serial murder victims.

Fantasy and Linking Criminal Events

The practical application of this information in the investigative process is the recognition of the fantasy-driven behaviors, which we call the **signature** element in the event. In *Practical Homicide Investigation*, 4th edition, the author (Geberth, 2006) described this phenomena as follows:

> The signature aspect of a violent criminal offender is a unique and integral part of the offender's behavior. This signature component refers to the psychodynamics, which are the mental and emotional processes underlying human behavior and its motivations.

However, in focusing on the **signature** aspect of the event, the investigator should not disregard the modus operandi (MO) of the offender. The MO is a learned behavior that changes as offenders gain experience, build confidence, or become involved with the criminal justice system. It also may reveal the level of sophistication of an offender. **Remember: Human behavior is repetitive. Certain actions engaged in at the scene by certain TYPES of PERSONALITIES will tend to repeat themselves.**

In investigative analysis, we look at signature and MO as well as the forensic evidence and its significance to the event.

Case #11: Linkage Blindness

A serial killer who was operating in two different states was able to elude police apprehension for a period of time because of "linkage blindness." Actually, the signature of the offender was that of a sexual sadist. Each crime was characterized by prolonged and sadistic assaults on his victims, whom he seemingly "played" with as he tortured them for hours. He selected each of his victims for the purpose of sexual and psychosexual gratification. The subject stated that bondage had aroused him since he was young. The suffering of his victims sexually excited him and the cruelty of the acts increased. The progression of his activities was consistent with sexual sadism.

In this particular case, one of the visible signature elements that allowed authorities to link the cases was that the victims had been found handcuffed or there were obvious handcuff marks on the victims' wrists (Figure 2.26). In addition, many of the torturous incision marks from the offender's knife were similar in each of the sexual assaults. The offender focused his attacks on specific body regions, particularly the breasts. He brutalized his victims and literally bit into their breasts (Figure 2.27). Investigation revealed that the offender had an intense interest in bondage and total control and submission of his victims including taping their mouths so they would be totally vulnerable and could not cry out in pain as he tortured them.

When the authorities in this case executed a search warrant at the subject's home, they discovered that he maintained a private room in the house. Even his wife was not permitted access. Inside that room, the detectives discovered a treasure trove of evidence. In fact, this room became known as the **Trophy Room** during the subsequent trials and prosecutions. Crucial evidence linking the subject to all of the murders was discovered in that room, from jewelry and clothing of his victims, which he took as trophies, to items as innocuous as nail polish and nail polish remover (Figures 2.28 through Figure 2.31). Among the many items recovered from this room was an extensive collection of bondage and discipline (B&D) materials and other pornography, which indicated the subject's intense interest in sadomasochistic activities.

The killer's need for bondage to obtain sexual arousal was graphically described by one of his surviving victims who told police that the subject told her how he derived sexual satisfaction and enjoyment from torturing and beating women. He told her that

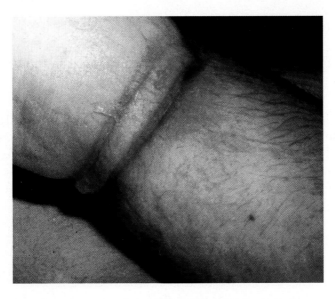

Figure 2.26 Handcuff injuries. One of the linking factors was the distinctive handcuff marks on the different victims' wrists. (Photo courtesy of Retired Lieutenant Frank P. Del Prete, Bergen County, New Jersey, Prosecutor's Office.)

Figure 2.27 Victim of serial killer. In this photo, we see a victim of a serial killer found in a New York City hotel. This victim had been tortured and sexually abused. The offender removed the breasts of the victim and placed them on the bed board to shock the police. (Photo courtesy of the author.)

Figure 2.28 Trophy room. The offender maintained a private room in his house that his wife was not allowed to enter. Note the bondage books. (Photo courtesy of Retired Lieutenant Frank P. Del Prete, Bergen County, New Jersey, Prosecutor's Office.)

Figure 2.29 Jewelry recovered. This piece of jewelry recovered in the trophy room was matched to one of the murder victims. (Photo courtesy of Retired Lieutenant Frank P. Del Prete, Bergen County, New Jersey, Prosecutor's Office.)

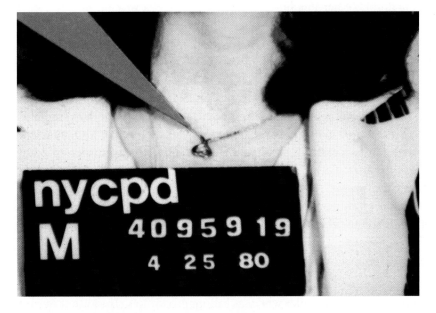

Figure 2.30 Victim identified and matched to jewelry.

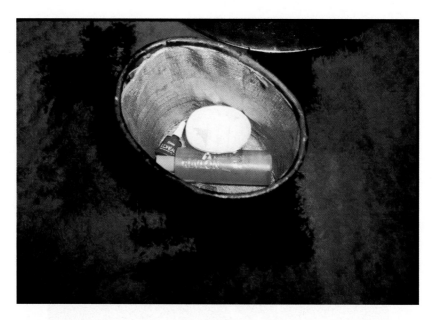

Figure 2.31 Trophies. Many of the trophies that the killer took were innocuous objects, such as nail polish and polish remover, along with costume jewelry. (Photo courtesy of Retired Lieutenant Frank P. Del Prete, Bergen County, New Jersey, Prosecutor's Office.)

he had done this before and that she (the victim) was a "whore." While torturing Leslie O'Dell, who was pleading for her life, he yelled at her, "You have to take it. The other girls did and you have to take it, too. You're a whore and you have to be punished." This became a very important "linking" statement in the subsequent prosecutions.

He was methodical and cunning and planned each of his offenses. He maintained a "murder kit" and props, which he used on his victims as well as handcuffs and restraints, and he taped his victims' mouths to control them. His MO was to pick up a prostitute and take her to a hotel. Or he would meet a woman in a bar, incapacitate her by slipping a drug into her drink, and then bring her to a location where he could torture her. Throughout his predation, he was constantly refining his MO and taking measures to avoid apprehension. He used fire to destroy the crime scenes in the New York City cases. In the New Jersey cases, he dumped his victims or left their bodies in motels. His "comfort" zone obviously was a particular motel in New Jersey. He not only brought three of victims there, but also took his girlfriend to the same motel.

The significance of his **signature,** along with his distinctive **MO,** enabled the district attorney to successfully prosecute this offender for a murder that authorities believe was his first victim, a next-door neighbor. This case became known as the "Signature Case."

The medical examiner testified that two of the cases were identical. The distinctive manner in which the subject had killed two of the women was the defendant's signature.

Case #12: Serial Killer—Fantasy Video

This case involved a serial killer who was killing prostitutes. The author became a consultant for the New Castle County Police and Delaware State Police in this case when

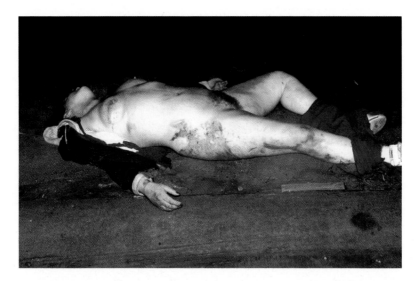

Figure 2.32 Serial killing. This female victim was sadistically tortured and killed by the offender. Note that the body is partially clothed, but has been arranged so as to expose the breasts and vagina. This homicide was the first in a series of killings by a sadistic sexual psychopath. (Photo courtesy of the Delaware State Police.)

the second body was discovered at a new construction site. There wasn't any doubt that the same killer was involved in a previous murder of a prostitute months earlier. His signature was quite identifiable. He would proposition his victims and take them in his van to a secluded location.

Once he completed the sex act, he stripped and tortured the victims for hours using his tools from the van. He would then display their bodies. The cases were linked by the distinctive injuries caused by the tools he was using as well as the killer's focus on causing pain to the victim's breasts. In addition, the first two murders were linked forensically by blue carpet fibers recovered from the bodies, which were matched to the suspect's van (Figure 2.32 and Figure 2.33).

The significance of fantasy in this case was graphically revealed when pursuant to a search warrant, detectives went to the killer's home and retrieved a number of items, which included a pornographic videotape entitled *The Taming of Rebecca*. This video-tape contained a number of scenes, which were similar to what the offender was doing to his victims. The breast assault and paddling activities appeared to be based on this sadomasochistic videotape, which seemingly fueled his increasingly sadistic activities. The offender used this videotape as a sexual turn on and then reinforced his fantasies by acting out the scenes with his live victims.

In Chapter 11 (Sex-Related Child Homicides and Child Abduction Cases), the author presents an investigation of a serial killer who was an extremely sadistic pedophile. He kept a diary and photos of his victims as well as notes about his fantasies to torture and terrorize his young victims.

The diary was the linchpin of the prosecution, which linked each of his crimes and illustrated the significance of fantasy in his criminal activities. In one of his drawings, he spells out a protocol for conducting exploratory surgery on his victims. He was planning on removing their sex organs in order to "make him a her" (Figure 2.34).

Figure 2.33 Serial killing. This was the second victim of the same serial killer. This offense took place approximately six months later. She also had been sadistically tortured and killed. However, note the progression of the offense. Sexual sadism is recognized as a progressive disorder. The injuries to this victim were even more severe than those of the first victim. She is totally nude and there is evidence of severe breast assault as well as additional injuries of torture, including paddling. The body has been provocatively displayed in a public area by the killer for the purposes of "shock value." There were, in total, five victims. (Photo courtesy of Retired Captain George 0. Haggerty, New Castle County, Delaware, Department of Public Safety.) *Author's note:* These offenses, which occurred six months apart, took place under the jurisdiction of two separate law enforcement jurisdictions: New Castle County and the Delaware State Police. Early in the case, I was invited to review the investigation with the respective lead detectives who had immediately recognized the murders as the work of a possible serial killer. Due to the cooperation and intelligent exchange of information among investigators and between the agencies involved, this case was effectively and successfully cleared.

Prosecution Presentation of Psychosexual Evidence

Deputy District Attorney John Trice of the San Luis Obispo District Attorney's Office was assigned to prosecute Rex Krebs, the serial killer depicted in Chapter 9. Krebs would bind his victims in an explicit manner, using sophisticated knots, which allowed him to maneuver and control his victim's movements. Trice wanted to present the significance of the defendant's fantasy-driven behavior and psychosexual dynamics of the sexual assault on one of the victims to the jurors. District Attorney Trice engaged the services of Medical Legal Art, which employs medical illustrators to prepare a demonstration graphics.

Medical Legal Art

Introduction
Medical Legal Art is a company that is the nation's leading provider of custom medical demonstrative evidence including illustrations, animations, anatomical models, and computer presentations. Many times, case presentation before a jury demands compelling, highly specific exhibits. Medical Legal Art has a full-time staff of medical illustrators, programmers, and customer support professionals to provide this service.

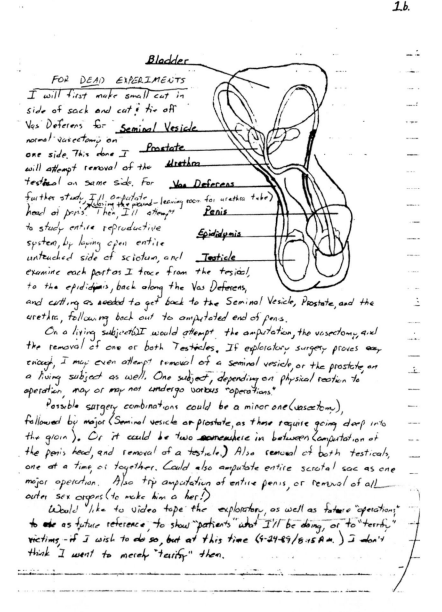

Figure 2.34 Experiment drawing. The offender had drawn a protocol for surgery, which he planned to perform on his victims. This was certainly investigatively significant and illustrated his sadistic fantasies. (Photo courtesy of Dr. Ronald Turco, Oregon.)

What Is a Medical Illustrator?

A medical illustrator draws and/or animates images of the human body in disease, health, surgery, and even after death for the purpose of educating a specific audience. Leonardo da Vinci is considered by many to have been the world's first medical illustrator because of his study and drawings of dissected cadavers.

Modern medical illustrators undergo rigorous academic and artistic training at only a handful of schools across the country in preparation for a degree, which can be either an undergraduate (bachelor's) or graduate (master's) degree. A typical curriculum includes human gross anatomy (including cadaver dissection), physiology, pathology, neuroanatomy, embryology, and surgical observation, along with a host of artistic and computer technology courses.

Contact Information: Medical Legal Art, 275 Shiloh Road, Suite 3130, Kennesaw, Georgia, 30144; Phone: 800-338-5954; Fax: 770-805-0430; E-mail: info@medicallegalart. com

The Rex Krebs Case

The district attorney based the graphic presentation on the condition of the body, when it was unearthed, coupled with the specific bindings, which were on the victim's body, and the medical examiner's reconstruction of these bindings. Deputy District Attorney Trice also had the statements of the defendant and the signature of his activities with his victims. The medical examiner was able to piece together the original knots and bindings that the suspect used to control his victim during the sexual assault. This was an excellent legal tactic, which provided the jurors with a visual representation of the horrific nature of this particularly brutal assault (Figure 2.35 through Figure 2.42).

Figure 2.35 Buried body. The offender had buried the bound body of the young woman in an isolated area. The bindings were very sophisticated and predicated upon the offender's intense interest in bondage. (Photo courtesy of Retired Assistant Chief Investigator Larry Hobson, Office of the District Attorney, San Luis Obispo, California.)

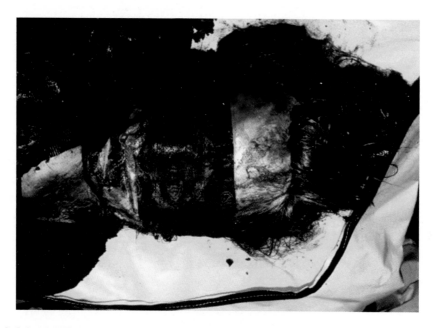

Figure 2.36 Blindfold over eyes. The offender would blindfold his victim as he led her around during the sexual assault. (Photo courtesy of Retired Assistant Chief Investigator Larry Hobson, Office of the District Attorney, San Luis Obispo, California.)

Figure 2.37 Victim's shirt. This was the shirt that the victim was wearing when she was abducted. (Photo courtesy of Retired Assistant Chief Investigator Larry Hobson, Office of the District Attorney, San Luis Obispo, California.)

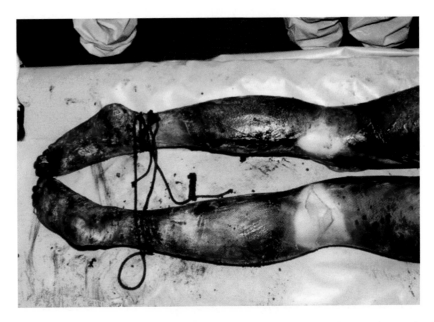

Figure 2.38 Bound legs. This autopsy photograph shows the leg bindings. The medical examiner reconstructed the leg and body bindings for the Medical Art experts. (Photo courtesy of Retired Assistant Chief Investigator Larry Hobson, Office of the District Attorney, San Luis Obispo, California.)

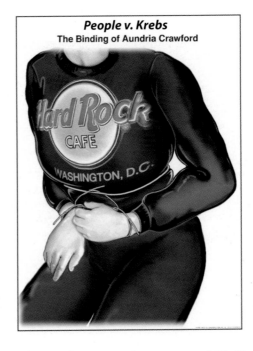

Figure 2.39 Medical Legal Art. The prosecution contracted Medical Legal Art to provide a graphic representation of the event for the courtroom. (Graphic courtesy of Medical Legal Art: Illustration © 2002 www.doereport.com)

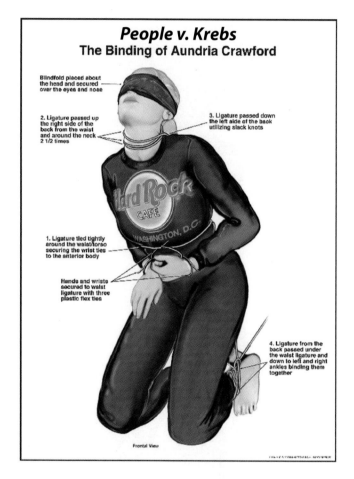

Figure 2.40 Medical Legal Art. This graphic shows from the front of the body how the victim was restrained. (Graphic courtesy of Medical Legal Art: Illustration © 2002 www.doereport. com)

Figure 2.41 Medical Legal Art. Shown from the back of the body in this graphic is how the victim was restrained. (Graphic courtesy of Medical Art; Illustration ©2002 www.doereport.com)

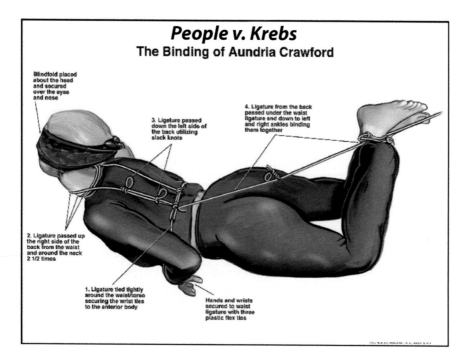

Figure 2.42 Medical Legal Art. This graphic shows the victim lying down and described the sophistication of the bindings. (Graphic courtesy of Medical Art: Illustration © 2002 www. doereport.com)

Domestic Violence Lust Murder: A Clinical Perspective of Sadistic and Sexual Fantasies Integrated into Domestic Violence Dynamics

Introduction

In a sex-related homicide inquiry, the investigator examines the actions and activities of the offender with the victim during the crime to determine and interpret his signature and attempt to understand how the individual person's mind played out the sexual act.

Realistically speaking, there is a very thin line between sexual fantasy and reality. Sexual perversions are premeditated in the obsessive fantasies of the offender. An offender who is not psychotic may experience a "psychotic episode" relating to a temporary condition brought on by, or in response to, an extreme stressor. **Sex is a stressor.** It is the author's opinion that **when an individual becomes thoroughly vested in sexually sadistic fantasy and begins to draw and script these fantasies, an insidious amalgamation develops in which fantasy and reality become blended.**

Domestic Violence Homicides

Domestic violence homicides are those murders that occur between men and women, husbands and wives, boyfriends and girlfriends, boyfriends and boyfriends, and girlfriends and girlfriends relationships. In fact, any murder between intimate partners would be considered a domestic violence homicide. They also may involve third-party relationships, such as "love triangles," former husbands or wives, and jilted lovers.

The author classifies domestic violence murders as Interpersonal Violence-Oriented Homicide. They are the most prevalent form of sex-related murder.

The rationale for classifying domestic violence as sex related is due to the fact that murder serves as the ultimate form of sexual revenge. And, in many instances, the homicides will include sexual assault or wound structures manifesting a sexual orientation.

It is important to note that the **motivation** in an interpersonal violence-oriented dispute may be obscured by what was done to the body of the victim or how the crime scene was staged or changed. Originally, what appeared to be a rape–murder, the work of a sexual psychopath, or a lust murderer is oftentimes based on interpersonal violence.

Case History: Domestic Violence—Lust Murder

POLICE RESPONSE

Police who had responded to an emergency call discovered a 37-year-old woman named Susan murdered in her home. Uniform police officers forced entry into the house, which was locked. They determined that the female victim was in fact dead. She had suffered numerous stab wounds to the frontal portion of her body. While clearing the house to assure that there were no other victims or offenders, officers discovered her 43-year-old husband, named Frank, in an upstairs bedroom. He was suffering from an apparent self-inflicted gunshot wound to the head fired from a .25-caliber automatic found next to his body. He was nude from the waist down and had blood on his legs and genitals as well as his arms and hands. He was rushed to a hospital where he died three days later from the head wound.

Susan had been shot four times in the chest with a .38-caliber handgun found at the scene and had been stabbed 57 times with a large hunting knife, which protruded from her chest. She was pronounced dead at the scene. According to the police report, Susan's co-workers had become concerned when she failed to show for work. They went to her house and after receiving no response looked into the front window and saw her nude body on the floor with a large hunting knife in her chest (Figure 2.43).

DETECTIVE INVESTIGATION

This case presented as a murder/suicide. The murder weapon was a .38-caliber revolver. Apparently, Frank had shot his wife with the .38 revolver and then used a .25-caliber semiautomatic to shoot himself. Police recovered the murder weapon and the gun that the husband had used to shoot himself in the head. In addition to these weapons, Frank had a .22-caliber semiautomatic, a .380- and a .45-caliber semiautomatic. The police also recovered hundreds of drawings and paintings of nude women. Frank had set up an art studio in one of the bedrooms where he apparently would spend his time drawing and painting his fantasies. According to friends and other family members, the couple seemed happy and there was no history of domestic violence. However, clearly depicted in the crime scene photographs was Frank's wedding ring jammed onto Susan's nose (Figure 2.44).

DESCRIPTION OF THE CRIME SCENE

Susan's body was in a supine position with her right arm extended above her head. North of her body was the chrome .380-caliber semiautomatic. Her legs were crossed and she was wearing high heel shoes. However, the rest of the body was totally nude.

Figure 2.43 Domestic violence lust murder. This is what the reporting witnesses saw when they looked into the window of the victim's home. The woman had been shot and killed by her husband, who then mutilated her body with 57 stab wounds directed to the sexual portions of her body. (Photo courtesy of Retired Detective Ken Roberts, East Lake, Ohio, Police Department.)

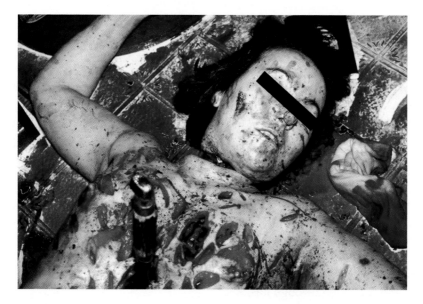

Figure 2.44 Wedding ring on nose. The husband had jammed his wedding ring onto his wife's nose. (Photo courtesy of Retired Detective Ken Roberts, East Lake, Ohio, Police Department.)

Figure 2.45 Drawing. There were hundreds of drawing and paintings of nude women who had been stabbed or shot. Many of the drawings had the woman's right arm extended in the air like the victim's arm. (Photo courtesy of Retired Detective Ken Roberts, East Lake, Ohio, Police Department.)

She suffered a number of stab wounds into her chest and breasts. The stab wounds continued down her chest into her pubis and pelvic area and her throat was cut. A telephone cord had been wrapped tightly around her neck. The extensive blood around the victim's body had been smeared. There were palm prints in the blood on the floor around the victim's body.

There were also footprints through the blood from the husband's feet and it was apparent that Frank had positioned his wife's body in a pose similar to some of the drawings police recovered (Figures 2.45 through 2.47). Approximately 18 of the stab wounds actually perforated her chest. The knife had literally been drilled into the linoleum floor after passing through her chest.

The hundreds of drawings and paintings that police recovered depicted women with gunshot wounds and/or knife wounds to the breast and chest. He also had a number

Figure 2.46 Impaled. The offender had drawn a number of pictures depicting women being impaled by various objects. (Photo courtesy of Retired Detective Ken Roberts, East Lake, Ohio, Police Department.)

Figure 2.47 Drawing blondes. Many of the drawings depicted blonde women being shot or stabbed in the chest. This was clearly a reference to Wendy. (Photo courtesy of Retired Detective Ken Roberts, East Lake, Ohio, Police Department.)

of centerfold photos into which he had stabbed or cut through and then added blood marks with a red ink pen. The injuries and mutilation of his wife's body, as well as the large knife protruding from her chest, bore an eerie resemblance to the drawings and paintings that the police recovered from the scene.

Frank was in an upstairs bedroom. His body was located between the right side of the bed and the wall. He was nude from the waist down. Blood on his genital area, which later was determined to be Susan's blood, would lead the consultant to conclude that he also attempted to engage in sexual activity with his wife. He had an injury to the right side of his head from an apparent self-inflicted gunshot wound.

There was a .25-caliber semiautomatic handgun found close to his body. This was the weapon he had used to shoot himself. One expended .25-caliber casing was found on the floor west of the bed. The .25-caliber projectile was lying on the bed. The phone in the bedroom was off the hook, lying in a puddle of blood.

There was a .38-caliber revolver found approximately three feet from the foot of the bed. It was lying in a piece of glass and had four empty .38-caliber shell casings with it. On the wall above the gun was a large poster picture of a seminude woman dressed in a short, black slip with one arm extended up and the other arm on her hip in a provocative pose.

This poster picture had been shot 15 times with both a .38-caliber and a .380-caliber through the chest area. The bullets traveled through the wall of a bedroom closet. Detectives recovered a total of eight shell casings from a .380-caliber semiautomatic, as well as spent rounds from a .38-caliber revolver and projectiles from the .380-caliber semiautomatic in the immediate vicinity of this bullet-punctuated poster picture. This indicated that this poster had been shot prior to this event. Investigatively speaking, the most current shooting into the poster picture most likely just preceded the homicide. In either event, it certainly provided some insight into the pathological dynamics of the marriage.

Additional shell casings were found on the bed, floor, and dresser. To the right of the headboard was the .25-caliber semiautomatic handgun. Detectives also discovered a black briefcase, which contained two additional weapons. There was a .45-caliber semiautomatic and a .22-caliber revolver along with numerous unexpended rounds of ammunition. To the north of the first bedroom (northwest corner of the house) was a second bedroom. This room was undisturbed. In the northeast corner of the house was the husband's art studio. On a dresser was an empty knife sheath consistent with the knife used on Susan.

VICTIMOLOGY

Susan was 34 years old and married for the second time. Frank was 43 years old. He had been married twice previously. Susan had a full-time job and worked every day to help support her husband. Frank drifted from job to job working as a male model and dance instructor. Susan had been married to Frank for approximately three years. Family and friends were seemingly unaware of any problems or incidents of domestic violence. Susan had lived in the house prior to her marriage to Frank. Following their marriage, Frank and Susan took over the mortgage on the house.

Friends described Susan as totally opposite from Frank. She was very down to earth and quiet, perhaps somewhat passive. Frank was very hyperactive. He wasn't afraid to state his opinions and was considered flashy. Frank taught dancing lessons.

Susan attempted to assist her husband by also working with him in an effort to assist him in his business. Detectives interviewed one person who stated that Frank was extremely intense about the dancing lessons and would chastise his wife severely if she made an error while dancing. This witness told police that Frank controlled Susan, who acted subservient.

FAMILY HISTORY

OPINIONS OF INTERVIEWEES

Police interviews of family and friends presented contradictory personalities. Some persons who were interviewed considered Frank a passionate and emotional man. Others described him as angry. Susan was very affection toward him. Based on further investigation, it was learned that neither his second wife nor his mother provided Frank with much love or nurturing. Ironically, Frank never got over his emotional attachment to his second wife. In fact, it was well known that Frank considered her as "the love of his life." He had often expressed this to Susan.

Several others who were interviewed found him to be effeminate due to a display of many feminine mannerisms. One acquaintance described Frank as having a "Hollywood" life style. He was very open-minded concerning sexual matters, outgoing and talkative. Other individuals who were interviewed stated that Frank drank excessively. He did not have a criminal record, but did have a domestic abuse complaint lodged against him by his former wife. The charge was dismissed when they were divorced.

It was also learned that Frank boasted that while he was at Kent State the CIA had recruited him. He told people that he had been part of a CIA assassination team operating in South America. He told others that he had martial arts training and owned a number of guns. He bragged about owning a .25-caliber Beretta, a .45 or 9 mm semi-automatic, and a .38-caliber or .357-caliber revolver as well as a shotgun and an assault rifle. He also proclaimed that he could kill someone and get away with the murder without getting caught.

Frank, who claimed to be a model, also boasted of other exploits, including his appearance in an episode of *Miami Vice*. In fact, he had held four separate jobs. He also tried to form his own company with his wife's assistance. As a result of his unsuccessful business ventures, the couple was experiencing financial difficulties.

Family members interviewed stated that Frank was a fairly good artist who concentrated on drawing well-endowed naked women. According to a female friend, Frank had told her he was beginning a project with another person. The project was to include drawings of various homicide scenes for a detective magazine. None of this was a reality.

Susan remained the primary breadwinner while Frank spent his days drawing pictures of nude women, fantasizing, and claiming he would soon be hired as a commercial artist. He had taken over the second bedroom of the house as an art studio.

Susan's father related the following to investigators. Four days before the murder, Frank and Susan had a fight. Frank told his father-in-law that Susan slapped him. Frank slapped her back and she left the house. Frank told him that they had been having financial problems and were behind on the house payments. Investigation revealed that the couple was two months behind in their mortgage payments. Frank also disclosed that he and Susan had been sleeping in separate bedrooms for approximately five months.

Frank explained that he and Susan were having problems. He mentioned that they were thinking about selling the house in the spring. It should be noted that Susan had lived in the house prior to marrying Frank and the house had been hers.

On the day of the murder, Susan's father received a call from Susan's mother, his ex-wife. She asked him to go and check on Susan. She thought there was something wrong. When he got to Susan's house, the police were already there. The investigators interviewed Susan's mother. She stated that she had called Susan's house 10 to 12 times and received a busy signal. She then went to the house and knocked on the door several times. She picked up the newspaper and placed it by the front door. She stated that she then walked around the house and looked in the window. She observed a body on the floor, but thought it was Frank sleeping on the floor. She then went home and called Susan's co-workers and her ex-husband.

Psychosocial History of the Husband

The police investigation revealed the following information about the subject. As a child, his mother physically and sexually abused Frank. He also witnessed domestic violence in his household as a child. His father deserted him, leaving the family because he couldn't deal with his wife, who was domineering and psychologically abusive. From age 11 Frank took over his father's position as the target of abuse. His mother basically controlled his life.

He was previously divorced and had remarried twice. His first marriage lasted 10 to 11 years. His first wife was a high school teacher. This marriage ended in divorce. During these years, Frank had a drug problem necessitating hospitalization. His first wife denied any abusive behaviors. However, Frank was controlling by nature, always wanting things his way. It was his idea to divorce. Frank had told her that he no longer wanted to be married and wanted to date other women. This is a prime example of an inability to commit to one individual in an intimate relationship.

He then began an eight-year relationship with his competitive ballroom dance partner, Wendy. After they married, he discovered she was having an affair with another woman. She was bisexual. Their marriage lasted only eight months.

He had a serious drinking problem during most of his adult life. Frank used alcohol to numb his thoughts and deal with his many losses. His best friend of 15 years left the area. His father died and the family estate was tied up. He had lost contact with most of his friends when his ex-wife Wendy left.

He felt isolated and abandoned and once again betrayed. He was eventually hospitalized for an attempted suicide. He then married Susan, who had been married once before. She was an old acquaintance. During the three years they were married, Frank started several business ventures. He had even attempted to form his own company with his wife's assistance, but was unsuccessful.

The consultant reviewed numerous notes written by the subject as well as correspondence from Wendy that he secretly kept with his art work. The subject would write down lists of his symptoms on notepaper. He kept these with his drawings. He complained of insomnia, nervousness, general depression, disorientation, anxiety, and fear, as well as nightmares and flashbacks. The notes and lists, as well as the written correspondence he had had with his ex-wife, display behaviors of a mixed personality disorder.

His pathology is consistent with child abuse victims, as they experience feelings of abandonment, betrayal, lack of trust, rage, chaos, and isolation. Frank's psychosocial history would reveal a fragile individual with low self-esteem as well as grandiose patterns of behavior.

INTERVIEW WITH HIS SECOND WIFE, WENDY

Wendy stated that they dated and lived together for about seven years before she married Frank. She stated that he was the kind of man that needed and thrived on being well liked. She described Frank as having a "love–hate" relationship with his mother. Wendy stated that they were married only eight months. She left him after he attacked her in their apartment. She stated that they had had an argument over her going to school. She walked away from him into another room. She said that he followed her and had a strange look in his eyes.

Wendy stated that he appeared to be staring off into space. Frank hit her and then began choking her. He hit her again and she kicked him and ran from the apartment. She was treated at a local hospital and made a police report. Following this explosive episode, she moved out.

She stated that Frank had numerous pornographic tapes including bondage. She also stated he liked to take nude pictures of her, which she agreed to pose for. She did not know that he had secretly videotaped them making love or that he secretly videotaped her taking a shower and getting dressed.

She was shocked when the detectives presented her with a photo of herself with numerous holes in it along with red paint on the holes simulating blood. She told the detectives that she thought she had taken all of her photos when she divorced him. She stated that, when they were together, she didn't remember any pornographic magazines in the house and Frank did not do any drawings like those found at the crime scene. However, there were porn tapes featuring bondage scenarios. She thought that he started getting stranger because he had a fascination with slasher-type and bondage movies. According to Wendy, he was constantly watching them.

She described her ex-husband as being dangerous and explosive. She said she was afraid of him. Later on, after their divorce, Frank would call her and complain that he was having problems with Susan. He stated that Susan wouldn't talk to him and she would overreact to everything he did.

CLINICAL ASSESSMENT OF DRAWINGS AND PHOTOGRAPHS

Frank had an art studio set up in the house containing hundreds of drawings and paintings. In addition to these paintings, he also had various fantasy stories on notepaper dealing with the CIA and sexual exploits. He also had scripted some of his drawings revealing his psychosexual attributes. In the opinion of the consultant, when someone begins to script his fantasy drawings, he has become "vested" in the fantasy and has effectively created an engram, which allows him to reinforce a specific sexual fantasy (Geberth, 1996). Furthermore, it is also the author's opinion that if an individual has vested in sexually sadistic fantasies, the fantasy drawings and scripts merge into an insidious relationship in which fantasy and reality become integrated into his everyday life.

Many of the drawings depicted blonde women who were being stabbed sexually (Figure 2.48) and the author believes that the subject was thinking of what he would want to do to his second wife, Wendy, who left him. The constant theme that Frank scripted was one of sexual sadism with the infliction of pain and suffering on

Figure 2.48 Blonde with ceremonial sword. (Photo courtesy of Retired Detective Ken Roberts, East Lake, Ohio, Police Department.)

his models accompanied with their scripted pleas. Much of his artwork was on poster paper measuring 2 × 3 ft. The subject spent many hours with his hobby, which most probably caused a great deal of friction between him and his wife.

The police discovered 115 drawings and 105 photographs of nude women. There were also 83 men's magazines, including *High Society, Gallery,* and *Penthouse.* Many of the magazines had loose pages removed, including pictures of centerfolds with stab marks. Frank also maintained an extensive collection of VHS and Beta pornographic videotapes as well as 16-mm movies. The numerous photos of nude women from men's magazines with knife holes and simulated bullet holes through the pictures obviously displayed his obsession with sexual mutilation of women. He then with red magic marker added blood marks on the models. He had literally stabbed through these photographs with a large knife (Figure 2.49). This very well could have been the same knife that was found in his wife's chest.

The drawings depict women with very large breasts who have been shot or stabbed in the breast area. The violence increases and progresses with multiple shots and cuttings. Inserted into the breasts, he would draw knives, arrows, swords, and darts, which represent phallic-like symbols.

In one of the more elaborate posters, a 2 × 3 ft one, he presents a series of 10 panels depicting a nude woman sitting in the bathtub, getting out of the tub, drying herself off, and dressing while a "shadow picture" of a voyeur is standing outside the bathroom window watching her (Figure 2.50). The consultant's opinion is that the shadow figure is actually the subject fantasizing about his own voyeuristic activities. Remember, Wendy, wife #2, was secretly videotaped showering and getting dressed.

Some of the drawings had been scripted to satisfy his fantasies depicting women as whores being punished and killed. There is a ritualistic and ceremonial context to the

Figure 2.49 Centerfold. The offender had ripped out the centerfolds of various men's magazines and then altered the models by stabbing through the paper and adding blood marks or, in this case, simulating bullet wounds. (Photo courtesy of Retired Detective Ken Roberts, East Lake, Ohio, Police Department.)

drawings, which indicates his rage and his desire to seek vengeance. There is also a very prominent lesbian theme in the fantasy stories.

The consultant found it extremely revealing that his drawings of the women for the lesbian theme were "true" blondes. His former wife, who turned out to be bisexual, was also a true blonde. Many of his illustrations reflected his obsession with women who were true blondes represented by coloring the pubis area yellow. Two to three of the drawings and paintings of a woman with black hair being stabbed and shot in the chest could have been Susan, as they were depicted in the same way as her body was positioned and posed in the crime scene.

SUMMARY AND CLINICAL ASSESSMENT

The wound structures clearly indicate a psychosexual orientation consistent with anger, lust, and rage. In fact, after the body was posed, in the position in which it was found, Frank then forced his wedding ring onto Susan's nose. Although there wasn't any official history of domestic violence, this behavior is a classic example of interpersonal violence.

Based on my extensive experience as a homicide and forensic consultant, I am of the opinion that one cannot separate the sexual component from a domestic violence episode. It is a manifestation of ownership and possession coupled with power and control.

Susan's murder was a sex-related homicide with classic "overkill" injuries directed to significant sexual parts of the body. The stabbing injuries into the breasts, chest, and vagina along with the evisceration and slashing of the throat are consistent with the psychodynamics of sexual sadism (Geberth, 1996, 2003, 2006)

Figure 2.50 Panel drawing. This was a 10-panel drawing depicting a voyeur peeking in on a woman taking a bath. Note the shadow figure in one of the panels. (Photo courtesy of Retired Detective Ken Roberts, East Lake, Ohio, Police Department.)

The consultant had the opportunity to review various pieces of the correspondence between Frank and his ex-wife Wendy as well as written materials and some personal papers. In addition, I reviewed all of the photographs, drawings, paintings, sketches, and fantasy stories that the authorities retrieved from the crime scene. Frank's psychosocial history coupled with the psychodynamics of the crime scene indicates that he could have been diagnosed with a personality disorder, which featured obsessive-compulsive personality traits and narcissistic traits. Individuals who are obsessive-compulsive tend to display a preoccupation with mental and interpersonal control at the expense of their own flexibility, openness, and efficiency. They are compulsive and repetitious in behavior, and practice rituals with lists, etc. and often self-critical. Frank had an obsession with nude women, which he drew and painted hundreds of times over. He also kept all of his drawings. He could not set priorities. He was prone to becoming angry, exploding when he felt he was unable to maintain control of his physical and interpersonal environment. A prime example was the poster picture with the bullet holes fired through the wall. He was also narcissistic, which was evident in the patterns of grandiosity in fantasy. He had a grandiose sense of self-importance and exaggerated achievements and talents indicated by his several business ventures. He also had the ideal love, Wendy, whom he labeled "the love of his life." In fact, he had told Susan how important Wendy was to him.

Frank was unable to hold on to one job and succeed. He told people that he was recruited as a member of the CIA's assassination team. He also claimed that he was going to be hired as an artist to draw covers for a detective magazine, etc. He had a pre-occupation with his fantasy of "power over women." He required excessive admiration. He was unwilling to recognize the needs of others nor could he relate to the feelings of others. Frank was unwilling to accept responsibility for his failures and most likely considered Susan to be weak.

Frank dominated Susan and demanded complete control of the family finances. Susan worked full-time and had a responsible position. Overtly, Frank probably appeared to respect his wife's ability to provide a steady income, which assisted him to launch his businesses and pay the bills. Internally, Frank probably resented his wife's stable position, particularly in view of his lack of steady work. Susan most likely complained about her husband's unemployment and grandiose ideas of becoming a commercial artist. It would be safe to say that, when Susan came home from work and found her husband engrossed in his drawings and painting pictures of nude women, there would most likely have been an exchange of angry words.

I also speculate that Susan's mother was aware of her daughter's distress, was concerned about her safety, and went to the house to check on her daughter. Actually, the investigation revealed that Susan's mother had gone to the house earlier when she did not receive an answer on the telephone. (The newspaper had been picked up and brought to the front door.) I believe that when Susan's mother didn't receive an answer at the door, she looked in the window and saw what Susan's co-workers had seen. She most probably went into both shock and denial. She immediately raced home and called Susan's co-worker and beseeched them to go to her daughter's house.

Frank was discovered nude from the waist down with blood on his legs and genitals. Susan was stripped of her clothing, with extensive and multiple stab wounds in her chest, breasts, and genitalia. In reconstructing the crime scene with an analysis of the victimology and history of the participants, I would suggest that there was a sexual confrontation.

Frank attempted to force his wife, with whom he had not been sleeping for months, into sexual relations. Susan denied his demands. When she refused, he became enraged and angry, showing his displeasure by firing the eight shots into the poster picture. Firing the gunshots set the stage for the escalation of his rage and anger.

In my opinion, during the course of this domestic argument with his wife, Susan, Frank became "out of control" and was extremely agitated resulting in a brief psychotic episode. This acute psychotic reaction would clinically be described as a temporary break from reality. During this break, Frank acted out his most primal and perverse sadistic fantasies. These actions were apparently predicated upon a perverse fantasy system fueled by his involvement with his drawings and his sadistic pornography and reinforced by the scripted fantasy stories depicting sexual sadism.

Under certain conditions, an otherwise normal individual may act out his most bizarre and primal fantasies on a victim. The sexual mutilation of the genitalia and breasts of the female victim are typical occurrences in lust murders. What is not typical is a domestic violence lust murder in which an offender acts out his most perverse and primal sexual fantasies on his wife's body. The crime scene was typically disorganized and the sexual mutilation of his wife's body suggested a brief psychotic episode.

At some point thereafter, upon coming out of this state and returning to normal consciousness, he comprehended what he had done to his wife's body and encountered the reality of his rage and anger. He then made a conscious decision to take his own life. He took a gun and shot himself in the head.

Fantasy and Search Warrants

In this chapter, we discussed how important fantasy was to the offender and how fantasy plays a major role in the offender's sexual behavior acting as the driving factor for sexual expression. In sexual predation, the underlying stimulus is expressed through sexual aggression, domination, power, and control. In Case #12, the authorities recovered a videotape, which portrayed the same sexual activities that the offender was replicating with his victims.

These individuals are aroused with thoughts and fantasies of sexual aggression that they reinforce through repetition illustrated by the use of sadistic pornography, drawings, video tapes, books, and women's lingerie and clothing, along with anatomically correct Barbie dolls and fantasy stories featuring sexual sadism.

In Case #11, the search warrant resulted in the recovery of evidential items that revealed not only the suspect's intense interest in sadomasochistic activities, but also the various "trophies" that the offender had taken from his victims.

The astute investigator should consider the offender's behavior with the victim along with what devices or materials were utilized to control the victim or enhance sexual arousal. As we have discussed, the sophistication of the murder or rape kits suggests prior sexual assaults. The materials that the offender used to control his victims and enhance his sexual fantasies are an integral part of the offense and can be introduced into evidence as an example of the role of fantasy. Therefore, the investigator should incorporate into his or her search warrant application a list of the types of materials one would expect to recover from the offender's residence or workplace.

Examples of items and locations that might be significant and should be cited in search warrant applications involving sexual sadism include the following:

- All processed and unprocessed film, video tapes, and audio recordings and recording equipment
- All paintings and drawings depicting sexual acts, torture, and bondage scenarios including commercial literature
- Drawings and/or pictures depicting S&M or B&D activities
- Items that can be used for body restraint, straps, etc.
- Coffins or boxes that can be used for body restraint
- Soundproofing materials
- Models and display cabinets depicting bondage scenarios
- Medications or syringes including hypodermic needles
- Badges and identification indicating law enforcement
- Homemade devices that could be used for torture
- Computers and hard drive memory as well as any disks
- Word processor and monitor

- Medical textbooks, manuals, or other documents depicting first aid and medical treatment
- Surgical instruments or other instruments that can be used to inflict pain and suffering to a person
- Tools including, but not limited to, shovels or digging devices
- Bank records, safe-deposit boxes, receipts for storage unit rentals and other properties
- Soil samples and examination of soil beneath structures
- Handwritten notes, checks, or other documents containing samples of the suspect's handwriting
- Documents that reflect vehicles that were previously owned or utilized by the subject
- Makeup kits including makeup, wigs, hairpieces, etc.
- Trace evidence including, but not limited to, hair, fibers, latent prints, discarded materials, cigarette butts, condoms, hygiene products, medical treatment materials, etc.

Conclusion

Detectives involved in the investigation of sex-related homicides and deaths should be aware of the role of fantasy in sex-related homicides and accidental deaths due to sexual asphyxia. Fantasy fuels the mental and emotional processes underlying human behavior revealed in the crime scene or accidental death event. The presentation in an autoerotic death case is oftentimes manifestation of a particular theme based on a sexual fantasy. Fantasy also serves as an indication of the signature of an offender, which enables detectives to link an offender to a particular series of crimes committed by that offender.

Sexual sadists rely heavily on fantasy and ritual to obtain sexual satisfaction. There is an element of compulsivity as well as an obsession on the part of the sexual sadist to keep trophies and recordings of the event. Photographs of the victims play a significant part in their rituals as well as their ability to recall their sadistic acts.

Therefore, the author recommends that any search warrant applications in these types of cases should certainly reference photographs as well as any records, scripts, letters, maps, diaries, drawings, audiotapes, videotapes, and newspaper reports of the crimes as possible evidence to be seized.

References

American Psychiatric Association. *Diagnostic and Statistical Manual of Mental Disorders, (DSM-IV-TR)*, 4th ed., Text revision, American Psychiatric Association, Washington, D.C., 2000.

Coleman, J.C., J.N. Butcher, and R.C. Carson. *Abnormal Psychology and Modern Life*, 7th. ed., Scott, Foresman and Company, San Antonio, TX, 1984.

DeRiver, J.P. *Crime and the Sexual Psychopath*, Charles C Thomas & Co., Springfield, IL, 1958.

Geberth, V.J. *Practical Homicide Investigation: Tactics, Procedures, and Forensic Techniques*, 3rd ed., CRC Press, Boca Raton, FL, 1996.

Geberth, V.J. Domestic violence homicides, *Law and Order Magazine*, 46 (11), 51–54, 1998.

Geberth, V.J. Domestic violence lust murder: A clinical perspective of sadistic and sexual fantasies integrated into domestic violence dynamics, *Law and Order Magazine*, 48 (11), 44–53, November 2000.

Geberth, V.J. *Sex-Related Homicide and Death Investigation: Practical and Clinical Perspectives*, 1st ed., CRC Press, Boca Raton, FL, 2003, pp. 68–83.

Geberth, V.J. The investigative significance of fantasy in sex-related incidents, *Law and Order Magazine*, 52 (9), 94–99. September 2004.

Geberth, V.J. *Practical Homicide Investigation: Tactics, Procedures, and Forensic Techniques*, 4th ed., CRC Press, Boca Raton, FL, 2006.

Geberth, V.J. Fantasy drawings and their significance in criminal investigative analysis, *Law and Order Magazine,* 56 (10), 114–118. October 2008.

McGuire, R.J., J.M. Carlisle, and B.G. Young. Sexual deviations as conditioned behaviour: A hypothesis, *Behaviour Research and Therapy,* 2, 185–190, 1965.

Roberts, K. Retired detective. Personal interviews, March 1998 and 2001.

Journal of a Serial Rapist
A Case Study

3

Introduction

In the previous two chapters, which address human sexuality and sexual deviance, as well as the investigative significance fantasy in sex-related incidents, the author presented both clinical and investigative perspectives to assist the detective in the analysis of such events. The author discussed the significance of fantasy in the analysis of these events and how this fantasy component, coupled with the presence of certain paraphilias, provides the **signature** of an offender, which enables detectives to link an offender to a particular series of crimes committed by that offender. Many times, the presence of paraphiliac activities is a clear indication of future sexual assault or perversion.

In this chapter, the author presents a case history involving a serial rapist who kept a journal in which he described his day-to-day life as well as his sexual thoughts and fantasies. In this journal of depravity, the offender's chilling personal accounts provided authorities with a graphic description of each of his sexual assaults. It also presents an unprecedented and comprehensive assessment of the thinking process of a serial rapist's mind, which validates much of the research on sexual predators.

The Suspect

Thomas SR (**serial rapist**), a 40-year-old computer programmer, was a serial rapist who sexually assaulted a number of women in the suburbs of Cleveland, Ohio. He managed to elude the authorities for years. Paradoxically, during the time he was eluding the police, he kept exquisite records of his predation on his computer. He referred to his activities as "hunting" and, just like a predator, he pursued his prey anonymously, stalking women in parking lots of retail stores. Miraculously, for his next would-be victim, Thomas SR was unsuccessful in his attempt to abduct a woman from her car. Thomas SR had attempted to enter the victim's car from the passenger side in a parking lot of a Super Kmart® center. He had been stalking her and planned to abduct her from her car. However, she fought him off and screamed for help, which alerted a store clerk. When the store clerk approached the victim's car, Thomas SR jumped out of the victim's car and fled in his own automobile. The store clerk got the license number of Thomas SR's car and called police. State troopers, who had received the call and description of the suspect and his car, spotted him on Interstate 90 and gave chase. The state troopers, as well as police units from three other departments, pursued him off of the interstate and into a driveway of a school in Avon where they had him trapped. Suddenly, Thomas SR took out his .45-caliber pistol and committed suicide while sitting in his car. Thomas SR was subsequently identified as a serial rapist who had committed at least five abductions and six sexual assaults. He also had a criminal record for two previous abductions of female victims.

When police searched his vehicle, they found his "rape kit" that consisted of duct tape, a knife and handcuffs, and rope and ace bandages for binding his victims. He also had goggles with the lenses taped over to blindfold his victims. He had a stun gun, which could be used to incapacitate or torture his victims, along with a ski mask to hide his identity, and latex gloves in order to prevent leaving fingerprints. In addition, Thomas SR had a Cleveland police badge and a fake police identification card (Figures 3.1 through 3.8).

Figure 3.1 Rape kit. 9 mm semiautomatic. (Photo courtesy of Detective Ray Adornetto, South Euclid, Ohio, Police Department.)

Figure 3.2 Rape kit. Shoulder holster. (Photo courtesy of Detective Ray Adornetto, South Euclid, Ohio, Police Department.)

Figure 3.3 Rape kit. Stun gun. (Photo courtesy of Detective Ray Adornetto, South Euclid, Ohio, Police Department.)

Figure 3.4 Rape kit. Tape, rope, and knife. (Photo courtesy of Detective Ray Adornetto, South Euclid, Ohio, Police Department.)

Figure 3.5 Rape kit. Tape and bindings. (Photo courtesy of Detective Ray Adornetto, South Euclid, Ohio, Police Department.)

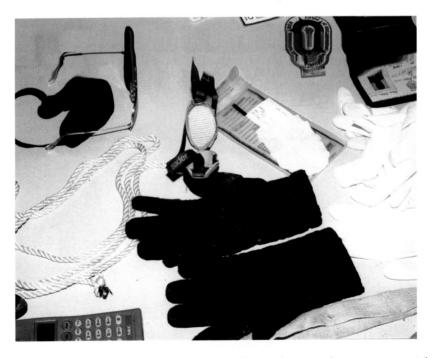

Figure 3.6 Rape kit. Gloves, badge, and cell phone. (Photo courtesy of Detective Ray Adornetto, South Euclid, Ohio, Police Department.)

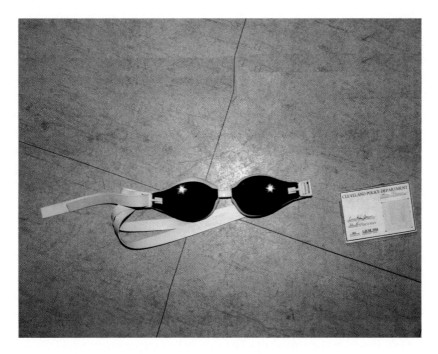

Figure 3.7 Rape kit. Swim goggles used as a blindfold. (Photo courtesy of Detective Ray Adornetto, South Euclid, Ohio, Police Department.)

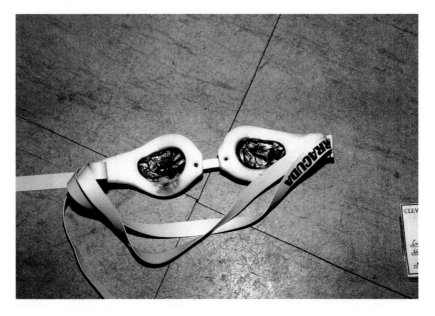

Figure 3.8 Rape kit. Swim goggles with duct tape over lenses. (Photo courtesy of Detective Ray Adornetto, South Euclid, Ohio, Police Department.)

Since the subject had a Cleveland police badge, Cleveland detectives were assigned to assist in the investigation. The detectives secured a search warrant for his apartment. When the police went to his apartment, they were surprised at the neatness of his rooms and the organization of his property, which included his personal computer and dozens of disks. In fact, it was Homicide Detectives Mike O'Malley and Robert Matuszny who convinced a lieutenant from one of the suburbs to seize the computer and disks. When I interviewed Detectives O'Malley and Matuszny, they told me that they "both just had a 'gut' feeling that Thomas SR's computer might contain evidence. The way everything in his apartment seemed so meticulous, it was only logical that the suspect, being a computer programmer, would enter data in his own home computer."

The homicide detectives' hunch proved to be crucial.

The Journal

Detective Ray Adornetto of the South Euclid Police Department had the first sexual assault case. He provided the author with copies of Thomas SR's 220-page journal as well as the investigative details of this serial rape case. In fact, it was Detective Adornetto and Lieutenant Dale Brady of the University Heights Police Department who first realized the similarity between the first two incidents and the significance of this particular offender's MO. The two investigators agreed that the same offender was probably responsible for both incidents. They based their conclusion on the words that the offender used with each of his victims, his approach in parking lots of malls, the use of the gun to threaten compliance, the fact that both victims had their hands taped behind their backs, as well as the similar sexual activities, which indicated a unique **signature**.

Thomas SR took his life as he was about to be apprehended for an attempted rape. Once he was identified as the unknown serial rapist who had terrorized women throughout the suburbs of Cleveland, Detective Adornetto, Lt. Brady, and their fellow detectives spent weeks going over the entries in his journal. They compared the entries with the information in the various police reports from all of the different jurisdictions that had experienced sexual assaults. The detectives reinterviewed the victims as well as some of the unsuspecting would-be victims who had been named or described in the journal.

The journal clearly identified Thomas SR as a serial offender. He had explicitly detailed each and every rape and sexual assault he had committed. He described in detail his stalking, as well as several attempts at abduction, in the journal recovered by detectives. As a result, he was subsequently linked to various sexual assault cases in Cleveland and the different suburban jurisdictions.

Thomas SR had meticulously detailed the most mundane details of his day-to-day personal life, his sexual fantasies about rape, and vividly described how he stalked dozens of women whom he planned on abducting and sexually assaulting. He was a man obsessed with his weight and looks, jogging, health clubs, strippers, pornography, and tennis. Throughout the journal, Thomas SR complains about his own physical appearance. He talks about being too short and overweight. Many of his entries began with an exact weight of the day. He experienced several failed relationships and was angry at being rejected. He dealt with this rejection by hunting for women whom he could rape and control. He referred to his stalking as "hunting" or "cruising" and he recounted within the journal his numerous excursions. In fact, Thomas SR recounted several attempts at abduction and sexual assault. During the assaults, he would talk to his victims and ask questions about their children or spouses and homes. In some instances, he would talk to them as if they were on a date. He also warned them of the dangers of leaving their cars unlocked and explained that this was why he chose them for attack. He also kept personal information in his journal. On other occasions, he was vulgar, threatening, and demeaning as he acted out his sexual perversions and fantasies, which included bondage, forced oral sex, and complete domination and control. His autobiographical exploits provided the authorities with his victim selection process and his distinctive **signature,** which was used to link the cases. He also was very methodical and followed a specific modus operandi (MO) spreading his crimes over several jurisdictions to avoid detection.

Journal Entries

In this section, I have provided specific examples of some of the journal entries for analysis and review. The MO involves actions necessary to accomplish the activity while the "signature aspect" represents the underlying emotional "needs" of the offender. I have bolded the **signature** and **modus operandi** entries for emphasis and review. I have also provided excerpts of the official police reports and complaints in the words of the victims for comparison with the journal entries. The vicious and cruel reality of the offenses as described by the victims is dramatically divergent compared with the subject's perception in his journal entries. The journal entries, which reveal his underlying fantasy-driven behavior, describe the events as sexual encounters and, in some instances, he would eroticize the attacks to fit his sexual fantasies.

The journal entries start off with a brief recap of his life in which he talks about vacation trips, his mom and dad catching a frog and keeping it in a bottle, how his uncle caught a tarantula-like spider, his crush on (*name withheld*) in kindergarten, a fishing trip, a crush on (*name withheld*) the girl next door, start on other relationships, high school, joining the army, getting arrested, his dad's death from cancer, Ohio School of Broadcasting, lists of different jobs, and then the rape.

Sexual Assault–Sodomy: Journal Entry

12-26: Went to the Revco at Mayfield and Plainfield. A blond woman went in and left her door unlocked. When she came back, **I got in the passenger side and forced her to drive** across the street to the bank lot. Her name was *Mary* — (*Author note: This is not her real name. But, in the journal, he lists both the first and last names of his victims.*) 46 and good looking. She started to escape out of the driver's door, but thought better of it when I put the gun to her head. **Taped her hands behind her back with duct tape** and forced her into the back seat. **Crossed and taped her ankles together and blindfolded and gagged her with duct tape.** Drove her over to the Center Mayfield parking lot and got in back with her. Unbuttoned her blouse and took her tits out of her bra. **Sucked on both of them, the nipples were red and tasty.** Forced her skirt up and pulled off her panties and panty hose, untaped her legs and played with her pussy. **Made her suck my dick for a while and made her get up on all fours so I could fuck her from behind. I forgot condoms, so I didn't fuck her.** Let her go after an hour.

Detective Ray Adornetto was assigned to this investigation, which had occurred in South Euclid, Ohio.

Police Report

The police report provides an insight into the offender's actual behavior during the crime as well as the remarks and statements that he made to his victim. He immediately threatened her with a gun and stated, *"Don't look at me,"* as he fixed his ski mask over his mouth. The victim reported that he was **very agitated and very nervous** as he gave her directions. He taped her hands behind her back. **He told her, *"Don't do anything stupid."*** He also stated several times *that if she did everything he told her, she would be okay.* When the victim offered her money and car to the perpetrator, he stated, *"It's not you car or your money I want, it's you."* As he was driving her to the location of assault, the subject said, *"You left your car unlocked—did you know that? Consider this your punishment."* The subject took her to an unknown location. When they got to this location, the offender said, *"If you are a good little girl and do everything I say all night long, you won't get hurt.* The victim reported that *he put both his hands around my neck, quite tightly, and said, "You're going to do everything I say and not make any trouble, aren't you?"*

The victim also reported that the subject told her **that if she didn't do what he said, he would kill her and throw her in the woods.** The offender ordered her onto her stomach and pulled her pants and pantyhose down and fondled her buttocks. She could hear him sigh. He then directed her to turn over on her back. She stated, *"He unbuttoned my coat and blouse and grabbed my bra and ripped it right off."* The victim stated that the offender fondled her breasts and nipples and put them in his mouth. She stated that when he removed the tape from her mouth, he appeared to become more at ease. He wasn't as nervous or agitated. *He told me, "If I screamed, he would kill me."* He then said, *"Kiss me—kiss me and do it like you mean it."*

The victim reported that the offender put his finger into her vagina as he continued to fondle her breasts. During this time, he asked the victim personal questions about her family and her children. The victim reported, *"He was carrying on a conversation and was very much relaxed."* He then said, *"I want you to suck my dick and, if you bite me, I'll kill you."*

She also reported that he stated, *"You're in luck, I'm not going to rape you—I didn't bring any condoms.* The offender then instructed her to suck his dick. He said, *"Lick it—lick it."*

The victim reported that the offender did not ejaculate. He asked the victim if she performed oral sex on her husband and stated, *"I bet he likes it."* When he finished, he said, *"I'm going to take you back to near where I got you and leave you and you're not going to file a police report on this."* The victim stated that he put his hands around her neck and repeated, *"You're not going to file a police report, are you?"* Then he said, *"If you do, I do worse than tonight—I know where you live."* He had gone through her wallet and asked if she still lived at the same address. The victim reported that the **perpetrator completely removed her panties and panty hose and took them**.

Analysis

The complainant's report confirms the journal entries. The difference between what the offender wrote and what the victim reported is the brutal reality of the incident. The victim stated in her report, **"When he bound and gagged me I thought that I would not live—that he would kill me."**

Thomas SR followed a specific MO. He stalked his victims in parking lots and watched for a target who had left her door unlocked. He wrote, "When she came back **I got in the passenger side** and forced her to drive across the street to the bank lot." **Taped her hands behind her back with duct tape** and forced her into the back seat. **Crossed and taped her ankles together and blindfolded and gagged her with duct tape.** He also apparently knew about forensic evidence and, because he didn't have a condom with him, didn't want to take the chance of raping his victim and leaving evidence.

The **signature** piece is revealed in what he does to his victims. **Unbuttoned her blouse and took her tits out of her bra. Sucked on both of them, the nipples were red and tasty.** The reference to him telling the victim, *"Kiss me—kiss me and do it like you mean it,"* is another element of interest. It almost seems as if the offender is on a date and wants his victim to like him. He also engaged in personal conversation with the victim. The offender then instructed her to suck his dick. He instructed her to "lick it." The victim reported that the offender did not ejaculate. This was certainly indicative of sexual dysfunction. He then asked the victim if she performed oral sex on her husband and stated, *"I bet he likes it."* In the offender's mind, a "putdown" as he humiliates her. Then he reveals his sadistic streak as he wrote, **"Made her suck my dick for a while and made her get up on all fours so I could fuck her from behind."**

The victim reported that the **perpetrator completely removed her panties and panty hose and took them**. He didn't mention this in the journal. This information is of investigative interest because it provides additional insight into an offender who was taking "trophies" to enhance and continue his fantasy at a later time using the victim's panties as a prop.

Sexual Assault: Journal Entry

1-22: Went to the Revco at Cedar and Green. A woman in a station wagon went in with her doors all unlocked. When she came back out **I got in and forced her to drive** over to the gas station where **I duct taped her hands behind her back**. It was not good enough, though, and she escaped. We struggled on the ground until I convinced her to get back in the car. **I taped her hands very tight behind her back, gagged her, blindfolded her, and crossed and taped her ankles.** Drove home, where the kids had come over to sleep! So I had to sneak the woman in through the back door into my room. I put her over my shoulder so her ass was right in my face, bumping her head along the way on a couple of walls and doorways. Got her into my room and laid her on the floor.

She looked so good there, helpless, bound hand and foot, gagged and blindfolded. Picked her up and sat her on the bed. Made her lay down and took off her shoes, socks, pants, and panties. I didn't ask her name and the gag never came out of her mouth. She was a mother of six children, but was in great shape. **She was 5' 2" and tiny. Perfect.** Untapped her hands and made her take off the rest of her clothes. **I ordered her to do it sexy and she did, striking a pose when she took off her bra. Women are so incredible when they are helpless!** Laid down with her nude body and licked and kissed her all over. **Sucked on her nipples, kissed and licked her beautiful little ass, legs and feet.**

Got her up on all fours and was ready to fuck her good when I lost my erection. It was because of the kids, and Mom being in the next room. Got her dressed and took her back to the Revco where I released her. **Got to buy handcuffs.**

Lieutenant Dale Brady was assigned to this investigation, which had occurred in University Heights, Ohio.

Police Report

The victim stated that the offender ran up to her car and opened the passenger door. She stated that she tried to put the car into reverse real fast and knock him down, but he got in and put a gun to her head and ordered her to **"drive over there."** The victim stated she did as she was told and said, *"Don't hurt me."* He told her to shut up and used duct tape to cover her eyes. He told her to open her mouth and gagged her with a piece of gauze, which he also duct taped. He then bound her hands but didn't do a very good job. He stated, **"Shut up. If you do everything you're told, you'll be okay."** The victim stated that he kept using the word **sodomy** and **"I'll sodomize you."** The victim attempted to flee after freeing her hands, but was running blind because her eyes were covered with duct tape. The perpetrator caught her and put the gun to her head and stated, **"You bitch. I'm going to kill you, you better listen to me."** He then threw her on the ground. He then taped her hands behind her back and put her in the back seat of her car.

He kept saying, **"I can't believe you did this, you bitch. You're going to pay for this."** The victim stated, *"Please don't hurt me I have six kids."* He replied, **"If you listen to me you won't get hurt."** He then gagged her again and taped her tightly. The offender then picked up the victim and put her into his vehicle. He then drove for approximately 5 to 8 minutes.

When he got to where he was going, he told her, **"Don't say anything or I will kill you. This won't take more than a few hours."** The victim stated that the suspect picked her up "like a sack of potatoes" and carried her up a narrow stairwell. **She stated that she was hitting her head against the walls and that he was huffing a lot.** He then laid her on a bed. She stated he was pacing the floor. He untaped her feet and took her socks off. He told her to lie on her stomach. He took her pantyhose and underwear off and tied her up again.

He stated, **"You screwed up, you tried to escape."** The victim reported that the **perpetrator used both hands to choke her,** stating, **"How does it feel not to have control."** The victim stated that she thought that he was trying to be perverted to get himself turned on.

She stated, *"He then untied my wrists and put a gun to my head and said he was going to shoot me if I didn't take my shirt and bra off in a sexy manner. He said it better turn him on."* He used twine to retie her hands behind her back. He told her he was going to use a condom. *"He then said that I would have to suck his penis."* The complainant stated to the investigators that she thought that he was trying to turn himself on. The subject turned her over onto her knees and was touching her breasts and vagina. The complainant stated, *"I could tell he was not hard enough. He kept saying it was my fault that I was not wet enough that's why he could not penetrate me. He started to choke me again … He started to kiss me and touch my breasts, playing with me … He tried again … He got real mad that he couldn't do it. I started to get scared."*

In the opinion of the author these observations as reported by the complainant are important since they suggest that the offender has a sexual dysfunction and must incorporate into the event certain behavior, which serve to identify a specific signature.

The victim stated that suddenly he got up and said, **"I can't do this to you. This is wrong. I'm really sorry. I'll take you back to the car."** He then untied her and ordered her to get dressed. She still had the blindfold on her eyes and a gag in her mouth. He then taped her hands behind her back. He guided her down the stairs and outside where he put her in the back seat of a car.

On the way back to the Revco parking lot, he stated, **"Don't go to the police."** The victim stated that she would not. **The subject was worried about police being by her car, so**

the victim suggested that he drop her off nearby and that she would face the wall so as not to see his license plate.

This strategy of cooperation on the part of the victim probably saved her. **He then said he was sorry** and said, *"You learned a lesson, keep your doors locked."* The victim told him to seek professional help. The perpetrator stated all he wanted was companionship.

When they got to Revco, he said there are people coming out of the store. He pulled over to another location, took her out of the car, and stood her up facing the wall. The victim waited until he pulled away. She ran to her car, went home and told her husband what had happened. They called the police.

Analysis

The modus operandi is the same and once again the victim was taken from a parking lot after the subject discovered that the victim had left her car door unlocked. He waited for her by her car, got in, put a gun to her head, and ordered her to drive. The words that he used during the event were similar, such as *"You learned a lesson, keep your doors locked."* In the first sexual assault, he stated; *"You left your car unlocked—did you know that? Consider this your punishment."*

His method of control is distinctive as well. **He tapes their hands tight behind their backs, gags and blindfolds them, and crosses and tapes their ankles.** His **signature** activities with his victims involve having total control over them. "**Women are so incredible when they are helpless!**" He wrote how he made her take off the rest of her clothes. "**I ordered her to do it sexy and she did.**" He engaged in specific activities. He wrote, "**Sucked on her nipples, kissed and licked her beautiful little ass, legs and feet. I got her up on all fours and was ready to fuck her good ...**" In the South Euclid case, he wrote; "**... made her get up on all fours so I could fuck her from behind.**" He reveals his victim selection choice in the journal stating: "**She was 5' 2" and tiny. Perfect.**"

The complainant's report confirmed the journal entries. However, once again the vicious reality of the assault and the victim's fear for her life are not recorded in Thomas SR's journal. The victim stated that the offender said, *"You bitch, why did you try to run away. Now I'm going to hurt you. I'm going to sodomize you, then kill you and throw you in a ravine."*

He stated, *"You screwed up, you tried to escape."* The victim reported that the perpetrator used both hands to choke her, stating, *"How does it feel not to have control."* The offender's anger at his victim does not appear in his journal entries, instead he erotized the event. However, he does make reference to not completing the sexual assault by stating, "**Got her up on all fours and was ready to fuck her good when I lost my erection.**" He explains that it was because of the kids, and Mom being in the next room. He also doesn't make any reference to his apology. However, the victim reported that he apologized to her and confided in her that all he wanted was companionship.

This was an extremely daring exploit on the part of the offender to actually take the victim to his mother's home and sneak her into the house and sexually assault her there.

In the South Euclid case, he wrote, "**I forgot condoms, so I didn't fuck her.**" In the University Heights case, he writes that he's "**got to buy handcuffs.**" It is apparent that he is researching and attempting to improve his predation by being prepared and having the "right" equipment.

In the opinion of the author, the offender was not only improvising his **rape kit,** but was progressing in his sexual activities, which is consistent with the elements of psychopathic sexual sadism.

The journal entries continue with his complaints about his weight (many entries are preceded by his weight of the day), some day-to-day activities at work, his tennis games, and his on and off relationship with a girl he names and how she dumped him.

Two months later, he wrote that while he was reading the paper, "… Saw an artist's rendition (of the suspect) that was pretty damn close to me." He wrote that the story said two women had been abducted and raped recently. He then makes the following entry: **"Both stupid bitches reported their rapes after I told them not to."**

In the opinion of the author, this was important information because it verified that this type of offender who is organized, follows the case and the police investigation in the newspapers and the media, and it also indicates that this type of offender is usually from the immediate area.

Sexual Assault and Sodomy: Journal Entry

6-4: Went to the Eastlake area. Followed several cars and finally found a white van with a pretty blond loading groceries. When the woman took the cart back, I checked the passenger door and it was unlocked. When she came back, she sat and lit a cigarette.

   I simply got in, pointed the gun at her head, and forced her to drive down to an isolated part of the parking lot. **I** *handcuffed* **her behind her back and forced her into the back of the van. Tied her feet, blindfolded, and gagged her.** Her name was **Jane.** (*This is not her real name. But in the journal, he writes her first name and describes her as a very pretty 32-year-old mother of three.*) Took her over to a bank parking lot and stripped her in her van and played with her. But there were too many people around, so I drove until I found a body shop on Vine and pulled into the back of it between two wrecked cars. There was even a cop across the street giving a ticket and no one saw us. **Ran my hands all over her beautiful body, licking and sucking on her tits and ass.** Took a tentative lick of her clit. Her pussy tasted very sweet! The tits were big C cups and beautiful. **A perfect ass, legs and feet made her quite a prize. She sucked me and I played with her for an hour or so. Made her stand outside the van so I could run my hands up and down her body. Played with her some** more before we parted company. I let her get dressed and took her back to the parking lot at Finest and got into my car and headed home. Now that's a good way to get over (*names the girl who broke up with him*). I think I'll go out to Mentor tomorrow and meet another woman out there.

This case occurred in Eastlake, Ohio, and was assigned to Detective Ken Roberts.

Police Report

The victim reported, "A man opened my passenger door and got in. He said, *'I'm not going to hurt you.'* But, he had a gun. He told me to do as he said and I wouldn't get hurt. I thought he wanted to steal my van. He told me to drive forward to a different part of the parking lot. He then told me to stop and told me to **do exactly what he said and I won't get hurt**. He took my arm and put **handcuffs on and I had to put the other arm around my back**. I was starting to panic now and then he put tape on my eyes and then put his sunglasses on me. He made me go to the back and lie on the seat and drove me to another spot. **While driving he asked me questions**. I told him I had three girls and not to hurt me, and they were home alone. He asked me what time I was expected home and I said 10:30. **He asked a lot of questions: age, married, kids ages, how far I lived from the store. When I didn't respond once, he told me to answer him when asked or he would hurt me**. When we stopped, he came around to the back and **told me he was going to rape me and if I cooperated I won't be hurt. He told me I left my door open and, if he was a murderer, I would be dead.**

He took my shoes, socks, pants, and underpants off. He pulled my shirt over my head and unhooked my bra. He told me I was going to do oral sex on him and I wasn't to bite him.

He pulled on my pubic hair and pinched my left nipple very hard while he stressed that I was going to obey him. He choked my neck to show me how he would kill me if I didn't do everything he wanted. He made me French kiss him and he sucked my breasts, did oral sex on me, kissed me on my butt and my feet. He even licked my feet.

Then he made me lay on the floor and he drove me to a second place. He made me get out of the van and stand outside and French kiss me. Then he made me get back in the van. He made me do oral sex on him. He was having me sit up and lay down on the seat and on the floor and turning me over. He was mad that there wasn't much room. When he was done, he said it was about 10:30 and that he was going to let me go. Before that he said that he wanted to keep me all night and wished he could keep me two or three days. He drove again and this time I was lying on the seat; that's when he told me to keep my head down and, if a cop saw me, I would be dead. He told me not to go to the police and not tell my husband. He also threatened that he would come back and get me if I reported it to the police. He told me when he let me go that he would take the handcuffs off and leave and that I was to lay still for a few minutes … I heard him get into a car next to the van and drive away. I got up and put my clothes on. I went to the Finest entrance and I carried my socks and shoes inside where I called the police.

Analysis

The offender has perfected his MO of stalking and approaching his victims in parking lots as they return to their cars. He wrote, **"I simply got in, pointed the gun at her head, and forced her to drive … I *handcuffed* her behind her back and forced her into the back of the van. Tied her feet, blindfolded, and gagged her."** It is interesting to note that he had added **handcuffs** to his rape kit. He also engages in similar dialogue with this victim as with the previous victims. Once again he tells the victim that, if she cooperates, she won't get hurt. He also warned her not to go to the police. He also told her that she left her car door open and, if he was a murderer, she would be dead. Similar to the remarks made to the previous victims. Suggesting that it was their fault for being attacked and that this attack should serve as a lesson to be more careful.

The **signature** piece is played out as he wrote, **"Ran my hands all over her beautiful body, licking and sucking on her tits and ass."** He engages in similar sexual activities with this victim, which included forced oral sex. He wrote in his journal that she had "**a perfect ass, legs and feet,** [which] **made her quite a prize."**

The complainant's report confirmed the journal entries. The victim's statement goes into details that the offender didn't mention in his journal. The victim's fear for her life is documented in the report. The victim stated that the offender said that **if I could see his face he would have to kill me.** *"Don't raise your head up because if a cop sees you and pulls us over, you'll be dead before they could get to me."*

The victim stated in her report that *"he pulled on my pubic hair and pinched my left nipple very hard while he stressed that I was going to obey him. He squeezed my neck until I couldn't breathe at all and I thought he was going to choke me to death right there."*

He doesn't mention that he caused her pain by pulling her pubic hair and pinching her left nipple very hard, as he ordered her to obey him. He also conveniently left out how he squeezed her neck until she couldn't breathe and that he choked her and threatened to kill her.

Once again the journal entries indicate his total control of the victim as he directed and ordered her to perform. He also revealed his anger at the recent breakup when he wrote, **"Now, that's good way to get over"** (*names the girl who broke up with him*). He then follows up with a reference about going out to Mentor, Ohio, for another **"hunt."**

The offender is clearly enjoying the assaults and acting out his anger against women in a brutal and degrading manner. The journal entries continued to eroticize the events and obviously served to fulfill his fantasies.

The journal entries continue on into October. During this time period, he is in and out of relationships. He complains about trying to lose weight, having erection problems, having a new job, meeting new people, etc. There is one particularly interesting entry in September, which indicates the offender's mobility. Thomas SR would drive around for hours looking for hunting places.

9-25: Rented a Mercury Cougar from Hertz and drive to Niagra [sic] Falls. Stayed less than thirty minutes, turned around and came home.

10-2: Subject was brooding over a breakup with another girl. Talks about trying to get over her.

10-3: "Mopped around the house all day feeling sorry for myself." Called another girl.

10-4: "No call from (names the girl who broke up with him)."

Attempted Rape: Journal Entry

10-5: Got up at 6 … I am still in pain over this whole (*names girl*) thing. I tried to cry last night, but only got a few tears to fall. The bitch is too screwed up to have anything to do with, yet I still have these strong feelings for her … Went to Willoughby and went to a kitchen cabinet store after-hours [sic] and **introduced** myself to a sweet young thing who was cleaning up. I took her into a back bathroom and **ordered her to take her cloths off.** She refused and started praying to Jesus! No matter how much I asked, she refused. I finally left after five minutes of trying to convince her to see things my way. Barely made it home. Injured the knee badly during the incident. It is swollen and stiff. I fantasized about the Retail Girl and what I would have done to her had she cooperated.

She was young, tall, and delicious, with nice tits and a great ass.

This case occurred in Willoughby, Ohio, and was assigned to Detective Gregory Knack. The original police report was unavailable for review.

10-6: Makes a comment about wanting to "fuck" the new neighbor. "A sweet little blond with big tits." He writes, "Hopefully I'll have my chance."

10-9: Lists his weight for the day. Writes, "Met the new file clerk (*names her*). I would like to nail this one."

10-22: Makes a reference to attacking his neighbor. "If I lose my job, the first person I'm going to **visit** is that little bitch! (*He fantasized about raping and killer her.*) He then wrote, "Went cruising. Checked out the real estate places and got a few leads. Went to Solon and checked out the K-Mart. Not too bad. But the best place I found was the Finest store in Salon. Just too many targets! All in minivans! Great location."

Analysis

The following entries referred to his "hunting and cruising" trips. Like most serial rapists, he is constantly on the prowl for new territory and locations to predate. He is also taking time breaks between the attacks and spreading his crimes over many jurisdictions, so as not to bring attention to one city or town. This technique effectively thwarted efficient police intervention.

10-29: Went **cruising** at 6:20. Went out to Mayfield and 306 and found a nice location. Saw a cute little girl who works at the Drug Mart come out to her car during her break to eat. She left all her car doors unlocked, which is a pretty dangerous thing to do these days. I think I'll go back out there next week and warn her about leaving herself open to abductions, rape, torture, and strangulation like that. Got home at 10:45 after checking out the Revco in Mentor, the Finest in Mentor, and the Revco in Willoughby. A lot of close calls, but nothing more than that.

On October 29, he was actively seeking out a victim. Take note that he "hunts" in places he has previously checked out. In the opinion of the author, this is classic behavior of the serial offender. Many times, offenders will go back to an area or location where they have been successful in the past. The reference about going back to Mayfield to "warn" actually means that he was thinking of abducting and raping that young woman.

11-22: Went out **cruising.** Went to Chester Township first and had a chance to **introduce** myself to a cute woman who left her van completely unlocked. But I didn't like the circumstances and passed on it. Went to Chagrin area and then to Salon. First to the K-Mart where nothing was happening and then to Finest where I had all sorts of opportunities.
    Followed a beautiful woman in a van to her home. **Almost met a cute woman who had left her van unlocked, but there were too many people around**. Went back to the Chagrin area, but again the pickens' [sic] were slim. Got home at 10:30

11-23: Went out to Garfield Heights Revco to look around. Almost met a young girl who left her car unlocked. Later almost met two teenage girls who left their car unlocked. I passed on it mainly because I didn't think I could handle two young girls like that.

11-25: Went **hunting** in Garfield Heights. The Revco offered up some tasty morsels, but the *guardia* [meaning security guards] *was in full bloom*. Went over to the Revco on Broadview Road. Nice location.

1-2: Went to check on my little girl in Middleburg Heights. She was there, in the attorney's office, working to 9. Went to the Finest up the street at State and Snow. Had the opportunity to meet a sweet young girl with short dark hair. She was driving a Jeep with unlocked doors. I passed because of the size of the Jeep.

    In retrospect, that would not have mattered, and I could have brought her home to spend some time with me. **I almost introduced myself to another woman with unlocked doors**.

She was cute and tiny, but in her late forties, so I passed. **I should have just asked** her to go someplace private with me to **give me a quick blowjob**. But I passed. Got home at 10.

The journal continues through to April with constant references to his weight, which he recorded to the ounce, his jogging, his golf, his tennis, along with his frustration in relationships and his anger at women. There are a number of entries in which the subject remarks about women he has met and what he would like to do to them. Whenever he got mad at a woman, he fantasized about raping and hurting her. He was constantly seeking out targets. These next entries are revealing as he documented how he did an "overhear" on a store clerk to obtain an address of a potential victim. He even drove to the area to locate her.

2-9: Saw a cute waitress. I'll got back and **talk** to her.

2-10: Saw a cute redhead there and stood next to her when she gave her address to the clerk! Went to South Euclid **to track her down, but could not find the address**.

Sexual Assault–Rape Sodomy: Journal Entry

4-6: Left for Warren at 1:00 PM. Got into the area at 2:30 PM and started **scouting** locations for my **night hunt for pussy**. After looking at places all over Warren and Niles, finally found a good place on Route 422 in Niles. Followed a girl home after opening her passenger door, but she was on to me and ran into her house before I **could introduce** myself. Had another girl, whose car I got in and unlocked the passenger door. She was a delicious tanned girl with curly black hair and a great body. I was ready to make the move, but there was a guy waiting in a jeep behind me, so I couldn't get to her. Followed her home, but couldn't get to her in time.

After a few hours of searching, I finally found a girl at a Super K-Mart. She left her door open and I prepared the car for her return, unlocking the passenger door and finding a parking place where I could surprise her from.

She returned to the car about 10:30, and sat there eating a taco. I started moving towards it, but another woman who was just pulling out thought my movements suspicious and stopped her car. So, I kept walking past the victim's car and pretended I was running across the parking lot. Came back after a few minutes and the woman was gone.

But the victim was still sitting there eating her taco. So I got in the passenger door, pointed the gun at her head and ordered her to drive.

She obeyed and I took her behind the Kmart. I handcuffed her behind her back and forced her into the back seat.

I decided to try the stun gun. I pushed it against her neck and hit the trigger. It did not have the desired effect. I really expected it to incapacitate her. Instead it just shocked her, making her cry. So much for fucking $50 stun gun.

I tied her feet, blindfolded and gagged her. Drove her car back near mine and made a flawless transfer, forcing her from her car to my car's backseat, and drove off, with no witnesses to her abduction. She had been somewhat calm up to that point, but once she realized she was being abducted and not carjacked, she began to panic, her gag muffling her cries. She tried to resist getting into my car for a second, but then did what she was told. She stayed quiet and didn't move. Drove to a motel and checked in quickly. Again, I got her inside the room with no witnesses. Once inside, I sat her on the bed and I told her to stay calm and she would be okay. I explained what was happening and told her straight out that I was going to rape her. Her long legs were shaking uncontrollably. I rubbed them and tried to calm her down. I took her gag off and asked her some questions about herself. Her name was *Betty* (*This is not her real name. But in the journal he names her and types in bold* "18-years old!!!") She was 5'9", had huge C cup breasts and a fantastic young little ass. She had sex for the first time at 13 and it was date rape! This time she was in for the real thing. She had a boyfriend and they had sex a few days ago. She became more calm as I rubbed her legs and she got used to her situation.

I asked her to strip nude for me, and I stripped while watching her. She took her blouse off, then her bra revealing those beautiful huge tits. Her shoes, socks and jeans came off next and then the panties. I made her wiggle her cute little ass as she took them off. I handcuffed her behind her back and made her lay down on the bed.

I got in with her and kissed, licked, and played with her body for a while. I made her kiss me and she kissed nicely, with her mouth open and her sweet little tongue darting all over the inside of my mouth. She said she was cold, so I turned the heat on.

It was fun having complete control over an 18-year-old girl, leading her to the bathroom, her being dependent on me to guide her every step because of the blindfold (*which was my swimming goggles covered with duck* [sic] *tape.*)

Took a shower with her washing her tits, belly, ass, legs and feet. Even washed her young little asshole, which looked very inviting. Licked her wet body, sucking on the tits and licking and kissing her wet little ass. Made her get on her knees and suck my wet dick. She had never sucked a man's dick before, so I was patient. She sucked real good for a beginner, licking and sucking like a pro. It was a great feeling knowing that my dick was the first dick she had ever tasted. For the rest of her life she'll know that the first dick she ever sucked belonged to me, her rapist! I stood there looking down at her. She looked so good nude, on her knees, her hands bound behind her back, with my dick in her mouth. I played with her big tits as she sucked my cock. Then I made her push her tits against my legs, rubbing the nipples all over. Took the handcuffs off and watched as she dried her body off. That was fun, watching her dry her beautiful, fresh, 18-year-old body.

Handcuffed her in front because she was so submissive and obedient. Took her to bed and made her get on all fours so I could explore her pussy and asshole from behind. I should have licked her from pussy to asshole. Played with her tits as they hung there helplessly.

I put her at the end of the bed on her back with her head hanging over the edge and fucked her mouth in the upside down position. I used some strawberry motion-lotion to try to make the taste better for her. She kept gagging because of the salty taste of my dick. But I kept fucking her sweet little mouth because it felt and looked so good.

I made her get back on the bed with her head on the pillow, on her back. I examined her beautiful pussy close up. I had never before had a chance to explore a woman's pussy up close and on my terms, so it was fun. It was so red and wet. The inner lips were so curly and cute. I opened them gently with my fingers and examined her clit. I then started licking her. She tasted great!

Now I know what I missed with the 15-year-old (*names a girl in the journal*) I wished I had buried my face in that pretty little fifteen-year-old muff!

In the opinion of the author, this entry revealed how the offender was constantly fantasizing about sex. As he described the current event, he suddenly goes back in time and equates this episode with an earlier fantasy and incorporates both into the journal.

I licked and sucked on her clit for a few minutes, but when I realized there was no way I was going to make her come, I gave up. But it was still fun licking a sweet, fresh 18-year-old cunt. She said that she had never been into oral sex that much and had a hard time cuming from a guy licking her. **Put a condom on and fucked her.** First in the missionary with her beautiful feet up by my head, which I kissed and licked [sic]. Then I turned her over and took her from behind. That sweet, young 18-year-old butt looked so good as I fucked her. The delicious asshole was so visible as I pumped her. The bad news was she started her period that day and as

I pumped there was more and more blood on the condom. It still felt great and I would have come, but the blood bothered me.

Her asshole was rimmed with blood from her vagina. Made her lie on top of me and rub her big tits and pussy and ass all over me. She dangled her tits above my face so I could suck her nipples. She had inverted nipples but it was still fun sucking those 18-year-old C-cup tities! [sic] **Put her on her tummy and tied her in different positions.**

Crossed her ankles and taped them tight, then tied her feet to her handcuffs. Her sweet little body looked great hog-tied like that. After that I just played with her for awhile [sic]. **Squeezed, kissed, and licked her firm, soft 18-year-old ass.** Licked her beautiful long legs and her sweet little feet. Kissed her toes and then worked my way back up her body and kissed her mouth for a while. **Made her suck my dick again, making her move that little mouth of hers faster and faster.** If she didn't keep stopping because of the taste, I would have cumed [sic] in her mouth. Laid there for awhile [sic] longer playing with the little 18 year old until 12:15. As I caressed her helpless body, I told her that she had been abducted because she had left her car door unlocked. I also told her that she was lucky I took her and not a guy who enjoyed torturing and killing young girls like her. Let her get dressed and took her back to K-Mart and released her.

Watched from a distance as she ran to her car to make sure she was okay and then I went back to the motel to check out. Hit the road at 1 am and got home at 2 am. Daylight savings time went into effect, so I had to turn the clocks ahead. Got to bed at 4 am.

This case occurred in Howland Township, Ohio. Detective Sergeant John Rumanisk and Captain Karl Compton were assigned to this investigation.

Police Report

"Got off work at Hooters about 10:45 PM. Went to super K-Mart. Was in store for only about 15 minutes. Left store and went to my car. Started the engine and was putting on my seat belt when the front passenger door flung open. There was a dark-haired man with a big black gun. He jumped in and told me to look forward and *drive and not do anything stupid*. He had me drive to the back of the Super K-Mart. **He put goggles on me, tied my ankles together, and handcuffed me behind my back.** *He put me in the back seat of my car and drove around the parking lot.* He had me get into his car's back seat. He covered me with a dark blanket and drove off. We got somewhere close by because it only took a couple of minutes to get there. He gagged me and got out of the car. He was gone for a couple of minutes and came back. He drove for a couple of minutes and parked the car. The car was a four door and had a stick. He unties my legs and ungagged [sic] me. He took me to a motel room. **Once inside he had me sit on the bed and he proceeded to tell me that he was going to rape me,** nothing more unless I got out of line. *He asked me if I was a virgin and if I have ever 'sucked' on a man's cock.* I lied to him and told him I have never performed oral sex. **But he told me I was going to do it anyways** [sic].

"He told me to stand up and strip for him. He told me to take my jacket off, then my shirt, then my bra. He told me to take off my shoes and socks and then my jeans. **Then he told me to shake my bottom when I take off my underwear.** I did what he told me to. He started touching me all over telling me what **a beautiful little girl I was** and if I **do everything right, I won't get hurt.** He had me lay down on the bed and he touched me all over. He told me to get up off the bed. He took me to the bathroom. He wanted to take a shower with me.

"We got in the shower, but he wouldn't let me get too wet. **Then he had me on my knees in the shower and made me suck his penis**. I stopped because I was going to throw up. He told me it was all right, that I could try later. We went back to the bed. He lay on top of me touching my breast and genitals. He got up. He said he was putting a condom on. **He came back and performed oral sex on me. Then stuck his penis in my vagina**. He only stayed in me a couple of minutes and pulled out. He was very caring about if he was hurting me or not. **When he pulled out, he laid next to me kissing my body and my mouth. Telling me what a good kisser I was and my boyfriend must love me.**

"**He tied my legs back together, then tied my legs to my wrists and said, 'I like my little girls hog tied.' He mentioned when hog-tying me that he likes to put the little girls that he takes in unique positions.** He touched me like that for a minute or two then untied me.

"**He had me get down on the edge of the bed so I could 'suck his dick again.'** He told me I could stop and then he lay next to me kissing me all over.

"He stopped and said he was going to let me go. He told me that I wasn't to report it because the cops won't do anything. He helped me get dressed and we left the motel. We went to his car. He put me in the back seat and he drove back to Super K-Mart. There was a cop out front, so he drove around the mall parking lot till [sic] the cop left. He dropped me off behind the Super K. He uncuffed me first then took off the goggles. He told me not to turn around or he'd shoot. He jumped in his car and I took off running. I got in my car and went straight to Hooters and told my manager. He called the Holland Police and I called my mother. My boyfriend took me to the hospital."

Analysis

The complainant's report confirmed the journal entries. However, the victim's report does not go into the detail that the offender wrote in his journal. The victim's fear for her life is documented in the report. The victim stated that the offender said, *"You have to do what I say or I will kill you." The victim stated that throughout the ordeal he threatened to kill her.*

The modus operandi was the same and once again the victim was taken from a parking lot after the subject determined her door was unlocked and he was sure that he could move without being observed. In fact, he had to avoid another customer who thought he was suspicious. He wrote, **"I handcuffed her behind her back and forced her into the back seat."** The journal entries indicated that he had added a new device to his rape kit. He wrote, **"I decided to try the stun gun. I pushed it against her neck and hit the trigger. It did not have the desired effect. I really expected it to incapacitate her. Instead it just shocked her making her cry."** The same MO continues: **"Tied her feet, blindfolded and gagged her."** This time he adds a new twist. It is quite apparent that this offender has progressed and there is an added intensity to both his descriptions and activities with his victims. He wrote, **"Drove her car back near mine and made a flawless transfer, forcing her from her car to my car's backseat, and drove off, with no witnesses to her abduction."**

He then takes his bound victim to a motel. He then interviews her and informs her that she is going to be raped. He writes, **"18-years old!!! She was 5'9", had huge C-cup breasts and a fantastic, young, little ass.** Once again he is in total control of his victim as he directs and orders her to perform. **"I asked her to strip nude for me."** He wrote, **"I made her wiggle her cute little ass as she took [her panties] off."** He wrote that he enjoyed the control over his victims and we also then learn that he has improved his rape kit with additional items. He had added a stun gun, the swimming goggles with duct tape, and the flavored lotion.

"It was fun having complete control over an 18-year-old girl, leading her to the bathroom, her being dependent on me to guide her every step because of the blindfold (which was my swimming goggles covered with duck [sic] tape.)"

His activities with the previous victims are repeated with him escalating his sexual assaults to include forced fellatio and the introduction of flavored lotion. **"Licked her wet body, sucking on the tits and licking and kissing her wet little ass."**

"I put her at the end of the bed on her back with her head hanging over the edge and fucked her mouth in the upside down position. I used some strawberry motion-lotion to try to make the taste better for her." He then adds, **"It was a great feeling knowing that my dick was the first dick she had ever tasted. For the rest of her life, she'll know that the first dick she ever sucked belonged to me, her rapist!"** He continues with the **signature** activities. **"Took her to bed and made her get on all fours so I could explore her pussy and asshole from behind."**

He reveals a further fantasy that he has had and because he has this victim totally under control, he writes, **"I examined her beautiful pussy close up. I had never before had a chance to explore a woman's pussy up close and on my terms, so it was fun."** He added another piece to his **signature** by trying out different bondage positions with his victim. He writes, **"Put her on her tummy and tied her in different positions. Crossed her ankles and taped them tight, then tied her feet to her handcuffs. Her sweet little body looked great hog-tied like that."**

In the opinion of the author, the journal entries have become more detailed than the previous entries he made with his other victims. He is clearly enjoying the event and reveals the fulfillment of his fantasies with the victim as he vividly described what he did and how it felt.

The subject went into much more detail with this event than in some of the prior sexual assaults. The journal entries compared with the police report are dramatically different. Although the victim's statements describe the actual sexual assault, the journal entries are filled with sexually explicit descriptions of the event depicting the victim as a willing participant who, in the mind of the offender, "must have enjoyed" the assault. The journal takes on the characteristics of a "fantasy story."

> **4-8:** Makes an entry regarding the previous rape indicating he was concerned about getting caught. He writes, "Whatever happens, it was worth it. To have a sweet young 18-year-old girl completely in my power was worth the price. The taste of that young, fresh pussy, the sight and feel of that delicious young body will stay with me a long time! It was worth it!

He continues to make entries in his journal each day. There are references to tennis matches, working out, and commenting about wanting to fuck some female acquaintances either because they look "hot" or to get even with them. There are a number of angry references, such as "(*name*) is no longer a friend. She is a potential victim … I'm going to fuck her right up her cute little ass."

> **5-4: Went to Brookpark to the adult bookstore. Got a fantastic bondage mag with incredible pictures of naked women bound hand and foot, gagged and blindfolded.**

In the opinion of the author, this journal entry is extremely important in the analysis of the cases. The offender is displaying an avid interest in sadistic fantasy and bondage materials, which he subsequently incorporated into his sexual assaults as he escalates the bondage fantasy. This element is consistent with the criteria of sexual sadism. Sexual sadism involves acts in which the individual derives sexual excitement from the psychological or physical suffering, which includes humiliation of the victim. Thomas SR certainly engaged in psychological suffering as he taped and bound his victims and threatened them with death. His attacks involved physical and sexual abuse and he sexually humiliated them during his attacks.

5-14: Makes mention of a rape victim who settled for $250,000. He mentions her by name and wrote, "I didn't think she reported it." Good for her.

He continues to make entries in his journal each day. Many of the entries are about his fantasies and what he would like to do to these women he meets. He even writes about getting aroused by the 12-year-old daughter of a family friend.

9-27: Went hunting at 7. The legal sec is still there at night … She left at eight though. Cruised the area around Brookpark and Broadview. Found great places on Brookpark to take a van to. Dark isolated places. Went to the Super K to hunt, seeing as how my last visit to a Super K in Warren got me (*name withheld*). And sure enough, another sweet little teenage bitch left her car unlocked. She was young, with big tits and a cute little face. But in the end, I turned her down. Too much risk, too little gain. Went to the 24-hour Revco at Snow and W. 150th. Saw a parade of beautiful young women, and everyone of them locked their car doors tight. Got home at 1.

10-19: Went **hunting**. All the way to Cuy. Falls. Could not find a decent hidden place to take the vic to until I got all the way up to 422 and 306. Had a couple of opportunities. One was a cute little teenager, with curly blond hair, who left her rear right door unlocked. I decided against it. There was a very cute, late 30ish woman in a jeep. I would have had to D-side her… (*meaning take her out of the driver's side*), but it was in an open place, so I let it go.

12-2: Weight 190.5 … Traded e-mail …Took (*name withheld*) to lunch. Talked with (*name withheld*). Couldn't take my eyes off her huge tits. The whole time I had fantasies about raping her sweet little ass.

12-4: Watched a good show on rape and how a woman was abducted and raped in her car for over five hours.

In the opinion of the author, the following entries are significant in the diagnosis of Thomas SR as a psychopathic sexual sadist. There were a series of entries in which he and a consenting partner had engaged in some S&M and bondage scenarios, which were remarkably similar to the activities he engaged in during his actual assaults and clearly represent the offender's **signature**.

1-10: I ordered her into the bedroom, stripped her nude, blindfolded her and taped her hands and feet. I forced her on her knees and made her suck my dick and I even fucked her mouth. She looked so incredible, nude and tied helplessly, forced to suck my dick like that. I put her in bed and touched and licked her helpless body and then I fucked her.

1-11: I ordered her to strip for me and made her wiggle her cute little ass as she took off her panties. Handcuffed her, forced her on the bed, tied her handcuffed wrists to the top of the bed frame, blindfolded and gagged her, then fucked her.

1-12: I handcuffed her behind her back, blindfolded and gagged her, tied her feet and knees, hogged [sic] tied her a little, tied her elbows together and played with her.

He then writes an interesting entry. "Got home at 11, jacked off to her helpless, bound and gagged image." In the opinion of the author, Thomas SR had constructed an engram of his playtime bondage activities, which allowed him to vividly recall that event as well as his crimes. He was able to fantasize himself to orgasm. More importantly, from an investigative perspective, we see the offender "acting out" his fantasies with a consenting partner. In cases of this nature, it is imperative that the detectives interview the significant other in an offender's life to gain insight into his actual crimes.

1-14: While dropping by his girlfriend's work place, he takes note of how the back area is so isolated and small. He writes, "**Any woman coming out of there is a good target.**"

1-17: Makes reference to an adult bookstore where he looked at gags, whips, nipple clamps, etc. He bought four satin cuffs and a satin blindfold and a cock ring to make him stay harder longer. Later that day he and his girlfriend act out another scenario.
   "**Bound and blindfolded her using the new "present" I bought. Gagged her tight and took her down to the basement licking and protesting. Tied her bent over to the ceiling pipe and spanked her hard enough to make her sweet little ass red. Pinched her nipples hard and ordered her to obey me. Retied her on her tiptoes with her hands stretched to the ceiling and spanked her again. Took her back upstairs and made her suck my dick. Ate her out for almost an hour and almost made her cum** [sic]."

2-15: Mentions a fight he had with his girlfriend. He goes **HUNTING**. "Almost took a couple of girls at Walgreen's at Pearl and Ridge. Passenger door unlocked on one of the girl's car. But I was fifteen seconds late in getting to her car and she drove off.

Sexual Assault–Sodomy: Journal Entry

2-21: (His girlfriend hadn't returned his calls.) **Went Hunting.** Checked out the salon place (he mentioned in the January 14th journal entry). One women left, the other, short woman stayed in the parking lot. I ran up and got into her car, **handcuffed her, gagged and blindfolded her.** Started to take her to my car and then decided to fuck her in the salon since I got her keys. **Took her inside and forced her to strip nude.** Her name was *Cindy* (*this is not her real name. But in the journal he names her and identifies her as a 34-year-old mother of two*).
   I handcuffed her nude and played with her huge C-cup tits with huge nipples. Made her knell [sic] **in front of me and suck my dick, which she did superbly.** I also held her head in place and fucked her cute little mouth for awhile [sic]. Made her lick and kiss and then French kiss me. She was very cooperative and funny, actually laughing at her predicament. Fingered her and she had the juiciest pussy I've ever seen … she was practically dripping all over everything. **Tied her in different positions and made her suck some more. Played with her sweet ass and tits, sucking them every once in a while, the huge nipples tasting good in my mouth.** Even her little asshole was cute. Convinced her that telling anybody or reporting it would not be good for her health. As I had her address.

Took $60 bucks [sic] from her and left her tied in a position where she could get loose in a few minutes … enough for me to get to my car and leave the scene. Waited around nearby to see what she would do, expecting the cops to come running any minute. They did not and she left 15 minutes later. I think I am in the clear on this one.

This case occurred in Cleveland, Ohio, and was assigned to Detective Robert Matuszny and Detective Michael O'Malley. The original police report was unavailable for review.

Analysis

The subject, who had developed a successful MO, had become even more confident. He returned to an area that he had previously checked out, stalking and approaching his victim as she returned to her car. He wrote, "**I ran up and got into her car, handcuffed her, gagged and blindfolded her.** Started to take her to my car and then decided to fuck her in the salon since I got her keys." The offender's **signature** activities, as well as his fantasies, are played out with this victim. He wrote, " **Took her inside and forced her to strip nude. I handcuffed her nude and played with her huge C-cup tits with huge nipples. Made her kneel in front of me and suck my dick. Tied her in different positions and made her suck some more. Played with her sweet ass and tits, sucking them every once in a while …".** The bondage scenario began to become an integral part of the fantasy.

In his entry, he fantasized that the victim enjoyed the attack. **"Fingered her and she had the juiciest pussy I've ever seen … she was practically dripping all over everything."** He also assumed that she didn't report it to the police. He based this on the fact that he had staked out the area and the police did not respond.

3-15: He wrote in his journal how he is thinking of raping and torturing a Chinese girl who works at a restaurant. He states, "Sweet little Chinese bitch! If I take her, I'll obviously have to snuff her. Can I do that? **We may find out soon, kiddies."**

In an obvious tone of escalation, his fantasies include killing to avoid detection.

4-5: We went to (*names*) diner for breakfast. The waitress *Sue* (*not her real name*) was a nasty little bitch, thin, little tits, cute face, and a great ass. **I immediately planned to abduct her and rape the shit out of her.**

4-9: Went out to Avon to check out **hunt** sites.

4-11: Went to Lorain to **hunt**. Cataloged some girls who work in some female stores. I'll take a closer look next week.

4-25: Went hunting. Cataloged the waitresses. The owner's wife is fucking beautiful and I want her. Another pretty waitress drives a Buick 4-door and is easily takable [*sic*].

4-30: Spent the rest of the night online, downloading bondage pictures.

5-2: His last entry, "Went hunting …," was at 6:30 on May 2nd. That was the evening he committed suicide after fleeing from the police in an attempted abduction.

Investigative Analysis and Opinion

In the opinion of the author, Thomas SR would best be described as a psychopathic sexual sadist. He certainly was unconcerned about the moral implications of his behavior. He felt no guilt or remorse about his actions. In fact, he justifies his sexual assaults because the women were "stupid" to leave the cars unlocked. After sexually assaulting and degrading his victims, he would warn them about the dangers of leaving the cars unlocked. He also wrote how what he was doing to his victims was fun and it felt good. **"She kept gagging because of the salty taste of my dick. But I kept fucking her sweet little mouth because it felt and looked so good."**

His behavior and conduct with his victims, as well as the control he displayed over his victims, including the forced oral sex acts, are key components of his **signature**.

His **modus operandi** was to stalk and then approach the victims as they entered their cars. This enabled him to quickly gain control. He became more adept in his MO as he gained experience with each event. The rape kit that he utilized became more sophisticated as he progressed and he began to experiment with his victims, using a stun gun, tying them up in different positions, making them perform as they were forced to remove their clothes, and examining their genitalia. He demanded submissiveness from his victims and he used restraints, blindfolds, gags, and handcuffs. He clearly derived sexual excitement from the infliction of psychological suffering including humiliation of his victims, whom he simply regarded as objects for his own sexual gratification. The following statements in his own words from the journal indicate his psychopathic sexual sadism:

> *She looked so good there, helpless, bound hand and foot, gagged and blindfolded.*
> *Untapped [sic] her hands and made her take off the rest of her clothes. I ordered her to do it sexy and she did, striking a pose when she took off her bra.*
> *Women are so incredible when they are helpless!*
> *She sucked me and I played with her for an hour or so.*
> *Made her stand outside the van so I could run my hands up and down her body.*
> *Made her suck my dick for a while and made her get up on all fours so I could fuck her from behind.*
> *I asked here to strip nude for me.*
> *I made her wiggle her cute little ass as she took them (panties) off.*
> *It was fun having complete control over an 18-year-old girl, leading her to the bathroom, her being dependent on me to guide her every step because of the blindfold.*
> *Made her get on her knees and suck my wet dick.*
> *It was a great feeling knowing that my dick was the first dick she had ever tasted. For the rest of her life, she'll know that the first dick she ever sucked belonged to me, her rapist!*
> *I stood there looking down at her. She looked so good nude, on her knees, her hands bound behind her back, with my dick in her mouth.*
> *Took her to bed and made her get on all fours so I could explore her pussy and asshole from behind.*
> *Took her inside and forced her to strip nude.*
> *I handcuffed her nude and played with her huge C-cup tits with huge nipples. Made her kneel in front of me and suck my dick, which she did superbly.*

Thomas SR was a **classic organized offender**. He planned his attacks and stalked his victims. He researched his craft. He personalized his victims with controlled conversation.

He revisited locations where he had been successful in the past. His victims were strangers. He controlled them through threats and force. He demanded a submissive victim. He maintained and utilized an effective rape kit. He transported his victims to comfort zones where he could act out his fantasies with them. Thomas SR had an above-average intelligence. He certainly was socially competent. He preferred skilled work. He was computer programmer. He was sexually competent and dated a number of young women. He maintained a controlled mood during his crimes. The precipitating situational stress seemingly was related to his failed relationships. Every time he experienced upset in his social life, he would go **hunting."**

Thomas SR fit well into society. He was contemporary in style. He worked out, played tennis, and had a very active social life. He seemingly was an outgoing person and the type you might want to befriend. However, as evidenced in his numerous failed relationships, it was quite apparent that he was a shallow, self-centered individual. In his journal, he constantly refers to his weight and how he looks, and talks about buying new clothes. On many of his entries, the first reference is to his weight that particular day.

He was a good communicator and was able to manipulate people into doing things. However, he was irresponsible and only cared about himself. He fancied himself a "ladies" man and was always bragging about his sexual conquests. He had multiple sex partners, one of whom he used to act out his sexually sadistic fantasies.

In many of his journal entries, he makes reference to his women co-workers. In his mind, he believed that they wanted him sexually. He fantasized about making love to them. However, if they turned him down, he wrote about **visiting** them, meaning attacking them. He used the words **visit** and **introduce himself** as code words for attacking and assaulting. He frequented a number of bars and lounges where there were a number of women.

He was methodical and cunning. He planned his assaults, stalked his victims, and conducted surveillance. If he didn't think the opportunity was worthwhile, he retreated. He was adept at avoiding detection and didn't take any chances. He was careful not to leave any evidence and he followed the crimes in the news media. His journal entries indicated that he was obsessive and compulsive in nature. They also pointed out that his every waking minute was devoted to his sexual fantasies. He was always on the prowl 24/7.

He traveled frequently, putting many miles on his car as he drove throughout the Cleveland suburbs selecting new sites and locations for his "hunts." The spontaneous trip to Niagara Falls is an example of this dynamic. Most of his crimes were well out of his area of residence.

He was known to have a violent temper and had lost jobs because of his outbreaks. There were a number of journal entries that go into detail about his relationship with co-workers and how they would avoid him if he were in a bad mood. When insulted or threatened, he responded with anger and violence. He would hold a grudge. Throughout the journal, he makes comments about **"visiting that bitch,"** meaning raping and assaulting a victim in a violent way.

He also wrote how he would have to **"kill the bitch"** so he wouldn't be identified. In one entry, he made reference to a boyfriend of a co-worker he desired. Thomas SR wrote, **"He is 6'2", but there is no way he can match my viciousness. No way he can equal my violence."**

Thomas SR could never accept criticism. It was always somebody else's fault at work and he would brood if reprimanded. If the reprimand came from a female, he would fantasize about raping and sodomizing her. **"I think I'll fuck the shit out of her."**

When he was caught the first time after abducting two women, he stated he was sorry and couldn't understand what came over him. He was sentenced to 4 to 15 years. However, the sentence was reduced and he received a 6-month term. As a result of this experience, he improved his MO, taking precautions not to get caught again. Although he did not kill his victims, the potential for murder is quite evident in his writings and his attitude toward women in general. He even wrote in his journal, **"If I take her, I'll obviously have to snuff her. Can I do that? We may find out soon, kiddies."**

There is no doubt in my mind that Thomas SR was a potential killer. If he found himself in a circumstance where he chose a victim who knew him or could identify him, he would kill to prevent this identification and continue with his sexual predation, which, according to the journal entries, dominated his entire existence. Thomas was a 24/7 sexual predator and a psychopathic sexual sadist.

It is quite apparent to a trained criminal investigator that if all of these offenses had been committed in one jurisdiction, the police would have immediately recognized the rape pattern based on the **MO** and the **signature** of this offender. He cleverly chose jurisdictions that extended over an 85-mile radius and with different time breaks between his attacks, thereby avoiding detection. Detective Ray Adornetto and Detective Lieutenant Dale Brady were convinced that their two cases were related and began to evaluate sexual assaults in neighboring jurisdictions. Eventually, the other cases would have been recognized as part of a distinctive rape pattern committed by an offender who was operating in various jurisdictions.

However, this case certainly showed the importance of communication between and among law enforcement agencies. In my opinion, as an expert in homicide investigations, the most viable alternative to VICAP (violent criminal apprehension program) is a series of statewide or regional systems that compile all serious crimes, such as rape, murder, and gang-related crime, into integrated databases that provide ready access to local law enforcement.

Acknowledgments

The author wishes to acknowledge the contribution of this information and materials in this chapter from professional law enforcement investigators representing various police departments who were involved in this major case investigation. Specifically, I wish to give special recognition to my friend, Detective Ray Adornetto, South Euclid, Ohio, Police Department and Lieutenant Dale Brady, University Heights, Ohio, Police Department; Detective Ken Roberts and Lieutenant Thomas Doyle, Eastlake, Ohio, Police Department; Detective Gregory Knack, Willoughby, Ohio, Police Department; Captain Karl Compton and Detective Sergeant John Rumanisk, Howland Township, Ohio, Police Department; Detective Robert Matuszny and Detective Michael O'Malley, Cleveland, Ohio, Police Department; Lieutenant Paul T. Romond and Police Officer Kevin Krugman, Avon, Ohio, Police Department; and Special Agent James Cioti, Ohio Bureau of Investigation.

Sexual Asphyxia and Autoerotic Fatalities

4

Introduction

Sex-related deaths due to solo sex-related activities, which usually involve asphyxia, are generally called **autoerotic fatalities**. These manners of death are not prevalent. Nonetheless, police and medical examiners, as well as coroners, in various jurisdictions have recorded a sufficient number of cases to make this phenomenon a concern in the accurate determination of manner of death. Therefore, the homicide investigator should be aware of them. In most instances, the mechanism of death is asphyxia by hanging, ligature, plastic bags, or chemical substances. Atypical asphyxial methods, such as chest compression, smothering, immersion/drowning, may be employed as well as electrocution, foreign body insertion, and other miscellaneous methodologies causing some other physiological derangement, which results in death. The manner of death, based on first observation, may be classified as either suicide or homicide, when in fact it is actually an accident that occurred during a dangerous autoerotic act.

Clinical Definition

Autoerotic deaths are normally classified as accidental deaths that occur during individual and, usually solitary, sexual activity in which a device, apparatus, or prop used to enhance the sexual stimulation of the deceased, in some way causes unintended death (Byard and Bramwell, 1991; Sauvageau and Racette, 2006a) (Figure 4.1).

Literature Definition

Autoerotic fatalities are deaths that occur as a result of or in association with masturbation or other autoerotic activity (Hazelwood et al., 1983).

However, it should be noted that in some cases the subjects will not be engaging in masturbation during the activity, but may postpone this until after the autoerotic activity. In some instances, they are bound in such a bizarre manner as to preclude masturbation. The author also has videotaped events in which the subject does not masturbate, but clearly acts out in a sexual manner consistent with autoerotic practice.

Most of the literature on the subject of autoeroticism analyzes the involvement of teenage boys and older men, who through certain ritualistic activities obtain some sort of sexual gratification.

The male victims have been discovered nude, attired in female clothing, or wearing a piece of female lingerie, or in normal attire. It should be noted that there are documented cases of female participants, who have been discovered nude, seminude, or in bondage as well as in normal attire.

The investigator confronted with a female victim found under these circumstances is cautioned to assess carefully all of the information available before jumping to any

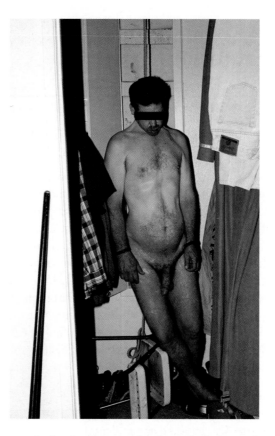

Figure 4.1 Typical autoerotic death. The completely nude male was hanging by a yellow rope, which was around his neck inside a clothes closet. The rope went around the victim's neck, up and over a 2 × 4 in the attic and back down to the ladder in the closet where it was tied off. The victim had black leather wristbands around each wrist with a black leather strap connected to each wristband. The leather strap was wound through his crotch from the front of his body to the rear. The victim was hanging, but his feet were touching the floor with a slight bend in his knees. There was a two-step folding stool, which was tipped over to the right of his legs. (Photo courtesy of Retired Detective Steve Mack, Huntington Beach, California, Police Department.)

conclusions. In some cases, there is evidence of self-abuse and other masochistic activities. Contraptions or ligatures with padding, to prevent visible marks of this activity, are often used to cause hypoxia.

Sex, Age, and Race

According to a study by Anny Sauvageau, her team examined 408 cases of autoerotic deaths. "There was a male predominance, with 390 male victims for 18 female ones (21.7:1 male to female ratio). The victims reported were aged from 9 to 77 years. Of the 408 cases, 334 were Caucasian, 7 were black, 5 were Asian, and 2 others (native or mixed). For the remaining 60 cases, there was no race specification" (Sauvageau and Racette, 2006a).

The author does have an autoerotic death case in file involving an elderly male who was 87 years of age. Presently, this case appears to represent the oldest known victim of autoerotic fatality.

Case History

This case involved an 87-year-old white male who was discovered after police went to his home on a request by the man's employer to "check on the welfare." The victim had failed to show for work and according to the employer, the victim was like an ox and had never missed a day of work. The police officers attempted to make contact with the resident by knocking on the doors and windows of the house, but didn't get any response. The officers also attempted to call, but there was no answer. A decision was made to force entry and the officers entered the kitchen as they called the resident's name. As the officers entered the living room area, they saw the man.

The victim was completely naked and bound from his lower legs to the midchest with three different ropes in a standing position. The ropes on the man's legs were looped around each other from the feet up to the chest creating a crisscross pattern. Two of the ropes were looped through and connected to a wrought iron room divider in the living room. These ropes held the man in a standing position. A fourth rope was tied to the same wrought iron room divider and was around the neck of the victim. The victim's hands and genitals were free from the bindings. There was a belt around the rope behind the man's head and a second belt was at the victim's feet. The rope around the victim's neck was loose but tightened when the victim's head was in a forward position. The victim could increase or release pressure by moving his head up and down.

The victim had apparently tied the first yellow rope around his ankles and then connected a second rope up his legs by looping each wrap as the ropes ascended to the waist. The rope was also looped through the wrought iron room divider and supported the victim's body. The third rope was connected to this series of ropes through the wrought iron divider up to the victim's midchest and then looped around his neck (Figure 4.2 and Figure 4.3). The ropes and bindings suggested that the victim was able to achieve this without assistance and had done this many times before. The detectives also discovered a suitcase in the victim's bedroom closet, that contained similar ropes and belts like the ones on the victim suggesting prior autoerotic activity on the part of the deceased.

The crime scene investigators used alternate lighting and discovered evidence of sexual activity. Semen was found on the floor in front of the victim as well as on the fingers of his right hand. Detectives and crime scene personnel examined the home, which was cluttered with boxes, old furniture, and various items and collectibles. There was no evidence of foul play or any criminal activity. The only damage or evidence of entry into the home was through the door, which had been forced open by the police officers who originally responded to the call.

Investigation at the scene and subsequent medical examination revealed this case to be a classic accidental death due to autoerotic activity. The unusual aspect of this case was the advanced age of the victim. Eighty-seven is the oldest recorded age of a victim of autoerotic death. The cause of death was asphyxia with ligature and the manner of death was accidental (Sauvageau and Geberth, 2009a).

Hypoxia

Hypoxia is defined as "an inadequate reduced tension of cellular oxygen characterized by cyanosis, tachycardia, hypertension, peripheral vasoconstriction, dizziness, or mental confusion" (*Mosby's Medical and Nursing Dictionary*, 1986).

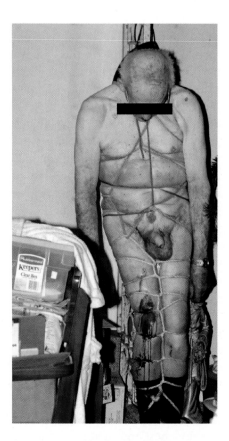

Figure 4.2 Older victim: This 87-year-old white male was discovered after police went to his home to "check on his welfare." The victim was completely naked and bound in a standing position from his lower legs to the midchest with three different ropes. The ropes on the man's legs were looped around each other from the feet up to the chest creating a crisscross pattern. There was a belt around the rope behind the man's head and a second belt was at the victim's feet. Detectives discovered a suitcase in the victim's bedroom closet that contained similar ropes and belts such as the ones on the victim suggesting prior autoerotic activity on the part of the deceased. (Photo courtesy of Detective Ronald Antonucci, Wayne Township, New Jersey, Police Department.)

H. L. P. Resnick, an author and researcher in this field, states that "a disruption of the arterial blood supply resulting in a diminished oxygenation of the brain … will heighten sensations through diminished ego controls that will be subjectively perceived as giddiness, light-headedness, and exhilaration. This reinforces masturbatory sensations" (Resnick, 1972).

A combination of ritualistic behavior, oxygen deprivation, danger, and fantasy appears to bring about sexual gratification for these people. According to Robert R. Hazelwood, a retired supervisory special agent, "Death during such activity may result from (1) a failure with the physiological mechanism, (2) a failure in the self-rescue device, or (3) a failure on the part of the victim's judgment and ability to control a self--endangering fantasy scenario" (Hazelwood et al., 1981).

The results of some 150 cases were the basis for an in-depth study and subsequent textbook, *Autoerotic Fatalities* written by Retired Supervisory Special Agent R. Hazelwood; Park Elliot Dietz, Professor of Law, Behavioral Medicine and Psychiatry at the University of

Figure 4.3 Bindings: A fourth rope was tied to the same wrought iron room divider and was around the neck of the victim. The rope around the victim's neck was loose, but tightened when the victim's head was in a forward position. The victim's hands and genitals were free from the bindings. The ropes and bindings suggested that the victim was able to achieve this without assistance and had done this many times. (Photo courtesy of Detective Ronald Antonucci, Wayne Township, New Jersey, Police Department.)

Virginia; and Ann Wolbert Burgess, Associate Director of Nursing Research, Department of Health and Hospitals, Boston, Massachusetts (1983). In my opinion, their text was one of the most thorough and comprehensive studies to date on the subject of autoerotic fatalities.

According to their 1983 text, approximately 500 to 1,000 people die from autoerotic asphyxiation each year in the United States. Many times this type of case has either been misclassified or gone unrecognized due to lack of knowledge, misinformation, or misguided efforts on the part of the surviving family to "cover up" what is perceived to be an embarrassing situation.

The 500 to 1,000 autoerotic deaths per year may no longer be valid and atypical cases may be underestimated according to a study conducted by Sauvageau in 2008 and published in *The Open Forensic Science Journal*, entitled Autoerotic Deaths: A Seven-Year Retrospective Epidemiological Study (Sauvageau and Racette, 2008).

In another recent publication, *Autoerotic Deaths in the Literature from 1954 to 2004: A Review* (Sauvageau and Racette, 2006b), encompassing a 50-year review of autoerotic deaths in literature, the authors evaluated 57 studies published in English and French analyzing 408 cases of autoerotic death. According to the authors, "The most frequent method of autoerotic activity was asphyxia by hanging or ligature, followed by plastic bag, chemical substances, or mixture of these." In addition, the authors identified some atypical methods discussed later in the chapter.

I have personally investigated and assessed over 200 of these investigations. Oftentimes, during a class presentation on the subject of autoerotic deaths, one of the participants will remark on how his department had a case like the ones being presented and that the death had been classified as either a suicide or homicide. In most instances, I have been afforded an opportunity to view the crime scene photographs and case reports that the investigators have supplied for my review.

I also have a number of videotapes, which graphically portray the dangers of autoerotic hangings and how quickly the hypoxia affects the victim's ability to control the onset of fatal cerebral anoxia. *Cerebral anoxia* is defined as "a condition in which oxygen is deficient in brain tissues caused by a circulatory failure. It can exist for no more than four to six minutes before the onset of irreversible brain damage" (*Mosby's Medical and Nursing Dictionary*, 1986). Therefore, the person who practices this sort of activity is certainly at high risk for sudden death.

I became involved in one particular case after reading a *New York Daily News* article that described the suicidal death of a 17-year-old. Based on my professional experience in the investigation of this type of death, I immediately recognized the possibility of an accidental autoerotic fatality. The following day, I called the detective commander of the local jurisdiction whom I knew and felt would be open to my speculations. He filled me in on the details of his investigation, which further assured me that this alleged suicide was in fact a tragic accident. In this incident, the crime scene had been changed. The brother of the deceased had discovered the body, removed the ligature from his brother's neck, and redressed him out of embarrassment. I learned that the detective supervisor had never heard of autoerotic fatalities. After I provided him with the necessary information, the case was properly reclassified. More importantly, the surviving family was made aware of the actual circumstances of their son's death. The family, who had been blaming themselves, could not understand why their son would commit suicide. We enlisted the services of a family priest to assist in explaining what had happened to their son. Although at first they were astonished and embarrassed (a typical response in this type of case), they were greatly relieved to learn that their son had not taken his own life due to some unknown personal or family problem, but had died accidentally. In fact, this family actually wanted to go public to warn other parents of this phenomenon. I counseled them against going public, but advised them they could work anonymously to accomplish the same objective without exposing their family to any further trauma.

Periodically, one will read a story in the local newspaper that focuses on one or more deaths believed to be teenage suicides. I remember one particular story in my area that made reference to a "teenage suicide epidemic." The series of stories that followed these initial events was directed toward warning the public about this devastating public health problem. There was a call for a renewed effort in bringing suicide prevention programs into the schools as public health officials sought a solution for what was perceived to be the contagious effect of suicide among teenagers. Parents, teachers, and public health officials were mobilized in an effort to identify a motive for these unexplained deaths. Ironically, it was discovered that half of the reported suicides were actually autoerotic fatalities. However, the focus of attention on this issue, although initially misinterpreted, was instrumental in identifying other potential problems and issues of concern regarding suicide. Some syndicated publications have reported on the phenomenon of autoerotic fatality quite accurately. Stories with headlines such as "Answers Sought in Unusual Deaths" or "Six Deaths in Past Year Stir Warning" or "Medical Examiner Concerned about Bizarre Fatal Accidents" actually provide a genuine insight into this type of death. Of course, there is always the possibility that publicity about this phenomenon may actually increase incidents. I believe, however, that persons predisposed to this type of behavior will neither be encouraged nor discouraged by the presentation of information on sexual asphyxia. Instead, I believe that certain details need to be made public for the purpose of alerting people to the dangers of this potentially lethal practice. As a result, I agreed to an interview with the Associated Press entitled, "Autoerotic Deaths—Shocking Practice Often Mistaken for Teen Suicide" (Raeburn, 1984).

Parents, who have the responsibility of raising their children, as well as educators and others responsible for the public welfare of society, have a right to information and the need to be educated about this phenomenon. I have investigated and consulted on a number of autoerotic deaths involving teenage boys. Teenagers, who are going through a period of sexual experimentation, are extremely vulnerable to peer suggestions. Teenagers have traditionally developed their own life styles, which involve different pleasures, amusements, and pastimes than those of their parents. They have their own slang, music, expressions, dancing, TV programs, movies, etc. Often parents are not even aware of their children's socialization into the teen culture. They are certainly not privy to their children's secret conversations, social groups, or risk-taking ventures, which explains their total shock, horror, and disbelief when advised of this phenomenon.

I supervised one investigation where a 16-year-old boy's mother showed him an article about autoerotic deaths in a newspaper so that he would be aware of the dangers. He offhandedly remarked to his mother, "Those kids are stupid. They don't know what they're doing."

His mother missed the significance of the remark. Her son was engaged in such activities himself and he was found dead two weeks later, the victim of an autoerotic fatality.

In most of the cases in which I was involved, the teenage victim was made aware of the practice through word-of-mouth. There have been cases, especially those involving adult practitioners, where the victim had learned of this activity through pornographic magazines, X-rated movies, underground publications, the media, and even novels.

Preliminary Investigation at the Scene

Every autoerotic fatality is unique because the circumstances surrounding this activity are based on the person's fantasy and perception of what is considered sexually stimulating. The death scene will vary according to the victim's age, resources, or sexual interests. However, there are some common denominators to suggest that the death may be accidental.

Hazelwood et al. (1981) describe five criteria for determining death during dangerous autoerotic practices:

1. Evidence of a physiological mechanism for obtaining or enhancing sexual arousal that provides a self-rescue mechanism or allows the victim to voluntarily discontinue its effect
2. Evidence of solo sexual activity
3. Evidence of sexual fantasy aids
4. Evidence of prior dangerous autoerotic practice
5. No apparent suicidal intent

The most common method practiced during this type of activity is neck compression or hanging, with some sort of padding between the neck and the ligature to prevent any markings from being left by the tightening noose or rope. However, more elaborate and exotic methods, such as chest compression, airway obstruction, and oxygen exclusion with gas or chemical replacement have been found.

Atypical Autoerotic Deaths

It should be noted that all autoerotic deaths are **not** attributed to sexual asphyxia. Some of the participants in autoerotic practice have devised some interesting and unique devices, which may or may not involve asphyxia. The author is aware of one particular case where the victim had constructed a long ceramic cone in the base of his "play toilet," which extended above the rim of the toilet seat (Figure 4.4). Over the toilet the subject had constructed a pulley system. He had affixed a wooden seat with a hole in the bottom that fit over the ceramic cone, which was lubricated with Vaseline. He pulled himself up and down with the ropes on the pulleys. As the subject would lower himself down over the toilet the seat, the ceramic cone would go into his anal cavity. The subject apparently didn't keep up with his maintenance on his system and one day one of the ropes, which had worn, broke. The subject was impaled on this device when discovered.

In a number of other cases that the author is aware of, subjects have resorted to mechanical equipment to stimulate themselves or have employed electricity with some devastating results.

One such case involved a 16-year-old male who was found with a cow's heart attached to his genitals. Wires had been attached and plugged into a wall socket. The boy died from electrocution and he was charred. Detectives found several pornographic magazines in the scene.

One of the magazines described a sexual toy that can be made from the fresh heart of a cow. Practitioners use a simple electrical circuit and some batteries to get the heart to beat and use the beating organ for sexual stimulation.

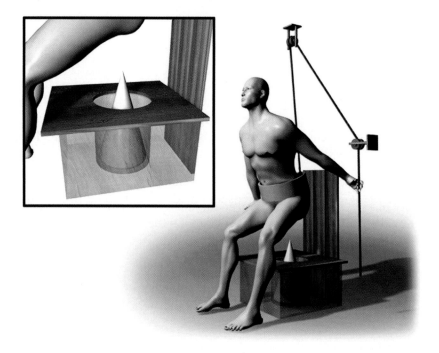

Figure 4.4 Play toilet: Subject created this contraption for sexual gratification. The concept was to stimulate himself anally by riding up and down on the ceramic cone. He used a series of ropes and pulleys. The ropes became frayed and apparently snapped during one of his activities. (Photo courtesy of Medical Legal Art, Illustration © 2009 www.doereport.com)

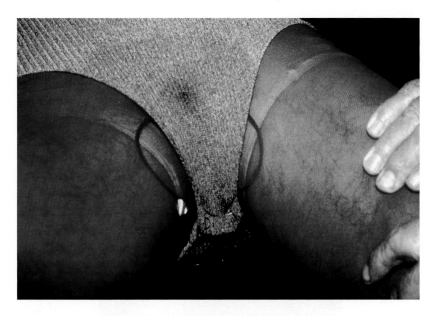

Figure 4.5 Copper wire: The victim had a copper wire in his crotch area where he would receive intermittent shocks from a device attached to a ceiling lamp.

In *Autoerotic Deaths in the Literature from 1954 to 2004: A Review,* Sauvageau and Racette (2006b) present several atypical methods, which are classified into five broad categories: electrocution (3.7%), overdressing/body wrap (1.5%), foreign body insertion (1.2%), atypical asphyxial methods (2.0%), which included chest compression, inverted or abdominal suspension, immersion/drowning, and miscellaneous (1.0%).

Electrocution

Sauvageau and Racette (2006b) cite 15 cases involving autoerotic electrocution. The victims were found with wires attached to their genitals or they had improvised a device to use with light dimmers or rheostats to produce intermittent shocks to their sex organs. I have included an example of electrocution in the case history where the subject had attached a copper loop of wire between his legs and connected the wire to an electrical apparatus with a timer, which sent intermittent shocks to the his genital area (Figure 4.5). Another subject hooked up electricity to shock his genitals and inadvertently stood in a puddle of water resulting in electrocution.

Overdressing/Body Wrapping

Sauvageau and Racette (2006a) cite six cases in which overdressing or body wrapping had been employed by the victim. I have included a bizarre example of this atypical autoerotic death (Figure 4.6).

Case History

A 64-year-old white male victim was found completely wrapped in duct tape from his head to his feet. At first it was believed to be a homicide involving a black female because the deceased was wearing a black wig and dark colored nylons. Due to the

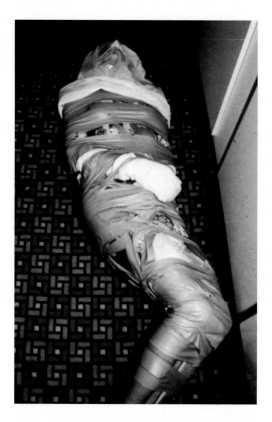

Figure 4.6 Duct tape victim: A 64-year-old white male victim was found completely wrapped in duct tape from his head to his feet. He was wearing a black wig and dark colored nylons. Due to the extensive duct tape, it was believed that someone must have taped the victim. However, a search of the victim's apartment revealed that he had done this himself and apparently had done this many times before. (Photo courtesy of Detective Terry Cousino, Toledo, Ohio, Police Department.)

extensive duct tape, it was believed that someone must have taped the victim. However, a search of the victim's apartment revealed that he had done this himself and apparently had done this many times before. In fact, one year earlier he was found outside his apartment tied up in ropes and tape seeking help. At that time, he told the responding officers that his friends had played a practical joke on him. Reconstruction of the event indicated the victim's ritual. He would first dress in women's clothing after putting a Tylenol bottle over his penis to catch the semen. He would put on makeup.

He then wrapped ribbons and duct tape around his legs. Next he wrapped his head leaving an opening for him to breathe through his nose. He also added a plastic bag over his head. He covered his hands with socks and duct tape. He then hopped to a doorway where he had rolls of duct tape on toilet paper holders, which were nailed into the door molding (Figure 4.7 and Figure 4.8). (Dozens of additional nail holes in the molding indicated habitual practice.)

When he was ready to escape, he hopped over to another doorway and used the ball ends of the empty hinge plates (the door was missing) to break the tape until he was loose enough to escape. There was a large amount of duct tape residue on and around the ball ends of the hinge plates. Apparently, this time he panicked and managed to make his way to the hallway and fell down the stairs where he crawled a short distance before

Figure 4.7 Duct tape rolls: He then hopped to a doorway where he had rolls of duct tape on toilet paper holders, which were nailed to the door molding. (Photo courtesy of Detective Terry Cousino, Toledo, Ohio, Police Department.)

expiring. At autopsy, the medical examiner discovered the Tylenol bottle attached to his penis and two nylon stockings were recovered from the victim's mouth. The cause of death was ruled asphyxiation. The medical examiner ruled the manner of death accidental due to autoerotic asphyxiation.

In one autoerotic death the subject used a commercial vacuum on his penis to simulate fellatio and died a horrible death. In another bizarre case, a man, who was discovered nude, had strapped himself into a harness and lowered himself into a septic tank. He died from inhaling the methane gases. This case was classified an autoerotic fatality based on his prior history and an examination of the crime scene.

Immersion/Drowning

Autoerotic deaths by immersion or resulting in drowning are very unusual.

Sivaloganathan (1984) reported an unusual autoerotic death of a man using submersion as an asphyxia method. The body was found in a river, dressed as a woman, a large stone tied to the right ankle. The following case history, which was reported in *A Journal of Forensic Science,* illustrated an extremely bizarre case involving aqua-eroticum, as reported by Sauvageau and Racette (2006a), where an individual was engaged in an autoerotic fatality involving a homemade diving apparatus.

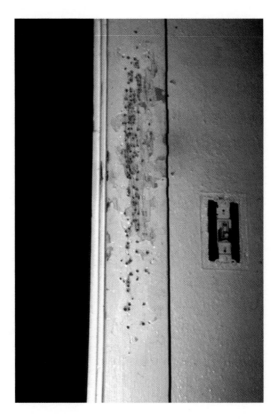

Figure 4.8 Nail holes: Dozens of additional nail holes in the molding indicated habitual practice. (Photo courtesy of Detective Terry Cousino, Toledo, Ohio, Police Department.)

Case Report

A 25-year-old man was found floating on a lake. He was wearing a hockey helmet equipped with a safety grid. His garments included a two-piece black snowmobile suit and beige ski boots. There was a complex bondage system joining together the waist, knees, and ankles of the victim comprised of metallic chains and straps and accessories usually used for horseback riding. All of the straps were interconnected by meshed metal chains. The entire bondage scenario was secured at the pubic region by a padlock keeping the man's legs tightly joined together. One of the chains was attached to the hockey helmet and straps were also present on each wrist (Figure 4.9).

A wooded board holding two ski bindings accompanied the body. It appeared that the victim's feet were attached to the board at the time of death. Under his winter garments, the victim was wrapped in a homemade, transparent plastic jumpsuit, which covered him from head to toe and was secured with duct tape. The only possible air supply was a black tube joined to the mouth and sealed to the suit with silicone. Under the leak-proof plastic, the man was totally nude. Another piece of plastic covered the penis and was secured with elastic. Autopsy and scene examination allowed for the reconstruction of this event. The man was completely immersed under water, his feet connected to the wooden board by ski bindings. The wooden board was linked to a floating pneumatic boat by an electrical cord. The victim had linked a long, black tube from his mouth to an open plastic container floating on the lake, thus creating a device for air supply. The open container allowed air to enter the black tube and get to

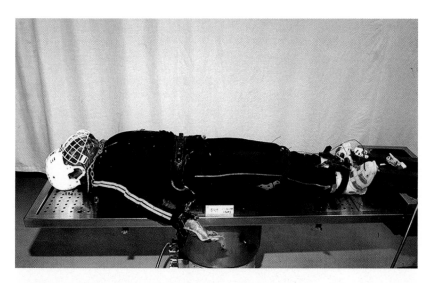

Figure 4.9 Aqua-eroticum victim. This victim was wearing a hockey helmet equipped with a safety grid. His garments were composed of a two-piece, black snowmobile suit and beige ski boots. (Photo courtesy of A. Sauvageau and S. Racette, *J. Foren. Sci.*, 51 (1), January 2006a.)

the victim (Figure 4.10). Unfortunately, this system required the victim to inhale and exhale through the same tube. The tube was too long to allow sufficient air exchange. Thus, most of the exhaled air in the tube was reinhaled causing a progressive diminution of the oxygen intake as well as a progressive uptake of carbon dioxide (CO_2). Death was attributed to an accidental asphyxia compatible with an autoerotic case. It was later determined that the deceased had been a member of an autoerotic practitioner's association and had shared experience online (Sauvageau and Racette, 2006a).

Case History: Chained and Burned

Police officers were summoned to a residence to check on the welfare of a man who had not reported to work for three days. There was no response at his home. Officers were able to enter the premises through a closed but unlocked window. The interior of the home, which was unkempt, was putrid. The victim's two dogs had relieved themselves throughout the home. Nothing appeared to have been removed or disturbed. When the officers checked the basement of the home, they discovered the dead 48-year-old, white male victim. He was found burned and chained to a metal support column beneath an I-beam. The deceased was chained in an upright position. He had Darby cuffs securing his feet with a chain running up from the cuffs to his handcuffed hands and then to the top of the metal support column where it was affixed to a padlock. Above his knees was another chain hooked with a clasp at his waist. A third chain wrapped around him and the pole and was secured with another small padlock (Figure 4.11).

There were severe burns to the waist, chest, and upper thighs, feet, and arms (Figure 4.12). A charred piece of cloth was wrapped around his penis with a remnant of burned cloth at his feet. Soot was present in the mouth, lips, and teeth as well as around his nostrils.

The Darby cuffs on his feet did not have a key and one could not be located in the area of the decedent. There also wasn't a key to the handcuffs. The crime scene was

Figure 4.10 Reconstruction. The wooden board was linked to a floating pneumatic boat by an electrical cord. The victim had linked a long, black tube from his mouth to an open plastic container floating on the lake, thus creating a device for air supply. (Photo courtesy of A. Sauvageau and S. Racette, *J. Foren. Sci.*, 51 (1), January 2006a; Medical Legal Art, Illustration © 2009 www. doereport.com)

searched and the following items were discovered on the floor by the decedent's feet: some burnt cloth and ash, medical forceps, a glass "crack" pipe, electrical cord, a tow strap, a paper cup, a plastic bottle, and a cigarette lighter.

There was a dresser next to the victim's body. On the top of the dresser was a candle and melted candle wax, a set of keys for the padlocks, and the dresser appeared to have been kicked back from its original position. The area in the basement around the victim contained the following items: a large mirror facing the deceased, a pair of pliers, a screwdriver, a hand drill, bolt cutters, cords, strapping material, and a weight bench.

The death was considered highly suspicious; therefore, the body was transported to the medical examiner's office with the cuffs still on the victim's ankles and hands and with the chains still attached. Toxicology indicated presence of cocaine in the victim's system.

Interviews of family members and neighbors revealed that the deceased had been caught in the past by his mother while he was engaged in sexual gratification using handcuffs.

The deceased basically kept to himself; he lived alone and did not date. On occasion he would have some friends from work in to play poker. Interviews also revealed that the deceased had been introduced to "crack" by his older brother. The detectives had a forensic analysis of his computer done, which revealed over 300 jpeg images of preteen boys from different Web sites.

The Darby cuffs had been ground out so that the victim could use the medical forceps instead of a key, which explained why there wasn't a key for the cuffs (Figure 4.13).

Figure 4.11 Chained and burned: Victim was found burned and chained to a metal support column beneath an I-beam. He had Darby cuffs securing his feet with a chain running up from the Darby cuffs to his handcuffed hands and then to the top of the metal support column where it was affixed to a padlock. There were severe burns to the waist, chest, and upper thighs, feet, and arms. Note the mirror in the background. (Photo courtesy of Detective Sergeant Steve Gurka, Dearborn Heights, Michigan, Police Department.)

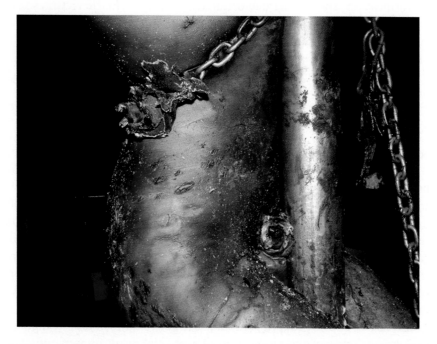

Figure 4.12 Severe burn: Note the severe burns and how tightly the victim is fastened by the chains to the pole. (Photo courtesy of Detective Sergeant Steve Gurka, Dearborn Heights, Michigan, Police Department.)

Figure 4.13 Darby cuffs: The Darby cuffs on his feet did not have a key, but the cuffs had been ground out so that the victim could use medical forceps instead of a key. (Photo courtesy of Detective Sergeant Steve Gurka, Dearborn Heights, Michigan, Police Department.)

He was quite adept at binding and releasing himself from the cuffs using the forceps. At the time of the event, he was engaged in autoerotic cordophelia behavior for self-gratification. The dresser had originally been close to the victim, so he could lean over and light his crack pipe. Apparently the candle ignited his sweatshirt, while he was under the influence of the crack. The victim had burned shirt material in one hand indicating his attempt to remove the burning shirt. The burning material fell onto his lap and ignited his shorts and socks. The manner of death was ruled accidental.

Asphyxial Deaths: The Pathology of Autoerotic Death

Asphyxiation is the end stage of significant interference with the exchange of oxygen and carbon dioxide. According to Dominick J. DiMaio and Vincent J. DiMaio (2001), both nationally renowned forensic pathologists, "Asphyxial deaths are caused by the failure of the cells to receive and/or utilize oxygen. This deprivation of oxygen maybe partial (hypoxia) or total (anoxia)." Fatal cerebral anoxia is an inadequate oxygen supply to the brain with consequent disturbance of bodily functions. The person loses muscle control and goes into spasms resulting in convulsions, which are sudden, violent, involuntary contractions of a group of muscles. The person experiences seizure-like activity.

Asphyxial deaths can be grouped into three categories: suffocation, strangulation, and chemical asphyxia. The most common form of asphyxial death in autoerotic fatalities is strangulation, which is characterized by the closure of the blood vessels and air passages of the neck from hanging or ligature. This results in vasoconstriction, which causes tachycardia, during which the heart beats more than 100 beats a minute to increase the oxygen to the cells of the body. Bradycardia develops because the heart muscle becomes anoxic and cannot maintain the pace. The person succumbs to fatal cerebral anoxia.

The suspension of the body may be complete or incomplete. In sexual asphyxia cases, the body is usually touching the ground. There may be elaborate bindings of the torso and hands of the victim. However, an analysis of these bindings will reveal that the victim was capable of binding him or herself.

Suffocation is the second most frequently occurring form of autoerotic death, which may result from covering the mouth and nose with a plastic bag or mask, or in what is described as proximal or positional asphyxia, such as in chest compression.

Case History

Detectives responded to a "check on the welfare" of a man who hadn't been seen for five days. They observed the deceased white male on a bed in the center of the room, in advancing stages of decomposition. The deceased was wearing a latex hood gas mask, with a yellow canister attached. (It was subsequently learned this type of mask is commonly referred to as a Soviet GP-5 rubber gas mask, readily available from a variety of online retailers). The victim was clad in a leather thong and was wearing black elbow-length opera gloves on both arms and black, support-type, thigh-high hosiery on both legs. Located beneath the crotch area of the deceased was a tube of hand cream. There was a silver-colored chain draped around the waist area up to and around to the back of the neck (Figure 4.14 and Figure 4.15). A search of the apartment revealed an assortment of S&M bondage devices, leather clothing, restraining devices, and an assortment of sexually related, adult-type latex toys. The entire apartment was filled with leather bondage equipment and paraphernalia. The deceased appeared to be living an alternative homosexual life style. The cause of death was suffocation. The manner of death was ruled accidental due to autoerotic activity.

Chemical asphyxia takes place when oxygen is excluded by inhaling noxious gases. The most common chemical asphyxial deaths involving autoerotic activities are with nitrous oxide.

The practitioners of this activity often are aware of the possibility of death and may even have taken precautions against a fatal act, but die as a result of a miscalculation. It would appear that the victim, who may be intent upon achieving an orgasm, misjudges the existent hypoxia already present and the time required to reach orgasm by masturbation. The victim loses consciousness and succumbs to the fatal cerebral anoxia.

Reality of Asphyxial Death: Videotaped Cases

I have included the description of five videotape cases in this chapter to indicate to the reader how suddenly one can lose his or her ability to survive such a dangerous game as sexual asphyxia. The Working Group of Human Asphyxia (WGHA) was formed in 2006 at the 58th meeting of the American Academy of Forensic Sciences (AAFS) to provide

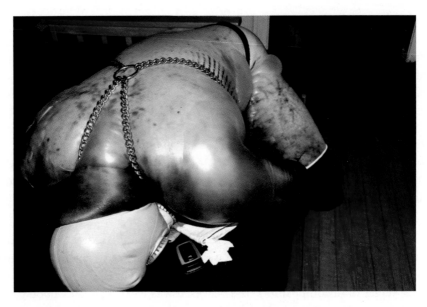

Figure 4.14 Suffocation case: Note the victim was engaged in S&M-type bondage involving chains and straps. (Photo courtesy Detective Mark Czworniak, Chicago, Illinois, Police Department.)

Figure 4.15 Victim's mask: Shown is a latex hood gas mask with a yellow canister attached. The man was breathing through this mask and suffocated during an autoerotic act. (Photo courtesy Detective Mark Czworniak, Chicago, Illinois, Police Department.)

new insight into pathophysiology of human hanging. As a member of this group, I have provided case examples including the filmed hangings discussed in this section. Despite the differences in the types of hanging, similarities have been revealed regarding the rapid loss of consciousness and the onset of convulsions, complex patterns of decerebration and decortication rigidity, and respiratory responses. My review of these particular videotapes has certainly validated my research into the dynamics of sexual asphyxia and the reality of fatal cerebral anoxia.

Anny Sauvageau, a forensic pathologist, and I conducted a workshop at the AAFS in Denver, Colorado, in February 2009, entitled "New Insight Into Asphyxia by Hanging: From Basic Hanging Deaths and Autoerotic Fatalities to Advanced Pathophysiology of Human Beings." The goal was to present attendees with new insight into asphyxia by hanging based on research from members of the WGHA. The presentation of our findings utilized actual videotapes of hangings, which included two filmed suicides and six autoerotic deaths. The hangings were of different types: free hanging, hanging with feet on the ground, hanging kneeling, and hanging almost lying face down. The hanging ligatures also varied widely, from cloth band to ropes with or without padding and electric cords. All of the victims were adult males.

Respiratory and movement responses to asphyxia by hanging were described in detail. With the time 0 representing the onset of hanging, rapid loss of consciousness was observed at 8 to 18 seconds, closely followed by the appearance of convulsions (10 to 19 seconds) in all of the cases. A complex pattern of decerebration and decortication rigidity was then observed in all of the cases (Figure 4.16 and Figure 4.17). Last isolated muscle movement occurred between 1 minute and 2 seconds and 7 minutes and 31 seconds. As for respiratory responses, we observed the onset of very deep respiratory attempts between 13 and 24 seconds and last attempt between 1 minute and 2 seconds and 2 minutes and 5 seconds (Sauvageau and Geberth, 2009b).

Figure 4.16 Decerebration. This is a video still photo of the first phase in a series of involuntary and complex patterns of decerebration and decortication. (Photo courtesy of the author.)

Figure 4.17 Decortication. This is a video still photo of decortication, which is another phase of the involuntary and complex patterns of decerebration and decortication. (Photo courtesy of the author.)

Equivocal Death Investigations

"Equivocal death investigations are those inquiries that are open to interpretation. There may be two or more meanings and the case may present as either a homicide or a suicide depending on the circumstances. The facts are purposefully vague or misleading as in the case of a **'staged crime scene.'** Or, the death is suspicious or questionable based on what is presented to the authorities. The deaths may resemble homicides or suicides, accidents or naturals. They are open to interpretation pending further information of the facts, the victimology, and the circumstances of the event" (Geberth, 1996).

Case History #1: Videotape, Cowboy Fantasy

This case is a classic situation in which the police are called to a scene to investigate what seemingly is a suicide involving a young man found hanging by the neck. Ironically, the case would have been classified a suicide had the authorities not found a videotape of the young man acting out a theme, which revealed the death to be an accident.

CASE FACTS

An older brother, who had gone to the garage to place a milk bottle in the trash, found the victim. Upon entering the garage, he observed his brother hanging from a rope, which had been tied to a 2 × 4 in the attic. The attic stairs were down. Another brother was called to the scene. He arrived about 10 minutes later. The two brothers untied the rope from the 2 × 4 and let the victim's body down to the floor. The brothers called the police and an ambulance.

The initial responding officers observed the young man's body lying on the floor of the garage. The victim was dressed in western clothing and had a blue bandana tied around his neck. The brothers had never seen the victim wearing this type of clothing before, and it was out of character for the victim to be dressed in this manner. A search of the residence was conducted. The police did not find any suicide note or anything else suggesting that the young man had intended to commit suicide. Interviews of family members indicated no history of depression. However, while searching the garage the investigators discovered a video camera positioned near the attic ladder. It was in the record mode when located. The videotape was seized.

The investigators reviewed the tape and discovered that the hanging incident had been captured in its entirety. The detectives had initially theorized that the death was likely a suicide. The victim was the youngest of three brothers. The two older brothers had excelled in athletics while in school and were very popular among their peers. It was determined that the victim was more interested in scholastic achievements than athletics and was more introspective than either of his brothers.

The theory was that perhaps the victim had dressed in this attire and strutted around smoking in a fashion like the Marlboro Man to exhibit some type of macho behavior or toughness that wasn't in his personality. Although some of the detectives were familiar with autoerotic deaths, they felt they needed an outside opinion.

REVIEW OF THE VIDEOTAPE

The tape begins with the subject posing and posturing for the camera. He is dressed in western wear, wearing a cowboy hat, and looking into the camera. He lights up a pipe and then blows smoke at the camera in a very macho fashion. The victim is obviously acting out a personal fantasy that does not appear to be sexual in nature. Yet, his actions and activities are significant in revealing an underlying psychosexual macho image that presents an "in control male" challenging the camera as he walks up really close showing his face and then suddenly stands up. He then turns his back to the camera, spitting to the side and walks away as if he is "walking into the sunset" in a movie script. The victim's facial expressions and gestures during this sequence of the tape replicated the Marlboro Man image, which was popular at the time of this event. The victim was portraying this image for the camera and his fantasy. This segment of the tape lasted approximately four minutes and was obviously part of a script that the victim had fantasized. **This fantasy component was taken into consideration in my analysis of the event.**

The next scene takes place in the garage. A review of the tape shows the subject carrying a rope up the attic stairs out of the range of the camera. He was apparently securing that rope, which had been tied into a noose, to a 2 × 4 in the attic. When he came down the attic stairs, he had the noose around his neck over the blue bandana. The subject was observed standing on the attic stairs adjusting his hat, which the rope had dislodged from his head. He then went into a full hang placing his hands behind his back in some sort of execution mode and hung there for a full six seconds during which time you could hear him choke and cough from the tightening of the noose around his neck and the restriction of the major blood vessels in his neck.

This was an extremely dangerous game and it was obvious to the author that the young man had no idea of how hazardous a full hang could be. The amount of pressure it takes to compress the jugular veins is 4.4 pounds. The amount of pressure to takes to compress the carotid is approximately 11 pounds. This young man weighed at least 160 pounds. Every time he stepped off the attic stairs, he was a "breath" away from death.

The victim then went back up the attic stairs out of view of the camera. He was still coughing from the first hang. He was apparently adjusting the rope so that the noose would be within the camera's range for the hanging. He then came down the attic stairs with the noose around his neck and proceeded to get in position to fully hang for a second time. He then stepped off the attic stairs and went into a full hang with his hands behind his back. Suddenly, within 9 seconds, he lost consciousness. His hat was dislodged and I observed his body go into a complex pattern of decerebration and decortication. He began to cough and choke as he went into fatal cerebral anoxia. He went into convulsions as he began seizure-like activity as his arms flailed in spasm and his fingers took on the classic claw-like spasm consistent with oxygen deprivation. His last muscle movement was observed at approximately 3 minutes.

It was absolutely amazing to observe how suddenly the hypoxia kicked in and the rapid onset of fatal cerebral anoxia. I can't impress upon the reader how dangerous these activities are.

This was a classic case of asphyxial death due to hanging.

Case History #2: Videotape, Execution Fantasy

CASE FACTS

I had the opportunity to review a case in which the victim, a white male, 38 years of age, had set up a video camera to record his autoerotic fantasy. The victim, who was married with children, had selected an area inside the garage of the family home to create some sort of execution scenario for his fantasy. He had placed a large sheet over the furnishings in the room to create a background for the camera. The entire scene was recorded on videotape.

The victim was discovered hanging in the garage by his mother, who had gone to the garage with one of her grandchildren to get a key to enter the house at 4 p.m. She reported to police that earlier that day she had tried to call her son at 10:30 a.m., but there was no answer. When they entered the garage, they encountered the body. They then ran down the street to her residence where she informed her husband, the father of the victim. The victim's father ran to the house, which was only four houses away, and discovered his son hanging with a pair of blue panties completely over his head. The father quickly removed the panties from his son's head and checked for life and found none. He then called an ambulance. The father reported that he had observed a VHS video camera near the overhead door, which was aimed toward the body. He took the camera down and placed it on a table. The father was asked whether or not there had been any problems. He stated that his son was not depressed, did not have any business problems nor did he have any enemies and, as far as he was concerned, everything was going great for his son, who was happily married and had three children.

The responding officers saw a man's body hanging from a rope, which had been placed over a beam, that was running east and west and was the second beam from the wall. This rope had been placed over a rafter beam and was tied to an adjustable post that ran to the center support beams, and the rope had been further tightened with the use of a screwdriver.

The victim was wearing a red, long-sleeved sweatshirt with red, short pants. He had a wristwatch on his left wrist and lividity was present. The body was also cool to the touch. Upon closer examination, a red cloth-type belt was observed protruding through the zipper fly of the victim. This cloth belt had been tied around the waist and the penis of the victim.

The investigators also noted that there was a pair of blue slippers on the floor and a small wooden stool beneath where the victim was hanging. A screwdriver was on the floor. The father stated he had knocked it down when he checked his son. There was a camera tripod near the garage door, which had held the video camera. The investigators located a box of pornographic periodicals in the living room along with certain hand-drawn sketches depicting sexual hanging scenes. This box also contained hand-written literature in reference to sexual hanging-type actions. There were also a number of porno magazines.

REVIEW OF THE VIDEOTAPE

A hangman's noose was secured over a rafter in the ceiling and was tied off to the side. Directly below the hanging noose was a small wooden stool, which the subject could stand on to place the noose over his head and around his neck. The subject was observed walking into the camera's view wearing a pair of women's panties over his head. In the background, a large white sheet covered the wall and workbench. He looked in the direction of the camera and placed the noose over his head and around his neck. In order to secure the rope around his neck, he had to stand on his toes. He then stood with his hands behind his back. The hypoxia began to take effect immediately because the noose had begun to restrict the blood flow to the head. He suddenly lost his balance and the noose became tightened around his neck. At this point, he could have saved himself by simply standing back onto the stool.

However, he was not aware of the impending danger and again placed his hands behind his back and continued with the fantasy. In seconds, he lost consciousness and began convulsions as the fatal cerebral anoxia developed.

This asphyxial death was a little different from the previously discussed case in that the victim was not in a full hang. His feet were touching the floor. However, the results were the same. His video production had gone from fantasy to reality in less than 4 minutes. This was also an extremely dramatic portrayal of the reality of sexual asphyxia.

Case History #3: Videotape, Homosexual Cross Dressing

CASE FACTS

This case involved a 28-year-old male homosexual who was heavily into S&M activities. His mother discovered him in the early morning hours. He was found hanging by his neck from a karate belt, which had been secured to a hook in the ceiling. He was nude, wearing black nylon stockings and black high heel shoes, and had a black hood over his head. This was interesting in that most victims of autoerotic fatalities are heterosexual males who play the part of a female victim in some sort of bizarre fantasy.

The value of this case from an investigative perspective was that the subject had an extensive collection of videos, which consisted of approximately 30 hours of autoerotic activities, as well as S&M events, in which he and a male partner would act out scenes. An example of these tapes was the subject dressed as a woman, wearing a wig, white mini skirt, a sequined bra, and long, white gloves. The subject, who pretended to be a female occupant all alone in her home, becomes the victim of a "home invasion," whereas the subject's partner pretends to be a burglar, who then sexually assaults the subject. The homemade videotapes are heavy-duty S&M involving beatings by fist, ligature restraints, bondage, and attaching battery clips to the abdominal skin of the subject. There is also oxygen deprivation. In one of the tapes the author viewed, the subject is bound on a couch. The subject's partner than slips a plastic bag over the head of the subject, who is visibly suffering the effects of suffocation. The partner monitors the subject's breathing and removes the plastic bag at the last minute as panic sets in.

The autoerotic tapes that the author viewed clearly show a progression from when the victim first began these activities up to the last tape where the subject dies during autoerotic practice. When the victim first began to practice these activities, he would wear a harness to prevent himself from hanging to death. Each of the tapes followed the same scenario. The subject videotaped himself as he walks into the room.

REVIEW OF THE VIDEOTAPES

In the room is a large, white sheet, which acts as a backdrop. There is a karate belt attached to a hook in the ceiling and a metal folding chair also covered with a sheet. The subject, who has a black hood over his head, walks onto the "set" wearing a black leather micromini skirt, a black bra, black nylons, and black high heel shoes. He poses and gestures in front of the camera. He then steps up onto the chair with his high heels. He has straps, which he uses to tie his knees and his hands behind his back. He then hangs there for a period of time. In the next few tapes, the subject begins to strip for the camera as he stands on the folding chair wearing the high heel shoes. He lifts the mini skirt up to expose his genital area, which is covered with the black nylons. In some of the tapes, the author observed that the subject was feeling the effects of hypoxia. The subject slipped a couple of times, but because he was wearing the harness, he was safe from hanging.

Other tapes depicted the subject wearing different costumes engaging in the same ritualistic scenario. Obviously, his fantasy entailed him depicted as a woman being directed through a striptease and then hanging to produce the hypoxia. In one tape, we can see the extent of the safety mechanism, as he was totally nude except for the nylons. The harness had a cross strap that fit across his abdomen and extended up under his armpits. Even if he fell from the chair, the ligature around his neck wouldn't constrict his breathing because the harness actually held him and prevented the noose from tightening.

REVIEW OF THE FATAL VIDEOTAPE

In the last tape, the subject is once again seen entering the room wearing the black hood, the black high heel shoes, and the black nylons. He is nude under the nylon stockings. Remember, he has done this a number of times without injury and it has become routine. This time, however, he is not wearing the harness. He stands up onto the chair and secures the karate belt around his neck. He engages in some posing and periodically tightens the belt around his neck. He does not have his hands behind his back this time. As he continues to tighten the belt, the hypoxia begins to take effect. He is clearly off balance. Within eight seconds, his foot slips from the chair and he drops to the floor on his knees. At this point, he is literally hanging to death. I observed onset of the fatal cerebral anoxia, the labored breathing, and the spasms. He stopped moving within two minutes.

Case History #4: Videotape, Nude and Masturbating

CASE FACTS

The victim was a white male, 30 years of age, who was living with his married brother and family. He had set up a video camera to record a sexual fantasy while the family was out of the house. The victim had selected an area in the second floor hallway beneath a set of attic stairs. The area was secluded and would afford him an opportunity to quickly stop if he heard someone enter the house from the ground floor. There was a room immediately off to the right where he could quickly exit the hallway if someone was coming. He had secured an electric extension cord to some rafters in the attic. The victim was in good physical condition and one would think that he would be able to prevent an accident from occurring by simply using his strength to stop the event.

REVIEW OF THE FATAL VIDEOTAPE

The tape clearly shows the victim as he enters the viewfinder of the video camera, removes his underwear, and proceeds to manually masturbate. The area is secluded and affords him an opportunity to quickly stop if he hears someone enter the house from the ground floor. The victim had selected an area in the second floor hallway beneath a set of attic stairs. He then walks over to the attic stairs, which are extended down to the floor. He steps up two rungs and places the electric cord noose over his head. As he does so, one can observe that he has an erection at this point, which clearly indicates that this event is an autoerotic event. He then steps down one rung and, as he does, he attempts to make some adjustments to the tightening wire cord around his neck. He appears at this point to be having some difficulty. He then steps down a second rung and, as he does, I observed a sudden abdominal spasm and, within less than five seconds, he lets out a guttural sound and proceeds to go into fatal cerebral anoxia. He experiences spasms and seizure-like activity, losing all muscle control. As the noose tightens, the tape continues to show the victim losing consciousness within 12 seconds as he goes into convulsions.

The tape then records the sounds of the victim's brother as he returns home with his two children. As the brother comes to the second floor, he suddenly sees the victim and yells to his older son to call 911. It is an extremely disturbing sight to observe the valiant attempts of the brother, who is a paramedic, trying to save the victim's life.

It is apparent from the conversation that the brother is having with relatives and the emergency operator that he believes that his brother has hung himself in a suicide attempt. The sounds of sirens and responding emergency units are heard in the background as the brother attempts to get a heartbeat. Although he was able to get a heartbeat using CPR, the victim had already suffered irreversible brain damage and died that evening at the hospital.

There wasn't any evidence of female attire, bindings, or other sexual paraphernalia present in the scene, and a search of the victim's room and vehicle produced no evidence of prior autoerotic behavior. The victim was reported to be sexually active with a female he had been dating for several months.

Without the videotape, which clearly shows the nude victim masturbating and putting the noose around his neck, the case most likely would have been classified as a suicide.

Case History #5: Videotape, Masochism and Masturbation

CASE FACTS

The victim was a white male, 35 years of age, who was married and had children. The evening before at about 11 p.m., the victim told his wife he was going to fix the kitchen sink, but had to purchase a pipe. She went to bed with the children. At about 5 a.m., she awakened and noticed that the garage light was on. She went to the garage and found her husband hanging. At first she was angry because she saw that he had knocked over a video camera. Then she realized that he was dead and that something horrible had happened. She immediately dialed 911.

The arriving police and medical personnel observed that he was wearing thong underwear and was hanging with a dog collar around his neck, which was attached to a chain affixed to a light fixture. The police observed a video camera attached to a video recorder. There were several lights pointing in the direction of the victim along with a large mirror against one of the garage walls. The police took the equipment and the videotape as evidence. According to family members, there was no history of marital or family problems and, according to the victim's wife, her husband certainly wasn't suicidal.

REVIEW OF THE FATAL VIDEOTAPE

The tape clearly showed the victim as he prepared the room for his fantasy. He was wearing thong underwear and was nude from the waist up. He attached the dog collar to the chain and then proceeded to look into the mirror as he beat his own buttocks with a paddle. He then attached some clamps to his buttocks as he paraded in front of the mirror. He is also observed attaching two foot-long bolts with clothespins to his nipples. He removed his penis from his underwear and proceeded to manually masturbate. This activity continued for approximately three minutes during which time one of the foot-long bolts slipped from his nipple. He removes the second bolt and proceeds to paddle his buttocks a second time. However, as he did this he leaned forward increasing the pressure on the neck and suddenly went into fatal cerebral anoxia.

The victim lost consciousness and went into convulsions and seizure-like activity. His fingers took on the classic claw-like spasm consistent with oxygen deprivation. The spasms and convulsions continued for approximately three more minutes until the man's body went limp.

Sexual Asphyxia: The Psychosexual Aspects of Autoerotic Activity

The purpose of this section is to acquaint the investigator with some of the clinical terminology used to define bizarre and deviant human sexuality. The psychopathology of this phenomenon is better left to the clinicians and other professionals trained in the fields of medicine and psychiatry. I refer the reader to the *Diagnostic and Statistical Manual of Mental Disorders (DSM-IV-TR)* (American Psychiatric Association, 2000), *Abnormal Psychology and Modern Life,* 7th ed. (Coleman et al., 1984), and Chapter 5 of *Autoerotic Fatalities* (Hazelwood et al., 1983).

The investigative interpretation of the psychosexual aspects of autoerotic activities can be found in a group of persistent sexual arousal patterns defined in *DSM-IV-TR* as **paraphilias.**

The essential feature of disorders in this subclass is that unusual or bizarre imagery or acts are necessary for sexual excitement. Such imagery or acts tend to be insistently and involuntarily repetitive and generally involve either (1) preference for use of a nonhuman object for sexual arousal, (2) repetitive sexual activity with humans involving real or simulated suffering or humiliation, or (3) repetitive sexual activity with nonconsenting partners. In other classifications, these disorders are referred to as **sexual deviations**. The term *paraphilia* is preferable because it correctly emphasizes that the deviation (*para*) is that to which the individual is attracted (*philia*). Because paraphiliac imagery is necessary for erotic arousal, it must be included in masturbatory or coital fantasies, if not actually acted out alone or with a partner and supporting cast or paraphernalia. In the absence of paraphiliac imagery, there is no relief from nonerotic tension, and sexual excitement or orgasm is not attained. The imagery in a paraphiliac fantasy or the object of sexual excitement in a paraphilia is frequently the stimulus for sexual excitement in individuals without a psychosexual disorder. For example, women's undergarments and imagery of sexual coercion are sexually exciting for many men; they are paraphiliac only when they become necessary for sexual excitement (American Psychiatric Association, 2000).

According to the *DSM-IV-TR*, there are nine (9) paraphilias. These are listed in Chapter 1 with brief definitions. However, for further information, I direct the reader to *DSM-IV-TR* (APA, 2000) and *Abnormal Psychology and Modern Life* (Coleman et al., 1984).

Case Histories

Hanging

A white male in his late forties, never married, living at home with his mother and sister, was found hanging in his basement workshop. He was wearing street clothing that covered women's garments: a bra stuffed with padding, women's panties, women's boots, and leather gloves. A mask, which he had apparently been wearing, was found on the floor beneath him. He was hanging by a rope affixed to a hook in the ceiling. There was a Polaroid camera positioned on the workbench and a number of photographs of the deceased participating in this conduct. There were a number of pornographic magazines depicting female bondage, lesbian conduct, and sadomasochistic behavior found in his room. In addition to these commercial products, police discovered sadomasochistic drawings depicting the deceased dressed as a woman. In these drawings, this "woman" is observed with an erect penis threatening and abusing other women. There were also a number of these sexually explicit drawings of nude and seminude women urinating. These "fantasy drawings" were further illustrated with words indicating that the deceased was actually verbalizing his sadomasochistic fantasies. Also discovered were two legal-size sheets of paper listing approximately 200 pieces of women's apparel and undergarments that the deceased had purchased. The victim had listed these items by number, description, price, and the name of the store

Figure 4.18 Fantasy drawing. The victim created a number of fantasy drawings, which depicted women in lesbian scenarios involving bondage and urophilia.

from which the item was purchased. He then had a separate column, which indicated whether or not he had photographed himself in the item. This individual's total sex life was involved with solo sexual activities. His drawings further suggested paraphilias of transvestism, sadism, and masochism with fantasies of necrophilia and urophilia (Figure 4.18 and Figure 4.19).

Hanging Case

The author had the opportunity to review a death investigation involving a white male in his forties who had died during an autoerotic event. I conferred with the lieutenant in charge of the investigation. The subject was a dentist, who was discovered in his office by an assistant after his wife had become concerned with his absence. When the man was discovered, he was wearing female attire and undergarments including dark stockings, a girdle, and high heel shoes. Inside the girdle were various hairbrushes turned in a manner to cause the brush to be against the skin. There was a plastic dildo inserted in the man's anal cavity. The man had padding to cushion his neck from a noose, which was around his neck. The noose was attached to a rope that was secured to a wall in the office.

During the search of his office, the authorities observed numerous precut ropes and bindings strewn about his office. There also was a five-drawer metal cabinet that contained hundreds of pornographic magazines, most of which dealt with bondage. The magazines dealt with heavy-duty adult pornography, titles, such as *Sensual Women, Bizarre in Rubber: Latex Lashers and Rubber Queens,* as well as a number of issues of *Bishop: The First Erotic Art of Bishop,* which dealt with discipline and BDSM (bondage and discipline, sadism and masochism). The subject had cut and pasted various objects and faces on the models

Figure 4.19 Fantasy drawing. In this drawing, the victim portrayed himself dressed in "La Femme" undergarments. Notice the penis protruding through the garments.

in the magazines. He had also created his own bondage fantasy by accenting the models pictures with objects placed into their sexual orifices. In fact, his alterations were done so meticulously that the conversion appeared to be an actual photograph of a dental instrument inserted through the breast, complete with shadow and blood drippings. Based on the number of magazines that were recovered, and the multiple alterations the subject had made, it was quite apparent that the subject had spent an inordinate amount of time with his fantasy. However, the most significant discovery was a black and white Polaroid photograph pasted onto one of the magazine pages. It depicted two women engaged in a bondage scenario practicing klismaphilia (paraphilia involving enemas), suggesting that the subject was involved with these activities with some playmates. This later proved to be of investigative significance in resolving whether or not this death was an autoerotic or group exercise event.

Although obviously embarrassing to the other participants who played these S&M games, the actual death was an autoerotic fatality. The authorities had properly classified the death as accidental. Cause of death: ligature asphyxiation. Manner of death was ruled accidental.

Suffocation

A white male, 66 years of age, was discovered lying upon his bed by police who had been called to the man's apartment. The deceased was wearing women's clothing, which consisted of a gray turtleneck sweater with crotch snaps and red panty hose. The upper torso was bound with straps and chains, which were interconnected by a series of locks. A rubber mask covered his face and the mask was connected to the bed board by rope. There was an electrical apparatus attached to a hook in the ceiling, which consisted of a timer and two wires. This equipment was plugged into a wall socket. One of the wires extended down to the crotch area of the victim. A copper wire loop had been fitted beneath the snaps of the turtleneck sweater and this could be connected to the electrical device. In the man's room, police investigators discovered three suitcases full of women's undergarments, wigs, and "falsies," as well as other sexual paraphernalia consisting of dildos, discipline masks, and pornographic materials. When the body was examined, the victim was found to be wearing women's undergarments. Under the head mask, duct tape covered his eyes, foam rubber was stuffed in his mouth, and a headband held a small rubber ball in each ear. He was totally in the dark and couldn't hear a thing, but all of the bindings and chains were within his grasp. His escape mechanism was a single lock, which secured all of the chains wrapped around his body. The deceased had held the keys for this lock in his right hand. He had apparently dropped his keys on the floor where the police discovered them. The duct tape and rubber balls in his ears certainly shut out any possibility of seeing the keys or hearing them drop to the floor. He had been bound to the bed in such a manner that he would not have been able to reach down to the floor even if he had heard the keys drop. The cause of death was suffocation. The police supervisor, as well as the detective investigating this case, had both been to one of my "Practical Homicide Investigation®" lectures. They immediately recognized the death to be an autoerotic fatality based on the above information. However, when the medical examiner of the jurisdiction arrived at the scene, he told the detectives it appeared to be a homicide related to biker gang activity. He obviously was not familiar with such cases and based his conclusion of homicide on the bizarre binding of the body (Figure 4.20 and Figure 4.21).

Chest Compression

The author reviewed a case involving a male who had constructed a device that would cause chest compression. The victim had used the blow end of a vacuum cleaner to inflate a plastic bag that he had placed inside a canvas laundry bag. The victim, who was wearing his wife's teddy and nothing else, had apparently crawled into the bag and was able to secure the bag by pulling a rope around his neck to secure the contraption. He then rolled over to the vacuum and turned it on with his nose. The vacuum then filled the plastic bag with air, which in turn caused the canvas bag to tighten around the subject's chest. The only problem with this device was that there wasn't any way for the victim to turn off the vacuum once the canvas bag had become inflated. He suffocated to death during his auto-erotic activity.

Suffocation: Plastic Bag, Chemical Substances

A deceased male was discovered lying on a bed in a rental cabin with a plastic bag over his head. This male had rented the summer cabin during the off season. The proprietor, who was checking on the rental, made the discovery when he entered the premises and noticed the nude body of the deceased on the bed. Police were called to the location and discovered an array of pornographic magazines opened to the centerfolds on the floor next to the bed. Also next to the bed was a canister of nitrous oxide. The investigators learned that the man, who had been involved with this activity in the past, had been sniffing the pure nitrous

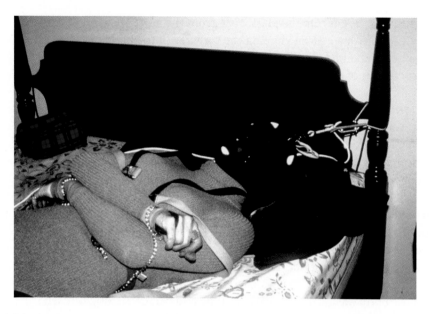

Figure 4.20 Autoerotic death suffocation: The man had dressed in female attire with a discipline mask over his head. His eyes were covered with duct tape, his mouth stuffed with foam rubber and a small rubber ball was in each ear. Beneath his outer garments he wore female lingerie. He had done this on many occasions and the release mechanism was a key to the lock that held all of the chains in place. The man apparently dropped the keys and was caught in his own fantasy. (Photo courtesy of Retired Detective Lieutenant Raymond Krolak, commanding officer, Investigations Division, Colonie, New York, Police Department)

Figure 4.21 Close-up of connected chains. All of these were interconnected to a single lock that he had gripped in his hand. (Photo courtesy of Retired Detective Lieutenant Raymond Krolak, commanding officer, Investigations Division, Colonie, New York, Police Department.)

oxide by releasing the gas into the plastic bag from the tank. He would then write down his sexual fantasies on a pad while viewing the pictures of the nude models in the magazines next to the bed. When he placed the plastic bag over his head, the lack of oxygen resulted in the asphyxiation of the victim.

Suffocation: Nitrous Oxide

The victim was a white male, 37 years of age, living alone in a large apartment complex. Police officers had responded to a call of the discovery of a deceased male. As the officers entered the master bedroom, they observed the nude victim in a supine position.

The body had begun to decompose and was bloated with skin slippage and swollen genitalia. Officers noted that the victim was wearing a pilot-type oxygen mask, which was attached to his mouth and nose (Figure 4.22). There was a long black hose that led from the facemask to a colored balloon. There were also several empty and full containers of N_2O cartridges. The victim had a black, nontransparent set of goggles covering his eyes. The victim was wearing a variety of jewelry, consisting of metal fingertip devices, rings, and bracelets on both hands and wrists. There was a Sony video camera pointed toward the victim, whose body was facing a mirror, as if he had been watching himself.

The officers reviewed the tape inside the camera and saw the victim lying on his back, masturbating with both hands. While he was masturbating, he was wearing the black Air Force–style facemask along with the nontransparent goggles. The victim also had a set of metal claws on his fingers.

The tape showed the victim leaning over and filling up the balloon with what appeared to be N_2O cartridges. The victim continued to masturbate for about a minute and a half. He then made an adjustment to the gas and, after about 45 seconds, he lifted his left arm to adjust his mask and lost consciousness. The video continued showing the victim gasping for air for the next few minutes, then all movement stopped. Examination revealed that the victim had been inhaling nitrous oxide.

Suffocation Case: Ether

A 62-year-old white male was found lying on his back in the center of his bed in the second-floor master suite with his legs dangling off the side of the bed. The victim had a gag around his face, consisting of an Ace™ bandage wrap and a green washcloth held in place with duct tape. This covered the lower part of his mouth and chin with his nose exposed.

The victim was naked, except for a black leather strap with two shackles on his wrists. His hands were cuffed with silver handcuffs with an Ace bandage beneath the cuffs to prevent bruising. There was a plastic, white zip tie connecting the black leather belt to the handcuffs. The key for the handcuffs was on the nightstand next to the victim. In the bathroom was a tan metal box containing dildos, leg restraints, hand restraints, lubricating jellies, and various other sexual devises. There was also a brown bottle containing a clear liquid, which examination revealed to be ether (Figure 4.23).

It was apparent that the victim had bound himself and placed the gag over his mouth. All of the towels and bandages were wrapped neatly around his face and wrists. The duct tape had been cut with scissors and carefully placed around the towels to hold them in place over his face.

Investigation revealed that the deceased would order Viagra™ and ether over the Internet and had becoming sexually obsessed with autoerotic activity. His wife was away on a trip when this event occurred. The death was properly classified as an accidental death.

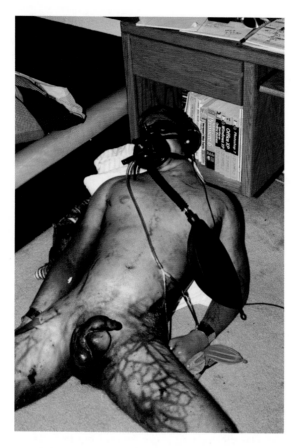

Figure 4.22 Nitrous oxide/gas mask: The victim was wearing a pilot-type oxygen mask that was attached to his mouth and nose. There was a long, black hose that led from the facemask to a colored balloon. There were also several empty and full containers of N_2O cartridges. (Photo courtesy of Retired Detective Steve Mack, Huntington Beach, California, Police Department.)

Female Victims of Autoerotic Fatality

Although most of the cases of autoerotic death involve males, it is important to realize that this type of practice is not limited to males. For example, what may appear to be a sex slaying, involving the bondage and suffocation of a female victim, may in fact be the accidental death of a female practitioner of autoerotic activities. Retired Special Agent Frank Sass of the FBI reported one such case. A 35-year-old female divorcee was discovered dead by her 9-year-old daughter. The woman was nude and lying on a small shelved space in the rear of a closet in her bedroom. She was on her stomach and an electric vibrator with a hard rubber massaging head was between her thighs and in contact with her vulva. The vibrator was operating when the victim was discovered. Attached to the nipple of her right breast was a spring-type clothespin, compressing her nipple. Immediately below her left breast another clothespin was found. Around the victim's neck was a hand towel. A nylon stocking went over the towel in loop fashion and was fastened to a shelf bracket above her head. The shelf and the victim's upper body rested on her arms, which were extended downward from her body in a pushup position, supporting the lower portion of the body. The clothespins were used to cause discomfort, the vibrator was used in a masturbatory exercise, and

Figure 4.23 Ether case: The victim had a gag around his face, with an Ace bandage wrap and a green washcloth soaked in ether held in place with duct tape. (Photo courtesy of Retired Detective Steve Mack, Huntington Beach, California, Police Department.)

the ligature reduced oxygen flow. She obviously intended to support her upper body weight with her arms, but she lost consciousness and the weight of her body, hanging from the nylon stocking, caused her to strangle (Sass, 1975).

It should be noted that the female victim of an autoerotic fatality, who has involved herself in binding and some sort of sadomasochistic scenario, presents authorities with circumstances that actually resemble a sex-related homicide.

Hazelwood et al. (1983) cite the following case. A 23-year-old black woman was found dead in her bathroom. The victim's upper torso rested on the edge of the bathtub, her face was in the water, and her knees were on the floor. The faucets were turned on, and the water had filled the tub, spilled onto the floor, and run throughout the house. There was vomitus in the tub water. A piece of rope had been doubled and looped around her on the left side of her neck, with the loose ends coming across and over her right shoulder. Her wrists were wrapped together in front of her body and the end of the rope securing them rested in her right hand. The decedent was nude, and a 9½-inch bolt was on the floor beside the body. There was a bruise on the left side of her forehead and drops of blood were found on the edge and side of the tub. Autopsy revealed the cause of death to be aspiration of vomitus.

This case was investigated initially as a suicide, based on statements by a relative and friend of the victim. It was also investigated as a possible homicide, with the boyfriend, who had discovered the body, as a primary suspect. Although this case had enough factors to support both possibilities, in actuality, the case was eventually classified as an auto-erotic fatality. According to the authors, "A theory that accounts for all of the facts in this case is that the victim had been drawing a bath while asphyxiating herself with the rope, intending to use the bolt for manual masturbation, or already having done so. Through asphyxiation, she lost consciousness, struck her head on the bathtub, and aspirated vomitus (Hazelwood et al., 1983).

Female Autoerotic Fatality Reported as a Homicide

The victim was a 34-year-old white female, who lived alone in an apartment on the north side of the city. She was a schoolteacher, single, heterosexual, and in good physical and mental health at the time of her death. On Saturday, she had spent the day with her parents who were house hunting. She had dinner that evening with them and agreed to meet them the next day to continue house hunting.

Her father told her he would call her for church the next day. Usually she went to church with them. However, she told her father to call her after church.

On Sunday morning after church, her father called her, but she did not answer. Knowing this to be strange, he drove to her apartment to check on her well-being.

He entered the locked apartment with a key she had given to him for emergencies. He called out her name and, when she didn't answer, began to search the apartment. He opened the closed bathroom door and found his daughter. She was hanging from the back of the door with a belt around her neck. She was nude with her breasts bound very tightly with rope and was hanging by her neck from the belt. The belt had been secured to a hook on the back of her bathroom door (Figures 4.24 through 4.26). The distraught man backed out of the apartment, locked the door, and called the police. Initially, the death appeared to be a sex-related homicide. There wasn't any forced entry, the apartment had been locked, and there were no signs of any struggle. The next suggestion was that the death was a possible suicide. However, that was quickly ruled out based on her victimology. Closer examination revealed the death to be accidental, involving autoerotic activities.

The rope used was nautical rope. Additional nautical rope was found in her closet. The belt came from a dress she owned and hadn't worn for some time. Directly across from the victim was a full-length mirror from which she could view herself from the door. The death was properly classified as accidental. Many of the considerations as outlined in this chapter were present in this particular case. This provided the authorities a basis upon which to make a determination of accidental death involving sexual asphyxia. (See below: Determining the Involvement of Sexual Asphyxia: Autoerotic Checklist.)

Female Autoerotic Fatality Reported as a Suicide

The body of a white female, 33 years old, who had recently been laid off from work, was discovered by an acquaintance, who became concerned when she couldn't contact her. The victim's friend, who had a key for the apartment, tried to get in, but a dead bolt had been secured, which could be unlocked only from the inside. She then notified another friend, who requested the maintenance man of the building to assist in the entry. The maintenance man used a ladder to climb to the second floor balcony and then entered the apartment

Figure 4.24 Female autoerotic. This case was originally reported as a sex-related homicide. (Courtesy of Retired Commander Tom Cronin, Chicago, Illinois, Police Department.)

through a sliding glass door. He opened the apartment door and the three individuals began to search the premises. They discovered the victim hanging from the top railing of the sliding glass shower door.

The victim was completely nude and was in a semistanding position. There was a restraint around the victim's torso, which held her arms close to her body. The witnesses left the apartment and called 911 and reported the death as a possible suicide. The first responders observed the woman hanging by the neck and determined that the victim had been dead for some time. Her body was cool to the touch and livor mortis was pronounced in her lower extremities. The responders did not cut her down or attempt any resuscitation, thereby preserving the death scene intact. The supervisor who noted that the victim's arms had been bound and her right wrist had a binding secured declared the death suspicious and designated the entire apartment a crime scene. All personnel were ordered out of the apartment and investigators were notified in accordance with excellent "Practical Homicide Investigation" procedure.

The reporting witnesses were interviewed. The victim's acquaintance advised authorities that the victim had been laid off from work about a week earlier. The company had given her a generous severance package and was assisting her in finding employment. The victim was last seen by the reporting witness the evening before and was in good spirits. The two of them had planned on going to a hockey game the next day. However, when the

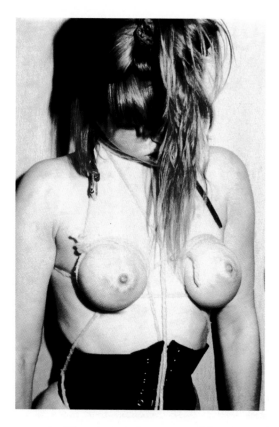

Figure 4.25 Female autoerotic. The victim's hair covered her face. There was a belt wrapped tightly around her neck. (Photo courtesy of Retired Commander Tom Cronin, Chicago, Illinois, Police Department.)

victim did not respond to several calls, the witness decided to check on her friend and made the discovery.

Investigators entered the apartment and examined the body. The victim was totally nude and hanging by the neck from the bathroom shower frame. The victim had a piece of cloth around her neck with a slipknot in it. The victim had another piece of cloth around her arms just above the elbows binding her arms to her sides. There also was a piece of cloth tied around her left wrist. On the bathroom floor behind the victim was a set of black nipple clamps. On the floor in front of the victim was a large vibrator. On the bathroom sink, there was a vibrator dildo shaped like a penis. A search of the apartment revealed a number of sex toys and numerous items relating to sexual asphyxia, bondage, and auto-erotic sexual activity. There were several pornographic magazines, bondage movies, and videos, which were sexually graphic.

The medical examiner conferred with the investigators and agreed that the death was an autoerotic fatality. The examination of the victim's body did not reveal an assault or trauma and the restraints used to bind the victim could easily have been put on and removed by the victim herself. It was hypothesized that the victim had bound herself and used the ligature around her neck to restrict the oxygen flow to heighten the sensations she would receive while masturbating with the large vibrator found on the floor in front of her

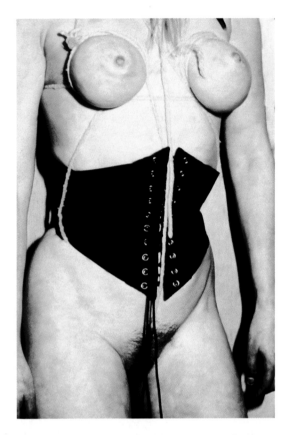

Figure 4.26 Female autoerotic. The ropes were wrapped tightly around each breast. One rope extended through the labia and gluteal fold. The corset was also tightly secured around her abdomen. (Photo courtesy of Retired Commander Tom Cronin, Chicago, Illinois, Police Department.)

body. She most probably intended to stand up to relieve the pressure on her neck from the noose, but had misjudged the hypoxia and lost consciousness and hung herself.

The case was properly classified as an autoerotic fatality and not a suicide as originally reported. The fact that the victim was discovered hanging nude in a bondage scenario and was heavily involved in solo sexual activity as evidenced by the number of sexual fantasy aids and sex toys recovered in the scene, coupled with the lack of any suicidal intent on the part of the victim, makes this case a classic sexual asphyxia event (Figures 4.27 through 4.30).

Atypical Female Autoerotic Case

The author consulted on a case involving two teenage girls who were discovered dead on one of the girls bed. They were under a large plastic bag and there was a canister of nitrous oxide on the side of the bed. Both girls were partially clothed and there was evidence of sexual activity. Apparently, they had been masturbating together and experimenting with the nitrous oxide gas when the gas overcame them. Although, technically speaking, this case would not be an "autoerotic" because there were two victims playing together, the same dynamics of sexual asphyxia were present to rule this death an accident.

Figure 4.27 Female autoerotic. This victim's body was discovered after her co-workers became concerned with her absence. The victim was suspended with ligature to the shower frame. (Photo courtesy of Instructor–Coordinator John J. Wiggins, North Carolina Justice Academy, Department of Justice, State of North Carolina.)

Equivocal Death Investigation

Many times while conducting homicide programs, participants will provide me with cases in order to get my opinion. One such case involved the reported suicide of a 17-year-old black female. The detective, who brought this case to my attention, was concerned that the medical examiner and other detectives had misclassified this case as a suicide.

He felt, based on his investigation into the background of the victim and what he observed at the scene, that the death might have been an autoerotic fatality. He was concerned that the family was blaming themselves for the daughter's death. I reviewed his case file and crime scene photos and provided the detective with a full report that he could bring to his superiors and the medical examiner for review. The report included the following information.

Crime Scene

The location of the incident was the basement of a single-family home occupied by the deceased and her family. The victim was home alone at the time of the incident. The area that the victim selected was secluded from the rest of the home. There was no evidence of

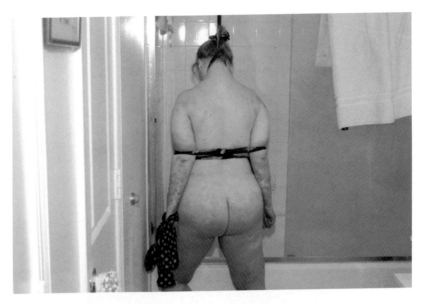

Figure 4.28 Female autoerotic. This close-up photograph shows the ligature around the victim's arms as well as the noose around her neck. The material hanging from her left wrist was probably used to secure her hands behind her back. (Photo courtesy of Instructor–Coordinator John J. Wiggins, North Carolina Justice Academy, Department of Justice, State of North Carolina.)

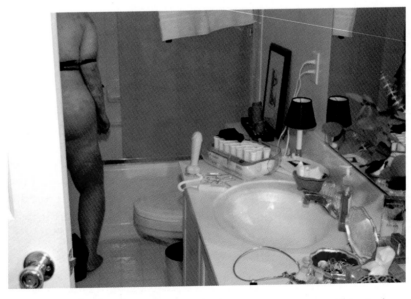

Figure 4.29 Interior view of bathroom. A penis-shaped, battery-operated vibrator was on the bathroom vanity. (Photo courtesy of Instructor–Coordinator John J. Wiggins, North Carolina Justice Academy, Department of Justice, State of North Carolina.)

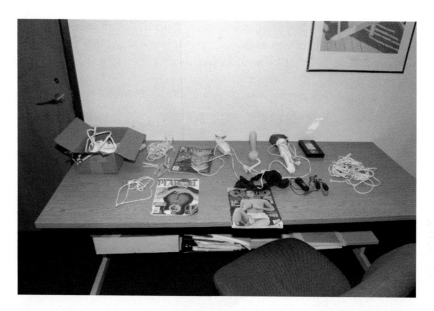

Figure 4.30 Sex toys. Various erotica and sex toys were recovered in the crime scene, such as vibrators, ropes, nipple clamps. (Photo courtesy of Instructor–Coordinator John J. Wiggins, North Carolina Justice Academy, Department of Justice, State of North Carolina.)

any break in or forced entry. The victim, who was found by her brother, was hanging from a wire noose, which had been affixed to a rusty metal clothes rod. There was a white towel wrapped around the victim's neck that would have formed padding between the wire and her neck. The victim was nude from the waist up and was wearing a pair of black sweat pants. A white T-shirt was observed approximately six feet away and appeared to have been discarded by the deceased. A white five-gallon bucket was observed lying on its side near the area where the deceased was found. Forensic examination of this bucket revealed latent prints, which were later identified as belonging to the right foot of the deceased. The material on the deceased's hands turned out to be rust from the metal pipe to which the wire had been affixed.

The deceased was a healthy and apparently happy 17-year-old young woman. The investigation disclosed that the deceased came from a good family background where both the mother and stepfather provided parental guidance and support. The family consists of the 17-year-old victim, her 19-year-old brother, the victim's mother, and her stepfather. In addition, the inquiry into the victim's background indicated that the victim maintained good social relationships with peers and was performing well in school. The interview of the deceased's best friend indicated that the victim was popular and well liked. The victim had two boyfriends and was sexually promiscuous with a young man. **There was no indication in the reports that the deceased was depressed or suicidal. In fact, from all indications** (*name withheld*) **was functioning as well both physically and socially as any typical 17-year-old teenager.**

Investigative Considerations

The teenage female victim was found partially nude in a secluded area of the house when no one was home. The location that the victim selected afforded her an opportunity to engage in a private fantasy. The most common method practiced in sexual asphyxia is neck compression or hanging with some sort of padding between the neck and ligature to prevent any markings. The suspension point was within the reach of the deceased (rust on hands) until the plastic bucket was knocked over. It is a known fact that most victims of suicide are not found partially or fully nude. In this case the victim's breasts were exposed (Figure 4.31 and Figure 4.32).

Figure 4.31 Equivocal death. This victim reported as a suicide was actually an autoerotic fatality. She had been standing on a plastic bucket, which slipped out from under her feet. She was found hanging from an electrical wire, which had been fastened into a noose. (Photo courtesy of Detectives Steven Little and Edward Dahlman, Columbus, Ohio, Police Department.)

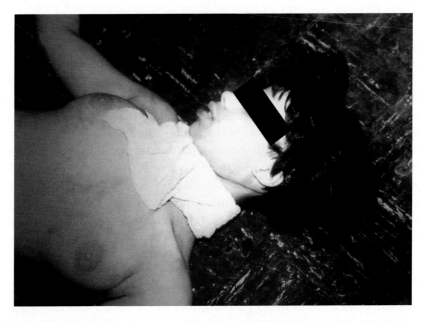

Figure 4.32 Close-up showing the padding. The presence of the padding was a crucial factor in the analysis of this case coupled with the victimology. (Photo courtesy of Detectives Steven Little and Edward Dahlman, Columbus, Ohio, Police Department.)

Remember, this is an investigative hypothesis. Don't get bogged down in theory and hypothetical speculation. In death investigations, there are no absolutes.

Opinion

In my professional opinion, (name withheld) died as a result of a tragic accident involving sexual asphyxia. The basis for this conclusion is twofold: (1) the indicators that were present at the scene and enunciated within this report, and (2) the lack of suicidal intent on the part of the victim. This fact is supported by the thorough police investigation into the background of the deceased. I recommend that the authorities confer with the medical examiner to reclassify this death as accidental and an **autoerotic fatality.**

Results

The detective took this report and conferred with his superiors and the medical examiner. Reportedly, the medical examiner's initial concern about classifying this case as accidental was that the deceased did not fit the stereotypical profile of a practitioner of autoeroticism because she was a black female. However, the professional in-depth investigation undertaken by the detective provided enough factual basis to have this case reclassified. My consultative report simply validated the detective's hypothesis. The important point here is that the detective's dedication to properly classify this case as accidental provided a measure of consolation to the surviving family. The family was advised that their daughter did not commit suicide.

Notification and Advising the Surviving Family of the Mode of Death

Advising surviving family members of the circumstances and nature of this type of death can be quite stressful and difficult. The tragedy is often compounded by survivor reactions, which range from guilt, shame, and humiliation to anger and rage.

As professional investigators, we are entrusted with a profound duty and responsibility not only to the deceased, but to the surviving family as well. It is imperative that we do all in our power to assist the surviving family by our professionalism. The official explanation of the circumstances of the death is best undertaken with the assistance of clergy or a professional practitioner after considering the family's ability to cope with the facts of the case. However, it is important to note that each case and set of circumstances will dictate the proper course of action.

The official classification of the manner of death is documented by the medical examiner. The manner of death can be homicide, suicide, accidental, or natural. In some cases, the classification may very well indicate that the death was due to sexual asphyxia.

In some instances, I believe investigators who recognize that a death was due to sexual asphyxia may make a conscious decision to spare the family further embarrassment and allow them to believe the death to be an accident due to something other than the sexual component.

I remember a case involving a family man, who was the town pharmacist and a deacon in his church and had expired during an autoerotic fatality. The investigators explained to the family that the man had died while playing a game of "Dungeons and Dragons" that was popular at the time, rather than go into the sexual details of the death and thereby spare the family.

Under certain circumstances this action might be an entirely appropriate alternative. I offer this personal advice as a veteran homicide cop. Whatever course of action you decide, "Just make sure you do the right thing." The "right thing" is to professionally and properly document the manner of death BUT spare the family the sordid details.

A Case History

Police were sent to the location to check on the welfare of a white male, 36 years of age. When the officers arrived at the scene, they observed what appeared to be a blond-haired female figure hanging from a weight bench by a chain attached to the neck. Upon entry into the premises, they ascertained that the victim was, in fact, a male wearing a blond wig.

The victim was discovered in the northwest bedroom. He was dressed in female lingerie, wearing the blond wig, facial makeup, and nail polish on his fingers. He was also wearing black fishnet hosiery, a black garter belt, a black corset, a black leather bra, and women's jewelry. In addition, he had a spiked leather collar, which was attached to a chain that was attached to the weight bench. A vanity mirror had been placed in front of the subject, which provided an opportunity for the subject to view himself from his position in the room. There was evidence of sexual activity in the scene and a possible suggestion of another participant. However, the officer noted that the premises were secured and there were no signs of forced entry.

During the search of the crime scene, detectives opened and looked into the victim's closet. They didn't notice anything unusual at first. However, on closer examination, they discovered numerous items of female attire secreted behind the regular clothing. The subject also had a number of pairs of women's panties in different sizes. He had women's large-size high-heel shoes, purses, and nylon stockings.

In the adjoining room, the detectives observed that there was a black rubber dildo attached to the bedpost of the waterbed with fecal matter on it. Underneath the dildo was a hand towel and an open jar of petroleum jelly.

There was a mirror placed on the floor with several Polaroid photographs. Some of these photos were of a female dressed in lingerie; glued onto these photos was a simulation of a penis and bondage bands around the wrists. There were also other Polaroid photos of the deceased wearing female attire and lingerie, being involved in bondage scenes and posing and simulating sexual activity. For instance, two Polaroids depicted the victim performing oral sex on a male partner. However, this turned out to be fabricated with a pair of stuffed jeans and a dildo. Apparently, the subject was using the dildo as a sexual stimulus as he bent over and viewed the photographs, which were on the mirror (Figures 4.33 through 4.36).

Many sexual devices, including various sizes of dildos, were recovered in the house. There were different types of chains, restraint devices, handcuffs, nipple rings, and leather whips. The subject also had numerous sex magazines and porno tapes as well as a nude anatomically correct Barbie doll. In addition, police discovered a number of firearms hidden throughout the house in secret compartments. In the opinion of the author, whenever there is have someone who is so thoroughly vested in pornography and this same person has access to a number of firearms, it is definitely a recipe for disaster.

Interview of Victim's Ex-Wife

When advised of her husband's death, the ex-wife stated that this incident was probably due to his obsession with deviant sex. She told detectives that he was always "kinky," but toward the end of their marriage, "she just couldn't handle it." His fixation on bondage and pain during sex frightened her. The witness stated that she left him after finding women's attire in her house along with photographs of her husband dressed in sexy lingerie and bondage. She stated that her husband took the pictures of her in lingerie, found at the crime scene, when they were married.

Case Disposition

The case was properly classified as an autoerotic fatality based on the following considerations:

Evidence of a physiological mechanism for obtaining or enhancing sexual arousal
Evidence of solo sexual activity
Evidence of sexual fantasy aids
Evidence of prior dangerous autoerotic practice
No apparent suicidal intentions
Statements by former wife relative to his "kinky" sex games as well as his past autoerotic practice
Photographs of the victim engaging in autoeroticism
Extensive collection of women's attire and lingerie

Figure 4.33 Male autoerotic. This was the view that the arriving police officers had when they responded to the call. It appeared to be a female victim. (Photo courtesy of Retired Lieutenant Mark Fritts and Retired Sergeant Pete Farmer, Hobbs, New Mexico, Police Department.)

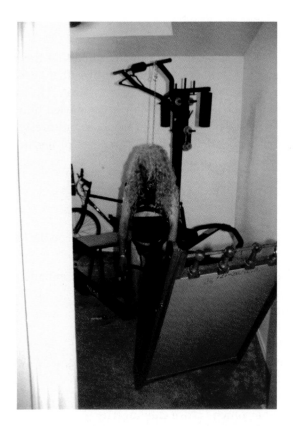

Figure 4.34 Male autoerotic. Note the positioned mirror. (Photo courtesy of Retired Lieutenant Mark Fritts and Retired Sergeant Pete Farmer, Hobbs, New Mexico, Police Department)

Figure 4.35 Male autoerotic. This view shows the body suspended from the weight bench in a kneeling position. The object on the floor is a clothespin with a fish weight on it. This had been attached to the victim's interior thigh to cause pain. (Photo courtesy of Retired Lieutenant Mark Fritts and Retired Sergeant Pete Farmer, Hobbs, New Mexico, Police Department.)

Figure 4.36 Male autoerotic. Note the makeup. The offender spent hours preparing for his events. This included makeup, female undergarments and outerwear. The mucous and protruding tongue are consistent with asphyxial death. (Photo courtesy of Retired Lieutenant Mark Fritts, Hobbs, New Mexico, Police Department.

Investigative Considerations

Although each autoerotic death scene may be unique, there are many common factors for the investigator to consider in making his or her determination of the mode of death. I have listed some of these considerations below.

Victim Profile

Research has indicated that most victims of this activity are white males ranging from 13 years of age to their late 30s. White females in their early 20s follow this group, next black males 20 to 40 years of age, and one reported black female in her late 20s. The victims are considered to be basically moral people, successful in their respective occupations. They may be considered shy by friends because they are not sexually or romantically active. However, they may be married or involved with a significant other person. Interviews and investigations do not disclose any indications of depression or suicidal tendencies.

Location

The location selected is usually secluded or isolated and affords the practitioner the opportunity to involve himself or herself in a private fantasy. Some examples include locked rooms at home, attics, basements, garages or workshops, motel rooms, places of employment during nonbusiness hours, summer houses, or outdoor locations.

Nudity

Most victims of suicide are not found in the nude. Although this is not a conclusive indicator, the discovery of a nude victim should alert the investigator to the possibility of an autoerotic fatality if other indicators, such as those listed below, are present.

Determining the Involvement of Sexual Asphyxia: Autoerotic Checklist

There are certain questions that the investigator should consider in determining whether or not the death is related to autoerotic activity.

1. Is the victim nude, sexually exposed, or—if a male—is he dressed in articles of feminine attire (transvestism), makeup, and wigs?
2. Is there evidence of masturbatory activity: tissues, towels, or hanky in hand, or in shorts to catch semen? Seminal fluids?
3. Is there evidence of infibulations: piercing or causing pain to the genitalia, self-torture, masochism, pins in penis, etc.?
4. Are sexually stimulating paraphernalia present: vibrators, dildos, sex aids, pornographic magazines, butt plugs, etc.?
5. Is bondage present: ropes, chains, blindfolds, gags, etc.? Are any constrictive devices present: corset, plastic wrap, belts, ropes, or vacuum cleaner hoses around the body, or chest constraints?
6. Is there protective padding between the ligature and the neck: towels, rags, or cloth to prevent rope burns or discomfort?
7. Are the restraints interconnected? Do the ropes and ties come together or are they connected? Are the chains interconnected through one another? Is the victim tied to himself, so that by putting pressure on one of the limbs the restraints are tightened?
8. Are mirrors or other reflective devices present? Are they positioned so that the victim can view his or her activities?
9. Is there evidence of fantasy (diaries, erotic literature, etc.) or fetishism (women's panties, bras, girdles, leather, rubber, latex, high heel shoes, etc.)?
10. Is the suspension point within reach of the victim or is there an escape mechanism (keys, lock, slip knot, etc.)?
11. Is there evidence of prior activities of a similar nature (abrasions or rope burns on suspension point); unexplained secretive behavior, or long stays in isolated areas; rope burns on neck, etc.?
12. Does the victim possess literature dealing with bondage, escapology, or knots?
13. Is there a positioned camera? (Check film and/or videotapes. Look for photos and view any videotapes in camera.)

While not all such deaths will involve the above characteristics, their presence will certainly alert the investigator to the possibility of death occurring as the result of sexual misadventure.

Summary

The investigation of sexual asphyxia and the appropriate determination of mode of death require that the investigator conduct a knowledgeable scene examination. This obviously means that the investigator should have an understanding of clues that may be present both at the scene and in the background of the deceased. The psychological autopsy can be helpful in resolving those cases in which it is not clear whether the motivational intent was suicidal or autoerotic in nature. As further information on this mode of death becomes available through research, the investigator will be afforded additional assistance in making this determination and properly classifying these cases.

References

American Psychiatric Association. *Diagnostic and Statistical Manual of Mental Disorders (DSM-IV-TR)*, 4th ed., Text revision, American Psychiatric Association, Washington, D.C., 2000.

Byard, R.W. and N.H. Bramwell. Autoerotic death—A definition. *American Journal of Forensic Medicine and Pathology*, 12(1): 74–76, 1991.

Coleman, J.C. J.N. Butcher, and R.C. Carson. *Abnormal Psychology and Modern Life,* 7th ed. Scott, Foresman and Co., 1984.

DiMaio, D. and V.J. DiMaio. *Practical Aspects of Forensic Pathology,* 2nd ed. CRC Press, Boca Raton, FL, 2001.

Geberth, V.J. *Practical Homicide Investigation: Tactics, Procedures, and Forensic Techniques,* 3rd ed. CRC Press, Boca Raton, FL, 1996.

Hazelwood, R.R., A. W. Burgess, and N. Groth. Death during dangerous autoerotic practice, *Social Science and Medicine,* 129–133, 1981.

Hazelwood, R.R., P.E. Dietz, and A. W. Burgess. *Autoerotic Fatalities.* Lexington Books, D.C. Heath & Company, Lexington, KY, 1983.

Mosby's Medical and Nursing Dictionary, 2nd ed. C.V. Mosby Co., St. Louis, MO, 1986, p. 562.

Raeburn, P. Autoerotic deaths—Shocking practice often mistaken for teen suicide. *Sunday Journal News,* December 2, 1984.

Resnick, H.L.P. Eroticized repetitive hangings: A form of self-destruction. *American Journal of Psychotherapy*, January 1972, p. 10.

Sass, F. Sexual asphyxia in the female. *Journal of Forensic Science,* 20 (1): 181–185, 1975; also in *Psychiatric Nursing in the Hospital and the Community,* 3rd ed., ed. A. W. Burgess, Prentice-Hall, Englewood Cliffs, NJ, pp. 316–319, 1981.

Sauvageau, A. and S. Racette. Autoerotic deaths: A seven-year retrospective epidemiological study. *Open Forensic Science Journal,* 1, 2008: www.bentham-mps.org.

Sauvageau, A. and V.J. Geberth. Elderly victim: An unusual autoerotic fatality involving an 87-year-old male. *Forensic Science, Medicine, and Pathology,* 5 (3):233–235, 2009a.

Sauvageau, A. and V.J. Geberth. Workshop #2 AAFS 61st Annual Meeting, Denver, CO, February 16, 2009b.

Sauvageau, A. and S. Racette. Aqua-eroticum: An unusual autoerotic fatality in a lake involving a homemade diving apparatus. *Journal of Forensic Science,* 51 (1), 137–139, January 2006a.

Sauvageau, A. and S. Racette. Autoerotic deaths in the literature from 1954 to 2004: A review. *Journal of Forensic Science,* 51 (1): 140–146, 2006b.

Sivaloganathan, S. Aqua-eroticum—A case of auto-erotic drowning. *Medicine, Science, and the Law,* 24 (4): 300–302, 1984.

Selected Readings

Adelson, L. *The Pathology of Homicide,* Charles C Thomas, Springfield, IL, 1974.

Burgess, A.W. *Psychiatric Nursing in the Hospital and the Community,* 3rd ed., Prentice-Hall, Englewood Cliffs, NJ, 1981.

Geberth, V.J. Sexual asphyxia—The phenomenon of autoerotic fatalities, *Law and Order,* 37 (8), 1989.

Harris, R. *Outline of Death Investigation,* Charles C Thomas, Springfield, IL, 1962.

Hughes, D.J. *Homicide Investigative Techniques,* Charles C Thomas, Springfield, IL, 1974.

Sauvageau, A. and S. Racette. Agonal sequences in a filmed suicidal ganging: Analysis of respiratory and movement responses to asphyxia by hanging, *Journal of Forensic Science,* 52 (4), 957–959, July 2007.

Schellenberg, M., A. Sauvageau, and S. Racette. Complex autoerotic death with full body wrapping in plastic body bag, *Journal of Forensic Science,* 52 (4), 954–956, July 2007.

Spitz, W.U. and R.S. Fisher. *Medicolegal Investigation of Death: Guidelines for the Application of Pathology to Crime Investigation,* Charles C Thomas, Springfield, IL, 1973.

The Crime Scene Investigation 5

The search of the crime scene is the most important phase of the investigation conducted at the scene. Decisions of the courts restricting admissibility of testimonial evidence have significantly increased the value of physical evidence in homicide investigations. Therefore, law enforcement personnel involved in the crime scene search must arrange for the proper and effective collection of evidence at the scene.

Physical evidence, which is often referred to as the "unimpeachable witness," cannot be clouded by a faulty memory, prejudice, poor eyesight, or a desire "not to get involved." However, before a forensic laboratory can effectively examine physical evidence, it must be recognized as evidence.

Practically speaking, *anything* and *everything* should be considered as evidence until proven differently. I cannot recall how many times I found myself and my detectives returning to a crime scene. This was after we received additional information, which revealed that some seemingly innocuous item was actually an important piece of evidence. That is why it is imperative to "hold on to" the crime scene as long as possible. Some item, which didn't seem significant on the first day of the investigation, may suddenly take on the intrinsic value of gold.

An excellent example of the "Practical Homicide Investigation®" principle that "anything" and "everything" should be considered as evidence is the case that involved serial murderer Danny Rollings, who became known as the "Gainesville Ripper." He had been staying in the woods at a campsite near an apartment where 18-year-old Christa Leigh Hoyt had been murdered. The police, who had been scouring the woods looking for anyone or anything suspicious, came upon Rollings and another male on their way back to a campsite. When the police ordered the two men to halt, Rollings ran away. The police questioned the other male who remained behind. He led them to the campsite where Danny Rolling and he were heading.

When the officers discovered the campsite, they found a number of items that would later link Rollings to five murders. However, the only item that seemed important at the time was a bag of cash covered with pink dye. There had been a bank robbery the previous day and the unknown white male who ran from the police matched the description of the bank robber, who turned out to be Danny Rollings.

The police collected and secured everything at the campsite, which included bedding, a gun, a ski mask, a cassette tape deck, and a screwdriver. Subsequent laboratory tests were conducted on these crucial materials retrieved from the campsite. The authorities were astonished to find that 17 pry marks at three of the murder scenes were matched to the screwdriver retrieved from Rollings' campsite. In addition, pubic hairs found through vacuuming the campsite matched Christa Hoyt through DNA analysis

Legal Considerations

Once an item is recognized as evidence, it must be properly collected and preserved for laboratory examination. However, in order for physical evidence to be admissible, it must have been legally obtained. The courts have severely restricted the right of the police to search certain homicide crime scenes without a warrant. The U.S. Supreme Court has rendered three major decisions that require police to obtain a search warrant to search a premises where the suspect and the deceased share a proprietary right to the premises.

In *Mincey v. Arizona* 437 US 385 (1978) the Supreme Court cited that the police had violated the defendant's Fourth Amendment rights. Mincey, who was a dope dealer, had shot and killed an undercover narcotics officer during a drug raid. Mincey was wounded and one of his companions was killed in the subsequent gun battle. The narcotics officers, following procedure, secured the premises and notified homicide. Homicide detectives conducted an investigation during which hundreds of pieces of evidence were seized by the police over a three-day crime scene search. Mincey was convicted of the murder of the undercover officer. The conviction was overturned by the Supreme Court, which maintained that Mincey's Fourth Amendment rights were violated and that the police who should have secured a search warrant. The Supreme Court basically informed law enforcement that "there wasn't any homicide crime scene exception" to the Fourth Amendment.

Did we in law enforcement get the message? No. In 1984, the Supreme Court once again stepped in to address the same issue in *Thompson v. Louisiana* 469 US 17 (1984). In the Thompson case, a woman who was reportedly depressed shot and killer her husband. She then took an overdose of pills in an attempt to commit suicide. She then suddenly experienced a "change of heart" and decided she didn't want to die. She called her daughter, who in turn called the sheriff's department, which dispatched an ambulance and deputies to the woman's home. The woman was transported to the hospital where she was treated. Investigators were called to the house and gathered evidence of the murder in the crime scene. The woman was subsequently charged and convicted in the murder of her husband. The U.S. Supreme Court ruled against the State of Louisiana citing the *Mincey* decision and the expectation of privacy provided in the Fourth Amendment. The woman's conviction was overturned. Once again the courts ruled that there was *no* homicide exception and that the police were required to obtain a search warrant.

Did we in law enforcement get the message *this* time? No. In 1999, the Supreme Court once again stepped in to address the same issues raised in the *Mincey* and *Thompson* cases. This time it was *Flippo v. West Virginia* 98 US 8770 (1999). Flippo was a pastor who reportedly was having a homosexual affair with a member of his congregation. His wife had discovered the relationship and was going to divorce him. Flippo convinced her that they should reconcile and talked her into going on a "camping trip." They went to a cabin in West Virginia that the pastor had rented. While at the cabin, the pastor reported that they had become victims of a home invasion during which his wife was fatally beaten and the pastor was slightly injured. The police were not impressed with Flippo's injuries. He was brought to a local hospital and patched up. Investigators, who were processing the crime scene came upon Flippo's briefcase. Inside the briefcase were various pornographic pictures of Flippo and his male lover engaged in sexual activities. These materials, which represented "motive" as well as the other evidence seized from the cabin were introduced into trial. Flippo was convicted of the murder of his wife. The conviction was overturned based on the same issues raised in *Mincey* and *Thompson*. The message is quite clear:

A Search warrant should be secured before any crime search is undertaken under these circumstances.

There is no "homicide scene exception" to the Fourth Amendment.

Any *extended search* of a *homicide scene*, without consent or exigent circumstances, requires a search warrant.

Homicides involving common-law relationships, husbands and wives, or family disputes may necessitate that the detective secure a warrant before a premises can be searched. The professional homicide detective must be aware of the legal requirements for a warrant dependent upon both Supreme Court decisions as well as state law and case law within their own jurisdictional purview. An additional consideration is the dynamics of the event, which may present legitimate search warrant exceptions. The courts have recognized certain circumstances that allow for exceptions to the requirement of a search warrant. These exceptions are emergency or exigent circumstances, evidence in plain view, postarrest search of an individual for weapons and contraband, and consent (Figure 5.1).

Warrantless Searches Where Suspect Shares a Possessory Right to the Premises

Almost every crime will constitute an emergency that *justifies* law enforcement's warrantless entry to the scene. Traditionally, courts have recognized three.

1. **Threat to life and safety**
2. **Destruction or removal of evidence**
3. **Escape**

Officers are authorized to do whatever is *reasonably* necessary to resolve the emergency. Once the emergency is resolved, the emergency exception is *negated*.

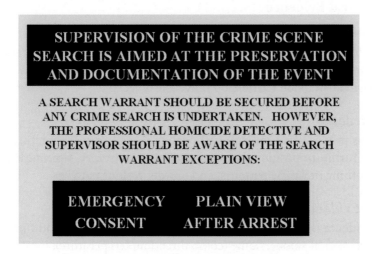

Figure 5.1 Search warrant exceptions. (From Geberth, V.J. *Practical Homicide Investigation: Tactics, Procedures, and Forensic Techniques*, 4th ed. CRC Press, Boca Raton, FL, 2006, p. 178. With permission.)

Practical Examples of Reasonableness

Officers arriving at the scene of a violent crime are permitted to do the following:

- Unquestionably **sweep** the premises in an effort to locate the victim, additional victims, or the suspect.
- If a body is found, take the medical examiner (ME) into the scene to view and collect the body.
- If there is probable cause to believe a crime scene contains evidence that will be destroyed if not quickly recovered, *that* evidence may be retrieved as part of the emergency.
- Follow *The Plain View Doctrine.*
- Preserve a crime scene, which is considered reasonable.
- Document the scene: photos, videotape, and diagrams

Physical Evidence

Physical evidence refers to any tangible article, small or large, that tends to prove or disprove a point in question. It may be used to reconstruct the crime, identify participants, or confirm or discredit an alibi.

Homicide and sexual assault crime scenes usually contain an abundance of physical or trace evidence. The systematic search, collection, and preservation of physical evidence is the goal of the crime scene search. Therefore, the detective supervisor should organize the crime scene search so as to collect as much physical evidence as possible. In addition, the search *must* be based on constitutionally legal grounds, and the evidence collected must be properly documented and handled so that it may be presented in court later. It is imperative that each piece of physical evidence be treated separately and carefully to avoid cross contamination.

Types of Physical Evidence

Transient Evidence: Temporary in Nature
This type of evidence is temporary in nature and can include odors, temperature, imprints, and indentations in soft or changing materials (e.g., butter, wet sand, snow, or mud), and markings (e.g., lividity, blood spatters on moveable objects).

Pattern Evidence
This evidence is produced by contact, such as blood splatter, glass fracture patterns, fire burn patterns, furniture position patterns, projectile trajectory, tire marks, modus operandi (MO), clothing or article patterns, and powder residue patterns.

Conditional Evidence
Conditional evidence is caused by an action or event, e.g., lighting conditions at the scene; odor, color, direction of smoke; flame (color, direction, temperature); location of evidence in relation to the body; and vehicle (locked or unlocked, lights on or off, window open or closed, radio on or off, mileage).

Transfer Evidence

This evidence is produced by physical contact and generally contact of persons or objects, or between persons or objects. It is characterized by the *linkage concept*.

Trace Evidence

There is a principle in homicide investigation that refers to a theoretical exchange between two objects that have been in contact with one another. This theory of *transfer* or *exchange* is based on Locard's "Exchange Principle." Edmond Locard, a Frenchman, who founded the University of Lyons' Institute of Criminalistics, believed that whenever two human beings came into contact, something from one was exchanged to the other, and vice versa. This exchange might involve, hairs, fibers, dirt, dust, blood, and other bodily fluids, as well as skin cells, metallic residue, and other microscopic materials. In "Practical Homicide Investigation," Locard's principle is summed up as follows:

1. The perpetrator will take away traces of the victim and the scene.
2. The victim will retain traces of the perpetrator and may leave traces of himself on the perpetrator.
3. The perpetrator will leave behind traces of himself at the scene.

The Concept of Linkage

Henry Lee (1994), a forensic scientist who is the director emeritus of the Connecticut State Crime Lab, developed the concept of linkage as the basis for any crime scene examination. A visible representation of this concept is shown in Figure 5.2.

The goal is to establish a link between the various facets of the crime scene, the victim, physical evidence, and the suspect. All of these components must be connected for the

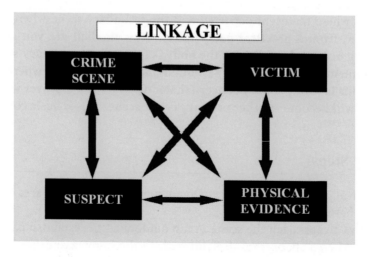

Figure 5.2 Linkage. (From Lee, H. *Crime Scene Handbook*. Academic Press, San Diego, CA, 2001, p. 114. With permission.)

successful resolution of the case. The basis of conducting such a four-way linkage rests on the principle of the *Theory of Transfer and Exchange.*

Remember: *Anything* and *everything* may eventually become evidence.

The Primary Crime Scene

The investigation starts at the point where the body was originally found. In "Practical Homicide Investigation," we refer to this as the **primary crime scene**. The person may have been killed there or dumped there. It really doesn't matter at this point in the investigation. Your *primary focus* in the crime scene process will be directed at this location. There is no such thing as a **secondary crime scene**. All crimes scenes are **primary**.

The practical rationale behind this primary crime scene concept is

1. That the police are usually called to this location by the person who discovers the body, a witness to the crime, or in some instances, the victim.
2. In homicide cases, the location where the body was discovered yields an abundance of physical evidence and serves as a base of inquiry.

There may be two or more crime scenes in addition to the primary crime scene:

1. Where the body was moved from; where the person was killed.
2. Where the original assault leading to death took place.
3. Where any physical or trace evidence connected to the crime is found. (This includes parts of the body.)
4. A vehicle used to transport the body.
5. The suspect: clothing, hands, and body as well as residence.

The author is keenly aware of some confusion that has been generated by the use of the term *primary crime scene*. I have heard some experts refer to the primary scene as the location where the event occurred and the secondary scene where the body was found. **However, from a practical perspective: "How the hell are you going to know where anything occurred on the day the body is found?" The primary scene for those in law enforcement is where the body is found and the location to where you respond when called. This is your primary concern. Later on when you discover where the event occurred, this will become another primary crime scene. This is basic common sense.**

Preliminary Steps

1. Upon arrival, ascertain boundaries. Do not move blindly into an area (always confer before acting).
2. Decide how to approach the scene. At an outdoor scene, establish paths of entry and exit. Always choose the difficult path to the body, assuming the offender used the most convenient path. This might result in locating some additional evidence that would have been damaged by police actions (confer with first officer or detective).

3. Conduct the initial survey. (Remember "The Escort." Use this opportunity to develop a mental image of the event and "absorb" the crime scene.

4. Ascertain whether or not any fragile evidence is present. (Assure the collection of these items before any contamination or loss.)

5. Prior to any crime scene process, Polaroid the scene. These become "work photos" that can be viewed by other officers and thereby limit crime scene intrusion.

Secure and Protect the Crime Scene and Area

The homicide supervisor and/or the investigator should stop and observe the area as a whole, noting everything possible before entering the actual crime scene for a detailed examination. The cardinal rule in homicide cases is to protect and preserve the crime scene. The first police representative at the crime scene is usually the patrol officer. His or her first responsibility is to determine whether or not the victim is alive. Upon confirming that the victim is dead, an assessment is then made to determine boundaries.

Practically speaking, at this stage of the investigation, it is next to impossible to know the exact boundaries of the scene. The best course of action for the officer to follow is

- Clear the largest area possible. The scene can always be narrowed later.
- Make a quick and objective evaluation of the scene based on
  - Location of the body
  - Presence of any physical evidence
  - Eyewitness statements
  - Presence of natural boundaries (a room, a house, hallway, an enclosed park)
- Keep in mind the possibility of multiple series of crime scenes.

If the crime scene is indoors, the job of making this determination and securing the scene is relatively easy to accomplish. If the scene is outdoors, the determination will have to be based on the type of location, pedestrian and vehicular traffic, crowds, paths of entry and exit, weather conditions, and many other factors peculiar to that specific location (Figures 5.3 through 5.6).

In any event, the first officer should not examine the contents of the scene. He or she should stabilize the scene by isolating the body and the immediate area, including any visible evidence, from *all* persons, including unnecessary emergency responders.

Realistically speaking, various units and additional personnel respond to homicide scenes. The toughest job confronting the first officers is the effective safeguarding of the crime scene from these additional police officers, emergency services personnel, and other officials. Obviously, certain persons must enter the crime scene in connection with their official duties. The first officers, who are safeguarding the crime scene, should identify and document the presence of these officials by maintaining a **crime scene sign-in** procedure as recommended in *Practical Homicide Investigation; Tactics, Procedures, and Forensic Techniques,* 4th edition (Geberth, 2006).

The purpose of having a **crime scene sign-in sheet** (Figure 5.7) procedure is to assure crime scene integrity and prevent unauthorized personnel from engaging in what I refer to as "crime scene sightseeing." During my over 40 years of experience, I have come to realize that "if anything can go wrong, it will go wrong at the crime scene."

Figure 5.3 Secure entire house. An excellent method is to secure an entire house as the crime scene. (Photo courtesy Detective Darrell Knutson, Rock County, Wisconsin, Sheriff's Office.)

Figure 5.4 Secure entire front and rear. An excellent method is to secure an entire house as the crime scene. (Photo courtesy Detective Darrell Knutson, Rock County, Wisconsin, Sheriff's Office.)

Figure 5.5 Outdoor crime scene. The first responding officers at this location took the entire square block surrounding the church and rectory as the scene of a double homicide. A trail of blood leading from the scene to the suspect's house was protected from contamination and loss. (Photo courtesy of Detective Ken Espinoza, Pueblo, Colorado, Police Department.)

Figure 5.6 Extended crime scene. The authorities, in this case, had a murder, which extended from one house to another with a large yard between them. The first responders secured the entire area. (Photo courtesy of the Kansas Bureau of Investigation.)

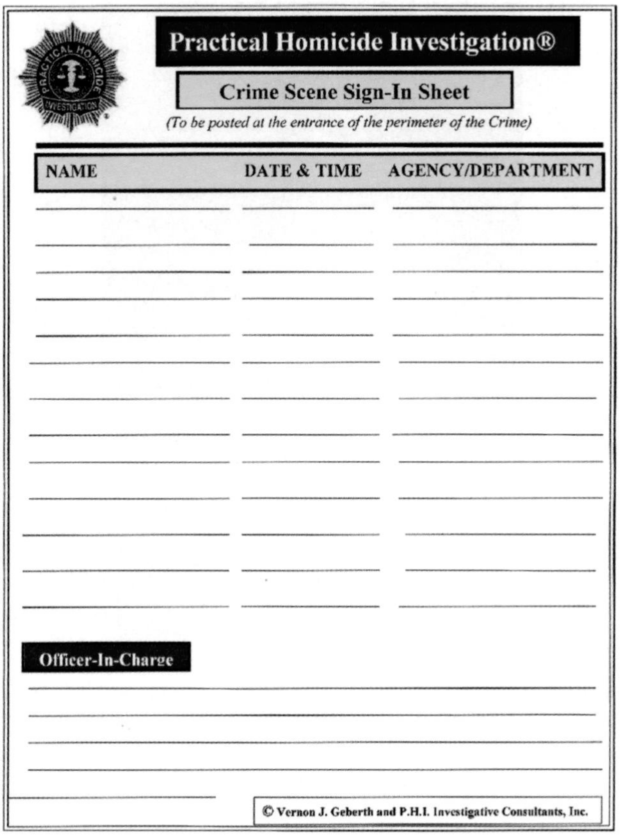

Figure 5.7 Crime scene sign-in sheet. (Courtesy of "Practical Homicide Investigation®".)

This is especially true for incidents that receive an inordinate amount of media attention. It seems as if every official (and his brother) feels the need to "show his presence" at the scene. My solution to this oftentimes impossible situation is quite simple. I suggest that the first officers establish *two* crime scenes.

1. The **first** or **primary** crime scene is the location where the body is found or where the actual event occurred, or the area where you expect to recover physical evidence. This is the real crime scene.
2. The **second** or **secure area** crime scene is an area set aside from the general public. This allows for all of those special dignitaries and high-ranking guests an opportunity to violate at least one police line in order to "validate" their importance. It will also keep them within an area where they will be "out of the way" of the actual crime scene operations and preclude any further contamination by official presence. This area can be called a **security zone.**

In conclusion, the police officer who is responding to or confronted by the homicide crime scene should prepare to take the five basic steps recommended in *Practical Homicide Investigation* (Geberth, 2006). Upon arrival, **ADAPT:**

A: Arrest the perpetrator, if possible.
D: Detain and identify witnesses and/or suspects for follow-up investigators.

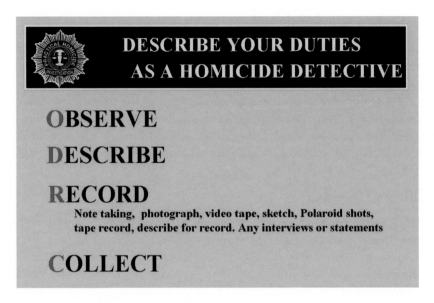

Figure 5.8 Duties of the detectives (Courtesy of "Practical Homicide Investigation®".)

A: Assess the crime scene. (What can I or my partner control?)
P: Protect the crime scene.
T: Take notes (document the scene and activities therein).

In "Practical Homicide Investigation®," the author describes the duties of a homicide investigator as follows (Figure 5.8).

Specific Duties of First Officers

There are a number of specific duties to which the first officer will need to attend. These concern the following:

The suspect in custody
Transporting the suspect
Examination of the suspect for evidence
Dying declaration
Victim removed to the hospital
Victim pronounced dead at the hospital
Officer's duties at the hospital
Victim confirmed dead at the scene
Handling witnesses at the scene
Additional officers at the scene
Handling news media personnel at the scene
Documentation of events by the first officer

For further in-depth information on these duties, the author refers the reader to *Practical Homicide Investigation* (Geberth, 2006).

Changing Sequence of Command

All officers should be aware of the changing sequence of command at homicide crime scenes. The first officer on the scene is in command until a uniformed officer of higher rank or an investigator arrives on the scene. The ranking uniformed officer will be in charge until the arrival of his superiors or an investigator. As soon as the investigator arrives, he/she will assume command from that point forward. An investigator of superior rank, in turn, will supersede him/her. Department regulations should provide for such shifts of command in these situations so as to avoid conflict and maintain a professional investigation.

Patrol Officer's Checklist

As a practical matter, the first officer's responsibilities in the preliminary investigation of homicide are divided into three specific duties:

1. Preserve life
2. Arrest the suspect
3. Protect the scene

The officer should record all homicide information in his memo book or notebook as soon as possible, preferably as it is obtained. This book should be retained for later court purposes and shown to the investigator when he arrives at the scene. All dead body calls should be handled as homicides in this preliminary stage.

I have provided the following checklist of first officer duties in order to assist the officer at the scene in refreshing his/her memory as to what vital information he/she should secure. Some of the information in this chapter may seem repetitive; however, it is meant to be. Based on my experience, some elements of investigatory procedure need to be reinforced by repetition.

Initial Call/Receipt of Information

- Record exact time and type of call patrol unit received. (In systems using modern computerized and recorded radio transmissions, unit can check with communications.)
- If first notification is received in person, detain this person for investigators. If unable to detain for some reason, obtain sufficient identification and information for follow-up investigator.

Arrival at the Homicide Crime Scene

- Record the exact time of your arrival and/or notify communications that you are on the scene.
- Enter the immediate crime scene area to view victim. (Only one officer should enter scene unless the call is an emergency call and the offender may still be on the scene. Use only one path of entry and exit.
- Determine if victim is alive or dead.

- Arrest the perpetrator if present.
- If there is a possibility of life, summon an ambulance and apply appropriate first-aid procedures.
- If circumstances indicate the victim is near death or dying, attempt to obtain a dying declaration.
- If an ambulance crew is present before your arrival, determine if the crew or anyone else moved the body or any items within the crime scene. If there were any items moved, record the following:
  - What alterations were made
  - When the alterations were made
  - Purpose of the movement
  - Person who made the alteration
- Record the names, serial numbers, and hospital of ambulance crew present at the scene.
- If the victim is dead, record the official time of pronouncement by ambulance attendant.
- If suspect has just fled the scene, initiate a wanted alarm.
- Record any alterations to the crime scene that were made as a matter of investigative necessity. For example:
  - Lights turned on or off
  - Door opened, closed, locked, or unlocked; body moved or cut down
  - Windows opened, closed, locked, or unlocked
  - Furniture moved; anything touched
  - Gas turned off, appliances turned off, motor of vehicle on or off

Protection of the Crime Scene

- Attempt to assess the entire crime scene, including paths of entry and exit, and any areas that may include evidence. *(Remember the possibility of a multiple crime scene.)*
- Establish a perimeter, secure and protect the scene by isolation and physical barriers, such as ropes, cones, and other equipment as necessary.
- Record names, addresses, dates of birth, telephone numbers, etc., of all persons present at the crime scene.
- Remove all persons from the immediate area. *(Be careful not to chase off witnesses or the perpetrator who may still be present.)*
- If victim is removed from scene by an ambulance, an officer should accompany victim to hospital, riding in rear with victim (for possible dying declaration).
- An officer should remain at the scene in order to provide for its security.
- If the victim's clothes are removed at the hospital, an officer should maintain control of them (victim's clothes are evidence).
- Request additional units as needed to protect the scene.
- If it is necessary that a clergyman or doctor enter the scene, have an officer accompany him through the designated path of entry and caution this person about contamination and/or alteration.

Notifications

- Make notifications by telephone or cell phone if possible (police radios are often monitored by the press).
- *Never,* unless absolutely necessary, use a telephone inside the crime scene. Such necessity would involve a life-or-death situation, the need for immediate transmission of alarms, or circumstances that require you to answer the phone, etc.
- Notify the investigators or homicide division.
- Record time of notification and who was notified.
- Establish a temporary headquarters away from central crime scene (preferably a location with two phones: one for incoming, one for outgoing).
- Broadcast any alarms for suspects or descriptions of perpetrators from command post to guarantee uniformity and possibility of verification.
- Notify communications of the telephone numbers of the command post to facilitate communications between the various units.

Preliminary Investigation

- Initiate and maintain a chronological log recording the names, shield numbers, and commands of any police officers entering the crime scene. In addition, record the names, addresses, etc., of any civilians who may have to enter, as well as names, titles, and serial numbers of any ambulance personnel. This log should reflect the entry and exit of any person who enters the crime scene.
- Isolate and separate witnesses or suspects. Do *not* permit any conversations relative to the crime. Hold witnesses and suspects for the investigators.
- Establish a path of entry and exit based on observation of scene.
- For any civilians at the scene, record identifying information and their knowledge of the crime.
- Do not touch, move, or alter anything in the scene. If you do, record it.
- Do *not* smoke in the crime scene.
- Do not flush toilets or run tap water in sinks or bathtubs. If it has been done, record it.
- Refer all newspaper and broadcast media inquiries to the investigators.
- Stand by for investigators and assist them as required.
- Advise and inform investigators of all that has transpired since arrival of the first officer.

Suspect in Custody

- Determine if the suspect is armed (search for weapons). If weapon is recovered, record description and location. Maintain custody, pending arrival of investigators who will instruct as to vouchering and disposition.
- Handcuff suspect and isolate him/her from any witnesses and/or associates. (Use rear handcuff method.)
- If suspect is arrested outside crime scene, *do not return him/her to scene.*
- If suspect is arrested inside crime scene, *remove him/her immediately. (Remember the possibility of scene contamination.)*

- Note and preserve any evidence found on suspect, advise investigators.
- Do *not* permit suspect to wash hands or use toilet (you may lose evidence).
- Do not permit any conversation between suspect and any other parties.
- Do not initiate any interrogation (wait for the investigators). However, in certain types of homicides, the first officer will take statements. *Make sure, however, that suspect has been warned of his/her rights* before taking any statement. As a general rule, do not interrogate.
- Carefully record all spontaneous statements *(Res gestae* [things done] rule).
- Observe and record behavior of suspect (e.g., nervous, erratic, emotional/unemotional, drunk, under influence of drugs, any unusual behavior).

Preliminary Investigation at the Scene

The Detectives

The purpose of this section is to provide the homicide investigator/detective with flexible guidelines to follow in the preliminary investigation of death. The principles set forth in this section are intended to help the detective and chief investigator at the homicide crime scene to systematically check and review all the facts applicable to the investigation. However, for more thorough and in-depth information on these duties, the author refers the reader to *Practical Homicide Investigation,* Chapters 4 and 5 (Geberth, 2006). The author also recommends the *Practical Crime Scene Processing and Investigation* textbook (Gardner, 2005) as an additional resource for the important considerations in crime scene processing. This book, which is in my Practical Aspects of Criminal and Forensic Investigations series, illustrates a number of practical and proven methods and procedures (Figure 5.9 and Figure 5.10).

Initial Receipt of Information

Homicide investigation is probably the most exacting task confronting the criminal investigator. It begins with the initial notification that a homicide has occurred. Investigators are rarely the first officers at the scene of a homicide. The body is usually discovered by friends, relatives, or citizens who in turn notify the police or call for an ambulance. The notification to detectives or investigators is usually made through department channels.

The response of the homicide investigator and detective supervisor must be methodical. In order not to overlook the obvious, the most basic details should be recorded. I personally recommend that the investigator start a separate steno pad or notebook for use in each homicide investigation.

The first entry should be the receipt of information that a homicide has occurred, including:

- Date and time of notification
- Method of transmission, e.g., telephone, radio, or in person
- Name, rank, shield number, and other data identifying the person who is reporting the information to detectives
- Complete details of the information and event

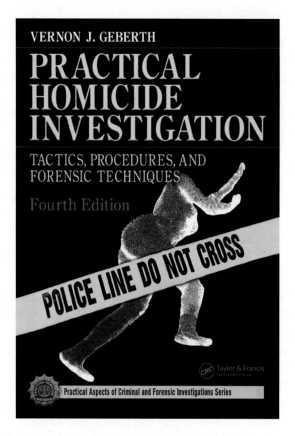

Figure 5.9 Practical Homicide Investigation. (From Geberth, V.J., *Practical Homicide Investigation: Tactics, Procedures, and Forensic Techniques*, 4th ed. CRC Press, Boca Raton, FL, 2006. With permission.)

Arrival at the Scene

When the investigator arrives at the scene, he should note the following:

- Time of arrival
- The exact address of the scene
- Persons present (officers, ambulance or medical people, relatives, friends, etc.)
- The condition and position of the body (personally verify death; see Chapter 2, First Officer's Duties on Arrival at the Scene, Geberth, 2006)
- Information concerning death
- Weather conditions
- Outside lighting conditions in nighttime situations
- Points of observation (locations where persons, such as the local busybody, could have observed what happened)

In addition, the investigator should stop and observe the area as a whole, noting everything possible before entering the actual crime scene for the detailed examination. Only the investigator and detective supervisor should enter the homicide crime scene, of course, with the exception of the first officers, and even then only to confirm death and observe scene conditions.

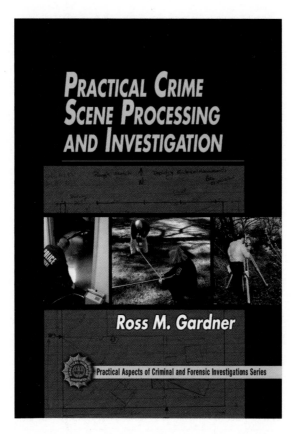

Figure 5.10 Practical Crime Scene Investigation. (From Gardner, R.M. *Practical Crime Scene Processing and Investigation*, CRC Press, Boca Raton, FL, 2005. With permission.)

Initiate the Canvass

A *canvass* is a door-to-door, road block inquiry or brief interview with persons on the street by which detectives attempt to gain information about a specific incident. It is an important investigative tool and a vital part of the preliminary investigation at the homicide crime scene.

The detective supervisor should assign investigators to conduct a preliminary canvass of the surrounding area including the approach and escape routes from the crime scene, while the case officer performs his functions at the scene. As the detectives conduct the canvass, their primary purpose should not be to conduct in-depth interviews, but to locate possible witnesses or persons who may have information about the crime. Canvassers should obtain the name and address of each person spoken to, whether the person provides information or not. Where no one is at home or there are additional residents who should be interviewed, this should be noted so that the parties can be reached during a recanvass. Likewise, locations that are negative should be recorded for the follow-up investigation. Because of the vast amount of information generated in a short period of time at the homicide crime scene, I recommend that everyone involved in the investigation possess a notebook. Each apartment, place, or person canvassed should be recorded in the investigator's notes for later official reports or a recanvass, as the case may warrant (Figure 5.11 and Figure 5.12).

At times it may be necessary to recanvass or extend the canvass to include additional areas. The thoroughness of the procedure is the determining factor of success. On the recanvass, a witness who was reluctant to talk the first time or someone who was inadvertently

CANVASS QUESTIONNAIRE

(Identify Yourself and Purpose of Canvass)

Name: (last) (first) (middle)	Date of Birth:

Address: Phone:

Employment (company name–type of work):   Address: Phone:

Other residents of This Address: (names and ages)

Did you know of the offense?   ☐ Yes   ☐ No

How did you first learn of it?   (when?)

Did you know the victim?   ☐ Yes   ☐ No

What was your relationship with the victim?   (if knew, date time, and location last seen or talked to)

Were you on the crime scene at anytime? (explain)

What knowledge do you have of the crime?

Typed stetement taken from this witness?   ☐ Yes   ☐ No

Reporting officer   (name)   (unit)   (date)   (time)

Figure 5.11 Canvass questionnaire. (From Geberth, V.J., *Practical Homicide Investigation: Tactics, Procedures, and Forensic Techniques*, 4th ed. CRC Press, Boca Raton, FL, 2006, p. 60. With permission.)

missed will be located. Also consider the physical location of the crime scene in relation to the area canvassed; i.e., don't miss the back of the building.

Also consider whether an immediate canvass is necessary. The type of crime or the hour of day or night may determine this. For instance, in an organized crime hit in an area frequented by persons friendly to criminal enterprise, it will probably be necessary to come back at a later time and talk to people out of the hearing or observation of criminal sympathizers and neighbors. A common mistake is to attempt a canvass in the middle of the night. You'll make a lot more enemies than friends if you start ringing doorbells at 3 a.m. Wait until a reasonable hour and then do the canvass.

Many homicides have been solved because a good canvass performed by a determined group of canvassers uncovered some vital information, including a motive or even an eyewitness. These canvassers were detectives who didn't just go through the motions, but took the time to effectively elicit information from the people canvassed. It is extremely important to keep in mind when instituting a canvass not to assign officers arbitrarily just because you are supposed to do a canvass. Usually at the homicide crime scene, there will be numerous personnel—sometimes more than can be effectively utilized. A common error committed by some supervisors is to indiscriminately assign these people to do a

CANVASS QUESTIONNAIRE

Street, Avenue, Road, etc. _____

Number (or name if no number) _____

If Apartment or Office Building (name) _____

Occupants (full name and age)   Questionnaire
                                                                           Completed

1. _____   Yes – No

2. _____   Yes – No

3. _____   Yes – No

4. _____   Yes – No

5. _____   Yes – No

6. _____   Yes – No

Officer Recording _____

Time _____ Date _____

Figure 5.12 Canvass questionnaire occupants. (From Geberth, V.J., *Practical Homicide Investigation: Tactics, Procedures, and Forensic Techniques*, 4th ed. CRC Press, Boca Raton, FL, 2006, p. 81. With permission.)

canvass, a practice that can do more harm than good. This is not to say that the supervisor shouldn't "shotgun" a number of investigators into an initial canvass, but the personnel selected should either be good at this investigative technique or have an interest in the particular investigation. The extra personnel can then be used for some of the other jobs that become necessary during the course of events at the scene.

The assigned detective or member of the team conducting the homicide investigation should conduct formal interviews with anyone located by the canvassers. Likewise, the detective supervisor should be kept up to date with any information uncovered by the canvassers. In this way, both the supervisor and the team will be aware of all developments in the case and be better able to put this information into proper perspective.

The correctly done canvass is an invaluable investigative technique that can provide

An actual eyewitness to the crime
Information about the circumstances of the crime
An approximate time of occurrence and/or estimate of time of death
Information about the deceased: identity, habits, friends, etc.
A motive for the crime

Preliminary Medical Examination at the Scene

In homicide cases, a medical examiner or coroner is responsible for performing an investigation to determine the cause, manner, and mode of death. The medical examiner's or coroner's office is responsible for conducting an autopsy later on. Ideally, the investigation at the scene should be carried out by the same pathologist who will later perform the autopsy. However, in jurisdictions that lack a medical examiner system or have a large number of homicides, this is not always possible. In most cases, the medical examiner at the pathologist's office or coroner must rely on the information provided by the medical examiner or medical investigator at the scene, and from the detectives investigating the homicide (Figure 5.13 and Figure 5.14). (For further information, refer to Chapter 9 in *Practical Homicide Investigation,* Geberth, 2006).

Because the physical aspects of the scene and the cadaver can never be replaced in quite the same manner after a body has been moved, the body, under ordinary circumstances, should not be moved before an examination by the medical examiner or coroner.

The preliminary medical examination should not, however, be undertaken until the crime scene has been photographed and sketched in its original condition. If the medical examiner arrives before the crime scene technicians or police photographer, he or she should be requested to delay the examination until after the scene documentation has been accomplished.

The medical examiner should be brought up to date on all aspects of the case as soon as he/she arrives. This includes any determinations or observations made by the investigators at the scene or in the course of the preliminary investigation. **Remember:** The teamwork aspect can never be overemphasized, especially in this preliminary medical examination at the scene.

Figure 5.13 Body dumped at scene. This photo depicts a body "dumped at the scene." The death appears to be a sex-related homicide. (Photo courtesy Detective Mark Czworniak, Chicago Police Department.)

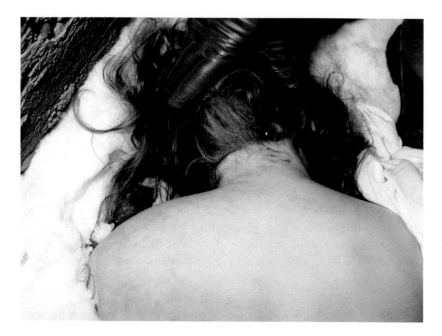

Figure 5.14 Preliminary medical examination. Shows the medical examiner making a preliminary examination at the scene, which verified manual strangulation. (Photo courtesy Detective Mark Czworniak, Chicago Police Department.)

The scene investigation by the medical examiner or coroner includes identification of the deceased, examination of the body, evaluation of the circumstances of death, and removal of evidence from the body. Therefore, it is important that these medical experts obtain as much information as possible about the facts surrounding the death so that later autopsy findings can be properly evaluated. For example, an ambulance may have responded and the attendants attempted resuscitation. This information could become important in evaluating rib fractures, facial trauma, or other internal injuries that could have been caused during the resuscitation attempts.

The medical investigation at the scene may indicate the following:

1. The apparent cause of death, by correlating the injuries with the manner in which they occurred. In homicide deaths, which are the result of stabbing or shooting, the determination of cause of death may be made at the scene. In some suspicious deaths, the medical examiner may observe *petechial hemorrhages* in the lining of the eyes and eyelids, alerting the police to asphyxial death.
2. Whether injuries are antemortem or postmortem.
3. Whether the deceased, after the initial injury, fell or struck other objects at the scene, thereby causing further injury.
4. Whether the body came to rest upon an object that, due to pressure, produced a postmortem injury (*artefact*), which could be erroneously interpreted as contributory or responsible for death.
5. The approximate time of death (indicated by such signs as loss of body heat, rigor mortis, lividity, etc.). (See Chapter 9, *Practical Homicide Investigation*, Geberth, 2006.)

The Initial Survey

The primary focus in this operation is to personally verify and confirm death. The initial survey or preliminary "walk through" is crucial in establishing the hypothesis and evaluating the nature and extent of the crime scene including the location of any fragile evidence, which might be lost, altered, or destroyed. During this phase, you can make a determination of what equipment and personnel you will require as well as what possible methods and techniques might be employed in the collection of this evidence. A procedure that I have found to be effective is to photograph the crime scene upon arrival. This is done most often with a digital camera (some may still use the Polaroid and single lens reflex (SLR) camera with built-in flash). The cameras are available at the homicide office and maintained for crime scene use. These preliminary photographs are **work photos** that can be viewed by other investigators and personnel who arrive at the crime scene later during the process. The work photos cut down on the type of crime scene contamination that usually takes place as additional personnel unnecessarily enter the crime scene to view the body or gather information.

Furthermore, photos taken during this preliminary phase represent a priceless record of *how* the scene appeared when the first investigator arrived. The crime scene photographer will take any number of photographs of the homicide crime scene, which will be submitted into evidence for prosecution.

Crime Scene Photographs

Crime scene photographs are permanent and comprehensive pieces of evidence, which may be presented in a court of law to prove or disprove a fact in question. During the preliminary stage of homicide investigation, it is impossible to determine all of the things that may become relevant or important later on. Therefore, it is imperative that photos be taken of the entire area and location where the crime took place, including any sites contiguous to the original crime. (For further information on crime scene photography, refer to Chapter 6 in *Practical Homicide Investigation*, Geberth, 2006). **Remember**: You only get one shot at the homicide crime scene, so obtain as much information and documentation as possible.

Value of Crime Scene Photographs

The old adage, "One picture is worth a thousand words," is certainly appropriate when considering the value of crime scene photography. Although an investigator can verbally describe the homicide crime scene, photographs are able to present the same facts in a more accurate and easily understood manner. In addition, photography enables the investigator to stop the clock at any given instant and obtain a durable record, which remains long after other more fragile evidence has dissipated. From an investigative point of view, crime scene photographs are practical and valuable tools, which can

1. Pictorially recreate the original crime scene
2. Refresh the investigator's memory and recall significant details, which may have been overlooked or forgotten
3. Be used to review particular aspects of the case
4. Provide a new slant on the case

Figure 5.15 Hallway. This photo shows the hallway that the victim entered and proceeded down the stairwell to go to work. The light bulb had been unscrewed to darken the hall. (Photo courtesy of the author.)

5. Refresh the memory of witnesses
6. Illustrate details of a scene and the relationship of objects to the crime
7. Provide proof of injury or wound
8. Make comparisons
9. Brief newly assigned investigators
10. Convey the crime scene and circumstances of the crime to a jury and serve as a *visible* piece of evidence (Figures 5.15 through 5.18)

Photos should be taken of the entire area and location where the homicide took place.

- Photos of contiguous areas
- Photos of witnesses (if applicable), e.g., crowds
- Photos of suspects (clothing and/or injuries)
- *In-situ* photographs of evidence

Admissibility of Photographic Evidence

The homicide investigator should have an understanding of the techniques and legal requirements necessary to ensure that the crime scene photos will be admissible in court.

The basic premise involved in crime scene photography is that the photographs are a true representation of the homicide crime scene as it was at the time the incident was reported. Therefore, before a detailed examination of the crime scene is undertaken, and before any items are moved or even touched, the crime scene must be photographed.

Remember: Do not draw any chalk lines or place markers in the crime scene until an original photograph can be obtained depicting the scene as it was when the police first arrived.

Figure 5.16 Light Bulb. The offender had loosened the light bulb in the hallway of a public parking garage waiting for the unsuspecting female victim to enter. (Photo courtesy of the author.)

Figure 5.17 Fire Hose. This crime scene photo shows the standpipe and fire hose in the hallway, which the victim entered to walk down the stairs. (Photo courtesy of the author.)

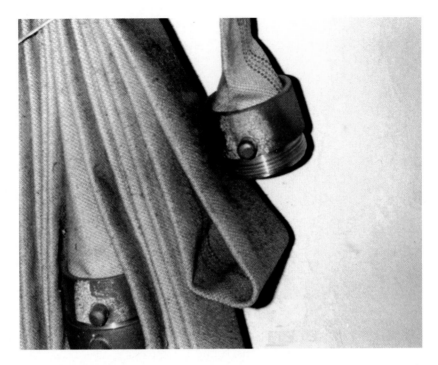

Figure 5.18 Missing hose nozzle. The offender had removed the nozzle from the hose to use as a blunt force instrument on his unsuspecting victim. This photo documents that the nozzle is missing from the hose. The bloody nozzle and the suspect's fingerprints were later found in garbage that the suspect had bagged. (Photo courtesy of the author.)

The photographer should show the relationship of one object to another by moving from the general to the specific. Several photos of the general view should be taken at eye level in a clockwise direction or from each point of the compass (north, south, east, and west). The photographer should start at the outside perimeter of the scene and work toward the central scene. In addition, the photos of the body should indicate its position in relation to some landmark or permanent point of reference. Do not delete images from the digital camera until they have been transferred to a computer and/or compact disk (CD). If using an SLR camera, shoot and develop the entire roll of film for one investigation.

Do not add any chalk marks or markers to the scene before a long shot and close-up detail shot are obtained. Defense counsel can argue that the crime scene photographs are not an accurate representation of the scene as it was upon discovery of the crime because the police have added markers or chalk lines. If chalk lines or markers are needed to pinpoint the location of a small item, such as bloodstains, hair, or similar articles, photos should first be taken without the markers and then additional photos taken with the markers (Figure 5.19 and Figure 5.20).

The number of photos taken is usually determined by the case. There is no limit on the number that can be taken. Practically speaking, it is always better to overshoot a scene than to miss some vital shots.

As each photo is taken, an accurate record should be made in the investigator's notebook. In addition, an entry should be made on an official photo log. Some agencies maintain logs or preprinted forms for use at crime scenes in order to assure the proper documentation of crime scene photographs. In any event, the following information should be recorded.

Figure 5.19 Blood at crime scene. The crime scene detective first photographed the blood *in situ* and then added the marker for evidence. (Photo courtesy of Lt. John Fallon and Detective Richard Peffall, Montgomery County, Pennsylvania, detectives.)

Figure 5.20 Blood at crime scene. The crime scene detective first photographed the blood *in situ* and then added the marker for evidence. (Photo courtesy of Lt. John Fallon and Detective Richard Peffall, Montgomery County, Pennsylvania, detectives.)

Documentation of Crime Scene Photographs
- Date and time photos were taken
- The exact location where photographs were taken.
- A brief description of the detail being photographed
- The compass direction (north, south, east, or west)
- The focus distance
- Type of film and camera utilized
- Any special equipment utilized
- Lighting and weather conditions
- Number of exposures
- Identity of the photographer

The photographer should keep possession of the digital picture card (or exposed film) for deliver to the laboratory for processing. After these images have been transferred to a computer or CD, the above information should be entered into the computer file or CD. (For film, add information to the back of each photo or on an appropriate form indicating each photo by number.)

The comprehensive log is necessary to assure the admissibility of the crime scene photos in court. The log includes the 10 points mentioned above, as well as the chain of custody from exposure to final disposition and storage of images (or film and negatives).

In addition, the police laboratory should keep an evidence log containing the following information:

1. Identity of the individual delivering the digital picture card or film for processing (name, rank, serial number, etc.).
2. Date and time the card or film was received for processing.
3. Results of processing.
4. Number of prints or CDs requested.
5. Location of original digital picture card or film negatives.
6. Identity of the person receiving digital picture card or developed prints and/or negatives if there is no central storage.

In the event that a commercial laboratory is used to transfer the data on the digital picture card or process the film, the management should be requested to cooperate in adhering to the rules of evidence handling. This should include limiting the number of personnel handling the evidence card or film, as well as guaranteeing the security of these items. Needless to say, the commercial firm utilized to process any evidentiary material should be a reputable establishment.

Photographing the Homicide Crime Scene
Recording the homicide crime scene is a major facet of the investigation. It is extremely important that this be accomplished before anything is touched or moved at the scene. Also, it is important while photographing the scene to eliminate persons or items—including officers and police equipment—that do not belong in the scene.

As mentioned earlier in the chapter, the photographer should attempt to show the relationships of objects to each other by shooting from the general to the specific, should take several photos of the general view, and should start at the perimeter and work toward the

Figure 5.21 Crime scene photo. This photo was taken before adding markers. (Photo courtesy of Detective Scott Mummert, Chambersburg, Pennsylvania, Police Department.)

body. This is followed by close-up shots of the body and any significant pieces of physical or trace evidence. Important items of evidence, such as weapons, should be photographed as they appear at the scene (Figure 5.21 and Figure 5.22). **Remember:** Do not add chalk marks or markers before you get a long shot and a close-up shot of the body and any other evidence. (For more thorough and in-depth information relative to the crime scene photography and the duties of the investigator, including videotaping, the author refers the reader to *Practical Homicide Investigation,* Chapter 6, Geberth, 2006.)

Describing the Crime Scene

A compete description of the body and the surrounding area should be taken during this preliminary walk through. (Although some of the points I have listed may seem quite obvious, I can assure you from my own experience that the obvious is sometimes overlooked, especially during this initial phase, as you attempt to cover all the bases.)

1. Sex, appearance, age, build, color of hair of the deceased, and a description of the deceased's clothing.
2. Evidence of injury and apparent cause of death.
3. Are the bloodstains wet or dry?
4. What is the condition of the body (lividity, rigor, etc.)?
5. Describe the color of the blood (bright red or brown).

Figure 5.22 Crime scene photo with markers. This photo was taken to show the location of blood drops before collection. (Photo courtesy of Detective Scott Mummert, Chambersburg, Pennsylvania, Police Department.)

6. Note any tears in clothing and evidence of gunshot or stab wounds.
7. Careful examination of the hands. Are there any wounds or a weapon?
8. Note whether or not there is any jewelry (rings, watches, gold chains, etc.). If there is no jewelry, make a negative notation. The defense has been known to resort to dirty tactics during trials. If they can make you appear like a thief to discredit your testimony, they'll do it.
9. Describe the immediate surroundings:
   a. Position of body in relation to articles in the room.
   b. Note doors, windows, furniture, etc.
10. If a weapon is nearby, take detailed notes. Do not handle.
11. Look for bullet holes or fired shells. *Note*: Do not collect at this stage of the investigation.
12. In poison and drug overdose cases, note presence of drugs, bottles, or glasses.

Implementing Crime Scene Procedures

The first thing that the investigator should do after confirming the death and conducting the initial survey is to take charge of the crime scene. The preliminary investigation at the crime scene is the most important and sensitive aspect. It sets the tone for the entire process. Therefore, extreme care must be exercised to preserve and protect the scene because even the smallest detail can suddenly assume vital importance in the case. Failure to implement proper crime scene techniques may irreparably damage the investigation. The author points to the Jon Benet Ramsey case as an example of this type of error. In the Jon Benet Ramsey case, the Boulder Colorado Police had been dispatched to the Ramsey household on a report of a possible kidnapping. When they arrived, they were advised that little Jon Benet had been kidnapped and that a ransom note had been discovered in the house. The initial responding police officers never thought to remove family members from the house nor conduct a thorough search of the premises for the missing child. The fact that the little girl was missing and there was an alleged ransom note found in the premises made the entire house a *crime scene*. No crime scene was established and the family members were not separated and individually interviewed relative to the event. Furthermore, neighbors who came to the residence were allowed entry and many persons came and went from the premises, which should have been secured. The police failed to conduct a thorough search of the premises for the missing child. Instead, her father discovered the body of the little girl in the basement. The father removed the body from the basement and brought the little girl's body upstairs where it was moved a number of times. The father covered the body of the little girl with a blanket. To compound this series of errors, the female detective who was supposed to be guarding the scene adjusted the blanket so the body was covered from the neck down. Someone else had placed a sweatshirt over the exposed feet. The father of the victim knelt beside his daughter's body and stroked her hair, then lay down and put his arm around her. Mrs. Ramsey, who was also present fell across her daughter's body, which further contaminated the scene. (Thomas and Davis, 2000).

Inexcusably, all of the transient, pattern, conditional, and transfer evidence was effectively compromised by these errors and, to this day, the murder of little Jon Benet remains unsolved.

If the crime scene is outdoors, a wide area surrounding the body should be cordoned off for later systematic examination. The patrol officer should be directed to isolate the body and secure the immediate surroundings from ALL persons.

If the crime scene is indoors, the job of securing the location is relatively easy to accomplish. It may be as simple as closing the door. The biggest problem is removing unauthorized persons from the scene. The investigation should begin with the walkway and front entrance to the structure. These areas and the location where the body lies should be considered part of the scene and appropriately secured. The homicide detective should determine what areas are to be included and/or excluded from the crime scene and decide whether or not the homicide involves multiple scenes.

Direction of Uniform Personnel at the Scene

The detective supervisor and homicide detective assigned to the case are in complete command at the scene of the homicide. They have the authority to exclude everyone including other police officers, the news media, and any unauthorized persons. Oftentimes, follow-up investigations of crime scenes have disclosed that valuable evidence was destroyed by the mere presence of police personnel.

Formulating the Crime Scene Search

The search for evidence begins with the isolation and protection of the scene. The searcher must ascertain that the scene is intact and then proceed to reconstruct the events that have transpired since his or her arrival. Obviously, the best places for obtaining physical evidence are nearest to where the critical incident occurred, such as in the immediate vicinity of the homicide victim. However, other areas related to the primary crime scene must not be overlooked.

The scope of the search is usually determined by a hypothesis agreed upon by investigators, based on their initial observations of the scene. The hypothesis emerges from a set of simple assumptions of how and why the homicide occurred and the sequence of events that followed. This hypothesis is utilized to guide the investigator in discovery of physical evidence.

However, remember that *anything* and *everything* may be evidence and become significant later on. Therefore, every item at the scene must be handled as evidence until determined otherwise.

The investigators must keep in mind that their hypothesis is provisional. If new evidence emerges that suggests a different sequence of events, the investigators must be willing to reassess and modify their hypothesis as the new facts dictate. I have been at many different scenes over the years and have seen initial theories or hypotheses change over and over again. The key to success in this phase of the investigation is *flexibility*. Practically speaking, use your common sense in this process. Don't get bogged down in theory and hypothetical speculation. Many times, the answer you are looking for is right in front of your nose. The problem is that with all the events going on at the scene, and some of the personalities that arrive with their own agendas, it is sometimes easy to miss a simple observation. Your instincts should not be discounted. They can bring you back to reality or direct you to a situation that would otherwise have slipped by, especially in staged crime scenes where the initial presentation might mislead you.

In formulating the search plan, there may be some critical areas that you will want to cover immediately, or there may be some question as to what is or is not evidence. Don't be influenced by the original report, the police call, or any initial statements. Note this initial information and then make your own determination based on the total information available.

Ask yourself the following questions:

1. Is the manner of death:
   a. Homicide
   b. Suicide
   c. Accident
   d. Natural causes
2. Do the facts, the scene, the statements, and the physical evidence support this explanation?
3. If the death is a homicide:
   a. What is the cause or agency of death?
   b. Is the homicide excusable or justifiable?

    c. Does it appear that any effort was made to purposely mislead the police? Example.
      i. A simulated burglary
      ii. An alleged "home invasion" and purported sexual assault
      iii. An arson
      iv. Murder made to look like suicide
      v. Suicide made to look like murder (insurance case)
      vi. Murder made to look like an autoerotic death
    d. Is there more than one possible cause of death?
    e. Are the witness statements consistent with the facts?
    f. Is the time element consistent with the condition of the scene?
      i. Are the bloodstains wet or dry?
      ii. Is the serum separating from the blood?
      iii. What is the condition of the body (rigor mortis, livor mortis, algor mortis, etc.)?
    g. Is there a weapon involved?
      i. Was more than one weapon used? What does this suggest?
      ii. Are the wounds consistent with the suspected weapon(s)?
      iii. Is the weapon from the premises?
      iv. If the weapon was a firearm:
        A. Are there any shell casings present?
        B. Are there any bullet holes or spent rounds present on the ground, the walls, the ceiling, etc.?
      v. Is there a weapon under the body?
      vi. Was the deceased armed?

During this self cross-examination, do not make any final evaluations because you are merely forming a hypothesis to assist you in planning the search. However, you should estimate as closely as possible the time and place of the homicide. In addition, you should have a general idea of how much evidence you plan to collect. During this stage, you will be depending on hard work, common sense, and keeping an open mind.

The Search

The most practical search method is to begin at the point where the body is first discovered and work in an outward direction until the entire room or location has been covered.

Remember: Do not smoke or dispose of any cigarettes, cigars, matches, gum wrappers, or any other item you brought into the scene that may be confused with evidence at the scene.

Once the search method has been determined, it is up to the detective supervisor to coordinate the efforts of the investigators in order to provide for location of physical or trace evidence, systematized search techniques, a chain of custody, and the recording of evidence.

The search should begin with an examination for latent fingerprints. Before any item is touched or moved, the crime scene technician should dust for prints. The supervisor should direct this phase by indicating what areas he wants examined. If possible, an attempt is made to determine points of entry and exit for latent impressions. In addition, any weapons or objects that were apparently handled by the suspect, as well as all door

Figure 5.23 Light bulb. This light bulb was observed lying on the floor. The offender had removed the bulb to darken the crime scene. He inadvertently left his fingerprints on the bulb. (Photo courtesy of Detective Scott Mummert, Chambersburg, Pennsylvania, Police Department.)

handles, telephones, windows, glasses, light switches, etc., should be dusted. Special attention should be given to objects that may have caused death, newly damaged areas, or items apparently missing from their original location. It is important to note that a good latent print will place the suspect at the scene (Figure 5.23 and Figure 5.24).

Remember: It's your case. You only get one shot at the crime scene, so make sure you do it right the first time.

Figure 5.24 Patent print. In this case, the offender, whose hands were covered with blood from dissecting the victim's body, went into a storage room and adjusted the light bulb, leaving a patent print in blood. (Photo courtesy of Kansas Bureau of Investigation.)

Direct the fingerprint people. If you do not direct that certain areas be dusted, they may not be. Tell the crime scene personnel or technicians what you want and then make sure that you get it. All visible details should be observed and described before dusting anything in the event that something might have to be moved. Note the location of any stains, weapons, etc.

During the initial search, each possible item of evidence should be measured from a fixed location. (See Chapter 7 in *Practical Homicide Investigation*, Geberth, 2006.)

The measurements, along with a complete description, should be entered in the investigator's notebook. This information should also be recorded on the crime scene sketch. Any latent prints located during this preliminary dusting should first be photographed and then lifted. The photo should be taken with an identifying label in order to document the lift, in case the lift fails. The photo can then still be used for identification and comparison.

Examination of the Body at the Scene

The actual examination of the body should not begin until all photographs and sketches are completed. In addition, a complete description of the body as well as any clothing must be obtained including

Sex
Race
Appearance
Age
Build
Color of hair
Evidence of injury and apparent cause of death
Condition of the body (rigor mortis, lividity, etc.)
Color of blood (wet or dry?)
Position of body relative to objects of significance at the location

The investigator should then concentrate on recording a complete description of the clothing as follows:

Position of clothes.
Condition of clothes (buttoned or unbuttoned, twisted sideways or pulled down, inside out, zippered or unzippered).
Damage to clothes (rips, tears, cuts, holes, etc.).
Stains: blood, saliva, vomit, semen, phlegm, urine, or feces. Where are they? What are they? Is there any direction of flow?

After a complete description of the clothing and any significant position, condition, damage, or stains have been noted, the investigator begins a careful examination of the body starting with the head and working down to the legs. This description will necessitate moving the body to look for any wounds or evidence of further injuries that are not visible in the origin position (Figure 5.25).

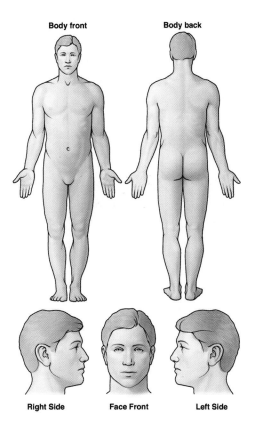

Figure 5.25 Wound chart. This chart can be used by the investigator to record observations of injuries to the deceased. (Courtesy of Medical Legal Art. Illustration ©2005 Medical Legal Art, www.doerport.com.)

1. The head:
   a. Are the eyes open or closed?
   b. Is the mouth open or closed?
   c. What is the position of the head in relation to the body?
   d. What is the color of the skin (lividity, etc.)?
   e. Is there any blood present? (Describe.)
   f. Are there any visible wounds? (Describe.)
   g. Is there any foreign material on the head (soil, mud, etc.)?
   h. What is the condition of the deceased's hair (neat or messy)?
   i. Any phlegm, saliva, or vomit present?
2. The trunk:
   a. The position of the trunk (twisted or bent over, on side or back, etc.).
   b. Any injuries. (Describe.)
   c. Presence of any stains (blood, semen, vomit, etc.).
   d. Presence of any hairs or fibers.
   e. Presence of any foreign substances on the trunk (soil, mud, grease, tar, paint, etc.).
3. Arms and legs:
   a. Position of each arm and leg.
   b. Presence of any injuries.

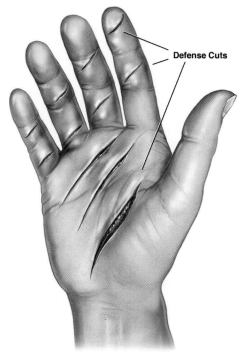

Right Hand, Palm Up

Figure 5.26 Sketch of defense wounds on hand. (Courtesy of Medical Legal Art. Illustration ©2005 Medical Legal Art, www.doerport.com.)

  c. Presence of any stains.
  d. Any foreign matter on the legs or arms?
  e. Are there any defense wounds on the hands, arms, legs, or feet?

Remember: Note the presence or absence of any jewelry—rings, watches, etc.—on the body, including any mark on the body indicating that such objects have been worn.

In most cases, it is good to bag the hands of the deceased with paper bags. This will preserve any trace evidence, which may be found under the fingernails later during autopsy (Figure 5.26). A paper bag is used because plastic tends to accelerate putrefaction, especially if there is any blood on the hands. In addition, plastic does not allow the skin to breathe and may even change the chemical composition of certain trace evidence.

The area under the body must be carefully examined bearing in mind that extensive bleeding may create pooling that conceals bullets, cartridge casings, or other small items of evidence. If the body has been lying on soft earth, bullets may be embedded in the soil. If any such items are found, they should be photographed in the position in which found before being collected and marked.

Remember: Appropriate notation should be made on the crime scene sketch and in the investigator's notebook.

Release of the Body

The body should not be moved until completion of the preliminary investigation at the scene. The medical examiner or coroner, if responding, should have the opportunity to view the body in its original position. This can be very helpful to these officials in carrying out their responsibilities. After the homicide investigator and medical examiners have completed their work at the scene and details noted, the question arises as to when the body can and should be released.

This decision is critical. Because the consequences of the decision are irrevocable, removal should be undertaken only after due consideration of several factors.

1. Before the body is removed, it should be wrapped in a clean sheet to preserve any evidence or residue for later analysis.
2. If the medical examiner is not going to conduct an immediate autopsy and the body will be lying in the morgue until the following day, there should be no rush to remove the body, particularly in cases of apparent homicide where there are no witnesses and no named perpetrator or arrests. If the body is not in a public place, the location can easily be secured. The reason for this procedure is that information may come to light during the canvass or while talking to witnesses at the station house that may require some additional photos or other police procedure with respect to the body. If the body has been removed hastily, this opportunity will be lost.
3. If an immediate autopsy is to be conducted by the medical examiner, then the removal should be directed only after conferring with the investigators doing the canvass and the interviewing teams at the station house, to determine if there is any new information that may require additional things to be done with the body.
4. If the body is in a public place and the medical examiner has completed his scene examination, and the crime scene work has been accomplished, the detective supervisor can release the body, usually after checking with his detectives at the station house and with the officers doing the canvass.
5. If the body is in a public place and the medical examiner is not responding, the chief investigator will authorize the removal after the crime scene work has been completed.
6. As previously discussed under conditions of violent crowds or public disorders, etc., the body may have to be removed immediately.

The Scene

A technique that I have found useful is to have someone who is thoroughly familiar with the scene go over it with you, bit by bit, first visually and then physically, being careful not to touch any items. This person can identify the usual positions of objects in the scene. You can then get a complete inventory on the spot. Instruct the person to take his time, and ask if he recognizes any inconsistencies or "foreign" material present. Have him point out the usual position of drapes, curtains, blinds, pictures, statues, ashtrays, etc. Obtain a detailed report. You may even want him to examine the scene along with an investigator so that he may point out new stains, signs of disorder, or any factor inconsistent with the life style of the deceased.

The ideal situation in any crime scene search is to have one officer designated the "searching officer," whose responsibility is to search and take evidence into custody. Other homicide detectives can assist by taking notes of locations where objects are found and even participate in follow-up searches. However, these officers assisting the searching officer should *not* handle any evidence. Instead, they can alert the searching officer, who

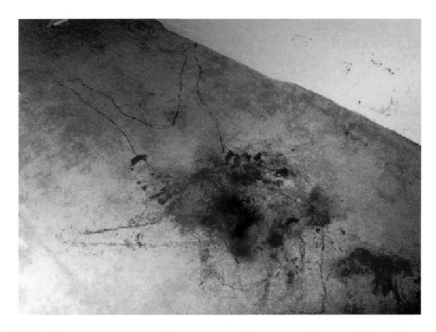

Figure 5.27 Crime scene process. This is an excellent procedure to follow. After you have taken the crime scene photos, outline the original location and position of the body on the carpet or rug. The laboratory can then focus their recovery efforts on this portion of the rug. In this case, an additional nine hairs were recovered. (Photo courtesy of Detective Sergeant Alan Patton, Grand Prairie, Texas, Police Department.)

will take significant evidence into custody. This procedure limits the chain of custody and makes the recording of evidence more uniform and professional.

Because items tend to fall to the ground, especially in a violent struggle or confrontation, the floor is the best place to begin the search after examining the body. As the search progresses, the investigators may move from the floor or ground to waist height, and from waist height to ceiling. The areas to be searched depend on the type of homicide. If the homicide is the result of a robbery or burglary, you will want to check the entire apartment or house for locations where the intruder searched for valuables. If the homicide was the result of a shooting, you will want to check the walls and ceiling for any bullet holes or spent rounds; any carpeting or rugs should also be rolled back or lifted up for examination.

If the murderer "cleaned up" after the crime, you must examine such additional locations as sinks and sink traps or garbage areas. If there are narcotics involved, you might have to locate a "stash" or secret hiding place. The murderer may have fixed something to eat, or may have taken something from a refrigerator. Did the killer turn the light off or on? Does the scene give an appearance of being ransacked? Was the door unlocked or locked? Are the windows open or closed? Where is the point of entry? These are all questions you should ask yourself (Figures 5.27 through 5.30). **Remember** the theory of exchange and transfer.

Locations where any physical or trace evidence may be found depend on the individual crime and the actions of the suspect or suspects at the scene, and will vary from scene to scene. However, certain areas and objects should always be given attention:

Under rugs or carpets	Elevator shaft
Under chair cushions	Tops of cabinets or furniture

Figure 5.28 Suspect used bathroom. The suspect, who had cut himself when he murdered his victim, cleaned up in the bathroom. He left blood on the floor in front of the sink and a bloody palm print on the cold water faucet. (Photo courtesy of Former Detective Sergeant Kurt Harrelson, Thibodaux, Louisiana, Police Department.)

Figure 5.29 Evidence from refrigerator. This case involved a rape and lust murder. The perpetrator had stabbed his victim multiple times. Upon completing his assault, he went into the refrigerator to get a cold beer. He had to move the wine box to get to the beer. His bloody hands left a perfect set of latent prints on the wine box, which placed him at the crime scene. (Photo by evidence technician Don Swanz and courtesy of Detective Alan Patton, Grand Prairie, Texas, Police Department.)

Figure 5.30 Evidence from refrigerator. A perfect set of latent prints left by the perpetrator was found on the back of the wine box. He also left a smudged blood print on the front of the box, which placed him at the scene. (Photo by evidence technician Don Swanz and courtesy of Detective Alan Patton, Grand Prairie, Texas, Police Department.)

Doorjambs	Chimney
Light fixtures	Gutters
Refrigerators	Roof
Behind drapes or curtains	Statues
Garbage pails or bags	Behind pictures or clocks
Wastebaskets	Sewers
Hampers or soiled clothes	Drainpipes
Ashtrays	Ventilation ducts
Ceilings	Behind desks set against walls
Suspended ceilings	Closets
Walls	Backs and bottoms of drawers
Under chairs	Inside ovens
Under beds	Inside cabinets
Mirrors	Kitchen or bathroom towels
Telephones	Sinks, toilets, or tubs
Signs of a party	Counter tops
Glasses	Windows
Stairs	Any newly damaged areas
Passages	Garments
Back yards	Mailboxes
Behind boxes or cartons	Any vehicles, cars, trucks
Boats	Docks
Computers	Computer disks
PDAs	Cell phones
Computer hard drives	Pagers

The ability to recognize and discover evidence at the crime scene is a prerequisite of a successful search. The acquired expertise of the homicide investigator and the detective supervisor will probably determine what trace evidence is found.

It is in this search phase that one can see the need for close cooperation between the investigators and the forensic scientist. It is imperative that the officers performing the search have a working knowledge of handling physical evidence (Figures 5.31 through 5.34).

Most major departments maintain a forensic or crime scene unit with trained personnel to assist in the search of major crime scenes. These officers have the expertise and equipment necessary to work under the detective supervisor for the proper retrieval of physical evidence.

Information sources, such as papers, personal effects, and address books, and any other property that may aid in the investigation should be taken by the homicide detectives for later perusal and disposition. The patrol or uniformed division should be responsible for the administrative search and safekeeping of any valuables or property of the deceased. These items can be vouchered and safeguarded at headquarters for later disposition to the property clerk, medical examiner, coroner, or family of the deceased.

Any photos of the deceased taken in life should be collected to use in the canvass to clearly identify the victim to persons interviewed as well as personal acquaintances or

Figure 5.31 Search of Garbage. Search revealed a torn letter written in Portuguese by the offender who had killed his American wife. Detectives, who had searched the garbage discovered this incriminating piece of evidence, which was used against the murderer. (Photo courtesy of Investigator Jack Henander, Larimer County, Colorado, Sheriff's Department.)

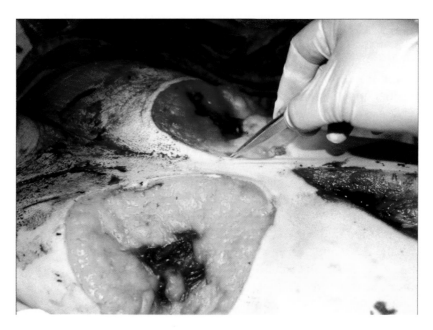

Figure 5.32 Recovery of hair evidence. Shown is the crime scene detective recovering the suspect's hair from the chest of the victim, who had been defeminized. (Courtesy of Chief Criminal Deputy Robin Wagg, Douglas County, Washington, Sheriff's Department)

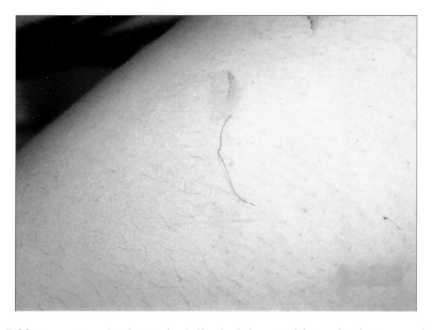

Figure 5.33 Suspect's pubic hair. The killer had deposited his pubic hair onto the leg of one of the victims. (Photo courtesy of Chief Criminal Deputy Robin Wagg, Douglas County, Washington, Sheriff's Department.)

Figure 5.34 Fiber evidence. Fibers from hospital gown that the suspect wore at the crime scene. (Photo courtesy of Chief Criminal Deputy Robin Wagg, Douglas County, Washington, Sheriff's Department.)

associates of the victim. If photos are not available at the scene, they should be obtained from the victim's family, friends, or employer, or from yearbooks or a driver's license. Photos should have a good likeness of the deceased just prior to death so as not to confuse a person to whom they are shown.

Examining the Outdoor Scene

The general techniques of a crime scene search apply to all homicide crime scenes; however, the outdoor scene poses additional problems for the investigator. For example:

1. The scene usually does not have easily defined borders.
2. The "floor" of the scene is usually rough and irregular and may be composed of hills, valleys, bodies of water, swamps, sand, or other natural contours.
3. The investigation is vulnerable to weather conditions. Rain or snow may have washed away much trace evidence, or the threat of a storm may force immediate procedures to collect evidence in a manner that precludes efficient collection of all evidence.
4. The investigator does not have the luxury of electricity, running water, telephones, or other common conveniences found indoors.
5. Daylight is limited; be prepared to return to the scene the following day.

The investigator's actions at outdoor scenes are usually determined by the weather and the time of day. I have provided some practical procedures to follow. However, they are presented only as a guide. Each individual case will dictate how an investigator will retrieve evidence.

Direct the following:

1. Rope off the largest possible area.
2. Establish a path of entry and exit.
3. Examination should be conducted as soon as possible before daylight ends or weather changes.
4. Surrounding area should be searched.
5. If weather changes, order evidence to be collected immediately.

Remember: Some evidence is better than no evidence.

Examples of Evidence Found Outdoors

1. *Pollen, vegetation, soil,* or *seeds* may be found on the suspect or the victim. The investigator should collect any foreign matter found on either the suspect or the body for later comparison. However, each individual item must be separately packaged and labeled in order to assure proper examination and admissibility in court later.
2. *Foot* and *tire impressions* may appear on the soil. In addition to gathering samples for laboratory analysis, these impressions must be sketched, photographed, and properly casted for later comparison purposes. When gathering this type of evidence, several control samples should be secured for later analysis (Figure 5.35).
3. *Trees, shrubbery,* and *fencing* should be examined for any trace evidence that may have been transferred during sudden contact. Fibers, hair, threads, and other material may be affixed to these objects and should be collected and preserved for later comparison with either the victim or the suspect.
4. *Bloodstains, seminal fluid, saliva* or *phlegm, brain matter, hair, feces,* and *any other biological evidence* are not only subject to rapid change and destruction, but are almost impossible to locate in heavily vegetated terrain. Likewise, these pieces of trace evidence are subject to insect activity and are likely to be washed away if it rains on the scene.
5. *Bullets* and *casings* may be located if the investigator closely examines any foliage or newly broken parts of shrubbery. In some instances, the bullet may have lodged in a tree, causing telltale damage to the bark, or there may be pieces of twigs or branches that are lying on the ground in the line of trajectory. The area immediately surrounding the body should be examined for any shell casings and bullets embedded in the ground under the body.
6. *Oil* or *gasoline traces.* When vehicles are driven through tall grass or weeds, there is a transfer of this material from the underside of the vehicle to the vegetation. This residue should be collected for later comparison.
7. *Crankcase traces.* If a vehicle has been driven through an area of heavy foliage or rocky terrain, there will be traces of this material on the crankcase that can be compared.
8. *Any foreign material at the scene.* Many times, a suspect unwittingly will leave traces of himself at the scene that may be gathered and compared later, e.g., cigarettes or cigars, toothpicks. In addition, there may have been some sort of struggle resulting in a lost item of clothing, such as a button or piece of jewelry that can link the suspect to the scene.

Figure 5.35 Tire impression. The offender left this tire impression at the location where the body was discovered. This impression was eventually matched to his vehicle. (Photo courtesy of Detective Corporal Arthur Clark, East Providence, Rhode Island, Police Department.)

9. *Foreign material found on the body.* Sometimes the body may reveal traces of evidence that come from a distinctive location. For instance, the body and clothing may indicate that the deceased was a mechanic or cement worker, or there may be traces of sawdust or coal dust on the corpse.

In the event that the body has to be moved before an extensive examination is conducted at the scene, I recommend that it be placed in a factory-wrapped disposable body bag or wrapped in a clean sterile sheet so that any trace evidence remaining on the clothing will be preserved for later inspection.

Examination of an Outdoor Scene at Night

Under ordinary circumstances, an outdoor scene is usually searched during the daylight hours.

1. Direct that the area be effectively secured and safeguarded.
2. Direct that the body be photographed prior to removal.
3. Direct that measures be taken to safeguard the body against additional damage.

The actual crime search for trace evidence should be postponed until daylight. However, consider pending weather conditions.

Figure 5.36 Outdoor scene (before). This outdoor scene was the site of a sex-related homicide. The authorities were trying to locate the murder weapon. Geberth (2006) recommends "deforesting" the area. (Photo courtesy of Capt. (Ret.) James Gannon, Morris County, New Jersey, Prosecutor's Office.)

The reason for postponing the search until daylight is that it is utterly impossible to detect minute traces of evidence under nighttime conditions. If some larger pieces of evidence are discovered that are not subject to dissolution, they should be covered or secured pending daylight because their significance can be better realized in connection with the overall scene. However, if you are faced with a sudden change in the weather, delaying the search until daylight may prove disastrous to the investigation. Obviously, there can be no set procedure to cover all possibilities, so, as in all other aspects of homicide investigation, be flexible and use common sense (Figure 5.38).

Physical Examination of a Suspect in Custody

The suspect and his or her clothing should be considered part of the homicide crime scene search. If the suspect is in custody at the scene, he or she should be immediately removed. If the suspect is apprehended a short distance away, he or she should not be allowed to return to the central crime scene. Instead, the suspect should be isolated for a preliminary examination for evidence.

Remember: if a suspect is allowed access to the crime scene, you will negate the value of any evidence found on the suspect, which came from the scene, or destroy the value of any evidence imparted by the suspect to the scene.

The examination of the suspect for evidence should be performed by the investigator assigned to the case or by an experienced detective assigned to the crime scene search. The examination must be conducted in a manner that precludes any possible destruction or loss of evidence. In addition, the search for evidence on the person of a suspect requires that the investigator be able to recognize certain materials and marks as related to the

Figure 5.37 Outdoor scene (after). This was the same crime scene after the "deforesting." The murder weapon was located in the heavy underbrush. (Photo courtesy of Capt. (Ret.) James Gannon, Morris County, New Jersey, Prosecutor's Office.)

Figure 5.38 Outdoor scene at night. The body of the victim was located at dusk in this wooded area. The authorities, following *Practical Homicide Investigation* (Geberth, 2006) techniques, suspended the crime scene search until the following morning so as not to lose any microscopic trace evidence. (Photo courtesy of Lt. John Fallon and Detective Richard Peffall, Montgomery County, Pennsylvania, Detectives.)

actual crime. This ability to recognize and recover trace evidence is a prerequisite to successful search of suspects.

The suspect's clothing and shoes should be closely examined for any trace material from the scene or evidence of the crime. These items should be seized and vouchered as evidence. If the suspect has any visible injuries or marks that might link him or her to the crime, such as bruises, bite marks, scratches, cuts, or injuries on the hands, face, or other parts of the body, photographs should be taken in both black and white and color, using a scale or marker. In certain jurisdictions the use of color film is considered inflammatory evidence and violates the right of the defendant.

Many homicides involve a struggle where both participants receive injuries. Color photographs of these injuries, both to the suspect and deceased, are valuable pieces of evidence, which can be presented in court.

It is important to note that once a person is under arrest, he or she has no reasonable expectation of privacy. Suspects under arrest can be subjected to a thorough examination and body search. Under certain conditions, if the case warrants, the investigator should have the suspect undress over a clean sheet or large paper to prevent the loss or destruction of any physical evidence on the clothing, and examine the suspect for any injury. Of course, female suspects subjected to body searches should be processed by female officers with no male officers present, and male suspects processed by male officers with no female officers present, in order to avoid any criticism or objection later.

If patrol officers have been assigned to transport a suspect to the police station or are assisting in the examination of the suspect for evidence, they should be cautioned to use extreme care and to preserve the suspect's clothing and shoes for examination for trace evidence. Furthermore, they should be instructed not to allow the suspect to wash his or her hands or engage in any activity that may alter or destroy any evidence. I have seen instances where suspects have "cleaned" themselves with urine and spittle to remove blood from their hands or bodies.

When evidence is located on the suspect, the same procedures utilized in other crime scene searches must be applied:

1. Photographs should be taken of the evidence *in situ*, and close-ups of the evidence.
2. The evidence should be described and documented in the investigator's notebook.
3. A sketch should be prepared of the area where evidence is found and the location noted on the sketch. This procedure is quite simple. If the evidence is found on the hands, for example, merely trace your own hand (right or left, depending on which hand of the suspect evidence is found) and indicate on the sketch where this evidence is located. The same procedure, without tracing, can be employed for the face and other parts of the body. Use a simple line drawing of the body part concerned, with appropriate notations.
4. The material should be collected in a manner that preserves its value (Figure 5.39 and Figure 5.40).

Release of the Scene

The decision to release the scene should be carefully considered. Obviously, the problem with releasing the scene prematurely is that soon thereafter information may come forth

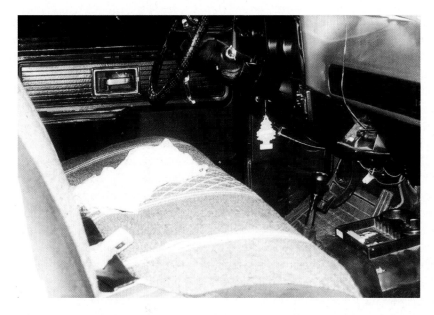

Figure 5.39 Proper vehicle search. This is a photograph of the truck before the search. (Photo courtesy of Chief Criminal Deputy Robin Wagg, Douglas County, Washington, Sheriff's Department.)

Figure 5.40 Proper vehicle search. A photo of the truck taken after the search. Valuable trace evidence was recovered. (Photo courtesy of Chief Criminal Deputy Robin Wagg, Douglas County, Washington, Sheriff's Department.

that would have required different photos or searching for and collection of other items. The scene should never be released before the initial canvass is completed, all the known witnesses interviewed, and the suspect in custody questioned fully. In some cases, it may be necessary to secure the scene and post a guard pending interview of witnesses who cannot be immediately located or, in other instances, to hold the scene until completion of the autopsy. This may not always be practical, but it is a recommended procedure in case additional examinations or searches are necessary as a result of information obtained during autopsy. Of course, if the autopsy is being conducted while the investigators are still at the scene, any such additional information can be immediately communicated to the chief investigator at the scene. Autopsy findings should always be made available to the homicide investigators as soon as possible to help them in their investigation and in questioning witnesses.

Before releasing the scene, the chief investigator should remember that any good defense attorney will visit the crime scene at his first opportunity. From this inspection, he will be able to gauge the nature, character, and extent of the investigation at the scene. He will be alert to things that may have been overlooked; to areas that have been dusted and not dusted; to the shape, pattern, and location of blood and other stains; to flash bulbs, film packs, and other debris that the investigators may have carelessly left at the scene. During police activities at the scene, the chief investigator should see that all waste materials from the lab work and photography are deposited in one container in a location that will not interfere with other activities, and that this container is removed before the scene is released.

The detective supervisor or chief investigator would do well to check over the entire crime scene from the point of view of the defense attorney before releasing it. Before abandoning the scene and securing it against reentry, make sure that you have all of your equipment and notes, including any portable radios and/or cell phones (that seem to have a way of disappearing at crime scenes). It would be embarrassing if you had to reenter the recently secured crime scene to retrieve something that was left behind. Especially in view of what an inquisitive defense attorney might suggest was your reason for returning to the scene after the crime scene was processed.

The Search Process

The search of the homicide or rape scene and the process of retrieving evidence from the body of the victim is the most important phase of the sexual assault investigation conducted at the scene and/or hospital. It begins with a two-fold purpose:

1. The complete documentation of events. Photographs (both black and white and color) and/or videotape, as well as crime scene sketches, should be accomplished prior to any other police procedures at the scene.
2. A careful and complete search conducted for any forensic materials and other evidence that might provide a clue to the identity of the killer.

Sex-Related Crime Scene Checklist

- Physical evidence in the form of seminal fluid must be collected as soon as possible before it is lost or destroyed. Samples can be allowed to air dry naturally or you can use a hair dryer on low speed. Wet samples can be drawn into an eyedropper and should be placed in a sterile test tube. Dry stains will have a stiff, "starchy" texture. If on clothing, submit the entire article, being careful not to break or contaminate the stained area. **Consider DNA testing technique requirements.**

- Blood (wet) should be collected using an eyedropper and transferred to a sterile container. The blood can be put into a test tube with EDTA (ethylenediaminetet-raacetic acid), an anticoagulant, and refrigerated. Small amounts can be collected using 100% cotton swab, #8 cotton thread, or gauze pad. Allow swab to air dry and place in sterile container. **Consider DNA testing techniques.**
- Blood stain, spittle, and hair (including pubic combings) should be obtained at the scene, properly packaged, and forward to lab. **Consider DNA testing techniques.**
- Trace evidence found on the victim and/or on the victim's clothing should be collected. Search for hair, fibers, and other microscopic evidence. Use forceps, a vacuum cleaner fitted with an inline canister attachment in the hose, or use tape. The best method to not contaminate samples is to use tape and forceps.
- Bruises and marks on the victim, including the presence of sadistic injuries, should be noted and documented in the investigative notes.
- Urine or feces may be left at the scene by the assailant. This evidence should be recorded and collected. Urine can be removed by eyedropper or gauze. Place in a sterile test tube or other container. If on clothing, submit entire article. **DNA testing can be performed on urine.**
- Fingernail scrapings should be obtained for an analysis of any blood, skin, or hair from the perpetrator. **Consider DNA testing technique.**
- Confer with the medical examiner and assure that specimens are taken from the body (e.g., hair from various areas of the body). A separate comb should be used for each area.
- In addition, vaginal washings, as well as anal, nasal, and oral swabs, should be requested for serological evaluation and examination. **Consider DNA testing technique.**
- Examine the scene for evidence of a struggle. The presence of torn clothing, missing buttons, ripped textiles, marks on the ground or floor, and blood splatters must all be photographed, documented, and collected as evidence.
- Homicides involving mutilation may yield clues, such as style of attack, the type of weapon used, the amount and location of mutilation, the position of the body. These items should be recorded.
- If a suspect has been taken into custody, his or her clothing should be taken and an examination conducted for any physical evidence. Examine for hairs and fibers.
- Each piece of evidence should be packaged in a separate container in order to prevent cross contamination.
- The suspect's body should be examined for any fingernail scratches, bite marks, or other indications of a violent struggle. Penile swabs for suspect offenders should be conducted to collect blood, epithelial cells, and any other evidentiary materials.
- Hair and blood samples should be obtained. **(Assure that any such samples are obtained legally.)**

- The body should be examined for the presence of bite mark evidence. Collect and record:
    - Saliva washing of the bite mark area for blood grouping and DNA. Use 100% cotton dampened in distilled water. *Important:* Obtain a control sample from another area of the body.
    - Photograph the bite mark. Obtain both black and white and color photos in case color photos are not allowed. Use a rule of measure and obtain an anatomical landmark.
    - Casting (if possible); use dental materials.

In sex-related homicide cases, basic evidence collection procedures acquire an increased importance. Human behavior patterns and psychosexual activities, not generally amenable to ordinary collection techniques, become additional factors to consider in determining the reason and motive for the killing. Practical experience in homicide investigation coupled with an understanding of human behavior patterns and human sexuality are important prerequisites in analyzing these types of cases.

The Investigative Checklist

The homicide detective faces a monumental task at the crime scene. A multitude of duties must be performed, and each event needs to be documented according to a routine procedure. This procedure is necessary so that valuable information or observations are not overlooked. Although each homicide is distinctive and unique, certain basic steps need to be pursued at all crime scenes. This investigative checklist is designed to be used by detectives involved in the investigation of sudden and violent death. Although extensive, it is not all inclusive. The investigator is advised simply to utilize this checklist as a guide to refresh the memory.

Remember: The fundamental rule in homicide investigation is the documentation of events in the investigator's notebook.

Documentation of the Initial Report

Initial Receipt of Information
- ☐ Record date and time of initial report.
- ☐ Record method of transmission — report received by.
- ☐ Record reporting party — officer, dispatcher, etc.
- ☐ Record complete details.

Arrival at the Homicide — Death Scene
- ☐ Record exact time of arrival.
- ☐ Record the exact address of the crime scene.
- ☐ Record outside weather/temperature conditions.
- ☐ Record outside lighting conditions.
- ☐ Interview the first officer and other police personnel at the scene to determine the sequence of events since their arrival.

- ☐ Note crime discovered by, date and time of initial call, complete details of initial police report.
- ☐ Determine the scope of the patrol officer's initial investigation at the scene:
  - ☐ Protection of the crime scene
  - ☐ Notifications, alarms, teletypes
  - ☐ Preliminary investigative results
- ☐ Record persons present at the scene:
  - ☐ Police officers and law enforcement personnel
  - ☐ Ambulance and/or emergency personnel
  - ☐ Family and/or relatives and/or friends of victim
  - ☐ Witnesses — including persons detained by patrol
    - ☐ Keep witnesses separated.
    - ☐ Provide for witness security and availability.

Preliminary Inspection of the Body at the Crime Scene

- ☐ Record victim pedigree, name and address if known (includes sex, race, and age).
- ☐ Record location of the victim: description of body and scene.
  - ☐ Have the patrol officer escort you through the scene to the body using same path used by responding police.
- ☐ Personally determine and verify death.
- ☐ Note condition of the body.
- ☐ Ascertain whether any suspects are in custody. (See "The Suspect in Custody" procedure.)
- ☐ Are there any additional victims?
  - ☐ Is this a multiple murder? (If "yes," establish separate case numbers and provide for additional documentation.)
- ☐ Officially assign investigator to case.
- ☐ If identity of victim is known, get a background check.

Implementing Crime Scene Control Procedures

- ☐ Determine the scope of the general crime scene — assessment.
- ☐ Make determination of police legal status in crime scene.
- ☐ Take preliminary photographs with an Instamatic, Polaroid, or digital camera to "freeze" the crime scene and provide for review by additional investigators as they arrive at the scene. (Polaroid or digital photos are preferred for immediate viewing.)
- ☐ Stabilize the scene by identifying and establishing perimeters.
  - ☐ If crime scene was not established by patrol, secure and protect the scene by isolation — ropes, barriers, etc.
  - ☐ Establish outside and inside perimeters — only authorized personnel allowed within respective perimeters.
  - ☐ Remember, the two-crime-scenes theory — the *general area* for police and other official personnel at the scene and the *forensic area* where the body as well as any other evidence may be located.

☐ Assign patrol officers as needed to safeguard scene effectively.
☐ Update and expand crime scene protection as necessary.
☐ Is this a *multiple scene*? Are there additional areas to protect?
☐ Establish a single path of entry and exit to the crime scene.
☐ Implement procedures to safeguard all evidence found at the scene.

Initiating a Crime Scene Log

☐ Assign an officer to obtain the names of all police and emergency personnel who responded to the original call.
☐ Assign an officer to record the names of all personnel and civilians involved in the investigation at the crime scene.
☐ Allow no entry to the crime scene except by authorized personnel involved in the official investigation.
☐ Record arrival/departure times of all officials. This includes the ME or coroner, state's attorney, crime scene technicians, etc.
☐ This crime scene log should be delivered to detectives upon release of the crime scene.

Establishing a Policy for Crime Scene Integrity

☐ Make a determination relative to obtaining a search warrant prior to any processing of the crime scene.
☐ Coordinate activities at the scene and direct investigators by fixing responsibility for the performance of certain duties.
☐ Do not touch, move, or alter anything at the scene until full documentation has been completed (observe, describe, record).
☐ Record any alterations to the crime scene that were made as a matter of investigative necessity or emergency police response.
  ☐ Lights turned on or off?
  ☐ Doors opened, closed, locked, or unlocked?
  ☐ Body moved or body cut down?
  ☐ Windows opened, closed, locked, or unlocked?
  ☐ Names of all parties who moved the body prior to and during the police presence at the scene.
  ☐ Any furniture moved or anything touched?
  ☐ Gas turned on or off? Appliances turned on or off?
  ☐ If vehicle is involved, is engine on or off? Is the motor cold, cool, warm, or hot?
☐ Do not use any telephones located inside the crime scene.
  ☐ Does the telephone have an answer machine or message capability? *Check messages.* Check the last number redial/listen to messages. Make recording/ seal original tape.
  ☐ Does the deceased have a beeper? *Check messages.* Check the last number redial/listen to messages. Make recording/seal any original recordings.
  ☐ Does the deceased have voice mail? *Check messages.* Check the last number and listen to any messages or check the answering service. Take recordings/ seal original tapes and document.

- ☐ Is there a computer at the crime scene? Check system — last date of use, documents, disks, hard drive. Consider forensic computer analysis.
  - ☐ Check computer for answering machine–message modem. *Check messages, e-mail, etc.*
- ☐ Is there a camera at the crime scene? Process and check film and/or diskettes. Search for photographs — deceased, friends, activities, etc.
- ☐ Is there a VCR? Check all tapes. Check tape in machine. Note rentals, personal tapes, etc. — secure for review.
- ☐ Implement procedures to protect the evidence from damage by weather or exposure, as well as the presence of police personnel.
- ☐ Do not allow smoking by anyone in the crime scene.
- ☐ Do not turn water on or off, do not flush toilets, do not use any facility in the scene.
- ☐ Record condition of lights, lamps, and electric appliances such as televisions, radios, and clocks.

Establishing a Command Post or Temporary Headquarters

- ☐ Select a location out of the central crime scene, preferably a location with two phones, one for outgoing and one for incoming telephone calls. Utilize cell phones for general communications. Use the land lines for security.
- ☐ Notify communications and/or the station house of the telephone numbers of the command post as well as those of personnel at the scene to facilitate communications among the various units concerned.
- ☐ Make notifications as necessary from this location to
  - ☐ Crime scene technicians
  - ☐ Medical examiner/coroner or representatives
  - ☐ Additional investigators or police personnel
  - ☐ Prosecutor/district attorney/solicitor's office

Emergency Medical Service (EMS) and Ambulance Personnel

- ☐ If ambulance or EMS personnel were present at the scene before the investigator's arrival, determine whether the crew or anyone else moved the body or any other items within the crime scene. If yes, record the following:
  - ☐ When the alterations were made
  - ☐ Purpose of the movement
  - ☐ Persons who made the altercations
  - ☐ The time of death as pronounced by the ambulance or paramedic crew
    - ☐ Consider taking fingerprints of the crew members if they touched or handled items in the crime scene.
    - ☐ Interview the EMS or ambulance crew for details of any action taken as well as their observations.

Initiating a Canvass

- ☐ Initiate a canvass of the immediate area by assigning sufficient personnel to locate any witnesses or persons who may have information about the homicide or death.
- ☐ Assign a supervisor or coordinator to organize the canvass.

- [ ] Use canvass control sheets.
- [ ] Assure that canvassers are provided with all information from the investigation and scene so they may properly solicit information from prospective witnesses. (This includes photos of the deceased taken in life, if available.)
- [ ] Have investigators check and record registration numbers of vehicles in the immediate area.
- [ ] Require official reports from canvassers indicating:
  - [ ] Negative locations (locations with no results).
  - [ ] Locations that have been canvassed, indicating the number of persons residing there to include possible visitors as well as residents.
  - [ ] Positive locations for possible follow-up and reinterview.
  - [ ] Information relating to the event being canvassed.
- [ ] Utilize the canvass questionnaire forms.
- [ ] *Note*: Attempt to conduct further canvasses on the same day of the week as the incident, at approximately the same time of the incident, in order to cover the behavioral patterns of persons to be canvassed.

Weapons

If a weapon is discovered, do the following:

- [ ] Do not attempt to unload firearm.
- [ ] Record where the weapon is located.
- [ ] Safeguard the weapon for forensic examination (this includes not only ballistics, but also operability).
- [ ] Have the weapon photographed before further examination.
- [ ] If weapon is a firearm, consider an examination of the suspect's hands for residue analysis (GSR) testing.
- [ ] Determine the origin of the weapon. (Does it come from the premises? Does it belong to the deceased, etc.?)
- [ ] Determine whether any blood or any other trace evidence is on the weapon.

The Suspect in Custody

- [ ] Remember that the suspect is part of the crime scene — "theory of transfer and exchange."
- [ ] If the suspect is arrested and present at the scene, make sure that he or she is immediately removed from the crime scene and not returned to the scene unless the clothing of the suspect is secured. This procedure is necessary to prevent crime scene contamination.
- [ ] Safeguard all evidence found on the suspect, including blood, weapons, debris, soil, proceeds of crime, etc.
- [ ] Ensure that the suspect does not wash his or her hands or engage in any conduct which may alter or destroy evidence.
- [ ] Note any injuries to the suspect and record them with black-and-white film with rule of measure included as well as color film indicating these injuries or marks with appropriate anatomical reference photographs.
- [ ] Record any spontaneous statements made by the suspect.

☐ Do not permit any conversation between the suspect and any other parties present.

☐ Guard your investigative conversations in the presence of the suspect.

Suspect in Custody: Interrogation at the Scene

If the suspect is in custody at the scene and circumstances indicate that immediate interrogation of the subject would be beneficial to the investigation, the following steps should be taken:

☐ Advise the suspect of his or her rights under the Miranda ruling prior to any custodial interrogation. (This should be done from a Miranda rights card or Miranda form.)

☐ Determine whether the suspect fully understands his or her rights.

☐ Obtain an intelligent waiver of these rights from the suspect prior to any questioning.

☐ Document this procedure in the investigative notebook.

☐ Allow the suspect to make a full statement.

☐ Reduce this statement to writing and have the suspect sign it.

☐ Keep the suspect isolated at all times from other suspects, witnesses, prisoners, and any personnel not connected with the investigation.

☐ Advise any officers transporting the suspect not to engage the suspect in any conversation or questioning. However, if the suspect makes any statement during transport, the officers should document this information.

☐ If the suspect is brought to the police station, he or she should be placed in a separate holding cell.

☐ Alibi statements should be documented and recorded in the investigator's notebook.

☐ Any self-serving statements should also be recorded and documented, in the event the suspect later changes his or her story.

A.D.A.P.T.

☐ Before beginning process, make an assessment regarding search warrant requirements.

☐ The crime scene search should not be undertaken until all photographs, sketches, measurements, dusting for prints, and written documentation have been completed except for emergency situations.

Documentation of Crime Scene Photographs

☐ Date and time photos are taken

☐ Exact location of photographs

☐ Description of item photographed

☐ Compass direction (north, south, east, or west)

☐ Focus distance

☐ Type of film and camera used

☐ Lights and weather conditions

☐ Number of exposures

- [ ] Identification of photographer
- [ ] Eliminate extraneous objects, including any police equipment.
- [ ] Show the relationship of the scene to its surroundings.
  - [ ] Outdoor scenes — fixed objects as they relate to the scene from eye level
  - [ ] Indoor scenes — objects in the room such as doors or windows to "fix" the body to the crime scene

Recommended Crime Scene Photographs

- [ ] The entire location where the homicide took place
- [ ] Contiguous areas and sites
- [ ] The crowd or any bystanders — surreptitiously
  - [ ] Suspect and/or witnesses, if applicable
  - [ ] Suspect's clothing and shoes
- [ ] Any injuries (body, face, hands, etc.)
- [ ] Take photos from the general to the specific.
- [ ] Front entrance of building
- [ ] Entrance to the room or apartment where the deceased is found
- [ ] Two full-body views
- [ ] A general view of the body and crime scene
- [ ] A close-up shot of the body
- [ ] Any visible wounds
- [ ] If the body has been removed, the body's original location
- [ ] Possible entrance or escape routes used
- [ ] Areas where any force was used for entry or exit
- [ ] Area and close-up views of any physical evidence such as bloodstains, weapons, shell casings, hairs, fibers
- [ ] Fingerprints (plastic, bloodstained, and latents) — as well as any "lifts"
- [ ] After the body has been moved, additional photos should be taken of
  - [ ] Areas beneath the body
  - [ ] Any additional evidence found beneath the body
- [ ] Note: Do not add any chalk marks or markers prior to taking the original crime scene photographs. Markers can be added later for close-up shots.

The Crime Scene Sketch

- [ ] Make a simple line drawing of the crime scene in the investigative notebook or on a separate sheet of paper. The following information should be included
  - [ ] Measurements and distance
  - [ ] A legend to identify any object or articles in scene
  - [ ] A scale to depict measurements used
  - [ ] A title block consisting of
    - [ ] Name and title of sketcher
    - [ ] Date and time the sketch was made
    - [ ] Classification of crime
    - [ ] Identification of victim
    - [ ] Agency's case number
    - [ ] Names of any persons assisting in taking measurements
    - [ ] Precise address of the location sketched and compass north

The Crime Scene Search

- ☐ Establish the perimeters of the crime scene and document this location by crime scene photographs and sketches, including written documentation.
- ☐ Reconstruct aspects of the crime in formulating the search.
- ☐ Ascertain the legal basis for the search prior to any seizure of evidence.
- ☐ Visibly locate any physical evidence and determine which evidence should be gathered before any destruction or alteration takes place.
- ☐ Establish the method of search based on your investigative theory, size of the area to be searched, and any other factors that arise while conducting this phase of the inquiry.
- ☐ Areas that should be processed include
  - ☐ The point of entry
  - ☐ The escape route
  - ☐ The suspect and his or her clothing, making note of injuries
  - ☐ The location of any physical evidence or weapons
  - ☐ A vehicle used in the crime
  - ☐ The suspect's residence
  - ☐ The location where the actual assault leading to death took place
  - ☐ The location from which the body was moved

Dusting for Fingerprints

- ☐ The following areas should be processed for latent prints:
  - ☐ Areas of entry and exit
  - ☐ Weapons or objects which were apparently handled
  - ☐ Door handles
  - ☐ Telephone instruments
  - ☐ Windows
  - ☐ Glasses
  - ☐ Light switches
  - ☐ Newly damaged areas
  - ☐ Objects that may have caused death
    - ☐ Objects missing from their original location
- ☐ Note that some areas to be processed may require the use of chemical reagents such as fluorscein, luminol, ninhydrin, amido black, tetramethylbenzidine, phenolphtalin, cynoacrylate in order to obtain latent print evidence. Consider these options before dusting.

Description of the Deceased

- ☐ A complete description of the body should be documented in the investigator's notes, including the following information:
  - ☐ The position of the body
  - ☐ Sex
  - ☐ Race
  - ☐ Appearance
  - ☐ Age
  - ☐ Build
  - ☐ Color of hair

- [ ] Description of clothing
- [ ] Presence or absence of any jewelry
- [ ] Evidence of any injuries (bruises, bite marks, wounds, etc.)
- [ ] Condition of the body:
  - [ ] Livor mortis
  - [ ] Rigor mortis
  - [ ] Decomposition (describe in detail)
  - [ ] Blood, wet or dry
  - [ ] Insect activity
  - [ ] Putrefaction
- [ ] Is the condition of the body consistent with known facts?
- [ ] Note and record the condition of the victim's hands for signs of evidence (defense marks, hairs, fibers, etc.).
- [ ] Note and record any creases and folds on victim's clothing.
- [ ] What is the condition of the victim's pockets?
- [ ] Examine the immediate area surrounding the body for evidence.
- [ ] Record the direction and size of any bloodstains.
- [ ] Check the clothing and shoes for any trace evidence.

Preliminary Medical Examination at the Scene

- [ ] Record the time of arrival of the coroner/medical examiner.
- [ ] Obtain a preliminary estimate on the time of death.
- [ ] Document the apparent cause of death after conferring with the medical examiner/coroner.
- [ ] Are injuries consistent with the suspected weapon involved?
- [ ] Release of the body:
  - [ ] Use a new or laundered sheet to wrap body before removal.
  - [ ] Bag the hands of the victim with paper bags (not plastic) to preserve any trace evidence under fingernails.

Victim — Hospital Information

- [ ] If victim was removed to hospital, dispatch investigators, if available, or patrol unit to obtain the following information:
  - [ ] Name, address, and phone number of the hospital
  - [ ] Name, address, and phone of attending doctor
  - [ ] Name of officer interviewing doctor
  - [ ] Doctor's diagnosis
  - [ ] If pronounced dead, get time and date.
  - [ ] If admitted at hospital, get time and date.
  - [ ] Was the victim interviewed — yes or no?
    - [ ] Name of officer conducting interview
    - [ ] Dying declaration?
      - [ ] Obtain witnesses, preferably doctor or nurse.
- [ ] Names, addresses, phone numbers of all emergency room and hospital personnel involved in treatment.
- [ ] Names, addresses, phone numbers of all ambulance or paramedic personnel involved in emergency and transport.

☐ Names, addresses, phone numbers of anyone who accompanied victim to hospital.
☐ For evidence obtained and/or impounded at hospital:
    ☐ Establish chain of custody — identity of person at hospital who impounded any evidence.
    ☐ Obtain for forensic examination any clothing worn by the deceased.
☐ Names of all police personnel at hospital.

Evidence Process and Control Procedures

☐ Ensure that all evidence is properly marked and packaged.
☐ Establish a chain of custody.
☐ Designate a "searching officer" to take charge of all evidence.
☐ Record the name and unit designation of all persons participating in the homicide crime scene search.
☐ Photograph all evidence in its original position (*in situ*).
☐ Record the position and location of all evidence on the crime scene sketch and in the investigative notebook.
☐ Record the name of any officer or person discovering any physical evidence and the location where it was recovered.
☐ Measure the location of any evidence found from two separate fixed points of reference.
☐ Note regarding weapons:
    ☐ Are any shell casings present?
    ☐ Are any bullet holes or spent rounds present?
    ☐ Determine how many shots were fired.
    ☐ What is the position of bullets in the revolver (record by diagram)?
    ☐ Is the safety on or off?
    ☐ Is the firearm loaded or unloaded? Are any bullets in the chamber?
☐ Are wounds consistent with the weapon suspected?
☐ Is any trace evidence on the weapon?

Release of the Homicide Crime Scene

This is a critical decision. Authorities should hold onto the crime scene as long as possible in the event that further processing, investigation, or review becomes necessary as additional information becomes available.

☐ Do not release the scene prior to the completion of the canvass and any interviews of witnesses or interrogation of suspects.
☐ Have the deceased's mailbox searched and note the date of any mail found there. Check with post office for undelivered mail and record all information.
☐ Note the telephone numbers of any phones at the scene.
☐ If the scene is to be abandoned temporarily during certain investigative procedures, provide for continued crime scene protection during the absence of investigators. The assignment of patrol officers to assist detectives at the crime scene is highly recommended.
☐ Before leaving the crime scene, look over the entire area from the perspective of the defense counsel to make sure you have covered all the bases.

☐ Gather all materials used in the crime scene processing, such as film packs, film containers, Polaroid negatives, notes, tape, evidence containers.
    ☐ Cause these materials to be removed from the scene for destruction and disposal at another location.
    ☐ Use large plastic garbage bags at the crime scene for disposal of materials generated during the search and dispose of at another location.

It is important to note that the extent of the crime scene search can be ascertained by examination of these types of materials if they are left behind at the crime scene by the authorities.

Suicide Investigation — Investigative Considerations

Important note: Most suicides occur as a result of depression. Therefore, the investigator should concentrate part of the inquiry into the clinical component of the event. However, keep in mind that some suicides are conscious decisions on the part of the victim and the particular motive for the event may never be ascertained.

Evaluation of the Wounds
☐ Could the deceased have caused the injuries and death?
☐ Was the person physically able to accomplish the act?
☐ Are the wounds within reach of the deceased?
☐ Are the wounds grouped together?
☐ Is there more than one cause of death?
☐ Describe the nature and position of the injuries.
☐ Are there any hesitation marks?

Psychological State of the Victim
☐ Obtain background of the victim from family and friends, including medical as well as social information.
☐ Were there any warning signs indicated by the victim? (Psychological autopsy is a collaborative procedure involving law enforcement and mental health experts who attempt to determine the state of mind of a person prior to the fatal act. By examining the victim's lifestyle and interviewing the victim's friends and relatives, they determine whether the death was accidental or involved suicide.)
☐ Were there any recent deaths in the family?
☐ Is there any indication of a recent upset or stress?
☐ Did the victim leave any notes?
    ☐ Request a sample of the victim's handwriting for a comparison analysis with any note found at scene.
    ☐ Request a sample of the victim's handwriting for an analysis in case a note is later discovered.
☐ Did the deceased have any close personal relationships, any close friends, etc.?
    ☐ Interview these persons as soon as possible.
☐ Conduct an immediate search of deceased's home and/or place of business for investigative data.

Any Prior Mental Disease or Defect
- ☐ Has the deceased been under any professional treatment?
- ☐ Had the deceased attempted suicide in the past?
- ☐ Has anyone in the family committed suicide?
- ☐ Was the deceased a heavy drinker?
- ☐ Was the deceased on any medication?
- ☐ Was there a history of drug abuse?

Recognized Warning Signs in Suicides
- ☐ A change in sleeping habits — sleeping more than usual or staying up much later — followed by sadness
- ☐ A change in eating habits — weight loss or lack of appetite
- ☐ A lack of interest in sex — a loss of the sex drive
- ☐ A sudden drop in grades or school attendance — young people
- ☐ A loss of interest in work — adults
- ☐ Loss of interest in favorite activities, hobbies, or sports
- ☐ Loss of interest in friends, family, etc. — isolation
- ☐ A preoccupation with death or an unusual interest in art or music dealing with death: teenagers — "heavy metal," rock, etc.; adults — preoccupation with death and afterlife
- ☐ Loss of interest in personal hygiene and appearance
- ☐ Involvement with drugs, including an abuse of alcohol

Extreme Danger Signs in Suicides
- ☐ Suddenly becoming cheerful or calm after a depression. A sudden euphoria or burst of activity could mean that the person has resolved the inner conflict by deciding to take his or her life. The decision has been made.
- ☐ Giving away prized possessions
- ☐ Speaking of life in the past tense — for example, saying, "I've loved you" or "You've been a good mother"

Autoerotic Fatalities (Accidental Asphyxia)

These are deaths that result during solo sex-related activities.

Investigative Considerations
- ☐ Is the victim nude or sexually exposed?
- ☐ If the victim is a male, is he dressed in feminine attire?
- ☐ Is there evidence of masturbatory activity?
- ☐ Are sexually stimulating paraphernalia present (vibrators, dildos, other sexual fantasy aids, pornography, etc.)?
- ☐ Is bondage present (ropes, chains, blindfolds, gags, etc.)?
- ☐ Are the restraints interconnected?
- ☐ Is there protective padding between the ligature and neck?
- ☐ Is there evidence of infibulation?
- ☐ Is there evidence of fantasy (erotic literature, diaries, fantasy drawings, etc.) or fetishism?

☐ Are any mirrors or other reflective devices present?
☐ Is the suspension point within the reach of the victim?
☐ Is there evidence of prior such activities (abrasions or rope burns on the suspension point, photographs, etc.)?
☐ Is there a positioned camera?
☐ Does the victim possess literature dealing with bondage, escapology, or knots?
☐ Is there any indication of suicidal intent?

References

Flippo v. West Virginia, 98 US 8770, 1999.
Gardner, R.M. *Practical Crime Scene Processing and Investigation*, CRC Press, Boca Raton, FL, 2005.
Gardner, R.M. and T. Bevel. *Practical Crime Scene Analysis and Reconstruction*, CRC Press, Boca Raton, FL, 2009.
Geberth, V.J., *Practical Homicide Investigation: Tactics, Procedures, and Forensic Techniques*, 4th ed., CRC Press, Boca Raton, FL, 2006.
Lee, H., *Crime Scene Investigation*, Central Police University Press, Taiwan, 1994.
Lee, H., *Crime Scene Handbook,* Academic Press, San Diego, CA, 2001.
Mincey v. Arizona, 437 US 385, 1978.
Thomas, S. and D. Davis. *JonBenét: Inside the Ramsey Murder Investigation*, St. Martins Press, New York, 2000.
Thompson v. Louisiana, 469 US 17, 1984.

Selected Readings

Bevel, T. and R. Gardner. *Bloodstain Pattern Analysis with Introduction to Crime Scene Reconstruction*, 3rd ed., CRC Press, Boca Raton, FL, 2008.
Geberth, V.J., Missteps at the homicide crime scene, *Journal of Professional Investigators*, 22 (3), 2008.
Geberth, V.J., 10 Most common errors in death investigations: Part 1. *Law and Order Magazine*, 55 (11), November 2007.
Geberth, V.J., 10 Most common errors in death investigations: Part 2. *Law and Order Magazine*, 56 (1), January 2008.
Guandolo, V., Munchausen syndrome by proxy: An outpatient challenge, *Pediatrics*, 75 (3), 526–530, 1985.
Meadow, R., Munchausen syndrome by proxy, *Archives of Disease in Childhood*, 57, 92–98, 1982.

Collection and Preservation of Physical Evidence in Sex-Related Death Investigations

6

Introduction

The recovery and collection of evidence in sex-related homicide and death investigations is of paramount importance to the overall investigation. Although the general principles of collection, chain of custody, and preservation remain the same, there are unique aspects to the types of evidence encountered in sex-related events. Sex-related homicides frequently result in various kinds of personal evidence including body fluids, such as semen, sperm, blood, and saliva, as well as hairs and fibers and other microscopic evidence, which may be lost or contaminated due to any number of variables ranging from the dynamics of the event and the environment of the scene to the actions of police personnel at the scene. This chapter will focus on the practical application of the collection, chain of custody, and preservation of evidence in sex-related homicide and death investigations.*

General Types of Evidence

Physical evidence
Testimonial evidence
Documentary evidence
Behavioral evidence

In *Practical Homicide Investigation* (Geberth, 2006), each of these general types of evidence become crucial in the identification, apprehension, and subsequent prosecution of offenders. However, the investigator should appreciate the nature of physical evidence

Physical Evidence

Physical evidence is any tangible article, small or large, that tends to prove or disprove a point in question. It may be used to:

---

* The techniques of collection presented in this chapter are based on the recommendations of Dr. Robert C. Shaler, who holds an MS and PhD in biochemistry from Pennsylvania State University. Dr. Shaler is currently at Penn State, has lectured at various universities and forensic symposia, and has published several articles related to forensic science. The author recommends the following textbooks for further and more in-depth information on criminalistics and forensic science: Lee, H., T. Palmbach, and M.T. Miller, *Henry Lee's Crime Scene Handbook*, Academic Press, San Diego, CA, 2001; R. Saferstein, *Criminalistics: An Introduction to Forensic Science*, 6th ed. Prentice-Hall, Englewood Cliffs, NJ; and Gardner, R.M. and T. Bevel, *Practical Crime Scene Analysis and Reconstruction*, CRC Press, Boca Raton, FL, 2009.

Reconstruct the crime
Identify the participants
Confirm or discredit an alibi

The proper collection and disposition of physical or trace evidence from the crime scene and the body of the deceased is of the utmost importance to the investigation and eventual court presentation. The evidence must have been obtained legally in order for it to be admissible. Therefore, it is imperative that both the legal authority to collect the evidence and the proper collection techniques be considered prior to the actual collection of the evidence.

Classifications of Physical Evidence

Class Evidence

Class evidence is that which cannot be forensically identified with a specific source to the exclusion of all others. Examples are non-DNA analyses of

Blood	Soil
Semen	Glass*
Saliva	Wood
Hair	Plant materials
Fibers	Animal materials

Individualistic Evidence

Individualistic evidence is evidence that can be positively and forensically identified with a specific source to the exclusion of all other sources. Examples are DNA analyses of

Body fluids and hair
Latent prints
Fracture matches
Bite marks
Specific handwriting

Types of Physical Evidence

Transient Evidence

Transient evidence is temporary in nature. Examples include odors, temperature, imprints, indentations in soft or changing materials (butter, wet sand, snow, or mud), and markings, i.e., lividity, blood spatters on moveable objects (Figure 6.1 and Figure 6.2).

---

* In certain instances, glass can now be positively and forensically identified with a specific source. Lasers zap the glass fragments, which evaporate the particles into smoke. Then a gas sweeps the particles into a hot plasma that allows the examiner to see a unique chemical makeup. The technique is so precise that some automobile glass particles can be traced to a specific manufacturer. For further information, call (515) 296-6372 or see the Web site: www.MFRC.ameslab.gov.

Figure 6.1 Transient evidence. License plate impression in snow. (Photo courtesy of the author.)

Figure 6.2 Impression evidence. In this view, the reverse impression of the license plate indicating four numbers, 5720, is evident. (Photo courtesy of the author.)

Pattern Evidence

Pattern evidence is produced by contact: blood splatter, glass fracture patterns, fire burn patterns, furniture position patterns, projectile trajectory, tire marks, modus operandi (MO), clothing or article patterns, powder residue patterns.

Conditional Evidence

Conditional evidence is caused by an action or event: lighting conditions at scene; odor, color, direction of smoke; flame (color, direction, temperature); location of evidence in relation to the body; vehicle (locked or unlocked, lights on or off, window open or closed, radio on or off, mileage).

Transfer Evidence

Transfer evidence is generally produced by physical contact of persons or objects or between persons or objects: The Linkage Concept.

Trace and Transfer Evidence   Practically speaking, there are two types of transfer evidence: trace transfer and pattern transfer evidence. Examples of commonly encountered trace transfer evidence include hair, fibers, blood, semen, glass, and soil. Examples of pattern transfer evidence are imprint and impression evidence. Many times transfer evidence is a combination of trace and pattern components, such as bloody shoeprints, hair and fibers, greasy fingerprints, or fabric impressions.

There is a principle in homicide investigation that refers to a theoretical exchange between two objects that have been in contact with one another. This theory of *transfer* or *exchange* is based on Locard's "Exchange Principle." Edmond Locard, a Frenchman, who founded the University of Lyons' Institute of Criminalistics, believed that whenever two human beings came into contact, something from one was exchanged to the other, and vice versa. This exchange might involve hairs, fibers, dirt, dust, blood and other bodily fluids as well as skin cells, metallic residue, and other microscopic materials. In *Practical Homicide Investigation* (Geberth, 2006) Locard's principle is summed up as follows:

1. The perpetrator will take away traces of the victim and the scene.
2. The victim will retain traces of the perpetrator and may leave traces of himself on the perpetrator.
3. The perpetrator will leave behind traces of himself/herself at the scene.

The goal is to establish a link between the various facets of the crime scene, the victim, physical evidence, and the suspect. All of these components must be connected for the successful resolution of the case. The Linkage Concept rests on the principle of the *Theory of Transfer or Exchange*. **Remember**: *Anything* and *everything* may eventually become evidence.

Direct Transfer—A direct transfer occurs when materials are transferred from the original source to another person or object. An example would be a bleeding victim's blood found on the suspect or his clothing. Or, a latent fingerprint of the suspect discovered at the crime scene and/or the suspect's semen recovered from the victim.

Indirect Transfer—An indirect transfer occurs when trace evidence, which was directly transferred to one location, is then transferred again to another location. An example would be rug fibers from the crime scene, which had been transferred to the clothing of a victim, are then found in the suspect's car after he transported the body to the dumpsite.

Procedures for Collection of Evidence

In order to be introduced as physical evidence in a trial, an article must

Be properly identified
Show a proper "chain of custody"
Be material and relevant
Meet all legal requirements

The crime scene technician or crime scene investigator who is summoned to the scene should have operational supervision over gathering, collection, and marking of evidence for identification. However, the investigator assigned to the case is still in charge of the investigation and should be consulted prior to any evidence gathering or crime scene processing.

The proper collection and disposition of evidence will be accomplished if the following guidelines are adhered to:

1. Each piece of evidence should be marked (on the container or item as applicable) to show its original position and location. This information should also be recorded in the investigator's notebook.
2. Each article should be marked distinctively by the searching officer to identify the person who found the particular piece of evidence. In cases of small or fluid specimens, this marking is done on the container.
3. Each item should be described exactly and completely with the corresponding case numbers affixed and the date and time of collection indicated.
4. Each item should be packaged in a separate, clean, and properly sized container to prevent cross-contamination or damage.
5. Each package should be sealed to retain evidence and prevent any unauthorized handling.
6. Each piece of evidence should show proper disposition:
   a. Police department laboratory
   b. Property clerk's office
   c. FBI laboratory
7. Proper records should be kept regarding each piece of evidence showing chain of custody. These records should reflect any movement of the evidence from the point of origin to its final disposition.

Remember: Each item should be photographed before it is collected as evidence. These photos should include a long-range view to show the relationship of the object to its surroundings and a close-range view to show the actual item being collected. (See Chapter 6 in Geberth, 2006.)

Field Test Reagents

Tests for the Presence of Blood

Phenolphthalein (Kastel-Meyer)

This test is performed by rubbing a cotton swab that has been moistened in a saline solution on the suspected blood stain. A drop is added to the swab then a drop of hydrogen peroxide 3%. A positive reaction will turn the swab pink to red within 15 seconds

Leucomalachite Green (LMG)

This test is performed the same way as above. A positive reaction is indicated by a greenish-blue color that will appear almost immediately.

Luminol

This reagent is sprayed onto the object to be checked. However, it must be viewed in total darkness. A positive reaction will luminesce violet within 5 seconds (Figure 6.3 and Figure 6.4).

BlueStar™

This relatively newer reagent has extreme sensitivity and is sprayed onto the area of testing. It is visible to the naked eye in darkness. It lasts for several minutes and will luminesce to an intense blue color. The luminescence intensity is higher than luminol. It lasts longer and does not necessitate total darkness. It also does not prevent reliable DNA typing (high frequency) and can be sprayed several times. BlueStar kit tablets dissolve in sterile water (Figure 6.5 and Figure 6.6).

Figure 6.3 Murder scene that has been "cleaned up." This is the crime scene photo of the bedroom floor where a woman has been stabbed to death. Her husband dumped the body and then cleaned the bedroom. (Photo courtesy of the Honolulu Police Department's Scientific Investigation Section, Captain Gary A. Dias.)

Figure 6.4 Application of luminol. This is the same view as the proceeding photo after the application of luminol, which shows where the blood had pooled. (Photo courtesy of the Honolulu Police Department's Scientific Investigation Section, Captain Gary A. Dias.)

Figure 6.5 BlueStar™. Bathroom area where an assault and murder took place, before the application of BlueStar™. (Photo courtesy Detective Mark Czworniak, Chicago Police Department.)

Figure 6.6 Application of BlueStar™. Same area of the bathroom after the application of BlueStar. (Photo courtesy Detective Mark Czworniak, Chicago Police Department.)

Ortho-Tolidine

This test is performed by rubbing a cotton swab that has been moistened in a saline solution on the suspected blood stain. A drop is added to the swab, then a drop of hydrogen peroxide 3%. A positive reaction is indicated by an intense blue color.

Tetra-Methyl Benzidine (TMB)

Another in a series of presumptive tests that is specific for blood. TMB is an enhancement reagent. The TMB reacts with the heme in the blood.

Spray the surface lightly two to three times about 10 inches away from the surface. The bloody imprint pattern should turn a greenish-blue. Overspraying may give a very dark blue pattern and mask ridge patterns.

Hemaglow

This is a protein reactant that does not ordinarily react with household cleaners like luminol does. Hemaglow also glows brighter and can be photographed with a flat plane camera.

Leucocrystal Violet (LCV)

A new positive blood identifier that turns permanently violet when in contact with blood. Leucocrystal violet can be testified to in court as a blood identifier at the scene without further testing to identify the stain as blood.

Tests for the Presence of Body Fluids

Semen: Acid phosphatase tests
Saliva: Amylase tests
Urine: Creatinine, urea tests

Fecal matter: Urobilinogen
Gastric contents: Gastric acid

Pattern Enhancement Reagents

Protein Enhancement Reagents   Numerous methods of staining are used to develop or enhance blood-contaminated latent prints. These methods depend on staining the protein components of blood to form a visible impression.

Ninhydrin   Ninhydrin detects trace amounts of amino acids associated with body secretions. The amino acids are transferred with the sweat from the pores of a finger, palm, or the sole of a foot. Amino acids are easily absorbed into absorbent and partially absorbent surfaces, such as paper, unfinished wood, cardboard, leather.

Coomassie Brilliant Blue (R250)   Coomassie brilliant blue is a general protein that works well with bloodstains. Coomassie is a more sensitive, general protein stain than crystal violet stains.

Crystal (Gentian) Violet   Crystal violet works exceptionally well on adhesive surfaces, such as tapes.

Amido Black   This is a protein reactant, which is sprayed onto the suspected area. Naphthol, which is the amido black powder, is mixed with glacial acetic acid and methanol. The formula is to mix 2 grams naphthol, 100 ml glacial acetic acid, and 900 ml of methanol.

   Procedure—Set the prints with methanol then spray the area with amido black. Rinse with 100 ml glacial acetic acid and 900 ml of methanol. Rinse with water. Clean with Clorox® bleach (Figure 6.7).

Figure 6.7 Amido black. Latent palm prints of the suspect raised from the victim's left arm by Detective Conley who used amido black with methanol alcohol rinse. (Photo courtesy of Retired Detective Rheta Conley, Gastonia, North Carolina, Police Department.)

Fatty Acid Elements and Compounds Enhancement Reagents
   Iodine fuming
   Small particle reagent
   Superglue (Cyanoacrylate) fuming

(For further information on the use of any of these reagents as well as a more in-depth explanation of the proper laboratory procedures, see Lee et al., 2001.)

Method for Diagnosing Abrasions, Lacerations, and Other Skin Disruptions in the Perineum and Perianal Areas

According to Frederick T. Zugibe, chief medical examiner, Rockland County, New York, an excellent procedure in determining sexual assault injuries can be visualized by the application of toluidine blue in .01% solution and/or methylene blue or azure.

Toluidine stains ground substance or mucopolysaccharides, which are found in abrasions as well as other skin injuries. The intact skin will not stain, but injured skin will be visualized with the application of toluidine blue or methylene blue or azure. This test is extremely effective in child sexual abuse cases. It can also be administered by doctors in hospital emergency rooms, who treat live victims of sexual assault to document the presence of mucopolysaccharides. A simple color digital photo taken before and after the application produces excellent documentation of sexual abuse, which can be used in trial. Toluidine blue is applied with cotton or gauze to the area of suspected trauma. The excess is wiped off with KY® jelly or a similar substance. The stain will remain in the area of trauma (Figure 6.8 and Figure 6.9).

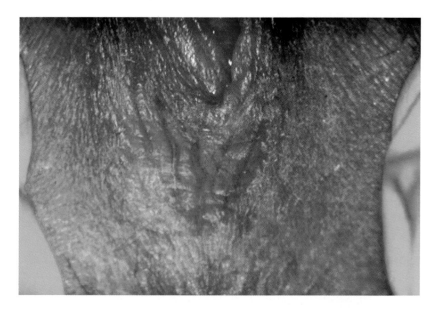

Figure 6.8 Toluidine blue. The perineum area of a homicide victim of a sexual assault. There are some visible lacerations present to the naked eye. (Photo courtesy of Tara Henry, Forensic Nurse, Anchorage, Alaska.)

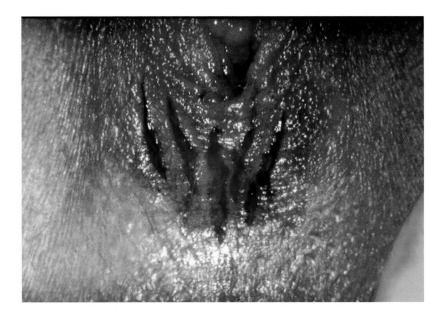

Figure 6.9 Toluidine blue. Note the purplish discoloration in the region of the vagina and perineum after the application of toluidine blue dye. Toluidine stains ground substance or mucopolysaccharides, which are found in abrasions as well as any other skin injuries. This photo shows that the application was positive for abrasive injuries in the perineal area. (Photo courtesy of Tara Henry, Forensic Nurse, Anchorage, Alaska.)

Collection of Specific Types of Evidence

The homicide investigator is usually confronted with the same general type of evidence in most murder investigations, such as blood, bullets, and fingerprints. The evidence ordinarily falls within three distinct categories: body materials, objects, and impressions.

This chapter will focus on the practical methods for collection of those types of evidence commonly found at the scenes of sex-related homicides. The more advanced and detailed methodologies have been purposefully omitted from this section because they are usually beyond the capability of the average investigator and are best performed by crime scene technicians and other experts who have been specially trained in forensic science techniques.

Body Fluids

Blood

Blood (Wet)
1. Large amounts or pools:
   a. Use an eyedropper or hypodermic syringe to collect the fluid and transfer to a sterile container (5 cc is sufficient for testing purposes).
   b. Transfer immediately to laboratory or refrigerate specimen. Generally, *do not freeze blood*. However, if the blood is to be shipped to a laboratory for DNA testing, it can be frozen for transport.

    c. In some instances, depending on the jurisdiction regulations, a chemical pre-servative, such as sodium azide or EDTA (ethylenediaminetetraacetic acid) can be used to prevent blood spoilage.

2. Small amounts of wet blood:
    a. Use a 100% cotton swab, #8 cotton thread, or gauze pad to collect specimen.
    b. Allow swab or gauze pad to air dry.
    c. Place in sterile test tube or other clean container.

Blood Stains (Dry)
1. Nonporous surface:
    a. If there is a sufficient amount of dry blood, it can be scraped from the surface with a clean razor blade or sterile scalpel. These scrapings should be saved into a sterile container.
2. Porous surface (fabric, unfinished wood, etc.):
    a. Collect and submit the article containing the stain to the laboratory as found.
    b. Wrap in separate and sterile container. If the article is too large or inappro-priate to transport, remove a portion of the material containing an adequate amount of the stain for transport to the laboratory for analysis.
3. Traces or smears that cannot be scraped into container:
    a. Moisten a 100% cotton swab or gauze pad with distilled water. Also obtain a control sample that should be forwarded to the lab for analysis with the specimen.
    b. Stain will soften and soak into swab or gauze pad.
    c. Allow to air dry.
    d. Place into a sterile test tube or container for laboratory.

Remember: Do not use a swab or other instrument to collect blood from more than one stain. Use separate swabs, razors, scalpels, or other instruments for each separate stain to be sampled. This is to prevent contamination of samples.

It is possible that the assailant's blood may also be present. If the same instrument is used to collect all samples, the evidence will be tainted. Furthermore, you should be careful not to touch the surface, which has contacted the blood sample because your own DNA and body secretions may contaminate the collected sample (see section below on Application of DNA Technology) (Figure 6.10 to Figure 6.13).

In the O. J. Simpson case, a review of one of the crime scene photos showed droplets of blood on Nicole Brown's back. The question is: "Could this blood have been deposited by her killer?" However, that blood was never tested because the coroner's office had washed the body prior to autopsy. I have personally investigated and reviewed numerous cases where an offender during a violent altercation had injured himself and left tracers of blood both in the scene and upon the victim's body.

Semen

Next to blood, semen and sperm is the physiological fluid most commonly discovered at sex-related homicide crime scenes. If a sexual assault is suspected, the investigator should

Figure 6.10 Bloody crime scene and weapon. A large bloody knife and bloodstains were found in this bedroom where an offender had sexually assaulted and killed a woman before attempting to kill her husband when he came home and interrupted the event. (Photo courtesy of Detective Scott Mummert, Chambersburg, Pennsylvania, Police Department.)

Figure 6.11 Crime scene. This crime scene photo taken at a double homicide indicated that someone had moved the phone after the murder. Note the absence of blood on the table where the phone originally sat. Note also the bloodstained chair where the telephone has been placed after blood has been deposited. (Photo courtesy of Detective Ken Espinoza, Pueblo, Colorado, Police Department.)

Figure 6.12 Recovery of blood droppings. The offender, who had cut himself during the attack hesitated by the front door before leaving the scene. These droplets of blood eventually led into the street. Bloodhounds were later used to follow the scent. (Photo courtesy of Detective Ken Espinoza, Pueblo, Colorado, Police Department.)

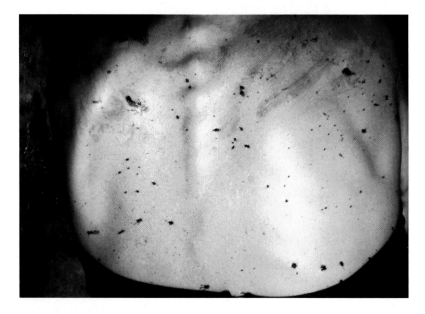

Figure 6.13 Blood droppings. Blood droppings on Nicole Brown Simpson's back at the crime scene, which were missed by the CSIs. (Photo courtesy of the author.)

carefully examine the body and clothing of the deceased prior to moving the body. If any stains are observed, procedures to collect this evidence should be performed at the scene. Later at autopsy, the medical examiner or coroner will take a vaginal swab or vaginal aspirant to obtain any semen traces from within the vaginal canal. In addition, oral and anal swabs may be taken, if sodomy is also suspected, and air dried immediately.

The following techniques should be employed at the scene.

1. Wet stain:
   a. Swab or wash (by medical examiner if possible).
   b. Draw the fluid into an eyedropper or hypodermic syringe.
   c. Place in sterile test tube.
   d. Use swab or cotton gauze pad for samples of smaller quantities that are still moist.
   e. Allow to air dry immediately and place in sterile container.
2. Dry stain:
   a. Dry stain will have a stiff, "starchy" texture.
   b. If it is on clothing, submit the entire article, being careful not to break or contaminate the stained area.
   c. On body, using 100% cotton gauze pad moistened with distilled water, gently remove stain and place in sterile test tube or container after allowing to air dry.

Sometimes an ultraviolet light or certain wavelengths of an alternate light source (ALS) can be used to locate seminal stains. However, in many instances, a false reading will be obtained due to the "brighteners" used in certain laundry detergents as well as the fact that numerous items also will fluoresce. It should also be noted that UV (ultraviolet) can and does disrupt the structure of DNA. In any event, caution should be exercised (Figure 6.14 to Figure 6.18).

Urine
1. Remove by eyedropper, sterile cotton swab, or 100% gauze pad.
2. Place in sterile text tube or other container.
3. If on clothing, the entire article should be submitted.

Saliva or Spittle
1. Remove with eyedropper, sterile cotton swab, or 100% gauze pad.
2. Place in sterile test tube or other clean container after drying.

Recovery of Saliva and Urine   The methods used in the recovery of saliva samples at a scene are dictated by the nature of the stain and the nature of the surface on which it is found. The surfaces on which such evidence is found might be porous or nonporous.

1. Porous Surfaces:
   a. Stains (wet or dry) on porous surfaces that can be removed along with ample surface area surrounding the stain should be recovered.

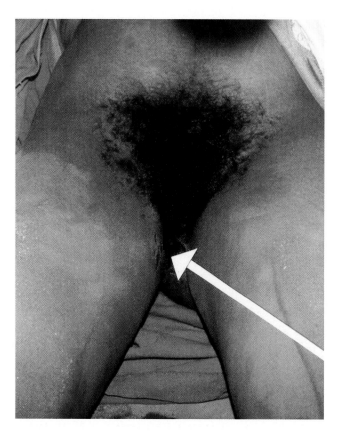

Figure 6.14 Dried semen. This close-up shot of the vaginal area of a rape–homicide victim disclosed traces of dried semen. Note the "starchy" appearance. This trace evidence should be gathered using 100% cotton moistened with distilled water, allowed to air dry, and then placed in a sterile container for delivery to the laboratory.

    b. Stains on surfaces that can be collected as an entire item should be collected whole.

    c. Wet stains should be allowed to dry before packaging.

    d. Surfaces, such as clothing, unfinished wood, paper, cardboard, and many more, fall into this category. Wet body fluids can be absorbed into the materials.

  2. Nonporous surfaces:

    a. Collection of the entire item and removal of a section of the surface bearing the stain along with ample material surrounding the stain are two preferred methods of collection.

    b. Nonporous surfaces bearing saliva stains may be susceptible to abrasive removal of the stain materials by packaging if the stain is not protected.

    c. Contamination through handling with uncovered hands or inadvertent rubbing should be avoided.

Remember: Saliva is more useful to the investigator today because DNA technology has become so advanced through the extreme sensitivity of techniques like PCR (polymerase chain reaction). DNA from epithelial cells that are present in saliva can be swabbed from the surfaces of the oral cavity of suspects and, in fact, have become the method of choice in

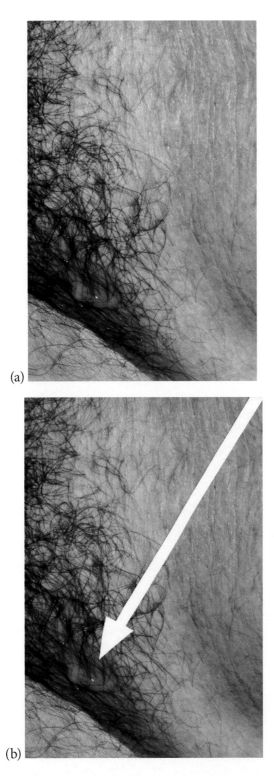

(a)

(b)

Figure 6.15 **(a) Wet semen.** This photo of viable wet semen is taken *in situ* from the victim's pubic area on a strangulation murder and sexual assault. **(b) Same area with marker.** This photo shows the same viable sperm *in situ* with an arrow marking the area of interest. (Photos courtesy of Detective Mark Czworniak, Chicago Police Department.)

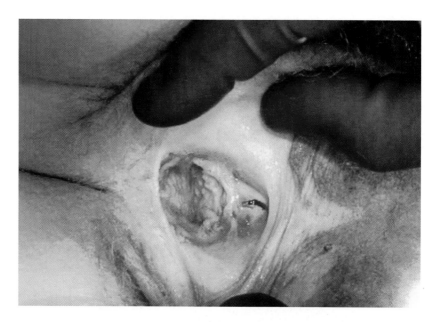

Figure 6.16 Recovery of semen. This photo shows the examination of a victim of a rape and sodomy. The injuries to the vagina are visible in the photo. Semen was recovered, which was linked by DNA to the subject. (Photo courtesy of Detective Sergeant Alan Patton, Grand Prairie, Texas, Police Department.)

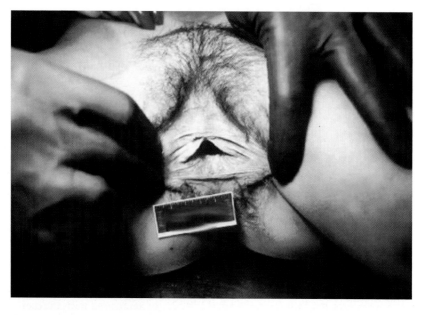

Figure 6.17 Autopsy examination. Semen recovered from victim's vagina. (Photo courtesy of Retired Detective Marsha Reed, Ft. Collins, Colorado, Police Department.)

Figure 6.18 Urine evidence. The offender, who was a fetish burglar, raped and killed a woman in her home. He then spent hours with her body. He masturbated, urinated, and defecated in the crime scene. (Courtesy of Retired Detective Marsha Reed, Ft. Collins, Colorado, Police Department.)

screening a number of suspects in an investigation. The swab method of extracting DNA is not as intrusive as taking blood samples and can be easily and quickly analyzed.

The author consulted on one particular sex-related homicide investigation involving the murder of a young boy who had gone to a carnival. There were a number of possible suspects, some of whom had criminal records. The authorities took over 50 oral swabs for buccal cells, which led to the positive identification of the offender (Figure 6.19).

Feces
1. Large amount:
   a. Remove with a small clean shovel. Allow to air dry.
   b. Place in sterile container.
2. Small amount:
   a. Remove with 100% cotton swab or gauze pad moistened with distilled water, then air dry or scrape into container.
   b. Place in sterile test tube.

Vomit
1. Remove with eyedropper or small shovel depending on the amount.
2. Place into a sterile container.

It should be noted that any physiological fluid found at the scene, such as urine, saliva, feces, perspiration, ear wax, nasal mucus, can be typed into the same grouping as blood providing the material comes from an individual who is a secretor. Secretors make up approximately 80% of the general population. Physiological fluids of these secretors can be blood-typed by the serologist.

Figure 6.19 Buccal cell recovery. This photo illustrates the proper method for collecting buccal cells from a suspect's mouth. (Photo courtesy of Detective Mark Czworniak, Chicago Police Department.)

Remember: DNA/PCR technology provides the possibility of an individualistic comparison to a suspect as well as other genetic factors, which can also be identified regardless of secretor status.

Tissue
1. Remove with tweezers.
2. Place in a glass container or sterile test tube.
3. Forward to the medical examiner.

Hair and Fiber Evidence

During crimes of violence, specifically against persons, certain trace materials, such as hair or fibers will be transferred between the victim and the perpetrator. These traces may also be left at the scene. Hair and fiber evidence, which is microscopic in nature, is oftentimes overlooked because it isn't as visible as blood and other *body materials, objects, or impression evidence* found at the crime scene. Therefore, effective crime scene process requires that the evidence technician vacuum the crime scene in order to retrieve hair and fiber evidence. The vacuum bag is then emptied onto a clean white surface and the hairs and fibers are collected by tweezers and placed in clear plastic envelopes for later analysis.

Hair is constantly being shed as new hair grows or as one simply runs a comb, brush, or fingers through one's hair. At any given time, there are about 300,000 strands of hair on the scalp of individuals who have not already suffered significant hair loss. Therefore, hair is among the most common physical evidence found at crime scenes.

In the Danielle van Dam abduction and murder case, the authorities discovered the little girls blood, hair, and fingerprints in the suspect's motor home. He was arrested after the blood and hair were matched to the victim through DNA analysis and the latent prints in the recreational vehicle (RV) were matched to the victim. Although the DNA analysis was crucial in determining the suspect's culpability, the little girl's hair became even more important to the prosecution.

The defense suggested that Danielle van Dam's fingerprints and DNA evidence, which the police had recovered from the suspect's motor home, could not be dated and might have been transferred to the suspect's unlocked motor home when little Danielle van Dam played hide-and-seek. However, Danielle had gotten her cut a few days before she vanished from her San Diego home. The hair that was recovered from the floor and in the sink of the suspect's RV was only eight inches long, which indicated that the victim would have to have been in the RV after her hair was cut. The authorities had already established that the suspect's RV had been parked miles away from the van Dam residence and there was no way that little Danielle could have innocently been in the RV after her haircut.

Often, hair provides the most valuable clues to the identity of the killer, especially in sex-related assaults where there is active physical contact between the nude bodies or the genitalia of offender and victim.

Sexual assault requires close contact between the attacker and the victim and even the most careful rapist or rape–murderer is unlikely to notice the loss of a few strands of hair. In addition to normal hair loss from the scalp, pubic and other body hairs are often torn loose during sexual assaults and left behind on the victim or on the sheets and other bed clothing.

I remember one serial murder case where the offender had left his pubic hairs on each of the victim's bodies or on the bed sheets at every crime scene. Had the authorities not been frustrated by their state crime lab's refusal to examine hair evidence without a comparable sample, they would have learned that their killer was in fact a black male and not the "imaginary" white male authorities were pursuing based on a defective FBI profile.

The case for the immediate and professional evaluation of forensic evidence has been dramatically brought to the forefront by some of the more sensational cases we have seen played out in the media. There is absolutely no reason for a crime lab to arbitrarily refuse to test hair samples because there aren't any comparable samples.

A single strand of hair subjected to forensic analysis can provide vital information about the identity of the subject. The color of hair is an obvious clue and many times the hair examination may reveal the race of the individual. In addition, hair can be used to provide information about the health of the individual and detect traces of drug use.

Drug molecules circulate in the bloodstream, seep into the hair, and stay there. It has been scientifically established that the hair is the body's garbage can. The drug molecules eventually find their way into the strands of hair. Analysis of these hairs using a mass spectrometer can provide authorities with a drug history of the offender.

Additionally, STR (short tandem repeats) DNA analysis can be performed on hair and could provide the authorities with the genetic fingerprint of the subject.

Another area where advanced methodologies have highlighted the significance of trace amounts of materials involves DNA analysis. Current techniques involving STR or analysis of mitochondrial DNA are highly sensitive and capable of yielding a DNA profile with minute amounts of DNA. Thus, the crime scene investigator must begin to evaluate a scene and implement search methods that take into consideration the fact that trace amounts of DNA-containing material may have been deposited during the crime.

Crime laboratory analysis and comparisons of fiber evidence have been greatly improved with the use of the microscopic and microchemical testing and other sophisticated equipment. An example of this sophisticated type of equipment would be the Fourier transform infrared spectrophotometer and gas chromatograph mass spectrometry (GC-MS). Recent analytical advances and increased sensitivities in instrumentation have further enhanced the significance of transfer evidence. For example, GC-MS analysis is capable of detecting accelerants at fire scenes in amounts in the magnitude of a few parts per million. The gas chromatograph is a criminalist's dream. The gas chromatograph burns a sample of the evidence. The resulting vapors are then separated to indicate the compound substances that make up the sample. In the forensic science lab, the gas chromatograph is connected to the mass spectrometer, which specifically identifies the substance.

In addition, the scanning electron microscope (SEM) is so powerful it can show atom spacing in molecules. Examination of fibers through microscopy will indicate origin, i.e., vegetable, animal, mineral, or synthetic.

Cross transfers of fibers between victims and offenders are particularly common in incidents of rape and other physical assault, and especially in homicides committed by strangulation, blunt force trauma, stabbing, and other means involving close physical contact.

Fibers and threads from clothing, blankets, rugs, and other common woven objects also have their own unique colorations and patterns that can be identifiable in meticulous detail during the laboratory process.

In the Stephen Pennel serial murder case in New Castle County, Delaware, the homicide investigators had discovered blue fibers on the first two bodies of Pennel's victims. These blue fibers were determined to be from the same source, which forensically linked the murders. However, someone in the FBI held a press conference and announced that the FBI laboratory had analyzed these fibers and this information appeared in the newspapers. The killer, reacting to the media, left his next victim in the Chesapeake Delaware Canal. Needless to say, there were no fibers recovered from this body (Figure 6.20 and Figure 6.21).

Eventually, a female undercover officer, posing as a prostitute was able to obtain some samples of these blue fibers from the offender's van when Pennel tried to lure her into his vehicle.

These blue fibers were microscopically matched to the fibers on the first two victims. Pennel, who was dubbed the The Corridor Killer, was subsequently convicted and eventually executed by the State of Delaware for this series of killings. The important point to note is that it was the fiber evidence that first enabled the authorities to link the two cases, and it was the fiber evidence that linked Pennel's van to the murders.

In another spectacular serial murder case, Roger Kibbe, who had been dubbed the I-5 Strangler, was linked to the murders of four young woman and the assault of a fifth victim strictly on the basis of "trace evidence." Retired Lieutenant Ray Biondi, a personal friend and colleague, who has investigated more serial murder cases than any other homicide cop in the country, shared with the author his frustration in this multijurisdictional nightmare. Lt. Biondi was confronted by a diabolical killer who would abduct young woman, some from their cars along I-5, take them to a location where he would rape and terrorize them before killing them by ligature strangulation.

He would transport their bodies many miles from where they had last been seen and make every effort to dispose of them so that the bodies either wouldn't be found or would be in such gross deterioration that the authorities would not be able to retrieve any significant evidence. What made this case so frustrating was the fact that the killer was

Figure 6.20 Body number two. In this serial murder case, the authorities were able to match the first two victims through carpet fibers from the vehicle in which they had been transported. However, an inappropriate news release by someone in the FBI alerted the suspect. He then began dumping the bodies in water to eliminate the blue carpet fiber evidence. (Photo courtesy of Retired Captain George O. Haggerty, New Castle County, Delaware, Department of Public Safety.)

Figure 6.21 Body number three. This was the killer's third victim. Her body was dumped into the Chesapeake–Delaware Canal to get rid of the fibers, which had linked the first two victims. (Photo courtesy of Retired Captain George O. Haggerty, New Castle County, Delaware, Department of Public Safety.)

multijurisdictional in his activities. The logistics alone were an investigative nightmare. More importantly, the other agencies involved either didn't want to believe that the cases were linked, or couldn't afford the resources that a serial murder case warrants.

The I-5 strangler was almost like a phantom. A seemingly unrelated arrest of Roger Kibbe for an attempted assault on a prostitute suddenly provided the authorities with a viable suspect. When Kibbe was taken into custody, he was in possession of a rape kit that included some white cord that was confiscated. Jim Streeter, a criminalist with the California Department of Justice, who had been handling all of the trace evidence from the murder series, realized the similarity between the cordage found on the victims and the cordage seized in the prostitute assault. However, he realized that a similarity was insufficient to positively match the cordage from the murder victims to Roger Kibbe. Criminalist Faye Springer, who was the leading forensic scientist in California, was requested to examine the cordage evidence as well as a series of carpet fibers that Streeter had recovered from the crime scenes and victim's bodies. It was Springer (and her scanning electron microscope) who broke this case wide open. She was able to positively link the fibers found on the victims to fibers from the suspect's cars. In addition, she was able to microscopically identify that the cordage used in the strangulation murders were the same as the cordage seized from Kibbe and also found in Kibbe's house.

Hair

Hair evidence prior to DNA/PCR technology was considered a class *characteristic*. Although it could not be identified as being absolutely identical to a given suspect's hair, it could be classified as similar to a known sample. Today, the DNA lab can provide specific genetic identifications with hair evidence, and hair can be used to exclude a suspect. However, from an investigative point of view, hairs or fibers can

1. Help determine the extent of the crime scene.
2. Place the perpetrator at the scene of the crime.
3. Connect the suspect to the weapon.
4. Corroborate statements of witnesses.
5. Determine the route to and from the crime scene.
6. Be located in any number of areas involved in the homicide:
   a. The victim
   b. The crime scene
   c. The weapon
   d. A tool
   e. A vehicle
   f. An article of clothing
   g. The suspect (Figures 6.22 through 6.25)

Class Determinations from Hair
1. Species: human or animal
2. Race: Caucasoid, Negroid, or Mongoloid (In certain instances, the determination of a combination of racial characteristics can be ascertained.)
3. Location of growth: body area from which the particular hair originated (head, thorax, chest, pubis, etc.)
4. Treatment: dyed, bleached, straightened, etc.

Figure 6.22 Recovery of hair evidence. Hair being recovered in crime scene. (Photo courtesy of Chief Criminal Deputy Robin Wagg, Douglas County, Washington, Sheriff's Department.)

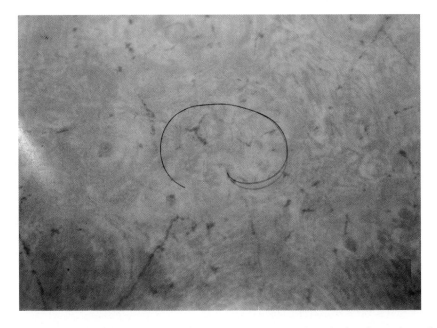

Figure 6.23 Pubic hair of killer. This pubic hair was recovered in the kitchen where the killer had retrieved some knives from the drawer. (Photo courtesy of Chief Criminal Deputy Robin Wagg, Douglas County, Washington, Sheriff's Department.)

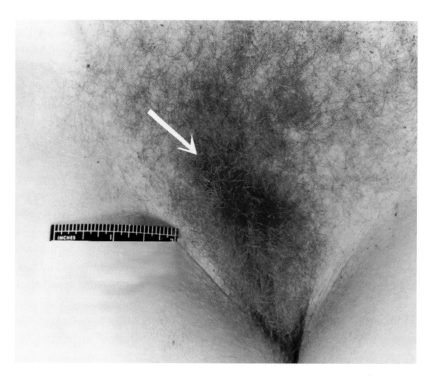

Figure 6.24 Evidence *in situ*. Note the trace evidence of black pubic hairs (arrow) discovered intertwined in the light brown pubic hairs of this victim of a rape–murder. (Photo by Don Swanz, evidence technician, and courtesy of Detective Alan Patton, Grand Prairie, Texas, Police Department.)

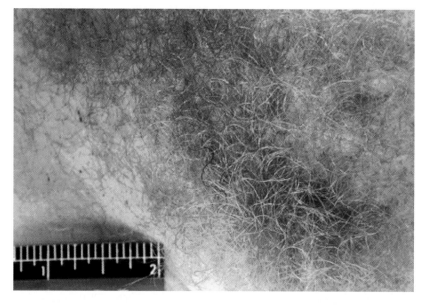

Figure 6.25 Evidence *in situ*. Close-up of pubic hair. (Photo by Don Swanz, evidence technician, and courtesy of Detective Alan Patton, Grand Prairie, Texas, Police Department.)

5. How it was removed: pulled, fell out, cut, etc.
6. Disease and/or damage.
7. Genetic information:
    a. PCR-STR DNA can identify the individual
    b. Blood type, from shaft of hair
    c. Other genetic markers, from roots of pulled hair
    d. Sex, from roots of pulled hair

It is recommended that a sample of hair from various parts of the body be obtained in all homicide cases. Even though hair evidence may not be crucial or known to exist in the early stages of the investigation, it may be discovered later even after the body has been buried or destroyed through cremation. Samples should always be taken from various parts by pulling or plucking so as to obtain a piece of the root. If pulling or plucking absolutely cannot be undertaken for some reason, cutting the hair close to the scalp will suffice. An ordinary sampling will comprise approximately 24 to 48 pieces of hair. Hair removed from the head should be taken as follows: front, back, left side, right side, and top. The sample roots should then be air dried.

Collection of Hairs from the Scene   Using oblique lighting to scan the surfaces of the crime scene, alternate light sources and lasers are useful techniques for observing and finding hairs at the scene and on the victim's or suspect's bodies and clothing.

1. If hairs or fibers are located, it is advisable to gather them by tweezers or forceps, being careful not to bend or break.
2. Masking or adhesive tape can be used to gather small fibers or hairs.
3. Place in a sterile container and seal. (Folded paper or envelopes may also be used.)

Conclusions from Hair Samples
1. Hair **did** come from unknown hair source.
2. Hair **did not** come from unknown hair source
3. Hair **could have** come from known hair source.
4. Hair sampling too limited for meaningful comparison.
5. No conclusion.

Objects

Fibers

Fibers, like hairs, may be transferred between the victim and perpetrator, and provide the investigator with an additional piece of class evidence, which can be subjected to microscopic and microchemical testing. Items, such as fabrics, thread, cordage, rope, or cloth, may also be found at the crime scene and should be collected for examination.

They should be collected the same as with hair evidence. Fiber evidence is searched for, collected, and packaged the same as hair evidence. Laboratory examination can identify the fiber type and determine the possible origin of the fiber from a fabric source.

Picking, tape lifting, and vacuuming techniques are used for the collection of fibers or threads. If there is fiber evidence adhering to a movable object found at the crime scene, then that entire object should be taken as evidence. If the object is too big, then a portion of that object should be cut out, wrapped, and packaged intact. It is important that the crime scene investigator remember that fabrics are easily caught or torn by broken windows, the edges of ripped screens, and other sharp materials.

1. Examination of fibers will indicate origin as follows:
   a. Vegetable: e.g., cotton and hemp
   b. Animal: e.g., wool and mink
   c. Mineral: e.g., glass wool and asbestos
   d. Synthetic: e.g., nylon and orlon
2. Examination of fiber evidence will determine if the fiber is similar to the control sample. Cuttings from carpets, fabrics, or other materials can be used as the known sample of the possible source.
3. Collect fibers as follows: forceps, tape, vacuum sweeping (it should be noted that this is the least desirable method because too many contaminants are also collected).
4. Collecting samples by using the sticky side of tape is considered the most practical method.
5. Evidence should be photographed *in situ* and before packaging.
6. Place samples in individual containers from each area gathered, mark appropriately, and forward to laboratory for examination.
7. If knotted cordage evidence is found at the crime scene, the knots should not be untied. The knot should be photographed intact. If removal of the knots and cordage is necessary for transportation, the cordage may be cut at its new location and marked by the person removing the cordage. Removal and cutting at the new location must allow the knots to remain intact.

Fabric

1. Pieces of fabric found at the scene can be examined in a manner similar to fibers to determine:
   a. Color
   b. Type of cloth and fiber
   c. Thread count
   d. Direction of fiber twist
   e. Dye
2. Class, as well as individual characteristics, can be obtained from fragments of fabric when matched by physically fitting the evidence pieces into its source.

Clothing

Each item of clothing collected as evidence should be individually wrapped in order to prevent cross-contamination. If the clothing to be collected is wet, it should be air dried before it is packaged. Clothing may provide the investigator with additional evidence (Figure 6.26 and Figure 6.27)

1. Stains on clothing may match stains from the scene, the victim, or the suspect.
2. A suspect's clothing may contain blood similar to the victim's.
3. The victim's clothing may contain saliva or seminal fluid from the perpetrator.

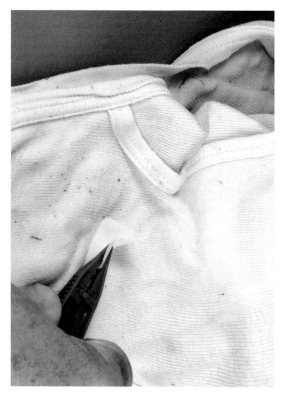

Figure 6.26 Suspect's bloodstained underwear. Investigators discovered some questionable stains on the offender's underwear in a rape case. They processed these stains with DISCHAPS™ a phenolphthalein blood test reagent. (Photo courtesy of Detective Mark Czworniak, Chicago Police Department.)

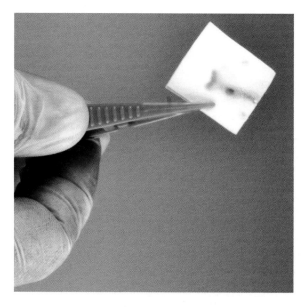

Figure 6.27 Positive reaction. The presumptive test for blood was positive. It was then matched via DNA to the victim. (Photo courtesy of Detective Mark Czworniak, Chicago Police Department.)

4. Hairs or fibers may be present on clothing that match similar hairs or fibers from a particular scene or location or from the victim.
5. Tears or cuts in clothing made by the weapon can be matched to show the position of the victim at the time of the assault.
6. The deposit of gunshot residue on clothing can be analyzed to determine the approximate distance from which the gun was fired.

Bullets

When a bullet is fired from a weapon, certain distinctive characteristics are imparted to the bullet by the gun. These markings can be examined through internal ballistics and provide the investigator with certain general information regarding the type of weapon used. In addition, ballistics evidence is highly individualistic, and a fired bullet recovered from the scene can be positively matched with the suspect weapon.

1. Bullets should be collected without damaging or marking the rifling (the series of grooves or lines on the interior surface of the barrel that cause the bullet to spin and travel forward through the barrel with accuracy). These grooves and lines are transferred to the bullet as it is fired and are used by the ballistics expert to make comparisons.
2. Bullets embedded in doors, trees, walls, etc., should be removed by taking out a portion of the object in which the bullet has become lodged rather than by probing or digging. Digging for the bullet may cause additional marks that may destroy the ballistics value of the evidence.
3. Recovered bullets should be examined for blood or other materials before packaging.
4. Bullets should be marked on the base or nose.
5. Each bullet should be packaged separately in an appropriate container, preferably one which will prevent any cross-contamination or accidental abrasion of the rifling marks.
6. The package should be marked to show identification and location of discovery.

Discharged Casings or Cartridges   The recovery of discharged shells may indicate the direction and location of the attack as well as how many shots were fired. In addition, certain class characteristics, such as make and caliber, can be ascertained. Furthermore, if an automatic weapon was used, certain ejector or clip markings may be present.

1. Recovered casings should be marked on the inside wall of the shell by the mouth end or, if this is not possible, as near to the opening as possible.
2. Never mark the recovered casing on or near the end that contains the primer cap because examination of weapon markings may be destroyed.
3. Always consider the possibility of fingerprints on the sides of these casings and take appropriate precautions to preserve them.
4. Package evidence in separate containers with proper documentation.

Shotgun Shells
1. Plastic or paper shotgun shells should be handled in the same manner as other discharged casings.
2. These items can be marked on the metal side part of the casing.
3. Never mark on the base of a shell casing.

Live Cartridges or Rounds of Ammunition
1. Examine for fingerprint evidence prior to marking.
2. Mark on side of casing.
3. Package, indicating the location of recovered rounds.

Shotgun Wadding
1. Recover and submit for laboratory examination.
2. Place in a separate container.

Weapons
1. Photograph and examine for fingerprints.
2. Examine for any serology or other trace evidence.
3. Place in a special container according to size to protect evidence and prevent handling.
4. Forward to serology or crime lab for further analysis.

Forensic Examination of Firearms and Ballistics

The Integrated Ballistic Identification System (IBIS®) developed by Forensic Technology, Inc. (Montreal, Canada) is an image analysis system for acquiring, storing, and analyzing the images of bullets and cartridge cases. IBIS is Forensic Technology's cornerstone product (Figures 6.28 through 6.30).

The system is composed of two modules:

Bulletproof® for bullets
Brasscatcher® for cartridge cases

The system captures video images of bullet striations and the markings left on cartridge cases, which produce an electronic "signature" stored in a database. Networking hardware and software allow transfers and comparisons of forensic evidence from different cities and countries.

- Unique characteristics of groove marks found on spent bullets.
- Unique characteristics left on cartridge cases recorded.
- Read by laser and coded for computer storage.
- Entered into the data bank.
- Comparisons with an entire database of fired bullets/cartridges.
- Networking hardware and software allow transfers and comparisons of forensic evidence from different jurisdictions.

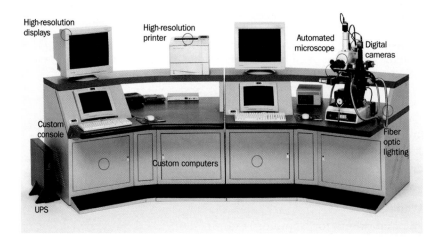

Figure 6.28 Integrated Ballistic Identification System (IBIS). This photo depicts the IBIS Hub, which comprises a Data Acquisition Station (DAS) networked to a correlation server and Signature Analysis Station (SAS). The DAS enables users to acquire images of bullet and cartridge case evidence using an automated microscope and digital imaging technologies. Images collected by DAS are given a unique "digital signature" and sent to the correlation server for comparison and storage. The correlation server mathematically compares digital signatures from the DAS and ranks them according to the degree of similarity. Correlation results can be reviewed on the SAS. The SAS provides examiners with the ability to view and analyze results from the correlation server. Proprietary software utilized by the SAS enables users to sort and filter massive amounts of ballistics evidence, concentrating on only the most likely matches. (Photo courtesy of Forensic Technology, Inc., 888-984-4247, www. forensictechnologyinc.com.)

IBIS BRASSTRAX™

This is an automated, desktop, cartridge case acquisition station for collecting digital images of cartridge case evidence for cataloging and comparison within an IBIS correlation server. Because of its simplified design, BRASSTRAX can be operated with little or no specialized training.

Advantages:
- Scalable cartridge case acquisition stations that can be added to an IBIS Hub or Data Concentrator.
- Gets evidence into the analysis process quickly.
- Minimal user training and expertise to operate.
- Desktop-size unit.
- Efficient Local Area Network and Wide Area Network connections.
- Increased automation reduces operator variances.

IBIS BULLETTRAX™*-3D*

This is a bullet-evidence acquisition station that uses the latest in three-dimensional imaging technology. BULLETTRAX-3D utilizes a specially designed microscope that can capture a digital image and create a 3D topographic model of the surface of a bullet. This information can then be sent to a centralized IBIS correlation server.

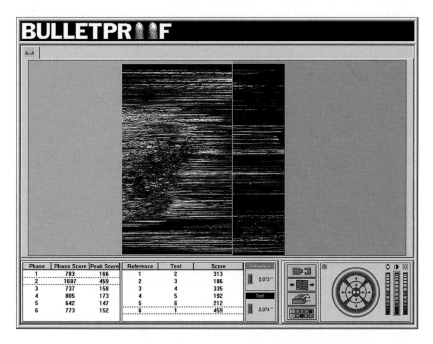

Figure 6.29 IBIS Bulletproof® for bullets. Screen depicting side-by-side comparison of bullet. (Image courtesy of Forensic Technology, Inc., 888-984-4247, www.forensictechnologyinc.com.)

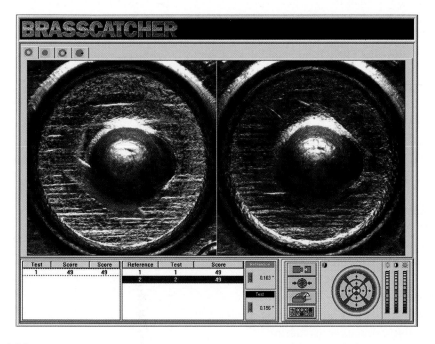

Figure 6.30 IBIS Brasscatcher® for cartridge case. Screen depicting side-by-side comparison of cartridge case. (Image courtesy of Forensic Technology, Inc., 888-984-4247, www.forensictechnologyinc.com.)

Advantages:
- Ability to take quantitative measurements of a bullet's surface.
- Scalable acquisition station that is compatible with other IBIS solutions.
- Minimal user training and expertise to operate.
- Environmental conditions (light intensity, orientation, type) can be modified after the acquisition process.
- Increased correlation accuracy.

Forensic Technology, Inc. can be contacted at www.forensictechnologyinc.com.

Firearms

1. Photograph in original position.
2. Examine for fingerprints.
3. Examine for any serology (e.g., blow-back of close-range firing may result in blood, hair, or tissue being transferred to weapon or in barrel of weapon).
4. Upon completion of preliminary examination for above, unload weapon and render safe before transporting.
5. Package individually in an appropriate container. (In circumstances in which the firearm must be transported for further examination at a proper facility, use a cardboard box. Draw a string through the trigger guard and attach this string at either end of the box, leaving the gun in a suspended position. For larger firearms, such as rifles or shotguns, cut a notch in each end of the box and lay weapon across container.)
6. Indicate the brand name, model designation, serial numbers, caliber, and number of shots the weapon is capable of firing, e.g., 5- or 6-shot revolver, in reports and on evidence containers. Also indicate the type of finish: nickel plate, etc.
7. All weapons recovered should be marked for identification as soon as possible in the following manner:
   a. Revolvers: mark on frame, barrel, and cylinder
   b. Rifles and shotguns: mark on receiver, bolt, and barrel
   c. Semiautomatic weapons: receiver (frame), slide, barrel, and any clips

Cigarette Butts and Ash Tray Contents

Cigarette butts and the contents of ash trays found at the crime scene, especially those with filter tips, can be examined for DNA (Figure 6.31).

1. Collect with forceps or tweezers and ensure dryness.
2. Place into separate containers to prevent cross-contamination.
3. Containers should be appropriately marked.
4. Forward to laboratory.

Displaced Furniture

1. Examine for any fingerprints or serology.
2. Useful in crime reconstruction.

Newly Damaged Areas

The presence of damaged furniture, objects, and any other newly damaged areas is indicative of some sort of violence or struggle.

Figure 6.31 Discarded cigarette butt. This cigarette butt was recovered from a drain in the basement sink of a crime scene involving a double homicide. A DNA profile was established and successfully matched to the offender. (Photo courtesy of Detective Mark Czworniak, Chicago Police Department.)

1. Photograph
2. Examine for serology
3. Process for fingerprints

Soil

1. Soil on shoes, clothing, tools, weapons, and other objects may be useful in placing a suspect at the scene and providing the investigator with additional evidence. Also microbiological comparisons in addition to mineral comparisons can be made.
   a. Color of soil may be distinctive.
   b. Minerals can be distinctive.
   c. Bacterial profiles can be distinctive.
   d. Vegetation (fungal spores, etc.) can be distinctive.
2. Collection of soil samples:
   a. Collect several samples at the scene from various locations since mineral and organic contents vary within short distances.
   b. Gather at least a cupful or handful from each location.
   c. Ensure dryness.

Figure 6.32 Sand. A detective located sand, fibers, and blood in the trunk of the suspect's car linking him to the body on the beach. (Photo courtesy of Detective Corporal Arthur Clark, East Providence, Rhode Island, Police Department.)

   d. Package in separate containers.
   e. Mark properly for identification and location (Figure 6.32 and Figure 6.33).

Tools

Tools suspected of being used in the crime should be examined as follows:

1. Examine for DNA, serology, or fingerprints.
2. If the tool contains any serological evidence, it must be carefully packaged to preserve this evidence.
3. If tool contains traces of certain materials that are to be matched up with known samples, care must be taken so that this material is not rubbed off.
4. Portion of tool to be matched must be protected.
5. Broken tools and/or knives can be fracture-matched to provide positive identification.
6. Never try to fit tool into tool mark or match broken pieces together.

Vehicles

1. Photograph and examine for serology
2. Process for fingerprints
3. Examine for other items of evidence
4. Search for weapons

Documents (Letters, Notes, Papers)

These items may be examined to ascertain authenticity, locate fingerprints, or determine authorship in suicide cases, or using more advanced techniques, such as psycholinguistic examination (see Chapter 20 in Geberth, 2006).

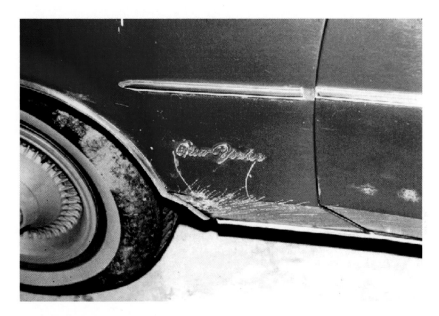

Figure 6.33 Sand on tire and panel. The police examined the suspect's vehicle. They observed sand on the tires and the rocker panel of the car, which matched the sand at the beach where the suspect had buried the body. (Photo courtesy of Detective Corporal Arthur Clark, East Providence, Rhode Island, Police Department.)

1. The primary consideration in handling this type of evidence is the preservation of any fingerprints, which may be on the item.
2. Evidence should be collected by using tweezers or forceps to gently pick up the paper.
3. Each item should be placed in a separate package. A package that is clear or see-through is best because it will allow the investigator to examine contents without contaminating the document with additional fingerprints.
4. If see-through packaging is not available, the object can be photocopied using forceps to place the object on the machine and later to transfer it to the evidence envelope. (This will allow for reading and other examination of content without disturbing evidence value of the original document.)
5. Marking this type of evidence depends on the type of examination to be conducted. In some instances, a mark can be placed on a back corner of the paper. In other instances, just the package in which the document is placed should be marked.
6. Documents should not be folded.
7. Examine for latent prints.
8. Saliva on envelopes can be blood-typed and sometimes analyzed for sex origin.

Examination of Documents The examination for latent prints on papers, documents, and other porous materials, such as wood, proceeds in a series of steps.

First step: Iodine fuming—reacts with oil or fatty fluids in latent print.
Second step: Ninhydrin—penetrates material and reacts with amino acids in perspiration. Heat should be applied and print will emerge.

Third step: Silver nitrate—reacts to salt in the perspiration. The document is then exposed to strong light.

Glass

Examinations can be conducted on glass and glass fragments using a *refractive index,* which proves that the known sample and the evidence glass may have come from a similar source. In addition, in certain cases, the fragments can be physically matched. Furthermore, the direction and sequence of bullet holes through glass can be determined by examination of radial and concentric fractures and may prove important in reconstructing the crime. Glass should be collected as follows:

1. Small pieces should be placed in a vial or pillbox.
2. Large pieces should be placed in a sturdy cardboard box with proper padding or protection to prevent further breakage during transport.

Impressions

Fingerprint Examination

The most valuable evidence that an investigator can obtain from the homicide crime scene is the fingerprints of the suspect. From an investigative point of view, any crime scene search should include a detailed examination for visible, plastic, and latent prints. It is important to note that the officer(s) performing this function should preserve all developed prints. Even partial prints, which may seem insignificant, may become valuable later when compared to prints taken from a suspect. It should be noted that fingerprint powders do not interfere with serological analyses. However, ninhydrin sprays and other chemical means to make prints visible may interfere with serology tests.

Types of Fingerprints Fingerprints are divided into three separate categories: plastic prints, visible prints, and latent prints.

1. **Plastic prints.** These impressions occur when the finger touches or presses against a soft pliable surface, such as putty, gum, a newly painted area, the glue on a stamp or envelope, wax, flour, thick dust, soap, grease, tar, resin, or clay. A negative impression of the friction ridge pattern is produced, resulting in a plastic print.
2. **Visible prints.** These prints occur when the fingers, palms, or feet, which have been contaminated with a foreign substance, come into contact with a clean surface and are pressed onto the surface, leaving a print. The most common type is the dust print. However, substances, such as ink, blood, soot, paint, grease, face powders, or oils, contaminate the friction ridges of the fingers; when they are pressed against another surface, an image is transferred.
3. **Latent prints.** These prints occur from the natural skin secretions, such as perspiration. When grease or dirt is mixed with the natural secretions, a stable print may be deposited on a surface. Latent prints, which are not visible, are usually found on objects with smooth or polished surfaces or on paper. The latent print is developed by dusting or chemical process. In some instances, these latent prints can be developed on rougher surfaces by using certain chemical processes.

Figure 6.34 Dusting for latent prints. (Photo courtesy of Polaroid Corporation.)

Development of Fingerprints The most common and practical method of developing prints at crime scenes is through the "dusting" technique. This is done by dusting or spreading fingerprint powder with a brush over the surface of the object suspected of bearing prints. The choice of the color of the powder to be used depends on the background of the object to be dusted. If the object is dark or black, a light powder is used, and conversely, if the object is light or white, a dark or black powder is used. The most common color powders are black, silver, grey, and white. However, fingerprint powders come in many other colors, which can be used to contrast with any background. The brushes available are composed of camel's hair, feathers, fiberglass, or nylon (Figure 6.34 and Figure 6.35).

1. A small amount of powder is poured onto a clean piece of paper.
2. The brush is drawn across the powder and then tapped with the finger to remove excess material.
3. The surface of object to be examined is then lightly brushed by the investigator who uses curved strokes to locate prints.

The fingerprint powder adheres to the material and forms the latent print. This latent print will first appear as a smudge and will require further treatment before it becomes a distinct print. This is done by brushing the powder parallel to the ridge structure of the print, being careful not to rub the print too hard. After the print is developed it should be photographed first and then lifted.

Another method of dusting is done with magnetic powders. The MAGNA Brush is dipped into the magnetic powder, which then adheres to the magnet in the brush. When the powder, which is actually fine iron fillings, is evenly distributed on the end of the brush, the investigator uses the applicator like any other fingerprint brush. The advantage of this method is that there is no mess or excess powder left on the object. The disadvantage is that the MAGNA Brush method cannot be used on ferrous metals and it is very expensive. The

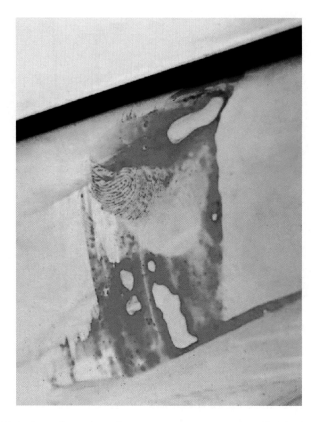

Figure 6.35 Visible print. Also referred to as a patent print. The offender left his bloody finger-print on the trunk of the car in which he had transported his victim's body to the crime scene. (Photo courtesy of the author.)

prints that are located are lifted in the same manner as those obtained with the regular fingerprint powder.

Preservation of Fingerprints   Prints found at the scene of a homicide should be immediately recorded by photography before any attempt is made to lift the print. This procedure is recommended in the event lifting is not successful or the print is damaged during attempts to remove it from the item on which it is found.

In addition, photography makes it easier to introduce the fingerprint evidence into court because parts of the object that contained the print can be seen in the picture. The method of photography used will vary with the expertise of the technician. I recommend that the investigator use the 1 × 1 or "fingerprint" camera (an application that takes a square or circle-shaped photo). Polaroid® produces a fixed-focus camera called the CU-5, which is ideal for this type of work.

It should be noted that in addition to latent fingerprints, *palmer* (palm), wrist, or *plantar* (foot, toe) skin designs may also be found at the scene.

Remember: These impressions or prints can also be used to positively identify suspects and should be preserved accordingly.

Chemical Processes   In addition to the powders, there is a series of chemical procedures, which can be employed to develop latent prints. Chemical processing methods for latent fingerprints can be used on dry and wet surfaces. The application of iodine fuming, ninhydrin,

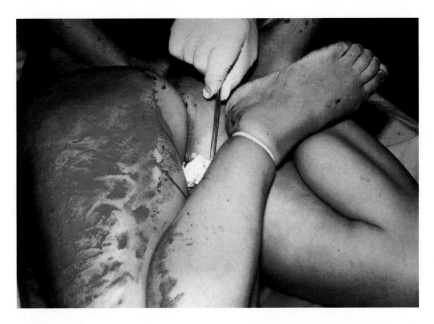

Figure 6.36 Plastic bags in vagina. The suspect had jammed white plastic garbage bags into the victim's vagina. They were removed at the autopsy for analysis. (Photo courtesy Detective Mike Essig, McLean County Sheriff's Department, Bloomington, Illinois.)

and silver nitrate are some examples. Various dye staining techniques, such as gentian violet, fluorescent dyes, or other laser-excitable dyes, followed by lighting or laser excitation, then photography of the developed latent fingerprints work on dry surfaces. There have been some remarkable results in developing latent prints by use of the laser. Practically speaking, the average investigator will not be employing these procedures. However, one should be aware of the availability of these methods in the event that further examination of evidence is necessary in order to discover and develop latent print evidence. (See section above on reagents—Tests for the Presence of Body Fluids) (Figure 6.36 and Figure 6.37).

Tire Tracks and Footprints

These impressions may be left in various types of material. The footprint is the most common impression left at or near the scene of a crime. A *footprint* is formed when the foot or sole and heel of a shoe become contaminated with some foreign substance, such as blood, paint, or dust. A *foot impression* is formed like a tire track, when the foot or tire treads are pressed into some type of moldable material, such as dirt, clay, or snow. Any such impression should be preserved and used for comparison with suspects or vehicles. Impressions may be identifiable by wear, damage, characteristic properties, or repair marks. Footwear impressions can be located and identified today with much more accuracy due to many of the newer techniques and methods presently utilized. The author highly recommends William Bodziak's excellent textbook *Footwear Impression Evidence: Detection, Recovery, and Examination,* 2nd ed. (2000) to the reader for an in-depth and practical understanding of footwear impression evidence.

Impressions should be collected in the following manner:

1. Photograph: Prior to photography, the impression should be cleaned of all foreign matter. Lighting should be employed so as to enhance the details. A scale

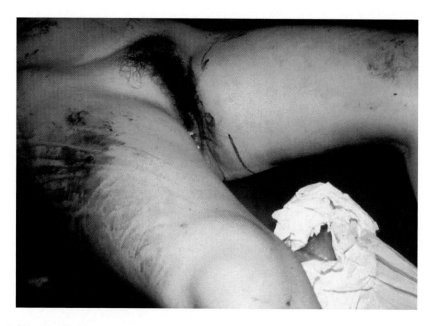

Figure 6.37 Plastic bags removed. There were two bags recovered from the victim's vagina. They were processed using cyanoacrylate fuming. Twenty-three latent prints of one of the suspects were obtained. (Photo courtesy Detective Mike Essig, McLean County Sheriff's Department, Bloomington, Illinois.)

of measurement should be included in the photo. Then, a long-range view and a close-up should be taken.

2. Casting: A casting kit should be available for use at the crime scene, which contains the following materials:
   a. Plaster of Paris (5 lbs)
   b. Mixing container (flexible for reuse)
   c. Stirring stick
   d. Reinforcement material (sticks, wire, etc., to hold form)
   e. Shellac or plastic spray (to form soft earth or dust)
   f. Oil spray (to serve as release agent)
3. Preparation for casting:
   a. Clean out the loose material without disturbing impression.
   b. Use plastic spray to fix soil prior to plaster.
   c. Build a form around impression to avoid run-off.
   d. Gently pour plaster of Paris over impression.
   e. Add reinforcement sticks as form builds.
4. Preservation of dust prints:
   a. Photograph first.
   b. Use a special lifter (black rubber with a sticky surface) placed sticky-side down over impression. Press on the impression and then remove lifter (Figures 6.38 through 6.41).

Tool Marks

Tool marks, like footprints and tire tracks, may contain minute imperfections, which are unique and can sometimes be microscopically compared to the tool or object in question.

Figure 6.38 Shoe impression in soil. This photo depicts a shoe impression in soil, along with a measurement scale. (Photo courtesy of William J. Bodziak, Retired Supervisory Special Agent FBI Laboratory Division and author of *Footwear Impression Evidence*, 2000.)

Figure 6.39 Bloody footprints. These bloody footprints were photographed and documented in connection with a brutal knife attack involving a sexual assault on the female victim. (Photo courtesy of Detective Mark Czworniak, Chicago Police Department.)

Figure 6.40 Bloody body Image. This victim's body impression can be seen on the floor where she was repeatedly stabbed by the offender. (Photo courtesy of Detective Mark Czworniak, Chicago Police Department.)

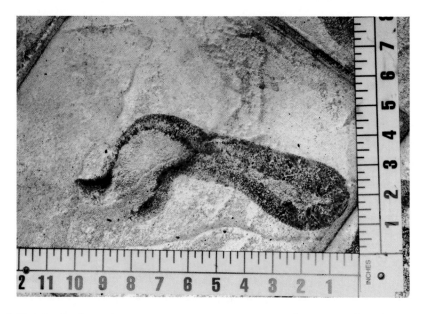

Figure 6.41 Bloody footprint. Crime scene investigators documented and recovered the offender's bloody footprint because he walked through his victim's blood. (Photo courtesy of Detective Mark Czworniak, Chicago Police Department.)

It is better if the investigator can remove the object that bears the tool mark. This can be done by removing the surface for submission to the laboratory. In instances where this would be impractical, the tool mark can be cast with a silicone rubber material. To collect tool marks:

1. Photograph (long-shot and close-up with 1 × 1 camera).
2. Cast with a silicone rubber casting after spraying surface with silicone release agent.

Bullet Holes
1. In walls or furniture, first photograph and then examine trajectory.
2. In garments:
   a. Photograph.
   b. Safeguard for examination for powder residue.
   c. Wrap (do not fold) and place in proper container. Direction of fire can be ascertained by using a color test to determine presence of lead (the Harrison test).

Newly Damaged Areas
The presence of damaged furniture, objects, and any other newly damaged areas are indicative of some sort of violence or struggle.

1. Photograph.
2. Examine for any serology or microscopic evidence.
3. Process for fingerprints.

Bite Mark Identification

The purpose of this section is to acquaint investigators with practical information and procedures to be employed in the investigation of homicides involving bite mark evidence. Bite marks are usually found in cases involving extremely emotional and violent episodes, such as child abuse, felonious assault, sexual assault, and sex-related homicides. However, in order for investigators to utilize this evidence, they must first be able to recognize and discover the existence of this type of wound. I have included various photos of bite marks herein to assist investigators in making this observation.

The homicide detective will obviously need the expertise of a forensic odontologist to interpret this type of evidence. Here we will look at certain basic steps that investigators must employ at the scene in order to assist the odontologist in his evaluations. Forensic odontology has become a highly important and technically complex area, as a medicolegal investigation of bite mark evidence has proved to be successful in many noteworthy cases, which have occurred in recent years.

The Bite Mark
Practically speaking, the bite mark should be viewed as an additional piece of evidence, which may be utilized to identify a suspect. The teeth are actually used by people as "tools," and, in the simplest terms, tooth marks are tool marks. It has been well documented that owing to such factors as size, shape, wear, rotations, restorations, fillings, loss of certain teeth, and accidental characteristics, such as breakage and injury, no two sets of teeth are

exactly alike. The relative positions of the teeth, their width, and the distance between them, together with ridges on the edges of the teeth and grooves on the back or front, vary for different individuals. These factors provide the forensic odontologist with specific and characteristic information about the person who has inflicted the bite mark and can be used to positively identify a suspect.

Generally, tooth marks come from the front teeth in the upper and lower jaws. The type of impression varies with the age of the individual. For example, children and young people have ridges on the lower edges of their upper front teeth, while persons over 20 years of age generally have upper front teeth that are smoother.

Bite mark identification is not limited to skin. Teeth leave impressions or scraping marks in the form of bite marks in chewing gum, cheese, fruit, chocolate, and similar materials. The discovery of a piece of discarded chewing gum at the scene of a homicide should certainly be considered a significant find. Its value is not only in its distinctive bite mark impressions, but also in its ability to yield additional information through serological testing to determine the blood grouping of the suspect who chewed the gum as well as a DNA analysis.

Direct contact between the suspect's mouth and the skin of the victim often results not only in a bite mark, but also in the presence of saliva in the immediate region of the mark. The recovery and forensic analysis of this saliva evidence can be of extreme importance, especially in cases where the bite mark alone does not exhibit sufficient clarity of detail for positive identification with the dental configuration of the suspect. While bite marks are likely sources of saliva, saliva may be deposited through licking, sucking, or nibbling such that no bruising or marks are left on the skin.

Most bite marks are found in the following types of homicides: (1) the homicide victim involved in sexual activity around the time of death, and (2) the battered child homicide victim.

Sexually-oriented homicides can be either homosexual or heterosexual and may involve voluntary sexual activity or forcible attack. Child victims may be either battered children or children murdered by other children in a single homicide assault.

There are two types of bite mark patterns:

1. Those that are inflicted slowly, almost sadistically, exhibiting a central *ecchymotic area* or "suck mark," and a radiating linear abrasion pattern surrounding the central area resembling a sunburst. This type is most often found in the sexually oriented homicide.
2. The second type more closely resembles a tooth mark pattern. This is a defensive bite mark and is seen most often in the battered child type of homicide.

Collection of Bite Mark Evidence at the Scene

The proper handling of bite mark evidence begins at the scene of the crime where the homicide investigator must initiate procedures to ensure that the evidence is not destroyed or lost.

The most important step in utilizing saliva in bite mark cases is the recognition of the mark and immediate protection of that location from contaminating or destructive activity. Care should be taken to avoid touching the area of interest with the bare hands.

The best course of action is to secure photographs of the bite mark wounds. If the material is other than skin, consideration must be given to casting the object. Bite marks are usually found in materials that cannot be kept for long periods of time; once the materials

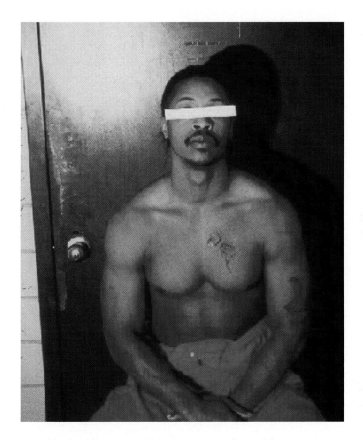

Figure 6.42 Homosexual robbery case. The suspect solicited his victim at a Greyhound Bus Terminal. He then went home with his victim for a sexual liaison during which time the victim was assaulted, robbed, and killed. The assailant took the victim's credit cards and his vehicle. (Photo courtesy of Retired Lieutenant Colonel James J. Hackett, Deputy Chief, Bureau of Investigation, St. Louis Police Department.)

have dried up or decomposed, the bite mark's appearance will change drastically and be of no value to the odontologist.

Therefore, it is imperative to obtain photos or casts of the bite mark before the material begins to change. The recommendation is to document the initial condition and location of the bite mark photographically (with and without a scale). Even if an object is to be cast, the bite mark should first be photographed in case the casting goes wrong. These first photos are usually taken by the police photographer at the scene, followed by medical examiner photos taken at autopsy. I recommend that the investigator take photos of any pattern of injury he or she observes on the body while at the scene, giving special attention to any ovoid-shaped wounds or marks that are less than two inches in diameter (Figures 6.42 through 6.46).

Photographs of the Bite Mark Wound
1. The best type of camera to utilize is the fingerprint type, which gives a 1 × 1 exposure or life-size photo of the wound.
2. Use a rule of measure in the photo to document size. The ruler used should not be white because this color is not conducive to enhancement (see example of dark rule in Figure 6.45).

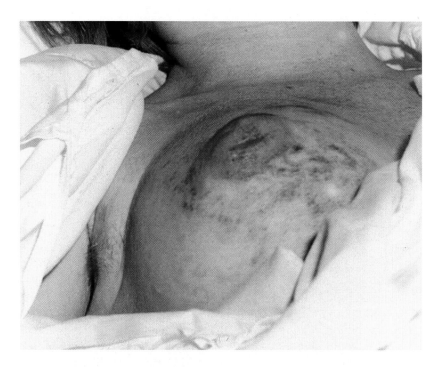

Figure 6.43 Breast assault. Multiple bite marks were inflicted upon the breast of this victim who survived an attack by a serial killer. (Photo courtesy of Retired Lieutenant Frank P. Del Prete, Bergen County, New Jersey, Prosecutor's Office.)

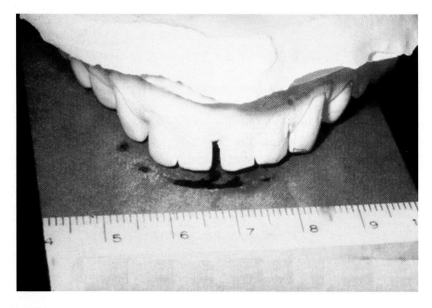

Figure 6.44 Victim's teeth. Reconstruction of bite mark using a mold of the victim's teeth placed over the wound on the perpetrator. (Photo courtesy of the late Dr. Arthur D. Goldman, DDS, forensic odontologist.)

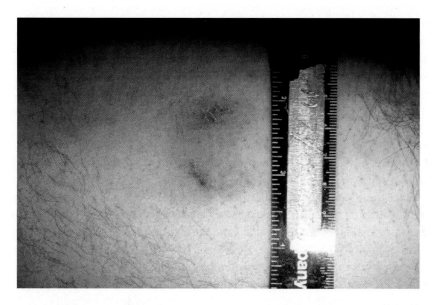

Figure 6.45 Fresh bite without detail. (Photo courtesy of the late Dr. Arthur D. Goldman, DDS, forensic odontologist.)

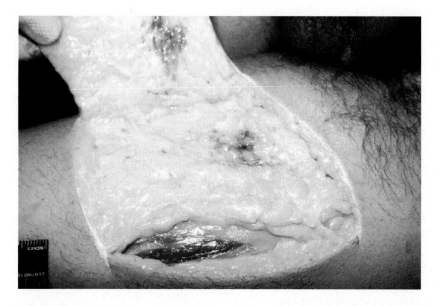

Figure 6.46 Same bite with tissue reflected. A subcutaneous view of the area shows capillary bleeding and detail of bite mark. (Photo courtesy of the late Dr. Arthur D. Goldman, DDS, forensic odontologist.)

3. Use oblique lighting to enhance bite mark.
4. Provide for an anatomical landmark in photo.
5. Take photos in black and white and color.
6. Take an overall photo and a close-up of each wound.
7. Do not delete, destroy, or throw away any "bad" shots, but save all negatives, disks, and photos. They are evidence.

Saliva Washings

1. Take a saliva washing of the bite mark area for a blood grouping and serological examination as well as STR-PCR DNA testing.
2. Washing should be done with distilled water and 100% cotton. Start at the periphery and work inward, use a separate swab for each bite mark. (If there is no distilled water available, use tap water, but take a control sample for examination.)
3. Air dry each swab.
4. Place each swab in a separate container, preferably a sterile test tube.
5. Take a saliva swab from victim for control.
6. Take a controlled swab from an area of the body other than bite mark.
7. Label each sample; keep items separate.

Remember: Always keep track of the chain of custody.

Interpretation of the Bite Mark Evidence

The interpretation of the bite mark requires the forensic odontologist to consider at least the following factors:

1. The teeth of the biter.
2. Distortion.
3. The mental state of the biter at the time the bite was inflicted.
4. The portion of the body upon which the bite was inflicted. Bite marks have been found almost everywhere on the body. However, certain patterns are most prominent in particular kinds of cases. For example, homosexual cases often involve bite marks of the back, arms, shoulders, axillae (armpits, face, and scrotum of the victim). Heterosexual cases usually involve the breasts and thighs. Battered children most often have randomly placed bite marks on the cheeks, back, and sides. However, bite marks on battered children have also been found on the abdomen, scrotum, and buttocks. In child cases, the biting seems to be done in a rapid, random, and enraged manner leaving tissue laceration, diffuse areas, and poor detail, as opposed to sexually associated bite marks, usually inflicted in a slow and sadistic manner and resulting in excellent detail.
5. Factors, such as size and shape, are helpful in establishing whether the bite mark was inflicted by a human being or an animal. If the bite mark is human, the time it was inflicted (antemortem or postmortem), tissue reaction of the surrounding area, and position of the body when found are all taken into consideration by the odontologist.

Examination of the Bite Mark

The examination of the bite mark by a forensic odontologist can generally provide the investigator with sufficient information to rapidly include or exclude a suspect in a particular investigation. For instance, in a case involving a battered child, only a limited number of persons would have the opportunity to bite and murder the child. The suspect in such cases might include one or two adults (the mother and father) and siblings. On the basis of the size of the arch, the forensic odontologist can usually determine whether the attacker was an adult or a child. In addition, there may be enough individual characteristics (wear, missing teeth, dental restorations, rotations, arch form, etc.) to exclude all but the perpetrator of the bite.

The forensic examination includes the following procedures:

1. Saliva washings of the area for blood grouping (using 100% cotton dampened in distilled water.
2. Photographs of the bite mark:
   a. 1×1 camera fingerprint-type model
   b.   Black and white and color photos
   c.   Rule of measure
   d.   Anatomical landmark
3. Examination of dental casts of possible suspects. Models of the teeth of all suspects, which will subsequently be used for comparisons, are taken only by informed consent or by court order. The models are made by either the forensic odontologist or another licensed dentist. This varies from case to case and from court order to court order. All models, however, are made according to accepted dental standards and labeled for evidentiary purposes.
4. Comparisons are made of the life-size photos of the bite marks with bite marks made in wax either by the suspect or by models of the suspect's teeth.
5. A report is prepared indicating whether the bite marks are or are not consistent with the teeth of the suspect.

The Detection and Documentation of Trace Wound Patterns by Use of an Alternative Light Source

Alternative light sources have been used by law enforcement to scan bodies and crime scenes to obtain evidence, such as fibers (with ultraviolet light), fingerprints, trace metals, and body fluids (blue light), not visible through other methods. A new method of detecting and photographing wound patterns on skin utilizes the fluorescent light emitted when skin is illuminated by ultraviolet or blue light. This technique is referred to as Narrow Band Imaging and is based on the fact that healthy tissue fluoresces and unhealthy, damaged, or diseased tissue does not. In this manner, a wound pattern appears as a dark image against an illuminated screen of healthy tissue. The image can be viewed or photographed through UV- or Blue-blocking filters and recorded on standard photographic film or videotape. (For more information on this subject, see Chapter 20 in Geberth, 2006.)

Remember: Bite mark identification represents individual characteristic evidence, which can positively identify a suspect.

Maggots

Flies are the most common insects to attack the body after death. However, various insects may eat the flesh of, or lay eggs on, the body of the deceased. Observation of insect larvae can aid in the estimation of time of death (Figure 6.47 and Figure 6.48).

Figure 6.47 Blowflies on body. These blowflies are seeking areas on the body to lay their eggs, which will become maggots. (Photo courtesy of Detective Mark Czworniak, Chicago Police Department.)

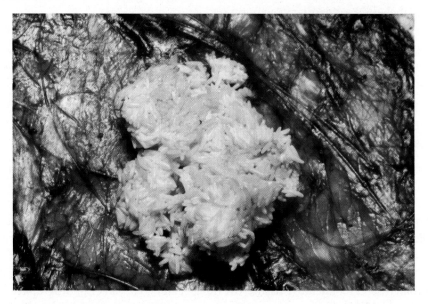

Figure 6.48 Blowfly eggs. A mass of freshly laid blowfly eggs. (Photo courtesy of Detective Mark Czworniak, Chicago Police Department.)

This is an example of the assistance that an *entomologist*—insect expert—can lend to the investigator. Many insects develop from eggs and then progress through growth stages before emerging as adult insects. The time element involved in this developmental stage is rather constant for any given species. For instance, the adult female housefly deposits eggs upon the remains, usually in the mucous membranes of the eyes, mouth, nostrils, but also in the wounds and bloody parts of the body. These eggs are white and measure about 1/16th of an inch long and are laid in clumps. The eggs develop into the larvae (maggots), which then feed off the body. The usual time span for hatching of the maggot is 24 hours. On a body lying indoors, the larvae usually come from the common housefly (*Musca domestica*) (Figure 6.49).

Development time varies among the various species of flies. Temperature and humidity play very important roles in this developmental stage, as do other factors. The larvae may even go into a period of suspended animation if conditions do not warrant further development (Figure 6.50 and Figure 6.51).

Figure 6.49 Maggot mass. Estimated to be developed from 5 to 7 days; 2nd and 3rd instars. (Photo courtesy of Detective Mark Czworniak, Chicago Police Department.)

Figure 6.50 Maggots migrating from food source. This photo shows the 3rd instar maggots leaving their food source in search of a place to hatch. (Photo courtesy of Detective Mark Czworniak, Chicago Police Department.)

Figure 6.51 Pupae. Hard shell-like casings or cocoons left behind after the maggot hatches and the adult fly emerges. (Photo courtesy of Detective Mark Czworniak, Chicago Police Department.)

The bluebottle or blowfly (*Calliphora erythrocephala*), green bottles (*Lucilia caesar*), and sheep maggot flies (*Lucilia sericata*) are the most common type found on remains discovered outdoors. The investigator at the scene and the medical examiner at the autopsy should collect some specimens for examination by an entomologist who can identify the specific insect and provide an estimated time frame based on the stage of growth or development of the larvae. In addition, the experienced entomologist can possibly identify the stage of the life cycle and ultimately the season of the year in which death occurred. The collection of maggots, which have been recovered from the body, can also be used to determine the DNA of the victim. After all, you are what you eat.

In order to assist the entomologist in making an accurate determination, the following procedure for collection and preservation of specimens is recommended:

1. Collect some maggots from the remains and place them in a KAAD (kerosene-acetic acid-dioxane) solution. (This is a mixture of kerosene and alcohol along with certain other ingredients for preservation.) If this solution is not available, place the sample in hot water first and then in a bottle containing alcohol, then seal it. The hot water bath will prevent the alcohol from shriveling the sample and maintain the specimen in a condition for examination.
2. Collect some live maggots as a control sample and place them in a separate container.
3. Collect any pupae (hard shell-like casings or cocoons) from around the site, under the body, and from the corpse. Keep the samples separated. The presence of pupae usually indicates a minimum time span of approximately two weeks. However, there may be several cycles involved, and the determination should be left to the entomologist.

Note that the type of maggots found on the body may be significant. For example, the presence of larvae from a housefly found on a body outdoors will indicate that the body had previously been indoors.

In addition to flies and maggots, a body is also subject to insect attack from different types of beetles that feed off the body (called carrion beetles), as well as ants and even worms that bore their way into the body. These are among a vast host of scavengers responsible for recycling decaying materials.

The recommended procedure for collecting all insect samples is to place them in 75% ethyl alcohol for preservation.

The forensic entomologist has knowledge of many of the habits of insects and other invertebrates most likely encountered on the corpse and/or in the immediate surroundings of the scene. Seemingly insignificant data to the untrained eye, such as insects not found on the body, habitat information, and climatological conditions, can be observed by the entomologist. This knowledge enables him to form certain determinations and opinions of how long the body has been at the scene.

In keeping with the team concept of homicide investigation, I recommend that an entomologist, if available, be brought to the scene to assist the investigators. The entomologist's expertise will ensure that proper entomological techniques are employed and the collection of specimens is conducted as it should be.

Application of DNA Technology

Introduction

Biological evidence retrieved from a victim or crime scene can now be examined at its most fundamental level—the deoxyribonucleic acid (DNA) molecule. There are several private corporations in addition to the FBI laboratory that perform forensic DNA analysis. (For a more in-depth discussion of the application of DNA technology, see Chapter 16 in Geberth, 2006.)

DNA profiling can be utilized to

1. Establish the link between evidential DNA with that of the possible suspect's DNA.
2. Identify whether the DNA in question is human or nonhuman.
3. Establish the sex of the specimen through the amelogenin gene.

Deoxyribonucleic Acid—DNA

DNA is housed in every nucleated cell in the body. Red blood cells are nonnucleated cells and do not contain DNA. These DNA molecules are often described as the body's blueprints because they carry the genetic codes that govern the structure and function of every component of the body. DNA has been described as the fundamental natural material, which determines the genetic characteristics of all life forms. Although there are portions of our DNA that are relatively conserved through the evolutionary process, as humans we share a human form that is basically human specific, while other classes of organisms share a DNA composition unique to that particular species, i.e., dog, cat, elephant, horse, cow, insect, fish, mouse.

In fact, the DNA molecule carries the genetic information that establishes each person as separate and distinct (the exception is identical twins). We as humans create progeny through the transfer of this DNA to our children. According to the genetic experts, the DNA molecule's configuration does not vary from cell to cell. Therefore, the billions of cells that make up each person contain the same molecules of DNA carrying the same codes in precisely the same sequence.

The Cell

The cell is the basic unit of all living organisms including humans, animals, insects, and plants. The human body has more than 10 trillion cells. The cell is composed of two parts:

1. Nucleus, which contains two structures: the chromosomes and the nucleoli
2. Cytoplasm, which is all of the material inside the cell membrane outside of the nucleus

The Nucleus

The nucleus contains the cell's genetic program, a sort of master plan that controls everything the cell does. The chromosomes within the nucleus are composed mainly of DNA and associated proteins. The chromosome stores and transmits genetic information. The DNA molecule is tightly coiled within the nucleus of a cell similarly to a ball of yarn. When unraveled, a molecule of DNA is approximately six feet in length. This DNA molecule is recognized by the scientists as a double-stranded helix.

Sources of DNA

Any biological materials containing nucleated cells are sources of DNA. These include

- Blood
- Body fluids: semen, saliva, vaginal secretions, urine, some fecal matter, perspiration, pus, and skin cells from point of contact
- Tissue
- Muscle
- Bone
- Tooth pulp
- Hair
- Maggots from the cadaver

Types of DNA

Nuclear DNA

Nuclear DNA is commonly referred to as the hereditary material of life due to its role in transmitting genetic information from generation to generation. Nuclear DNA is inherited in a diploid fashion, with half of our DNA inherited from our mothers and the remaining half from our fathers. Normal humans have 46 chromosomes organized as 23 pairs. The 23rd pair is specific to the sex chromosomes where an X or Y chromosome is inherited from the father and an X chromosome is inherited from the mother. In its native

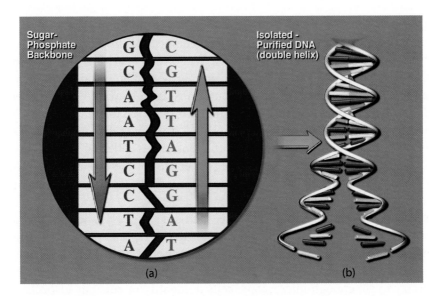

Figure 6.52 DNA molecule. (a) Double-stranded DNA in its uncoiled form resembling a ladder structure representation of A-T G-C base pairing. (b) DNA in its native helical form. (Figure courtesy of Medical Legal Art, Illustration © 2005 Medical Legal Art: www.doereport.com. With permission of *Practical Homicide Investigation*, 4th ed., CRC Press, Boca Raton, FL.)

form, DNA exists as a double-stranded helix composed of a series of nitrogenous bases known as nucleotides with a sugar and phosphate backbone. There are four bases: two purines (adenine (A) and guanine (G)), and two pyrimidines (thymine (T) and cytosine (C)). If one could envision the DNA helix uncoiled, it would resemble a ladder with sides (Figure 6.52).

Mitochondrial DNA

Mitochondrial DNA is 16,569 base pairs in length; it typically exists as a circular molecule. The mtDNA genome has been completely sequenced. Mitochondria are organelles that reside in the cellular cytoplasm and contain their own DNA. Every cell in the human body may contain from 10 to thousands of mitochondria, the energy-producing center or the power plants of cells. Mitochondrial DNA is inherited in a haploid fashion and is passed from the mother to the child. Thus, lineage can be traced through the maternal line: grandmother to her children to her daughters' children, staying in the female line.

There are many more copies of mtDNA than nuclear DNA. The advantage of mtDNA typing over nuclear DNA is the added sensitivity in cases where nuclear DNA is significantly degraded or scarce, such as from bone fragments, hair without root, teeth, and other biological evidence that may be limited.

Y-Chromosomal DNA

The human Y chromosome is approximately 60 million base pairs in size. Unlike nuclear DNA, Y chromosomal DNA is inherited from father to son and is transferred along the paternal lineage; commonly referred to as a haploid fashion of inheritance. The Y chromosome plays a central role in human biology. The presence or absence of this chromosome determines gender. Therefore, the presence of a Y chromosome in a developing embryo results in a male child, while those without it become female.

Touch DNA

Recent technology, such as Touch DNA, which is named for the fact that it analyzes skin cells left behind when assailants touch victims, weapons, or anything else in a crime scene. Touch DNA doesn't require you to see anything, or obtain any blood or semen at all. It only requires seven or eight cells from the outermost layer of skin. Humans shed tens of thousands of skin cells each day, and these cells are transferred to every surface with which skin comes in contact. When a crime is committed, if the perpetrator deposits a sufficient number of skin cells on an item at the scene, and that item is collected as possible evidence, Touch DNA analysis may be able to link the perpetrator to the crime scene. Touch DNA has been successfully sampled from countless items including gun grips, steering wheels, eating utensils, and luggage handles, just to name a few.

Investigators recover cells from the scene, then use a process called polymerase chain reaction (PCR) to make lots of copies of the genes. Next, scientists mix in fluorescent compounds that attach themselves to 13 specific locations on the DNA and give a highly specific genetic portrait of the person. Analysts scrape or swab surfaces, such as clothing or food, to try to get enough microscopic cells to identify or rule out suspects in violent crimes, robberies, and burglaries. Unlike other DNA methods, Touch DNA is used on surfaces without a visible stain, such as blood, but that investigators suspect might contain genetic material.

Since Touch DNA is usually deposited in smaller amounts than the DNA found in bloodstains or other body fluids, it is more difficult to obtain DNA profiles from Touch DNA samples. The key to obtaining successful Touch DNA results depends on recognizing items that may be suitable for Touch DNA analysis and using the sampling technique that will recover the highest number of skin cells.

DNA Amplification (Polymerase Chain Reaction)

PCR was discovered in 1983 by an American chemist named Kerry Mullis who was later awarded a Nobel Prize in 1993. The basis of PCR is that it mimics the cell's ability to replicate DNA. With this technology, unlimited copies of DNA can be duplicated from trace quantities of DNA in the laboratory using an instrument known as a thermal cycler. This breakthrough in technology has revolutionized forensic science and the way crimes are being investigated and solved (Figure 6.53).

Short Tandem Repeats (STR Technology)

STR is an abbreviation for a "short tandem repeat." This test looks for short sections of DNA that have unique patterns of nucleotides. STR loci are polymorphic genetic markers that are well distributed throughout the human genome. These repeated STRs are unique to each person and can be used for positive identification of individuals. These patterns can be extremely helpful in solving crimes.

STR DNA testing can often be performed on small or degraded samples that are often the only materials available at the crime scene. Such are usually done in conjunction with DNA amplification using PCR procedures. Many STR tests can be analyzed at once. Further, the interpretation is simplified and nonsubjective due to the discrete sizes of the STR repeats.

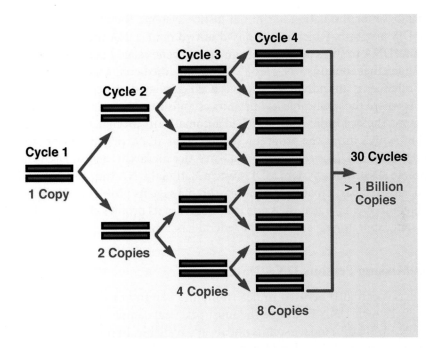

Figure 6.53 Schematic representation of the DNA duplication process of PCR. Following four cycles of PCR, 8 identical copies of the original DNA region are produced. Because DNA is replicated in exponential fashion, cycle 5, 6, and 7 will produce 16, 32, and 64 copies, respectively. At the completion of a 30-cycle reaction, greater than 1 billion copies are duplicated. (Information by Dr. Pasquale Buffolino, Director of Department of Forensic Genetics, Nassau County Medical Examiner's Office. Figure courtesy of Medical Legal Art, Illustration © 2005 Medical Legal Art: www.doereport.com. Reproduced with permission from *Practical Homicide Investigation*, 4th ed., CRC Press, Boca Raton, FL.)

What Exactly Is an STR?

It may contain repeating units of three to seven building blocks. For instance, CATT is a 4 repeat STR. CATTCATTCATTCATTCATT is a 4 repeat STR randomly repeated 5 times. The number of times the core sequence is repeated represents the "type" of an individual.

Advantages The small size of STR loci improves the chance of obtaining a result. The small size range of STR loci makes them ideal for multiplexing, which allows the examiner to look at multiple DNA locations (loci) simultaneously. Multiplexing allows fast analysis with high discriminating power. Interpretation of STR types is simplified through the use of computers, which analyze the sample. The STR primers tagged with fluorescent dyes are incorporated into the STR during the polymerase chain reaction (PCR). Fluorescent dye technology increases the number of tests performed with each PCR run. Currently, 9 STRs and amelogenin (X,Y) can be identified in one test run. The STRs are sized under electrophoretic conditions and analyzed using state-of-the-art software.

CODIS

The national DNA database known as the COmbined DNA Index System (CODIS) began as a 14-state pilot study in 1990. The program expanded nationally as a result of the 1994 DNA Identification Act (Public Law 103 322) giving the FBI legal authority to establish a DNA database for the nation's criminal justice system. Today, all 50 states participate in the CODIS program, which is composed of two main DNA indexes: a Forensic Index that contains DNA profiles developed from crime scene related evidence and a Convicted Offender Index that contains DNA profiles from qualified convicted offenders. A qualified convicted offender is an individual who has been convicted of a crime in federal, state, or local courts where the applicable law permits establishment of a DNA record for the convicted person. The two indices are searched automatically for matching DNA profiles.

The FBI, which funds the program, requires that all participating laboratories utilize the same 13 STR. CODIS is structured as a three-tier hierarchy: a local DNA Index System (LDIS), a State DNA Index System (SDIS), and a National DNA Index System (NDIS). With this approach, each participating laboratory can manage its profiles in accordance with its own legal requirements, but at the same time compare its profiles electronically with other local and state laboratories, and with the federal laboratory.

National Missing Persons DNA Database

DNA databases can also be used to determine the identity of a missing person. Ideally, the individual's own DNA would be the most practical sample to determine an identity; however, DNA from missing persons is not always available. In these type of cases, familial DNA from parents can be used to identify individuals through DNA. A National Missing Persons DNA Database has been established through CODIS. DNA from unidentified remains are compared to a database of DNA samples given voluntarily by family members to establish genetic links.

Collection and Preservation

The most crucial role is the examination of biological evidence. The integrity rests with the crime scene investigator to assure proper collection procedures. Biological evidence may contain hazardous pathogens, such as hepatitis viruses and HIV.

Crime scene investigators must use precautions. The same universal precautions that protect the crime scene investigator from biological pathogens also protect the integrity of DNA. Tyvex® jumpsuits, respirators, and latex gloves minimize the contamination from external sources.

There are essentially three methods of collection: (1) swabbing, (2) cutting, and (3) recovery of the entire item. Regardless of the method of collection, all stains, swabs, and other wet evidence must be thoroughly air dried before packaging.

1. For dried stains, the cotton swab should be moistened with sterile water.
2. Biological evidence should be collected by cutting when swabbing is not possible, such as on porous surfaces.
3. When faced with blood soaked items, which will soak through paper, they may be packaged in plastic containers for the purposes of transport.

Civil Applications of DNA Testing
Paternity testing
Child support enforcement
Human rights issues

Immigration issues
Missing person identification
Breed identification
Historical interests

Application in Forensic Medicine

Victim Identification

DNA profiling has been successfully used in a number of criminal investigations to positively identify the deceased. In one particular case, scientists were able to confirm that the brain matter found in a missing woman's vehicle belonged to the victim, who was identified through her DNA and the DNA of her parents. Skeletonized remains (bone marrow), body parts, and other materials that contain nucleated cells can be analyzed for DNA and provide authorities with an identification.

Forcible Rape

DNA offers the criminal justice system an unprecedented opportunity to obtain the strongest possible evidence from semen specimens. Prior to DNA technology, the best that forensics scientists could provide was an exclusion or suggestion of inclusion based on specimens that had been analyzed for blood type and protein polymorphic enzymes. Semen would be mixed with the vaginal fluids, which also contain proteins. This would make determining identity by protein analysis difficult. In other cases where there were multiple assailants, several semen samples would become intermingled making any determination of identity by protein analysis almost impossible.

DNA profiling, however, can provide close to positive individual identification. Because it is possible to physically separate sperm cells from vaginal epithelial cells, and because each contains its own DNA, mixtures can be sorted out and interference by bacteria eliminated. It is also applicable to old stains. It's like the criminal leaving his name, address, and social security number at the scene of the crime. The evidence can then be submitted to the national CODIS database to ascertain if there is a match to profiles of convicted offenders or other unknown DNA from crime scene related evidence.

Investigation of a Series of Crimes

DNA profiling is useful in investigations of a series of similar crimes. If several rapes have been committed in the same general area, forensic experts can test the semen specimens from the victims and know whether they should be looking for one suspect or multiple suspects. When evidence from one crime scene is compared with evidence from another using CODIS, those crime scenes can be linked to the same perpetrator locally, statewide, and nationally.

Forensic scientists in public and private DNA laboratories have provided forensic evidence in a number of serial rape and murder cases and provided prosecutors with crucial evidence in many other cases as well.

Reopening Unsolved Cases

Because DNA maintains its integrity in dried specimens for prolonged periods, DNA profiling can be utilized on old evidence. In my capacity as an investigative consultant, I have reopened a number of cases for DNA analysis. I conferred with the detectives in a case, which was approximately 12 years old to consider this forensic technique. The authorities in that jurisdiction now have forensic evidence linking a serial killer to crimes a dozen years old.

DNA patterns from old evidence can also be compared with DNA patterns of recently apprehended suspects. Or, cases from the past, in which evidence was inconclusive, can now be tested using DNA technology.

The Green River Killer: A Cold Case Investigation

The Green River Killings, which began in 1982 and abruptly ended in 1984, involved some 49 victims. The women, some of whom had histories of prostitution, started disappearing in 1982. Many were last seen along Pacific Highway South near to Sea-Tac Airport (Seattle, Washington). Countless leads and the scarce evidence they had to deal with frustrated the police. Most of the bodies that were recovered were in various degrees of decomposition or had been skeletonized.

The Green River Killer seemed like a phantom striking at will and leaving hardly a trace. He reached his peak in 1983, murdering as many as five women a month. Fishermen, bikers, nature hikers, people walking their dogs, etc., were finding the bodies of these victims in a wide area around Sea-Tac. Many times when the police arrived to examine a body in the woods, they would come across the remains of several others nearby.

The police requested an FBI profile of this elusive killer and were told by Quantico that the subject "… felt humiliated by women, was an outdoorsman who knew the local countryside well, and may have some religious motives." Obviously, the profile was too broad to be very useful.

In 1984 the Green River Task Force was set up to investigate the series of crimes. More than $15 million was spent, thousands of suspects were checked out, and more than 750 binders were filled with millions of facts. However, the police still did not have a suspect.

However, in 1987, a suspect who was reportedly seen by witnesses with two of the victims prior to their deaths was interviewed. His name was Gary Ridgeway. The police ascertained that he had been arrested in 1982 on a "prostitution sting" after he approached a female undercover officer and asked for sex. In 1984, a prostitute reported Ridgeway after she became uneasy about the way he approached her for sex on Pacific Highway.

The police felt that Ridgeway was available as a suspect and suspicious enough to warrant further investigation. The police obtained a search warrant and executed the warrant on his residence and vehicles. They also took hair cuttings and had Ridgeway bite down on a piece of gauze to obtain saliva, which contains buccal cells. However, all of the evidence was at best circumstantial.

The Green River Task Force began to wind down in the 1990s and by 1991 only a single detective, Jim Jensen, was assigned to basically monitor any new information and keep track of all of the information that had been collected. It appeared that the entire case was in a permanent state of limbo and whoever the murderer was would probably remain free.

In 1997, Dave Reichert, who had been a detective when the case first began, became Sheriff of King County. In April 2001, he called a meeting of detectives who had been assigned to the Green River case to reexamine what they might be able to do in light of the advances in DNA technology. Sheriff Reichert had been discussing with Jensen the possibility of using newly developed DNA testing on samples of semen taken from three of the victim from 1982 and 1983 and comparing these to the buccal cell sample taken from Ridgeway in 1987.

The new technology that Reichert had been discussing with Jensen was called Short Tandem Repeat testing or STR, which only became available in 1997. STR testing has revolutionized DNA analysis because of its unprecedented accuracy. STR measures 13 tiny repeating sections in a DNA sample, which effectively represent a unique bar code on any individual's genome. STR loci are polymorphic genetic markers that are well distributed throughout the human genome.

In March 2001, the laboratory began testing the evidence. In September, the Washington State Crime Lab was able to match Ridgeway to three of the murder victims.

On November 30, 2001, 52-year-old Gary Ridgeway was arrested for murder. The authorities were able to match Ridgeway's DNA to three of the victims. The fourth victim was matched through circumstantial evidence.

Sheriff David Reichert stated that he was not ready to declare that he had captured the Green River Killer. However, he is convinced that Gary Ridgeway is responsible for some of the deaths of women on the list of Green River victims. The investigation into the Green River cases will continue as the King County investigators sift through thousands of reports and over 10,000 pieces of evidence. The bottom line is that 20 years after these murders, a suspect has been charged in connection with four of the slayings due to advances in DNA technology (Reichert, 2001, personal interview).

Cold Case Ruse

In 1982, little 13-year-old Kristen Sumstad was raped and strangled by an offender who left her body dumped in trash in a large, brown, cardboard box behind a store in Seattle, Washington. The offender John Nicholas Athan, who was 14 at the time, was a suspect, but the police did not have sufficient evidence to charge him. He was seen pushing a hand truck and a large brown box down a street in the city's Magnolia neighborhood the night before Kristen's body was found in a television box behind a store about four blocks away. Athan told investigators he had used the hand truck to steal firewood from his neighbors. He remained a suspect as the case went cold. Athan and his mother later left the area and went back to New Jersey where Athan found employment as a construction worker.

Detective Richard Gagnon (Gagnon personal interview, 2006) and his partner Gregg Mixsell, who were assigned to cold case investigations, knew that 10 years later, scientists at the Washington State Patrol crime laboratory tried and failed to extract a DNA profile from the sperm that had been recovered from the little girl's body in 1982. The two detectives decided to have the sperm retested with the newer STR/PCR technology in 2002. However, the detectives would need a sample of Athan's DNA to compare it to their evidence. One of their colleagues suggested a bogus class action lawsuit, and another detective drafted the letter with a stamped self-addressed envelope for the suspect to lick and seal. Athan got the official-looking letter about a class-action lawsuit filed on behalf of people who had been overcharged on parking tickets. If he wanted to take part in the case, he was told that he had to sign and return the enclosed form. He licked the self-addressed envelope, sent it back hoping to get some money. The saliva on the flap of the envelope was matched genetically to semen taken from the body of 13-year-old Kristen Sumstad. Athan, who was 35 years old, was arrested on murder charges on May 21, 2002.

The letter was part of ruse devised by detectives to get a sample of Athan's DNA and connect him to a slaying that had gone unsolved for nearly 21 years. Athan's defense attorney claimed invasion of privacy and violation of his clients constitutional rights and claimed that the sample was involuntarily taken. That was overruled when the prosecutor explained that the detective was listed as a "partner" in the law firm. Police ingenuity and creativity was instrumental in solving this case.

Police have long used deception to get evidence or information from suspects. It's not unlike a time-honored ruse in which police bring a suspect to the station for a friendly conversation and offer a drink of water. After the suspect leaves, the glass is dusted for prints. Or, the bottle is swabbed for DNA. DNA samples and other evidence collected in public places are not protected by the Fourth Amendment prohibition on warrantless searches and seizures. Just because you were outwitted doesn't mean it was not voluntary.

DNA John Doe Warrants

Sometimes cases are solved only by advances in science, for example, the Green River Case.

Nationally, prosecutors in several states have used these warrants to avoid losing a case due to the statute of limitations. The DNA print identifies the offender. Scientists match up 13 "core loci" on a person's chromosomes, or STR.

The probability of a random or false match is 1 in 3 trillion, according to federal scientists. DNA evidence is almost as accurate as a fingerprint. Identical twins do share the same DNA, but not fingerprints. Also it's important that DNA as a science has no emotions, no prejudices, and no biases. "Killer is still nameless, but not unknown." He is better known as John Doe or, by the 13 loci of CODIS as:

D3S1358: 15/16, vWA: 17/17, FGA: 22.5/ 25, D8S1179: 12/13, D21S11: 30.2/31, D18S51: 13/ 14, D5S818: 12/12, D13S317: 11/12, D7S820: 7/9, D16S539: 10/11, THO1: 6/9, TPOX: 8/11, CSF1PO: 11/11 and DQ alpha 4/4.

DNA Evidence Conclusion

DNA and genetic fingerprinting represent the most important breakthrough in crime detection since the discovery of the fingerprint. DNA technology represents the future of forensic medicine and the experts have only begun to scratch the surface with this technology. It is a powerful tool that protects the innocent just as surely as it pinpoints the guilty. Genetic identification takes the "gamesmanship" out of the trial—it either is the defendant who committed the crime, or it is not.

References

Bodziak, W.J., *Footwear Impression Evidence: Detection, Recovery, and Examination*, 2nd ed., CRC Press, Boca Raton, FL, 2000.

Gagnon, R., personal interview, April 2006.

Geberth, V.J., *Practical Homicide Investigation: Tactics, Procedures, and Forensic Techniques*, 4th ed., CRC Press, Boca Raton, FL, 2006.

Lee, H.C., T. Palmbach, and M.T. Miller, *Henry Lee's Crime Scene Handbook*, Academic Press, New York, 2001.

Reichert, D., personal interview, August 2002.

Saferstein, R., *Criminalistics: An Introduction to Forensic Science*, 6th ed., Prentice Hall, Englewood Cliffs, NJ, 1998.

Shaler, R., personal interview, August and September, 2002.

The Star Ledger, Many WTC dead may go unidentified, July 13, 2002, p. 3.

Further Reading

Bodziak, W.J. *Tire Tread and Tire Track Evidence,* CRC Press, Boca Raton, FL, 2008.

Frye v. United States, 293 F. 1013 at 1014 (D.C. Cir. 1923).

Jeffreys, A.J., V. Wilson, and S.L. Thein, Individual-specific fingerprints of human DNA, *Nature*, 316: 76–79, 1985.

New York Post, DNA effort may close with 800 never ID'd, July 13, 2002, p. 6.

People v. Wesley, 73 NY2d, Albany, NY, 1988.

Interpersonal Violence-Oriented Disputes and Assaults and Sex-Related Domestic Violence Murders

7

Introduction

Sex-related homicides cover interpersonal-oriented disputes and assaults, which include domestic violence homicides involving sexual assault, rape–murders, serial murders, killings that involve anal and oral sodomy and other acts of sexual perversion, and sexually oriented interpersonal violence cases.

A homicide is classified as "sex-related" when there is evidence of sexual activity observed in the crime scene or upon the body of the victim. This includes the following:

1. The type of, or lack of, attire on the victim.
2. Evidence of seminal fluid on, near, or in the body.
3. Evidence of sexual injury or sexual mutilation.
4. Sexualized positioning of the body.
5. Evidence of substitute sexual activity, i.e., fantasy, ritualism, symbolism, or masturbation.
6. Multiple stabbings or cuttings to the body. This includes slicing wounds across the abdomen of the victim, throat slashing, and overkill-type injuries, which are considered highly suggestive of a sexual motivation (Geberth, 1986).

The victims of these crimes are usually females and young children, and the killer is most often a male. However, it is important to note that sex-related homicides involve homosexual as well as heterosexual relationships.

The homicide might have sexual implications even without an overt sex act or observable sexual activity at the crime scene. It is important to note that unlike other murders, the motive or reason for the killing may not always be readily discernable or as "clear cut" as is presented in a robbery–homicide, a drug-related murder, or an organized crime "hit."

Practically speaking, if the body is that of a female and it is found nude or partially clothed, the investigator should think "sex crime."

Classifications

In my professional opinion as an expert in the sphere of homicide investigation, sex-related homicides should be classified into *four distinct categories* based on their frequency of occurrence and statistical probabilities.

My opinion of the FBI Classification of Crime, as found in the *Crime Classification Manual (CCM)* (Douglas et al., 1995) is that it does not facilitate or assist in the solving of criminal offences. These *CCM* classifications serve no purpose other than to allow "alleged experts" to testify to the data and statistical information compiled in a research project. In fact, the *CCM* not only confuses the investigative process, it actually allows for an interpretation of events that may not conform to state, county, and local government legislation as it applies to the specific crime.

According to the Preface in the *Crime Classification Manual,* the purpose of classifying crimes is fourfold:

1. To standardize terminology within the criminal justice field
2. To facilitate communication within the criminal justice field and between criminal justice and mental health practitioners
3. To educate the criminal justice system and the public at large to the types of crimes being committed
4. To develop a database for investigative research (Douglas et al., 1995)

I believe that the FBI attempted to produce the equivalent of a *Diagnostic and Statistical Manual of Mental Disorders (DSM-IV-TR)*–type publication (APA, 2000), which is fine for research and theoretical analysis of criminal events in the area of clinical research, but lacks the **practical application** necessary in the investigative practice.

In the "real world" of death investigation, we do not need to complicate the investigative process by constructing theoretical definitions and subclassifications for computer analysis. I believe in keeping things simple. I have instructed, proposed, and recommended that the criminal investigator approach sex-related death investigations by considering the **practical** statistical significance of the *four classifications of sex-related homicides.*

1. Interpersonal violence-oriented disputes and assaults, which include domestic violence homicides
2. Rape- and sodomy-oriented assault
3. Deviant-oriented assault commonly referred to as a lust murder or psychotic killing (In these situations, the motive for the murder may not be readily discernible.)
4. The serial murder

I will address each of these specific categories in this and the following chapters. I list them in their frequency of occurrence. In other words, before I go out looking for a serial killer, I would consider the possibilities of the previous classifications with a view toward the victimology.

Remember: National surveys to date indicate that most women are raped by someone they know.

Interpersonal Violence-Oriented Disputes and Assaults

The most common type of sex-related homicide originates from interpersonal violence. *Sexual domestic disputes* involve husbands and wives, men and women, boyfriends and girlfriends, boyfriends and boyfriends, girlfriends and girlfriends, and even on occasion, siblings. They may also involve third-party relationships, such as love triangles, former husbands or wives, and jilted or would-be lovers.

Practically speaking, whenever a man reports the sudden death of his wife, girlfriend, lover, or associate, or makes a report of a "missing person" from one of those relationships, a smart homicide cop should immediately consider him a possible suspect until the facts prove otherwise.

Who kills women in our society? Men. The author bases this conclusion on statistics. In fact, experienced murder cops usually take a good, hard look at the husband, lover, or boyfriend to scrutinize their behaviors as they report the event.

Are they too demonstrative in their grief? Have they surrounded themselves with concerned relatives? Or, do they have their act together and seem to be going through the motions. The subject who uses all the right words and comes across as overly confident or nonchalant would be a good candidate for further investigation.

In my experience, the innocent husband or wife may go into shock and remain in shock for a considerable period of time. Their grief rings true and their actions and behaviors are in sync with the event. The experienced detective will immediately recognize the difference.

The author includes domestic violence homicides within this category because murder serves as the ultimate form of sexual revenge and accounts for a number of sex-related homicides.

In some instances, the death may not appear to be sexually motivated. However, upon an examination into the background and relationships of the victim, a new possibility soon presents itself to the authorities.

The O. J. Simpson case was a classic domestic violence homicide coupled with the unfortunate murder of Ron Goldman, who just happened to be in the wrong place at the wrong time. Simpson had a history of domestic violence incidents involving his wife, Nicole.

The police were certainly correct in looking at Simpson as a suspect. However, the case became politicized and sensationalized and common sense went out the window (Figure 7.1).

Figure 7.1 O. J. Simpson crime scene on Bundy Drive. The body of Nicole Brown was found lying in blood at her home. Ron Goldman's body was found a short distance away. Evidence indicated that there had been a violent struggle and that the offender had most likely cut himself while struggling with his victims. (Photo courtesy of the author.)

"The trail of blood" theory, based on the DNA analysis, indicated that blood drops at the scene of the double murder of Nicole Brown Simpson and Ron Goldman, as well as blood in O. J. Simpson's Ford Bronco and in his residence positively identified O. J. Simpson as the suspect. The DNA analysis of three stains on the console of Simpson's Ford Bronco indicated that droplets were a mixture of blood from Simpson, the blood of his ex-wife, Nicole Brown, and the blood of Ron Goldman. The famous "bloody gloves" that were presented as evidence provided the crucial linkage. One glove was found at Bundy Drive, the scene of the double homicide. The matching right-hand glove was found at O. J. Simpson's estate. DNA testing of the glove found at O. J. Simpson's estate indicated that blood matching Simpson and the two murder victims "linked" him to the murders. DNA testing of the blood on the glove at Bundy Drive matched O. J. Simpson. The ski cap found near Ron Goldman's body had fibers like those from the carpet in Simpson's Ford Bronco. Goldman's shirt contained a head hair, which matched O. J. Simpson. However, Judge Ito did not allow that evidence into the trial. The socks found in O. J. Simpson's bedroom bore traces of blood from O. J. Simpson and his ex-wife, Nicole, who was one of the murder victims (Figures 7.2 through 7.4).

The defense claim of police misconduct and introduction of race into the trial played upon the emotions of the predominantly black jury. The murder trial was turned into a race trial.

Figure 7.2 Bloody glove found at Bundy Drive. Left-hand glove was found at Bundy Drive. (Photo courtesy of the author.)

Figure 7.3 Bloody glove at Simpson's estate. The matching right–hand glove was found at the Simpson's estate. (Photo courtesy of the author.)

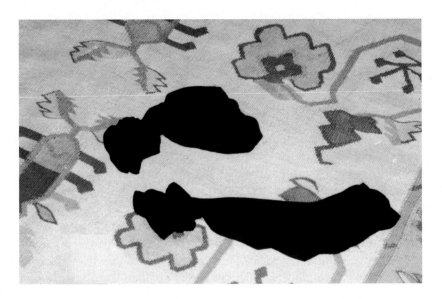

Figure 7.4 Bloody socks. Bloody socks with blood matching the victims were found in O. J. Simpson's bedroom. (Photo courtesy of the author.)

Despite the overwhelming physical and forensic evidence linking O. J. Simpson to the murders, the jury rejected good, solid physical and forensic evidence and rendered a "not guilty" finding.

In my opinion, the DNA analysis of the evidence in this case overwhelming inculpated Simpson. The reality of this physical evidence was proven in the civil trial where he was determined to be responsible for the murders.

I remember a case in which a 36-year-old female executive was found shot to death "execution style." She had been shot three times in the head at close range and her body was left in her automobile, which was found parked under the George Washington Bridge (between New Jersey and New York City). The police investigation revealed that the victim had an ongoing lesbian relationship with a 31-year-old female bartender. Detectives ascertained that the deceased had become embroiled in an argument with her lesbian girlfriend over another woman. The victim had met this woman at an East Side singles bar. When the "other woman" arrived, the argument began and the three ended up leaving the bar together. The deceased drove the auto with her "new friend" sitting in the front seat and her lesbian lover sitting in the rear seat. The argument continued as they drove. During the argument, the jealous lover shot her friend in the head from the back seat. The woman passenger fled the scene as the shooter exited the vehicle and got behind the wheel. She then drove the victim's car and body to the location of discovery. The witness/passenger eventually came forward and police arrested the jealous lover, who was hiding at another woman's Manhattan apartment. Initially, this case did not appear to be a sex-related homicide (From the author's files).

I recall another case in which two boys, who were taking a short cut through a baseball field and found the nude body of an unidentified female. The offender had apparently used a vehicle to transport the victim's body, which was dumped at the site. Detectives located tire mark impressions in the dirt. The body had tumbled down an embankment and rigor had set in.

There was no identification. However, the victim was wearing distinctive rings on her hands. The victim's age was estimated to be between 20 and 30 years of age. The decedent had sustained 31 stab wounds to the chest as well as blunt force trauma to the head and face. The cause of death was multiple stabbing and blunt force traumas. The case appeared to be a rape–murder perpetrated by an unknown offender. After killing his victim at one location, he dumped her body at another. The immediate problem for the investigators was the fact that the victim was unidentified and there were no missing persons reports matching her description (Figure 7.5).

The detectives at the scene documented and collected the tire marks left by the vehicle used to transport the victim to the dumpsite. The crime scene technicians recovered red cotton fibers, which were vacuumed from the victim's body at the scene.

The medical examiner retrieved a blue paint chip from the neck area of the victim's body during the autopsy. In addition, blood pattern evidence on the victim's leg was documented and photographed.

A sketch of the victim, along with a description of her jewelry, was distributed throughout the metropolitan area to law enforcement and the news media in an attempt to identify the unknown female. Three days later, the distinctive rings worn by the victim led to her identification.

A friend of the deceased, who recognized the description of the rings, was located. She identified the body. The friend was also able to provide the police with crucial information about the victim, who was an exotic dancer in a strip club in an adjoining county.

Figure 7.5 Dumped body. This case was first thought to be a rape–murder where the offender had dumped the body. It was, in fact, an interpersonal domestic violence case. The jealous boyfriend of this young woman killed her during a domestic argument and dumped the body in an adjoining county. (Photo courtesy of Captain James Gannon, Morris County, New Jersey, Prosecutor's Office.)

The police learned that she divided her time between two domiciles. She stayed at her boyfriend's house and also had an apartment that she shared with another exotic dancer. Search warrants were obtained for both locations as well as a vehicle owned by the boyfriend. The police recovered the following evidence from the boyfriend's home and his vehicle:

- Police searched his automobile. The tires were matched to the tire marks at the crime scene.
- Blue paint chips were recovered from the trunk. This matched the paint chip on her neck.
- Red cotton fibers found in the garage matched the fiber evidence vacuumed from her body.
- Blood pattern on leg matched that of carpet in the car.
- Piece of wood was matched by blood type to the victim.

The investigation and interviews of the victim's friends revealed that her boyfriend was extremely jealous of her dancing at the club. Police learned that he had had a violent fight with her in his home.

During this fight, he stabbed her and struck her with a blunt instrument. After she was dead, he then stripped her body and put it in the trunk of his car and drove to the adjoining county to dump her body (From the author's files).

A Case with a Twist

I remember responding to a report of a rape–murder in the South Bronx. The nude body of the victim was discovered in her apartment after a neighbor had rescued her baby. The child was observed hanging from the window gate on the fifth-floor window. A crowd had gathered and was calling to the child to hold on. A fourth-floor neighbor had climbed up the fire escape and kicked in the locked window of the victim's apartment to rescue the baby and discovered the body. The victim's body was in an advanced state of decomposition. Apparently the child was trying to escape the noxious odors of the decaying corpse and had climbed up to the windowsill. The woman's nude body was lying on her back on the bed with her legs open. She had suffered numerous stab wounds to the chest and there also was evidence of blunt force trauma. There was a gag around her mouth and neck. On the bed was a plunger with blood on it, suggesting that it had been used in the sexual assault. There also was evidence of a struggle. The victim's panties were around her right leg. A man's ball cap was found next to the body and there were numerous blood splatters on the wall and ceiling in the room. There was no weapon found at the scene (Figure 7.6).

It appeared that she had been sexually assaulted on the bed. The apartment had been locked and the only way in was through a window, which was also locked.

In addition to the plunger, there was a doll and a baby's toy on the bed next to the body. Eventually, we determined that the victim's 18-month-old daughter had probably brought these items to her mother as she attempted to "awaken" her. It was a very sad scenario. The baby had been in this locked apartment with the decomposing body of her mother for three to four days. The baby, who was suffering from malnutrition and exposure, was rushed to the hospital.

The victimology indicated a moderate to high-risk life style. Detectives learned that she had filed a rape charge in connection with a sexual assault one week earlier that had occurred at a club that she frequented. We also learned that she had just recently gotten her baby back from Bureau of Child Welfare (BCW) due to her inappropriate social activities. She reportedly had a boyfriend whom we could not locate, and the neighbor, who saved her baby, had three prior rape charges against him. We had more than enough suspects. Our first suspect was the man against whom she had filed rape charges. We were able to eliminate him immediately. He was still in jail.

We conducted a canvass of the building and spoke to a number of neighbors. No one had heard anything. However, we did locate persons who saw her with the baby on Saturday; her body was found on Monday. Some people were not interviewed because they weren't home. This included her downstairs neighbor.

We interviewed the hero neighbor, who provided us with a detailed description of how he became aware of the event, his entry into the apartment, the rescue of the baby, and how he discovered the body. He provided information about the victim's personal life and a description of her boyfriend, whose name was Junior. He also told us how the victim had recently gotten her child back from BCW and how he had helped her move her bed against the bedroom wall to make room for the crib. In fact, he had a lot of information about the victim, which included the fact that the victim told him she was upset because her boyfriend, Junior, had a set of keys to her apartment.

Figure 7.6 Sex-related homicide. This case appeared to be a rape–murder. It actually was an interpersonal violence-oriented dispute and assault.

Although he provided an elaborate account of his activities at the scene, he was less than forthcoming about his personal life and his extensive arrest record, which included three charges for rape. *He remained a suspect.* However, we needed to locate the victim's boyfriend. It took us two more days to identify and locate an address for Junior, who never seemed to be home when the police went to his apartment. Finally, I decided to put our Night Watch crew on him and he was picked up at 6 a.m. as he left the housing projects for the subway station. When Junior was questioned as to why he was avoiding us, he replied that he was working two jobs and was planning on getting married. He was asked about his relationship with the victim and he stated that she was just a friend and that he hadn't seen her in over a month. Junior was asked about the keys to the victim's apartment. He stated that he had forgotten he had them and handed over the keys to the detectives. One of the detectives brought the keys back to the crime scene and discovered that the locks had been changed. Apparently, the victim had changed the locks without telling anyone. Junior, who was still being interviewed by other detectives at the police station, had volunteered his fingerprints and hair samples to the investigators. In fact, he was extremely cooperative. He had given the detectives the name of his fiancé, who he said could vouch for him. He provided an in-depth statement, which seemingly eliminated him from suspect status. Especially, since the keys didn't fit and he had told detectives he hadn't seen the victim in over a month.

This brought us back to the "hero neighbor," who couldn't or wouldn't provide us with his whereabouts on Saturday evening. We had determined the murder had occurred on that Saturday evening or early Sunday morning. When he was told that we had recovered latent fingerprints in the apartment, he stated, "I told you I was in the lady's apartment and helped her move the bed against the wall." We then asked him what other rooms he had been in. At which time, with a big smile on his face, he answered, "Every room, officer." It was apparent that he had been through a police interrogation before. It looked like a stalemate.

We had been continuing the canvass of the building that the deceased lived in since earlier in the week in an effort to locate everyone who might have information. Detectives were in that same building Saturday evening for the first time.

Author's note: I cannot emphasize enough how important it is for you to conduct your canvasses on the same day of the week as the day of occurrence. Many times, persons you would not ordinarily have an opportunity to interview on other days, in fact, will be home the same day of the week as the day of the occurrence. This principle also applies to roadblock scenarios. Certain days are travel days for different folks and it behooves you to be out there on the particular day of the week that they travel. Especially, if that particular day is the same day of the week as the day the murder occurred.

On Saturday evening, the people in the apartment directly below the deceased's apartment were home. When detectives knocked on their door, they were startled. At first they stated that they didn't want to get involved in anything because they were both married to others and that they just used this apartment on weekends. However, it was too late, they had already indicated that they knew something. Detectives learned that at about midnight last Saturday they heard sounds of a terrible fight upstairs with people running back and forth and yelling and screaming. They told the detectives they heard a female voice scream out, "No, Junior. Stop. Don't," and suddenly the fighting and screaming stopped.

We were floored. Junior seemed like such a nice guy and certainly had cooperated in the investigation. We immediately took a look at the statement the Night Watch detective had taken from Junior during that early morning interview. The Night Watch detective, who had never been to the crime scene, was very meticulous in his reports. In order to clarify his discussion with Junior, he asked him to describe the layout of the victim's apartment as well as locations of various pieces of furniture in the apartment based on the last time he had been there. When we read the page where Junior described the bedroom the last time he was in the apartment, *supposedly one month earlier,* Junior put the bed on the wall where it had been moved to the day before the murder by the downstairs neighbor. We had just cleared the guy we really thought was our suspect. In homicide investigation, "little things mean a lot."

We picked up Junior and brought him in for a reinterview. We confronted him with his earlier statement, which showed that he had lied to us and then advised him of the downstairs neighbors. He broke down and confessed.

It wasn't a rape. They had consensual sex in the bedroom and when they had finished, the victim asked Junior when she would see him again. Junior told her that he was getting married and that he wouldn't be able to be with her anymore. Junior stated that the victim got very angry with him and ran into the kitchen and got a steak knife and began chasing him through the apartment. Junior stated he used a child's toy baseball bat to hit the knife away and grabbed it from the victim. He then stated that he "blacked out." We asked him what happened when he blacked out and he stated he stabbed and hit her in the head with the baseball bat until she wasn't moving anymore. He then left the apartment through the window, which he closed behind him. The window locked in the down position. He then carried the bloody knife and the toy bat down the fire escape. He disposed of these items in a sewer one block away from the apartment (From the author's files).

Atypical Interpersonal Violence Homicides

It should be noted that in some instances, the interpersonal violence-oriented dispute and assault-type case might appear to be a lust murder, depending on what was done to the victim's body. I remember responding to a call from my Night Watch detectives at an apartment in the South Bronx and supervising the investigation of a case that appeared to have been committed by a lust murderer or a psychotic killer. The partially clad body of a 22-year-old black female, who had been beaten and sexually mutilated, was discovered in her apartment. She had been savagely beaten on the head with a baseball bat and her throat had been slashed.

Next to the body was a blood-stained drinking glass. I observed a lip print in blood on the rim of the glass, suggesting that the glass had been used to drink blood. On the coffee table in the living room were a number of kitchen knives, which had been used to slice the victim's body. All the utensils were lined up on the coffee table like an operating room in a hospital (Figure 7.7 and Figure 7.8).

The victim had been eviscerated and a large soda bottle had been thrust into her abdominal cavity. Her intestines could be observed inside of the clear plastic bottle. There were a number of postmortem slicings to her breasts and chest. In addition, the killer had also carved diagonal wounds into both of the victim's legs.

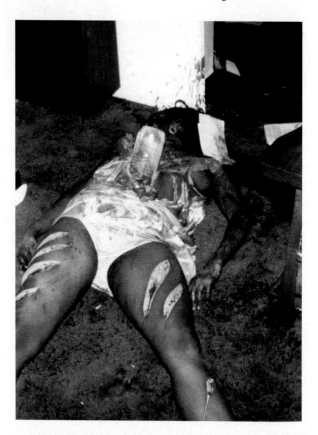

Figure 7.7 Lust murder. Anthropophagy and postmortem mutilation of body. The victim had been hit in the head with a baseball bat. Her throat was cut and there are multiple cuttings to the breasts and legs of the victim. A soda bottle was placed into the eviscerated abdomen and there was evidence that the offender drank the victim's blood.

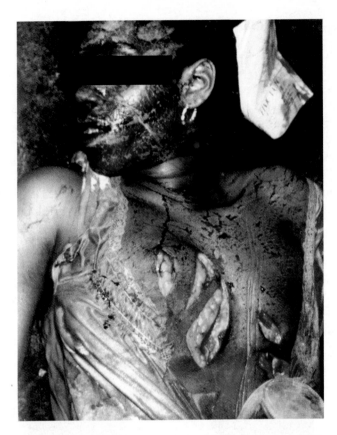

Figure 7.8 Lust murder. This photo shows multiple cuts to the chest and breast.

The case appeared to be the classic disorganized lust murder perpetrated by someone who had used a "blitz-style" attack to render his victim unconscious and then engaged in postmortem mutilation. The investigation revealed that this murder was actually committed in a fit of rage during a domestic dispute by the victim's live-in boyfriend. He had a fight with her during which time she slapped him across the face. He went berserk and hit her with the baseball bat. He then proceeded to engage in these bizarre activities, which included drinking her blood. During his confession, he told us that he drank her blood so that it would flow in his veins. Needless to say, we were quite surprised by that turn of events (from the author's files).

Stalker Murder: A Mother's Nightmare

Joely Ann, a beautiful, young, 23-year-old woman, became the victim of a stalker murder when she attempted to escape the unwelcome advances of a would-be suitor named Robert. In the opinion of the author, Robert had a classic psychopathic personality based on the description of psychopathy by R. D. Hare (Hare, 1993). Robert believed that he was entitled to a relationship with this young woman and when she did not respond to his amorous advances, he became enraged with his loss of control and set out to destroy what he couldn't have.

Joely Ann, a recent college graduate, was sharing an apartment with Robert and another young woman in Metairie, Louisiana. It is noted that at some point Joely Ann became concerned about Robert's obsession with her. He was constantly asking her where she was going and what she was doing. Apparently, Robert wanted more than just to share expenses. On March 31, Joely Ann hastily packed some of her belongings while Robert was temporarily out of the apartment.

She had called another male acquaintance in Thibodaux, Louisiana, and asked him if she could stay there for a while until she could get her own place. He came and drove her to Thibodaux. She left a note behind indicating that she needed to leave. Joely Ann was ultimately attempting to avoid a confrontation with Robert.

The Stalking

Robert reported her missing to local police on April 2 when he realized Joely Ann was not coming back to the apartment. Robert cleverly used the police in an attempt to locate her. Through filing the Louisiana Missing Persons report, he was able to ascertain that Joely Ann's actual residence was in Houston. He then contacted the Houston police in an attempt to locate her. Robert eventually contacted the victim's mother, Dee Ann, whom he repeatedly called asking her if she had heard from Joely Ann or knew her whereabouts. Robert was calling Joely Ann's mother 10 to 15 times a day. Initially, Dee Ann appreciated Robert's concern for Joely Ann. However, the incessant and frantic calls from Robert on a daily basis began to really disturb Dee Ann and make her more concerned about her daughter's safety.

Joely Ann Contacts Her Mother

Dee Ann had not been in contact with Joely Ann since March 31. It was not like her not to be in contact with her mother. When Dee Ann finally heard from her daughter on April 2, she was greatly relieved. Dee Ann, who had "call waiting," was in conversation with Joely Ann when she received a beep indicating that a caller was trying to get through. Robert was on the line and she told him that she was talking to Joely Ann and that she was all right. She also told Robert that Joely Ann was staying with a friend in Thibodaux, Louisiana, and she provided Robert with the person's name. She had given this information to him before she had an opportunity to hear what Joely Ann had to say about Robert and why she left Metairie. When she found out that Joely Ann had left Metairie to get away from Robert, she realized her mistake. Joely Ann then told her mom about Robert and how he made her extremely nervous. Dee Ann asked her, "How in the world did you get involved with him?" Joely Ann told her mother, "He seemed nice when I first met him and there was another girl living at the apartment. I just needed a place to stay for a few days before I got my own apartment." Joely Ann then related to her mother how "he acted so crazy." She told her mother that she felt she couldn't even breathe without him asking her what she was doing. He put roses on her pillow before she went to bed. When she was in the bathroom, he would knock on the door and ask her if she needed toilet paper.

While they were talking, Dee Ann's phone kept beeping indicating that someone was trying to get through. Joely stated, "Oh, mom, it's him again, don't pick up the phone."

Dee Ann then told Joely Ann that Robert had reported her as a missing person to the Jefferson Parish sheriff's office. Joely Ann told her mother that she was going to back to Metairie with her male companion to pick up her things and advise local police that she was *not missing*.

When Joely Ann arrived with her male companion to gather the rest of her belongings, Robert didn't say anything to her in the presence of the other male. What Joely Ann did not realize was that Robert had secreted her driver's license so that he would have an excuse to contact her.

Robert then began calling her in Thibodaux from April 2 to April 5. He would say, "How could you leave me; I've been nothing but nice to you; I can't believe that you left me." He then told her that he would bring her driver's license up if she gave him the address. She told him not to worry about it; she would go to Motor Vehicles and take care of it.

Robert used the driver's license and the missing person's police report and was able to trace her to Thibodaux. Robert actually convinced a supervisor in the telephone company to provide the address in Thibodaux so that he could return her "lost" driver's license.

Lying, deceiving, and manipulation are natural talents for psychopaths (Hare, 1993). Robert was so clever that he had used the police to get information on Joely Ann and then was able to manipulate the telephone supervisor into providing him with confidential information that police officials oftentimes have difficulty obtaining.

The Confrontation

On April 5, Robert borrowed a car from a friend and drove to Thibodaux. He did this so Joely Ann wouldn't recognize his auto. He watched the house and waited until the male resident left for work. When he was sure that Joely Ann was alone, he approached the house on foot and knocked on the front door. Joely Ann answered the knock and was confronted by an angry Robert, who demanded that she come back with him to Metairie. There was a physical struggle and Joely Ann received a black eye. Robert then tried to coerce her into leaving with him. At some point in the discussion, Robert tried to physically remove her from the residence. There was another struggle. At this time, Robert grabbed a knife from the kitchen and began stabbing her in the chest (Figure 7.9).

Figure 7.9 Interpersonal violence. This victim was stalked by a male friend and killed when she spurned his advances. She was stabbed 22 times with 6 different knives. (Photo courtesy of Retired Detective Sergeant Kurt Harrelson, Thibodaux, Louisiana, Police Department.)

Joely Ann was stabbed 22 times with 6 different kitchen knives. In fact, some of the blades were broken off from their handles. Robert, who cut himself during the attack, attempted to "clean up" and then staged the crime scene.

"Staging a scene occurs when the perpetrator purposely alters the crime scene to mislead the authorities or redirect the investigation" (Geberth, 2006).

Robert removed a couple of the knives from the victim's body, placed them on the floor, and left a knife handle on the rug. He then placed a large plastic baggie of marijuana, which he found secreted in the house, on the living room floor to make the event appear to be drug-related.

The Arrest

Robert was fleeing from the scene when he came upon a roadblock. He saw a uniformed officer blocking the roadway with his emergency lights on. Robert thought that Joely Ann's roommate had somehow returned home, discovered the body, and called the police. He thought the roadblock was for *him*. Actually, the roadblock was already in place and the officer was blocking the road for the "Way of the Cross" procession. Good Friday fell on April 5th that year.

The author has personally spoken with Dee Ann many times since this tragedy. Dee Ann states that she believes it was fate that intervened that Good Friday and provided police the opportunity to apprehend this evil person.

Robert told the officer that he was a witness to a murder and had been injured by the killer. Robert told the police that he had gone to the victim's home to return her driver's license, which she had left behind when she moved from Metairie. Robert stated that he, Joely Ann, and a white male named Rick were all smoking marijuana in the living room. Robert stated that he went to the bathroom and, when he returned, he saw Rick stabbing Joely Ann. He said he tried to stop Rick and he was stabbed. Robert told the police that Rick then fled out the back door and Robert closed and locked it. At this point, Robert realized that the detectives would probably find his fingerprints on the knives. Robert stated that he pulled the knives out of Joely Ann to try and save her. He thought this information would explain how his fingerprints would be found on the knives.

Robert was taken to a hospital while other units responded to the crime scene.

The Crime Scene

Officers who had responded to the house found the victim lying on her back in the kitchen in a pool of blood. Joely Ann was wearing a white bra and black shorts. Her T-shirt, which was inside out, was lying a short distance from her body. Apparently, as she tried to get away from Robert, he grabbed her by the shirt and ripped it from her body. A steak knife handle and a fingernail were found in the living room. Three other steak knife handles, a steak knife, and a butter-style knife were located in the kitchen area.

Two knife blades were imbedded in the victim's body. One blade was in her back and the other one jammed into her left leg.

The victim had defensive wounds on her right arm, cuts on her forehead, and patches of hair had been pulled from her head.

The position of her body was such that the back door could not be opened (Figure 7.10). This proved to be vital because the suspect had stated that the killer had run out the back door.

Figure 7.10 Body position. When the offender gave his statement he didn't realize that the door couldn't be opened with the victim's body blocking the doorway. (Photo courtesy of Retired Detective Sergeant Kurt Harrelson, Thibodaux, Louisiana, Police Department.)

Detectives saw bloody footprints as well as blood droppings leading from the body to the bathroom. There was evidence that someone had cleaned up using a towel from the bathroom, which was then refolded and found on the kitchen counter.

There was only one set of bloody shoe prints on the floor, which led to the bathroom *not* the back door, as Robert had stated.

The position of the victim's body prevented the back door from being opened. Therefore, the supposed perpetrator Rick would not have been able to exit the house as Robert had stated.

Blood evidence indicated that only two persons were present. There was also evidence that someone had attempted to clean up in the bathroom.

In his second statement, after being confronted with the discrepancies in his story, Robert told the detectives that he had located the residence by calling the telephone company. He stated he had borrowed a friend's car to drive to Thibodaux to return the victim's driver's license. He stated that, when he arrived, he and Joely Ann talked for a while. He told the detectives that Joely Ann suddenly got angry and demanded that he leave the residence. When he did not comply, she pulled a steak knife on him.

He stated he disarmed her and then picked up the knife to *defend* himself. Robert stated that the argument started in the living room and then Joely Ann ran to the kitchen. He was asked how many times he stabbed her. He stated six or seven times.

When asked why he had used different knives, he stated, "Because they kept breaking." Not only did he attempt to minimize his actions, he had the audacity to blame the victim for the attack. Robert stated that when he stopped stabbing her, she was still alive and he heard her saying that she was sorry. He believed that she was apologizing to him. Just like a psychopath, it was all about him. Possibly Joely, who realized she was near death, was attempting to make her last Act of Contrition, as she had been taught to do when she was a youngster.

The Autopsy

- The victim had 22 stab wounds; three of the fatal wounds were to the heart.
- In addition to the stab wounds, she suffered bruises to her face as well as a black eye indicating she had received this antemortem wound prior to the stabbing.
- This finding ruled out any chance of the suspect obtaining a manslaughter plea.
- The beating had been followed by a cooling-off period and then the fatal stabbing had occurred.

The Evidence

- Seventy-eight items were located and secured by investigators.
- Robert's fingerprints were located on one of the knife blades, the cold water handle of the bathroom faucet, the interior door knob of the back door, and the living room telephone.
- Robert's bloody palm print was found on the utensil drawer containing the knives.
- In addition, blood evidence was found on his clothing and his shoes, which matched the footprints in the scene.
- During the assault, he cut himself on the hand.
- His blood was also found on the victim.

On April 5, Thibodaux Police arrested Robert for second degree murder.

Background Information

All of the Thibodaux, Louisiana, Detective Division had been through the "Practical Homicide Investigation®" seminars conducted by the author. The detectives believed that Robert was trying to con them into thinking that he was just a good guy. In the words of one of the detectives, "He was just too damn polite: 'Yes sir, no sir,' etc. He just didn't seem like the 'killer' type." First, Robert told the detectives that he had recently been released from the Marine Corps to take care of his sick mother. When they checked with the Marines, they found out he had been dishonorably dismissed for going AWOL. This occurred when he had stalked a young woman from California to New Orleans, Louisiana. The detectives didn't locate any criminal history for Robert in Louisiana. However, they discovered that he had been arrested in Texas. He had threatened a woman with death over the phone when she attempted to end a relationship. The police had taped that call. Eventually, detectives located four previous female acquaintances. All four of these young women provided accounts of stalking, harassing, and threatening phone calls as well as physical abuse. In fact, one woman was knocked unconscious when she attempted to end their relationship. The author interviewed each one of these young women who provided a graphic description of the abuse they endured as they tried to end an abusive relationship.

Court Disposition

Robert's trial was scheduled for December 9. However, without explanation, he decided to plead guilty on December 5.

He pled to a mandatory life imprisonment rather than face the jury. There was a rationale for this sudden turn of events. While in the Lafourche Parish jail awaiting court proceedings, Robert had the audacity to contact one of the young women, he had tormented in their relationship. He demanded that she come to visit him at the jail and provide him with companionship. In fact, he was calling this young woman's home 10 to 15 times a day.

The young woman, whom I will refer to as Renée, then called the detectives in Thibodaux to advise them that she was receiving these harassing calls. The detectives told her they would alert the authorities at the Lafourche Parish jail and advised her to get an answering machine to screen her calls. The young woman then had the phone number of the La Fourche Parish Jail blocked so that Robert would not be able to get through. But, Robert was not to be deterred. He made a third party call into the young woman's residence. While waiting for her to pick up, there was a conversation between his cell mate and the cell mate's brother who provided the third party phone. The cellmate's brother asked Robert, "Are you the guy who killed that girl (meaning Joely Ann)." Robert stated, while the answering machine was recording, "Yeah, I killed her and she deserved it and I really messed her up. And this 'bitch' [meaning Renée] got her phone blocked so I can't call." This taped conversation was damaging and Robert knew it. That was why he pled guilty.

On December 9, he was sentenced to life imprisonment at hard labor in Louisiana State Prison in Angola.

Court Grants Appeal: Approves Retrial

A liberal activist female defense attorney petitioned the courts for an appeal and retrial, which was granted in March 2000. The family of Joely Ann, especially Dee Ann, were psychologically devastated to think that this nightmare was about to begin all over again.

The defense attorney, who was aware that the State had some compelling witnesses ready to testify, including the young woman who had been harassed by Robert and provided authorities with that damaging recording, kept delaying and requesting continuances into 2001.

The retrial took place in February 2001. During the trial, the defense attorney contended that Robert should not have been charged with second degree murder because it was an act of passion and rejection brought on by Joely Ann's provocation because she attacked Robert, who was defending himself. The defense attorney also tried to present that Joely Ann was high on drugs and crack cocaine and had been the aggressor.

The State strategically presented the toxicology evidence to refute this ridiculous assertion. The State also contended that the slaying was an act of premeditated murder and that Robert had "specific intent" to kill her, stabbing Joely Ann 22 times.

Final Disposition

Robert was convicted of second degree murder and sentenced to life in prison without parole.

Victim Impact Statement

Dee Ann (Joely Ann's mother) was finally given an opportunity to speak and she made a very dramatic statement in the courtroom. "I have been so filled with grief over you murdering Joely Ann that I almost quit living. I was not a wife, a mother to my sons, a daughter, a sister, or a grandmother to our precious grandson. Joely Ann never got to see him, except from up in heaven. You took all that away from us. After five years, I have finally gotten justice for Joely Ann " (From the author's files).

Summation

Robert presented as narcissistic and arrogant. He viewed the young women he became involved with as nothing more than objects to be used for his own gratification. Initially, Robert appeared to be a respectful and caring individual as he manipulated women into a relationship. However, as soon as he became involved in a relationship his true personality "leaked out." Each of the young women I interviewed provided accounts of stalking, harassing, and threatening phone calls as well as physical abuse. When Joely Ann attempted to distance herself from his control, he could not accept the rejection. He told her, "How could you leave me; I've been nothing but nice to you. I can't believe that you left me."

In Joely Ann's case, Robert hunted her down like prey and killed her in a brutal knife attack. His lack of remorse is quite obvious. He even attempted to convince the police and the jury that the murder was an act of "self-defense."

Interview of One of the Young Women Who Survived by Ending Her Relationship with Robert Bone

The young woman that Robert had attempted to persuade to visit him at the Parish jail provided the author with her personal experience. I will refer to her as Renée, a pseudonym to protect her anonymity. Renée's experience furnishes an excellent example of the type of personality that stalks. I have included her description of the events in her own words.

One Saturday evening, I joined my closest friends for a night visiting local hangouts. Upon our first destination point, I ran into Robert Bone. Although his first name was Robert, his friends called him "Bone." I had met Bone briefly in the past through mutual friends, so when I ran into him that night, we had no trouble conversing. I was single at the time and was enjoying life as any young woman in her early twenties would. Bone was very interested in what I had to say, and quite honestly, I had a good time talking to him that night. We even shared a few laughs. When my "crew" decided to move on to the next destination, I parted ways with Bone, but not before fulfilling his wishes to get my telephone number and permission to call.

The following evening, I received a call from Bone. After talking for an hour or so, he asked me out to a movie. He was very chivalrous, for not only did he pick me up (I lived about 45 minutes away), but he also opened the car door for me. I thought, "Wow, do men really behave like this anymore?" Needless to say, I was very impressed. The movie we saw was *Dead Man Walking*. I was indifferent about the choice of film, but he seemed to be interested in this particular film. I had no idea why, but hadn't focused on it.

After the movie, we drove to the lakefront and talked for about two hours. I could not believe that this guy was so interested, nice, and that he listened so well. At this point, I considered leaving the single life and decided to see him more. I figured I would take it slow, that way we both would not be seriously committed if something went awry.

Robert Bone was a relatively attractive young man. He was tall, approximately 5'9", and had blond hair. His style was not flashy, in fact, quite mild. He was in the U.S. Marines and stood very proud at times. Although he wouldn't turn a head on the street, his personality and kindness assisted his overall appearance. The flattery didn't hurt either. He was well spoken, drug free, and an occasional drinker. He attended Catholic school and college briefly. He lived in a nice home with his mother, and he drove a new truck. I assumed from this that he appreciated having nice things.

As I mentioned, he told me he was a U.S. Marine, which I thought was his source of money. I had no prior knowledge of any stable work history. This is not exactly something you dig into when you casually begin a relationship. About two weeks into it, he told me, as we were hanging around his house, that he wasn't exactly an active Marine. He then went into this long, drawn out story of how he thought he was to return to California for training on one day when actually, he was supposed to return much earlier then he thought. He then told of how military authorities came to his house and arrested him, but that everything was quickly straightened out once the misunderstanding was explained. It seemed plausible, in detail, and to me it made sense. I knew nothing otherwise. I had introduced him to my sister and our friends, and they thought the same thing that I did. In fact, one friend commented that he was "too good to be true."

The following week, our 3rd week together, was the week of Valentine's Day. I had no idea what he would get for me; perhaps I was hoping for some nice flowers. Instead, I was told to dress nicely for a surprise evening out. He picked me up and drove me to a local airport that offers charter flights. A pilot flew us to the Gulf Coast where a stretch limousine was waiting for us. The limo brought us to a fine dining establishment and waited to drive us along the coast back to New Orleans. I was very surprised, but not very happy.

This was too much for me to handle at the time. I appreciated the effort immensely, but I had only been seeing him for three weeks, and certainly was not ready for this level. On the drive back, he became very affectionate and extremely touchy. Point blank, he wanted to have sex. I did not and pushed him away on every approach.

He became very angry with me, and turned his back and ignored me like a child the entire drive home. When we reached the city, he directed the driver to drive to a local bar where his mother was so that he could show her what he had done for me. After leaving the bar, he asked me if we could drive around for a little while longer.

I directed the driver to my friend's home, where my sister and 10 other girls and guys were visiting. Once we arrived, everyone wanted to ride in the limousine. All 11 of them piled in the limo, pushing Bone aside. The limo drove us to a local hangout where we stayed for a few drinks. Needless to say, at this point, he was very unhappy. He moped in the corner of the bar, and then instructed everyone to get in the limo for it was time to leave. We dropped everyone off home and returned to the airport to get his car.

When we arrived at the airport, it was like the nice guy I knew was gone. He did not open the car door. He would not speak to me. He would not even look at me. When we pulled off, I changed the radio station a few times and he lashed out at me because it was "annoying" him. I decided this was more than I was ready for and that I would not bring any more commotion into this evening; rather, I would break the news to him the following day.

The following day, we were scheduled to meet my friends on a parade route where we would hang out all day. I had not said anything about ending our relationship. The timing just didn't feel right. I hung out with my friends all day at the parade route. Bone disappeared, although no one missed him. He returned at the end of the parade extremely intoxicated and acting obnoxious. We had an ice chest that had nothing left in it at the end of the day but a few blocks of ice. Bone pulled a large outdoor knife out of his back pocket and began chopping the ice. We had no idea why, and equally we were all embarrassed.

The next day my friends and I had decided to attend another parade in the city. I had to work earlier that morning, so we were going to meet some time after 3 p.m. when I was done. I didn't tell Bone about our plans, in fact, I just avoided his calls. I asked my boss not to accept any phone calls for me after explaining the situation. Bone called repeatedly. Thirty-three times to be exact; we counted.

My name is pronounced the same way by everyone I know except for my father, who addresses me by a nickname. Bone called my place of work for the 34th time, only this time he asked for me by nickname. I answered the call. I shouldn't have; he was really frightening me. I lied to him about what my plans were for the evening; he was insistent on seeing me. I told him that I was going to spend the evening with my brother and sister at my brother's home. Actually, I was going to a parade and then out later with my sister and some friends.

We walked into a local hangout and, much to my surprise, I saw Bone sitting at the bar with another girl and another couple. I, in truth, felt a sigh of relief, as though he might have moved on and I didn't even have to go through a breakup. I was wrong. He immediately jumped up, cornered each of my friends, male and female, and questioned them on where I was all day. I thought I had covered my bases, but I was clearly busted. He then grabbed my arm, pulled me into the doorway, and pointed at my face as he sternly said, "If you ever cheat on me, I will kill you." I asked, of course, if it was a threat or a promise, and he replied, "A promise; believe me that it's a promise."

This certainly seemed like a bad time to break up with him, but I tried anyway. I apologized for lying and while crying tried to tell him every reason why I couldn't see him anymore and why I lied. I told him I was an alcoholic. He said he'd get me help. I told him I had mental problems. He also had an answer. I told him I needed to think. He just laughed at me. I tried every excuse short of telling him I was a lesbian to get this guy to leave me alone. Nothing worked. Nothing. He finally left, and my sister and I went to another late night hangout. I ran into an old friend whom I had not seen in years. She asked me if I was still seeing Bone because that's what she had heard. I updated her on my situation. She then told a few details about Bone's past that seemed radical to me, but slightly believable.

She said that he had tormented his ex-girlfriend, whom I also knew, in a very serious way. He followed her, stalked her, even broke into her house, stole her personal belongings, kidnapped her, and drove her to a location where he dumped her belongings into the lake. Wow. I was speechless, but looked to the next day to assist me with this crazy situation.

I worked again the next day. I was a waitress at a local restaurant while I attended college. I had decided that I was going to end everything with Bone that night after I finished my shift, at his house so that we were not in public. As fate would have it, Bone's ex-girlfriend, the girl I was informed about the previous night, dined in the restaurant that same night. I wanted so bad to approach her and ask if what I had heard was true, but then I thought I would be way out of line. I did it anyway, but I waited until she finished eating. I walked up to her table and introduced myself; she remembered who I was. I told her that I was dating Bone and that I had heard that she had dated him, too.

This poor girl looked at me like she was going to drop dead from fear as soon as I said his name. No kidding, I have never seen a look of fright in someone in my life. I quickly told her why I was inquiring so as to calm her suspicions, whatever they were, and that I was going to end my relationship with him that night.

My reasoning was that if what I had heard was true, then perhaps there was a few things I needed to consider before going to his home to break up with him. She told me everything about her relationship and the horror she experienced with him. It was very bad even involving police intervention. Trust me, he was a sick person. What stuck with me was that she said that he just stopped bothering, following, stalking and calling her around the end of January. Keep in mind, I met up with him at the end of January. Did he move on to me? Was I his next victim? These questions scared me, but they also angered me. How dare he do this to me? I did not go over to his house that night.

I avoided his telephone calls at all costs for the next few days until I thought things through. I was consistently harassed at work and found notes on my car saying things like, "Call me, Bone." I knew I would have to get closure to this at some point, but was hoping that maybe he would just go away. I was scheduled to begin a job at another restaurant later that week.

On my first day, I was driving to work when I saw Bone driving one car behind me. Remember that I lived 45 minutes away from him, so it made no sense as to why he would be in the area I spotted him in, except that he was following me. I really didn't want him to know that I had a new job. So, I weaved in and out of streets and circled corners, but to no avail. He found me. He called me later that morning around 1 a.m. demanding an explanation for my behavior (driving) earlier that day. I couldn't say a word.

I went out to his apartment the next day to finally put an end to this madness. When I knocked, he shouted, "Come in." Not sure as to why he didn't get up to answer the door, I entered. What I experienced next is the worst thing I think I have ever been through in my life, aside from seeing him at trial. Bone was sitting on his sofa polishing a gun. He said it was his new Ruger. There was a large, silver briefcase open on his coffee table with bullets laid out and lined up. He looked like a kid playing with a toy and seemed very mesmerized by the gun.

He picked up a regular bullet and told me, "You see this bullet; it's a regular bullet. It will shoot right through you and come straight out." He then picked up the other kind of bullet and said, "You see this bullet, It's called a cop killer. You see the open tip, it will shoot right through you, and blow you apart." He then turned the gun to my forehead and said, "Do you think that you could ever kill anyone?" I turned the gun slowly back toward his head and said, "Yes. As a matter of fact, this feels pretty good." I don't know how I managed to do this without shaking, crying, or just plain old fainting.

He quickly picked up the gun, bullets and all, and put it away. I ran out of the apartment after that and sped off. What the hell was going on?

Amazingly, I would only hear from Bone after this through an occasional telephone call, usually late at night, and my entire family knew that, if he called, not to answer the phone.

About two weeks after the episode with the gun, I saw Bone at a nightclub where he was working. I was with a group of friends and he was across the room playing pool with a girl who had long, brown hair.

He moved over our way and stopped to talk to me. The conversation was not nice. He pointed to the girl and said, "That's my new girlfriend. I do not need you anymore." I went to the bathroom and decided that, when I had the opportunity, I was going to pull her aside and tell her what I knew about him. When I came out of the bathroom, they were both gone. I never saw her again. Later, I found out that her name was Joely Ann and she was his murder victim." (From the author's files; personal interview, 2002.)

Domestic Violence Homicides

Domestic violence homicides are among the most prevalent interpersonal violence murders committed in the United States. The author, who served on New York Governor Pataki's Commission on Domestic Violence Fatalities from 1996 to 1997, was afforded an opportunity to participate in an in-depth analysis of the problem of domestic violence fatalities within New York State. However, the dynamics of domestic violence murders are universal.

Domestic Violence Defined

Domestic violence is defined as a pattern of behaviors involving physical, sexual, economic, and emotional abuse, alone or in combination, by an intimate partner often for the purpose of establishing and maintaining power and control over the other partner. The origins of domestic violence are in social, legal, and cultural norms, some historical and some current, including acceptance of violent behavior by men as the heads of households. While domestic violence occurs in all types of intimate relationships, it is overwhelmingly a problem of violence perpetrated by men against women (Commission on Domestic Violence Fatalities, 1997).

Domestic Violence Homicides Defined

Domestic violence homicides are those murders that occur between men and women, husbands and wives, boyfriends and girlfriends, boyfriends and boyfriends, and girlfriends and girlfriends. In fact, any murder between intimate partners would be considered a domestic violence homicide. They may also involve third-party relationships, such as love triangles: former husbands or wives and jilted lovers.

In *Practical Homicide Investigation: Tactics, Procedures, and Forensic Techniques* (Geberth, 2006), these murders are classified as sex-related homicides in the category of interpersonal violence-oriented disputes and assaults or lust murders depending on what was done to the victim. The motive in this category of slayings is most often based on elements of rage, hate, anger, jealously, or revenge. The psychological dynamics involved in such violent interpersonal disputes and assaults oftentimes present scenarios that involve violent actions and the classic statement: "If I can't have you, then nobody will have you." This is most common in sexual domestic dispute cases (Figures 7.11 through 7.14).

Opinion: Based on the victimology that was reviewed the event was predicated on an interpersonal violence scenario.

There wasn't any forced entry, suggesting she allowed the offender into her apartment. The offender knew the victim. He had most probably had a personal relationship with the victim and was upset with her life style. The rape and sodomy were done to "punish" the victim. Her body was then purposefully displayed to degrade her in the eyes of whoever found her. The attack to the throat was indicative of the offender's knowledge that she had a good voice and sang for the choir. The offender "destroyed" that throat by stabbing and cutting. He then purposefully placed the knife on the throat of the woman to indicate his disdain for her.

Dynamics

In most instances, the event is initiated when the woman attempts to end the relationship or petitions the court for an Order of Protection or Restraining Order. The court order directs the other partner to stay away from the petitioner and refrain from any further

Figure 7.11 Rape and sodomy—interpersonal violence. The nude body of the 22-year-old victim was discovered on the bed in her ground-floor apartment. She had been raped and anally sodomized. (Photo courtesy of Detective Sergeant K. W. Bonsal, Pasadena, Texas, Police Department.)

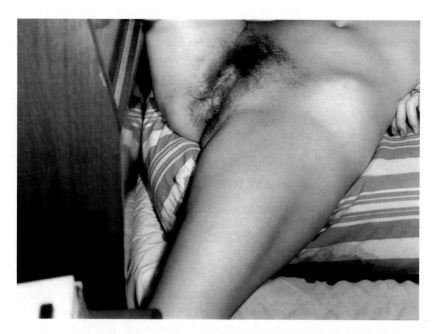

Figure 7.12 Rape and sodomy—interpersonal violence. The victim, who had been raped and anally sodomized showed bruising to the vaginal area as well as rectal tears. The vaginal and rectal smears were positive for spermatozoa. (Photo courtesy of Detective Sergeant K. W. Bonsal, Pasadena, Texas, Police Department.)

Figure 7.13 Rape and sodomy—interpersonal violence. There was a pair of female pantyhose wrapped tightly around the victim's neck. Her neck had been cut open with a large butcher knife, which was then placed across her throat. The victim apparently led a double life and was reportedly sexually promiscuous with a number of both male and female partners. She was a schoolteacher who also sang in the church choir, but at the same time frequented local bars and was into the drug scene. (Photo courtesy of Detective Sergeant K. W. Bonsal, Pasadena, Texas, Police Department.)

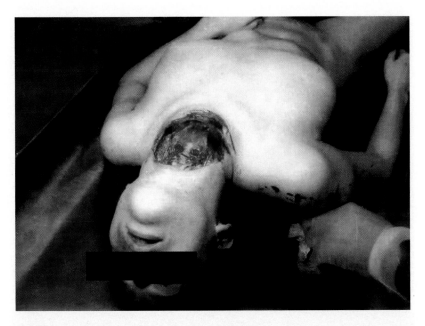

Figure 7.14 Rape and sodomy—interpersonal violence. Autopsy showed that she had also received 10 stab wounds into the throat. The pantyhose were imbedded in the wound structure suggesting that they had been in place prior to the stabbing and that the offender had used the stockings as a ligature to control the victim. (Photo courtesy of Detective Sergeant K. W. Bonsal, Pasadena, Texas, Police Department.)

harassment. The man becomes enraged with his loss of control and the attempt by the woman to "break the relationship" and engages in various acts of harassment, which include stalking, threats, assault, or other subtle forms of "psychological warfare."

This may culminate in a violent homicidal episode in which sexual aggression is evident in the crime scene. Every year, thousands of women are killed in the United States in these interpersonal scenarios. Current and former husbands, lovers, and friends commit most of these murders. And, it is important to note that domestic violence homicides involve homosexual as well as heterosexual relationships.

The author classifies domestic violence murders as interpersonal violence-oriented homicide. They are the most prevalent form of sex-related murder. The rationale for classifying domestic violence as sex-related is due to the fact that murder serves as the ultimate form of sexual revenge. And, in many instances the homicides will include sexual assault or wound structures manifesting a sexual orientation.

Case History

Police had taken a domestic violence report from a young woman, who stated that her ex-boyfriend tried to choke her into submission as he attempted to tape her hands. She was able to escape, and the suspect fled and was not apprehended.

The subject, who knew police were looking for him, subsequently committed suicide. His body was found in his home by the police who were investigating the report.

The detectives discovered a locked storage room in the basement that was completely padded and carpeted. The walls were five to six inches thick. The sophistication of the construction, which involved sound proofing and the installation of various recording

Figure 7.15 Exterior door to play room. The view is from outside the room. (Photo courtesy of Detective LaVern Brann, Battle Creek, Michigan, Police Department.)

equipment, a camera, and a VCR indicated that he had constructed this "play room" in the basement of his home to fulfill his bondage fantasy. The room contained binding materials, restraints, duct tape, and petroleum jelly.

During the search, the detectives located several porno tapes including one of the subject engaged in B&D (bondage and discipline) with an unidentified female in this "play room." This offender was planning on kidnapping his former girlfriend and her two-year-old son and keeping them in the room (Figures 7.15 through 7.18).

Prevention of Domestic Violence

Realistically speaking, domestic violence homicide is the one category of murder that is actually preventable. Early intervention by law enforcement, social services, and the criminal justice system can effectively deter future violence. However, in order to attain success, there must be a goal of zero tolerance in the community. This requires that all elements of the community respond with a consistent, clear message that domestic violence is *not* tolerable.

Law enforcement agencies alone cannot eliminate domestic violence. Domestic assault must be confronted on many fronts. Schools must educate children on the existence and danger of domestic violence; members of the clergy must send an unequivocal message from the pulpit that domestic violence is unacceptable; and neighbors, friends, and co-workers of domestic violence victims must be alert to the potential danger.

However, law enforcement is usually the first to respond to domestic violence incidents. Therefore, the police are in the best position to initiate intervention. The police are able to arrest the offender and make a determination of who was the "primary aggressor."

Figure 7.16 Looking into room. This photo shows the view inside. Note the baby toy. (Photo courtesy of Detective LaVern Brann, Battle Creek, Michigan, Police Department.)

Figure 7.17 Equipment. Pictured are the VCR, TV monitor, and binding ropes. (Photo courtesy of Detective LaVern Brann, Battle Creek, Michigan, Police Department)

Figure 7.18 Interior view. This photo shows the view from inside looking out. (Photo courtesy of Detective LaVern Brann, Battle Creek, Michigan, Police Department.)

They determine what charges are possible and ensure the safety of the victim and any children present.

In addition, there is also a link between domestic violence and child abuse, which is well documented in clinical literature. The police may decide to remove the batterer from the home, as well as request social services to offer the woman and child shelter services. In most instances, the police intervention is unannounced and spontaneous. Therefore, the police may observe other conditions, which put the children or mother at risk, such as the precipitating factors of alcohol and drug abuse.

Case History

Police responded to calls from neighbors indicating domestic abuse. They discovered that a man had been holding his wife and children prisoner in their apartment. He had beaten her, broken her eye socket, and threatened her with a gun. The husband was arrested for assault, unlawful imprisonment, possession of a gun, and menacing actions. The case went to trial. However, the woman refused to testify against her husband. The district attorney's office took the case to trial without the cooperation of the witness. The husband pled guilty and was supposed to serve one year. However, the judge released him in a plea agreement, which was supposed to include supervision and an order of protection. The district attorney's office objected to his release. Although the wife feared her husband, she told her friends that "her sons need a dad." She allowed him to return to their apartment. Within one month, the man butchered his wife and one of his sons as the other son called 911. The boy could be heard yelling in the background: "Daddy! Daddy! Don't, Daddy!" The man used a hatchet and knife to decapitate his wife and son. He attacked the other son who escaped and managed to survive his injuries. The husband then slit his wrists, but did not die. Had the man been incarcerated and the woman and children afforded shelter, this homicide could have been prevented (*New York Daily News*, 1997).

The uncooperative victim, who refuses assistance, creates a dilemma for the police, social services, and the criminal justice system.

Case History: Classic Domestic Violence Attempted Murder; Perpetrator Killed by Cops

On August 28, 2002, a suspect was shot and killed by police while holding his wife hostage at knifepoint. He had been released from jail only hours earlier for a previous attack on the same woman. The woman had previously gotten an order of protection in 1999 for domestic violence. However, she had gone back to him and they were living together. On August 14, her husband attacked her in their apartment. He slapped her across the face, choked her with a telephone cord, and shoved her face into a bathtub filled with water.

Despite the subject's violent history against his wife, Brooklyn Judge Betty Williams set bail at only $500. The woman, who feared that her husband would hunt her down, went to her apartment with some friends and bolted the front door. However, her husband had already gained entry to the apartment and attacked the woman. Her friends managed to escape, but the woman couldn't get away. By the time the police arrived at her apartment, she had already been stabbed five times and the suspect was holding her hostage with a knife at her back and a knife at her chest.

When the officers ordered the man to put the knives down, he stated, "You're going to have to kill me. I'll put the knife in her back down, but I'll stab her in the heart." When it was apparent that the woman faced imminent death, a police officer fired on shot striking the suspect in the chin instantly killing him. The woman was transported to Kings County Hospital in critical condition (*New York Daily News*, 2002; *New York Post*, 2002).

In the opinion of the author this entire incident never should have happened. The man was obviously dangerous. He had attempted to kill his wife in the past. The authorities had arrested him for a violent assault. Why would the judge release this individual on such low bail?

Case History: Staged Crime Scene/Domestic Violence

The police department received a 911 from a frantic male stating that his wife had been stabbed and he needed help. Police arrived and met a male with blood on his clothes and hands. He led them to the basement of his home where they discovered a woman's body.

The woman, whom the man identified as his wife, was found lying on her back. Her pants had been ripped open and her panties had been pulled down to reveal her pubic area. Her sanitary napkin was pulled away. Crime scene officers retrieved an unused condom from between her legs (Figures 7.19 through 7.22).

The husband stated that he had left his house to go jogging. When he returned and walked in the back door, he was attacked by a male dressed in black and covered with blood. The husband reported that the male had cut him with the knife while they were

Figure 7.19 Staged crime scene. The husband of the victim reported that his house had been burglarized by an unknown intruder who killed his wife during a sex attack. He had thrown these objects around the floor to indicate a "burglary" had occurred. (Photo courtesy of Investigator Jack Henander, Larimer County, Colorado, Sheriff's Department.)

struggling. He said that the unknown male then fled by running down the driveway and jumping into a dark colored auto and sped away.

The husband stated that after he chased the attacker, he returned to his house where he got a band-aid for the cut on his knee. He told police that the attacker had cut and stabbed him during their struggle. He indicated that he had been injured and showed the officers some superficial cuts and puncture wounds on his body.

The husband stated he then began to check the house to see what was missing. When he went to the basement, he discovered his wife's body.

He told the police that he got blood on himself when he cradled his wife's body before calling police. The man was transferred to the emergency room of the local hospital for treatment.

BLOOD EVIDENCE

The blood evidence at the scene indicated the attack had been initiated outside and continued into the house.

The deceased had apparently been taken by surprise as she was working outside. She received stab wounds to the top of her head and face. The blood evidence also indicated that she had attempted to flee into the house to escape.

Figure 7.20 Female victim's body at scene. Note that the body has been moved and positioned to present as a sexual assault. (Photo courtesy of Investigator Jack Henander, Larimer County, Colorado, Sheriff's Department.)

The assailant apparently had managed to push his way through the door, forcing the victim into the basement.

Detectives used luminol throughout the crime scene and located a number of areas that indicated that there had been blood present or someone had "cleaned up" blood. Blood evidence was collected from the bathroom, office, master bedroom, stairwell, and basement. The majority of blood found in the upstairs area belonged to the husband. The majority of blood found in basement belonged to the victim.

STAGING

The male showed the officers evidence of a burglary, which consisted of items being tossed on the floor and perfume bottles being turned over on the dresser in the master bedroom. However, there was nothing missing. Interestingly, the "burglar" very carefully handled the husband's possessions. Yet, the wife's side of the room was trashed and her possessions were strewn about the room.

Although the presentation of the female body in the crime scene suggested a sexual attack, the circumstances of the event, as well as the inconsistent statements of the husband, indicated this murder to be based on an interpersonal-oriented dispute and assault scenario. There was no evidence of sexual assault. The crime scene had been

Figure 7.21 Staged scene to appear sex-related. The husband tore open his wife's pants and exposed her pubic area to make the event appear to be a sexual assault. He also placed an unused condom between her legs. (Photo courtesy of Investigator Jack Henander, Larimer County, Colorado, Sheriff's Department.)

staged. The husband was charged with his wife's murder based on the police investigation as well as the blood evidence and DNA testing.

RECONSTRUCTION

The subject had attacked his wife from behind while they worked in the garden. She managed to escape to the house, but was trapped into going to the basement where she received the fatal stab wounds. The women had 16 stab wounds, including a deep penetrating wound of her left jugular vein and left carotid artery. The woman had received multiple stab wounds to the back of her head, the side of her neck, and to her chest. The husband had four superficial wounds, including a cut on his pinky that he received as he was stabbing his wife.

The husband had attempted to make the crime appear to be a sexual assault by ripping open her pants and placing a condom between her legs. However, when he ripped her panties, he left a drop of his own blood from his cut pinky finger on her leg.

It should be noted that family members, who were interviewed by the police after the murder, reported that the victim had been in fear of her husband because of his physical and sexual abuse. Had there been intervention, this woman would still be alive (Geberth, 2006).

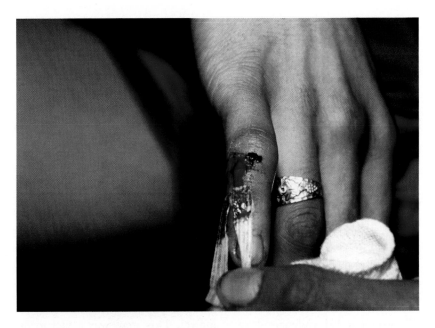

Figure 7.22 Offender cut himself. Photo shows an incised injury to the right finger of the husband, who cut himself during the vicious attack on his wife. In fact, he left his blood on the victim's right leg while he was "staging the scene." (Photo courtesy of Investigator Jack Henander, Larimer County, Colorado, Sheriff's Department.)

Case History

The partially clad body of a middle-aged male was found slain in his apartment. His throat had been slashed and there were multiple wounds into his chest. His face was covered with a towel. Someone had smashed all of the knick knacks and figurines in the apartment. Witnesses, who had called the police, saw the victim's roommate, leaving the apartment with a suitcase. Patrol officers, who had been given a description of the male leaving the apartment, located the suspect at a bus station. He was about to leave town. Investigators learned that the police had been called to the premises in the past in connection with domestic disputes. The disputes usually involved the young man, who was 20 years younger than his partner, and stayed out and partied most of the night. The older male, who was paying the bills, objected to the younger man's activities. They had gotten into a shouting match during which time the younger man was smashing the knick knacks and figurines. When the older male tried to stop him, the young man grabbed a kitchen knife and began stabbing him in the chest. He then cut the older man's throat before packing his bags and leaving the apartment (From the author's files).

It is important to note that domestic violence homicides can be homosexually oriented as well as heterosexually oriented (Figure 7.23 and Figure 7.24).

Considerations

Homicides involving domestic violence *can be* prevented through early intervention by law enforcement, social services, and the criminal justice system. Even victims who are reluctant to press charges due to lack of resources—emotional, physical, financial, or

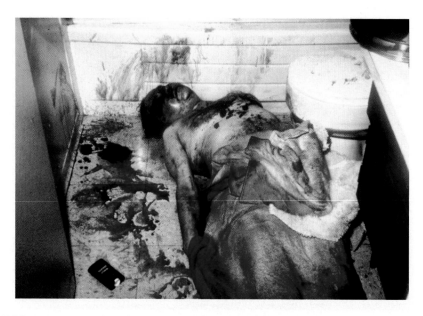

Figure 7.23 Interpersonal violence—lover's quarrel. This man was a victim of a dispute involving his younger male partner. After his lover had killed him, he covered the victim's face with the bloody towel. (Photo courtesy of the author.)

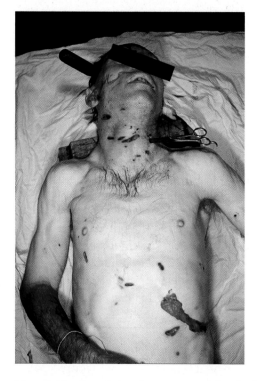

Figure 7.24 Homosexual homicides involving lover's quarrels, slashing and cutting to the throats of victims. Note the increased level of violence and "over kill"-type injuries that are common in homosexual homicides. This type of violent wound structures to the throat and chest of victims is attributed to the dynamics of two biologically engineered sexual aggressors involved in an emotional conflict with elements of rage, anger, and revenge. (Photo courtesy of Dr. Dominick J. DiMaio, former chief medical examiner, City of New York.)

psychological—can be assisted once they have been identified and removed from the hostile environment.

Persons who abuse their partners are potentially dangerous and some are more likely to kill, especially when certain conditions exist. These conditions or indicators pose the potential to kill.

I have provided a listing of **lethality indicators** from *The Pennsylvania Coalition against Domestic Violence* (Hart, 1997) as a reference. Obviously, the more indicators present or the greater intensity of the indicators, the greater the potential for domestic violence homicide.

Lethality Indicators

1. **"Ownership" of the battered partner**: The batterer who states "Death before divorce!" or "You belong to me and will never belong to another!" or the old standby, "If I can't have, you nobody will!" may be stating his fundamental belief that she has no right to life separate from him. A batterer who believes he is absolutely entitled to a woman's services, obedience, and loyalty, no matter what, may be life endangering.

2. **Centrality of the partner**: A man who idolizes his partner, or who depends heavily on her to organize and sustain his life, or who has isolated himself from all other community, may retaliate against a partner who decides to end the relationship. He rationalizes that her "betrayal" justifies his lethal "retaliation."

3. **Depression**: Where a batterer has been acutely depressed and sees little hope for moving beyond depression, he may be a candidate for homicide and suicide. Research shows that many men who are hospitalized for depression have homicidal fantasies directed at family members.

4. **Repeated intervention by law enforcement**: Partner or spousal homicide almost always occurs in a context of historical violence. Prior intervention by the police indicates elevated risk of life-threatening conduct.

5. **Escalation of risk taking**: A less obvious indicator of increasing danger may be the sharp escalation of personal risk undertaken by a batterer when he begins to act without regard to the legal or social consequences that previously constrained his violence. The chances of lethal assault increase significantly.

6. **Threats of homicide or suicide**: The batterer who has threatened to kill his (ex) partner, himself, the children, or her relatives must be considered extremely dangerous.

7. **Fantasies of homicide or suicide**: The more the batterer has developed scenarios about who, how, when, and where to kill, the more dangerous he may be. The batterer who has previously acted out part of a homicide or suicide fantasy may be invested in killing as a "solution to his problems."

8. **Weapons**: When a batterer possesses, collects, or is obsessed with weapons and/or has used them or has threatened to use them in the past in assaults on women, the children, or himself, this increases his potential for lethal assault. If a batterer has a history of arson or the threat of arson, fire should be considered a weapon.

9. **Timing**: When a batterer believes that he is about to lose his (ex) partner or when he concludes that she is permanently leaving him, if he cannot envision life without her, this may be when he chooses to kill. That is not to say that all batterers kill

when they conclude that the battered woman is separating from him. Some kill long before they have any idea that the battered woman may be thinking about leaving. So, it is not safe to assume that because she hasn't made plans to leave, the batterer will not be dangerous. In one study of spousal homicide, over half the men were separated from their victims when they murdered them (Barnard et al., 1982). Women are most likely to be murdered when attempting to report abuse or to leave an abusive relationship (Sonkin et al., 1985; Brown, 1987).

10. **History of antisocial behavior**: A batterer who has demonstrated aggressive behavior to the general public, such as bar fights, gang-related violence, job-related violence, vandalism, repeated unlawful behavior, or illegal occupation is likely to be more dangerous.

11. **Hostage taking**: A hostage taker is at high risk of inflicting homicide. Between 75 and 90% of all hostage takings in the United States are related to domestic violence situations.

12. **Drugs and alcohol**: Men with a history of problems with drugs and/or alcohol show a higher risk. In addition, regardless of their drug and/or alcohol history, intoxication at the time of the assault shows significant risk to partners.

13. **Violence in his family of origin**: The more severe the violence either experienced personally or observed in the family of origin, the greater the risk.

References

American Psychiatric Association. *Diagnostic and Statistical Manual of Mental Disorders*, 4th ed., Text revision (*DSM-IV-TR*), APA, Washington, D.C., 2000.

Barnard, G.W., H. Vera, M.I. Vera, and G. Ne, Till death do us part: A study of spouse murder. *Bulletin of the American Association of Psychiatry and Law,* 10, 271–280, 1982.

Brown, A., *When Battered Women Kill*. The Free Press, New York, 1987.

Commission on Domestic Violence Fatalities, Report to the Governor of New York State, the Honorable Jeanine Pirro, Westchester County District Attorney, and Commission Chairperson, October 1997.

Douglas, J.E., A.W. Burgess, A.G. Burgess, R.K. Ressler, and J.E. Dougles, *Crime Classification Manual*, Lexington Books, New York, 1995.

Geberth, V.J. The investigation of sex-related homicides. *Law and Order Magazine*. July 1986, p. 40.

Geberth, V.J., *Practical Homicide Investigation: Tactics, Procedures, and Forensic Techniques*, 4th ed., CRC Press, Boca Raton, FL, 2006.

Hare, R.D., *Without Conscience: The Disturbing World of the Psychopaths among Us*, Pocket Books: A Division of Simon & Schuster, New York, 1993.

New York Daily News, June 10, 1997, p. 7.

New York Daily News, Freed, he stabs his wife, August 28, 2002, p. 6.

New York Post, Wife-abuser had just got out on bail, August 28, 2002, p. 7.

Hart, B. Pennsylvania Coalition against Domestic Violence, 1997.

Personal interview, with Renee, whose real name will remain anonymous and is in the author's file, September 13, 2002.

Sonkin, D.J., D. Martin, and L.E.A. Walker, *The Male Batterer: A Treatment Approach*, Springer Publ., New York, 1985.

Rape- and Sodomy-Oriented Murders

8

Introduction

In this category of sex-related homicide, the offender's primary intent is to rape or sodomize the victim. The offense may be heterosexual or homosexual depending on the circumstances of the crime. Usually the victims are females and young children, and the killer is a male. However, it is important to note that sex-related homicides involve homosexual as well as heterosexual relationships. Two aggressive homosexual serial killers named Walter Kelbach and Myron Lance were sadistic thrill killers. They would anally rape their male victims, who were not homosexual, because they enjoyed inflicting pain on their victims.

Sex-related homicides occur under the following circumstances:

1. The assailant has used excessive force in overcoming the resistance of the victim and progressing the sexual assault.
2. The death is intentional because the victim knows the assailant. These cases are extremely brutal. The assailant kills to prevent the victim from identifying him and to assure that the victim will not be able to testify to the attack.

The victim may be choked or strangled into submission, or the mouth and nose may be held tightly in order to stifle the victim's screams, thereby causing asphyxia. Blunt force injuries may be present when the killer has attempted to beat the victim into submission. The assailant may have used a weapon, usually a knife or firearm, to threaten and then kill his victim. In addition to the brutality of the attack, a victim may also die of shock or other trauma. This is particularly evident in young children or older persons.

In some cases, the offender may actually attempt to mislead the authorities by staging the crime scene to make it appear to be something other than a sex crime. For instance, I remember a case where the police were requested to respond to a "possible suicide." When they arrived, EMS (emergency medical services) personnel were attempting to revive a partially clothed female. The EMS personnel advised the officers that when they arrived they observed the unconscious female with a ligature around her neck. Her body was partially suspended by this ligature, which was affixed to some molding. However, upon closer examination of the death scene, the officers noticed signs of a struggle. The officers noticed that the victim's blouse had been ripped open. They also observed some buttons on the floor along with a broken wristwatch, which belonged to the deceased. In addition, a closer examination of the victim's neck revealed concentric fingernail marks, which would be consistent with a manual strangulation. The officers immediately initiated basic crime scene procedures and notified detectives. As a result, additional evidence was located and a proper crime scene investigation conducted (From the author's files).

Investigative Strategy

The usual intent of the offender in sexual assault is to rape or sodomize. The offender in this category generally does not receive any sexual satisfaction from the murder. Therefore, as a *practical* matter, the police are dealing with a rapist who has killed and not a murderer who rapes.

Investigatively speaking, it has been my experience that a rape–murder is usually preceded by other sexual offenses including fetish burglaries, indecent exposure, peeping Tom cases, and rapes or sodomies where the victim has not been killed. The investigative approach should be to first ascertain whether or not other sex-related events and cases involving a similar modus operandi have taken place in the jurisdiction. This can then be expanded to include other jurisdictions within the immediate area. This avenue of inquiry can then be expanded to research records for similar offenses committed in the past by persons who have since been released from prison.

If you have recovered semen or sperm evidence from the homicide victim, you should consider submitting the DNA results into the FBI's national computer system CODIS (COmbined DNA Index System) for comparison with convicted offender databases.

Cold Case Homicide Linked through CODIS

On August 31, 2003, Katie left a house party in Las Cruces, New Mexico, which was approximately a half mile away from her residence. She had gotten into an argument with her boyfriend after she caught him kissing another girl at the party. She could not find her purse so she decided to walk home. Her partially nude and partially burned body was found the next morning in a rather remote desert area approximately a mile and a half from her residence. She had been manually strangled, anally and vaginally raped, and we recovered DNA from her fingernails and her vaginal vault. She had been battered, but there was no evidence of severe anger, it looked like just enough force to control her. There were two diamond rings and a watch removed from her body (Figure 8.1 and Figure 8.2).

Katie did not have her keys or her cell phone because they were in her purse. The investigation focused on the boyfriend for several reasons. He was in possession of her purse and cell phone, yet he kept calling her cell phone and leaving her messages. It appeared as if he was trying to set up an alibi. By his own admission, he drove by her residence looking for her and we knew that she was assaulted at her residence, and he refused to give us DNA. For some reason, however, the District Attorney's Office refused investigator's requests for a search warrant and it took them three months to surreptitiously collect her boyfriend's DNA. When the authorities finally did get the sample, it proved he wasn't the offender.

During those three months, Gabriel Avila was arrested in what I believe to be a second attempt at a sexual homicide. He was arrested with a knife and he had obviously been watching and stalking this victim because of the location of her residence. Fortunately for her, he did not anticipate that her roommate was home. He was caught in the act of breaking into her residence and convicted of aggravated burglary. He was eventually transferred to the Department of Corrections. That was when investigators received a CODIS hit on Katie's homicide.

As authorities were concentrating their efforts on one subject, Avila had remained under the radar. Avila's attempt at a sexual assault was thwarted only because there were

Figure 8.1 Body at scene. The victim's body was face down when found in the foothills about two miles from her residence. (Photo courtesy of Detective Mark Meyers, Las Cruces, New Mexico, Police Department.)

Figure 8.2 Sex-related homicide. The victims had been vaginally and anally raped. Authorities recovered DNA. (Photo courtesy of Detective Mark Meyers, Las Cruces, New Mexico, Police Department.)

two girls at home. When he was caught in what obviously was an attempt at a sexual assault, the authorities should have realized the significance of this arrest. The fact that two different jurisdictions were involved as well as the behavior of the "primary suspect" complicated and confused the investigation.

After receiving the CODIS hit, investigators were able to track down the vehicle he used and we were able to find a transaction with one of the local tire stores where he traded out the tires that he had on the truck. Unfortunately, the public information officer (PIO) released the fact that we had tire impressions at the dump site. Investigator Mark Meyers interviewed Avila's ex-wife and to his amazement she was in possession of one of the diamond rings that was taken from Katie.

After Avila was convicted of the above-mentioned aggravated burglary, he was allowed to remain out on bond. He took the opportunity to flee to Mexico, but before he left, he parked his truck at a local McDonalds and got word to his wife that it was there. When she retrieved it, she decided to sell it in an attempt to recoup some of the lost bond money. When she were cleaning out the truck, she found the ring in the ashtray. Avila's ex-wife decided to keep it just in case she needed to pawn it for some emergency cash.

Detective Mark Meyers and another detective interviewed Avila in prison and were able to get him to confess. He stated that he was in Katie's neighborhood by chance. He advised us that he had just scored some cocaine and was driving home when he almost ran her over. He asked her if she needed some help or a ride and she refused his assistance. He stated that he followed her home to her residence and he noticed her by her front window, so he asked her again if she needed some help. She asked him if he could help her get into her window because she was locked out and she didn't want to wake her roommate's mother (something only the killer would know). Avila stated that he took the screen of the window and when he did, something just came over him and he turned and attempted to hug Katie. At that time, Katie pushed him and he punched her in the face and took her down to the ground. He stated that he used his forearm to apply pressure to her throat so he could get her pants down. Avila stated that she scratched him, fairly deep, on his forearm. As a matter of fact, he even looked at his arm, thinking he might still have a scar (Figure 8.3).

Avila went on to explain that he raped her anally and vaginally. After the assault, he stated that he looked up at his truck and he recalled it looking as if it was very far away. He knew it wasn't, but it seemed that way to him. Avila stated that he was afraid that if he just left she would make enough noise that he might get caught, so he decided to strangle her. He stated that he choked her until she quit moving. He picked her up and carried her to the front seat of the truck and placed her in the passenger's seat. He stated that when he got in, she slumped forward and this scared him. Avila took her out and put her in the bed of the truck and took her to the desert. Avila stated that he dumped her in the desert and he had some alcohol in the truck, which he used to set her on fire. He stated that he though that she would burn up beyond recognition. Avila refused to tell us why he picked that location and refused to admit that he positioned the body.

Katie's Law

The parents of Katie have become outspoken advocates for victim's rights and were directly responsible for the passage of a bill in New Mexico and other states known as Katie's Law. The law will allow states to immediately take a DNA sample from anyone arrested for one

Figure 8.3 Victim's fingernails. Authorities also recovered DNA from the fingernails. She had apparently scratched her assailant. (Photo courtesy of Detective Mark Meyers, Las Cruces, New Mexico, Police Department.)

of a group of specified felonies. This legislation will not only help solve crimes, but will save lives and also absolve the innocent (Figure 8.4).

In March, 2006 Katie's Bill, which requires DNA for most felony arrests, was signed into law and went into effect on January 1, 2007, as Katie's Law (www.katieslaw.org and www.dnasaves.org). Presently, a number of states have passed similar legislation. By passing arrestee DNA legislation, law enforcement officials can catch criminals sooner, save more lives, and use DNA to its full potential. Collected at the same time as fingerprints, DNA testing requires only a simple cheek swab upon arrest.

If New Mexico had required a DNA sample for Avila's felony arrest in November of 2003, Katie's murder would have been solved three years sooner. More importantly, Gabriel Avila would have remained in police custody rather than being released to flee justice. Avila's activities are largely unaccounted for during the time he was missing. It is unknown if there are other lives that he jeopardized or other crimes that he committed during that time.

Motivation

The motivation of the offender is an important consideration in the investigation of rape- or sodomy-oriented homicides. "Did the offender target this specific victim?" This could suggest a stalker or an offender who has preselected his victim and has spent some time planning the event. Or, "Are you dealing with an opportunistic rapist?" The opportunistic rapist is usually an offender who, during the course of a burglary or robbery, encounters a female victim. He becomes sexually aroused and impulsively rapes or otherwise sexually assaults her. The investigator should take into consideration that this type of offender probably has an arrest record for burglary or robbery. The death investigation should then be expanded to include these types of suspects.

Figure 8.4 Katie's Law. A photo of Katie provided by her mother, who has been an advocate for victim's rights. (Photo courtesy of Detective Mark Meyers, Las Cruces, New Mexico, Police Department.)

I recall investigating a case where a young female housekeeper was confronted during a home invasion. During the robbery, the offender tied the young woman's hands behind her back causing her blouse to become unbuttoned exposing one of her breasts. The offender suddenly changed his mind about the robbery. Instead, he removed the victim's pants and underwear and vaginally assaulted the woman, whom he left tied up on a couch. The victim was able to untie herself and call the police. I responded with the detectives to what was reported as a home invasion robbery. However, during the interview of the victim by the detectives, I noticed that she was very nervous and embarrassed. In fact, based on my experience with victims of sexual assault, I was sure that there was more to this event than "robbery." I asked the detectives to hold off on the robbery interview. I provided her with some privacy and then discretely asked her if I could speak to her alone. She agreed and seemed genuinely relieved by this confidential approach, considering five or six men had just extensively questioned her about the details of the robbery. I asked her if the offender had touched her or had done anything sexual to her. She immediately broke down and cried. She was obviously waiting for an opportunity to tell what had happened to her, however, not to a crowd. The victim told me how the offender had come to the door and forced his way into the premises. She was told not to scream and she wouldn't be harmed. He stated he was only after the valuables. As he tied her up he became sexually aroused. So he removed her clothes and raped her. When he finished, he allowed her to redress and then apologized for raping her. As she provided me with the details of the event, it was quite obvious that this sexual assault was a classic opportunistic rape. We were looking for a robber/burglar. Interestingly, as we were conducting the interviews and processing the scene, the offender called the premises. A female sex crimes detective, whom I requested to respond to the crime scene to conduct the formal interview of the victimized woman, answered the phone. The offender, thinking it was the victim, once again apologized for raping her. When the detective asked him why he had done this, he stated he didn't know why. He said he was a burglar and had only come to rob the house. She told him if he was really sorry, he should surrender to the police. He began cursing and swearing and hung up the phone (From the author's files).

In the investigation of rape/sodomy-oriented homicides, remember that you are dealing with a sexual offender. Sexual offenders usually have a history and more than likely have a criminal record. Modus operandi (MO) and "signature aspects" of the offenses are important detective considerations in developing specific rape patterns, linking these events, and providing strategic investigative information. Larger and more progressive police departments usually maintain specialized operations, such as homicide, robbery, and sex crimes units. The investigators in these specialized units have a unique advantage. They become experts within their respective fields and are able to gain an insight into certain criminal behaviors that the average generalist detective will not experience. Furthermore, when a specific MO or signature reemerges within their jurisdiction, they may have an idea as to who the offender may be based on their intelligence and prior offense record-based systems. Sex offenders do not retire after doing time for an offense. Sadly, they use their jail time to reeducate themselves. When they do get out of prison, they become even more proficient at predation. Sex offenders are cognizant of the value of evidence to the law enforcement inquiry and will attempt to avoid leaving biological fluids by using a condom or forcing the victim to bathe.

I remember one case that I consulted on in which the offender had a very distinctive MO as well as signature. The suspect entered the victim's home through a ground floor window. He climbed into the bed and placed a knife to her throat and woke her. He instructed her to be quiet. He threatened to hurt her and her child if she didn't do as he told her, as he demanded cash and property. He brought electrical zip ties with him, which he used to bind the victim's hands behind her back. He also placed tape over the woman's mouth. He walked her through the house as he looked for valuables. He then put the victim on the floor and raped her. After he completed the rape, he made the victim get into the bathtub where he attempted to wash her vagina. He was wearing gloves to avoid leaving fingerprints. He wore these gloves as he washed out her vagina and caused her additional injuries and pain. The offender washed her head and shirt to destroy any fiber evidence. He then took her to her bedroom and tied her feet and hands with nylons and cut off pieces of her hair, which he sprinkled around the bed and the area of the floor where he had raped the young woman. He also squirted hair conditioner on the floor and sprinkled dry chocolate over her and in the crime scene. He took body lotion and ketchup and put it into her vagina. All of these actions were obviously done to destroy biological and fiber evidence. It was apparent to the detectives that they were obviously dealing with an offender who had been arrested in the past for sexual assault and this offender was being extremely careful not to leave any evidence.

Two days later, a woman was raped and killed six blocks away from where the first rape had occurred. She had been repeatedly stabbed. This time the offender had started multiple fires in the premises in an obvious attempt to destroy any evidence. However, the MO was basically the same as in the first rape case. The suspect had entered the victim's house through an unlocked bedroom window and attacked her in her bed. However, this time the victim had been stabbed repeatedly. The body was discovered by firefighters who had

Figure 8.5 Victim's burned and charred body. The victim had been burned after being bound and stabbed multiple times. (Photo courtesy of Detective Todd Park, Salt Lake County, Utah, Sheriff's Office.)

responded to the house fire. She had been bound with her hands tied behind her back and a sock had been placed in her mouth. Although her body was severely charred, the medical examiner was able to retrieve sperm using the vaginal swab technique. The authorities had enough biological fluids to obtain DNA (Figure 8.5 and Figure 8.6).

They requested a comparison of the DNA with the DNA from the other rape case that had occurred in the same area, and the evidence matched. The investigators then submitted the DNA for comparison with any sex offenders in their database. The suspect, who had been arrested and convicted of rape some years before, had had his blood sample taken for entry into the database as a sex offender. Ironically, due to a backup of cases, his blood sample and DNA not yet been entered into the system. However, an investigator who kept profiles of parolees charged with rape thought that this subject might be a good suspect in these cases based on his past MO. When the suspect's blood was compared to the DNA from the rape victim and the murder victim, there was a positive match.

A review of his MO and signature along with the DNA linked him to both the rape and the murder. Significantly, he was identified as the perpetrator of an additional rape when the DNA was compared to open cases. He had gotten away with the other rape by washing his victim's vagina in the bathtub while wearing gloves and inserting lotion and ketchup in her vagina and cutting her hair. Because he believed that this had been successful, he continued this practice (From the author's files).

I have listed both his MO and signature below for review.

Modus Operandi

- Entry was made through lower floor or basement window.
- He used a knife to gain compliance of his victims.
- He wore cotton work gloves.

Figure 8.6 Chest plate. Victim's chest plate showing the location of the stab wounds inflicted before the body was charred and burned. (Photo courtesy of Detective Todd Park, Salt Lake County, Utah, Sheriff's Office.)

- He walked his victims through house to find valuables.
- He told his victims *not* to look at him.
- He tied the victim's hands behind the back.
- He raped the victims on the floor.
- He cut the victim's hair and spread it around scene.
- He made his victims bathe and washed their vaginas.
- He put lotion on them and spread it on floor where he had raped them to destroy evidence.

Signature
- The perpetrator stalked and targeted his victims.
- He planned his attacks, selecting victims he could control.
- The subject climbed into the victim's beds as they slept and took them by surprise.
- He put the knife to their throats and gave them specific instruction.
- He raped his victims while their hands were tied behind their backs.
- The binding and gagging are psychosexual.
- When he forced them to bathe, he manipulated their vaginas.
- He forced his gloved finger into them to cause them pain.
- He exercised total control over them.

I personally think it is good procedure to assign a member of the Sex Crimes Unit to work with the homicide detectives on sex-related homicide investigations. In fact, on major case investigations involving a series of rapes or homicide, I recommend that teams of sex crimes and homicide detectives work together in a **task force**–type operation. I believe in specialization and professionalism within the criminal investigative process. It takes literally years of experience to learn the many details and nuances of homicide and sex crimes investigation.

Categories of Rapists

According to Groth et al. (1977), there are four categories of rapists. I will list the categories with a brief description. They are power reassurance, power assertive, anger retaliatory, and anger excitation.

Power Reassurance

This type of rapist assaults to assure himself of his masculinity. He lacks the confidence to interact socially and sexually with women.

Indoor type
Victim can negotiate
Victim alone with small children
Takes a souvenir
Local victims
Probably is married
Attacks victims as they are asleep
Weapon only for show
Uses ski mask or pillow or makes his victim turn over
Maintains guilt
May call the victim
Loner type, dominant mother
Will kiss victim
May keep a diary or scrapbook
Wants to please her
Nonathletic
Underachiever

Power Assertive

This type has no doubts as to his masculinity. He uses rape to express his dominance over women. He also uses force.

Same age as victims
Sports minded
Cruises for victims
Flashy vehicle

Resides in area near crime
Body conscious
Selects victim of opportunity
Tears clothing
Short time span between attacks
Oral assault
Prior institutionalization
Direct approach
Selfish actions
Commits crime outdoors
Poor record if in the service
Alcohol user

Anger Retaliatory

This type is getting even with women. He uses sex as a weapon to punish and degrade and is anger-oriented.

Strikes out at women; may select prostitutes or elderly
Selects symbolic victims
Tears clothing
Does not spend much time
Uses alcohol
Blitz style of attack
Random times (no pattern)

Anger Excitation

This type is sexually turned on by the victim's response to the infliction of physical and/or emotional pain. The sexual acts will be varied and experimental and are intended to cause pain.

Might work with an accomplice
Into S&M activities
No mental or health problems
No remorse
Uses auto
Brings weapon
Uses degrading language
Good I.Q.

I included these typologies in all of my textbooks as a guide for criminal investigators to assist them in ascertaining motivation in rape–murder cases. I recommend the textbook *Practical Aspects of Rape Investigation: A Multidisciplinary Approach* (Hazelwood and Burgess, 2009) for further information and case studies of these types of offenders.

Keppel and Walter (1999) published a paper entitled *Profiling Killers: A Revised Classification Model for Understanding Sexual Murder* in which the authors proposed that the four original classifications of rape as described by Groth et al. (1977) be extended to include the classification of sexual murders. They then selected specific cases as examples of the above typologies and suggested that the typologies could be used to develop suspect profiles.

I likened it to placing round pegs into square holes and vice versa. Unfortunately, their typologies of the specific cases they used had only descriptive value for those specific cases. Their extended classifications of categories of rapists *could not* be applied to all sex-related homicides.

Homicide investigators very rarely use crime classifications or typologies in solving a particular murder, and Keppel and Walters even admitted that in their study. Many of the cases in this textbook are a direct result of my professional consultation with other practitioners, and I can state unequivocally that most homicide investigators don't use terms like power reassurance, power assertive, or anger excitation in their description of sex-related murder. (See Chapter 14, which defines and presents investigative considerations, patterns and clusters of behavioral information, as well as specific typologies of offenders.)

In my opinion, only one of the original Groth et al. (1977) classifications can be effectively applied to sex-related murders. The anger/retaliatory model can be applied to the type of murderer who kills out of sexual revenge or retaliation. Their classification of rapists was based on empirical research.

In 1987, Hazelwood and Burgess refined those categories to define a classification of rapists not murderers. I interviewed Dr. Ann Burgess on July 27, 2009. In that personal interview, she stated, "The typology of the four classifications were developed based on interviews of convicted rapists. The classifications were never intended to be applied to sex-related homicides."

Typical Sexual Killer

Typically, sexual killers start out by fantasizing murders based on pornography and/or their own private imaginings. Eventually, they "graduate" to acting out these fantasies, sometimes with a willing partner as practice and then eventually with a real victim. In the violent, highly sexualized fantasy life of the killer, the victim is simply a prop. There isn't any power reassurance, power assertive, or anger excitation model in play. It is **fantasy-driven** behavior that motivates the sexual killer.

Case History: Neighbor Rape

CASE FACTS

On May 5, 1998, at approximately 9:17 a.m., Wichita, Kansas, officers were dispatched to a small, one bedroom, duplex apartment on a report of a deceased person. The house was divided into two apartments: one in the front and one in the back of the house. The victim lived in the back portion of the duplex. The officers were met by Ben Gray, the father of the victim, Regina Gray, 28 years old. The father reported that he had gone to check on his daughter because her co-workers at the Kansas Cancer Center had called and were concerned because she had not shown up for work that morning.

According to Regina's co-workers, this was very strange because she was never late to work and was generally the first one in the office. Co-workers later stated she had planned on bringing biscuits and gravy for breakfast to share with her co-workers.

THE CRIME SCENE

Officers found Ms. Gray lying on the floor of her living room partially dressed. Emergency medical personnel reported to the responding officers that it appeared she was dead from blunt force trauma to the head. Officers cleared the other rooms in the house and established a perimeter. Homicide detectives were notified.

The police obtained a search warrant before processing the scene. The partially clad body of the victim was face down on the living room floor. She was covered with a blue robe and beneath the robe was a maroon blouse. Her arms were out to the side and her legs were apart. There was also evidence of a struggle in the apartment. Detective Kelly Otis noticed a blood impression on the carpet, which appeared to be from a large knife. Detective Otis also noted the presence of a bread maker and thought it strange that there wasn't a knife with the bread maker. A bloody footprint was observed on a calendar next to the victim's head. Two buttons, apparently ripped from the victim's clothing were found on the bedroom floor. Later examination showed they were torn from the garment.

When the body of the victim was examined, it was determined that she had a large, gaping wound to the throat. No sharp knives were recovered in the residence. Gray's purse was in the kitchen; however, her billfold was missing. The autopsy indicated that Gray had been sexually assaulted. DNA was recovered from semen found during the examination (Figures 8.7 through 8.9).

Figure 8.7 Body in scene. The victim's body was found covered with a robe and face down on the living room rug. (Photo courtesy of Lieutenant Kenneth F. Landwehr, Homicide section, Wichita, Kansas, Police Department.)

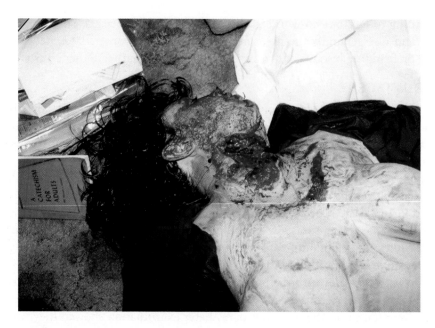

Figure 8.8 Throat cut. The victim's throat had been sliced open to the spine and into the vertebrae. (Photo courtesy of Lieutenant Kenneth F. Landwehr, Homicide section, Wichita, Kansas, Police Department.)

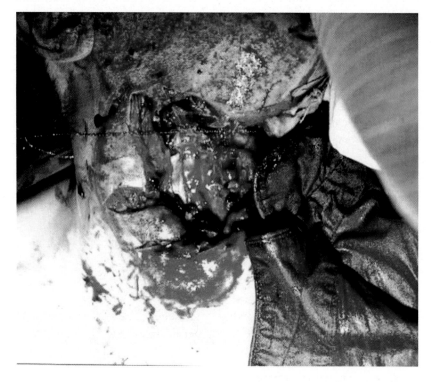

Figure 8.9 Close-up of cut throat. Suspect claimed that the police showed him crime scene photographs of the deceased. He was able to accurately describe the injuries. (Photo courtesy of Lieutenant Kenneth F. Landwehr, Homicide section, Wichita, Kansas, Police Department.)

Figure 8.10 Attic crawl space. The offender had apparently broken through the fire wall, which separated the two duplex unit apartments, thus being able to gain access to the victim's apartment through the attic. (Photo courtesy of Lieutenant Kenneth F. Landwehr, Homicide section, Wichita, Kansas, Police Department.)

Investigators worked into the late evening hours documenting and collecting evidence from the scene. When the officers, who were processing the scene, went into the attic, they observed that the firewall between the two apartments was broken and entry into the victim's portion of the duplex was possible (Figure 8.10).

EARLY LEAD

As detectives and additional officers arrived, they began contacting neighbors. Detective Dana Gouge arrived at the scene and was immediately advised by a patrol officer, who was speaking to a neighbor, to stop a gray Honda four-door that was driving past the residence.

The detective's car was not equipped with red lights and siren, so Detective Gouge followed the car several blocks, calling in the location on the radio. The car stopped at a nearby car wash. Detective Gouge identified the driver as Stanley Elms, an 18-year-old white male. It was determined Elms, who was driving with a suspended license, lived with his girlfriend. She resided in the front portion of the same duplex where the deceased lived. The patrol officer at the scene observed him drive by and then quickly drive away after seeing the police activity. That was the reason that the patrol officer alerted Detective Gouge to stop the gray Honda. Detective Gouge directed patrol officers to take Elms into custody for driving with a suspended driver license. Detective Gouge advised the patrol officers that he wanted to interview Elms after he reviewed the crime scene.

BACKGROUND INFORMATION

Detectives Gouge and Otis learned that Gray was engaged to be married. Detective Gouge interviewed the victim's fiancé, Thomas, who told the detective that he and Gray had been to catechism class the night before, May 4. He said that they had planned on getting married in November. According to Thomas, they had not engaged in sex and were waiting until they were married. Gray was last heard from when she spoke to a relative on the telephone at approximately 10 p.m. on May 4.

DETECTIVE INTERVIEW OF SUSPECT

Detectives Gouge and Otis returned to the police station to interview Stanley Elms, who had been charged with driving with a suspended license. At this time, Elms was considered a possible suspect, but the police didn't have any physical evidence, so the interview was basically conducted for background information. During the interview, Elms made statements about the victim being a good person and stated he had never had any problems with her. He was questioned about the victim's habits and friends, but little information was gained. He also denied any physical or sexual contact and said he had not been in the victim's apartment for almost a year. Elms voluntarily gave up DNA standards to Gouge in the form of oral swabs and also gave up head and pubic hair.

Detective Gouge noticed that Elms had feces and hair stuck to the toe of one of his shoes. Gouge asked Elms to allow the lab to process the shoes. Elms gave Gouge the shoes, which were taken to the Wichita Police Lab. Detective Gouge returned to the interview room and told Elms the shoes would be returned to him after processing, but it could take awhile as the lab personnel were very busy. Elms elected to be taken to the booking desk and to retrieve his shoes later.

Elms was released on the charge of driving with a suspended license and was picked up at the police station by his live-in girlfriend's mother.

THE INVESTIGATION

The following morning, Detective Gouge took the shoes and calendar, along with several known standards of DNA from different people, including Elms, to the Sedgwick County, Regional Forensic Science Center.

On May 7, results from the examination of the tennis shoes and comparison to the impression on the calendar were completed. Elms' shoes could not be eliminated as having made the print. The detectives contacted the Kansas State Parole Office and inquired about Elms and his status on parole; he was on parole for burglary. The parole officer told detectives that Elms had been found to have a dirty urine analysis several weeks prior. The detectives also learned that Elms had been arrested for driving under the influence (DUI). The detectives requested parole authorities to arrest Elms for a parole violation.

On May 9, Detective Otis interviewed Elm's girlfriend's mother. She told the detective that she had picked up Elms from the county jail on May 5, following his arrest for driving on a suspended driver license. She said he told her the police had shown him photographs of the crime scene during his interview. He described the wounds in detail and stated it looked as though someone had sawed back and forth on her neck with a knife used to cut frozen meat. He said he could see the only thing holding her head on was her spine. It was later discovered that Elms had told this same story to several people including his girlfriend and his sister.

On May 9, Elms was interviewed again and gave the same statement. However, when the detectives confronted him with the information they had developed and the results of the laboratory analysis of some of the evidence, Elms immediately invoked his Miranda rights.

THE ARREST

Later DNA testing showed that the semen recovered from Gray's vagina matched Elms' DNA. Elms' tennis shoes were also tested by the Kansas City, Missouri, police lab for fibers and compared the fibers to the insulation in the attic, but no insulation was found on the shoes. However, the bloody footprint impression on the calendar in the victim's apartment matched the suspect's tennis shoes. Stanley Elms was charged with capital murder, rape, aggravated burglary, and theft.

While in jail awaiting trial, Elms confessed to two inmates. They later provided this information to detectives. The inmates told the detectives that Elms had told them he knocked on the front door and the victim let him in. He also claimed he had contacted another person who assisted him in the clean up of the scene.

DISPOSITION

At trial, Elms testified that Gray had invited him over for a sexual interlude. He testified that a drug dealer he knew, named Rico Rojas, came over and accompanied him to Gray's apartment. Elms stated that he had consensual sex with Gray and then Rojas killed her. The jury did not believe him and he was convicted of capital murder and was sentenced to be executed. The sentence was later changed to life in prison with no possibility of parole for 40 years. (From the author's files.)

ACKNOWLEDGMENTS

Recognition goes to Detective Dana Gouge, Detective Kelly Otis, and Lieutenant Ken Landwehr, Wichita Police Department.

Case History: Serial Rapist

CASE FACTS

On June 14, an unknown offender abducted Tina from her rural home in front of her five-year-old-son. Her nude body was discovered the next day in a wooded area. She had been shot in the head with a large caliber weapon. Her residence and a large yard were bordered on all sides with trees. There were plenty of locations where someone could watch her undetected from the tree line (Figure 8.11).

Tina had just returned home from work after picking up her son, Jonathan, from day care. She entered her home and changed. As Tina and Jonathan walked out of the house to feed their dog in the dog pen, a strange man walked from the wood line and forced Tina at gunpoint into her red Ford Escort.

Her son, Jonathan, ran to the uncle's house and told him that a white man with brown hair, white jeans, with a large silver gun, had taken his mother in her car and left him behind. The uncle immediately called police.

VICTIMOLOGY

The victim was an attractive 26-year-old woman, 5'3", 130 lbs, with blond hair and hazel eyes. She lived alone with her five-year-old son. She had been married and divorced,

Figure 8.11 Victim's rural home. The house was surrounded by trees in a very rural area. (Photo courtesy of Investigator Rusty Clevenger, 7th Circuit Solicitor's Office, Spartanburg, South Carolina.)

but had no contact with her ex-husband. She worked as a sales associate for a local tool company.

There were men who were interested in dating her. They were interviewed extensively and none were suspect. She didn't socialize or date often because of a medical problem that many didn't know about. At the time she gave birth to Jonathan, a part of her colon was torn, which left her incontinent at times. If she got excited or scared, she would void her bowels. The young woman was obviously very self-conscious of her condition and avoided dating and socializing.

THE INVESTIGATION

Detectives entered the victim and car information into the National Crime Information Center (NCIC) because Tina's residence was near a major highway, and it was thought that someone may have carjacked her and her vehicle in order to escape or leave the area in a hurry.

An aerial search was initiated and all police agencies in the area were put on alert. Family members and friends were interviewed. Tina had been married, but hadn't been in contact with her husband for some time.

There was no sign of the victim or her car. The initial search continued until 4 a.m. The following morning, the search was resumed and all alarms were retransmitted. Police requested that Jonathan be reinterviewed by a child psychologist using play therapy to gain a better description of the unknown white male and the sequence of events.

The victim had a cell phone in her car and the number was called repeatedly with no answer. Detectives requested a trace for any calls made from this instrument. Detective Rusty Clevenger received a call from a wildlife officer, who reported that he saw the victim's car on a small road that was an entrance to a deer hunting club. He noted the plate number and thought the car belonged to a deer hunter. The next day he heard the alarm and checked his notes and notified police.

A helicopter was dispatched and detectives rushed to the scene. The victim's body was found within 30 yards of her vehicle. She had been shot once in the head and left at the scene (Figure 8.12 and Figure 8.13).

Detective Clevenger asked a police officer, who was a long-time resident of the area, if he knew of any possible suspects who might be considered. The officer named David Duke as a known sex offender. The detective immediately requested any intelligence information on Duke.

Figure 8.12 Victim's car. The victim's car was recovered in the adjoining county. (Photo courtesy of Investigator Rusty Clevenger, 7th Circuit Solicitor's Office, Spartanburg, South Carolina.)

Figure 8.13 Victim's body. Tina's body was found about 30 feet away from her vehicle, which the offender had left at the scene. (Photo courtesy of Investigator Rusty Clevenger, 7th Circuit Solicitor's Office, Spartanburg, South Carolina.)

CANVASS OF THE AREA

The initial canvass of the area yielded two witnesses who saw a white male standing on the side of the road near the victim's car. This was within an hour of the abduction. Their description of the man matched David Duke, who was now considered a potential suspect.

Residents in the area were able to identify Duke, whom they saw walking from the area of crime scene to his residence. Additional witnesses were located who saw Duke near the victim's residence the day of the abduction. Witnesses who lived next door to Duke saw a small, red car drive by their residence with a white female hanging from the passenger side yelling and screaming for help. Their description of the female matched Tina and her car was red. In addition, the crime scene detectives found Tina's cell phone in the vicinity where the witnesses saw Duke.

INITIAL INTERVIEW AND INVESTIGATION OF SUSPECT

When detectives finally located Duke, they noticed he was limping. He refused to give any information on how he had gotten hurt. However, he did provide an extensive alibi.

One of the recommended tactics of *Practical Homicide Investigation* (Geberth, 2006), is to get the suspect to talk by not interrupting him with questions. Allow the suspect to expand on his alibi and seemingly go along with his story as preposterous as it sounds. There is no way that the offender will be able to corroborate this concocted story. Instead, the authorities will be able to use the words of the offender to trap him in his own web of deceit.

He stated he had been driven to work that day by a man who later told police that Duke asked to be let out about a mile from the victim's home. Duke told this witness that his boy was sick and he had to visit him at the hospital. This turned out to be untrue. Detectives had ascertained that Duke was a smoker, who exclusively smoked Winston cigarettes. This was significant because an empty pack of Winstons and Winston cigarette butts were found in the area of the victim's residence at the tree line. Later, DNA was extracted from these discarded cigarette butts and matched to Duke, who also told the detectives that he had gone drinking the day of the abduction. He identified his drinking buddies as two men: Terry and Ricky. The investigators were unable to locate any such persons.

In his statement to police, Duke stated that he had never been near the victim's car. This proved to be extremely important since the police had actually located a single fingerprint of the suspect *inside* the victim's car. Also Duke's footwear was matched to impressions recovered at the crime scene in the vicinity of the victim's car.

The investigation revealed that Tina had been shot with a .357. Detectives learned that Duke had possession of a .357 pistol some time earlier after taking it from the owner.

SIGNATURE ASPECT AND MODUS OPERANDI

There was a distinct *pattern of behavior* to the suspect. The suspect was a serial rapist, who 20 years earlier had raped a young mother at gunpoint in LaGrange, Georgia. Detectives discovered a number of similar rapes by the suspect, some of which were not originally reported. In each case Duke would stalk his victims and plan out his crimes. He reportedly had raped two of his wives and had taken one wife to the same area where Tina's body was found. Duke usually targeted a woman with a small child. He picked a certain type of victim with similar looks. He would look for a woman who was timid, vulnerable, and submissive and, because of her child, would cooperate with his demands.

DISPOSITION

Tina was actually killed because she had a medical problem, which caused her to suffer from incontinence. Her killer, who obviously had made detailed plans to abduct and sexually assault her, became outraged when she soiled herself. In his rage, he shot her to death. A young woman was slaughtered and a young five-year-old boy was left without a mother.

Duke pled guilty to the murder and received a life sentence.

The author has reviewed other cases where an offender, who had planned out an attack with an obvious sexual fantasy, gained control over his victim only to have some unforeseen circumstance emerge. In one particular case, a young woman, who was taking a purgative had been stripped and bound in her bed. She obviously was extremely frightened and voided her bowels. In this case, it was the victim's incontinence that enraged and angered the offender because it ruined his sexual fantasy. In other cases, it was a victim who was menstruating at the time of the attack. In any event, it is another element to take into consideration during the investigation.

Case History: Victim Killed to Prevent Identification

CASE FACTS

A black subject was stopped by a police officer when he observed the subject squealing his tires and flashing his lights at the car in front of him. The police officer pursued the subject who attempted to speed away. When the officer asked for his license and identification, he noted that there were stolen plates on the vehicle. The subject also had an outstanding warrant on him.

The subject was arrested for possession of stolen license plates. Pursuant to standard search procedure, the vehicle was impounded and searched. When the officers opened the trunk, they discovered the nude body of an unidentified, white, female victim. At this point, the police realized that they had a potential murder suspect in custody. The victim was subsequently identified as "Pamela" (Figure 8.14).

Pamela owned the Cadillac, which the subject had stolen. The victim had left her apartment on a Tuesday morning to get gas and have the car washed. She was a regular customer at this car wash.

The manager, who had been waiting for an opportunity to sexually assault her if there was no one else around, directed her to drive into the garage. When she drove her car into the garage, the manager closed the doors. At gunpoint, ordered the woman to strip. He then raped and anally sodomized her in the garage. The manager then forced the nude victim into the trunk of her own car where she remained trapped in a virtual tomb.

The suspect then drove over to his girlfriend's house and told her the Cadillac was a gift from his mother. He then drove the girlfriend and another girl to Royal Oak, Michigan, which is about 15 miles south. While they were in the car, they heard Pamela pleading to get out. He told the girls it was only a tape recorder that he used in his undercover work. The suspect had been previously arrested for impersonation of a police officer.

He gave the car to his girlfriend to use Wednesday and Thursday. On Friday, the girlfriend's two children heard Pamela pleading to get out of the trunk. The children ran to

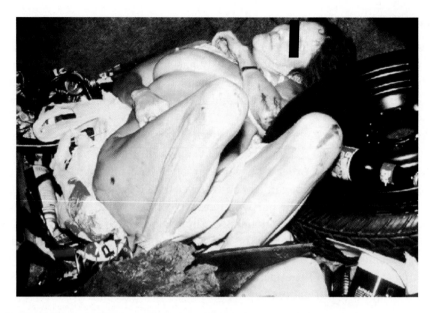

Figure 8.14 Victim's body in trunk. The officers discovered the nude body of the victim in the trunk of her car. (Photo courtesy of Chief John B. Dean, Waterford Township, Michigan, Police Department.)

their grandmother, who "spoke" to the voice in the trunk. In fact, detectives had ascertained she heard the voice saying, "Please help me." She never even thought to call the police. Instead the grandmother told the subject about the voice in the trunk and he told her the same story about the tape recorder. She later told police that she believed him.

The subsequent police investigation revealed that over 30 persons had heard or spoken to Pamela while she was trapped in the trunk of her car, where she had been for six days.

The victim, who couldn't even turn around to relieve herself, died a horrible death. She was so thirsty and desperate to survive that she drank windshield washer solvent from a container in the trunk. As a result of ingesting this fluid, Pamela went into convulsions and eventually lost consciousness and died. The mechanism of death was hypothermia and dehydration.

DISPOSITION

The subject was found guilty and received three counts of "natural life" in Michigan State Prison, which translates to life in prison without parole (From the author's files).

Case History: Rape Murder—Attempt to Dispose of Body by Mutilation and Disarticulation

---

INITIAL POLICE REPORT

On February 21, 1997, at approximately 4:09 p.m., the Pottawatomie County, Kansas, Sheriff's Department took a missing person's report on a 66-year-old woman named Rose. The missing woman's daughter was the reporting witness. Rose was a lifelong native of Kansas and had been married twice; however, each of her husbands had

Figure 8.15 Blood stain. Officer noticed a blood stain and a piece of human flesh at the back door. (Photo courtesy of the Kansas Bureau of Investigation.)

predeceased her. She was the grandmother of 26 and a great grandmother of five. She had never remarried and had lived in Westmoreland, Kansas, for 25 years. Rose kept herself busy with the grandchildren and had a part-time job as a waitress at the Leisure Lounge in Westmoreland. The last time Rose was seen was when she left the lounge after work at approximately 12:30 a.m. to go home.

A neighbor became concerned when noticing that Rose's vehicle was still parked at her residence at 3 p.m. The neighbor knew that Rose would normally be at work. The neighbor contacted Rose's daughter who went to her mother's residence to check on her well-being and noticed "that things were not quite normal."

The reporting witness told the deputy that her mother's blinds were not pulled up throughout the residence. She added that the bedroom and bed appeared as if they hadn't been used and there was no indication that the mother had made her traditional morning coffee or daily iced tea. The daughter also noticed that her mother's purse and car keys were missing.

The deputy entered the premises and noticed a red stain on the bottom portion of the back door (Figure 8.15). He also noticed a piece of bone or tooth on a concrete pad just outside the back door. He notified detectives to respond to the scene.

ADDITIONAL INFORMATION

Rose was considered to be friendly, happy, and helpful toward her friends and neighbors. However, she was not trusting. She maintained a continued fear of burglary to her home. The daughter further advised the deputy that her mother's neighbor, James Martin, had been outside earlier when she had arrived to check on her mother. According to the daughter, Rose knew Martin, who lived directly south of her place, and she had told her neighbors and her family that Martin "acted weird" and that she had expressed concern about him. She also told the deputy that Martin had been carrying a can of gasoline and appeared to have been intent on burning a large brush pile on his property.

Ironically, the deputy who was taking this missing person's report had taken a complaint against Martin the night before. On February 20, at approximately 10:57 p.m., Jennifer Martin had called the Sheriff's Office to complain that her husband James had threatened (via telephone) to kill her. According to Jennifer, James was at the Leisure Lounge in Westmoreland and had been drinking since 5 p.m. Jennifer had been at the lounge with him earlier in the evening. While at the location, James and Jennifer got into an argument and James cursed Jennifer. Rose, who was working at the location confronted James about his abusive language.

The Sheriff's Deputy advised Jennifer Martin that he would forward the complaint to the County Attorney and would make contact with James Martin. Jennifer advised the deputy that she was going to spend the night with her parents. The deputy drove to the Leisure Lounge where he learned that Martin had left approximately 30 minutes earlier. The deputy attempted to make contact with Martin at his residence, where a light was visible inside. However, he was unable to contact Martin.

The deputy, who had been advised that Martin had been outside earlier when the complainant called the police, went to Martin's residence. Martin, who was dressed in multicolored boxing shorts, invited the deputy inside. Martin, who was mopping his kitchen, told the deputy that he didn't know his neighbor Rose and had not seen her. The deputy noticed that the kitchen was extremely clean compared to the rest of Martin's residence. The deputy reported his observations to detectives. Martin told the deputy that he had to go to work and was allowed to leave pending the arrival of the Kansan Bureau of Investigation (KBI) and other investigators.

THE INVESTIGATION

On February 21 at approximately 7:45 p.m., James Martin was arrested for the criminal threats against his wife, Jennifer, made on February 20. Martin was arrested at his place of work in Westmoreland where he worked as a part-time cook. Martin was interviewed regarding the criminal threats and for any information on the disappearance of his neighbor, Rose.

Martin told the detectives that he had been drinking at the Leisure Lounge on February 20 from 5 p.m. until he left at about 10:30 p.m. He stated that he arrived home at approximately 10:45 p.m. and went directly to bed. Martin acknowledged that he knew Rose from the Leisure Lounge, but did not associate with her as a neighbor. It was during the interview that the detectives noticed that Martin used the past tense when he described Rose. The investigators asked the suspect if they could examine his clothing, which Martin voluntarily submitted to them. Martin further agreed to allow agents to search his residence as long as he could be present during the search.

In the interim, unbeknownst to Martin, officers had brought in a human tracking canine to ascertain whether or not the dog could locate the missing person. The dog tracked a scent, associated with Rose, to the Martin residence.

THE SEARCH

A search warrant was issued for the Martin residence at approximately midnight on February 21, 1997. Supervisory Special Agent Ray Lundin of the KBI led the search, which was completed on February 24. During the search, a black plastic bag containing the victim's purse and identification were located.

Figure 8.16 Body parts. Investigators located body parts in a Ziplock® bag inside a large, black, plastic garbage bag along with other items belonging to the victim. (Photo courtesy of the Kansas Bureau of Investigation.)

In addition, the authorities discovered human body parts, a steam iron with cut cord, and bloody clothing inside the plastic bag (Figure 8.16). The search of the residence also located bloody clothing belonging to Martin. The authorities seized a .22-caliber rifle and ammunition, photographs depicting James and Jennifer Martin and others who had been bound in electrical cord, assorted pornographic materials, and marijuana.

At approximately 8:15 a.m. on February 22, a search party located the torso (head, arms, and legs missing) wrapped in a blanket and multicolored afghan under tree roots on the west bank of a creek approximately 200 yards east of Rose's residence (Figures 8.17 through 8.19).

An initial search of the missing woman's residence revealed it to be extremely clean. However, a detailed forensic search did yield additional trace evidence. This evidence included blood in the kitchen sink trap, blood under the floor tiles in the kitchen, and human tissue in the toilet.

THE SUSPECT

James Martin was a 28-year-old ex-convict. He had an extensive arrest record and had been imprisoned in California several times. His charges ranged from DWI to assault and battery, grand theft auto, burglary, possession and selling of stolen property, aiding a felon, and resisting arrest. While in prison, he met his wife, Jennifer, through a pen-pal arrangement. James and Jennifer met in person several times while he was incarcerated. They married when his was paroled.

Throughout their marriage, James and Jennifer lived with friends and/or family at various residences. They had a volatile marriage with each of them battering the other. Jennifer claimed that James bound her arms and legs and raped her anally within two months of their marriage. According to Jennifer, James had a low overall sex drive and initiated sex with her less than once a week. Jennifer also advised the investigators that James had confided in her that his mother physically and sexually abused him.

Figure 8.17 Torso. The victim's torso was found wrapped in a sheet inside of an afghan and floating in a creek behind the suspect's home. (Photo courtesy of the Kansas Bureau of Investigation.)

Figure 8.18 Torso. The torso was unwrapped at the medical examiner's office and identified as the deceased. (Photo courtesy of the Kansas Bureau of Investigation.)

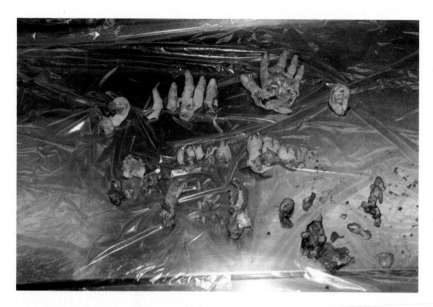

Figure 8.19 Body parts. The suspect cut off the identifiable parts of the woman's body. (Photo courtesy of the Kansas Bureau of Investigation.)

James Martin rarely worked and when he did it was only part-time. The longest period of time that he was able to hold a job was five months. All of the jobs involved low skilled labor. According to his wife, James enjoyed watching horror-type movies and pornography. They had moved from California to Westmoreland, Kansas, in 1996, so that Jennifer, who was originally from Kansas, could be near her family.

THE CONFESSION

On February 22, James Martin was reinterviewed after authorities had executed the search warrants and recovered a number of pieces of evidence, including the victim's disarticulated body and other body parts. During this interview, Martin admitted shooting the victim and then provided police with an extensive statement, which was obviously self-serving and attempted to portray the innocent victim as a willing participant.

Note: The author has experienced this circumstance many times. An offender will attempt to minimize his responsibility by either blaming the victim or suggesting that the victim encouraged the behavior or was a willing participant in the event. The offender will then construct an elaborate alibi or story that has kernels of truth interspersed in the story. These "kernels of truth" seemingly explain some of components of the event and some of the evidence that the authorities have uncovered. However, when placed in context, the statement doesn't ring true in its entirety. Many times the investigator needs to allow the suspect's subterfuge in order to maintain dialog and at least gain some admissions that can be focused on in subsequent interrogations.

Martin stated that he had gone to the victim's residence after she arrived home from work. He claimed that he was outside playing "Rambo" with his .22-caliber rifle prior to going to Rose's home. Martin claimed that once inside Rose's house, they both drank beer and smoked cigarettes and talked. Martin claimed that Rose asked him, "Do you want to fuck?" after changing into a negligee. Martin claimed that Rose asked him to tie her up. Martin stated that he bound her hands with electrical cord from an iron. (*This iron was a Christmas gift from one of her children and had been recovered during the search secreted in a black plastic bag.*)

Martin stated that they then had consensual sexual intercourse, which didn't last long. According to Martin, he had been overcome with guilt having violated his marriage vows. Martin stated that the cord binding Rose's hands had become loose, so he then tied Rose's hands and feet together and placed a towel over Rose's face. Martin then claimed that he attempted to leave the residence, but then returned with his rifle in hand to the bedroom where Rose was bound. Martin stated that, while attempting to untie Rose, the rifle accidentally discharged striking Rose in the head.

Martin claimed that he tried to save Rose to the point of performing CPR. He told the investigators that he was afraid to call the paramedics because he thought that people would not believe him, so he decided to dispose of her body, but claimed she was too heavy to lift. Martin stated that he then decided to dismember Rose. He told the investigators that he used a serrated-edged knife to remove Rose's head, arms, and legs. Martin stated that he wrapped the torso in blankets and used electrical cord to bind the blankets. He then carried the blanket-wrapped torso to the creek and threw it in.

Martin told the investigators that he then returned to Rose's residence and cleaned the house. Martin directed KBI agents to an area behind the co-op where he had hidden the arms and legs in a big red bag. The location of the co-op was approximately 150 yards north of the restaurant where Martin worked. The bag contained a black shirt, a car seat cover, and a white plastic bag, which contained a fragmented skull, scalp, eyebrows, skinned feet, skin, arm and leg bones, and leg flesh.

REINTERVIEW AND CONFESSION

James Martin was reinterviewed on February 23 and 24. He was confronted with the discrepancies in his previous statements as well as the evidence that the KBI agents and police had recovered and analyzed. Martin acknowledged that the sex with the victim was not consensual. However, he continued to maintain that the gunshot was accidental. Marin explained that once he determined that Rose was dead, he needed to remove the bullet from her head so that it could not be traced back to him. Martin told the investigators that he put his finger in the bullet wound, but could not feel the bullet.

Martin said that he looked in Rose's mouth and couldn't find the bullet. He stated that he then used a small hammer, screwdriver, and knife to make a hole in her skull. He stated that he stuck his hand inside the victim's head and tried to find the bullet, but could only find pieces of bone. Martin then stated that he pulled the brains out and placed them on a plastic bag and continued to look for the bullet, but couldn't find it. (*It should be noted that the forensic pathologist located bullet fragments during the autopsy.*)

Martin stated that he removed Rose's head, arms, and legs and disposed of the torso as he had previously described. Martin told the investigators that he used bleach to clean traces of semen from Rose's vagina and stomach. Martin stated that after he disposed of the torso, he returned to the victim's residence and carried the other body parts back to his residence using the kitchen trashcan. He then returned to Rose's house and cleaned the residence using bleach and a mop. Martin stated that he hid the trashcan containing the body parts next to the air conditioning unit outside his residence. He told the investigators that he then entered his residence, took a bath, and went to bed at approximately 5 a.m.

Figure 8.20 Flesh. The suspect had cut the victim's flesh from the bones. (Photo courtesy of the Kansas Bureau of Investigation.)

Martin stated that he awoke about five hours later. He said that his wife, Jennifer, had returned to the residence, but then left again at approximately 1 p.m. to go to work. Martin stated that he brought the remaining body parts into his residence and sectioned them into smaller pieces as he attempted to remove identifiable parts and accelerate decomposition by removing the skin tissue from the bones. He told the police that he finished sectioning the body between 2:30 and 3:30 p.m. (Figure 8.20).

Martin told the investigators that he noticed people in Rose's yard and knew that they were looking for her. So, he returned to the creek where he had disposed of the torso and held it under some tree roots with a rock. Martin then returned to his residence and cleaned the kitchen area with Joy dishwashing soap and Pine-Sol® cleaner. Martin also advised the investigators that he had been arrested approximately 30 minutes after he had placed the big red bag behind the co-op.

DISPOSITION

Martin pled guilty to capital murder and burglary. In return for his guilty plea, the State of Kansas agreed not to seek the death penalty. James Martin was sentenced to 40 years for the capital murder and 102 months (8 ½ years) for the burglary. The sentences were to run consecutively.

ACKNOWLEDGMENTS

The author wishes to acknowledge the contribution of the information and materials to this particular chapter of professional law enforcement investigators who were involved in this major case. Specifically, I wish to give special recognition to my long-time friend Special Agent-in-Charge Larry Thomas, KBI, who had been through many of my "Practical Homicide Investigation®" classes prior to this case and realized the significance of including this particular case in the book. I also wish to thank the following investigators: Senior Special Agent Raymond Lundin; The Pottawatomie Sheriff's

Department; and Westmoreland, Kansas, primary investigators, Sheriff Greg Riat and Detective Gerald Schmidt.

Case History: Rape–Murder—High-Risk Victim

CASE FACTS

On June 30, an unidentified victim's body was found buried on a beach. A passerby, who was walking with her child, observed a woman's hand sticking out of the sand and called police. Detectives observed two human hands sticking out of sand. The hands appeared to be those of a white female.

A large Dunkin' Donuts® coffee cup, which seemed relatively clean, was located approximately two feet away. There were fresh tire impressions in the sand near where the body had been buried. Apparently someone had recently driven onto the beach. There were also footwear impressions around the gravesite. The grave appeared to have been dug sometime after a rainstorm because the sand around the grave was loose. The sand outside this area was packed down by rain.

The scene was photographed and sketched. When the medical examiner arrived, authorities began to exhume the body. In accordance with the recommendations of *Practical Homicide Investigation* (Geberth, 2006), all of the sand was removed from the grave for sifting and the body was removed and placed on a sterile white sheet before transporting to the morgue.

The body was that of a white, female, with brown hair, a thin build, and was dressed in a reddish satin-type dress, white pantyhose, bra, and high heel shoes. She was approximately 30 years old. It appeared that she had been beaten about the face and head. There were markings on her neck area as well as blunt force trauma to the head. There were also defense-type wounds on her hands and arms. Authorities, who had sifted through the sand, recovered three press-on fingernails similar to the victim's other nails. They also recovered a clump of human hair consistent with the victim and a Ramsey brand condom wrapper. The decedent had sustained multiple wounds and abrasions to the face, head, arms, and hands caused by a hatchet-, shovel-, spade-, or ax-type instrument. There were six chopping wounds. The cause of death was due to brain injuries from sharp force trauma to head. There was also an incised wound to the victim's back consistent with sexual sadism. The rape kit was positive. There was also vaginal trauma. The stomach contents indicated that the victim was killed within three hours of her last meal, which placed the event around midnight. The victim was apparently still alive when buried. The authorities found sand in the victim's mouth. The victim's panty hose were ripped in the crotch area and her bra was not hooked properly in the back (Figure 8.21 and Figure 8.22).

Police were notified that a man reported that his wife, Kendra, was missing. Police were dispatched to take a report. They interviewed the husband and another male, who stated that he was Kendra's boyfriend and Kendra was supposed to meet him there. This case was certainly taking on a few twists. The husband stated that his wife had gone on a date with another male named Gary. Apparently, the husband knew that his wife would make dates with men through the personal ads in the local newspaper and he didn't object.

Figure 8.21 Hand. The victim's hand was sticking out from the sand. She had been buried alive. (Photo courtesy of Detective Corporal Arthur Clark, East Providence, Rhode Island, Police Department.)

THE SUSPECT

Gary was located by investigators and interviewed. He told detectives that he had met Kendra about a month earlier through her personal ads. He stated they were supposed to meet on June 29, but Kendra cancelled. He signed a consent form to search his auto. He then gave a statement. However, subsequent statements by Gary indicated he had used his mother's auto.

He then changed his story. He said that he did meet Kendra that night and they had sexual intercourse. He stated that he had killed her by mistake after they had an argument.

Gary agreed to take the investigators to the location where he had disposed of the blanket, the shovel, and other evidence. Detectives recovered this additional material, which linked him to the crime. After the detectives had searched his car and recovered the items he had disposed of, Gary gave a full statement to the police regarding the murder of Kendra. Detectives recovered blood, hairs, fibers, and sand from the blanket that the suspect used.

The victim's blood was on the recovered shovel. The suspect's mother's auto was searched. Additional blood and sand were recovered along with a napkin from the Dunkin' Donuts shop where he bought the coffee.

Figure 8.22 Victim's body. The victim had been sexually assaulted and struck in the head with a shovel. She was still alive when the offender buried her on the beach. (Photo courtesy of Detective Corporal Arthur Clark, East Providence, Rhode Island, Police Department.)

DISPOSITION

The subject was charged with first degree murder. He was sentenced to life without parole because torture and aggravated battery were inflicted upon the victim. (From the author's files.)

Case History: Gang Rape–Murder

CASE FACTS

On Tuesday June 23, at approximately 6:10 p.m., a farmer tending his fields discovered the body of a female. The body had been wrapped in white plastic garbage bags and was left under a culvert in Bloomington, which is a rural area of McLean County, Illinois. The farmer initially thought someone had dumped garbage on his property. When he drove over to the culvert and looked more closely, he saw the chest of a female, who also had been hog-tied and wrapped in plastic bags. He immediately notified the county police.

POLICE RESPONSE

McLean County police responded and met the witness at the culvert. They secured the crime scene and notified detectives to respond. It was ascertained that the witness was the only person to have entered the area beneath the culvert. He had not touched anything nor had he disturbed the scene other than to walk close enough to observe that the plastic bags contained a human body. The initial hypothesis on the part of the investigators was that possibly a trucker, or a serial killer, had dumped the body along this rural route.

The rationale for this hypothesis was that Bloomington is located halfway between Chicago and St. Louis, Missouri, and is a truck route. Also, the detectives had investigated several homicides that had occurred in these two cites and the bodies had been dumped in this county.

DESCRIPTION OF THE CRIME SCENE

Detective Mike Essig was assigned as the primary detective on this case and was assisted by Detectives David Deerwester and Howard Springer. The female body had been wrapped in white plastic bags. One bag covered the head of the victim and another covered the lower extremities of the body. The chest area was exposed and one could observe three stab wounds to the middle of the chest (Figure 8.23 and Figure 8.24). A fluorescent green shoelace had been used as a ligature to bind the ankles together, pull the victim's feet back to her buttocks, and then from the ankles the ligature was secured around the victim's neck. The ligature was tied on the outside of the garbage bags. Detective Essig requested that the Illinois State crime scene unit respond to assist in processing the scene. After Technician Ed Kallal photographed the scene, the three investigators examined the body and the immediate area. When the plastic bag covering the head was removed, the investigators found a woman's shoe with blood on the toe and side.

Lying outside the bag were two used condoms. Detective Essig observed that the other bag, which covered the victim's lower torso, had a hole punched through the bag at the location of the victim's vagina and he could see white plastic stuck in the victim's vagina. When the body was turned over, the detectives observed a pair of panties with a flower pattern lying midway between the victim's waist and head. The body was nude and there was no other clothing found at the scene. Also beneath the body was an empty blue Trojan condom wrapper.

Detectives observed what appeared to be knee impressions in the soil on the east side of the body, and a small indentation near the buttocks of the body, indicating that the soil had been pushed away from the body. Soil samples were taken. It should be noted that the space below the culvert was not high enough for a person to stand.

At the foot of the body there were several leaves, which were later identified by the Biology Department at Illinois State University (ISU) to be Common Burdock weed (*Arctium minumus*). The leaves were collected because there did not appear to be any other plants of this type at the scene. It was the opinion of the investigators that these leaves were trace evidence and probably had been transported to this location along with the body.

It was apparent to the investigators that the victim had been killed elsewhere and dumped into the culvert. Several pubic hairs, fuzz leaves, and other microscopic evidence were collected for laboratory analysis.

Also found at the scene was a large, beige-colored purse with embroidery on the front. Inside the purse the investigators retrieved several forms of identification. There was a passport issued from the Republic of Korea to a woman we will call "Sue." The

Figure 8.23 Dumped body. Victim was discovered under a bridge of a highway within a rural area in McLean County, Illinois. This particular highway served as a truck route between Chicago and St. Louis. At first, authorities felt they were dealing with a serial killer due to the location of discovery. This location was obviously a disposal site. The body was hog-tied and bound in plastic bags and there were two used condoms found at the location of discovery. An examination of the body indicated that there was a hole in the plastic bags in the area of the perineum of the victim. It appeared that the offenders had sexual intercourse with the victim's body after she was bound. (Photo courtesy Detective Mike Essig, McLean County Sheriff's Department, Bloomington, Illinois.)

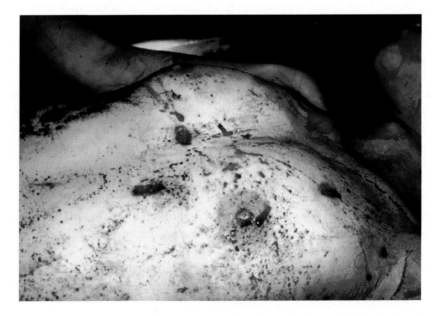

Figure 8.24 Body at autopsy. There was evidence of multiple stabbings to the chest area, which is consistent with sex-related homicides. (Photo courtesy Detective Mike Essig, McLean County Sheriff's Department, Bloomington, Illinois.)

passport had been issued at Seoul, Korea, and indicated a residence in the United States. This passport contained a photograph.

There was also a Resident Alien card with a photograph issued to a Sue (*last name withheld*) and a U.S. military ID issued to Sue. This showed the cardholder to be 4'8", 90 pounds, with the same date of birth. The ID also indicated that the sponsor of this person was a U.S. Army sergeant. (Investigation later revealed him to be Sue's ex-husband.)

In addition, there was another form of identification. A uniform vehicle law citation issued from the State of Michigan to Sue on June 18 at 0725 hours by a Michigan state trooper for "Pedestrian on a Freeway."

This citation indicated that she had been in Michigan five days earlier. Other items in the purse included notebooks, makeup, and a bar of soap. No money or credit cards were found in the purse. The items of identification were held as evidence and the purse was sent to the laboratory for latent print follow-up.

On completing the crime scene process, Detective Essig directed that a deputy be assigned to conduct surveillance of the scene and record all vehicle traffic and interest in the area of the crime scene by anyone.

This is standard procedure, according to *Practical Homicide Investigation* (Geberth, 2006). Whenever the investigation involves a body, which has been dumped at a remote location, the authorities, upon completing the crime scene process, should assign officers to maintain surveillance on the location. Many times the offender feels the need to return to the scene to ascertain whether or not the body has been discovered or to assure that there is no evidence at the scene that could possibly be used to identify him.

INVESTIGATIVE CONSIDERATIONS

After establishing a possible identification from the materials found in the beige purse, an alarm was dispatched countywide for any information regarding "Sue." Bloomington police immediately responded that they had contact with this person, who was transported by local police to the Home Sweet Home Mission on June 22 at approximately 9 p.m. Detective Essig directed the officer to meet him at the morgue to ascertain whether or not this was the same person. The police officer identified the body as Sue, the person he took to the Mission on June 22. The police officer stated he was dispatched to the Pilot Truck Stop in response to a woman wearing only a T-shirt for a dress. Employees at Pilot advised the officer that a trucker had dropped Sue off at the truck stop after picking her up hitchhiking in Chicago. The trucker also told the employees that Sue told him that she was going to Miami.

At this point in the investigation, it appeared that the victim was a transient, who had received a summons for hitchhiking in Michigan. She had been hitchhiking in the Chicago area and apparently had been picked up in the county and dumped in Bloomington.

VICTIMOLOGY

Detective Essig made contact with the victim's ex-husband, John (*not his real name*), who was visibly upset and provided the investigator with the following information.

He stated that he had met Sue while he was in the service stationed in Korea. Sue had come back with him to the States when his tour of duty ended. He told Detective Essig that they had been married approximately eight and one-half years and had a nine-year-old son from this marriage. They were divorced a year earlier. He also stated that his last contact with Sue had been in January. John went on to state that Sue was not happy in this country and wanted to return to Korea. He stated that Sue had been heavily involved in the Korean church and had made a lot of friends. However, toward the end of their marriage she had gone through several religious changes; she was sour toward people, did not trust a lot of people, and became stubborn and did not want to talk to people. John told the detective that Sue would wear a lot of makeup and stated, "She couldn't grasp the concept of a 'little went a long ways.'" He also advised the detective that he did not believe that Sue used any drugs, but she had been arrested twice for DUI after their divorce.

Investigation and interviews revealed that the deceased had been living as a homeless transient. She was reportedly suffering mental and emotional problems and apparently sustaining herself through prostitution at truck stops. She carried all of her possessions in the cloth bag that police recovered at the crime scene.

AUTOPSY

On June 23, a medical examination was conducted on the deceased. The medical examiner determined that the victim had been stabbed eight times. One wound penetrated the heart, two wounds penetrated the heart and lungs, three pierced the lungs, and four wounds penetrated the stomach and pancreas. The body also bore shallow puncture wounds from the point of a knife, described as "torture"-type wounds. Anal, vaginal, and oral swab samples were taken as well as pubic, body, and head hair samples. Two separate white plastic bags, which had been jammed into the victim's vagina, were removed from the victim.

PRELIMINARY INVESTIGATION INTO VICTIM'S ACTIVITIES

Wednesday, June 24, Detectives Essig and Deerwester went to the Home Sweet Home Mission in Bloomington to interview the case manager who was on duty when Sue was brought to the mission. The manager told the detectives he had attempted to find out what specific needs Sue required and provided her with two pair of dark jeans and tan-colored jacket. She provided her military identification and explained that her sponsor, identified as John, was her ex-husband. She was requested to register at the mission, but declined the offer. Instead, Sue requested directions back to the truck stop.

While Sue was at the Mission, she met a male identified as Tarone Smith (*fictional*). The detectives were able to establish that Tarone was possibly the last person to see her alive on June 22. Tarone was identified as a known sex offender with a recent history of mental illness. Tarone, who was also homeless, stayed at the mission as a part-time resident. When he wasn't at the mission, he would stay in an abandoned house in Bloomington.

There were several leaves at the crime scene, which were later identified by the Biology Department as ISU to be Common Burdock weed (*Arctium minumus*). When the detectives checked the yard of the abandoned house where Tarone was staying, they found this particular leaf growing all over the yard. A search warrant was secured for these premises.

However, the actual killing site could not be established. The suspect, Tarone, was located and brought to the Sheriff's Department for questioning. He denied leaving with Sue or bringing her to the abandoned house, stating he had only talked to her. He was then released and placed under 24-hour surveillance.

On Thursday morning, June 25, a witness reported to police that she had seen the victim on Tuesday morning at approximately 8 a.m. in downtown Bloomington. This witness stated that she had seen Sue get into a pickup truck driven by a white male. They then drove out of town. They were heading in the direction of Hudson, Illinois, which is a small town just west of Bloomington. Incidentally, there was a carnival in this town. The witness stated that she could identify the truck and the driver. Several detectives were sent to the carnival with a description of the truck and driver. The detectives reported that they had found the vehicle and the driver, a "Carney," identified as John Waldo (*fictional*). They also discovered that fluorescent green shoelaces, like the ones used to bind Sue, were also sold at the carnival.

John was brought to the Sheriff's Department for questioning as search warrants were secured for his truck and trailer.

Detective Essig established that John had stayed at a local motel on Monday evening. The police searched this premises for any evidence.

While searching the suspect's trailer Detective Essig found a wallet belonging to Mr. Waldo. This wallet contained several seminude pictures of Asian women. John told the detectives that the women in the photographs were Korean women and stated that his father was in the Korean War. This suspect also had an extensive criminal record, which included sex crimes.

As with Tarone, John certainly appeared to be a viable suspect. This was based on the evasiveness of his answers, compounded by the circumstantial nature of the fluorescent shoelaces, which were sold at the carnival. These facts, plus the information reported by the eyewitness who saw him accompanying the victim, made him appear to be a possible suspect. John was questioned for several hours and given a polygraph, which he passed. However, both gentlemen remained suspects.

BREAK IN THE CASE

Detective Essig and his team concentrated their efforts on these two suspects. However, a phone call on Saturday morning, June 27, changed the entire course of the investigation. A local attorney had called the State Attorney's Office and advised that he was representing a 22-year-old young man named William (*last name withheld*).

William was a witness to a homicide. The attorney was going to bring his client in to the Sheriff's Department to give a statement.

Before providing the detectives with a statement, William was advised of his *Miranda* rights in the presence of his attorney. William would become a state's witness and not be prosecuted for his involvement in concealing the crime in return for his cooperation.

According to the witness, the victim was killed to cover up a gang rape at a fraternity house in Normal, Illinois. The suspects were identified as Jeffrey Glen Whitehead (23-year-old white male) who was the actual stabber, Kevin Rittenhouse (22-year-old white male), and Shaun Chaszar (20-year-old white male).

Ironically, the offenders were not hardened criminal types usually associated with brutal sexual assaults, but, in fact, had all come from upstanding families and were students at Illinois State University.

WITNESS STATEMENT OF EVENTS

William stated that on Monday night, June 22, at about 8:45 p.m. he picked up Kevin Rittenhouse. They then went to a bar in Bloomington. While at the bar, Jeff Whitehead showed up at approximately 11 to 11:30 p.m. At about 11:30 p.m., Whitehead and Rittenhouse went to another bar in Whitehead's red Camaro. In the interim, William, who had been given a key to Whitehead's residence at 408 N. School Street, went out to get 12-pack of beer. William stated that when he arrived at 12:45 p.m., June 23, Whitehead's roommate "Mike" was home. Mike worked nights and was about to get ready for work.

At approximately 1:15 a.m., Rittenhouse and Whitehead arrived at the location with an Asian woman. He was introduced to the woman who was wearing a blue skirt and tan jacket.

William stated that they talked for a while and then he and Rittenhouse left and went to Shaun Chaszar's house on Fell Street. William stated that when they arrived, Chaszar was there with his roommate "Eddie." He stated that he stayed and talked with Eddie while Rittenhouse told Chaszar that there was an Asian woman at the School Street apartment. Chaszar and Rittenhouse then left to go to Whitehead's house on School Street while William and Eddie continued their conversation. William stated he was at the Fell Street location for at least an hour. (This was later verified through police interviews of other persons who were present). William told Detective Essig that he returned to the School Street location.

When he entered the house through the rear door, he was met by Rittenhouse, who told him, "They are doing her; they are raping her." Rittenhouse then shut and locked the door. William stated he told Rittenhouse that he was going to leave because he didn't want anything to do with what was going on. According to William, Rittenhouse told him that he wasn't going anywhere and to be "cool." They would take care of it. Rittenhouse also told William that he couldn't leave and had to stay because, he (William) was Rittenhouse's ride home.

William stated that while he and Rittenhouse were in the kitchen, Chaszar came out of Mike's bedroom and asked for a rubber. William had one in his wallet and he gave it to him. William stated that he insisted that Rittenhouse go into the bedroom and make Whitehead and Chaszar stop what they were doing and get rid of the woman. According to William, Rittenhouse said, "Okay," and then went into the bedroom. Rittenhouse came back out and said they would get rid of her as soon as Chaszar finished. William stated he did not see what was going on and sat down in the living room. He stated that from where he was sitting, he could hear the woman moaning and saying "no." William also stated to the detectives that he heard Chaszar tell the woman, "to get on your knees." He also reportedly gave other sexual commands.

William stated that at this time all three men (Rittenhouse, Chaszar, and Whitehead) were in the room. William stated he thought Rittenhouse had gone into the room twice, but didn't remember whether or not Rittenhouse was turning the lights on and off.

After the second time Rittenhouse went into the bedroom, he came out and told him that the victim was dead. Rittenhouse told William, "It's done, it's over, she is dead."

William stated that he got up off the couch and headed for the kitchen door and said he was going to leave. William stated that Rittenhouse stopped him and told him he couldn't leave.

At this time, according to William, he was walking around in a dazed condition. William said the offenders were trying to decide what to do next; this was when William first observed Sue. William stated he saw Sue lying on the couch nude and Whitehead walked by him with blood on his hands. At this point, according to William, everyone was trying to figure out what to do. William stated that he did not actually see Whitehead with a knife; however, he did see the bag with the murder weapon. William stated that he believed that the murder weapon was a butterfly knife that he had seen in Whitehead's possession in the past.

William stated that the one and only time he saw Sue after she was killed was when her body was on the couch and everyone was trying to decide what to do. William stated he did not see her bound and that he was told to get garbage bags. He ran upstairs to another apartment and grabbed a handful of garbage bags. William stated, when he got downstairs, Whitehead and Chaszar were getting dressed and everyone was still "kind of fumbling around." At this point, someone had moved Sue to the floor. William handed the garbage bags to someone, he doesn't recall whom, and he left the room. William stated he emptied a large garbage can, which was used to hold a keg of beer. He said he saw Whitehead and Chaszar putting Sue in garbage bags and then putting her into the garbage can. According to William, Whitehead and Chaszar then carried the garbage can with Sue's body out of the apartment and put the can in the back of Whitehead's red Camaro. Whitehead and Chaszar then left with the body to get rid of it.

William stated that he and Rittenhouse were left at the apartment to clean up what was left and pick up other evidence. William stated that this other evidence included items that had blood on them. William explained that these items included a cushion off the couch, the murder weapon, and some of the victim's clothes.

William stated that after they had gathered up the evidence, he and Rittenhouse returned to Rittenhouse's residence on Lincoln Street. According to William, when they got back, Rittenhouse went into the garbage and picked up some old beer cans. He threw them around the back yard and also put out some lawn chairs to make it appear that they had returned from the bar and were "partying" in the back yard.

William stated that this was the alibi that they were going to tell Amy who was Rittenhouse's girlfriend. Amy lived with him at the Lincoln Street address. They then went into the house and slept on the living room floor.

According to William, the next day he pulled his car around to the driveway of Rittenhouse's garage. They took the evidence out of the trunk of his car, and he and Rittenhouse put the evidence upstairs in Rittenhouse's garage. Later that day, William stated that he and Rittenhouse went back to Whitehead's apartment to ask what Whitehead and Chaszar had done with the body. Whitehead stated they got rid of the body somewhere northwest of Normal. William stated that he, Whitehead, and Rittenhouse went out to get something to eat and then went to another location to play volleyball. William told the detectives that while they were playing volleyball, Mike, Whitehead's roommate showed up and started yelling at Rittenhouse and Whitehead.

He wanted to know who had messed up his apartment by leaving clothes on the floor. Who had broken the door to his room, where were some of his clothes, and who had stolen his cushions. Rittenhouse made up some sort of story and promised to take care of everything. William stated that when he, Rittenhouse, and Whitehead went back to Whitehead's apartment, someone saw some of Sue's clothes on the floor. William stated that Whitehead picked up the clothes and put them into a paper bag and dropped the bag in a dumpster that was located down the alley from the School Street apartment.

William stated that as he was getting ready to leave, Whitehead was telling him and Rittenhouse that the body wasn't hidden very well and plans were being made to return to the crime scene and bury the body. Later that day, Tuesday June 23, Rittenhouse and Whitehead went to William's house. They stayed awhile before leaving to get shovels to bury the body. William estimated that Whitehead and Rittenhouse left his house around 9 p.m.

William stated he didn't see Whitehead or Rittenhouse until Wednesday, June 24. Rittenhouse showed William the newspaper article. He was burning evidence and sweeping up the garage. Rittenhouse then told him that when they went back to bury the body, they couldn't because an unmarked police unit followed them.

This information proved interesting and was corroborated by the fact that an unmarked police unit had been detailed to conduct surveillance of the scene and record all vehicle traffic or interest in the area of the crime scene by anyone. That evening, a deputy, who reported the incident, observed a red Camaro with California plates occupied by three white males in the area of the crime scene.

According to William, Rittenhouse told William that he had to take the rest of the evidence and get rid of it. William stated that Rittenhouse was holding a bag, which William believed contained the victim's purse and the murder weapon. William stated that Rittenhouse insisted that he take the stuff because Rittenhouse believed the police were going to show up at anytime. William refused. Rittenhouse allegedly stated, "Damn it, Bill, you gotta [sic] take this stuff or I'll kick your ass right here." William stated he refused and Rittenhouse took off running through the alley with some of the evidence. William stated he left the rest of the evidence in the driveway. He got into his car and left. William stated to the authorities that this was the last time he saw Rittenhouse or Whitehead.

On Thursday, June 25, William said he called Rittenhouse prior to Rittenhouse and Whitehead leaving for The Grateful Dead concert in Chicago. William told Rittenhouse he could not take it anymore. William stated that he told Rittenhouse that he was going to get an attorney and go to the police.

William stated that he told Rittenhouse that sooner or later Mike was going to figure out what happened and would probably go to the police. William told the detectives that Rittenhouse said, "You gotta do what you gotta do."

This was the last time William spoke to Rittenhouse. Before ending the interview with William, Detective Essig asked William if anyone asked why the woman was killed. William stated that right after it happened, and when William went into the bedroom, he was hysterical and asked Jeff Whitehead why he had killed her. William stated that Jeff replied, "She was saying our names and everything and said she was going to go to the police. We had to kill her."

INVESTIGATIVE CONSIDERATIONS

Detective Essig realized the importance of corroborating William's statement and securing search warrants for the School Street location where the rape–murder had occurred and the Lincoln Street location, which was the residence of Rittenhouse, where evidence had been stored. In addition, the police would secure a search warrant for the red Camaro. This car was owned by Whitehead and had been used to transport the body. Detectives immediately attempted to locate the three primary suspects, two of whom were reportedly out of town.

INTERVIEW OF SUSPECT CHASZAR

On June 27 at approximately 6:15 a.m., Detectives Essig and Deerwester located Shaun Chaszar at his residence on Fell Street in Normal, Illinois. He was asked to come to the Sheriff's Department for an interview. Chaszar was advised of his *Miranda* rights and agreed to speak to the detectives without an attorney. He was asked if he had met a Korean woman on Monday evening at the School Street apartment. He stated he had been there for only 45 minutes and then returned to his apartment and hung out with his roommate, Eddie. Chaszar was confronted with the facts known by the detectives. He agreed to tell what really happened that evening. He told the detectives that Rittenhouse had come to his apartment and told him to come over to the School Street location because Whitehead and Rittenhouse had picked up a foreign girl and he wanted Chaszar to check her out. While at the apartment, he stated Rittenhouse was poking the woman trying to keep her awake and Whitehead was asking the woman if she liked to have sex and other stuff. Chaszar stated that Whitehead started to touch the woman's leg, hands, and arms and then asked her if she wanted to go into the bedroom.

The woman stated she only wanted one boyfriend. Whitehead then led her into Mike's room. Whitehead was in the room with Sue for approximately 20 to 30 minutes. According to Chaszar, Whitehead then came out of the room and told Chaszar he could go into the bedroom indicating it was his turn with the woman. Chaszar stated that when he entered the bedroom Sue was on the couch naked. Chaszar stated he began touching her breasts and thighs. Chaszar said he had sex with the victim on the floor and that while he was having sex with the victim, Rittenhouse and Whitehead were coming into the room and flicking the lights off and on like a strobe light.

Chaszar stated while this was happening, he was trying to find his clothes and Whitehead was standing behind him. Chaszar stated that this was when he heard the sounds of hits. He told the detectives he heard Whitehead hit Sue 5 to 10 times and witnessed the last blow. Chaszar stated that, after the last blow, he, Rittenhouse, and Whitehead walked out of the bedroom. This was when he saw Whitehead go to the bathroom and wash the blood off his hands. Chaszar stated that during this time Rittenhouse and Whitehead were laughing. Chaszar stated that Rittenhouse and Whitehead told him to go in and check on Sue. Chaszar stated that there was blood all over the victim.

Chaszar said he told Rittenhouse and Whitehead that she was dead. According to Chaszar, Rittenhouse and Whitehead were laughing and calling Sue a bitch and a whore. The next thing that occurred was that they were deciding what to do with the woman. Chaszar stated that Rittenhouse gathered up all the stuff in the bedroom and it was decided that Chaszar would go with Whitehead to get rid of the body. Chaszar stated Whitehead and Rittenhouse "hog-tied" Sue using a florescent string from the shorts that Whitehead was wearing. Chaszar then stated that after Rittenhouse and Whitehead had tied the woman up, Whitehead put a garbage bag over the woman's head and put her headfirst into the garbage can.

Chaszar stated that after Sue had been placed in the garbage can, her knees and crotch were exposed. Chaszar stated that because he didn't want to look at her, he put a garbage bag over her knees and crotch area. He said that Rittenhouse was the last person to be alone with the body. Detective Essig asked Chaszar if he had placed the plastic bags into the victim's vagina. He denied placing the bags in Sue's vagina and also denied seeing anyone else do this. Detective Essig asked Chaszar who he thought might have done this.

Chaszar stated he thought Rittenhouse probably put the bags there because Rittenhouse had been "mean" to the girl throughout the evening. Chaszar stated that after Rittenhouse came out of the bedroom, he and Whitehead placed the body into the back seat of Whitehead's Camaro. They drove about 10 miles out of town. When they came to a bridge, Whitehead decided that this would be a good location to dump the body. They pulled off the road and carried the body down under the bridge into the culvert.

Whitehead was thinking about digging a hole for her, but Chaszar told him that it was beginning to get light out and someone might see them. Whitehead then dropped Chaszar off at his apartment. The next day, June 33, Chaszar stated he went to his mother's house and stayed there until early evening.

He said that at about 8 p.m., June 23, Rittenhouse and Whitehead came to his apartment. However, they didn't talk much about what had happened because his roommate was there. Chaszar stated the only conversation they had was that just before Rittenhouse and Whitehead left Chaszar's apartment. They made a comment that "they would do whatever it took not to get caught." Chaszar stated that he took this as a threat and also as the group staying together. Chaszar stated that this was the last time he saw Rittenhouse and Whitehead.

Chaszar told the detectives that he knew that Rittenhouse and Whitehead were going to Chicago for The Grateful Dead concert, which was on Thursday and Friday.

At no time during the interview did Chaszar mention the presence of William or the fact that William was at the School Street apartment during the course of events on Monday night and early Tuesday morning.

After the interview was ended, Detective Essig asked Chaszar if he would agree to take a polygraph examination. Chaszar stated that he would. After Chaszar took the polygraph, the examiner advised Detective Essig that Chaszar did not pass on three particular questions. The questions Chaszar could not prove truthful on were: "Whether or not the sex he had with Sue was consensual," "If William was present during the incident," and Chaszar's knowledge of who put the garbage bags into Sue's vagina.

Chaszar was interviewed a second time concerning the above questions. Chaszar admitted that William was present at the apartment and that he didn't want to involve him in the crime because they are friends. Chaszar also told the detectives that William didn't have sex with the victim. Chaszar insisted that the sex he had with Sue was consensual on her part and denied any knowledge of the bags in her vagina.

Chaszar was given a second polygraph. He admitted that he did force the woman to have sex, but he still denied any knowledge of the plastic bags in the vagina.

EXECUTION OF SEARCH WARRANTS

At approximately 10:40 p.m. on June 27, McLean County Sheriff's Police executed a search warrant at the School Street address. Lieutenant John Brown, Lieutenant Brett Beyer, Detective Howard Springer, and Illinois State Crime Scene Tech Ed Kallal processed the scene.

At approximately 11:13 p.m., the red Camaro was towed to the McLean County Sheriff's Department for processing by CST Kallal. At approximately 1:15 a.m.,

Lieutenants Brown and Beyer, Chief Deputy David Goldberg, Detective Springer, and CST Kallal executed the search warrant for the Lincoln Street address.

Rittenhouse's girlfriend, who was present at this location, was interviewed and a statement was obtained. Also during this same time period, detectives located and interviewed Mike, Whitehead's roommate, and Eddie, Chaszar's roommate. Statements were taken from both individuals, which revealed how the events leading up to the murder unfolded that evening.

More importantly, these interviews corroborated the statement of William, who would eventually be called as a State's witness. The authorities now had a firm timeline and synopsis of exactly how the event unfolded.

LOCATION OF THE OTHER TWO SUSPECTS

In the interim, police received information regarding the location of Rittenhouse and Whitehead. The Chicago police were requested to pick up Whitehead, who was attending the concert in that city. The investigators, through interviews of friends and associates, learned that Rittenhouse had gone to New York State and was staying at his mother's house. The New York State Police were requested to pick up Rittenhouse.

On Sunday, June 28, in the early morning hours, Detective Essig spoke with Senior Investigator Ed McKenna of the New York State Police. He advised Investigator McKenna that he had an arrest warrant for Kevin Rittenhouse, who was staying at his mother's house in Neversink, New York.

At approximately 6 a.m., Investigator McKenna notified Detective Essig and advised him that Kevin Rittenhouse had been arrested at his mother's house and was in custody at the Sullivan County Jail. Investigator McKenna advised Detective Essig that when Rittenhouse was placed under arrest for murder, he made the comment, "I know something about the case, but I didn't kill her." The recording of this *res gestae* comment by the murder suspect at the time of his arrest was an astute observation and documentation on the part of the New York State Police Investigator. It showed guilty knowledge and would later be an admissible statement under law.

On June 28 at approximately 5:30 p.m., after being picked up in Chicago, Jeffrey Whitehead was returned to the McLean County Sheriff's Department. Detective Essig advised Jeffrey Whitehead of his Miranda Rights after taking the preliminary arrest information. Whitehead stated that he understood his rights and invoked his right to counsel.

On Monday, June 29, Detectives Essig and Deerwester drove to the Sullivan County Jail in Monticello, New York, to interview Kevin Rittenhouse and bring him back to McLean County if Rittenhouse waived extradition. When they arrived, Rittenhouse passed them a note stating he would not talk to them without first talking to his attorney. On Tuesday, June 30, Detectives Essig and Deerwester went to the New York State Police Barracks and conferred with the State Police Investigator regarding this matter.

During the day, the investigators were unsuccessful in their attempts to make contact with members of Rittenhouse's family. Later in the day, they were contacted by the family attorney who advised them they were not to speak to any family members. The investigators spent the next two days in New York waiting for Kevin Rittenhouse to make a decision whether or not to waive extradition. On July 2, Rittenhouse waived extradition and was turned over to the McLean County detectives for transport back to Illinois. He was advised of his rights and made no further statements.

INTERVIEW OF KEVIN RITTENHOUSE

On July 3, Rittenhouse met with his attorney and agreed to take the detectives to various locations where evidence had been placed. At each of the two dumpster sites, the trash had been collected. However, at the third location, which was a storm drain, the investigators observed a knife. Rittenhouse identified the knife as the one he had thrown into the drain. This butterfly knife was the murder weapon.

The detectives interviewed Rittenhouse in the presence of his attorney. He provided the same basic story William did. However, he minimized his participation in the crime and placed the blame on Whitehead. Rittenhouse did state that he saw Whitehead swing at the woman four or five times and saw the knife in Whitehead's hand.

Detective Essig asked Rittenhouse if he knew who put the bags in the victim's vagina. Rittenhouse stated that he remembered Chaszar making the comment; "Did you remember the bag stuffed in her pussy?" Rittenhouse also recalls Chaszar making the comment "We hog-tied that bitch." Rittenhouse also admitted that he, Chaszar, and Whitehead went back to the crime scene to bury the body. Rittenhouse told the detectives that Chaszar was the only one who knew exactly where the body was. All three went together, but they couldn't bury the body because an unmarked police car followed them.

The detectives elicited some additional information from Rittenhouse during this interview. For example, Rittenhouse stated that Chaszar was making comments to Sue, such as "Fucky, fucky, sucky, sucky, love you long time. …" Rittenhouse stated that during this time, Sue was telling Chaszar, "No," in a timid voice. Rittenhouse admitted going into the bedroom and seeing Whitehead getting off Sue. He stated Whitehead was naked and Sue had her shirt pulled up and her skirt was pulled up. Rittenhouse stated he saw Chaszar take off his pants and try to get Sue to the middle of the floor and she resisted. Rittenhouse stated Whitehead told her to do what she was told. Rittenhouse told the detectives that Sue was holding her legs together.

According to Rittenhouse, Chaszar said. "Open your legs, bitch. Spread your legs, bitch." Sue refused and Whitehead grabbed her by the hair and pulled her head back so that she was looking up at him. Rittenhouse stated that Whitehead then said to Sue, "Do it." And Sue did what she was told. Rittenhouse stated that at about that time William came in the back door and asked where everybody was, Rittenhouse told him, "They are in the room and they are fucking that girl." This statement corroborated the statement that William had originally given the detectives.

Rittenhouse agreed, through his attorney, to take a polygraph test. According to the polygraph examiner, Rittenhouse was not telling the truth about whether or not he had any knowledge there was going to be some type of criminal activity involving Sue at the School Street location. Rittenhouse also failed the question of who put the garbage bags into the victim's vagina.

EVIDENCE

- The investigators had recovered the murder weapon, which contained the blood of the victim matched through DNA.
- The red Camaro with the California license plates was found to contain microscopic evidence linked to the crime scene and the victim.
- Blood samples from the crime scene were matched to Sue.
- Pubic hairs found at the scene matched the suspects.

- Pubic hair of the victim found at the crime scene.
- Additional forensic evidence retrieved from crime scene.
- DNA analysis on semen found in the used condoms found at the dumpsite matched Chaszar.
- Fingerprints recovered from the plastic garbage bags, which had been stuffed into the victim's vagina, were matched to Chaszar.
- Plant material similar to the plant material at the dump site matched plant material at the School Street location.

CRIMINAL CHARGES AND DISPOSITION

Jeff Whitehead, who was the "stabber," was charged with first degree murder, aggravated criminal sexual assault, obstructing justice, and concealing a homicide. He was found guilty after trial and sentenced to 65 years.

Shaun Chaszar was charged with first degree murder, aggravated criminal sexual assault, obstructing justice, and concealing a homicide. He was found guilty after trial and was sentenced to 38 years.

Kevin Rittenhouse was charged with first degree murder, aggravated criminal sexual assault, and concealing a homicide. He was found guilty after trial and was sentenced to 20 years.

Reconstruction and Opinion

This was a classic case of gang rape. The individuals involved in this crime started out drinking and smoking marijuana. There was no planned attack. However, when the victim, who was looking for a ride, appeared to be available, Rittenhouse and Whitehead decided to take her to their fraternity house and take advantage of the situation. When the victim got into their car, the sexual fantasy had already begun. When they got to the fraternity house, the pack mentality of gang rape dynamics began.

In the words of one of the offenders, "I'm going to rape this bitch." Rittenhouse told the detectives he heard Whitehead state, "Now we are going to fuck this girl, or at least get blow jobs." Rittenhouse, who emerged as the leader of the group, left the victim with Whitehead as he went to get Chaszar to join in. When Chaszar arrived at the fraternity house, there were three males, who had been drinking, all with one thing on their minds, "Are we going to get laid?" Rittenhouse began by taunting the victim and setting the stage for a sexual confrontation.

He then distanced himself, as the event got physical. The sex talk that Whitehead engaged in with the victim, as well as his touching of her breasts and thighs, fueled the group fantasy.

The eventual intercourse, first by Whitehead and then by Chaszar, escalated when, according to Rittenhouse, Chaszar said, "Open your legs, bitch. Spread your legs, bitch." Sue refused and Whitehead grabbed her by the hair and pulled her head back so that she was looking up at him. Rittenhouse stated that Whitehead then said to Sue, "Do it," and the victim complied.

This is a classic gang rape pattern. The victim was reduced to an object and the assault became justified by her lack of cooperation. Sue was referred to as a "bitch and whore." Suddenly, without warning Whitehead took out his butterfly knife and stabbed the victim to death. They then attempted to justify this killing to each other because she was going to report them.

The reference to the statement, "We are all in this together," certainly summed up the group thinking at the time.

This is a group dynamic with the purpose of protecting the group from discovery. The cleaning up of the crime scene, the destruction of the evidence, and the disposal of the body were all acts carried out as a group exercise. It was Rittenhouse who directed the "clean up" of the scene.

It was Whitehead and Chaszar who provided for the disposal of the body. The group members were Chaszar, Whitehead, and Rittenhouse. The group plan was to rape the girl. Chaszar and Whitehead carried out the rape exercise, but Rittenhouse, who gave up his leadership role to Whitehead, never actually participated in the rape. William, who was a reluctant participant in the "cleanup," went along because of the group dynamics.

Interestingly, the stabber, Jeffery Whitehead, had been in the U.S. Navy and had been stationed in San Diego, California. According to the police investigation, he had attempted to enlist in the Navy Seals, but was rejected and took a job as an administrative assistant to the Seal Commander. While he was at this station, there were two unsolved stabbing attacks on Asian women that bore striking similarities to this case.

I mentioned this because of the statements made by his co-conspirators, along with his loner personality, and his fascination with knives and death. It was Whitehead who told the group after the killing that they were all pussies and needed to be tough like in the military. He emerged as the group leader when Rittenhouse took a secondary role and distanced himself from the physical act.

In a final act of outrage, Chaszar had sex with Sue's corpse at the dumpsite by penetrating her body through the tear in the plastic bags.

The interview strategies employed by Detective Essig were excellent. The corroboration of the witness statement and the supporting information from collateral witnesses set the stage for the first interview with Chaszar. As Chaszar began his story, minimizing his participation, the authorities already knew that he was lying and were able to confront him with his falsehoods. This coupled with the effective use of the polygraph enabled the detectives to obtain a valuable confession. When Rittenhouse was finally interviewed, the detectives had a pretty good idea of what had transpired at the fraternity house that evening as well as the suspects' attempts to cover up the crime. Once again, the effective use of the polygraph on Rittenhouse indicated where the suspect was lying to minimize his participation and protect his own interests. These interviews and interrogations were the key to successful prosecution of all three of the defendants.

Detective Essig, who had attended one of my "Practical Homicide Investigation®" classes, contacted me right after this investigation. He told me that the *Practical Homicide Investigation* textbook had certainly come in handy for him. He stated, "This case could have come right out of your book, just like the other cases we learned about during your class." He stated, "At first I thought that we had a serial killer, who had dropped a body on us. Then, we had the first two suspects, both of whom looked guiltier than hell. Then we went from the low end of society to the high end with three suspects, who turned out to be college students. It's like you told us in class, 'Things are not always as they appear to be.'" Essig told me that during the entire investigation "I had in the back of my mind, I am working for God and will solve this case." The motto of *Practical Homicide Investigation* is, "We Work for God" and Detective Essig certainly was "working for God" as he brought justice to the victim and her family.

Case History: Gang Revenge Rape–Sodomy–Murder

CASE FACTS

On Tuesday, July 11, the nude and battered body of Margaret, a 43-year-old, white female, was discovered in the basement of her home by her 21-year-old son, Jeremy. Her daughter, Angela, became concerned when she couldn't reach her mother by phone. She had gone to the house earlier that day. When she did not receive an answer to her knocks on the door, she contacted Jeremy. Jeremy, who had moved out of the house on Friday, July 7, had relocated in an adjoining town, and had a key to the house. Responding to Angela's call, Jeremy went to his mother's house. Using his key, he entered through the back door, which had been locked. He proceeded into his mother's bedroom and found the room in slight disarray with various dresser drawers open. The telephone was on the bed with the cords ripped out. He also noticed that one of the pillowcases from the victim's pillows was missing. He then walked through the house looking for some note or message from his mother. When he entered the basement area, he discovered his mother's nude body lying on the basement floor with a pillowcase over her head and her hands and feet bound. He immediately realized that she was dead and called 911.

POLICE RESPONSE

The initial response to the crime was by the Pontiac Police Department, who subsequently requested the Oakland County Sheriff's Department to assist both in the crime scene process and the subsequent major case investigation. The Pontiac Police Department worked jointly with the Oakland County Sheriff's Department on all major crimes. Detective Sergeant William Harvey of the Oakland County Sheriff's Department eventually became the officer in charge of the homicide investigation, which occurred in the City of Pontiac, County of Oakland, in the State of Michigan.

DESCRIPTION OF CRIME SCENE

The scene was described as a single story, white house located on the north side of Peacock Street. The victim was described as a white female, later identified as Margaret. Her body was found in the southeast corner area of the basement floor. The victim was lying on her right side. Her body was totally nude and a multicolored pillowcase had been wrapped around her head and tied at the neck area with a telephone cord. Her hands were tied very tightly with telephone cord, which had been knotted. Her feet were also tied tightly together with telephone wire. There was a pooling of blood, which appeared to emerge from the head area (Figure 8.25 and Figure 8.26).

There were also signs of a struggle in the area where the victim's body was lying. The north-side basement window, above a washtub, was found open and a dark-colored paint chip was found on the basement floor just in front of the washer.

The basement wall, just below the opened basement window, had spray painting on it, which was recognized by investigators as some type of gang graffiti. There were also signs of a struggle in the northeast bedroom:

Figure 8.25 Body at scene. The victim's body was totally nude. Her head was covered with a pillowcase and her hands and feet were bound. (Photo courtesy of Donna Pendergast, Assistant Prosecutor, Michigan State Attorney's Office.)

Figure 8.26 Body examination. The pillowcase on the victim's head was saturated with blood. She had been stomped to death. (Photo courtesy of Donna Pendergast, Assistant Prosecutor, Michigan State Attorney's Office.)

- The phone and answering machine were lying tossed on the bed with their cords removed and/or ripped out.
- There was a brown wallet-type purse on the bed, which appeared to have been dumped onto the bed. The contents were strewn across the sheet.
- There was one pillow missing, a pillowcase at the side of the bed, and another pillow with a multicolored pattern on top of the bed. This matched the pillowcase tied on the victim's head.
- It also appeared that the dresser drawers had been gone through in the northeast bedroom.
- Investigators observed a pair of light-colored flowered panties and a black negligee lying on the bedroom floor next to the bed.
- There was a phone base, missing its cord, which had been apparently ripped from its connection.

The rest of the house was neat and clean with no signs of forced entry except for the basement window.

A number of items of evidence were recovered from both the victim's body and the crime scene. Among these items were hairs, including suspected pubic hair, swabs from the victim's buttocks area, blood samples from the crime scene and victim, and hairs and fibers from the basement window. Preliminary examination revealed multiple hair types foreign to the victim.

VICTIMOLOGY

Margaret was a single, attractive, 43-year-old woman with two grown children. She had been married in the past and had a number of relationships, some of which were with abusive men who often walked out of her life. She was a recovering alcoholic and had recently gotten her life back together, apparently taking good care of her physical appearance as well. She had always maintained her parental responsibilities to her two children. Margaret was a survivor. She lived in this tough neighborhood and in this particular house most of her adult life. Her daughter lived at another location in an adjoining city and her son, Jeremy, had just moved from the house the Friday before to the same city in which his sister lived. A neighbor last saw Margaret on Saturday, July 8, at about 1:30 p.m. as she was cutting her lawn. When she wasn't working, she would often sunbathe in her back yard and usually cut her lawn while wearing her two-piece bathing suit. The victim had a youthful figure. The initial police investigation revealed that Margaret had a telephone conversation with a close friend on Saturday, July 8, in the early evening hours. An investigative canvass indicated that no one had seen or heard from Margaret after Saturday evening.

AUTOPSY

An autopsy was conduced on July 12 by a Deputy Chief Medical Examiner for the Oakland County Medical Examiner's office. The cause of death was listed as blunt force head trauma. The autopsy findings are listed as follows (Figure 8.27):

1. Blunt force head trauma with
   a. Abrasions and lacerations on face
   b. Extensive subscalpular hemorrhage

Figure 8.27 Autopsy photograph. The brain edema and herniation were suggestive of survival following impact on the head. Note the large amount of hemorrhaging. (Photo courtesy of Donna Pendergast, Assistant Prosecutor, Michigan State Attorney's Office.

    c. Skull fracture
    d. Bilateral subdural and subarachnoid hemorrhage
    e. Brain contusions
    f. Brain edema and herniations
  2. Small focal areas of hemorrhage in the soft tissue of neck.
  3. Contusions in vagina and anus. The vagina had contusions near the introitus as well as on the middle part of the posterior wall of the vagina. The anus has contusions all around the external opening.
  4. Abrasions and contusions on back and extremities.

OPINION

Margaret died of blunt force head trauma. Although there were small areas of hemorrhage in the soft tissue of the neck, there was no fracture of laryngeal cartilage or hyoid bone and there was no evidence of conjunctival petechiae indicating strangulation. The injuries in the vagina and anus were indicative of sexual assault. The medical examiner further opined that the brain edema and herniation were suggestive of survival following impact on the head. This meant that the victim lay there suffering on the floor for some time after the assault.

The manner of death was determined to be homicide.

PRELIMINARY INVESTIGATION INTO THE VICTIM'S ACTIVITIES

Detective Sergeant Harvey established the following information from the Pontiac Police Department, who conducted the preliminary investigation. Margaret had informed a friend that she had called the Pontiac Police on Thursday, July 5, to complain about ongoing drug sales occurring in the DeJesus residence located at 639 Peacock Street. Two Hispanic males identified as Melvin DeJesus, 20 years of age, and his brother George, 18 years of age, lived at this address. They and their friends had an informal affiliation with a Pontiac Street gang known as Los Capones and the DeJesus home had become a "drug hang out." The DeJesus home was next door to the victim's house. Margaret's son Jeremy had hung around with the DeJesus brothers while growing up. In fact, Margaret had even babysat for the DeJesus boys when they were young. However, as they grew up, there was increasing friction between Margaret and the DeJesus boys, especially Melvin. Sergeant Harvey learned from a confidential source that Margaret had a physical confrontation with Melvin resulting in her slapping him across the face in front of other gang members. This confrontation resulted from her concern regarding her son, Jeremy. However, what she didn't realize was that this physical confrontation became a major affront to Melvin's ego. Most probably, from her perspective, since she had provided childcare to the DeJesus boys, she felt that she could still discipline them. This incident, coupled with the fact that she wanted her son to get away from the DeJesus brothers, and that Jeremy had recently began to distance himself from the gang, set the stage for this brutal attack.

According to Sergeant Harvey, the reason that Jeremy moved away was to satisfy his mom. Early on, Detective Sergeant Harvey realized the significance of this information. The DeJesus brother and their friends, as well as Margaret's son, Jeremy, had this affiliation with the Los Capones street gang. Jeremy had recently broken his association with the gang and Margaret had reportedly informed the police about drug activities at the DeJesus house.

The victim had been brutally beaten to death after being raped and anally sodomized. The preliminary investigation and condition of the crime scene suggested more than one assailant.

Detective Sergeant Harvey, who had been involved in several gang-related investigations, specifically gang-related homicides, had become familiar with their behavior and practices as well as gang psychology. Harvey believed that the entire motive for this crime was gang revenge.

DETECTIVE INVESTIGATION: INTELLIGENCE GATHERING

In September, Detective Sergeant Harvey brought Jeremy in for an extensive reinterview establishing the following information. Jeremy admitted being a member of the Los Capones, a local street gang in Pontiac, Michigan. His mother's home was in the heart of known Los Capones territory. Melvin DeJesus and George Dejesus were both members of the Los Capones street gang.

He also identified another member, a black male, named Brandon Gohagen, as a member of the gang. Sergeant Harvey was well acquainted with Gohagen, who was a known rapist. However, he had never been arrested because several females had refused to press charges. Harvey was also aware of Gohagen's penchant for anal sex. This would be the "signature" element to the case.

(According to *Practical Homicide Investigation*, Geberth, 2006, Chapter 21, "The signature aspect of a violent criminal offender is a unique and integral part of the offender's behavior. This signature component refers to the psychodynamics, which are the mental and emotional processes underlying human behavior and its motivations.")

The anal sodomy aspect of the Margaret case coupled with the information that Gohagen hung out with the DeJesus boys further enhanced Harvey's suspicion toward Gohagen as an additional suspect.

Detective Sergeant Harvey learned that Jeremy had intended to leave the Los Capones and move out of the area. About a week before Margaret was killed, Jeremy told his mother that he intended to leave the gang and the area.. Margaret indicated to friends that she was fearful of the DeJesus brothers who lived next door to her.

Harvey also learned that George DeJesus, Melvin DeJesus, and Brandon Gohagen had been in Jeremy's home many times. In fact, they would socialize in the same area of the basement where Margaret's body was found. They were also aware that entry to the house could be gained through the north basement window or though Jeremy's first floor bedroom window, which did not latch.

Jeremy also told Detective Sergeant Harvey that he had lost three sets of house keys in the past year. Each time the keys came up missing, he was with the Los Capones. As a member of the Los Capones, Jeremy had been witness to several "punch ups" or assaults. During these assaults, it was the practice of Melvin DeJesus to stomp the heads of his victims. This element would be considered the modus operandi and would link Melvin to the murder.

According to *Practical Homicide Investigation* (Geberth, 2006, Chapter 21), "From an investigative perspective, it is important to note an offender's mode of operation or way of doing things. The MO is a learned behavior that changes as offenders gain experience, build confidence, or become involved with the criminal justice system."

Harvey also learned that the DeJesus brothers and Gohagen were aware that Jeremy intended to leave the Los Capones without being formally "V'ed" out. Harvey ascertained that being "V'ed" was an initiation into as well as an exit from the gang. The gang code required the member, who wanted membership or exit, to take a beating. A time limit was set by the gang leader who determined whether "two minutes" or "three minutes" would satisfy the "V." During this time frame, all the members of the gang would beat, stomp, kick, or punch him. However, no weapons could be used.

Jeremy told Sergeant Harvey that the other gang members had watched him from the DeJesus house as he packed his belongings and moved out of his mother's house on Friday, July 7. Jeremy told Sergeant Harvey that he was aware that the DeJesus brothers and Gohagen resented his leaving the gang and that he (Jeremy) was in violation of their code. In addition, Harvey learned that Jeremy called Melvin DeJesus on July 11 asking him to check on his mother after his sister, Angela, called to tell him that she couldn't make contact. However, Melvin refused. Harvey also determined that since the murder, Jeremy had had limited contact with neither the DeJesus boys or Gohagen.

INVESTIGATIVE TACTICS

Detective Sergeant Harvey began an intensive gang intelligence gathering, which included the interviews and interrogations of every gang member in Oakland County, specifically those involved with the Los Capones. This took months of intelligence analysis and investigative operations to elicit information from gang members, who ordinarily would not provide police with information unless the police had "something on them" to get them to agree to cooperate. An experienced detective involved with gang-type offenders realizes early on that most of the information elicited by the police during gang-related investigations will be either bogus or provided with an attempt to gain favor or misdirect the investigation. Detective Sergeant Harvey was well aware of this possibility and utilized his informants and street information effectively. Eventually, this tactic began to pay off. One informant provided information that

George DeJesus had fresh scratches on his face at the same time as the murder. There were also rumors on the street among gang members that the DeJesus brothers were involved in Margaret's murder.

Sergeant Harvey also learned about the street confrontation between Margaret and Melvin and how Melvin was "pissed off" that she had "dissed" him in front of his boys and how Melvin had promised to "get even" for this.

Eventually, Sergeant Harvey was able to establish probable cause through these interviews and the evaluation of forensic evidence gathered at the crime scene, which included the autopsy information and the evidence from the victim's body. Sergeant Harvey was able to secure search warrants for nontestimonial evidence on each of his primary subjects, specifically Melvin and George DeJesus and Brandon Gohagen. The most important evidence would be the apparent seminal fluids found in the perianal area of the victim as well as the foreign pubic hairs gathered at the crime scene. The establishment of probable cause for the execution of these warrants was not developed until November, four months after the murder.

Detective Sergeant Harvey established that the Los Capones gang ruled by fear and intimidation. When Margaret reported drug sales from the DeJesus home to the Pontiac Police Department, the gang claiming authority to this territory, considered this as a direct assault to their turf.

As mentioned earlier, Sergeant Harvey had learned that gang members were initiated into the gang through a process called "V-ing." The "V-ing" process differs for each gang. The typical "V-in" for the Los Capones gang included Melvin DeJesus stomping on the person's head. The autopsy indicated that Margaret's head had been brutally stomped.

In addition, all of the gangs have a structured hierarchy and each member must obey the commands of someone above him. Melvin and George DeJesus were higher ranking members than Jeremy. The gangs also have behavior codes. A violation of these codes results in a beating or other retaliation. The codes, including that of the Los Capones gang, were that a member cannot just walk away. He had to be "V-ed" out of the gang.

Detective Sergeant Harvey was able to establish through his investigation and information, from confidential sources, that the motive for the murder of Margaret was gang revenge. The revenge was twofold. The report of drug dealing to the Pontiac Police by Margaret and the fact that Jeremy walked out on the gang in violation of the Los Capones code of conduct were the most obvious. In addition, the personal insult to Melvin DeJesus when Margaret slapped him across the face exacerbated the tensions. The gang code demanded retaliation.

Detective Sergeant Harvey had all three of his primary subjects brought in for execution of the warrants. The purpose was not only to gather evidence, but more importantly to psychologically stress the subjects. Whenever there is more than one subject involved in a particularly heinous crime, an attempt is made to identify the "weak" or less enthusiastic member of the group to turn "state's evidence." Search warrant executions are particularly effective.

Immediately after the execution of these search warrants for blood samples, saliva samples, and hair samples from the subjects, Brandon Gohagen left the jurisdiction and went to a town in Texas, where he had relatives. The two DeJesus brothers remained in town and continued their activities as if nothing had happened.

Ironically, two members of the Oakland County Sheriff's Department, who were in Texas on an unrelated matter, ran into Gohagen while he was in a phone booth. The two detectives, who were aware of Gohagen's status as a primary suspect in Margaret's murder, took advantage of the fortuitous meeting and interviewed him with the intent of indicating that he was under surveillance. According to Harvey, who was in touch with a number of his informants, "This really spooked him." He was on the phone every day calling back to Pontiac and asking if the police had been around and what was going on. This chance meeting in Texas "set the stage" for a later interview with Gohagen, who eventually returned to Pontiac, Michigan, when things seemed to quiet down. The immediate problem for the investigators was that there was a limited amount of semen recovered from the victim's buttocks and the sample was too small for the RFLP (restriction fragment length polymorphisms) DNA testing. The sample had to be sent out for a polymerase chain reaction (PCR). The basis of PCR is that it mimics the cell's ability to replicate DNA. That is, by using this tool, forensic scientists have the ability to take a small sample of DNA and make more, essentially copying it a millionfold. The PCR has discrete steps, which are basically the same, but specific parameters for different loci may be different. All PCR procedures have basic steps: DNA extraction, amplification, and detection.

The test results were not completed until the spring of the following year. By this time all of the subjects felt confident that they were free and clear and resumed their day-to-day activities. However, Sergeant Harvey was actively monitoring their activities looking for any information that might stimulate the investigation. Every gang member who was arrested in Oakland County was interviewed by Harvey or one of his detectives. In addition, a number of confidential sources were developed that assisted in enabling the police to monitor their prime suspects.

Donna Pendergast, a no-nonsense prosecutor in Oakland County, took an interest in the case. Pendergast, who is the daughter of a Detroit homicide cop, had a "tough-as-nails" reputation in the Oakland County Prosecutor's Office. She had been involved in a number of high profile cases and was an excellent trial attorney.

I remember when I first met her at one of my "Practical Homicide Investigation®" seminars in Michigan. I asked her if she was "just passing through," which meant, was she in the District Attorney's Office as a prelude to becoming a defense attorney or was she in it for the long run. She replied, "I'm a prosecutor for life." I immediately provided her with a "We Work for God" plaque and designated her a "disciple" of the Practical Homicide Investigation mission, "May Justice Prevail."

After much delay and discussion Pendergast was able to convince the District Attorney to allow her to provide Sergeant Harvey with an arrest warrant for Brandon Gohagen.

The DNA had been positively matched to Gohagen and the investigators thought that they might have enough leverage on Gohagen, who had fled to Florida, to build a case against the two DeJesus brothers. An arrest warrant for Gohagen was issued on September 18 after Detective Sergeant Harvey was able, through his street informants, to locate Gohagen in Hillsborough County, Florida. Sergeant Harvey also had the address where Gohagen was staying. Sergeant Harvey called the authorities in Florida and advised them that he had an arrest warrant for Brandon Gohagen for murder. Florida sheriff's detectives went to the location and arrested Gohagen on September 19.

Five days later, Detective Sergeant Harvey and a partner traveled to the Hillsborough County jail.

STATEMENT OF CO-CONSPIRATOR

On September 25, Detective Sergeant Bill Harvey and his partner Mark Goodrich interviewed their primary suspect, Brandon Gohagen, whose DNA had been matched to the victim. Gohagen, who had been picked up by Florida authorities on an arrest warrant issued by the Oakland County Prosecutor's Office, agreed to talk to Sergeant Harvey. During this interview, which took place in the Hillsborough County Jail in Florida, 14 months after the brutal murder of Margaret, Sergeant Harvey would for the first time be provided the horrific details of the last moments of Margaret's life.

Gohagen, after being advised of his rights, first wanted to know whether or not he would be provided protection from the DeJesus brothers. As a gang member, he didn't want to be branded as a "snitch" and end up in jail with them. Gohagen stated that he wanted to "do the right thing" by Margaret and that he felt bad about what had happened. Detective Harvey, who is an excellent interviewer, assured him that he would be fine if he told the truth and that Gohagen was answering for the victim. Harvey told him that "to make things right, Brandon shouldn't lie, shouldn't embellish, and not try to put it on someone else."

Harvey also told him that he could see that Brandon was upset about his situation and that was understandable. He advised Brandon that he could stop at any time and collect himself.

Detective Sergeant Harvey realized that this interview was going to be crucial in linking the events that had occurred. He was not about to try and rush Gohagen or cajole him into making statements that did not support the forensic findings as well as what the sergeant had learned from his street sources during his investigation.

Gohagen started out by stating, "I don't know exactly what night it was, but we [meaning he and the DeJesus brothers] used to sit out in the tent behind Melvin's mother's house." "We'd sit and drink and stuff, you know and you're out there pretty late."

"Melvin got to talking about how he don't like Margaret. Melvin said they use to fall out all the time. Something about how she always fought him for stuff that Jeremy do to her. Melvin said how Margaret told him she don't want Jeremy to the house no more." Sergeant Harvey asked Gohagen, "Who was in the tent when Melvin was saying this?" Gohagen answered, "Me, Melvin, and George [Melvin's brother]." Gohagen stated that Melvin said he wanted [to] go over there [meaning Margaret's house] and 'mess with her.'"

Gohagen stated, "The next thing I knew Melvin was in the house. Melvin got in through the back somehow and he was calling me [Gohagen] and George to come over."

Harvey asked him how late it was and whether or not the lights were off in the victim's house. Gohagen stated that it was late and that the victim was sleeping.

Harvey asked Gohagen if they knew that Margaret was alone in the house. Gohagen stated they knew she was alone because they knew that Jeremy had moved out. Harvey asked Gohagen, "What happened after everybody [Melvin, George, and Gohagen] was in the house?"

Gohagen stated, "I didn't want to be there, I was getting nervous, I knew we had been drinking and stuff." Harvey then asked him what he had been drinking and Gohagen stated a couple of 40s (40-ounce beers). Harvey then asked, "Who opened Margaret's bedroom door." Gohagen stated, "Melvin." Harvey asked, what could he (Gohagen) see?

Gohagen stated that "you could see her hair sticking out from the covers." Harvey asked Gohagen, "What happened?" Gohagen stated, "Melvin grabbed her by the hair and told her, 'Wake up, bitch.' Margaret was like startled, she knew who we were and she started like trying to talk to Melvin."

Harvey asked Gohagen, "What did she say?" Gohagen stated, "Like, what are you doing, how did you get in here? She said a whole bunch of stuff." Sergeant Harvey then asked Gohagen, "Okay, let me ask you a question, a very, very, very important question. Don't lie and don't embellish. Tell me the God's honest truth, was anybody armed?" Gohagen stated that he and Melvin both had guns. Harvey then asked; "Did anyone pull out a gun and did Margaret know you were armed?" Gohagen stated that no one pulled out a gun, but Melvin let Margaret know he was armed. Gohagen stated; "Melvin told her if she didn't shut up that he was going to shoot her." Harvey asked; "Did that quiet her down." Gohagen stated, "Yes." Sergeant Harvey then asked Gohagen what happened next? Gohagen stated, "I [unclear] moved her around there and take off her clothes." Gohagen then stated that Melvin said, "Go ahead and knock her off." Sergeant Harvey asked Gohagen what Melvin meant by "knocking her off." Gohagen explained that this meant "to have sex with her." The sergeant asked Gohagen if he had intercourse with the victim and Gohagen said, "I didn't want to, he, we here now." Sergeant Harvey pressed him on the intercourse and whether he was able to obtain an erection. Gohagen stated, "Not at first. That was how I tried to get out of it by telling Melvin I couldn't get hard." Sergeant Harvey asked Gohagen what happened. Gohagen stated, "Melvin made her, told her to suck." Harvey then qualifies that answer by stating to Gohagen, "He told her to orally copulate you?" Harvey then asked Gohagen, "Okay what did Melvin say specifically, I know those weren't the terms you used." Gohagen stated, "Melvin said 'Suck my boy's dick, bitch.'" Harvey asked Gohagen what happened and Gohagen stated, "She did it and I got hard." Harvey then asked Gohagen, "What happened then?" Gohagen stated that Melvin told him to go ahead and climb on top of her.

Harvey asked him if he did and Gohagen stated that he hesitated and Melvin got mad. Gohagen then admitted to violating her vaginally, which had been established forensically.

Sergeant Harvey asked Gohagen if the victim was lying on her back and Gohagen stated, "Yes, yes." Gohagen then proceeded to explain how Melvin got a rope or something and then George and Melvin tied her up. Gohagen stated that he couldn't really see what they were using to tie her up, but he was adamant that Melvin and George did the tying and he did not participate. Harvey asked Gohagen if the victim had said anything to him while he was having sex with her. Gohagen stated, "She said, 'Don't, not to listen to Melvin.'" Harvey asked Gohagen why he listened to Melvin, and Gohagen stated he was scared, not only of Melvin, but of his brother George as well. The sergeant asked Gohagen if Melvin threatened him and Gohagen stated, "Not in words, but just the looks, how he said it." Sergeant asked Gohagen, "What happened after Melvin and George bound her." Gohagen stated that George carried her down to the basement. Melvin and George were in the basement while Gohagen got dressed. Gohagen said that when he came downstairs they had her on the floor and he heard her saying something, but it wasn't clear. Harvey asked, "What happened next?" Gohagen said,

"Something about, just go, she wasn't gonna say nothing to nobody." Sergeant Harvey asked Gohagen if anybody answered her. Gohagen stated, "Melvin said, 'I know you ain't gonna say nothing to nobody.'" Gohagen stated that the two DeJesus brothers began kicking and hitting the victim who was on the floor.

Gohagen told Sergeant Harvey that as Margaret was being beaten she kept telling them, "I'm not going to say nothing, just don't hurt me." Gohagen said that's when George jumped in and started kicking her two or three times. Gohagen then said that George didn't beat her as bad as Melvin, who "thumped" her in the head. Gohagen then stated that it got quiet in the basement and all he heard was the victim moaning. Sergeant Harvey asked him what happened next and Gohagen stated he ran from the house.

Detective Sergeant Harvey then returned the questioning to the anal penetration, which Gohagen failed to mention earlier in the interview. At first Gohagen didn't want to admit the anal sex stating, "I didn't stick nothing in her butt." Harvey asked him, "Did you penetrate her anally, you know what I mean by anally?" Gohagen then said, "In the butt, right?" Harvey answered, "Yes."

Gohagen then said, "I might of, I might of." Sergeant Harvey then stated to Gohagen, "You have to remember. I'm using science and with a medical exam it tells me. I don't want to put words in your mouth, I'm not saying you did it, but if you did, you must tell me now. Somebody penetrated her anus. Somebody stuck something in her butt. Was it you?" Gohagen then stated, "I didn't stick nothing in her butt." Sergeant Harvey then asked him, "Did you stick your penis in her?" Gohagen answered, "I said it." The sergeant then questioned Gohagen as to whether anybody else had sex with the victim and Gohagen told him, "No."

Gohagen was apparently very concerned about admitting anal sex with the victim. Detective Sergeant Harvey kept at him until finally Gohagen confessed to the anal sex as well. Sergeant Harvey said to Gohagen, "Okay, you had sex with Margaret, but Melvin barked out the commands on what he wanted to see next; now, is that accurate?" Gohagen stated, "As far as I, I mean as far as I could tell, it was a command." The investigator said to him, "He told you he [Melvin] wanted to see oral sex." Gohagen replied, "Yea, well he told her her cunt don't work." The interview revealed that Melvin was directing the sexual assault including the rape and subsequent anal sex when he ordered Margaret to roll over on her stomach and told Gohagen "to do her." Gohagen agreed to take a polygraph and the interview was concluded.

The authorities now had sufficient evidence to charge the DeJesus brothers if they could convince the Oakland District Attorney's Office to provide Gohagen with a plea bargain.

Donna Pendergast, who would be in charge of the prosecution, wanted to assure that Gohagen was telling the truth. She directed that Gohagen be polygraphed on the veracity of his confession, as well as the fact that he didn't place a single kick or punch to the victim. Gohagen passed. This was important because the only evidence against the DeJesus brothers, who were still out on the street, would be the testimony of Gohagen.

The Sheriff's Department came to Pendergast's office and made their pitch for a deal for Gohagen. They wanted a plea bargain down to second degree murder with no agreement as to sentence. The Oakland County District Attorney was reluctant because they had Gohagen cold on first degree felony murder. In other words, Gohagen would be the state's sole witness tying the DeJesus brothers to the murder and would logically have every motive in the world to lie and save his ass. After much thought and urging by both District Attorney Donna Prendergast and Sergeant Harvey, the prosecutor agreed to the deal and the trial was set. Both DeJesus brothers were convicted as charged in a jury trial in which the summation lasted less than three hours.

The two DeJesus brothers, through their attorneys, immediately filed for an appeal. A couple of state appellate defenders characterized Donna Pendergast as the devil incarnate. They criticized the prosecutor for referring to the victim as "Margaret" rather than the body. They accused Pendergast of prosecutorial misconduct for referring to the two defendants as "two brutal savage murderers," and telling the jurors that they would be terrified and haunted by the facts of the case. According to the two defense attorneys, Ms. Pendergast further prejudiced the defendants when she told the jurors that when they left the courtroom, "They will have looked square into the face of evil, not once but twice."

The Court of Appeals affirmed the defendants convictions much to the dismay of their defense attorneys. Melvin and George DeJesus will spend the rest of their lives in prison. Gohagen was ultimately sentenced to 35 to 80 years in prison for his crimes. And justice did prevail.

Reconstruction and Opinion

Sadly, the victim's fate was sealed when Jeremy left his mother's home in Pontiac, Michigan, distancing himself from the gang. The fact that Margaret had stood up to Melvin, which was witnessed by other gang members, and was successful in convincing her son to leave the gang, was certainly enough to put her at risk. Margaret's report of drug dealing at the DeJesus house to the Pontiac Police Department was another direct insult to Melvin and the Los Capones gang. Melvin, in his mind as the leader of the gang, had lost "respect" because of "this woman." As Melvin, George, and Brandon sat around drinking beer and smoking pot, the discussion eventually turned to Margaret and how she had "disrespected" Melvin.

For Melvin, it was a spur of the moment decision without any thought to the consequences of his actions. Psychopaths demonstrate this impulsivity all of the time. Statements, such as "I did it because I felt like it" are quite common. These sorts of impulsive acts are aimed at instant gratification, pleasure, or relief. In this case, it was Melvin's need to extract revenge.

It was Melvin who announced his intention of "messing" with Margaret, and it was Melvin who broke into the victim's house.

Once Melvin had gained entry, he called the others over to the house. Upon entry, the group dynamics emerged. Melvin was the recognized leader. Melvin was aware of Gohagen's sexual assaults and rapes on women as well as his penchant for anal sex. Melvin directed that Gohagen engage in sex with Margaret, and he and George watched as Margaret was degraded.

In my opinion, it is possible that Melvin couldn't engage in sex with Margaret because she had been in a parent position to him as a child. Margaret babysat these evil gang members and changed their dirty diapers when they were toddlers. I'm positive that Margaret believed she had some authority over them, as demonstrated when she slapped Melvin across the face during an earlier confrontation.

Melvin ordered the victim to perform oral sex on Gohagen. He then directed Gohagen to rape her, and then ordered the victim onto her stomach so that Gohagen could anally assault her. These sexual acts were intended to "put her down." The words that he used as he instructed Gohagen were also intended to degrade and dehumanize her.

The covering of her head with the pillowcase was a further act of depersonalization and removed any sense of emotion or feeling for the victim. She was reduced to an object. The beating was brutal and severe. The kicking of her head and the blows to the body were inflicted with vengeance and hate.

Although they had left the victim for dead, the autopsy findings clearly indicated that after the beating, Margaret remained alive for some time as she slowly bled to death.

This was a particularly brutal crime orchestrated by Melvin, a criminal psychopath. Psychopaths are much more likely to be violent and aggressive than other criminals. Their violence is callous and their motives are strictly for personal satisfaction. Melvin DeJesus directed Gohagen to sexually assault the victim as a punishment. However, he also acted as a voyeur and most probably enjoyed watching the victim suffer the ultimate indignation, vicariously achieving gratification. Psychopaths display a general lack of empathy and are indifferent to the sufferings of others. Melvin and his brother, George, savagely beat and stomped their victim to death as she pitifully pleaded for them not to hurt her anymore. And, we know through Gohagen's statements that when the victim told Melvin that she wouldn't say anything to anyone, Melvin responded, "I know you ain't gonna say nothing to nobody." At this point, he had already consciously decided to kill her. Psychopaths are amoral and asocial and characterized by their irresponsibility, lack of remorse or shame, perverse or impulsive (oftentimes criminal) behavior, and other serious personality defects. Melvin degraded and destroyed this woman without feeling remorse or any sense of guilt as he carried out his heinous attack and revenge.

Conclusion

In the opinion of the author, sexual assaults and rapes have drastically increased and there are many more incidents of stranger rape then heretofore thought. Many serial rapists have become serial killers as they attempt to thwart identification and apprehension by murdering their victims. In reality, women are at risk of sexual assault simply because they are women. Most men do not have to worry about being sexually assaulted as they go about their business. Under certain circumstances, women may find themselves at risk while on a routine business trip. A woman traveling alone to a major city and staying at a large hotel could very well be the target of a sexual assault. I purposely selected a number of cases within this chapter, which depict the classic scenarios encountered in rape and sodomy murder. These cases have served as excellent examples of effective tactics, procedures, and forensic techniques.

It is quite apparent that the detective investigating sex-related homicides must concentrate on locating the microscopic evidence consistently associated with sexual assault as well as the behavioral aspects of the event focusing on MO and signature. The ability of the investigator to elicit from the suspect an account of what actually occurred and then corroborate this information with the physical evidence is the benchmark of professional criminal investigation.

Therefore, I recommend that detectives afford themselves the opportunity to attend practical interview and interrogation schools. Two schools that have proven to provide practical and effective techniques are John Reid & Associates (Chicago) and SCAN (U.S. Army Laboratory for Scientific Interrogation).

References

Burgess, A.W. Personal communication, July 27, 2009.

Geberth, V.J. *Practical Homicide Investigation: Tactics, Procedures, and Forensic Techniques*, 4th ed., CRC Press, Boca Raton, FL, 2006.

Groth, N.A., A.W. Burgess, and L.L. Holmstrom. Rape: Power, anger and sexuality. *American Journal of Psychiatry*, 134: 1239–1243, 1977.

Hazelwood, R.R. and A.W. Burgess. *Practical Aspects of Rape Investigation,* 1st ed., Elsevier Science Publ., New York, 1987.

Hazelwood, R.R. and A.W. Burgess. *Practical Aspects of Rape Investigation: A Multidisciplinary Approach*, 4th ed., CRC Press, Boca Raton, FL, 2009.

Keppel, R.D. and R. Walter. Profiling killers: A revised classification model for understanding sexual murder. *International Journal of Offender Therapy and Comparative Criminology,* 1st ed., 43 (4): 471–437, 1999.

Lust Murder and Deviant-Oriented Assaults

9

Anatomy of Lust Murder

Definition

Lust murders are homicides in which the offender stabs, cuts, pierces, or mutilates the sexual regions or organs of the victim's body. The sexual mutilation of the victim may include evisceration, piquerism, displacement of the genitalia in both males and females, and the removal of the breasts in a female victim (defeminization). It also includes activities, such as "posing" and "propping" of the body, the insertion of objects into the body cavities, anthropophagy (consumption of blood and/or flesh), and necrophilia. (Geberth, 1998)

Lust murders are predicated on the obsessive fantasies of the offender. It is not enough for these type killers just to kill, they have a compulsive need to act out their fantasies with their victims and their victim's bodies. This would be the **signature** component of the crime (Geberth, 1998).

A psychological perspective of the development and effects of deviant fantasies and behaviors can be found in the psychosexual disorders, specifically sexual sadism and other paraphilias as they are listed in the *Diagnostic and Statistical Manual of Mental Disorders* (*DSM-IV-TR*, 2000).

Lust murder may be classified as organized or disorganized depending on the psychopathology manifested in the crime scene and the killings. In addition, lust murders may have a homosexual as well as heterosexual orientation. In the case of Jeffrey Dahmer, all of the psychodynamics of lust murder were acted out on his male victims, some of whom he cannibalized.

In the case of an organized lust murderer, there will be penis assault as well as torture inflicted on the live victim consistent with controlled rage. In the case of a disorganized offender, the victim will be immediately rendered unconscious or dead by a "blitz" style of attack and there will be evidence of symbolic and postmortem sexual activities.

In both instances, however, the cutting, mutilation, and overkill-type wound structures will be directed toward those parts of the body that the offender finds sexually significant to him and serve as a sexual stimulus. This is consistent with sexual sadism, which is a chronic and progressive disorder. Sadism is a compelling element in some lust murders; in others, arousal is not derived from the infliction of pain and suffering of the victim, but rather from the act of killing itself.

Lust murderers also can be distinguished from other sex-related homicide offenders by their involvement in necrophilia. In fact, the dynamics of lust murder and necrophilia are intimately connected. The Jeffrey Dahmer and Ted Bundy cases are examples of this dynamic.

Psychodynamics

- The lust murderer, who engages in necrophilia, may not witness any prolonged degree of suffering on the part of the victim. However, he is likely to call upon his imagination and fantasy to supply him with the necessary engram to satisfy his craving for his depravity.
- The lust murderer may also torture victims before killing them, and then recall an after-image engram of the sensation produced by the physical torture and mutilation. This sadistic scenario is thus conjured in the imagination, be it a recreation of the actual crime scene or the product of fantasy.
- Most lust murders are viewed as behaviors of sadistic sexual psychopaths. This is the type of offender who tortures and kills for sexual gratification and characterizes the prototypical serial killer, which is an organized offender.

However, it should be understood that disorganized offenders are also capable of similar behavior and engage in related sadistic activities with their victims as well.

The primary difference between the organized and disorganized lust murderer is the inability of the disorganized offender to repeatedly escape apprehension. In fact, most disorganized lust murderers are apprehended at the time of the event or shortly thereafter.

Organized Offenders

The organized offender is usually above average in intelligence (Geberth, 2006). He is methodical and cunning. His crime is well thought out and carefully planned. He is likely to own a car, which is in good condition. The crime is usually committed away from his area of residence or work. He is mobile and travels many more miles than the average person. Fantasy and ritual are important to the organized-type personality. He selects a victim, which he considers the "right" type, someone he can control (either through manipulation or strength), usually a stranger. Most of his victims will share some common traits.

He is considered socially adept. He uses his verbal skills to manipulate his victims and gain control over them until he has them within his "comfort zone." He is fully cognizant of the criminality of his act and takes pride in his ability to thwart the police investigation. He is likely to follow news reports of the event and will oftentimes take a "souvenir" from his victim as a reminder, which is sometimes used to relive the event or continue with the fantasy. (The souvenir is referred to as a "trophy" when describing this particular action by the organized offender.)

He is excited by the cruelty of the act and may engage in torturing the victim. Sexual control of the victim plays an important part in this scenario. He avoids leaving evidence behind and usually brings his own weapon. He is aware of police procedures. The body is often removed from the crime scene. He may do this to "taunt" the police or to prevent its discovery by transporting it to a location where it will be well hidden.

Disorganized Offenders

The disorganized offender is usually below average intelligence (Geberth, 2006). He is generally a loner type, usually not married, living either alone or with a relative in close proximity to the crime scene. He experiences difficulty in negotiating interpersonal relationships and is described as socially inadequate. He acts impulsively under stress and will usually select a victim from his own geographic area. In most instances, this type of offender will not own a vehicle, but will have access to a vehicle. Generally, he will avoid people. He is described as sexually incompetent without any meaningful sexual relationships. He uses a "blitz" style of attack, which catches the victim off guard.

This spontaneous action in which the offender suddenly "acts out" his fantasy does not allow for a conscious plan or even a thought of being detected. This is why the crime scene will be disorganized.

In homicide investigation, we call these events a clustered crime scene. "A clustered crime scene involves a situation where most of the activities take place at one location; the confrontation, the attack, the assault and sexual activity, etc" (Geberth, 2006).

The disorganized offender usually depersonalizes his victim by facial destruction or overkill types of wounds. Any sexually sadistic acts are performed postmortem. Mutilations to the genitalia, rectum, breasts of females, neck, throat, and buttocks are performed because these parts of the body contain a strong sexual significance to him.

There are significant differences between the organized and disorganized offender. However, there are no situations where the organized and disorganized offenders are mutually exclusive. Both types of murderers are capable of all types of behavior.

Case Histories of Lust Murders

An Organized Offender

Case History

The following case is from the author's files. A young woman discovered the bodies of her mother and sister. She had become concerned when she couldn't get an answer from their telephone. She decided to go to her mother's residence to check on them. She discovered her mother and her sister dead in the home. Both victims had been murdered and sexually mutilated. Her screams alerted neighbors who called the police.

CASE FACTS

Douglas County Sheriff's officers responded to 911 calls from neighbors and entered the residence. They quickly checked the victims for signs of life and searched the house for any additional victims as well as suspects. Upon "clearing" the premises, they secured the crime scene and requested detectives to respond. The reporting witness, who was the mother's older married daughter, stated that she last had contact with her family about 10 p.m. the prior evening. She stated that the front door was locked. She entered the house through the unlocked rear sliding door, which she knew to be unlocked. She first went to her mother's bedroom and discovered the mutilated body of her sister. She had thought that the body was her mother. (It was actually her sister, Amanda.) She then ran hysterically from the bedroom to the front door into the family room passing the mutilated body of her mother as she ran out the door.

INVESTIGATIVE CONSIDERATIONS

Chief Criminal Deputy Robin Wagg was in charge of operations. Crime scene security measures were implemented along with a crime scene log. The First Officer provided detectives with a walk-through showing exactly where he had walked and what he had touched. A designated walkway to each victim was established after making a determination of any trace evidence.

The crime scene and bodies were videotaped and photographed with both 35 mm and Polaroid® film. Chief Deputy Wagg directed that Polaroid photos were to be taken in accordance with tactics and procedures recommended in the text *Practical Homicide Investigation* (Geberth, 2006). These "work photos" were utilized to brief the additional detectives who would be arriving at the scene thereby reducing any further scene contamination.

Chief Deputy Wagg had requested the Washington State Crime Scene Response Team to respond and assist Douglas County. This is good policy and makes sense in major crime scene investigations, especially when the agency of record does not have the required resources for such an event. A command post was established with logistical support. The entire area surrounding the crime scene was secured and searched for additional evidence. A canvass of the area was undertaken along with a request for all incident reports for the previous 24 hours.

Without disturbing the bodies, the medical examiner conducted a preliminary testing of core body temperature. Time of death was estimated to be between 11 p.m. and 2 a.m. During the examination of the bodies at the scene, it was observed that apparently Rita's wristwatch was broken during the struggle with her assailant. The watch was stopped at 11:35 p.m. The medical examiner described the mutilations as very skilled, nearly surgical in nature.

When the suspect was finally apprehended, it was learned that he had worked as a butcher and had also engaged the torture and mutilation of animals including cats.

SPECIAL PROCEDURE TO FOLLOW IN SPECIFIC CASES

The author recommends that in certain cases the medical examiner/coroner be requested to allow the body to remain at the scene during the crime scene process in order to recover crucial microscopic evidence that would have been lost in the removal or transport of the body. In fact, as part of the "Practical Homicide Investigation Seminar®" series, I have illustrated this procedure to alert investigators to the possibility of utilizing this course of action in specific cases. These specific types of cases are usually sex-related homicides, homicides in which the offender stabs, cuts, pierces, or mutilates the sexual regions or organs of the victim's body.

These cases involve evisceration, piquerism, displacement of the genitalia in both males and females, and the removal of the breasts in a female victim, and include the posing or propping of the victim's body, insertion of objects into body cavities, and sexual mutilation.

These events are predicated on the obsessive fantasies of the offender. It is not enough for these types of killers just to kill, they have a compulsive need to act out their fantasies with their victims and their victim's bodies. Thus, their personal interactions with the body many times result in the transference of microscopic evidence. If the body is moved or transported, valuable evidence can easily be lost, contaminated, or destroyed in the process.

EXCELLENT CRIME SCENE PROCESS

In this case, a decision was made by Chief Criminal Deputy Robin Wagg to follow the above "Practical Homicide Investigation®" model. He requested the medical examiner to conduct a preliminary review of the condition of the bodies at the scene and then allow the bodies to remain in the scene while crime scene investigators processed them for microscopic evidence. The chief deputy had the heat in the residence turned off and supervised the crime scene process within the house. The crime scene team processed the scene and the bodies over the next two and half days, recovering hairs and fibers, which were eventually matched to the suspect. These microscopic traces may have been lost had the bodies been transported (Figure 9.1 and Figure 9.2).

VICTIMOLOGY

The mother, Rita, was a 48-year-old divorcee who worked as a sales representative. She had a relationship with a male friend. However, she did not live with him because of her daughter. She resided in a single-family home in a rural area with her 14-year-old daughter, Amanda, who was a high school student and played on the school softball team. Unbeknownst to the family, the offender had stalked them for months with the intent of sexually mutilating and killing them. Teenager Amanda was the intended focus of his lust.

Figure 9.1 Mother's body. Killer placed victim's body on couch to display her. Note the evisceration and the defeminization. (Photo courtesy of Chief Criminal Deputy Robin Wagg, Douglas County, Washington, Sheriff's Department.)

Figure 9.2 Daughter's body. Killer positioned the victim's body on the bed after engaging in sexual activities. He jammed the baseball bat into her vagina. (Photo courtesy of Chief Criminal Deputy Robin Wagg, Douglas County, Washington, Sheriff's Department.)

AREA

The crime scene was within a rural area in East Wenatchee (Douglas County), Washington. The residence was located in a quiet neighborhood and the surrounding area consisted of a number of single-family homes.

THE CRIME SCENE

Both victims were murdered and mutilated inside their residence. It was believed that the killer entered the residence using the same unlocked rear sliding door that the reporting witness used to enter the house. Amanda's body was on the master bed in the north bedroom. Rita's body was on the couch in the family room in the south end of the residence. The mother's breasts were removed and transported by the offender from the family room to the north bedroom and placed near the daughter's body. It was determined that the mutilations were done postmortem.

Amanda suffered severe blunt trauma to the left side of her head. Her body was in the mother's bed in a supine position. She was totally nude and there was evidence that the killer had undressed her. She had been eviscerated from near the vaginal area to her chest. The skin surrounding the vaginal area had been excised from her body and placed on the right side of her face. In addition, there were numerous stab wounds into the anterior portion of her neck. Her legs had been spread and her arms were near her side. A baseball bat had been jammed into her vaginal cavity. The mother's breasts had been placed on a dresser and headboard beside the daughter's body (Figure 9.3).

Rita suffered numerous defense-type wounds to her forearms and wrists. She also suffered several stab wounds into the upper portion of her body. She was found lying in a supine position on a couch in the family room. She was naked except for a nightgown, which the killer pulled back to expose the body and there was evidence that

Figure 9.3 Breast. The killer placed the mother's breast on an end table. (Photo courtesy of Chief Criminal Deputy Robin Wagg, Douglas County, Washington, Sheriff's Department.)

the killer had undressed her as well. The offender had also removed her panties and a tampon. Rita had been eviscerated from the vaginal area to midchest, which exposed some internal organs. Both of the victim's breasts had been excised from her chest and taken into the bedroom. Rita's vaginal area, including pubis, had been excised from the body and placed into her mouth. The killer had posed the body on the couch with her legs spread and her arms by her side (Figure 9.4 and Figure 9.5).

THE AUTOPSY

Rita had received 31 stab wounds to the chest, arms, left leg, neck, and back consistent with a knife attack. Cause of death was multiple stab wounds causing massive internal and external bleeding. The autopsy revealed postmortem excisions of the breasts and excision of the skin and underlying tissue of the right pubis, vulva, and perineum; incision of the abdomen and peritoneal area; evisceration.

Amanda suffered massive left cerebral contusions causing immediate death as well as 16 penetrating stab wounds of the anterior neck. Cause of death was massive cranial and cerebral trauma secondary to blunt impact to the left side of the head. Also found were postmortem excision of the skin and underlying tissue of the pubis and upper half of external genitalia; a baseball bat jammed up through the vaginal vault; abdomen and peritoneal sac incised; evisceration.

THE SUSPECT

Chief Deputy Robin Wagg was advised that a patrol officer had stopped a person named Jack Owen Spillman, III, at 2 a.m. on suspicion of burglary. Spillman was driving a dark-colored Chevy pickup truck with large tires and a roll bar. He had parked near a trash receptacle in the parking lot of a VFW Hall, which was closed for the night. This VFW Hall was in the vicinity of the crime scene. When the officer had approached Spillman, the suspect raised his hands in a position of surrender. The officer thought

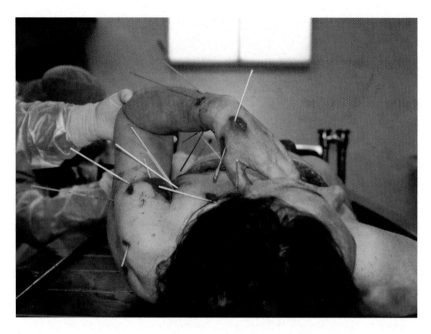

Figure 9.4 Defensive wounds. The woman had attempted to fight off her attacker and received numerous sharp-edged instruments wounds. (Photo courtesy of Chief Criminal Deputy Robin Wagg, Douglas County, Washington, Sheriff's Department.)

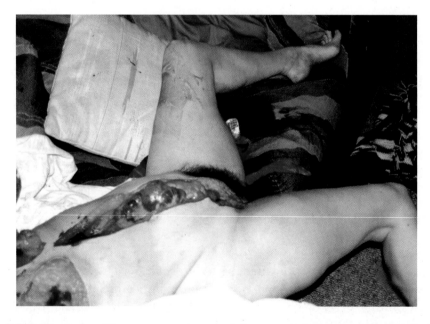

Figure 9.5 Evisceration. The suspect eviscerated the woman from the vagina to the breasts. (Photo courtesy of Chief Criminal Deputy Robin Wagg, Douglas County, Washington, Sheriff's Department.)

that the suspect, who was dressed in black, was a burglar. Finding no sign of a break-in, Spillman was properly identified and released. Investigators were dispatched to the VFW hall where the patrol officer had confronted Spillman. The detectives subsequently located what was eventually determined to be one of the murder weapons lodged in the bottom of a trashcan near where Spillman had been parked.

Investigators also located another witness who stated that he had seen a dark-colored Chevy pickup truck with large tires and a roll bar parked in an elementary school parking lot about 250 feet from the rear of the murder site at about 11:30 p.m. The truck was backed in off the street with a clear view of the rear sliding door of the family's house.

Spillman was immediately put under surveillance while other detectives obtained further information and gathered evidence from the scene. The suspect had an extensive record for burglary, rape, and indecent exposure. He also was a suspect in a rape attempt involving another mother and daughter living alone in the same area as the murders. The surveillance team reported that they saw Spillman throw something into the dumpster outside his apartment. Chief Deputy Wagg directed Waste Management to pick up the dumpster, which had been kept under surveillance by detectives, and had it brought to the Sheriff's Office where it was searched. Inside the dumpster was a bloody ski mask, which was matched to the suspect.

Subsequently, investigators learned that Spillman drank Amanda's blood and had gotten the blood on his mask.

ADDITIONAL INFORMATION ABOUT THE SUSPECT

Amanda's softball coach reported that he had seen the same dark-colored Chevy pickup truck, identified as Spillman's, several times at the softball field during practices when Amanda was present. A week prior to the murders, another woman, who lived a block west of the victims, reported that she saw Spillman driving that same truck in the area of her residence. He had asked her if she was married and had a daughter.

Authorities in Okanagon County, Washington, which borders Douglas County, reported that Spillman was the primary suspect in the disappearance and murder of a 10-year-old named Penny. The little girl was originally reported missing by her mother, who at the time was living with Spillman. Spillman had also participated in the search. It should be noted that this is classic behavior for the organized offender who wants to experience a psychological high by interjecting himself into the police investigation. These offenders sense a feeling of superiority over the police and at the same time gain an opportunity to monitor the police investigation. When the body was found, Spillman left the jurisdiction. This victim had also been eviscerated. Photos of the body position when it was recovered were remarkably similar to the "posed" position of Amanda (Figure 9.6 and Figure 9.7).

Spillman was arrested two weeks after the murders. Authorities executed a search warrant on his person and premises as well as his truck. The authorities learned that Spillman had placed the bloody gloves and clothes he had worn during the attack on the front seat of his truck when he left the crime scene. The suspect immediately invoked his *Miranda* rights and refused to make any statements to the police. The suspect was held without bail. The suspect's girlfriend, as well as other witnesses, could not account for his whereabouts at the time of the murder.

The blood on the recovered knife was matched through DNA to the victims. The hairs and fibers found at the crime scene were matched to Spillman. It was also learned

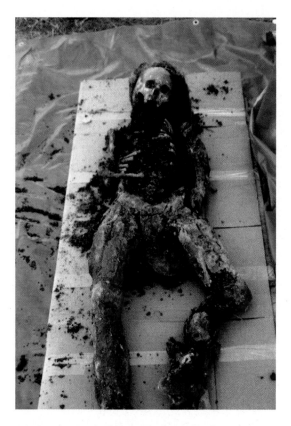

Figure 9.6 Little girl. Body of little girl who was buried positioned similar to the manner that Mandy was discovered. (Photo courtesy of Chief Criminal Deputy Robin Wagg, Douglas County, Washington Sheriff's Department.)

that Spillman had worn hospital gowns and gloves with tape during his sexual assaults to prevent trace evidence from being discovered during crime scene process. The fibers found at the crime scene matched these surgical gowns.

POLICE INTERVIEWS OF SPILLMAN'S CELLMATE

The authorities decided to interview Spillman's prison cellmate. Investigators had learned that while Spillman was in jail he was bragging about his crimes. The cellmate provided additional information about his strange behavior. The inmate, with no prior knowledge of the crime scene, precisely described the manner of death and the crime scene. Spillman bragged that his ambition was to be the most famous serial killer in the country.

Spillman also read and studied a number of serial murder cases and used the prison library for his research.

He also planned on avoiding detection by following some rules he promulgated from his reading.

Spillman talked of shaving his body hair and wearing ninja-type clothing. He told how he would tape around his feet and socks and wears rubber gloves, which he would tape to his sleeves to avoid detection. Spillman told his cellmate if he committed the crime in the bedroom, he was going to remove all linen and bedding. In any room where the acts occurred, he was going to remove as much material as possible

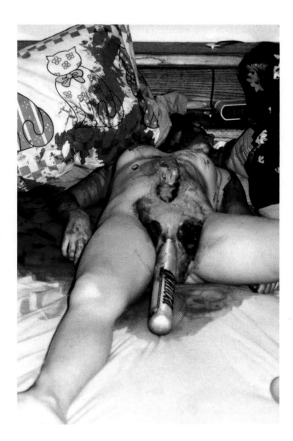

Figure 9.7 Body position. Similar to Penny Davis. (Photo courtesy of Chief Criminal Deputy Robin Wagg, Douglas County, Washington, Sheriff's Department.)

and bring it to another location to burn. He also stated that he would burn the entire house down to destroy any trace evidence. He told his cellmate that he would never do anything in his hometown because, according to the FBI reports he had read, this was how many serial killers got caught. Spillman had gleaned from the FBI materials he read that most of the serial killers had a burglary conviction in their backgrounds. He also told of knocking his victims out with a baseball bat or heavy piece of pipe and then taping their mouths so they couldn't make any noise while he took them to another location to torture them. According to the cellmate, Spillman would probably get so emotionally wrapped up in his own frenzy that he would start by breaking his own rules.

Spillman revealed his sexual fantasies of being anally sodomized by a large male while torturing and mutilating young girls. According to the cellmate, Spillman would fantasize so intensely on this that he would experience an orgasm. The cellmate stated that there was an emotional intensity in Spillman's eyes once he started talking about his sexual fantasies. On one occasion, Spillman reportedly drank his own blood after he cut his arm with a razor blade. This wound later required stitches.

Spillman's sexual fantasies included sexual assault, evisceration, and sexual mutilation of young girls. He wanted to cut off his victim's breasts and vaginas and shove beer bottles and other instruments into their sexual orifices. He planned on cutting out the hearts of his victims during the peak of the sexual attack and then eating it.

Spillman told his cellmate that he wanted to build underground caves out in the woods where he could keep his victims alive for a week or two before killing them. These caves would have "play rooms" where he could act out his fantasies with his slaves. He was also going to construct long escape tunnels in order to avoid apprehension. Spillman also fancied himself a werewolf. He talked about stalking his victims and waiting until they were alone or out of sight where he could knock them out and carry them off. He revealed that he had stalked his victims for months prior to the attacks.

ADDITIONAL INFORMATION

The authorities learned that the 10-year-old victim in Okanagon County was not his intended target, but he couldn't separate the older girl, who was about 13 years old, from the other children. When he convinced the 10-year-old to go with him, he carried her on his shoulders so there wouldn't be any footprints to follow. When he got her into the woods, he tied her to a tree. He then started to cut on her with a knife. He continued torturing her as she was screaming. This turned him on. He then plunged the knife into her abdomen and she died. He complained that she died too quickly. He stated he enjoyed the cutting and the screaming. He then had sex with her dead body. After killing the 10-year-old, he placed her body in the river, but her body kept coming back up. He then buried her. He revealed that he had sex with her body a number of times by digging her up and engaging in necrophilia.

DISPOSITION

The suspect was allowed to plead guilty to the three counts of aggravated murder, as well as robbery and burglary in the Douglas County case. He received life without the possibility of parole plus 116 years.

Reconstruction and Opinion

The offender had intended to knock Amanda out with the baseball bat and then sexually assault and mutilate her as she regained consciousness. However, he used too much force and the blow resulted in her death.

He then attacked Rita as she lay dozing on the couch. During this attack, Rita was able to get to her feet and attempted to fend off the blows. She received numerous defensive wounds to her forearms, wrists, and right leg as she valiantly fought to protect herself and her daughter from this intruder. One of these blows broke Rita's wristwatch stopping it at 11:35 p.m. He opened her nightgown to expose her breasts and undressed her before stabbing into her chest. After killing Rita, he placed her body back onto the couch in a supine position with her legs spread and her arms at her side. He pulled the nightgown back to expose the body and removed her panties.

He then removed a tampon, from the victim's vagina and threw it on the floor next to the couch. He eviscerated Rita from the vaginal area to her midchest exposing some of her internal organs. He excised the skin around Rita's vaginal area, which included her pubic hair and inserted this flesh into Rita's mouth.

He then removed both of her breasts and transported them to the bedroom where Amanda's body was located. He placed one of Rita's breasts on a dresser beside the daughter and placed the other breast on the headboard next to the daughter's body.

The offender had engaged in sexual activities with Rita's body, which included drinking some of her blood. The body was positioned for "shock value." This propping and posing of the victim in a grotesque manner satisfied his sexual needs.

Amanda, who had been lying on her stomach when he hit her with the bat, suffered severe blunt force trauma, which resulted in her immediate death. Her body was discovered on her mother's bed. The offender rearranged her body in a supine position as he engaged in his sexual perversion. The offender removed Amanda's bed clothing and panties, which he rolled off her legs. He then eviscerated her nude body from her pubic area to her chest, which exposed her internal organs.

He excised the skin around her vaginal area and placed the pubis on the side of her face. The offender also inflicted 16 postmortem stab wounds into her throat. An aluminum baseball bat had been jammed 12 to 16 inches inside her vaginal cavity. Amanda's legs were spread open and her arms were near her sides.

Once again, the offender engaged in sexual activities with Amanda's body, which included drinking some of her blood. The offender remained in the residence for hours while he mutilated his two victims and engaged in his sadistic fantasies.

This type of behavior would be described as psychopathic sexual sadism. Jack Spillman, who had sexual fantasies about sexually assaulting and mutilating young girls, engaged in this postmortem activity with his victims creating an engram, which is a mind picture that is conjured up in the imagination and/or fantasy. Or it may be predicated on a mental recreation of an actual event.

Clinical Assessment

This is a classic case of an organized offender who is a lust murderer and a serial killer. These were his second and third murders. His first victim was the 10-year-old daughter of his live-in girlfriend. He had eviscerated her body and engaged in necrophilia in his postoffense phase. Although he was a suspect, the authorities did not have sufficient evidence to charge him and he left the jurisdiction. In the above case, we see an offender who had preplanned the event, stalked his victims, brought his own weapon, and left very little evidence at the scene. He had stalked the family over a period of two months in an attempt to gain access to the daughter. He already had decided to kill the mother first and then "enjoy" himself with the girl.

Lust murderers who torture their victims before killing them and then recall an after-image engram of the sensation produced by their activities are an example of this dynamic. The pathological sadist can only receive sexual gratification if mutilation is performed on the victim.

It should be noted that his first victim's injuries were very similar to those inflicted on the 14-year-old. Although fantasy and ritual were extremely important to him, he remained in complete control and was fully aware of his actions and his need to avoid detection.

A Stalker Case

CASE FACTS

Angela, a white female, 26 years of age, had been raped and sodomized in her garden apartment. On August 28 at approximately 11:30 a.m., her father discovered her body. The father had gone to Angela's apartment because he hadn't heard from her and was concerned that she did not answer her telephone. Her front door was locked from the inside and her car was parked in the parking lot of the complex. Her father contacted the building manager and accompanied him back to his daughter's apartment. Together, they entered her locked apartment by using a security pass key and discovered her dead body on the floor covered in blood.

POLICE RESPONSE

Grand Prairie, Texas, police responded to the 911 call from the building manager. After determining that the victim, in fact, was dead from apparent stab wounds, they secured the crime scene. The building manager and father of the victim were questioned by uniform patrol and were requested to await arrival of the investigators. During this initial patrol inquiry, the officers elicited information from management concerning some incidents that Angela had complained about and the names of three possible suspects, which were provided to the arriving detectives.

DESCRIPTION OF THE CRIME SCENE

The deceased occupied an apartment on the second floor of a two-story garden apartment complex. The body of the victim had been positioned in a supine position just inside the front door with her legs spread. Near her head lay her bloody panties. Her blouse had been ripped open exposing a blood soaked bra. The bra had been pushed up to expose her breasts. Except for the bra, she was nude. The condition of the apartment indicated that there had been a furious struggle. A trail of blood extended from the victim throughout the apartment indicating that she had fought with her assailant as she attempted to ward off the attack and escape. Furniture had been knocked over and a telephone answering machine was on the floor next to the victim's body. There were numerous stab wounds into the victim's chest and breast area as well as obvious defense wounds on her hands and arms. There was also a blood splatter pattern on the wall near where the body lay. In addition, her throat had been cut with numerous slashes across the neck. There were incised wounds across her eyes and eyelids (Figure 9.8 and Figure 9.9).

The detectives were able to substantiate that the offender had spent a significant amount of time in the victim's apartment. There was evidence in the bathroom, which indicated that he had washed the blood off his hands and cleaned up in the bathroom. There were bloody tissues in the sink and an empty beer bottle in the trash receptacle similar to the brand found in the victim's refrigerator. First officers also discovered a blood drop on the stairs leading to the apartment suggesting a possible injury to the offender. However, this turned out to be the victim's blood, which had probably dropped from the murder weapon as the offender left the apartment.

VICTIMOLOGY

Angela was 26 years old at the time of her murder. She was an attractive single, white female who lived alone in this garden apartment complex. Angela also worked part time as a model and aspiring actress. People who knew Angela described her as an out-going person who loved life and liked people. She dated regularly and had a number of female friends and ex-boyfriends; however, she did not want a serious relationship until she had established her career. According to the interviews of her friends and ex-boyfriends, a lot of guys wanted more of a relationship than she was willing to give. She was studying for her nursing degree at Texas Women's University and had been afforded a Navy Nurse

Figure 9.8 Rape victim. The victim's body was discovered by her father inside the apartment. The victim had been stabbed 114 times. The killer had also slashed across her eyes with the blade of the knife. (Photo courtesy of Detective Sergeant Alan Patton, Grand Prairie, Texas, Police Department.)

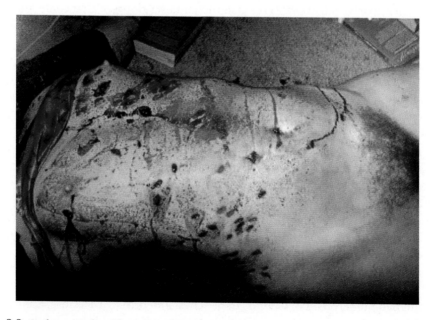

Figure 9.9 Stab wounds. Close-up of stab wounds into victim's chest: lust murder. (Photo courtesy of Detective Sergeant Alan Patton, Grand Prairie, Texas, Police Department.)

Commission. She had already received orders to work in Okinawa after graduation as a commissioned officer and registered nurse in a midwife program, and was excited about the opportunities. Angela had previously served in the U.S. Army as a medic after graduation from Arlington High School, but had joined the Navy for a nursing career.

INVESTIGATIVE CONSIDERATIONS

Detective Alan Patton of the Grand Prairie Police Department was assigned as the primary investigator on this case. Detective Dennis Clay and Evidence Technician Don Swanz, who processed the crime scene under the supervision of Sergeant Bob Wilbanks, assisted Patton. It was evident that the homicide was sexually motivated. The crime scene was processed with the objective of obtaining as much microscopic evidence as possible to link a suspect to the crime.

THE INVESTIGATIVE HYPOTHESIS:

It was suspected that the victim might have known her attacker because she had apparently allowed the offender into her apartment. There was no evidence of a break in or forced entry. It was obvious that the offender spent a considerable amount of time in the apartment. The offender even locked the door upon leaving the premises.

The investigation revealed that the victim's father had spoken to her by telephone the previous evening. At that time, the victim indicated that she did not feel well. In fact, that was the reason he had gone to his daughter's apartment the next day. He had called that morning, but there was no answer. He became concerned and drove over to the apartment complex. He made contact with the building manager and requested him to use the passkey to enter the apartment. When the door was opened, he saw the nude and bloodied body of his daughter on the living room floor.

Detectives began a canvass of the apartment complex and the immediate neighborhood. They discovered that a neighbor had seen the victim letting a man carrying fast food into her apartment. Authorities obtained a description of that male and issued a plea for this man to come forward to assist in the investigation. It was unknown whether or not that male was a suspect in Angela's killing.

Detectives were also able to determine that two of her neighbors heard "screams" at about 11:15 p.m. on Thursday, August 27. One of her neighbors, who resided below Angela, heard a woman scream upstairs and then heard the sound of running in the apartment above her. The other neighbor who resided directly across the hallway also heard screams about the same time. However, they did not think to call the police when silence suddenly followed the screaming. The neighbors returned to sleep.

An autopsy later found that the victim's trachea had been cut preventing her from crying out. Ironically, the victim's sister had called about the same time. Of course, there was no answer.

It was during this time that the offender was sexually assaulting and killing Angela. Sadly, had either of the neighbors called 911, the victim may have been saved and the offender apprehended at the scene.

CRIME SCENE PROCESS

The victim had numerous stab wounds in her chest and breast. Therefore, according to *Practical Homicide Investigation* (Geberth, 2006), this case would be properly classified as a lust murder.

She also had extensive defense wounds on her arms and hands, which she sustained attempting to fight off her attacker. The blood spatter on the rugs, as well as the drainage blood from her torso, indicated that the offender had manipulated her body by turning her over onto her stomach. He then repositioned her body in a supine position before leaving the scene. The victim's chest and breast area bore the rug pattern in blood from lying on the blood-soaked rug. In fact, you could literally see the pattern of the wounds from her chest in blood, which had drained onto the carpet. Also, some of the wounds had drained as the body was turned indicating that the victim's body had been turned to the left onto her back.

When the body was turned over by the detectives, they observed additional stab wounds in her back. These wounds were shallow and more consistent with torture-type injuries. The detectives also observed blood on the soles of her feet indicating that the victim had run through her own blood as she attempted to escape her attacker. In addition, investigators found evidence that the killer had taken a wet towel from the wash and had "cleaned" the pubic area of the victim prior to engaging in vaginal sex (Figure 9.10).

A close examination of the body revealed the presence of "foreign" pubic hairs caught in the pubis of the victim. These hairs were black in color and contrasted against the lighter hair of the victim's pubis. A crime scene photo was taken of this evidence *in situ*. The evidence in the crime scene indicated that she had been raped and anally sodomized. This was later verified by the medical examiner.

Before the body was removed, the crime scene investigators outlined the original position of the body on the carpet and then had the entire carpet removed for

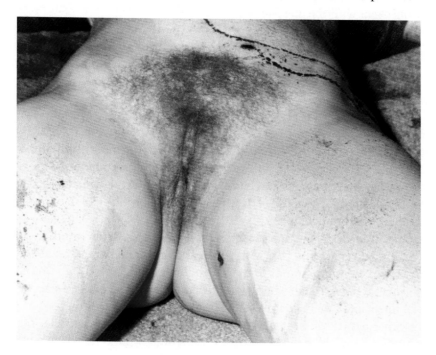

Figure 9.10 Perpetrator cleaned the body. Investigation indicated that the offender had taken a wet towel from the laundry and used it to clean off the blood on the victim's abdomen before raping her. (Photo courtesy of Detective Sergeant Alan Patton, Grand Prairie, Texas Police Department.)

microscopic analysis. An additional nine pubic hairs were recovered as a result of this crime scene procedure. A total of 11 pubic hairs were recovered. They were determined to be Negroid in origin and eventually matched to the suspect.

It was apparent that the offender had taken a beer from the victim's refrigerator and brought the beer into the bathroom where he cleaned up. It was also determined that the offender had wiped the beer bottle clean of any fingerprints and had wiped down the scene.

The detectives had learned during the canvass that a male had been seen entering the victim's apartment carrying fast food. The refrigerator was checked and a box of Church's Chicken® was located. They processed the box for fingerprints with negative results. However, more importantly, when they opened the refrigerator door, they observed a smudged print in blood on the front of a wine box. Immediately to the rear of that same wine box was a clear fingerprint in blood. Apparently, when the offender moved the wine box to get himself a beer, he left a perfect patent print in blood on the container.

According to "Practical Homicide Investigation®," an excellent recommendation is that after the crime scene has been processed, "have someone, who is thoroughly familiar with the scene, go over it with you, bit by bit, first visually and then physically, being careful not to touch any items. This person can identify the usually position of objects in the scene. You can then get a complete inventory on the spot. Instruct them to take their time and ask if they recognize any inconsistencies or 'foreign' materials present. Have them point out the usual positions of drapes, curtains, blinds, pictures, statues, ashtrays, etc. Obtain a detailed report" (Geberth, 1996). What you are looking for is any factor inconsistent with the lifestyle of the deceased.

Upon processing the crime scene, the Grand Prairie detectives, who had attended the author's courses, requested the family to ascertain if anything was missing from the apartment. The police learned that a portable TV and a 35 mm camera were missing from the apartment. An alarm and advisory were initiated in the event someone attempted to pawn these items.

AUTOPSY

On August 29, an autopsy was performed on the body of the victim. She had been stabbed 113 times. Her throat was cut and there were incised wounds across her eyes and defensive wounds on both arms and hands. The weapon was estimated to be approximately four inches long. The cause of death was ruled to be multiple stab wounds of the chest and abdomen: homicide.

She had received 16 stab wounds to the right upper chest, 4 stab wounds to the right upper arm, 37 stab wounds to the right side of abdomen and flank, 32 stab wounds to the left upper chest, 5 stab wounds to the left abdomen and flank, 3 stab wounds to the right forearm and hand, 5 stab wounds to the left forearm and hand, 9 stab wounds to the back of torso, and 3 stab wounds to the inner aspect of the left thigh.

Internal wound tracks indicated two wound tracks into the left ventricle of the heart, four to six entered each of the lungs, with the remaining wound tracks penetrating the liver, stomach, and peritoneal cavities.

In addition to the stab wounds, there were numerous incised wounds to the face, neck, and throat of the victim as well as numerous defensive-type wounds on her hands. There was also injury to the interior aspect of the vaginal vault. Her trachea had been cut, which prevented her from screaming. The autopsy revealed that the victim had been raped and anally sodomized. A rape kit procedure was employed and it was determined that there was a sufficient amount of genetic material to do a DNA analysis.

DETECTIVE INVESTIGATION

The first officers had established from management and neighbors that within the last three months the victim had complained about some unwanted attention and contact by male residents. There were three incidents that the detectives were interested in pursuing. One involved a male neighbor who had come to her door in the middle of the night and woke her wanting to come into her apartment. Another incident involved a male, who was apparently psychotic. He believed he was a former government agent and that people were watching and following him. He also believed that women were "evil" and "prostitutes." The victim had complained to management about him looking at her very strangely. Then there was another incident involving a former resident of the apartment complex, named Kenneth Renord Smith, a 32-year-old black male. According to Angela's complaint, he had been leaving notes on her car indicating that he wanted to date her. She had complained to management and friends about these unwanted solicitations. However, because Smith had moved from the complex in June, the manager advised the complainant that they couldn't intervene for her.

In fact, she had subsequently confided in a male professor, who was also black. She told him about the Smith incidents and had sought his advice on how to deal with this individual without appearing to be prejudiced. He had advised her to treat Smith like any other unwanted suitor and request that he leave her alone.

Although the Smith incident had been the most recent, detectives were more interested in the unknown male who had delivered some fast food to the apartment the night the victim died. Initially, they could not locate or identify this unknown male.

Detectives had been looking into all aspects of the case when they received information that the "unknown pubic hairs" were Negroid in origin. At this point, they began to look more closely at Smith.

On September 10, Detective Alan Patton interviewed Smith. He stated that he had left the complex in June after divorcing his wife and had moved several miles away. He also denied leaving any notes on the victim's car and he voluntarily provided the authorities with his fingerprints.

On September 11, detectives contacted Smith's employer and ascertained that he had worked on Thursday, August 27, from 6 a.m. until 11 a.m. and did not return to work until August 28 at 4 p.m.

The detectives also contacted Smith's wife, who stated that they had been separated and that Smith was living alone at another apartment complex several miles from the scene.

On September 13, other detectives who had been checking the deceased's telephone calls located a U.S. Marine pilot who was stationed at Pensacola Naval Base. Telephone records indicated that he had had telephone contact with Angela earlier in the month.

He was interviewed and he recalled talking to the deceased on Thursday, August 20, a week prior to her murder. The deceased stated to him during their conversation, "The guy that has been leaving the notes on my car is at my door. I'm not going to answer." She then described Kenneth Renord Smith to the Marine.

On September 15, Smith was invited back to the station house for a further interview. Detective Patton wanted to establish whether or not Smith had ever been in the apartment. The fingerprints that detectives had obtained from the subject on September 10 established that the left middle finger of Smith matched the bloody patent print on the wine box. This was extremely important evidence, especially if Smith said he had never been in Angela's apartment. How did his bloody fingerprint end up on a wine box in the victim's apartment? Detective Patton needed to establish that Smith had never been in the apartment prior to the murder. After engaging in nonthreatening routine dialog with Smith, Detective Patton suddenly confronted Smith in the interview room, stating, "Had you ever been in Angela's apartment at any time?" Smith stated to Detective Patton that he had never "crossed the threshold" of the deceased's apartment.

At that time, Detective Patton informed Smith that his bloody prints had been found in the apartment in the refrigerator when he took out the beer. At this point, Smith was formally charged with Angela's murder. Kenneth Renord Smith invoked his rights under Miranda. Rape and sodomy charges would be added later after conferring with the laboratory.

Detectives obtained a search warrant for exemplars of hairs and blood for DNA analysis. Smith was unable to present a verifiable alibi for his whereabouts at the time of the crime. Additionally, since the subject had driven to the police station voluntarily for the interview, the detectives decided to get a search warrant for his automobile to look for further evidence.

The detectives located a Hershey's Kisses™ candy tin containing the victim's military collar brass and other military unit crest and insignia that the deceased's family identified as being in her apartment. Detectives also located a piece of paper in the suspect's jacket pocket with the deceased's name written on it in her own handwriting. Smith claimed he had found these items at a basketball court in Dallas. Although, the subject could have gotten rid of this damning evidence, he felt the need to hold on to these items, as these were his trophies.

Eventually, detectives were able to locate the unknown male who had brought the Church's Chicken to the deceased's apartment. He had contacted the deceased through work and come over to her house with the fast food only to find that she wasn't feeling well. He made a date to return and left shortly thereafter. He was cleared of any involvement in the death of Angela.

FORENSIC FINDINGS

The search warrants executed on Kenneth Renord Smith for physical specimens of blood and hair proved to be valuable. Eventually, all of the hairs found on the victim were matched to Smith.. The semen and sperm found in the victim was analyzed by Southwest Institute of Forensic Sciences and matched through DNA analysis to Smith.

INVESTIGATIVE FINDINGS

In addition, Detective Patton was able to establish that Smith had pawned a Bentley portable TV and a 35 mm camera at a pawnshop in Irving, Texas, on August 29 at 4 p.m. Detective Patton provided a photo array to the pawnshop employee. The store clerk positively identified Smith as the person who had pawned the stolen items. Subsequently, the family identified the items as those belonging to the deceased.

FINAL DISPOSITION

The subject was allowed to plead guilty to capital murder to cover the indictment. In February of the following year, he received a life sentence and must serve 35 years before possibility of parole.

Reconstruction and Opinion

Kenneth Renord Smith had stalked Angela with the intent of sexually assaulting her after being repeatedly rejected by the victim. He had left numerous notes on her car in the parking lot of the apartment complex indicating he wanted a relationship with her. She wasn't responding and was actually ignoring him. This angered the offender, who began stalking her.

If he couldn't initiate a relationship, then he would have her sexually. When he came to her apartment complex the evening of August 27, he brought a weapon. He clearly anticipated the assault. He may possibly have seen the other gentleman come to Angela's apartment and then waited for him to leave. When he came to her front door, he was prepared to force his way in if necessary. I believe that Angela probably thought that she could explain to him her lack of interest without personally offending him and this might very well have been the initial conversation. Suddenly, he lashed out at the victim threatening her with the knife. She screamed and he realized he would have to "shut her up." The incised wound across the victim's throat effectively cut her voice box. She continued to struggle running through the apartment. He knocked her to the floor and continued to stab into her chest and breasts. This is the rationale for labeling this attack a lust murder (Geberth, 1998, 2006). He then mounted her from the rear, anally penetrating her and stabbing into her back. After turning the body onto its back, he went to the laundry where he removed a wet towel and "cleaned" the blood off her abdomen. He then engaged in penis–vaginal assault leaving two of his pubic hairs ensnared in the victim's pubis.

Upon completion of his attack, he went to the refrigerator and removed a cold beer with his bloody hands leaving a patent print in blood on the wine box. He then went into the bathroom to clean the blood from his hands and wash up. He wiped the bottle down to remove his prints.

These actions are similar to other cases that the author has investigated and provided an assessment. First, he violates the victim and then violates the victim's personal space. He helps himself to a beer in the refrigerator. He then uses the bathroom to "clean up." He basically makes himself at home. When he was satisfied that he had removed any evidence, he looked out to make sure no one was around and then exited, locking the apartment as he left. In one final outrage, he left the victim's body positioned on the floor with her legs spread.

Kenneth Renord Smith is a sexual psychopath who had no regard for his victim's life, only his sexual desire and lust. The overkill injuries speak volumes about his anger and his retaliation over being rejected. The location of these penetrating wounds into the victim's chest and breasts manifest the psychosexual nature of the crime. The anal sodomy was perpetrated to degrade the victim and the torture-like stab wounds to the back were to punish her for rejecting him.

He had a stalker mentality. He left messages on the victim's car. He repeatedly attempted to communicate with her despite her lack of interest. He was fully aware of the effects of these actions and engaged in this conduct as a prelude to his attack.

Taking possession of Angela's Hershey's Kisses candy tin that contained her military collar brass and other military unit crest and insignia, along with a piece of paper with the deceased's name written on it in her own handwriting, is an example of taking a "trophy" of the event. These items took on a psychological significance and served as "engram," which enabled him to recall the event and fantasize about his sexual conquest over the victim.

When the police asked him to come in for an interview, he traveled to the police station with the Hershey's Kisses candy tin in his car. This is yet another example of how the psychopath would demonstrate that he is superior to the police. He probably thought that this was quite funny. As the police were interviewing him about the murder, he had the "evidence" of the crime located right outside in his car.

The piece of paper with the victim's handwriting on it is another example of an offender keeping something personal that belonged to the victim as a physical reminder of the event. An important investigative consideration is that it is not the value or worth of an item taken by an offender that is of great consequence, but the psychological significance of this item to the sexual psychopath (From the author's files). (See Chapter 20 in *Practical Homicide Investigation*, Geberth, 2006.)

A Disorganized Lust Murderer

CASE FACTS

The following comes from the author's files. The female victim, who lived alone in a rural area, was found murdered in her home. Her body was discovered by a deputy who was checking on her welfare.

Her nude body had been mutilated and there was evidence of sexual activity at the crime scene. Two weeks earlier, on February 27, she had confronted a burglar in her home who was stealing her panties. She chased him out with a fire poker and reported the crime to the police, who took a burglary report. Their primary suspect was a "fetish burglar" known by people in the community, who considered him a nuisance.

The next day, on February 28, the suspect appeared at the store where the victim worked. He made verbal contact with her, knowing she would recognize him. He apparently wanted to see her reaction. The victim got his description and wrote down his license plate number when he left. She conferred with friends and ascertained the suspect's name. She advised the police. The deputy who had investigated the burglary obtained an old arrest photo from records to show the victim.

On March 3, the deputy showed the victim a photo array. However, the victim wasn't sure she could identify him. The deputy decided to interview the suspect and get a more current picture of him. On March 9, the victim informed a friend of the break in and named the suspect. That same day, the friend watched the victim as she drove away toward work and saw the suspect following the victim in his orange Chevy Citation. On March 11, the suspect was waiting for the victim to come home from work. The suspect had hidden in a wood closet on the porch of the victim's home waiting for her to return from work. As the victim unlocked her door, she was attacked "blitz style" with a knife.

She was repeatedly stabbed in the breast and chest area and suffered a number of defense wounds. The victim had desperately fought with him on the porch as was evidenced by the obvious disturbance and the defense wounds she received (Figure 9.11 and Figure 9.12).

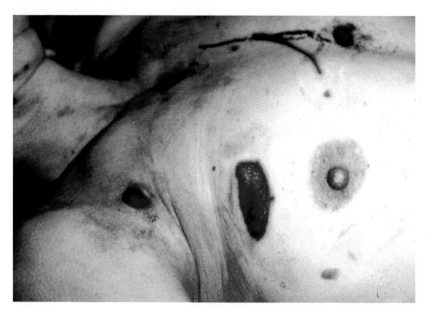

Figure 9.11 Lust murder. This victim suffered a "blitz attack" by a fetish burglar who was waiting for her to return from work. Note the attack to the breast and chest area. (Photo courtesy of Detective Bryan Skordahl, Clark County, Washington, Sheriff's Office.)

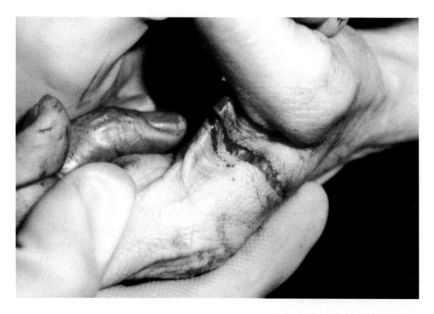

Figure 9.12 Defense wounds. Classic defense wound pattern on victim's hands as she tried to ward off the attack. (Photo courtesy of Detective Bryan Skordahl, Clark County, Washington, Sheriff's Office.)

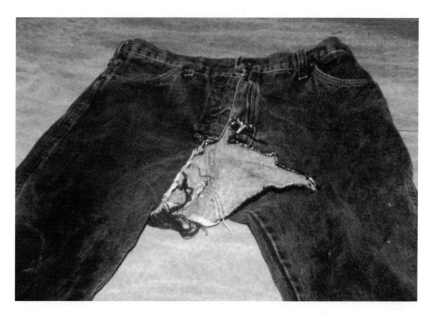

Figure 9.13 Victim's jeans. The offender had cut out the crotch area and then disrobed her body by cutting the garments off of her body. (Photo courtesy of Detective Bryan Skordahl, Clark County, Washington Sheriff's Office.)

The suspect then carried the victim's body into the house where he began a bizarre 18-hour sexual ritual. The suspect cut out the crotch area of the victim's pants and then began disrobing her by cutting all of the garments from her person. He then dressed in the victim's undergarments complete with makeup, water balloons for breasts, and padding from a pillow he cut open. He also took a pair of the victim's high heel shoes and cut the heal portion out so that he could wear them as well. He glued false fingernails on and then polished his "new nails" with red nail polish. He inserted objects into her vagina and masturbated on the victim's body. While in the victim's residence, he made a number of phone calls to a 1-900 service, which totaled $643. The suspect managed to escape out a rear door when police arrived at the victim's home. However, he was quickly located and taken into custody by officers who found him hiding in a closet in another home in the area (Figures 9.13 through 9.17).

CLINICAL ASSESSMENT

This is a classic case of a disorganized offender who is a lust murderer. The subject had started his fetish burglaries as a youngster. He progressed from panty theft, which was substitutive sexual behavior, to physically confronting some of his victims.

The police retrieved magazines and articles on gender change as well as cross-dressing and a large collection of pornography in the suspect's home. Police interviews revealed that he had previously molested his own sister and had stolen her panties. The sister was forced to sleep with her door locked because she was in fear of her own brother.

The suspect was a classic sexual deviant whose past behavior as well as his activities with the victim in the crime scene clearly demonstrated his sadistic progression and potential dangerousness. He interacted with the victim's corpse as if she were alive as he called upon his imagination and fantasy to supply him with the necessary engrams

Figure 9.14 Victim's bra. Note that the bra has been cut. (Photo courtesy of Detective Bryan Skordahl, Clark County, Washington, Sheriff's Office.)

Figure 9.15 Victim's high heel shoes. The offender cut out the heel portion of the victim's high heel shoes so that he could wear them. (Photo courtesy of Detective Bryan Skordahl, Clark County, Washington, Sheriff's Office.)

Figure 9.16 Water balloons. The offender simulated breasts with these two balloons, which he filled with water and wore with the victim's bra. (Photo courtesy of Detective Bryan Skordahl, Clark County, Washington, Sheriff's Office.)

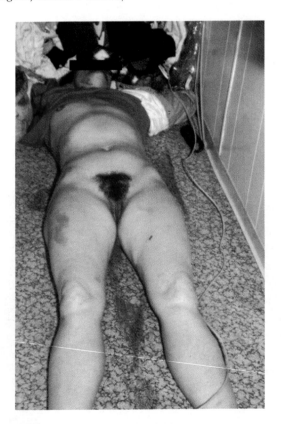

Figure 9.17 Victim's body. The offender then spent an 18-hour sexual ritual with the victim's body as he inserted objects into her vagina and masturbated on her. While in the premises, he made a number of telephone calls to a 1-900 service, which totaled $643. (Photo courtesy of Detective Bryan Skordahl, Clark County, Washington, Sheriff's Office.)

to satisfy his craving for his depravity. The necrophilia and interaction with the victim's body were clearly enhanced by the 1-900 calls. In fact, he was so engrossed with his fantasy, he was almost caught in the house.

He manifested the paraphilias of sexual sadism, which was the driving force, and necrophilia coupled with the substitutive paraphilias of voyeurism, fetishism, transvestic fetishism with apparent gender dysphoria, and telephone scatologia.

Lust Murder: Offender with Sexual Dysfunction— Disorganized Offender Acts Out with Victim's Body

CASE FACTS

Police received an anonymous call reporting a body of a female in an area used as an illegal dumpsite. Patrol officers responded and stopped any vehicles within the area. The officers upon their arrival observed a nude, light-skinned, black female, who appeared to be approximately 25 to 35 years of age. There was evidence of mutilation.

THE CRIME SCENE

The officers observed tire marks from a vehicle suggesting that the body had been transported to the scene. There was only about a half pint of blood found beneath the neck area of the victim. The victim had been cut open from the vagina to the sternum. She had deep slashing wounds to the throat and inner thigh. The body was lying spread-eagle on her back. A dismembered breast was lying on the left side of her face. The other breast was placed on her abdomen with an apparently used condom placed on it. An unused condom was located between the victim's feet. The surrounding area was immediately cordoned off and detectives were notified. All vehicles traveling in the area were stopped and the drivers were identified.

POSSIBLE SUSPECT

One of the occupants of a vehicle stopped by police appeared to be intoxicated. When the officer asked for identification the subject had difficulty producing his license.

When the officer requested the occupant to exit his vehicle, he observed a gun and a bloodstained knife in the compartment in the door. The subject was arrested at the scene for DWI and possession of a loaded firearm.

The suspect, after being provided with his Miranda warnings, gave an extremely detailed statement that had him traveling from place to place and purchasing pints of vodka and drinking throughout the day. When officers asked him about the gun, blood, and the bloodstained knife and ax found inside his vehicle, he stated he didn't know anything about them. Later on, investigators discovered that the subject had bought the gun on the street a few weeks earlier.

THE CONFESSION

The suspect was brought to the Michigan State Police to take a polygraph test. The suspect confessed to the state police investigator. He admitted to picking up a prostitute, who offered him oral sex for $20. When the victim entered his car, they went to a location to engage in sex and, according to the suspect, she raised the price to $40. There was an argument and a physical altercation. During this argument, the victim was shot and according to the suspect fell to the ground. He stated that he realized she was dead and removed all of her clothes. He then got the knife and ax out of his vehicle and used the knife to cut off her breasts and the ax to chop the victim's neck and pubic area. The suspect stated he used the victim's clothes to wipe the blood off the ax and rear seat of his vehicle. He stated that he threw the bloodstained clothing out of the window of his car as he drove away. He stated that he had driven back to the scene to see if anyone had discovered the body when the uniform officer stopped him. Investigators located the several pieces of bloodstained clothing along the route the suspect told police he had traveled.

CLINICAL ASSESSMENT

This is a classic case of a disorganized offender, who became a lust murderer as a result of being unable to sexually perform. He then acted out a perverse fantasy with the victim's body. His confession was obviously bogus based on the forensics and not consistent with the facts of the case. This victim had been transported to the dump location after death and was mutilated postmortem with the implements he had in his car. He removed her breasts and placed them in a position that was significant to him in connection with the dynamics of this event. The deep cuts into her throat are highly suggestive that he was destroying the voice that ridiculed him as he revealed his impotence and couldn't perform. The position of the body splayed out with the arms over her head and the legs spread open is an important consideration in understanding his need to dominate her sexually. He had eviscerated the woman with a deep cut, which ran from her vagina to her upper chest. He created a sexual presentation and wanted the body discovered to show his superiority over her. The deep cut into her upper right inner thigh was a pathologically sadistic wound. The placing of one of the woman's breast over her face was an act of depersonalization. Axing out the vaginal area and then placing the other breast over the pubis with a used condom on top was another act of defiance and highly suggestive that he was unable to sexually perform and was "making a statement" that he had sexually conquered her by his presentation of the woman's body. Placing her body at a dumpsite was a further act of humiliation and degradation (Figures 9.18 through 9.20).

Deviant-Oriented Assault: A Classic Disorganized Offender

CASE FACTS

On a Sunday evening, September 10, at approximately 6 p.m., a baby's body was found by hikers and a doctor as they were jogging in a wooded area of Valley Forge National Historic Park. The body was an unidentified white female approximately two years old. The people who had discovered the body alerted a Pennsylvania state trooper who was passing through the park on patrol. The trooper called for assistance and established a crime scene. CPR was begun on the infant, who was then transported by ambulance to Phoenixville Hospital where she was pronounced dead. The child had been strangled to death.

POLICE RESPONSE: CRIME SCENE NUMBER #1

This area of the park was near the Montgomery and Chester County border in Pennsylvania. The Upper Merion Police, and the Park Rangers responded to the scene.

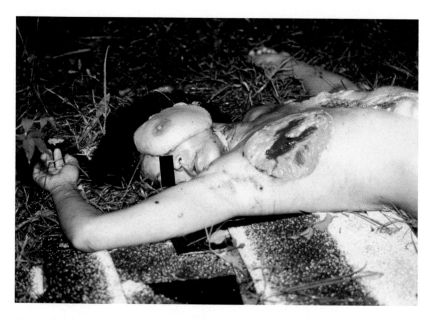

Figure 9.18 Lust murder. The offender had severed the victim's breasts from her chest. He placed one breast across her face. (Photo courtesy of Detective Marc Abdilla, Township of Van Buren, Michigan, Department of Public Safety.)

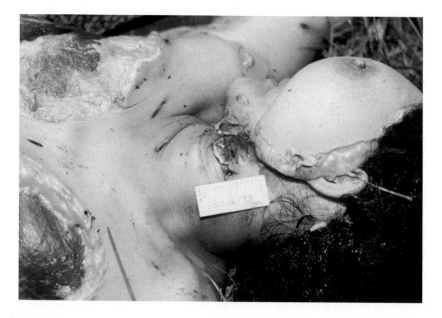

Figure 9.19 Lust murder. Close-up of severed breast on victim's face. (Photo courtesy of Detective Marc Abdilla, Township of Van Buren, Michigan, Department of Public Safety.)

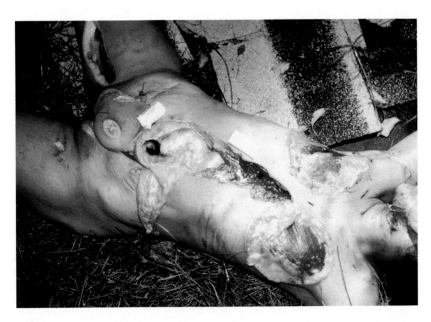

Figure 9.20 Lust murder—gross mutilation. The offender, who told police that he had muti-lated the body at the place of discovery, had severed the victim's breast and placed them on her body. There was about a pint of blood found at the scene. This body was obviously placed for shock value after having been killed elsewhere. However, the offender was acting out some underlying psychosexual need in what he did. (Photo courtesy of Detective Marc Abdilla, Township of Van Buren, Michigan, Department of Public Safety.)

The actual jurisdiction of incident was determined to be in Upper Merion within Montgomery County. The Montgomery County District Attorney's Office was noti-fied and County Homicide Detectives County Detectives Lieutenant John Fallon and Detective Richard Peffall were dispatched to assist Upper Merion Police Detective Bruce Saville in the investigation and to respond to Phoenixville Hospital.

INVESTIGATIVE CONSIDERATIONS

The crime scene was within a wooded area of the park and darkness was settling in. The initial search concentrated on locating additional victims and any obvious items of evidence within the immediate area where the baby's body had been found.

In accordance with "Practical Homicide Investigation®" techniques, a decision was made to postpone any detailed search until the next morning due to the geography of the scene and the increasing darkness. Upper Merion Police and Park Rangers guarded the crime scene area throughout the night.

While at the crime scene, detectives were informed that a man had reported to police that his wife Lisa and their 19-month-old baby daughter, Devon, had not returned home from a shopping trip to a shopping center in Collegeville, Pennsylvania. Detectives met the husband and relatives at the Phoenixville hospital and requested him to look at the body. The husband refused to look at the body. Family relatives identified the body as the missing 19-month-old child. Since the husband had refused to view the body and the mother of the child was still missing, police considered the husband a suspect.

CRIME SCENE NUMBER # 2: SEPTEMBER 10, 10 P.M.

On Sunday evening, September 10, at approximately 9:20 p.m., the Collegeville Police located the missing woman's 1988 Pontiac Firebird in a parking lot in the Collegeville Shopping Center in Collegeville, Pennsylvania. The car was parked in front of a card store and a children's clothing store. The police immediately secured the car and established a crime scene around the area of the car. Detectives were notified and proceeded to process the auto and the scene.

The car was unlocked and the driver's side window was down. There were no signs of any forced entry into the vehicle. The front seat was pushed forward. There was a baby car seat in the back. The victim's empty purse and her identification were recovered in the car. No cash was found.

INVESTIGATIVE CONSIDERATIONS

Upper Merion and Montgomery County detectives began questioning family members and friends. There were no leads as to Lisa's whereabouts. At this point, the full thrust of the police investigation concentrated on the family. The husband remained a suspect. However, the police were also focusing on the possible involvement of the mother in her daughter's death. It was unknown if Lisa was alive or dead, a victim or a perpetrator.

MAJOR CASE ERROR

According to "Practical Homicide Investigation®" techniques, when a major case is initiated, all information needs to go through a central command and no independent actions are initiated or taken without consulting the command post and the lead detective. To do otherwise could possibly jeopardize the efficiency and integrity of the overall inquiry.

Independent of the county police, Collegeville police contacted the owner of the children's clothing store. She told them that the clerk on duty, before closing, was her 21-year-old son, Caleb. She stated that her son wouldn't be home until early morning since he was at a nightclub in Philadelphia. On Monday, September 11, at 1:15 a.m., Caleb called the Collegeville police as requested and spoke to a desk sergeant. He reported that he had closed the store at about 5:30 p.m. on Sunday afternoon. The sergeant gave Caleb a physical and clothing description of Lisa and her daughter, Devon. Caleb stated he didn't remember them because he had seen several women in the store that day, wearing similar black blouses. Caleb then volunteered information to the desk sergeant that while he was at the downtown Philadelphia nightclub, his face was scratched during a fight that Sunday evening. The desk sergeant never thought he should immediately notify the detectives. He simply filled out a report

INVESTIGATIVE CONSIDERATIONS

On Monday morning, September 11, the media had been alerted of this incident. In order to enlist public assistance in locating Lisa and her baby, they were provided photographs of Lisa and her car. Media representatives were present at Valley Forge National Park and the Collegeville Shopping Center covering this breaking story.

CRIME SCENE NUMBER #1: VALLEY FORGE NATIONAL HISTORIC PARK

On Monday morning, an extensive crime scene search was initiated in the area where the child's body was found. Hundreds of firefighters, Park Rangers, and police officers scoured Valley Forge Park for signs of Lisa and evidence. In addition, since the park is federal property, the FBI provided an infrared tracking device and helicopter. The Pennsylvania State Police also provided a helicopter and tracking dogs. Detectives recovered forensic evidence, but there was no trace of Lisa or her body.

AUTOPSY

Although Phoenixville Hospital is in Chester County, the Chester County coroner yielded jurisdiction over the child's body. On Monday, September 11, the autopsy was performed in Lansdale, Pennsylvania, by Dr. Isadore Mihalakis. The cause of death was asphyxia with evidence of suffocation and strangulation.

INVESTIGATIVE CONSIDERATIONS

On Monday morning, Detective Bruce Saville, who was assigned as the primary investigator from Upper Merion, became aware of the Collegeville patrol sergeant's report on the store clerk. He immediately realized its significance as well as the potential harm this action might cause the investigation. *The Collegeville police had never informed the detectives that they were calling the business owners at the shopping center. This was a major error and violation of protocol.*

Detective Saville was aware of several contacts with the store clerk, named Caleb, and the Upper Merion Police. In fact, Caleb had been identified in connection with sexual harassment of female joggers, indecent remarks, and other incidents. However, the victims had been reluctant to press charges and Caleb was never prosecuted. Detective Saville and Detective Rich Peffall, from Montgomery County Police immediately went to the children's clothing store to interview Caleb while other investigators continued to search for Lisa.

Caleb was requested to accompany the detectives to the Upper Merion police station for an interview. Caleb called his mother to tell her he was closing the store temporarily and was going to the police station to give a statement. During the interview, the detectives noticed that he had makeup on his face. He told them that he had gotten his face scratched by someone during "mosh dancing." He was requested to remove the makeup. Detectives observed several fingernail-type scratches on his face (Figure 9.21). There were also scratches on his wrists. Caleb then gave a voluntary statement and an extensive alibi after being advised of his rights.

CRIME SCENE NUMBER #3: THE CHILDREN'S CLOTHING STORE

Investigators had obtained written consent from Caleb to search the children's clothing store. The story had attracted a great deal of media attention. Because Lisa's car had been recovered in the Collegeville Shopping Center, there was a substantial media presence there when crime scene investigators arrived to search the store and surrounding area.

A local television reporter approached the officers and reported that earlier that morning he had seen a young white male vigorously vacuuming and cleaning the rear of the store. He had only seen him through the window, but he accurately described the store clerk named Caleb. Although the authorities had originally obtained written consent to search the store, they petitioned the court for a search warrant when they determined the clerk's possible involvement and culpability. An extensive search of

Figure 9.21 Suspect's scratched face. (Photo courtesy of Lieutenant John Fallon and Detective Richard Peffall, Montgomery County, Pennsylvania, detectives.)

the store and the suspect's car produced several items of evidence, including hairs and fibers as well as blood, semen, and sperm.

INVESTIGATIVE CONSIDERATIONS

Detectives Saville and Peffall continued to question the store clerk about the scratches on his face. He voluntarily answered their questions. Caleb had told some people that his face was scratched during a fight at the downtown Philadelphia nightclub. However, he had told others he scratched his face during mosh dancing. When Caleb's father was interviewed, the detectives learned that the father had also remarked to his son that his face "looked like he had raped a woman."

As the interview proceeded, other detectives were running down leads, locating witnesses, and uncovering forensic evidence. The store clerk provided the names of alibi witnesses as well as an extensive itinerary of his activities on Sunday unaware that his story was falling apart as detectives questioned these witnesses.

CANVASS OF THE COLLEGEVILLE SHOPPING CENTER

The canvass and media exposure provided the following information to investigators. Four to five customers remembered seeing Lisa and her child in the children's clothing store between 3:45 and 4 p.m. Two people remembered seeing a CLOSED sign on the door of the store at 4 p.m. The store was supposed to be open till 5:30. A storeowner remembered seeing a maroon car parked behind the store at about 4:30 in the afternoon. The suspect's car was maroon.

Detectives located another customer who went to the store at about 5:15 p.m. and found the store closed. She then saw a "fat" subject driving a maroon car from behind the store. This witness eventually identified Caleb in a police lineup. The police also interviewed another woman who told of being followed around the store by the clerk, whom she described as weird.

INVESTIGATIVE CONSIDERATIONS

Detectives Saville and Peffall felt they had developed enough evidence and sufficient discrepancies in Caleb's alibi to challenge him. Detective Rich Peffall, Montgomery County Police, confronted Caleb after his statement, stating, "I don't believe you scratched your face during 'mosh' dancing at the dance club. I think Lisa scratched your face when you attacked her in the store." The detective then placed a "birthday" picture of the little girl in front of the suspect. Peffall then told him, "The family needs to know where Lisa is. It isn't fair to put them through this additional pain. Tell us where Lisa is for the family's sake."

The store clerk stared at the detective. His eyes began to fill up with tears and his lips began to quiver. The detective thought he was going to confess. The suspect suddenly stated, "I don't want to talk to you anymore." He then invoked his right to counsel. The interview was then terminated and the suspect was placed under arrest for the murder of the little girl.

Although he remained a suspect in the disappearance of the baby's mother, the police could no longer question him.

LEGAL TACTICAL DECISION AND INVESTIGATIVE CONSIDERATIONS

District Attorney Michael Marino, realizing the value of the potential DNA evidence to be gained if Lisa's body was found, was able to reach an agreement with the suspect through his attorney at about 6 p.m. Monday evening. Twenty-four hours had passed since the little girl's body had been found in Valley Forge Park.

"A deal with the devil had been struck." If Caleb would reveal the location of Lisa's body, the Commonwealth of Pennsylvania would not seek the death penalty in a capital murder prosecution.

Caleb Fairley, through his attorney, told the authorities that he dumped Lisa's body in a wooded area near an industrial park in Upper Merion, Pennsylvania. On Monday evening, at 6:30 p.m., Detectives Bruce Saville and Rich Peffall discovered the missing woman's body.

CRIME SCENE NUMBER #4: SEPTEMBER 11, 6:30 P.M.

Detectives found the victim's nude body in a wooded area near an industrial park in Upper Merion approximately four miles from where her baby, Devon, had been found. When her body was found, she was wearing only her T-shirt, which was pulled up to expose her breasts. Her body had been positioned on her back with her legs spread. Her long black hair was brushed down across her face to cover her eyes. She had been manually strangled (Figure 9.22).

AUTOPSY

On Tuesday, September 12, 1995, at 1 a.m., Dr. Ian Hood performed the autopsy in Lansdale, Pennsylvania. The cause of death was manual strangulation.

FORENSIC FINDINGS

Autopsies indicated that both Lisa and Devon had died from manual strangulation. Although semen was found on the floor of the store, none was recovered from her body.

Figure 9.22 Victim's body. The offender had positioned the victim's body with her legs spread and her top pushed up over her breasts. He then brushed her hair over her face. (Photo courtesy of Lieutenant John Fallon and Detective Richard Peffall, Montgomery County, Pennsylvania, detectives.)

Lisa had not been raped. Her fingernail clippings and samples of her known blood along with the suspect Fairley's blood were immediately sent out for DNA analysis. The crime scene process resulted in over 138 pieces of evidence being recovered from the bodies, the crime scenes, and the suspect.

- The blood found on the floor and wall of the store was matched through DNA analysis to the victims Lisa and Devon.
- Lisa's head hair and pubic hair were found in the suspect's car.
- The vacuum cleaner bag contained hair and fibers from Lisa.
- Lisa's blouse and bra contained blue carpet fibers from the store carpet.
- Lisa's fingernail clippings revealed Caleb Fairley's DNA.
- Semen stains from Fairley were found on the carpet in the store.
- A piece of blue carpet from the store contained blood and saliva from Devon, which was identified through DNA analysis.
- Dirt and vegetation from Fairley's car matched the dirt and vegetation from the crime scenes.
- The suspect Fairley's head hair was found on Lisa's blouse and bra.
- Rubber gloves recovered from a storm drain had carpet fibers from Fairley's car on them.
- A towel from Fairley's car had fibers, hair, and blood from the baby Devon.
- Semen stains from Fairley's undergarments found in the laundry matched semen stains at the store.
- And, finally, an oil swab from Fairley's car was similar to the oil stains found at one of crime scenes.

THE SUSPECT

A search of the suspect Fairley's room pursuant to a search warrant revealed his obsessive interest in pornography. A number of S&M-type adult videos were found.

Detectives also located three adult videos in the backroom of the children's clothing store. The suspect also had a plastic vibrating dildo with gels, a used rubber vagina, a battery-powered testicle vibrator, sexual magazines, and pornographic cards and photos. Fairley also had several previous complaints of sexual harassment from women. He also had a shirt depicting a vampire ravaging a beautiful young woman with long black hair. **This shirt had such a striking resemblance to Lisa on it that the District Attorney introduced this shirt at trial.**

DISPOSITION

Caleb Fairley was charged with two counts of murder, robbery first degree, two counts of aggravated assault, theft by unlawful taking, and abuse of a corpse. First Assistant District Attorney Bruce Castor was assigned to prosecute the case. The case generated so much publicity in the Philadelphia area that a jury panel was brought in from Harrisburg. Fairley was found guilty after trial of the two counts of first degree murder and all of the related offenses. He is presently serving two life sentences in a Pennsylvania correctional facility.

Reconstruction and Opinion

This case is a classic example of the disorganized offender. The offender who was so absorbed in his perverse fantasy world that he never considered the consequences of his actions. The crime scene was his mother's clothing store where he was the only clerk on duty. Lisa was the classic victim of opportunity, who happened to be at the wrong place at the wrong time. In this case, a mother–daughter clothing store, which under ordinary circumstances would have been a safe place.

The offender never considered that other customers might come to the store while he was attacking the woman. He certainly didn't think about the baby when he assaulted the mother. He never considered what he would do after his attack or what he would do with their bodies after he killed them. When he did dispose of their bodies, he didn't make any effort to hide or conceal them. He simply dropped them off in secluded areas.

This entire episode was based upon a sexual fantasy, which resulted in a spontaneous eruption of sexual violence at the place of occurrence. Obviously, the offender wasn't thinking about forensic evidence. Consequently, the clustered crime scene provided the authorities with abundant physical evidence.

The investigation revealed that Lisa and her daughter had gone to the store to purchase some clothing. As other customers began to leave the store, the offender surreptitiously locked the front door to the store and put up a *closed* sign. Lisa and her daughter were in the back of the store at the time. Lisa didn't see the clerk as he came up from behind and suddenly attacked her. However, the offender didn't realize how strong she was. Lisa put up a fierce struggle and she was able to severely scratch his face before she succumbed to the strangulation.

The offender then removed her clothing and undergarments as he tried to rape her. It appeared that he masturbated over her body as she lay dead on the floor. Semen and sperm were recovered from this location on the floor of the store. After the attack on Lisa, Caleb strangled the little girl.

He attempted to get rid of the obvious evidence of the attack by transporting the bodies in his car to a disposal site. However, he didn't have time to clean up the store. He placed Lisa's body in the trunk. He then wrapped Devon in his black jacket and placed the baby's body on the back seat of his car. He drove to Valley Forge Park and dropped the baby in the woods. He saw a car coming and couldn't dispose of Lisa's body. He then drove to King of Prussia, which is near a health club he belonged to. Here he disposed of Lisa's body after posing her with her legs spread and her long black hair brushed across her face. He then fabricated two different stories about how his face was scratched. However, the police were able to locate these witnesses who refuted the suspect's alibi.

The history of the offender depicted a loner type personality who was an underachiever with a poor self-image. Although he was 21 years old, he was sexually incompetent. He didn't date and lacked interpersonal relationships with young women his age. Many people who were interviewed by the police described him as weird.

Masturbation compensated for his lack of interpersonal relationships and S&M pornography served to reinforce his sadistic sexual appetite. The items recovered from his room certainly suggested a heavy reliance on solo sex-related activities, which obviously included voyeurism at the store. The suspect had made a peephole in the woman's dressing room so he could watch the woman customers undress from the back storage room. There was a VCR in the back room of the store where he could watch his S&M videos while at work. In addition to the extensive collection of pornographic videos and magazines, his sexual paraphernalia included a plastic vibrating dildo, a used rubber vagina, and a battery-powered testicle vibrator. The varied sexual devices and pornography found in his room, as well as his place of work, clearly attests to his sexual obsession.

The police investigation revealed that he had attempted to manipulate another woman into the back room on the very same day that he attacked Lisa and Devon. It is my opinion that Caleb Fairley was actively seeking a victim to satisfy his perversions on that particular day.

When Lisa, who resembled the beautiful young woman on the "vampire" shirt, came walking into the store, Caleb made a conscious decision to sexually assault her. He had no plan. He had an intense sexual desire predicated upon his obsessive fantasies. Thus, he committed the assault in a classic "blitz style" of attack in an attempt to quickly quiet his victims. What the offender did not realize when he attacked Lisa, was how strong she was and how courageously she would fight to protect herself and her baby. As a result, the police were able to retrieve extensive physical and forensic evidence from the crime scenes (From the author's files).

Deviant Oriented Assault: Disorganized Offender

CASE FACTS

I remember participating in an investigation in which a nude body of a 26-year-old woman had been discovered on the roof landing of her Bronx building. She had been the victim of a classic lust murder. The young woman's jaw and nose had been broken suggesting a "blitz style" of attack. She had been manually strangled with a strap from her purse and her panties had been placed over her face (depersonalization). Her body had been placed in a grotesque position. (A position that was probably sexually

Figure 9.23 Classic lust murder. Sex-related homicide, disorganized offender. After postmortem mutilation and sexual abuse, the body was positioned in a sexually provocative manner significant to the offender. Note the postmortem bindings as well as penis substitution into the vaginal canal with foreign objects. (Photo courtesy of the author.)

significant to the offender.) Her nylon stockings had been loosely tied around her wrists suggesting evidence of symbolic postmortem binding (fantasy and symbolism). The items used to create this postmortem binding came from the victim and included a belt, which was draped across her abdomen representing bondage.

The killer had cut off her nipples and placed them on the her chest. An umbrella and a pen had been inserted into the dead girl's vagina (penis substitution) and a comb was placed in her pubic hair. The words, "Fuck you," were written upon her abdomen and, on the inside of her left thigh, the killer had etched in pen, "You can't stop me." In addition, there were postmortem bite marks on the victim's thighs. This offender was classified as disorganized based on the analysis of the crime scene information (Figure 9.23).

The profile, which was prepared by the FBI, matched all of the suspects developed during the police investigation. However, one suspect, who was the son of the superintendent of the building, was of particular interest to the detectives. This suspect was a patient at a local psychiatric hospital. The suspect claimed to have been in the hospital on the day of the murder. Although the authorities knew that the suspect had been absent from the institution on the day of the murder, the hospital records did not indicate his absence. This created an additional problem for the police, who were attempting to obtain a court order for teeth impressions of the suspect.

When the court order was finally approved, the suspect's teeth impressions were compared to the bite mark evidence. Three forensic dentists agreed that the suspect had inflicted the bite mark wounds on the victim's body.

The suspect was arrested after an exhaustive 13-month police investigation. The bite mark evidence was crucial in the outcome of the case. The suspect was found guilty and is presently serving 25 years to life in a New York State facility (From the author's files).

Deviant Oriented Assault: Organized Offender

CASE FACTS

James Allen Kinney, suspected by Washington police to be an interjurisdictional serial killer, was charged with the lust murder of 20-year-old Keri Lynn in Whatcom County, Washington. Kinney was also a suspect in three bank robberies. Keri, who was visiting relatives in Bellingham, Washington, had gone on a day outing to a city park near Mt. Baker. However, she never came home. Her friends described Keri Lynn as an innocent, trusting, and carefree young woman who was "free spirited." She had never been to the West Coast and was considering attending college the next semester at Western Washington University.

POLICE INVESTIGATION

Investigators, who reviewed her diary, noted she had engaged in some sexual affairs with strangers, whom she met during her travels, including some men she had met on the bus ride out to Washington. This factor certainly raised her risk level.

On October 2, Keri left her aunt's house at about 11 a.m. with her backpack to go to Lake Padden, a city park that has a three-mile trail that goes around the lake. When she did not return home and did not call her relatives, the police were notified.

A missing person's report was filed and a search and rescue operation was conducted. The news media had also broadcast an appeal.

As a result of the news broadcast and description, numerous calls came in placing the victim at a bus stop in the park at about 4 p.m. She was presumably on her way home.

On the evening of October 4, Keri's battered and nude body was found by two boys who were riding their bikes on a trail in a remote section of Whatcom County near Mt. Baker.

The victim had been posed with her legs spread open and held open with a vine.

There was evidence of blunt force trauma to her face and manual strangulation. However, the strangulation did not cause her death. She had received blunt force trauma to the face and head from a pair of lopping shears used by gardeners. The police recovered the blood-stained lopping shears at the scene.

There was evidence that the killer had spent time with the victim after she was killed. There were also several beer cans and field-stripped cigarette butts found at the crime scene.

An examination of the body at the scene indicated that the offender had forcibly inserted a stick into her vagina with such force that it broke off inside the victim (Figure 9.24 and Figure 9.25).

There was also evidence of anal penetration. However, no semen was recovered on the body. In addition, the offender had apparently shaved off a small area of the victim's pubic hair.

The next day, on October 5, while traveling back to the crime scene, Detective Mark Joseph discovered a landscaping truck parked on the side of the road about a mile from the crime scene. The truck was mechanically disabled.

In the bed of the truck was all the equipment a landscaper would use (lawnmower, weed-eater, rake, leave blower, trimmers, etc.). More importantly, in the cab of the truck was a beer can of the same brand found at the crime scene and several field-stripped cigarettes, which were the same brand as the ones found at the crime scene.

Figure 9.24 Lust murder. Offender had posed the body at the scene to degrade her and engaged in deviant-oriented assault. (Photo courtesy of Detective Mark A. Joseph, Whatcom County, Washington, Sheriff's Office.)

Figure 9.25 Lust murder. The offender had jammed a stick into the victim's vagina. (Photo courtesy of Detective Mark A. Joseph, Whatcom County, Washington, Sheriff's Office.)

Detective Joseph contacted the owner of the truck and landscaping business. The owner stated that the truck was driven exclusively by one of his employees whom he hired from Labor Ready, a temporary labor agency. He identified the driver as James Allen Kinney.

The owner indicated that he had last seen Kinney on October 2 when he came to pick up his check. He told Detective Joseph that when Kinney came to pick up his check, he was with a young woman named Keri. The owner identified a photo of Keri that the detective showed him.

The owner of the landscaping business advised Detective Joseph that Kinney told him he was trying to find Keri a job and that they left his house together at about 10 p.m. He stated that Kinney was taking Keri to see Mt. Baker, where her body was later discovered.

Police retrieved the video surveillance tape from the bank where Kinney cashed his check on October 2. The tape clearly showed Kinney and Keri in the bank together.

Additional witnesses were also located who saw Kinney and Keri eating dinner together in a restaurant near the bank. Police then obtained another video surveillance tape. This tape showed Kinney and Keri together in a local casino from 11:50 p.m. to 1:45 a.m.

SEARCH WARRANT

Kinney had fled the jurisdiction. Investigators believed that he would resort to his usual modus operandi (MO) and head for a major city where he would seek refuge in a homeless shelter or Veteran's Administration hospital. Investigators obtained a search warrant for Kinney's apartment and located a number of informational items that would assist in locating the fugitive. During the search of Kinney's room, a number of adult pornographic magazines were located. Interestingly, in one of the porno magazines, Kinney had hand-drawn some restraints on the legs of the woman who was posing with her legs spread open. The adulterated porno pictures with the hand-drawn restraints were almost exactly like the pose that Keri had been positioned in by Kinney (Figure 9.26). In the opinion of the author, this was very significant in the analysis of the psychosexual motivation of the offender (see Chapter 2, The Investigative Significance of Fantasy in Sex-Related Incidents).

THE SUSPECT

The authorities discovered that Kinney had been a transient since he was discharged from the Army in 1973. He had traveled all over the United States, staying at VA hospitals, clinics, and homeless shelters. He did menial jobs working for temporary employment agencies. Persons who were interviewed stated that Kinney was a pathological liar. Authorities in Dubuque, Iowa, where Kinney had stayed at a mission, were requested to assist the Whatcom County authorities. Captain Mike Sullivan, who had attended my "Practical Homicide Investigation®" training, was able to supply additional intelligence on the subject. Captain Sullivan's detectives secured some personal belongings of the suspect and the only usable photograph of the suspect, who had regularly stayed at a mission in town. Detective Joseph was advised that Kinney used the alias, Jerome Porrevechio, aka "Tugboat." *America's Most Wanted* was enlisted to broadcast this information along with Kinney's photograph and personal information. The authorities realized that Kinney could be anywhere and during the broadcasts persons reported seeing him in various locations.

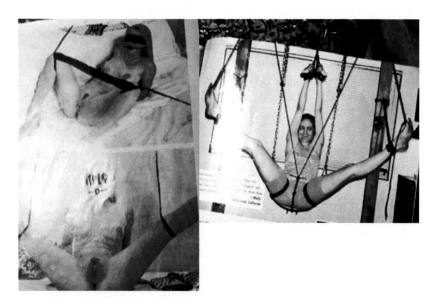

Figure 9.26 Fantasy pornography. The offender had drawn restraints on the female models in his pornography collection that looked very much like the presentation at the crime scene. (Photo courtesy of Detective Mark A. Joseph, Whatcom County, Washington, Sheriff's Office.)

Interviews of persons who knew Kinney described him as a "bull shitter" and a con man. Police also interviewed an ex-girlfriend of the suspect who provided authorities with personal information.

Kinney reportedly told several women that he was heir to the Kinney Shoe fortune. He told others he was on the Board of Directors for The Disney Corporation. Kinney also told women he had attempted to date that he owned several businesses and offered them jobs. These women stated that he was sexually dysfunctional and had trouble maintaining an erection, which made him very angry.

ARREST AND CAPTURE

On March 3, Kinney's story was re-aired on *America's Most Wanted* and two tips immediately came in from listeners that he was in Elizabeth City, North Carolina. He was using the name Julius Goldman and purported to have been a rabbi. He had been staying at a mission and recently moved in with a woman. The FBI didn't arrest Kinney until March 6. When the FBI agents went to the location, they found local police already at the scene maintaining surveillance on Kinney.

At first Kinney denied that he was the fugitive; however, once his fingerprints were matched, he admitted it. On March 6, Detective Mark Joseph and Special Agent Chris McMurray flew to North Carolina where they obtained a full confession.

CONFESSION

Kinney admitted killing Keri. He told Detective Mark Joseph that Keri allegedly offered him drugs as they "made out" in his truck. Kinney showed no remorse as he told his side of the story. Kinney stated, "After she was knocked out, I saw a stick on the ground and rammed it up her vagina." He told the detective that he poured gasoline on her, but didn't remember shaving her pubic hair. Kinney stated, "At that point, she meant nothing to me. She was just another dead drug dealer."

When the authorities questioned him about other murders, he denied being a serial killer. However, he expressed an intense interest in both Bundy and Bianchi. Kinney ended his statement by telling Detective Joseph that he didn't remember killing anyone else because he was on lithium. But if he did remember, he would consider talking to him.

FINAL DISPOSITION

The suspect was allowed to plead to life in prison without the possibility of parole. On January 14, 2002, James Allen Kinney was sentenced to life without parole (From the author's files).

Reconstruction and Opinion

Kinney had apparently approached Keri while she was at the bus stop and engaged her in conversation.

Based on his known MO, he probably lured her with the promise of helping her get a job. She accompanied him to cash his check and was seen in the bank video. Eyewitnesses reported that Kinney and Keri had dinner together.

The video from the local casino showed Kinney and Keri talking and socializing together between 11:50 p.m. and 1:45 a.m. on October 3. In fact, authorities learned that Kinney had introduced Keri as his daughter. This was the last time Keri was seen alive

Kinney and Keri left the casino together at 1:45 a.m. Kinney apparently took Keri in his truck to a remote location and proceeded to engage in sexual activity with her.

This preliminary sexual activity might very well have been consensual on the part of the victim. However, Kinney was known to have sexual dysfunction.

The questions are: "Was he unable to perform?" "Did the victim laugh at him?" The apparent outburst of physical violence and the brutal beating to the face certainly indicated rage and anger. The savage jamming of the stick into the victim's vagina would be consistent with these dynamics. The sexual posing of the body, which resembled the pornography that Kinney had adulterated, was extremely significant. This psychosexual element and the overkill injuries are consistent with lust murder.

Lust Murder: Offender Goes from Organized to Disorganized

CASE FACTS

On November 3, a man and a woman encountered a gunman on the front porch the two shared with their neighbors. The man was shot and killed and his fiancée was left for dead. The woman called 911 after hearing the gunman flee in a vehicle. The police responded and found one male dead and another male seriously injured. Police also discovered the body of a woman inside, who was the wife of the injured male.

Detective Sergeant Dianne Kelso, and Detectives Scott Mummert, Matt Cody, and William Frisby of the Chambersburg Police Department began their investigation of what appeared to be a double homicide and two attempted murders.

Officers found two males lying in front of the residence. The one calling for help was lying on the porch. The other was lying on his back in the front yard. The woman who had called the police advised the 911 operator that her fiancé, named Jim, had been shot

Figure 9.27 Victim at scene. Police arrived to a call of "shot fired, man down." One man was dead at the scene, the other man was transported to the hospital. (Photo courtesy of Detective Scott Mummert, Chambersburg, Pennsylvania, Police Department.)

and that the offender was outside the house. The other injured male was identified as Travis. He had been shot and stabbed and was soaked in blood.

Jim and his fiancée had just returned home from dinner (Figure 9.27). They exited their car and walked toward their porch at #395.

Suddenly the door to #391 opened quickly and a white male pointed a handgun at them. The subject fired toward Jim, who was standing behind his fiancée. She covered her head and fell to the floor. The male then fired a second shot at her. She played dead and held her breath.

POLICE RESPONSE

The responding officers asked the injured Travis where the gun was and who the actor was. He said nothing, but motioned toward Jim. Travis was taken to the local hospital and later flown to another hospital due to his severe injuries.

While being transported, he was questioned as to what had taken place. He said he didn't want to talk about it.

The front door of 391 was standing open and the responding officers observed a large amount of blood on the stairs and walls leading to the second floor. Police did an emergency sweep of the residence for additional victims and/or perpetrators.

Officers entered the master bedroom where there appeared to have been a violent struggle. Officers observed something on the bed covered by a comforter. The comforter was pulled back revealing the nude body of a woman later identified as Christine, who was Travis' wife.

Her body displayed a severe laceration across her chest. Her hands and wrists had been bound and secured to the headboard of the bed with duct tape. Her head and face were wrapped in duct tape covering her eyes and mouth. She was dead.

The reporting witness told the detectives that, when she heard the car drive away, she ran into her house and locked her door as she called 911. While on the phone, she heard pounding on her door and believed that the offender had returned. At that time she believed that the offender was Travis since the man who shot her fiancé and shot at her had come out of Travis' residence. She advised the police that the shooter had driven away in Christine's Jeep Cherokee (Figures 9.28 through 9.30).

PRELIMINARY INVESTIGATION

A trail of blood led from the foyer across the living room and into the kitchen. In the kitchen, the blood pooled in an area beneath an empty wall-mounted phone base. Bloodstains were observed on the linoleum floor in the kitchen as well as the stairs leading up to the master bedroom. Two bullet holes were observed in the living room ceiling, originating from the master bedroom. A bullet hole was observed in the left side of the doorframe of #391 where a bullet had been fired at the reporting witness. There were a number of blood smears on the carpet upstairs in the bedroom and spare bedroom and blood smears on the walls. Preliminary investigation indicated that Christine had been raped, murdered, and sexually mutilated in her home.

Detectives surmised the offender either had a key to the house or was allowed entry into the scene and that Christine knew her attacker. At this point in the case, the logical suspect appeared to be the dead woman's husband, Travis, based on the observations at the crime scene, the statements of the reporting witness, and Travis' initial refusal to discuss what happened.

Figure 9.28 Bedroom. Police entered the house to look for any other victims and/or offenders. There had been a bloody altercation in the bedroom. (Photo courtesy of Detective Scott Mummert, Chambersburg, Pennsylvania, Police Department.)

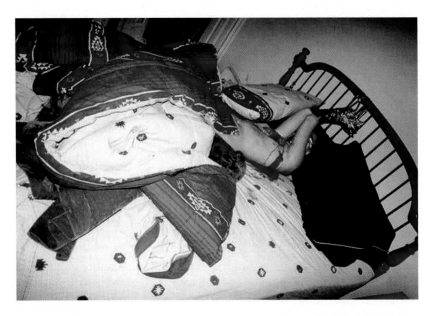

Figure 9.29 Lust murder. The woman was secured to the bed with duct tape and covered with the bed covers. (Photo courtesy of Detective Scott Mummert, Chambersburg, Pennsylvania, Police Department.)

Figure 9.30 Lust murder. The victim had been eviscerated and her hands were tied over her head with duct tape to the bed board. (Photo courtesy of Detective Scott Mummert, Chambersburg, Pennsylvania, Police Department.)

THE CRIME SCENE PROCESS

Due to the complexity of the scene, it was decided to process the event in stages starting from the outside with the first victim and then work into the interior crime scene. The area in front of the two residences and the body of Jim were processed by 2 a.m.

Detectives then moved into the interior of the scene and collected samples from the ground floor and stairway. This process was completed by 8 a.m.

The coroner agreed to allow Christine's body to remain at the scene until detectives gathered all of the evidence from the floor areas leading to her bed.

This is a procedure recommended by "Practical Homicide Investigation®" if the outside and indoor temperature are conducive and will not allow for rapid decomposition. In the Douglas County case, discussed earlier in this chapter, Douglas County detectives followed the same procedure resulting in the retrieval of additional hairs and fibers, which were crucial to linking Jack Owen Spillman to the murders.

SPECIAL PROCEDURE TO FOLLOW IN SPECIFIC CASES

The author recommends that in certain cases the medical examiner/coroner be requested to allow the body to remain at the scene during the crime scene process in order to recover crucial microscopic evidence that would have been lost in the removal or transport of the body. In fact, as part of the seminar series, I have illustrated this procedure to alert investigators to the possibility of utilizing this course of action in specific cases (From the author's files).

The crime scene investigators had recovered a minimag flashlight, rolls of duct tape, and a buck knife that had apparently been brought to the scene. A seminal stain found on the carpet next to the bed and two light bulbs, which had been removed from the ceiling fixture, were deposited on the floor.

The victim had suffered a large laceration to her chest, which extended from the right side across her left breast downward at an angle across her abdomen. She had also received a stab wound to the left side of her chest and multiple stab wounds to the left side of her neck and throat area.

The comforter and bedclothes were collected and processed separately. A bloodstain on the left side of the fitted sheet showed that both sides of a knife blade had been wiped on it. It was at this time that the extent of the duct tape bondage was realized.

There were massive amount of duct tape wrapped around her hands, therefore, the investigators used a reciprocating saw to cut the headboard around Christine's hands so that the wrappings could be brought intact to the autopsy.

INITIAL SUSPECT INFORMATION

The parents of Michael Singley appeared at the crime scene and advised detectives that their son, Michael, who was suffering from depression, might be involved. They advised the detectives that Michael knew that his cousin, Travis, had a gun and the family thought he may have gone to the house to get the gun to commit suicide. It was later determined that Michael had called his fiancée to advise her that he loved her and had implied during that call that she would not see him again. Michael Singley emerged as a viable suspect as additional information became available.

At 1:45 a.m., Sargeant Dianne Kelso located the public phone that Michael had used to call his fiancée. She found bloody fingerprints on the receiver and bloody napkins in a trashcan beside the phone.

The phone and the trashcan were transported to the station house for processing. As officers were preparing to set up surveillance on Singley's residence, they located Christine's Jeep in a field in a construction area about a block away from Singley's home.

DETECTIVES OBTAIN A STATEMENT FROM TRAVIS

On November 4, Travis identified his assailant as his cousin, Michael Singley. He didn't understand why Michael stabbed and shot him. Travis also didn't know that his wife, Christine, was dead. Travis stated that he arrived at his residence and saw his wife's Jeep parked out front. He called his wife's name and there was no answer. He proceeded upstairs where his cousin Michael, who pointed a gun at him, confronted him. Michael ordered him into the bedroom and then told him to lie on the floor. He then began to stab him. Travis, realizing he would be killed, struggled with his cousin, who grabbed the gun and shot him. Michael then fled the residence.

Travis told the detectives that he tried to call for help, but couldn't find the phone. Travis slid down the stairs and went to the kitchen, but that phone was also missing. He got his car keys and was going to drive for help. As he opened the front door, Travis saw a body on the ground and assumed it was Michael. Travis saw that Christine's Jeep was missing and believed that his wife had been able to escape. Travis began to beat on the neighbor's door for assistance and then collapsed on the front porch.

Travis was transported to the local hospital and subsequently transported to another hospital where he was treated for gunshot wounds to his left chest and arm. He also had received stab wounds on his left palm, right cheek, chest, upper right back, and a long laceration from the base of his skull down his back.

HYPOTHESIS

Christine was the obvious focus of this lust murder. She was totally nude and her clothing had been cut from her body. Her hands and wrists were bound with large amounts of duct tape. Duct tape covered her eyes and mouth leaving her nose exposed. Her legs and feet were also bound. The offender knew that his cousin, Travis, would not be home until later that evening.

Michael went to the house with the intent of sexually assaulting his cousin's wife and then staging the scene to make it appear that a stranger had perpetrated the crime. Singley had removed the light bulbs from the ceiling fixture and had covered the body with a comforter prior to Travis returning home. He was in the process of staging the scene for discovery.

SUSPECT ARREST

While detectives were processing the master bedroom at the crime scene, Michael Singley was taken into custody. He was hiding at his house, which was surrounded by tactical officers. Detective Sargeant Kelso had made contact with him by telephone and was negotiating with him to surrender. Shortly before 2 p.m. he surrendered to tactical officers who were outside his residence.

Detective Sergeant Kelso, who was supervising this aspect of the investigation, requested a search warrant, which was executed at about 6 p.m. on November 4. A Smith & Wesson .44 magnum was recovered along with ammunition and the keys for

Christine's Jeep. In addition, notes written by Singley to his family and fiancée requesting they visit him in prison were found. Bloodstained clothing and his sneakers, which matched the sneaker print in the master bedroom, were also seized.

ADDITIONAL EVIDENCE

Singley's Toyota was discovered parked one block away from the murder scene. Detectives secured a search warrant for Singley's car and an additional 20 items of evidence were seized including one roll of duct tape, a buck knife box, an empty Kmart® bag with a receipt dated September 3 at 2:57 p.m. for the purchase of three rolls of duct tape, an empty Walmart bag with receipt dated September 3 at 3:19 p.m. for the purchase of a knife, ammunition, and gloves, along with a ballot stub dated September 3.

SUSPECT'S STATEMENTS

Detective Sergeant Kelso interviewed Singley at the police station during which time he made statements. He believed all four persons were dead and claimed that he was having dreams about hurting people. He stated that he had planned on killing himself after killing Christine and Travis.

Singley refused to discuss what happened to Christine. He only admitted that he killed her and that she was dead prior to Travis returning home. Singley stated that he had purchased the duct tape, knife, and shells for Travis's gun that afternoon. He drove to the area of his cousin's residence and parked. He knew that Travis was in school that evening. He went to the residence and told Christine that his car had broken down and that he needed assistance. Christine allowed him into the house and then went upstairs to change. Singley entered the bedroom while she was changing. He began to struggle with her, knocking her to the floor.

Singley stated that he wrapped duct tape around her arms and legs to secure her and removed the phone from the bedroom. He said he then went down to the kitchen and removed that phone. When he returned to the master bedroom, he discovered that Christine had gotten free and had locked the door. He stated that he kicked in the door and again struggled with her, subduing her, and taping her to the bed. Singley would not discuss anything else involving her.

Singley then described Travis returning home unexpectedly and the ensuing assault during which he suffered a stab wound to the leg. He described the shooting of the neighbors and leaving the scene in Christine's Jeep, which he abandoned. He stated he hid in a shed behind his house until he could get in.

PHYSICAL EXAMINATION OF THE SUSPECT AT THE POLICE STATION

Singley had a fresh cut on his right thigh that he had received while fighting with his cousin Travis. He also had scratches on his fingers from scraping against the bones of Christine's ribs as he sliced her open.

CHARGES

Singley was charged with two counts of criminal homicide and two counts of attempt to commit homicide. He was also charged with rape, criminal trespass, and theft of a motor vehicle.

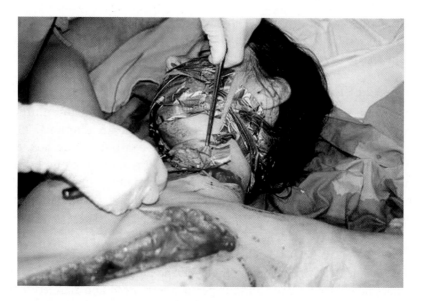

Figure 9.31 Autopsy. The victim's throat was cut and she had suffered numerous stab wounds to her body including a long laceration from her breast to her abdomen. (Photo courtesy of Detective Scott Mummert, Chambersburg, Pennsylvania, Police Department.)

THE AUTOPSY

The victim had multiple stab wounds and had a gaping sharp force injury to her chest and abdomen. The medical examiner ruled the cause of death as multiple stab wounds of the chest and lungs. The stab wounds had penetrated into the heart and lungs. The downward portion of the evisceration wound measured over a foot long and penetrated some six inches. The wound was consistent with a sawing motion. Four postmortem incisions of the neck, facial injuries and hemorrhage of her scalp were also recorded (Figure 9.31).

EVIDENCE

Evidence recovered by the detectives consisted of spermatozoa found on vaginal swabs from Christine, which were matched to Singley. Bloodstains on the clothing collected at Singley's residence matched to Singley and Travis. Bloodstains on the fitted sheet identified as Singley's. Bloodstains collected outside the residence were identified as Travis' and the other man's. Bloodstains collected from the Jeep were matched to Singley. Seminal fluid was matched to Singley. The .44 magnum was identified through ballistics. Singley's fingerprints and palm prints were found on

- Duct tape from Christine's head and face
- Duct tape attached to headboard
- Wall phone from victim's kitchen
- Roll of duct tape from spare bedroom
- Ammo box from Jeep
- Pay phone receiver from Municipal Park
- Light bulb from master bedroom

And Singley's left shoe was matched to a blood print at the crime scene.

SUSPECT MANIPULATIONS

During his interrogation, Singley alluded to the fact that he was depressed and wanted to commit suicide. Lawyers used expert testimony to suggest a psychosis in order to present a diminished capacity tactic. The defense presented that Singley thought that he needed to commit a horrific crime in order to kill himself and that's why he killed Christine and then attacked his cousin, Travis.

However, the overwhelming evidence that investigators gathered linking Singley to the crimes coupled with the statements of witnesses made for a strong case and showed premeditation.

DISPOSITION

The jury in the penalty phase decided Singley was guilty of first degree murder with aggravating circumstances and recommended death. The judge sentenced Singley to death in the killing of Christine and life imprisonment for the murder of the other victim, who was shot as the offender fled from the rape–murder scene.

Reconstruction and Opinion

The murder of Christine was clearly a premeditated lust murder.

- The presentation of the body at the crime scene suggested a fantasy-driven motivation.
- The final binding of her legs after the rape is representative of a bondage fantasy.
- Christine's clothes had been cut from her body, which has as its basis a psychosexual dynamic.
- She was nude.
- She had been rendered helpless.
- She was blindfolded with tape over her eyes and the tape over her mouth so that she couldn't scream or talk.
- Her arms were drawn up over her head and taped to the headboard making her extremely vulnerable (Figure 9.32).

Case Facts

- Singley had planned this event knowing that the husband was in school and that Christine would be alone in the house.
- He purchased the items he needed for his rape kit.
- He purchased ammunition for the gun at the house.
- He parked his car a block away so it wouldn't be seen.
- He purposely stopped taking his medication because it inhibited his normal sexual response.
- He took the phones so no one could call for help.
- This sexual fantasy had been rehearsed in his mind.
- If he really intended to commit suicide, he had plenty of time as he cleaned his wounds and hid at his house trying to avoid apprehension.

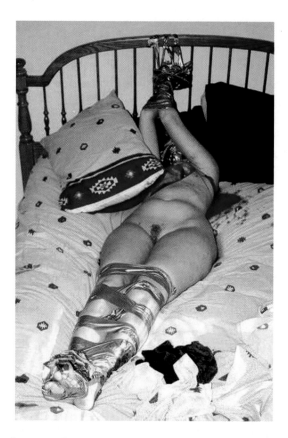

Figure 9.32 Bondage fantasy. The victim's clothes had been cut from her body. The final binding of her legs after the rape was the fantasy component in this event. The presentation of the body at the crime scene was fantasy driven. The offender had bound the young woman's hands over her head and secured them to the headboard to make her vulnerable. The killer had intended that her husband discover the woman's body when he came home. (Photo courtesy of Detective Scott Mummert, Chambersburg, Pennsylvania, Police Department.)

In this particular lust murder, we have an offender who, for all intents and purposes, is organized and has planned a sexual assault based on a sexual fantasy. He had taken precautions to hide his car and brought the items he needed for his rape kit. He had removed the telephones so that they couldn't be used to call for help. He raped his victim and then bound her in a fashion to satisfy his fantasy. He had complete control of the victim and the premises, when suddenly the husband of the victim returned home. At that point, a very organized offender became disorganized as he realized that he was about to be seen and identified. The abundance of evidence that was recovered was a direct result of this disintegration and consistent with disorganized offender dynamics (From the author's files).

Conclusion

Lust murders are primarily heterosexual and intraracial, yet there are recorded instances of homosexual lust murder as well as interracial lust murders.

The offender usually lives or works in close proximity to the crime scene. This type of killer, who acts on the spur of the moment, is obsessed with some sort of perverse fantasy.

In his own mind, he has planned the event. However, when the opportunity presents itself, this type of offender does not have a plan for avoiding detection. He either panics or becomes so involved in the fantasy that he is totally oblivious to the fact that he is leaving evidence behind.

Lust murders can be classified as *organized* or *disorganized* depending on the psychopathology manifested in the crime scene as well as the ability of the offender to repeatedly elude apprehension. The common denominator is sexual sadism, which is a chronic and progressive disorder. Lust murders are carried out in an obsessive manner as the offenders attempt to translate their perverse sexual fantasies into reality by inflicting sadistic sexual violence upon the bodies of their victims.

References

American Psychiatric Association. *Diagnostic and Statistical Manual of Mental Disorders*, (*DSM-IV-TR*), 4th ed., Text revision, APA, Washington, D.C., 2000.

Geberth, V.J. *Practical Homicide Investigation: Tactics, Procedures, and Forensic Techniques*, 3rd ed. CRC Press, Boca Raton, FL, 1996.

Geberth, V.J. Anatomy of lust murder, *Law and Order Magazine*, 46 (5): 98–102, 1998.

Geberth, V.J. *Practical Homicide Investigation: Tactics, Procedures, and Forensic Techniques*, 4th ed., CRC Press, Boca Raton, FL, 2006.

Serial Murder 10

Definition

The definition of serial murder, according to *Practical Homicide Investigation* (Geberth, 2006) is "Two or more separate murders where an individual, acting alone or with another, commits multiple homicides over a period of time, with time breaks between each murder event" (pp. 475, 971).

Most individuals who strictly research homicides have never actually investigated a homicide. Obviously the basis for their classifications is found in their research models and not on the practical aspects of criminal investigation and the dynamics involved in an operational setting.

As a homicide investigator you should focus on the similarities of cases as you develop a hypothesis. If you have a second victim killed in a similar fashion with a modus operandi (MO) and signature that is consistent with the other case, then you must think of the possibility of a serial killer.

According to the Federal Bureau of Investigation (FBI), "Serial murder is the killing of three or more separate victims with emotional time breaks between the killings" (Ressler et al., 1988). These breaks or "cooling off" periods range from days to weeks or months between victims.

I concur with the emotional time breaks between the killings and the "cooling off" periods in their definition. I do take issue with waiting around for the third incident before some "expert" decides whether or not it is a serial murder case.

In my professional opinion as an expert in homicide investigation, one of the most complete studies and research into the serial killer can be found in *Sexual Homicide: Patterns and Motives* (Ressler et al., 1988).

In addition, Geberth and Turco, a forensic psychiatrist, conducted a comprehensive study of the psychopathology of serial killers in the United States (Geberth and Turco, 1997).

The FBI changed their definition of serial murder in 2005 to the "Practical Homicide Investigation®" model, now in its fourth edition. The Serial Murder Symposium Working Group, which met in Quantico, Virginia, in 2005, published their findings in a government publication entitled, *Serial Murder: Multi-Disciplinary Perspectives for Investigators*. The FBI Behavioral Analysis Unit now defines serial murder as: "The unlawful killing of two or more persons by the same offender(s) in separate events" (U.S. Department of Justice, 2005).

Introduction

There has been a great deal of public interest generated about the phenomenon of serial murder, and a number of books and articles have been published on the subject. There have been television documentaries as well as major Hollywood movies, such as *Silence of the*

Lambs, Hannibal, and *Red Dragon,* as well as real serial murder cases presented on A&E and the Discovery channel.

In the case of the psychopathic killer who is a serial murderer, I would suggest, based on my own personal experience and research into these types of offenders, that they kill because they like to kill. Psychopathy is a personality disorder manifested in people who use a mixture of charm, manipulation, intimidation, and occasionally violence to control others, in order to satisfy their own selfish needs (see Chapter 15, Psychopathic Sexual Sadism: A Clinical Study).

Interpersonal traits include glibness, superficial charm, a grandiose sense of self-worth, pathological lying, and the manipulation of others. The affective traits include a lack of remorse or guilt, shallow affect, a lack of empathy, and failure to accept responsibility. The lifestyle behaviors include stimulation-seeking behavior, impulsivity, irresponsibility, parasitic orientation, and a lack of realistic life goals. The relationship between psychopathy and serial murder has been well documented. Psychopaths who commit serial murder do not value human life and are extremely callous in their interactions with their victims. This is particularly evident in sexually motivated serial killers who repeatedly target, stalk, assault, and kill without a sense of remorse.

According to Ressler et al. (1988), "These men have conscious, detailed plans for murder. Often these plans are improved upon with each successive killing; each new experience gives the offender insight into his next murder."

Serial killers have been described as intelligent, charismatic, streetwise, charming, and generally good looking. They are mobile individuals capable of traveling any number of miles in search of the "right" victim. I analyzed one case in which the killer cruised a local strip for three hours and put over 120 miles on his van while searching for a victim. In another case that I have reviewed, the offender drove hundreds of miles as he cruised looking for victims in an area away from his home, which he referred to as his "hunting grounds." Serial killers often target a certain type of victim. They are attempting to fulfill a fantasy and within that fantasy there is a specific type of victim. They look for someone who is vulnerable and easy to control. Their victims may be males or females. They may select children, vagrants, prostitutes, etc. If the victim is female, she may resemble other female victims in some aspect (long hair; blond, brunette, or redhead; prostitute; coed; nurse; waitress; female executive; etc.).

Serial murder, for the most part, involves strangers with no visible relationship between the offender and the victim, which is frustrating to the police who usually focus on the relationships closest to the murder victim. In serial murder cases, the detective needs to focus on the killer's motivations to narrow the investigative focus.

Homosexual Serial Killers

Serial killers can be heterosexual or homosexual. Homosexual serial murders involve sadomasochistic torture, lust murders, thrill killings, and child killings as well as robbery–homicides, which are homosexually oriented. Homosexual serial killers have most frequently chosen young boys or gay men as their victims.

Homosexual serial killers can be loosely divided into three groups:

1. The homosexual serial killer, who exclusively targets other male homosexual victims
2. The homosexual-oriented serial killer, who attacks heterosexual and homosexual victims
3. The male pedophile homosexual serial killer, who attacks young males and boys (Geberth, 2006)

The homosexual serial killer poses a unique problem for law enforcement in that he functions within a subculture of a subculture. Cruising or tricking by male homosexuals, who hang out at gay bars, gay baths, restrooms, bus stations, amusement parks, truck stops, and other kinds of public places looking for casual sex, represents a high-risk victim group. Serial killers who "work" these locations can operate anonymously among their victims. The impersonal nature of cruising where participants meet to engage in sexual acts with complete strangers affords the clever serial murderer a number of killing fields of opportunity.

It should be noted, however, that these three categories presented by the author are not mutually exclusive due to victim opportunity and victim availability. For instance, John Wayne Gacy and Wayne Williams, who were basically homosexual male pedophiles, sexually assaulted and killed children and young adult males who were heterosexuals as well as homosexuals. Jeffrey Dahmer, solicited homosexual young men, but he also was charged with the death of a heterosexual male as well.

For a more in-depth discussion of homosexual homicide including homosexual serial murder, see Geberth (2006), Chapter 15.

The Serial Killer Profile

The original FBI theory that serial killers were white males in their late 20s to early 40s has proved to be wrong. Practically speaking, known serial killers are heterosexual, homosexual, and bisexual. Most serial killers are men (95%). Female serial killers are extremely rare and most women, who have been charged with serial murder, usually are in partnership with a male. A few examples of male/female serial killing couples are Charles Starkweather and Carrill Ann Fugate, Alvin and Judith Neelley, Alton Coleman and Denise Brown, Douglas Clark and Carol Bundy, Paul Bernardo and his wife Karla, Gerald Gallego and his wife Charlene, and David Parker Ray and his wife Cindy Hendy, as well as his daughter, Glenda, who are the subject of Chapter 12 in this book.

Serial killers can be white, black, Hispanic, Asian, or Native American. In fact, serial killers can be from any ethnic grouping. Serial killers can come from all races, cultures, nationalities, educational levels, economic levels, genders, and sexual orientations. Statistically speaking, serial murderers in the United States are predominantly white. However, there has been an increase in black male serial killers, most of whom have a history of rape or other sexual assault, who kill to prevent identification.

In fact, there have been a number of serial murder cases involving black males who have targeted prostitutes within the inner city, such as in New York, Detroit, Chicago, St.

Louis, Atlanta, Baton Rouge, and New Orleans. In fact, the author has a listing in files of 72 black serial killers who were responsible for the sex-related murders of 574 victims.

Serial killers may or may not have superior intelligence; however, most are street-wise. This is what enables them to function very effectively and repeatedly avoid apprehension. Serial killers are methodical and cunning. They plan and research their crimes and display a complete indifference to others because they are self-centered and thrive on self-gratification, whether it is sexual gratification or to fulfill a fantasy. In some instances, the murders are to express control. In other instances, the murders are for the pleasure of possessing the power of life and death over another person.

The author was the first person to publicly use the metaphor of the great white shark to describe the serial killer in a *PrimeTime Life* presentation of "Serial Murder" on June 13, 1991.

The serial killer travels through society just like a great white shark swims through the ocean. The shark is a predator and a 24/7 killing machine. The psyche of a serial killer is also 24/7 and, like a great white shark, he is constantly on the prowl for a victim. The reporter, Dianne Sawyer, asked the author to provide a description of a serial killer. I answered, "You go to an aquarium and you look at a shark swimming around that shark pool, look at that bastard's eyes. That's a serial killer. A 24-hour-a-day killing machine."

I used the metaphor of the shark and the dark eyes to indicate that the shark's eyes were devoid of feeling. Persons who have survived a serial killer have often described the eyes of the offender as hollow, dark, or black. Apparently, the behavioral science crowd liked the metaphor so much that they adopted it as their own. I later received a call from the producer of *PrimeTime*, who told me that the network had received a complaint from some sort of animal rights groups that objected to the author referring to the shark as a bastard when I pointed out the significance of the predator's eyes.

In a June 21, 2009, AP report, there was an article entitled, "Great white sharks hunt just like Hannibal Lector" (Borenstein, 2009). The article described the similarities of great white shark attacks to serial killers. According to the report, "They don't attack at random, but stalk specific victims, lurking out of sight. The sharks hang back and observe from a not-too-close, not-too-far base, hunt strategically, and learn from previous attempts, according to a study being published online Monday in the *Journal of Zoology*. Researchers used a serial killer profiling method to figure out just how the fearsome ocean predator hunts." According to Kim Rossmo, a professor of criminal justice at Texas State University-San Marcos, "The great whites and serial killers have the same objective, which is to find a target or prey or victim … they have to lurk. They want to be efficient in their search" (Borenstein, 2009).

Serial killers are extremely manipulative. Often, they are able to talk their victims into what has been described as their "comfort zone." This is a location where they feel comfortable and safe and can control the victim. Many times they use a ruse to gain access to a potential victim. They have posed as appliance repairmen, utility workers, or someone in need of help.

Ted Bundy used a cast on his arm. John Wayne Gacy offered young men jobs in his construction business. David Alan Gore, Freddie Waterfield, Jr., and Michael Ross, as well as others, offered hitchhikers a ride. In the case of Christopher Wilder, he posed as a talent scout and offered modeling assignments. Kenneth Bianchi and Angelo Bouno, as well as others, have posed as police officers, etc. The serial killers continually perfect their ruse and seem to have an uncanny knack at recognizing potential victims. They are quickly able to gain the victim's confidence with their verbal skills.

Many serial killers have a fascination for police procedure. Some have even worked as police officers, reserve officers, or security guards using their experience to avoid detection. Some have been known to frequent police hangouts and eavesdrop on police conversations during a case. They may even interject themselves into the investigation or offer to assist authorities in some manner, which will give them an opportunity to monitor the investigation.

In some instances, serial killers have gone back to the crime scene or location where the body was discovered either to assess the police investigation or to taunt police with additional clues. I remember one case where the killer complained that the police had discovered the body sooner than he had anticipated. He was upset because he hadn't had time to make sure he hadn't left any evidence behind.

The serial killer, despite his outward facade, is a very insecure individual. He is powerless unless he is in control. This is reflected in his personal life and in his behavior. He is at his "peak" when he has a victim under his control. Serial killers enjoy the publicity of their crimes for the same reason. It's all about power and control.

The FBI Highway Serial Killer Initiative

The FBI launched the Highway Serial Killer (HSK) initiative to track slayings and suspect truckers after local law enforcement requested assistance on similar cases where unidentified or out-of-state victims' bodies had been found discarded at locations near interstates or highways.

Terri Turner, a senior criminal intelligence analyst for the Oklahoma Bureau of Investigation, was working on a string of seven slayings along I-40. She had determined that all of the victims were truck stop prostitutes, whose bodies had been left at roadside locations.

Turner contacted a fellow analyst at VICAP (Violent Crime Apprehension Program), who was able to locate additional roadside victims and, as a result, the HSK project was begun to assist local law enforcement by creating a national crime database on similar cases.

The author interviewed Unit Chief Mike Harrigan, who supervises the program, to obtain information on how local law enforcement can participate in this project. The Unit's number is (800) 634-4097.

Presently, the FBI has identified about a dozen persons of interest, some of whom had been charged on the local level, but, in fact, may be suspects in unsolved or cold case homicides.

The information and timelines can be of value to local law enforcement investigating cases, which may involve highway serial killers. Authorized users have the ability to enter their own case information and retrieve information on other similar cases.

The News Media Influence

Serial killers are likely to follow news events of their crimes very closely and gain satisfaction in the knowledge that they have defeated the police. There is no doubt in my mind that when some police officials issue press releases and make statements to the media about an ongoing serial murder case, they do more harm to the investigation than they realize. The serial killer makes adjustments as he reads about the police investigation. I have a number of cases in my files that demonstrate the damage that is done to the investigation by inappropriate news releases, for example, telling the press where the police will be setting up surveillance or announcing that the police have discovered evidence and what that evidence entails.

Some serial killers communicate with the press. David Berkowitz, "The Son of Sam" serial killer in New York City, communicated with authorities by sending cryptic messages to a major metropolitan newspaper. Another serial killer, who referred to himself as "BTK," sent messages to the press demanding that they acknowledge his killings by affording him a title like other serial murderers. (See Chapter 13, The BTK Investigation.)

In St. Louis, Missouri, a serial killer named Maury Travis was captured after sending a letter to a reporter directing him to the location of his 17th victim. Travis committed suicide in jail before authorities could learn more about him and his activities. However, it was estimated that he was responsible for approximately 20 homicides of black female prostitutes and drug users in Missouri and Illinois.

Students of Serial Murder

My research has indicated that many of these serial killers are aware of police techniques. They are aware of evidence and how the police use evidence, such as DNA, to identify them. I remind the individuals who attend my classes that "We are not the only people watching *Forensic Files*, *The New Detectives*, The Discovery Channel, and all of the other programs devoted to criminal investigation." Today there are more forensic programs available for viewing than ever before: *CSI*, *Law and Order*, *Law and Order Special Victims Unit*, *Criminal Minds*, *NCIS*, *48 Hours*, *First 48*, *Crime Stories*, *Watching the Detectives*, *Criminal Law*, and *Cops*, to name just a few. Perpetrators of crimes will change their modus operandi as they become more familiar with police procedures and more sophisticated in their criminal activities.

Some criminals even read specialized journals to learn about law enforcement techniques. Many of the serial killers within my study followed the police investigation in the newspapers and media. They would adjust their activities and change their modus operandi to thwart the police investigation.

In fact, many of these serial murderers were "students" of serial killings and had read about the activities of other serial murderers in the many popular books detailing these cases (From the author's files). I have cases in which serial killers have replicated the activities of other serial killers in an attempt to enhance and expand on their own psychosexual needs.

Organized Serial Killer Activities

The serial killer engages in purposeful postmortem mutilation of the corpse as opposed to the disorganized offender who engages in sexual or exploratory mutilation. The organized offender will employ mutilation to hinder identification, for shock value, or to allow ease of transport of the body. Remember, both organized and disorganized offenders commit lust murders (see Chapter 9, Lust Murder and Deviant-Oriented Assault).

In one of the New York City serial murders, the offender removed the heads and hands of two prostitutes in order to prevent the identification of the victims. In another case, this same offender removed the breasts of one of his victims and left them on the bed's headboard for police to find. Some serial killers have posed their victims' bodies or left them in an open area.

The serial killer who displays bodies and body parts does so for the shock value. In the Gainesville, Florida, case, in which a serial killer named Danny Rollings terrorized an entire college community, the police were confronted with posed bodies, which had been horribly mutilated. In one particularly grotesque murder scene, Rollings had eviscerated the nude victim and had sliced off both of her nipples. He then decapitated the young woman's head and propped it up on a bookshelf. The first officer who entered the scene would see the head with its eyes closed (Philpin and Donnelly, 1994) (Figure 10.1 and Figure 10.2).

Serial killers may choose to leave the body of their victim for discovery to satisfy some psychological need or go through elaborate detail to assure that the body is never found. Robin Gecht, a serial killer operating in the Chicago area, came up with a unique way of hiding his victim's bodies. He would watch the local cemetery for an excavation in connection with a burial. He and his cohorts would pick up a prostitute and then torture her to death. Gecht would take the body to the local cemetery that night and place it in the new grave. He covered the body with a little dirt. The next day, during the burial, a casket would be placed into the hole on top of the body. He was responsible for approximately 18 murders. Despite the fact that his cohorts turned state's evidence against him, most of the bodies were never found.

Serial killings are considered by a number of experts in the field of psychology and psychiatry to represent the ultimate extension of violence. From a rational standpoint, serial killings are completely senseless acts. However, in the mind of the serial killer, he experiences great pleasure in exerting power and control over his victim including the power of life and death. The sex act is secondary. He is excited by the cruelty of the act and will engage in physical and psychological torture of the victim. He derives his pleasure by watching the victim writhe in pain, as she is humiliated and tortured to death.

Richard Ramirez, dubbed the "Night Stalker," terrorized Southern California during 1984 and 1985. He was responsible for the rape, sodomy, mutilation, and murder of 13 victims. Ramirez perpetrated unspeakable horrors upon his helpless victims, which included women, men, and children.

Figure 10.1 Victim's head on bookshelf. (Illustration courtesy of Medical Legal Art, Illustration © 2002 Medical Legal Art: www.doereport.com.)

Figure 10.2 Victim's head on bookshelf. (Illustration courtesy of Medical Legal Art, Illustration © 2002 Medical Legal Art: www.doereport.com.)

Robin Gecht, who was mentioned earlier, certainly fits the author's description of a psychopathic sexual sadist. He was a serial killer and the ringleader of a gang of like-minded sexual psychopaths, Eddie Spreitzer, and two brothers, Andy and Tommy Kokoraleis. They would target prostitutes. Their victims would be handcuffed and their breasts would be mutilated. Gecht would then have sex through the open wound in the woman's chest and then with the severed breast. Other times, they would insert their penises into the open wounds of their victims, force wine bottles or wooden handles into the women's vaginas, torture and stab their victims in the abdomen as they tortured their helpless victims to death (Fletcher, 1995).

Tommy Kokoraleis, one of Gecht's cohorts, told the police about a bizarre series of rituals that he called ceremonies. Tommy said, "Robin, Eddie, Andy, and he would kneel around a table that Robin had fixed up as an altar in his attic. Robin lit candles and read from the Bible. Each of the men took turns masturbating into the flesh portion of the breast; first Robin, then Eddie, Andy, and Tommy. After they were finished, Robin would cut the breast into pieces and they ate it." Tommy Kokoraleis said that he personally had participated in 10 to 12 of these ceremonies" (Fletcher, 1995).

Kenneth Bianchi and Angelo Bouno (dubbed "The Hillside Strangler" because authorities were not aware that there were two killers) sexually violated and brutally murdered 12 young women between them. They would tape and gag their victims and proceed to torture and sexually abuse them. Bianchi and Bouno experimented with various techniques of torture, such as injecting them with Windex, smothering them with gas from the stove, subjecting them to electrical shock, and then eventually killing them by strangulation when they tired of their perverse and inhuman entertainment (O'Brien, 1985).

The serial killer operates in an emotionally detached manner. It is almost as if he is following a script (see Chapter 12, Sex Slave Torture and Serial Murder Case). The script is usually based on a sadistic fantasy. Police investigations of serial murderers have revealed intricate and precise planning on the part of the serial killer. In some instances, detectives have seized recorded evidence of the offense, such as audio tape recordings of a victim's screams of pain, writings, photos, and even videotape segments of their sadistic activities. The videotapes depicting the atrocities committed by Leonard Lake and Charles Ng in Calaveras County, California, are an example of the depravity of a sadistic serial killer.

Lawrence Bittaker and Roy Norris, however, provide the most graphic example of evil. These two psychopaths, who met in prison, shared a mutual interest in female domination, rape, torture, and murder. They eventually murdered five young women using a combination of methods, which included stabbing them through the ears with an ice pick and strangling them manually and with wire coat hangers, which were tightened around the victim's necks with pliers. They tape recorded two of their torture sessions while they repeatedly raped, sodomized, and tortured the young women (see Chapter 14 for a case history on Bittaker and Norris).

In each of these examples, the conduct displayed by the offenders suggests that the sex act is secondary. Instead, the offender is sexually excited by the cruelty of the acts and engages in physical and psychological torture of the victims. They obtain their gratification through the humiliation and torture of their prey. The murder itself is an expression of power and control. Necrophilia is an extension of their control and sadistic quest for complete and total domination.

Other offenders have used a variety of torture techniques, such as biting, whipping, burning, electrical shock, and forcing the victim to ingest a caustic cleaning fluid.

Many of these serial killers seemingly maintained a respectable life style and engaged in sexual relations with a primary female in their lives. However, they really don't have any type of satisfactory relationship with anyone. They are totally vested in self-gratification to a point where nothing else matters.

Most of the serial killers who were interviewed by the FBI's Behavioral Science Unit or by psychiatrists conducting independent examinations reported that they had been victims of child abuse, usually at the hands of a female parent or parent figure. Many of the offenders were reportedly under the influence of alcohol or marijuana while committing the crime, which tended to exacerbate their sadistic fantasies.

The serial killer tends to increase his killings. It appears that they have to kill more often to maintain an equilibrium. The fantasy and psychic high that they obtain through their conduct induces bold and more frequent attack sometimes with a complete disregard of risk. Consequently, many of the country's most notorious serial killers were caught either by accident or during some independent police action not related to the murder investigation. New York serial killer Joel Rifkin, who was responsible for the murder of 18 young women, most of whom were prostitutes, was apprehended by two alert New York State troopers on routine patrol. They observed Rifkin's vehicle operating without headlights and missing a rear license plate. He attempted to flee. However, when the troopers captured him, they found the rotting corpse of one of his victims in the rear of his truck. This routine vehicle and traffic incident uncovered one of New York's most prolific serial killers.

Disorganized Serial Killer Activities

The disorganized serial killers, who would fit the clinical description of psychotic, are in the minority because they lack the ability and wherewithal to repeatedly escape apprehension.

An excellent example of the disorganized offender is the case of Richard Trenton Chase, which is fully presented in Geberth (1996).

Richard Trenton Chase was known as "The Vampire Killer." Chase, who may have also committed additional homicides, was conclusively linked to the murders of six individuals, five of whom were killed in one week.

His first known victim, a 51-year-old man who had exited his house to retrieve groceries from his car in the driveway, was shot once in the chest with a .22 caliber automatic.

The police were perplexed by this murder, which was apparently random and motiveless and they certainly didn't have any suspects.

His next victim was a 22-year-old housewife. She had been shot and then savagely mutilated. The victim's blouse had been pulled up over her chest, her pants forced down to her ankles, and fecal matter (later determined to be human) had been placed into her mouth.

The killer, using steak knives taken from the kitchen, had opened up the midsection of his victim and removed her intestines. He then stabbed her through her left nipple. He smeared her blood over his own face and licked his fingers. He then smeared the blood along the inner thighs of the victim. In addition, the victim's blood had apparently been scooped out of her body cavity with a paper cup, which had been discarded at the scene.

The investigation into this murder had hardly begun when later that same week, five blocks away, another even more grisly discovery was made.

The dead woman, who was 36 years of age had been shot three times and had been eviscerated. Her 52-year-old boyfriend, who had been visiting, had died of gunshot wounds to the head; the woman's 6-year-old boy had been shot dead. A 22-month-old baby, who the woman was babysitting, was missing from a bloodstained crib.

The investigation indicated that the offender was most probably a psychotic individual who lived or worked in the neighborhood and was committing the crimes and murders on impulse or opportunity. All of the murders, as well as other bizarre incidents, had occurred within a one-mile radius.

When the subject was apprehended at his apartment, the police recovered a number of items of evidence. There was dried blood caked on the suspect's mouth and hands, and additional evidence indicated that he had cooked and eaten his victim's body parts and drunk blood. In the refrigerator was a can containing brain matter. The remaining steak knives, which he had taken from the residence of the first victim, were found in the suspect's apartment.

According to the suspect, the reason for his vampire-like activity and grisly behavior was that flying saucers were drying up his blood through some sort of radiation and that in order to survive he had to replenish his supply. This was a classic disorganized offender (Figure 10.3).

David Berkowitz, the infamous "Son of Sam" murderer is another example of this type of serial killer. Berkowitz terrorized New York City for 13 months. The killings began in July 1976. Berkowitz preferred young women with long dark hair. His victims were usually parked in cars when they were attacked. The police, at first, were baffled by these seemingly unrelated shootings and murders. However, once the ballistics were matched and notes were

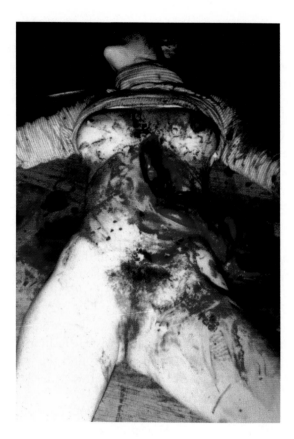

Figure 10.3 Chase victim. This eviscerated body was one of the victims of Richard Trenton Chase, who was known as the "Vampire Killer." He fits the category of a disorganized serial killer. (Photo courtesy of Retired Lieutenant Ray Biondi, Sacramento, California, Sheriff's Department.)

left at the scenes, the authorities knew they had a serial killer on their hands. Berkowitz, who used the name "Son of Sam," was communicating with the press. In these communications, he claimed to be getting messages from his neighbor's dog, which ordered him to kill. By the time Berkowitz was caught, he had killed six victims and wounded seven others.

Albert Fish, who could be clinically diagnosed as psychotic, was a multiple killer, a child molester, and a cannibal. Fish underwent a marked change in personality and fell into a pattern of bizarre behavior after his wife left him for another man. He cultivated an interest in cannibalism and saved news stories about such people as Fritz Haarmann, the "Hanover Vampire."

Fish was also a masochist. He enjoyed the experience of physical pain and often pleaded with his own children to beat him. One of his favorite pastimes was to insert sewing needles into his scrotum, savoring the unbelievable agony. He claimed to have molested hundreds of children. Many children found themselves the victim of unspeakable tortures practiced by this sexual sadist.

Fish was convicted of the murder of a little 10-year-old girl that he lured to a supposed party. Fish strangled the child and then beheaded and dismembered her with a meat cleaver. He then cooked her body parts into a stew seasoned with onions and carrots. Fish then consumed this cannibal meal. Six years later, he wrote the little girl's family a letter explaining what he had done.

Fish was arrested and tried. The jury discounted his insanity plea and sentenced him to death in the electric chair. Fish was executed at Sing Sing in New York in 1936.

Ed Gein, who was the basis for the movie *Psycho* and *The Texas Chainsaw Massacre* was a classic disorganized offender. Gein's mother was a domineering woman who kept a tight emotional rein on both of her sons. She preferred that her boys remain unmarried. To her, women were evil things that trafficked in the sins of the flesh. His mother and brother both died early and Gein was left alone. He withdrew from realty. His mind developed strange fantasies. He became a voracious reader of anatomical texts, and he developed a new interest in women. Then, without explanation, he sealed off all of the farmhouse except for his bedroom and the kitchen. Gein began to pursue a new vocation: grave robbing. Between 1950 and 1954, Gein haunted three local cemeteries, opening an estimated 9 or 10 graves in his nocturnal raids. He might remove whole corpses or settle for choice bits and pieces.

He would exhume the bodies of women buried in the remote areas of graveyards and drag them to his farm. In a shed attached to the main house, Gein would draw and quarter his prized trophies as if they were slaughterhouse cattle. Portions of the quartered corpses often wound up on his dinner table.

At home, he used the ghoulish relics as domestic decorations. Skulls were mounted on the bedposts. Gein used severed skullcaps as bowls. He fashioned hanging mobiles out of noses, lips, and labia, sporting a belt of nipples around the house. Human skin was variously utilized for lamp shades, the construction of waste baskets, and the upholstery of chairs.

Gein had been ambiguous about his masculinity from an early age. He actually considered amputation of his penis on several occasions. The famous transsexual, Christine Jorgenson, was much in the headlines at the time. Gein considered transsexual surgery, but the process was costly and frightening. He obviously thought that there must be a way of "turning female" on a part-time basis.

Gein saved other parts of bodies for his own use to wear at home. He wore a human's scalp and face, and a skinned-out "vest" complete with breasts, and female genitalia, which he strapped above his own organs. Gein would dance in the moonlight dressed as the opposite sex. He amused himself with these macabre adventures for a while and then began to hunt live women.

On December 8, 1954, 51-year-old Mary Hogan disappeared from the tavern she managed. Authorities found a pool of blood on the floor, an overturned chair, and one spent cartridge from a .32-caliber pistol. Foul play was the obvious answer, and although deputies remembered Ed Gein as a suspect in the case, no charges were filed at the time. (Three years later, the shell casing would be matched to a pistol found in Gein's home.)

On November 16, 1957, 58-year-old Bernice Worden disappeared from her Plainfield hardware store under strikingly similar circumstances. There was blood on the floor, a thin trail of it leading out back.

Worden's son recalled that Gein had asked his mother for a date the day before. The deputies went looking for their suspect. What they found would haunt them all for the remainder of their lives. Inside a shed, behind Gein's house, the headless body of Bernice Worden hung from the rafters, gutted like a deer, the genitals carved out along with sundry bits of viscera.

The investigators couldn't believe what they found in the cluttered house. Worden's heart was found in a saucepan. Her head, which had nails inserted into both ears with twine attached had been turned into an ornament. Her other organs were in a box.

Gein readily confessed the Hogan and Worden murders, along with a series of unreported grave robberies. However, there may have been more that the authorities missed. The search of Gein's home turned up two "fresh" vaginas, removed from young women that could not be matched to existing cemetery records. Two women, who had been reported missing, had never been found.

A judge found Gein insane and packed him off to Central State Hospital in Wisconsin. In 1968, Gein was found innocent by reason of insanity and was returned to the State Hospital, where he died in 1984 (Newton, 1990).

A Clinical Perspective

In clinical terminology, a serial killer may be defined as either psychotic or psychopathic depending on the information supplied during the examination and the facts as presented to the clinician. In the experience of the author, serial killers are rarely psychotic. They are more properly defined as *sexual psychopaths* or *psychopathic sexual sadists* depending on the circumstances of the homicide and what was done to the victim. They obviously have a profound personality disorder, but are keenly aware of their own criminality and certainly not out of touch with reality. If serial killers were psychotic, they probably wouldn't be as successful in eluding the police (see Chapter 15, Psychopathic Sexual Sadism: A Clinical Study).

In the case of the *psychotic killer,* one could propose that he kills because his psychosis drives him to kill. An example of this type of serial killer was Joseph Kallinger, whose exploits were detailed in *The Shoemaker* (Schreiber, 1983). Kallinger reportedly was acting under orders from God to kill his victims. Kallinger's hallucinations had God commanding him to "destroy mankind" and to "kill three billion people." According to Schreiber (1983), Kallinger could not obtain an erection without the thoughts and images of mutilation of sexual organs. From an early age, Kallinger associated sex with violence and fantasized about cutting the sexual organs of both males and females. Kallinger eventually involved his 12-year-old son Michael, who enthusiastically agreed to help his father in this bizarre mission.

Serial killers display aggressive and antisocial behaviors during their childhood, which escalate and take on elements of sexual sadism in adulthood. There is also a style and pattern to their killings that involve domination, control, humiliation, and sadistic sexual violence. Their murders are committed without the least sense of guilt or shame, and the killers display a total lack of remorse. The victims are chosen at random and the murders carried out in almost an obsessive manner. The behaviors of these subjects can appropriately be described as *psychopathic sexual sadism* (Geberth, 1995, 1997).

In any event, it is not the purpose of this chapter to present psychiatric information or engage in an in-depth psychological analysis of the serial murderer. Instead, I present this information from an investigative perspective with clinical references for the purpose of analyzing the sex-related murder investigation.

Investigative Considerations

Most serial offenders are sexually motivated and, therefore, may have prior arrests for sex-related incidents or burglary in their backgrounds. Investigators should have access to all criminal records as well as parole information and registered sex offender files. These types of offenses do not occur in a vacuum. Many times, the actual murders have been preceded by some other sex-related incident, such as a voyeurism complaint or a fetish burglary.

In addition, any reports of a missing person, especially those involving women or children, have to be investigated with an eye toward the possibility that the missing person was the victim of a sexual offender. In many serial murder cases, the offender has been able to effectively avoid apprehension by burying or hiding the body from discovery. Rex Krebs, Michael Ross, Leslie Allen Williams, David Alan Gore, and Freddie Waterfield, Jr. are examples of this type of serial killer.

Another way that serial killer cases come to the attention of the authorities is when a victim escapes from the killer during an abduction, escapes from captivity, or is left for dead by an offender. In the Robert Yates case, one of the victims was able to get out of his van and run for help. In the David Parker Ray case, the captive was able to escape from the house (see Chapter 12). In the Robin Gecht case, one of the prostitutes, who had been tortured and had her breasts cut off, was left for dead in an alleyway. She survived by some miracle and lived to testify against her attackers.

The most common serial killer encountered by law enforcement is the offender who targets prostitutes. In the investigation of prostitute murders, I recommend that investigators conduct thorough interviews of the associates of the victim as well as other prostitutes "working" the area. Many times, the killer will have had occasion to use the services of other prostitutes and may even have attempted to kill one of them, who was able to escape. The reality of the world of the prostitute is that it is a dangerous occupation. Many of the prostitutes are drug users and, therefore, dependent on this life style. The average prostitute is not going to make a police report because some "john" assaulted her or was acting "weird." The nature of the business is that these girls talk to one another about the "johns" that they meet and which ones they try to avoid. Many times during a serial murder investigation, investigators are surprised to learn some of the lurid details and the bizarre activities that "johns" require from the prostitutes. The interviews reveal what some of these women endure day-to-day as they provide their services.

It has been my experience that most prostitute serial murder cases are solved through a combination of interviews of prostitutes about their customers coupled with an undercover "sting" operation during which time the police are able to identify the population of "johns."

I recommend that the police saturate the area where the prostitute victim was "working." In addition to the interviews of the prostitutes and the undercover operations, the police can also do routine vehicle stops for the purpose of identifying potential suspects.

The Green River Killings, which began in 1982 and abruptly ended in 1984, involved some 49 victims. The women, some of whom had histories of prostitution, started disappearing in 1982. The police had formed a task force. Suspects were identified and eliminated or put on hold pending further developments. The case began to wind down in the 1990s and it looked like the murders would remain unsolved. During the investigation, the police developed a suspect named Gary Ridgeway. Witnesses who were interviewed reportedly saw him with two of the victims prior to their deaths. The police also ascertained that he had been arrested in 1982 on a "prostitution sting" after he approached a female undercover officer and asked for sex. In 1984, a prostitute reported Ridgeway after she became uneasy about the way he approached her for sex. In 1987, the police took hair and buccal cell samples from the suspect. The evidence that the police had acquired was at best circumstantial. However, in 2001, DNA technology had advanced to new levels. The buccal cells taken from Ridgeway in 1987 were submitted to the state laboratory.

On November 30, 2001, 52-year-old Gary Ridgeway was arrested for the murders of four of the Green River victims: Opal Charmaine Mills, 16; Marcia Faye Chapman, 31; Cynthia Jean Hinds, 17; and Carol Christensen, 21. The authorities were able to match Ridgeway's DNA to three of the victims. The fourth victim was matched through circumstantial evidence (see Chapter 6, DNA Application of DNA Technology).

Case History: The Spokane Serial Killer

CASE FACTS

Robert Lee Yates, Jr., who became known as "The Spokane Serial Killer," was responsible for the murders of 18 women. The killings, which began in 1990 had the authorities believing that they had another Green River Killer operating within the Spokane, Washington, area.

The police were quick to match the killings. The similarities of the victims' deaths, the fact that a small caliber gun was used, and the fact that all were engaged in prostitution left little doubt in the investigators' minds that they were dealing with a serial killer. However, there were no suspects. Two years passed without any additional victims being found that could be attributed to the Spokane serial killer. In May 1992, a nude female body was found. The victim had a history of prostitution and the cause of death was determined to have been gunshot wounds.

More than three years passed before the next victim attributed to the Spokane serial killer was found. Her body was found on August 25, 1995. Although, she wasn't a prostitute, she was a street person and had been shot with a small caliber gun. This killing was linked to the elusive "Spokane Killer."

On Friday, June 14, 1996, another prostitute's body was discovered. Like all the others, she had been shot to death. Tuesday, August 26, 1997, two more bodies were discovered. The first body found that day was that of a 20-year-old known prostitute. She had been killed by gunshot. In another location, a member of the Spokane serial murder task force investigated the discovery of the body of a 16-year-old Asian female, who was subsequently identified as Jennifer, a prostitute. This time the police recovered a used condom.

A prostitute witness told police that she last saw Jennifer traveling eastbound in the company of a white male, approximately 30 to 40 years old, in a car believed to have been a white Corvette.

SUSPECT EMERGES

As part of the investigation, detectives and undercover officers were frequenting those areas where prostitutes were known to work. A police officer on routine patrol made the first contact with Robert L. Yates, Jr., 45. Yates was driving a 1977 white Corvette with Washington license plates. The police officer stopped him for a minor traffic infraction at 12:45 p.m. on Wednesday, September 24, 1997. However, the connection between Yates' Corvette and the murder of Jennifer was not noted immediately because the patrolman had mistakenly written in his report that Yates had been driving a Camaro. Yet, this contact would prove to be of importance.

The killings continued with five more bodies being discovered before the end of the year. Once again, each of the victims had been shot to death and all were known prostitutes.

On Sunday, February 28, 1998, the body a known prostitute and drug user was discovered. She had died of gunshot wounds and three plastic bags had been placed over her head. On Wednesday, April 1, 1998, the body of 34-year-old known prostitute was discovered under similar circumstances. On Tuesday, July 7, 1998, a white female body identified as a 47-year-old prostitute was recovered. Cause of death was gunshot wounds.

On Tuesday, October 13, 1998, the Pierce County Sheriff's Department found a badly decomposed body, which had three plastic bags placed over the head. The body was identified as a 35-year-old prostitute named Connie. Because of the ongoing investigations of murdered prostitutes in several counties that were obviously linked to the Spokane serial killer, who was clearly traveling across the state to carry out his murders, Pierce County detectives promptly notified the Spokane cops of their discovery. The discovery of Connie's body brought the official body count attributed to the Spokane serial killer to 17. There were likely many others that were not yet found or linked to the elusive killer.

ROBERT YATES

On Tuesday, November 10, 1998, the Spokane serial killer task force operatives were out in numbers as they had been for some time. It had been less than a month since Connie's body had been found on the other side of the state. Based on the killer's prior activities, the cops knew that it would be only a matter of time before he struck again.

It was 1:25 a.m. when Spokane officers observed a man driving a silver 1985 Honda Civic, Washington license plate identification 918AJH, pull over and pick up known prostitute Jennifer Robinson on the corner of First and Crestline, another area of Spokane well known to be frequented by working prostitutes. The officer identified the driver of the Honda Civic as Robert L. Yates, Jr., and his encounter that evening would be the second time his name came up during the task force investigation.

When Yates was confronted by the police officer, he told the officer that he had been instructed by Jennifer Robinson's father to drive to the area, find his daughter, and bring her home. With Robinson acknowledging that she knew Yates, there was little that the officer could do. Unable to hold either one of them, the officer took a field report of the incident, which made its way to the task force. Robinson probably didn't realize it at the time, but she was one of the lucky ones because the officer's intervention and ability to identify Yates precluded him from killing her.

POLICE REPORT

As the investigation into the prostitute murders continued into 1999, task force detectives became aware of a report that had been filed on August 1, 1998. According to the report, 30-year-old Christine L. Smith had been the victim of an assault and robbery while working as a prostitute on East Sprague. According to what Smith told the police, she had been picked up by a "date" near E. 124 Short Street driving a 1970s model black van with orange coloring on the passenger side exterior. She described the van as having dark brown vinyl seats, with a wood framed bed with a mattress in the back. She described the driver as a white man, approximately 50 years old, about 5'10" tall, 175 pounds, with a medium build.

After negotiating a price for her services, she told her "date" to drive to a parking lot behind a clinic on E. 400 Fifth Street. While enroute to the location, the "date" told her that he was a helicopter pilot with the National Guard. Smith said that she asked the man if he was the "psycho killer," and he had responded that he was not. He told her that he had five kids and would not do something like that.

After arriving in the parking lot, the man paid her $40 for oral sex. They went to the rear of the van and got onto the raised mattress, where the man pulled down his pants and she performed oral sex on him for approximately 5 to 7 minutes. During the entire time, she said, his penis did not become erect. At one point after the 5 to 7 minute period, the man hit her over the head with something, but she wasn't sure what he hit with. The blow caused her to nearly lose consciousness. She fell backward and struggled to keep her senses intact. The man told her to return his money to him, and she struggled to find a door handle to the sliding side door. She made her way to the front and out of the van. Fleeing for her life, Smith made it to a hospital where she received three stitches to close a 1/2" long wound above and behind her left ear. After leaving the hospital, she contacted the police.

SUSPECT YATES

The investigation began to take on momentum as the task force detectives became more convinced that Yates was their man. He fit the general identification of the suspect who had attacked Smith, including age and appearance, right down to the pockmarked face; he drove a white Corvette and a Honda Civic; and, they learned, he was a member of the Washington National Guard and served in the capacity of a helicopter pilot.

In addition, they had the two police contacts of Yates while he was in the company of a known prostitute and in the vicinity of the locations from where the women had been taken.

On Wednesday, September 15, 1999, task force detectives met Robert Yates at the Public Safety Building. When Yates showed up, detectives greeted him in the lobby. They immediately noted that he had light brown hair and observed that he was sweating profusely. After being taken into an interrogation room, the detectives advised him that his name had surfaced in connection with the serial murder investigation. They told him that he was not being considered a suspect at that point, that he did not have to answer any questions, and that he was free to leave at any time. Yates acknowledged that he understood.

Yates was first questioned about the contact he had made with the woman and the police on November 10, 1998, and he basically repeated the same story that he had told the police officer that stopped him. The detectives bluntly confronted Yates by telling him that they didn't believe his story.

Next they asked him about any contact he may have had with prostitutes. He said that he had not been involved with any other prostitutes in Spokane, but admitted that he had hired prostitutes in Germany several years earlier while serving in the military.

Yates was then asked if he would voluntarily provide a sample of his blood to the detectives to help eliminate him as a suspect. He stated that he wanted to discuss the issue with his wife first and would call them with his decision. He then left the building, but called back later to say that he would not be providing the requested blood sample.

EVIDENCE

The police eventually obtained a warrant for Yates' blood for DNA testing. However, in the interim, they had put together a compelling case against Robert Yates. They had recovered fibers from his vehicles, which were matched to some of the victims. The police located blood in his van, and blood in his Corvette, that he had sold. This blood was matched through DNA to the victim named Jennifer. In addition, a latent fingerprint, which had been developed from a plastic bag found on the head of a victim was matched to Robert L. Yates. The police also located a spent Magtech .25 bullet casing, the same brand and caliber of ammunition used in some of the murders.

THE ARREST

On Tuesday, April 18, 2000, Robert L. Yates, Jr. was arrested for the murder of Jennifer. A search warrant executed at the time of his arrest enabled authorities to obtain blood samples from Yates, and a subsequent DNA analysis was found to match the DNA profiles of sperm samples taken from eight of his victims.

There was another murder that Yates was suspected of committing. A 43-year-old known drug addict named "Melody" was last seen on May 20, 1998. Yates was a prime suspect in her disappearance and murder because she matched the profiles of the other victims. However, there was no body and no evidence that linked Yates to Melody. That would soon change.

On Monday, October 16, 2000, faced with the insurmountable evidence against him and the almost certainty of receiving the death penalty if convicted of the charges against him, Yates, through his attorneys, announced that he was ready to strike a deal.

In exchange for receiving life in prison, Yates said that he was willing to plead guilty to 13 counts of first degree murder and one count of attempted first degree murder, but would not plead guilty to the charges facing him in Pierce County. He also said that he would lead the cops to Melody's body. Yates sketched out a map of the yard of his home. The detectives found Melody's remains buried about eight inches below the surface in a bark-covered flowerbed near what used to be Yates' bedroom window.

DISPOSITION

Yates pled guilty to 13 of the murders that the task force had been investigating. He was then sentenced to 408 years in prison for one of the worst murder sprees in U.S. history. In 2002 Yates was convicted and sentenced to death in Pierce County for the murders of two other women. A judge had ruled that evidence used to link Yates to the multiple slayings in Spokane would be admissible in his Pierce County trial (King, 2000).

Case History: The Bi-State Strangler Investigation (Maury Travis)

CASE FACTS

Maury Travis, a 36-year-old black male, was a serial killer from the St. Louis area who was killing victims in both in Missouri and Illinois. He was suspected in a series of killings of at least 11 women from the St. Louis area and an additional number in Illinois. All of his victims were black females, most of whom were drug addicts or prostitutes.

Their bodies had been dumped along roadways on both sides of the Mississippi River. Some of the victims had been strangled and bound with rope. St. Louis Homicide Detective Roy Douglas, who had been in my "Practical Homicide Investigation®" classes and had my textbook, was kind enough to tell me that the detectives and agents had used my text and the information they had received from my classes to investigate this serial murder case.

The investigators, who conducted this inquiry, are proud of their work and what they learned during the course of their investigation: what tactics, procedures, and forensic techniques were applicable and what could have been done to make their case more effective. This is what the St. Louis Police Department's Homicide Section and the Illinois State Police want to share with others in the law enforcement community.

THE INVESTIGATION

On July 31, 2000, the body of an unidentified black female was discovered at 20th and Piggott in East St. Louis. She was last seen alive the previous day. The case remained unsolved until a series of killings began on March 24, 2001. Trooper C. Jones and Special Agent Jim Peterson of the Illinois State Police were assigned to investigate a decomposed body off Highway 64. The body was subsequently identified and authorities learned the victim had a criminal history in Illinois and Missouri for drug use and prostitution (Figure 10.4).

On March 24, 2001, Illinois State Police were directed to Interstate Highway 64 to investigate a homicide involving a black female dumped alongside the roadway. The nude body was identified as a young woman with prostitution arrests in Missouri and Illinois (Figure 10.5).

On April 1, 2001, Special Agent James Walker, Illinois State Police, was assigned to investigate a dumped body of an unknown female. This victim also had a history of prostitution and was known to frequent the prostitution-prone North Broadway stroll area in the city of St. Louis (Figure 10.6 and Figure 10.7).

On April 4, 2001, another prostitute, who survived an attack was found nude in an area of East St. Louis in Illinois. She was unable to assist in the investigation due to her mental state and the trauma she suffered during the attack. However, Special Agent Walker learned that she too had frequented the North Broadway stroll area in the City of St. Louis.

Special Agent Walker contacted the St. Louis Homicide Section and advised them of the facts of his investigation. Homicide Detective Roy Douglas was assigned to assist.

On May 15, 2001, St. Charles County had a homicide involving a nude black female, who was subsequently identified as a known prostitute from the North Broadway (Baden neighborhood) stroll area in the City of St. Louis.

On May 30, 2001, City of St. Louis Homicide was assigned to investigate a nude female body in a rear alley within the City of St. Louis. A visual inspection of the body revealed apparent evidence of bondage. Investigators also observed what appeared to be tire impressions on her legs. Apparently, the killer had driven over the body when he dumped it at this isolated location. Once again, the victim was identified as a known prostitute who frequented the North Broadway (Baden) stroll area in the City of St. Louis (Figure 10.8 and Figure 10.9).

Figure 10.4 Dumped body. The unidentified body was dumped in East St. Louis, Illinois, in July 2000. This case was possibly the first in the series and subsequently linked to a serial killer from the St. Louis, Missouri, area. (Photo courtesy of Detective Roy Douglas, homicide section, St. Louis, Missouri, Police Department.)

Figure 10.5 Dumped body (Illinois State Police case Highway 64). This victim was subsequently identified as a prostitute and drug user with arrests in both Illinois and Missouri. (Photo courtesy of Detective Roy Douglas, homicide section, St. Louis, Missouri, Police Department.)

Figure 10.6 Dumped body case (Illinois State Police). This case had similarities to the highway case. (Photo courtesy of Detective Roy Douglas, homicide section, St. Louis, Missouri, Police Department.)

Figure 10.7 Tire mark evidence. Investigators obtained tire mark impressions at the scene of the dumpsite. (Photo courtesy of Detective Roy Douglas, homicide section, St. Louis, Missouri, Police Department.)

Figure 10.8 St. Louis victim. This victim's nude body was dumped at a location within St. Louis. There was evidence of sexual assault and binding. (Photo courtesy of Detective Roy Douglas, homicide section, St. Louis, Missouri, Police Department.)

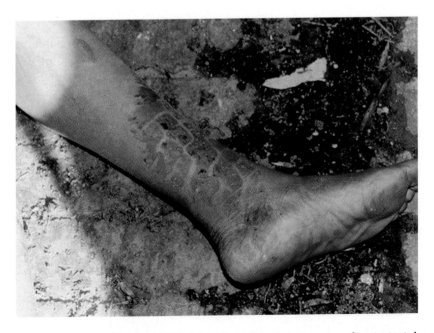

Figure 10.9 Tire mark evidence on body. The offender had driven over the victim's leg and left an excellent tire imprint, which was later matched to the suspect's vehicle. (Photo courtesy of Detective Roy Douglas, homicide section, St. Louis, Missouri, Police Department.)

Figure 10.10 Decomposed body. In St. Charles County, another black female's nude body was found dumped along a highway. This case was linked to the other cases. (Photo courtesy of Detective Roy Douglas, homicide section, St. Louis, Missouri, Police Department.)

On June 13, 2001, The St. Charles Sheriff's Office was called to Missouri State Highway 367 to investigate a decomposed body found along the highway. This victim also turned out to be a known prostitute from Illinois, who was known to frequent the North Broadway (Baden) stroll area in St. Louis (Figure 10.10).

THE LINKAGE

In July 2001, Special Agent Walker, Detective Roy Douglas, and Crime Analyst Aaron Kustermann of the Illinois State Police convened a meeting of investigators from Illinois State Police, City of St. Louis Homicide, St. Charles County Sheriff's Office, and East St. Louis, Illinois.

At the meeting, the facts of each incident were compared, which revealed several similarities in the victims: their profession, their habits, the location where they applied their trade, the way the bodies were disposed of, the location where the bodies were left, and evidence of bondage and torture.

It was decided that one individual was responsible for the aforementioned incidents and that he was placing the bodies in the various jurisdictions in an attempt to confuse the investigators.

At this point, it was determined that a multijurisdiction investigative team, consisting of Illinois State Police; East St. Louis Illinois Police; St. Charles County Sheriffs Office; St. Louis Police Homicide Section; Alton, Illinois, Police; and the Jennings, Missouri, Police Department should be established. It was agreed that Aaron Kustermann, crime analyst, would establish and coordinate the monthly meetings starting in September 2001.

(This procedure is recommended in *Practical Homicide Investigation*, Geberth, 2006. In any case, where there are multiple investigators working in a multijurisdictional setting there is a need for one person to be designated as coordinator. The task force should be housed under one roof with all of the information coming into on location and distributed among each and every member so that everyone is one the same page.)

On August 25, 2001, East St. Louis had another nude black female body. This body bore evidence of ligature marks around the wrists and blunt trauma. The victim was subsequently identified as an East St. Louis prostitute with an arrest record in St. Louis and known to frequent the North Broadway (Baden) stroll area in St. Louis. This case was added to the multijurisdiction investigative team task force.

THE BI-STATE STRANGLER INVESTIGATION

In September, the multijurisdiction investigative team had their first official meeting. Each agency presented the facts of its cases including the scene investigation, the victim's information, arrests, and life style, habits, associates, and family members.

All of the evidence that had been recovered at each and every scene was cataloged, referencing exactly what evidence had been recovered from each of the victims, i.e., semen, hairs, fibers, residue of any materials.

A request was made for an update on all of this evidence. The information request included a determination of what stage the processing of the evidence was at or when it was expected to be completed. This included any results of the evidence that had been completed.

It was determined the detectives should continue to narrow the time frame from when the victims were last seen to when they were discovered. It was decided to try to cross-check and interview associates, friends, possible customers, to find out where the victims purchased their drugs, and what locations the victims frequented more often than others.

In addition, the members were asked to identify and locate any possible suspects, conduct record checks, and locate and interview associates about if they use the services of prostitutes, drug use. The investigators would attempt to secure buccal swabs for DNA comparison from the individuals by written consent and each agency would submit the buccal swabs to its respective labs.

It was agreed to review any incidents that may have occurred previously in the stroll areas for each jurisdiction. This would include a review of sex crime incidents and any suspects who were arrested. The task force was instructed to contact the patrol officers for the stroll areas, advise them of the investigation, and keep them updated and informed. Patrol would be asked to assist the task force in locating any individuals who needed to be interviewed. Furthermore, investigators were advised to solicit any information the patrol officers might have relative to prostitution activity. This would include any assaults that may have occurred where a potential customer of a prostitute may have assaulted her.

A case management system was established and, as each lead/interview was completed, it would be forwarded to Aaron Kustermann who would place the information on a compact disc (CD). Copies of the CDs would then be supplied to each of the investigating agencies.

On October 8, 2001, East St. Louis Police and Special Agent Walker were directed to 15th Street and Converse Avenue in East St. Louis, Illinois, to investigate the partially nude body of a black female found lying along the roadway. Special Agent Walker observed that the victim was nude from her head to her ankles with a pair of jeans around her ankles. The body evidenced ligature marks around the wrists and the ankles; however, no other evidence of blunt trauma was observed. The victim, who had an arrest history in both Illinois and St. Louis for prostitution and drug use, was identified. Once again, it was determined that she would also frequent the North Broadway (Baden) stroll area in St. Louis.

The bi-state strangler investigation continued its efforts from October through January 2002.

On January 31, 2002, Illinois State Police were dispatched to an area off Interstate 64 after a highway crew discovered skeletal remains. Although the body was not identifiable, the medical examiner ruled that the remains were that of a black female. This case was also added to the investigation.

On March 11, 2002, a second set of skeletal remains was uncovered by highway workers. Once again the identity could not be determined. However, the medical examiner determined that the remains were that of a black female in her 30s or 40s. This case was also added to the task force investigation.

On March 28, 2002, highway workers discovered the skeletal remains in a creek along Illinois State Route 3. The medical examiner determined that the victim was a black female between 28 and 45 years of age. The medical examiner estimated that the victim had been dead six months to one year. This case was also added to the task force investigation.

It should be noted that as each skeletal remains was recovered, artist Joe Siefferman, Forensic Science Laboratory, Illinois State Police, Charleston, Illinois, prepared a facial reconstruction of each of the victims. Copies of the drawings were packaged as evidence. This is an excellent procedure, which is also recommended in *Practical Homicide Investigation* (Geberth, 1996).

In April 2002, Captain Harry Hagger, Commander, Crimes Against Persons Division, St. Louis Police Department, determined that two detectives should be assigned to the bi-state strangler investigation on a full-time basis. He detached Detectives Jocelyn Mercier, Central Patrol Detective Bureau, and Brian Van Nest, North Patrol Detective Bureau, to the homicide section. Detectives Mercier and Van Nest were updated on the status of the investigation and supplied copies of all materials that had been written up to that point.

On May 8, 2002, Metro East Forensic Science Laboratory advised that they had a DNA match on two of the homicides and that the profiles from the spermatozoa recovered were, in fact, from the same individual.

At the conclusion of the monthly meeting, it was determined that FBI Special Agent Jimenez would contact the FBI National Center for the Analysis of Violent Crime (NCAVC) and advise them of the investigation. She spoke with Supervisory Special Agent Robert Morton and requested assistance in determining a possible profile for the suspect. Morton advised that he needed additional information about the investigation. He was informed that St. Louis Homicide would contact him.

May 24, 2002, the police caught a "break" in the case when an anonymous letter was sent to a reporter at the *St. Louis Post-Dispatch*. At approximately 7 p.m., Illinois State Police, received a phone call from William (Bill) Smith, reporter for the *Post-Dispatch*. He said that he had received a letter in the mail from an unknown individual who wrote that he liked his story the week prior about one of the homicide victims named Teresa. The letter requested the reporter to write another story about a victim. The anonymous person wrote, *Dear Bill, nice sob story about Teresa Wilson. Write one about (writer names victim) write a good one, and I'll tell you where many others are to prove im [sic] real here's directions to number seventeen search in a fifty yard radius from the "X," put the story in Sunday paper like the last.*

The reporter also advised the police that there was a computer-generated map enclosed along with the letter. Smith said the envelope was addressed to him at the *Post-Dispatch* with a return address of I Thralldom 325/331 Lafayette St., New York, NY 10012. The reporter stated that the stamp was upside down and the postmark was dated May 21 (Figure 10.11 and Figure 10.12).

The *Post-Dispatch* withheld a number of details pending the police investigation. The return address on the envelope included the words, "I Thralldom," which referred to slavery or enslavement. The *Post-Dispatch* informed the investigators of a possibly related Web site that shows graphic pictures of partially dressed and nude women in chains and assorted torture devices. The site is located at www.thralldom.org.

The map directed detectives to Highway 67 and St. Charles St. Detectives responded to the location indicated on the map along with the St. Charles County Evidence Unit. On May 25, 2002, the investigators immediately located a human skull just south of the location indicated on the map. A further search of the area to the south of where the skull was located revealed the rest of the remains with the exception of the hands and feet bones. The remains were void of any tissue and had apparently been there for an extended period of time. The medical examiner advised the authorities that the remains were that of a black female approximately 30 to 40 years of age, approximate

Figure 10.11 Envelope. This was the envelope containing the letter to the reporter. (Photo courtesy of Detective Roy Douglas, homicide section, St. Louis, Missouri, Police Department.)

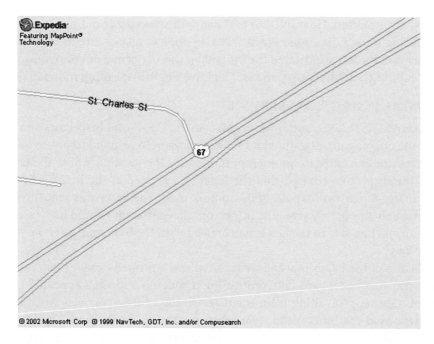

Expedia
Featuring MapPoint©
Technology

St Charles St

67

© 2002 Microsoft Corp © 1999 NavTech, GDT, Inc. and/or Compusearch

Figure 10.12 Download. This was the map downloaded by the serial killer that led to his arrest. (Photo courtesy of Detective Roy Douglas, homicide section, St. Louis, Missouri, Police Department.)

height 5'4" to 5'8" and weight 130 to 140 pounds. This case was added to the task force investigation.

The letter, envelope, and map were conveyed to the homicide section where they were processed for fingerprints and any DNA. This proved to be negative. FBI Profiler Morton was contacted and supplied with the information.

FBI PROFILE STRATEGY

Special Agent Morton recommended compliance with the demand of a follow-up article. The FBI agent recommended that the *Post-Dispatch* reporter, Bill Smith, be replaced as contact person in the eye of the suspect, with a law enforcement official. Morton indicated that this strategy had worked in other incidents, thus eliminating any risk to persons outside law enforcement and giving more control of the evidence and leads to the investigating agencies.

The proposed strategy called for the substitute contact person to attempt a direct dialog between the letter writer and law enforcement. The strategy called for a telephone contact, local address, and e-mail address to be published in the newspaper and given to electronic media in addition to a short compliance or teaser article to be written in the newspaper.

ANALYSIS OF LETTER

FBI Agent Morton stated the return address on the envelope (I Thalltron) indicated the individual who wrote the letter was informing the world that he held the victims and controlled them. He kept them for bondage at his pleasure. The return address was used to spark attention. He wanted to make sure the newspaper did not just ignore the letter. Placing the stamp upside down was also done to attract attention. In addition, the contents of the letter indicated the individual was of normal or above normal intelligence, cunning, and deceptive, and was a native English-speaking individual.

U.S. POSTAL INSPECTIONS SERVICE

On Monday, May 27, 2002, authorities contacted the U.S. Postal Inspectors and advised them of the ongoing investigation and requested them to respond to police headquarters to examine the letter in an attempt to identify the location where the letter was mailed. The inspectors advised that the letter had arrived at the main post office at approximately 8 p.m. on May 22, 2002, in bulk mail. The letter was sent through the bar coding machine at 8:27 p.m. The inspectors stated that they could not trace the letter back any farther due to the fact it had arrived with the bulk mail after 3 p.m. of the business day.

On the top of the paper that the writer used was a printed design that consisted of a floral array that had a yard rake protruding through it and what appeared to be the handle of a shovel protruding from the rear. On top of the array was what appeared to be a straw hat that one would wear while gardening. Investigators had contacted to various print shops, office supply stores, specialty shops, paper manufacturers, and lawn and garden shops in an attempt to identify the manufacturer of the paper or the organization who used the logo.

TRACING THE COMPUTER-GENERATED MAP

On May 29, 2002, the FBI conducted a detailed search of Internet mapping Web sites and found an exact match of features displayed on the map sent to the reporter. The mapping company was determined to be Expedia. On May 30, 2002, Expedia.com informed authorities that all records of access to the map Web site could be tracked through Microsoft, Inc. The FBI obtained a Grand Jury subpoena directing Microsoft, Inc. to present all data, graphic files, log files, user account information, and session information associated with this file from May 18 through May 21, 2002.

On June 3, 2002, Microsoft, Inc., provided the FBI with a computerized spreadsheet showing that only one person accessed the Expedia.com mapping Web site and searched the area of West Alton, Missouri. Analysis of the spreadsheet by the FBI revealed that the person using the Internet Protocol (IP) address ####### was the only person who accessed Expedia.com on the evening of May 20, 2002, and mapped the area of West Alton, Missouri. Further analysis showed that the person who used IP ######### zoomed in on the map of West Alton, Missouri, area approximately 10 times in a chronological order to end with the exact match of the map printed on the second piece of paper enclosed in the envelope that was sent to the *Post-Dispatch*.

On June 4, 2002, UUNet Technologies, Inc. provided the FBI with the name of the user with the IP address of ###### on the evening of May 20, 2002. The user was MSN/maurytravis. The account information revealed the subscriber to be Maury Travis at 1001 Ford Drive, Ferguson, Missouri, home telephone number 314-000-0000.

SUSPECT BACKGROUND

Maury Travis had an extensive record and was on probation for various felonies. A photo was obtained from the department files. Further processing Maury Travis through the Department of Revenue for the State of Missouri revealed that he had a driver's license, which was issued to the Ford address. The Department of Revenue also indicated that the suspect had a 2000 Mitsubishi Eclipse registered to him.

Interestingly, Travis's mother resided in Alton, Illinois, and three of the bodies were located in West Alton, Missouri. Further investigation revealed that Travis' father, Michael, maintained an apartment in close proximity to where the body of another victim was located. The father's house in East St. Louis, Illinois, was also in close proximity to where the bodies of two other victims were discovered.

THE APPREHENSION

On June 4, 2002, Captain Hegger directed a 24-hour surveillance be established on Maury Travis due to the nature of the incidents (homicides) while affidavits in support of a search warrant were being prepared.

In the early morning hours of June 6, 2002, Detectives conducting surveillance on Travis observed him to carry a bag of trash out of his residence and place it at the curb. Later that morning, the detectives observed a Midwest Waste trash vehicle. Following "Practical Homicide Investigation®" tactics, they stopped the vehicle and advised the driver of their investigation. The detectives informed the driver they needed the trash from 1001 Ford as evidence. Detectives cleared an area in the rear of the truck and Detective Van Nest entered the cab area of the truck.

The sanitation driver continued his duties and when he collected the trash from 1001 Ford, he placed it in the cleaned area of the truck and later relinquished it to Detective Van Nest. Detective Van Nest retained custody of the bag of trash and later relinquished it to Detective Douglas and Special Agent Walker who conveyed it to the homicide office. At the homicide office, the trash bag was opened and the contents were examined, photographed, and placed in an evidence bag. Later, it was conveyed to the department laboratory for further examination.

On Friday morning, June 7, 2002, at 6 a.m., St. Louis homicide detectives accompanied with FBI agents and an FBI Evidence Recovery Team (ERT) went to the suspect's house in Ferguson, Missouri. They had a search warrant for the house and wanted to question Travis in connection with this series of killings.

Special Agent James Walker, Illinois State Police, and Detective Douglas approached the front of the residence. Detectives Mercier and Van Nest responded to the rear of the residence. The officers knocked on the front door and announced, "Police, Search Warrant." At this time, someone inside the residence looked out the window. The individual was advised to open the front door and he complied. Authorities entered the residence and asked the black male subject who opened the door if he was Maury Travis and he said he was. He was secured and advised that the officers had a search warrant for his residence.

Special Agent Morton and Sergeant Sachs advised Travis that he was not under arrest and was free to leave if he so desired. Travis wanted to know why the detectives were serving a search warrant on his residence and he agreed to be interviewed. Travis was told the reason for the search warrant had to do with a letter sent to the *St. Louis Post-Dispatch* newspaper regarding an article written about a murder victim. When Travis was told the search was related to the acquisition of the map using the Internet. He refused to comment any further.

He never admitted anything, but he didn't deny anything either. He seemed more interested in how the police caught on to him. When they told him he had a problem and that they knew he had downloaded the map that was sent to the reporter, he cursed the computer and the Internet. Travis was arrested and brought to the police station.

A PSYCHOLOGICAL INTERROGATION TECHNIQUE

An excellent strategy to utilize in an interrogation setting is to convince the offender that the police have a good case against him prior to beginning the interview. *Practical Homicide Investigation* (Geberth, 2006) recommends that you prop the room and "set the stage" for the interrogation by providing the subject with the opportunity to get an eyeful of the amount of work and effort that has gone into "his case."

The authorities in St. Louis placed all of the charts, graphs, crime scene photos, photos of the victims, and files in interview room #2 as if the detectives had been working in the room around the clock as they hunted for this serial killer.

When the detectives brought Maury Travis to the police station, they were directed to an interview room area. Travis was purposely directed into interview room #2 so that he could see the enormity of the investigation on which the detectives were working. After a few seconds, Travis was informed that they were in the wrong room as if a major error had occurred in letting him see the "operations room." Travis was then placed in another interview room. Although, Travis didn't confess to the murders, this tactic certainly resulted in some interesting *res getae* comments that Travis made during the day he was with the investigators, such as, "I got fucked by the computer," "I'm toast," and "What do I tell my mother?" Travis also told Detective Douglas, "You guys are going to bury me or lock me up forever, aren't you." He was informed that it was a possibility.

THE SEARCH

St. Louis police forensic teams seized numerous items from the suspect's home. They seized his computer, ligatures, ropes, belts spattered with what appeared to be blood, women's underwear and wigs, and videotapes. Investigators believed that Travis held several of his victim's captive in the basement of his home before killing them.

He was charged with two federal counts of kidnapping pending the state charges of homicide. The federal complaint also listed six women who were tortured and then strangled. Semen was recovered from the bodies of two other victims. There were indications that as many as 20 victims in the St. Louis area, many bound with ropes or handcuffs, might be linked to Travis (Figure 10.13 and Figure 10.14).

However, before the police could even begin to investigate the extent of Travis's crimes, something happened. Travis was found dead Monday night, June 10, in his cell at St. Louis County Jail. Travis had hung himself in an apparent suicide. He left a suicide note. In the lower right hand corner of the letter, Travis wrote the following: "To whom it may concern; please give this to my mother; it's also proof that you guys didn't kill me."

THE EVIDENCE

The authorities had retrieved numerous items of evidence including materials that were later matched to the suspect through DNA analysis. The suspect's automobile tires matched the tire imprint impressions from an East St. Louis crime scene. The tread

Figure 10.13 Travis' house. He brought his victims here where he tortured and killed them before dumping their bodies in various jurisdictions. (Photo courtesy of Detective Roy Douglas, homicide section, St. Louis, Missouri, Police Department.)

Figure 10.14 Downstairs area. This was where most of the victims were killed. Police located a hidden compartment in this area where the "wedding tape" had been secreted. The authorities also recovered numerous items of women's clothing and undergarments, along with porno tapes and S&M paraphernalia. (Photo courtesy of Detective Roy Douglas, homicide section, St. Louis, Missouri, Police Department.)

design pattern of the B.F. Goodrich tires on his other auto matched the design pattern on the left leg of another victim.

Travis had gathered materials and plans for constructing a torture chamber in his basement. He had written out explicit instructions for dealing with his captives. He marked off locations where he could pick up victims as well as locations for disposal.

The suspect's computers were seized pursuant to the search warrant. The forensic examination of the computer hard drive revealed further evidence inculpating Travis in these series of murders.

Travis had an extensive collection of written materials, which dealt with bondage and sexual slavery. He had also made plans to build a concrete block cell in his basement. While conducting the search of the basement, the detectives located a secret wall. Upon checking behind the wall, they located a VHS tape, which investigators dubbed, "the wedding tape," along with an 8 mm porno videotape. Ten other videotapes were also seized, which contained various sexual acts; however, there was no bondage or physical abuse on the tapes.

"The wedding tape" provided the most compelling evidence. Travis had recorded his sexual assaults and tortures on the VHS tape using the wedding footage as a cover. The actual wedding lasted approximately 1 hour and 26 minutes. The remainder of the tape contained video showing Travis torturing and killing a young woman. The tape then continued with various video clips, which depicted Travis torturing a series of victims, who were subsequently identified as homicide victims Travis had dumped in Illinois and Missouri (Douglas, personal interview, 2002).

ACKNOWLEDGMENTS

The author wishes to acknowledge the contribution of the above information and materials from this particular case from the following members of the St. Louis Homicide Section, St. Louis, Missouri, Police Department: Captain Harry Hegger, Detective Roy Douglas, Detective Jocelyn Mercier, Detective Brian Van Nest and the Illinois State Police: Special Agent James Walker and Crime Analyst Aaron Kusterman.

Case History: David Alan Gore and Freddie Waterfield, Jr.— A Killing Team

---

CASE FACTS

David Alan Gore and Freddie Waterfield, Jr., were two psychopathic sexual sadists, who enjoyed hunting and stalking human prey and sadistically murdering their victims.

The suspects, who were cousins, lived in Indian River County (Florida) their entire lives and had a number of relatives living and working in the area. Many of their relatives worked in the citrus business. Gore worked as a day foreman in the orange groves. He knew the area well since he had to drive into various groves to check on the workers and report any problems. Gore also worked as a part-time sheriff's deputy on night patrol in Indian River County.

The line was that Freddie Waterfield was the "brains" behind the activity. Waterfield would play the good guy and Gore the bad guy or enforcer. However, I believe that Gore was an extremely vicious sadist, who was very seriously underestimated with his 275 pound frame and his stereotypical Southern "redneck" demeanor.

STALKERS

The suspects hunted their victims like prey. Their sadistic game involved abduction, rape, torture, and eventually death to cover their tracks. They mutilated and dismembered their victim's bodies, which they dumped in alligator-infested canals or buried in the extensive acreage of Florida's citrus country. Gore, who knew the orchards, handled the disposal. Waterfield's ugly temper and taste for violent sex perfectly meshed with Gore's sexual sadism. Gore and Waterfield also worked the areas around Orlando and Daytona cruising for potential victims. There were two verified incidents involving prostitutes.

OFFICIAL RECORD

The suspects were officially charged with the rape and murder as well as abduction of six women. They also were charged with attempted murder for the victim who survived capture.

THE REALITY

The cousins are actually suspected in many more killings that will probably remain unsolved due to the manner in which they disposed of their victims. They only confessed to what the authorities could prove. Gore bragged in a letter that he had killed 32.

MODUS OPERANDI (MO)

The suspects would disable an unsuspecting women's vehicle, wait for her to return to the car, and then pretend to be good Samaritans. They also cruised A1A picking up hitchhikers as "prey." In addition, Gore would cruise around in his reserve officer's uniform looking for potential victims. In one incident, Gore, who had disabled a young woman's car, was waiting for her to return. When he pulled up to offer help, the woman recognized him as a part-time officer in the adjoining jurisdiction. Gore, backed off.

RECORDED ATTEMPTS OF ABDUCTION

The suspects had followed a young woman, who was traveling alone, out to a rural area. As they were driving, they shot out the tires of the young woman's car. They stopped to offer help and then suddenly threw her into their car. She jumped from their car and ran into the highway. A passing motorist rescued the victim. Later, they followed another woman from Vero Beach to Miami, but gave up the pursuit when she parked on a busy street. Their first successful rape took place near Vero Beach, and while the victim notified police, she later dropped the charges to avoid embarrassment in court.

MURDER VICTIMS NO. 1 AND 2

While prowling the groves, Gore spotted a 17-year-old girl disembarking from a school bus. He had watched the young girl for a few days to get her routine down, plotting a way to capture her. He flashed his badge and convinced her to get into his truck. He then drove her home. Gore didn't know that the girl's mother had just arrived from Taiwan and was home. He told the mother and the daughter that he was with the Sheriff's Department. But, the mother became suspicious of his motives. He then pulled out his gun and handcuffed the two women together. Gore told them they were under arrest. He then forced them into his truck and drove out to the groves to meet Waterfield. While waiting for Waterfield, he decided to sexually assault the young girl. He had her handcuffed to the mother, who began to yell and scream to leave her daughter alone.

Gore took out his gun and shot the mother in the head. He then continued on with the rape of the young girl, who was forced to lie there with her dead mother cuffed to her.

When Waterfield arrived, Gore had already removed the handcuffed mother from her daughter. The young girl was sexually assaulted again and tortured by both offenders before being shot and killed. The two cousins then dismembered the two bodies. Gore removed one of the young girl's breasts and took it with him. The body parts were placed in large drums and buried the next day in the groves with a backhoe by Gore. Waterfield took the victim's clothes and disposed of them. The husband and father of the victims reported his wife and daughter missing. A missing person's case was opened. Their bodies were not recovered until the suspects gave each other up as they attempted to manipulate the court system.

MURDER VICTIM NO. 3

Gore was stalking the beach area when he spotted the 35-year-old victim sunbathing by herself on the beach. He went into the parking lot where he disabled her vehicle and waited. When the woman came back to her car, Gore appeared and offered to help.

He feigned trying to start the woman's car. He then offered her a ride. When he got her in his truck, he drove to another rural area, pulled his gun, and threatened to shoot her. Gore handcuffed her hands behind her back. He then took her to his mobile home, which he called his "lair." He kept her there all weekend where she was horribly tortured and sexually assaulted. He removed her breasts and then threw her body parts in a canal for the alligators.

GORE DISMISSED FROM THE SHERIFF'S PATROL

Gore, who had been under suspicion in connection with complaints from female motorists, was dismissed from the sheriff's patrol after a local man reported that a deputy had stopped his teenage daughter on a rural highway and attempted to hold her "for questioning." Gore was dismissed from the department.

Gore was then arrested a few days later when officers found him crouched in the back seat of a woman's car outside a Vero Beach clinic. Gore was armed with a pistol, handcuffs, and a police radio scanner. He had planned on abducting her.

He was convicted of armed trespass, and was sentenced to a five-year prison sentence. However, he was out of jail within two years.

THE KILLINGS RESUME: MURDER VICTIMS NO. 4 AND 5

As soon as Gore got out of prison, he and Waterfield resumed the hunt, this time preying on hitchhikers. They abducted two 14-year-olds. Both girls were sexually assaulted and raped in their van.

When they finished torturing and "playing" with the two young girls, Gore drove the bound girls to the grove. Gore used the groves as a dumpsite. He shot both of them in the head, and then he decapitated one of the girls.

VICTIM NO. 6 AND ATTEMPTED MURDER

Gore and Waterfield were stalking the beach area when they spotted two teenage girls hitchhiking along A1A. Lynn, 17, and Robin, 14, had been thumbing a ride when the cousins pulled up and offered to take the girls out to the sand dunes to show them how the truck performed. They offered the girls a beer and then asked them if they wanted to smoke pot. At first the girls thought they were nice guys until Gore suddenly pulled a gun and pointed it at them.

Gore said to Waterfield, "Let's take these two home and have fun with them." Lynn started screaming and Robin was crying. Waterfield was "playing" the good guy and told the two frightened girls to "just do what he says." Gore told them, "Shut up or I'll kill you." He ordered them to put their heads between their legs and their arms behind them. He handcuffed them together.

Waterfield drove the truck out to the groves to Gore's place because Gore's family was away for the weekend. The house was hidden from the road by a long driveway. They knew that no one would be at the house. While they were driving, Waterfield's sister spotted them and he panicked. He helped bring the girls into Gore's house and then told Gore that he would be back after he went to the shop in case his sister or mother showed up. Gore had Robin's hands cuffed behind her back. He had tightly tied Lynn with rope, which cut into her wrists. He then cut off the girl's bathing suits (Figure 10.15).

Gore spent the next hour going back and forth between the frightened girls brutally and repeatedly molesting them and threatening to kill them. He viciously shoved his penis down Robin's throat until she thought she would suffocate.

While Gore was forcing oral sex on Robin and preparing to rape her, Lynn kicked loose from the ropes and with her arms still tied behind her back she ran nude from the house. Gore heard her making an escape and grabbed his .22-caliber gun. He chased after her and fired a shot.

Lynn fell down and was yelling for help. A 14-year-old boy saw the nude girl being chased by a nude man and watched as the nude man grabbed her by the arm and dragged her several feet. She was still yelling. Gore shot her two times and ran back

Figure 10.15 Victim's cut clothing. The offender had sadistically cut the girl's bathing suits from their bound bodies. (Photo courtesy of Lieutenant Andy Bradley, Indian River County, Florida, Sheriff's Department.)

to the house and got the keys to his mom's car and drove down to get Lynn's body. He opened the trunk, picked up her body, and tossed her into the trunk (Figure 10.16 and Figure 10.17). She was still breathing.

Gore raced the car back to the carport and ran inside to see if the witness called the police. He listened to a police scanner and then called to report that a man with a gun had run through his yard.

Figure 10.16 Victim's body in trunk. Gore had jammed the girl's body into the trunk to hide her. Note the bindings. (Photo courtesy of Lieutenant Andy Bradley, Indian River County, Florida, Sheriff's Department.)

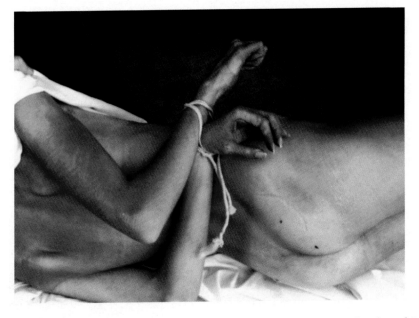

Figure 10.17 Victim's bound hands. This was Gore's signature. He wanted to keep his victims helpless during the sexual assaults. (Photo courtesy of Lieutenant Andy Bradley, Indian River County, Florida, Sheriff's Department.)

Indian River deputies were dispatched to the Gore residence as a result of the 14-year-old witness's report. When Gore also called to make his report, deputies in the area who knew his reputation suspected the worse. They had surrounded the house and spotted a car in the garage and saw a pool of blood. Lynn's dead body was discovered in the trunk. She had been shot twice in the head with Gore's .22-caliber pistol, which was recovered in the house.

The police attempted to make contact with Gore, but he wouldn't respond. Finally a female relative was brought to the scene to talk to him and Gore meekly surrendered to police.

Officers entered the house to conduct a sweep and located the hysterical 14-year-old girl screaming from the attic. The officers freed the sobbing, trembling girl and gave her clothing from the closet so she could cover herself. Little 14-year-old Robin turned out to be an excellent witness in the subsequent murder and kidnapping cases. David Alan Gore and Freddie Waterfield, Jr., were arrested by Indian River sheriff's officers and subsequently charged with rape, murder, and abduction of the six murder victims and the attempted murder and abduction of the 14 year old, who was rescued by the police. The trials lasted several years as Gore and Waterfield manipulated the courts with their changing stories of what actually happened and how many were actually killed.

DISPOSITION

David Alan Gore was sentenced to die in the electric chair. The judge ruled that his crimes were especially wicked, evil, atrocious, and cruel. However, he was later granted a stay of execution. Freddie Waterfield was first convicted of manslaughter because of credibility factors raised by Gore's changing testimony. Waterfield ultimately was sentenced to two life imprisonments.

Buried Bodies

The hardest serial murder cases to solve are those involving buried or hidden bodies. In some instances, offenders have preselected burial sites in rural areas. This type of killer frequently disposes of the body of his victims at a secluded location or places it where the body will not be found. This provides him with an opportunity to return to the scene and monitor investigative operations. It also furnishes him with an opportunity to return to the scene to fantasize and relive the event as he savors his trophy.

The next three case histories will describe the dynamics of this type of offender.

Serial Murder Case: Michigan—Leslie Allen Williams: Serial Killer

MISSING PERSONS CASE FACTS: MICHELLE AND MELISSA

The following is from a personal interview with Detective Sergeant Eric Schroeder in July 2002.

On September 30, 1991, troopers from the Michigan State Police in Brighton were dispatched to a residence on Hartland Road in Livingston County on a report of two missing female juveniles. The mother reported that her daughters, Michelle, 16, and Melissa, 14, were missing. They were last seen on September 29 at approximately 4 p.m. when, after eating dinner, they left their residence to go for a walk.

The mother advised the troopers that her daughters had run away from home together in July of 1991 and had been gone for the weekend, then returned home voluntarily. She had contacted the Livingston County Sheriff's Department in response to this earlier incident and filed a runaway report with that department.

The mother told the troopers that, when her daughters had run away in the earlier incident in July, they had packed and taken a their belongings. She was concerned because all they had was the clothing they were wearing when they left the house. In fact, Michelle had even left without taking her purse, driver's license, and money. Furthermore, neither girl had taken a coat. In light of these facts, the mother stated she was particularly worried about her daughters and felt that they may have run into some trouble and been victimized in some way. Detective Sergeant Robert Swackhammer (now retired) was assigned as the lead investigator.

At this point, the responding troopers initiated a missing person's report and entered both girls into LEIN/NCIC (Law Enforcement Information Network/National Crime Information Center) as missing juveniles and began their investigation. No substantial leads surfaced during the investigation and the case remained unsolved until May 24, 1992, when officers from the Oakland County Sheriff's Department arrested Leslie "Les" Allen Williams.

ARREST OF SERIAL MURDER SUSPECT

Les Williams' arrest was a textbook example of how an alert patrol officer can make all the difference in a major case investigation. According to Geberth's (2006) experience, many serial murder cases are resolved by the independent police action on the part of alert patrol officers, which has nothing to do with the actual serial murder investigation.

Williams had abducted a female victim and was transporting her to an Oakland County cemetery where he intended to rape and murder her. A witness happened to be in the cemetery and observed Williams fighting with his victim. The witness approached and asked Williams what he was doing. Williams advised the witness to mind his own business, then added, "Can't you see we're making love." The witness, who realized that something was very wrong, took down the license plate number, left the cemetery, and flagged down an Oakland County Sheriff's Deputy. When the witness advised the deputy of what had just occurred, the deputy immediately went in search of Williams.

The deputy entered the cemetery area and observed Williams attempting to leave the area in his vehicle. When the officer attempted to initiate a traffic stop, Williams raced off and a high-speed chase ensued. During the police pursuit, Williams lost control of his vehicle and crashed into a tree, effectively ending the pursuit. When the officers opened the trunk of Williams' car, they found the victim bound and unconscious, but alive. Williams was lodged in the Oakland County Jail on charges of kidnapping, criminal sexual assault, assault with intent to murder, carrying a concealed weapon, and fleeing from police. At the time of his arrest, Williams, a habitual offender, was on parole for previous charges of kidnapping and sexual assault.

During the subsequent custodial interviews conducted by detectives from the Oakland County Sheriff's Department, Williams made many statements and admissions concerning the incident for which he was currently under arrest.

In addition to these statements, Williams also advised detectives that he was responsible for other kidnappings, sexual assaults, and murders in the local area over the past nine months. These included the kidnap, rape, and murder of Kami Marie, 18 years old, of South Lyon, Michigan, who disappeared on September 19, 1991; Michelle and Melissa, who were kidnapped, raped, and murdered on September 29, 1991; and Cynthia Marie, age 15, of Milford, Michigan, who was kidnapped, raped, and murdered on January 4, 1992.

THE INVESTIGATION

When the detectives from Oakland County ascertained that Williams was involved in the disappearance of the two sisters, they immediately contacted the lead investigator in the case, Detective Sergeant Swackhammer in Brighton. A multiagency investigation was implemented to coordinate the homicides in the various jurisdictions where the four homicides had occurred.

On May 27, 1992, detectives from the Oakland County Sheriff's Department, the Livingston County Sheriff's Department, and the Michigan State Police escorted Williams as he directed investigators to the locations where he had abducted and murdered victims and where he had buried their bodies. While escorting Williams to the different crime scenes, detectives were afforded the opportunity to conduct additional interviews with Williams. During these interviews, Williams very frankly and candidly described how he abducted, raped, and murdered his young female victims.

WILLIAMS' TAPED CONFESSION IN THE MICHELLE AND MELISSA CASE

I had driven the [unintelligible] frequently and I had noticed the [two sisters] girls taking a walk. And they usually walked around a certain area. At some times I'd drive by. They'd be walking in front of the store. Sometimes they'd be back on the dirt road. Sometimes they'd be on the paved road. Access road along the expressway. So I was familiar with the—the semiregular route that they took.

On the day in question, I cannot remember the date. I observed the girls walking by the store and beginning to walk down the dirt road. And I assumed that they were probably going to walk the same path. Same track that they normally did. So I drove up ahead of them and I pulled into the woods up a dirt road. When they walked by, I jumped out with a knife and informed them that this was an armed robbery, to be quiet, to step into the woods with me. Which they did without making a sound.

After they were in the woods about 15 to 20 feet, I had them lay down and I bound their hands with wire ties. I had them both stand up and I walked them back to my car, which was parked about 50 to 60 yards further back. I got them behind the car and I laid out a blanket. Then I attempted to put one of them in the trunk with the intention of having sex with the other one while one was in the trunk so I didn't have to watch them both.

They both assured me that they would not run, but I undid their hands and I had two flex cuffs or whatever you call them. I had two of them left and I put on around each of their ankles to bind their feet. Prior to that—prior to putting it around their feet, I had them strip down. From the waist down so that it would be easy to have sex with them.

Melissa, the younger one—the 14-year-old—tried to convince me to just have sex with her because she was experienced and her older sister Michelle was still a virgin—and that she (Melissa) could do everything that Michelle could do. So she had me lay on my back and she gave me oral sex—in a way kind of instructing her sister how to do this and how to do that. Because at this point I told her that it didn't matter—I was gonna do both of them anyway. But if she wanted to be first, that was fine. After about 5 or 10 minutes of oral sex from Melissa, I had attempted to have intercourse with her, but the twisted ties prevented me from getting between her legs properly without it hurting her ankles. So I cut the ties off and I had intercourse with her.

When I was done, I insisted that I put her in the trunk and she said okay—as long as I didn't close the trunk. So she kind of sat there in the trunk—kneeling in the trunk—looking down on us and then, kind of telling Michelle what to do cause Michelle was then giving me oral sex. After a few minutes and I had achieved another erection and I had intercourse with Michelle. And she was indeed a virgin and, ah, didn't cry or scream. But she was in pain. When that was done, I didn't have anything to tie either one of them up again so I used some type of cloth or what I believe was a piece of chamois that I had used to wash the car. I cut it into strips and then I bound Michelle and—ah—Melissa. Then I picked Michelle up and I took her back about another 40 to 50 feet. I told them that I was going to separate them—or excuse me—before that I have to back up here.

I had some starter fluid and a rag in the car and I told them what I was gonna do was, ah, the starter fluid had ether in it and I was going to place a rag over their face, and it was going to put them to sleep. And when they woke up, I was going to be gone. I handed the rag to Michelle and she just put it over her face and laid face down. Melissa, I held it over her face and it didn't work. She more or less went into a hallucinogenic, ah, shaking and trying to get up. After a few minutes, I realized that it wasn't going to work so I told them I was going to tie them up and then separate them. That way I could take off. I didn't have to worry about getting caught.

I had no intention of letting either one of them go. I wanted to render them immobile with the starter fluid, with the ether, so that I could suffocate them without all the, ah, kind of not wanting to be putting them through a knowing pain as well as the pain it is to suffocate someone. It's an ugly thing.

I took Michelle back further. I came back and Melissa was on her face and I took her t-shirt and a rag and I placed it over her nose and mouth and I laid heavy on her. She was fully dressed then—I let her get dressed. I let them both get dressed before I tied them back up. And I laid on Melissa and I held the rag to her face until she quit moving and I held her for a couple minutes more. Then I went back and did the same thing to Michelle. It was a lot harder to asphyxiate Michelle and I think I may have done some neck twisting and stuff on her cause she didn't pass that easy.

When I was sure that Michelle was no longer living, I went back and I dragged Melissa's body back to Michelle's. I got back in my car and backed it further into the area to make sure no one could see it. Then I went about looking for a place to bury the girls. I went up on the ridge and I tried to dig a hole but the ground was too hard. I went back further into the field and tried to dig a hold, but the root system was also prohibitive from digging.

So I went back down and at that time I pulled the pants off of Michelle one more time and had sex with her. When that was done I put them both in the trunk of my vehicle and put a blanket over the top of them, and I drove to the cemetery in downtown Fenton. And I buried them in the, ah, cemetery.

The following excerpt was William's response when the investigator asked if there was anything else he'd like to add at the end of the interview.

Mention details of conversations that I have had with some of the girls, ah, in respect to their previous sexual experiences or abuse. Melissa was not a virgin, she was 14. She was, ah, more than experienced in oral sex. She was, on a scale of 1 to 10, you could say she was about a 9 ½ or a 10. She was absolutely, ah, a girl of 14 should not act the way that she acted in my opinion. The feeling I got was that a family member or a relative was engaging in some type of sexual activity with her. She was not a virgin. [But] Michelle was definitely a virgin.

It was also interesting to note that at the time of his arrest, detectives found two Polaroid® photos in William's wallet. These photos depicted females with their legs spread and using their own hands to spread their genitalia. Williams had altered these photos. Williams had cut out any facial or identifying features of the subjects so they couldn't be identified. When questioned by detectives as to the origin of these photos, Williams indicated that these were photos of Michelle and Melissa. Williams had taken these photos just prior to him murdering the girls.

Williams was ultimately sentenced to life in prison with no possibility of parole.

(The author provided only the Michigan State Police's case not the local jurisdiction's in this case history.)

Serial Murder Case: San Luis Obispo, California—Rex Krebs: Serial Killer

CASE FACTS: RACHEL NEWHOUSE

The following is from interviews with Assistant Chief Investigator Larry Hobson in July 2002.

Rachel Newhouse, of 2425 Gerda Street, San Luis Obispo, was reported missing by her roommates on November 13, 1998. She was last seen at a fraternity party at the Tortilla Flats Tavern around midnight. Newhouse was a 20-year-old college student from Irvine, California, attending Cal Poly State University in San Luis Obispo.

Investigators found blood and blood droppings on the Osos-Jennifer Street Bridge and a path leading into a parking lot. They believed that the victim had been attacked on the bridge while walking home from the Tortilla Flats Tavern. Investigators suspected that the victim had been abducted from this location because blood and head hair were also found in the parking lot. The San Luis Obispo police formed a task force, which included investigators from the District Attorney's Office, Parole, Probation, Department of Justice, and the FBI.

On December 19, 1998, investigators were advised that blood found on the Osos-Jennifer Street Bridge on November 13 belonged to Rachel Newhouse (Figure 10.18).

From November 13, 1998 to March 12, 1999, the task force investigators continued to follow hundreds of leads established through the computerized Law Enforcement Agency Data System (LEADS) system. During this investigation, all known sex offenders registrants in San Luis Obispo County were being interviewed.

AUNDRIA CRAWFORD

On March 13, 1999, Aundria Crawford of 420-B Branch Street, in San Luis Obispo, California, was reported missing by her mother. Aundria's mother usually spoke with her daughter every day. She hadn't heard from her since March 11. Aundria was a

Figure 10.18 Bridge crossover. Rachel was last seen heading for this bridge. Detectives found the victim's blood on the bridge. They also found her blood and hair in the parking lot and on the walkway. The case was an apparent abduction. (Photo courtesy of Assistant Chief Investigator Larry Hobson, Office of the District Attorney, San Luis Obispo, California.)

20-year-old student from Fresno, California, who was attending Cuesta Community College in San Luis Obispo, California.

Investigators, who responded to her residence, determined that she was abducted from her duplex apartment sometime during the early morning hours of March 11. The point of entry into her apartment was determined to be through a small window located above the shower, approximately 12″ × 18″ in diameter. The offender had to squeeze through this small transom-type window and twist himself around so that he could lower himself to the floor (Figure 10.20).

The police found blood on the floor suggesting that Aundria had been injured. Investigators determined that someone had taken a TV, VCR, tapes, and some CDs. The mother reported that Aundria's 8-ball key chain was missing and that someone had locked her unit door.

A BREAK IN THE CASE: A PAROLEE WITH A SIMILAR MO

On March 16, 1999, Parole Officer David Zaragoza decided to check up on one of his parolees, Rex Krebs. Krebs was a 35-year-old convicted rapist and ex-con.

The parole officer had read an article in the local paper about the abduction of Aundria Crawford. He recognized several similarities in the MO in the Crawford case that matched one of Krebs' prior sexual offenses:

- Stalking and selecting his victims for sexual assault
- Breaking into single women's homes in the middle of the night
- Overpowering his victims while in their beds
- Threatening them with a weapon or beating them using brutal force

Figure 10.19 Rape scene. Police later ascertained that the killer had taken his captive to this abandoned A-frame in the heavily wooded area in Davis Canyon where he raped and killed her. (Photo courtesy of Assistant Chief Investigator Larry Hobson, Office of the District Attorney, San Luis Obispo, California.)

Figure 10.20 Second victim's home. Aundria Crawford was abducted from her home in the early morning hours after an intruder entered her residence by crawling through the transom window in the bathroom. (Photo courtesy of Assistant Chief Investigator Larry Hobson, Office of the District Attorney, San Luis Obispo, California.)

SUSPECT BACKGROUND: FIRST KNOWN VICTIM

Rex Krebs committed his first sexual assault in February 1984 when he was 18 years old. He raped a 13-year-old girl named Jennie in Sandpoint, Idaho. He was with her and two acquaintances. He had offered her some vodka to drink. When the other two persons left, he attacked her after pushing her into some bushes. He punched her and hit her head against the ground and started to strangle her before running off. Krebs was charged with attempted sexual assault, but was allowed to plead out so that the 13-year-old wouldn't have to testify. When he was paroled, he moved to California where he lived with his mother.

SECOND KNOWN VICTIM

On May 24, 1987, three years later, when he was 21 years old, he raped his second known victim. This time his victim was a 22-year-old young woman. Krebs had followed the woman home from a coffee shop. He waited until the lights went off and then he broke into her home and jumped onto her bed and threatened her with a kitchen knife. He asked her if she thought this knife could kill her. She told him, "yes." He then took out his own knife and told her this could kill her even quicker. He then cut off her sweats. He raped and anally sodomized her during the attack. During the time he was with her, he bound her with ropes and hogtied her. Krebs was into bondage and enjoyed tying up his victims with intricate knots, such as truck hitches.

THIRD KNOWN VICTIM

On June 15, 1987, he attacked his third known victim, a 31-year-old woman named Anishka. After spotting her in a neighborhood where he was installing a garage door, he began to stalk her. He approached her and asked if she was interested in having her garage door repaired. She told him, "no." However, while talking with her, he learned that she lived alone in the house with her 7-year-old daughter. He broke into her house in the early morning hours by forcing open the garage door. He then cut the phone lines both inside and outside the house. The woman heard him breaking in and tried to call the police, but the phone line was dead. She locked herself and her daughter in the bedroom. Krebs kicked in the bedroom door and attacked the woman threatening her with a knife. However, she managed to fight him off, suffering severe lacerations to her right hand and arm. As they fought on the bed, Krebs pulled a clump of hair from her head and attempted to stab her. She grabbed his knife and wouldn't let go. Krebs bit into her finger severing a tendon. He left his knife behind as he fled.

He was apprehended a short time later and charged with attempted rape, burglary, and assault, and identified as the assailant in the May 24 incident. He was convicted and sentenced to 20 years.

In September 1997, Krebs was paroled to San Luis Obispo County after serving 10 years of a 20-year sentence for the rape and sodomy of the May 24, 1987, victim and the attempted rape of the June 15, 1987, victim.

In September 1998, Krebs moved to Davis Canyon to live in a barn house in a rural area on Davis Canyon Road.

PAROLE OFFICER VISIT

Parole Officer Zaragoza visited Krebs at his residence, which was a converted barn located in an isolated, rural mountain area of Davis Canyon. During the brief visit,

Zaragoza noticed that Krebs was walking funny. When the parole officer asked why, Krebs told him that he fell off the retaining wall onto his woodpile and injured his ribs. Zaragoza didn't believe the story and became more suspicious when he examined Krebs' ribs and saw no signs of abrasions or external bruising. In fact, Krebs had injured his ribs while entering Crawford's home through that small transom window. In order to get through the window, he had to arch his back and he ended up pulling his back muscles.

Zarogoza reported his suspicions to the task force investigators. Krebs' name was on the list of sex registrants, but he had not been interviewed because he lived out of the city limits in a rural area of San Luis Obispo County.

On March 19, 1999, investigators from the task force and Parole Agent Zaragoza conducted a search of Krebs' house. Under California law, a parole officer can search a parolee's residence without a warrant if he suspects that there is a violation of parole. During the search, .22 caliber pellets were found. Krebs acknowledged he used them in a pellet pistol he kept at work at 84 Lumber to shoot birds that fly inside the work areas.

The parole officer and task force members also found an 8-ball key chain, minus the keys. This 8-ball key chain was similar in description to the key chain and keys that belonged to Aundria Crawford that her mother told police were missing. They also discovered 84 Lumber receipts with the names and addresses of women customers.

Subsequently, during the follow-up investigation, Investigator Hobson ascertained that some of these women had reported late night prowler incidents to the police department.

On March 20, Krebs was arrested at 84 Lumber by Parole Agent Zaragoza for possessing the .22-caliber pellet pistol that looked like a .45-caliber semiautomatic handgun. This was a parole violation.

SUSPECT INVESTIGATION: INTERVIEW STRATEGY

On March 21, 1999, Rex Krebs was interviewed by Investigator Larry Hobson at the San Luis Obispo Police Department. Hobson asked Krebs about the 8-ball key chain. Krebs told Hobson that when he was in Soledad prison working out in the iron pile, he found the 8-ball key ring and decided to keep it as a souvenir. What Krebs did not know is that Hobson had checked with prison authorities as to whether or not a prisoner could keep such an item. This type of item would be considered contraband and would have been taken away from Krebs during one of the many "shake-downs" at Soledad.

Krebs denied any knowledge or involvement in the disappearance of the two coeds. He provided investigators with an alibi on or about March 11, 1999, but was unable to remember where he was on or about November 13, 1998, because it was so long ago.

Krebs gave permission to have his home and vehicles searched and stated he was willing to do whatever it took to prove that he was not involved. During the interview, Krebs was vague and evasive about his criminal history and claimed he had left all of that behind him when he paroled from Soledad State Prison.

The investigators continued to look into Krebs as a possible suspect. They even obtained permission from his girlfriend to allow investigators to tape record telephone conversations between her and Krebs from the county jail. The investigators provided the girlfriend with questions to ask Krebs to clear up her suspicions. He was very evasive with her. But more importantly, he didn't even talk about his arrest.

On March 24, Investigator Hobson interviewed Krebs again. Krebs again was extremely cooperative and told Hobson that he wanted to do whatever he could to prove his innocence. Once again, Krebs gave the task force investigators permission to search his house and all his vehicles. Krebs told Hobson that he was willing to assist him by viewing the crime scenes and providing information on the unknown suspect based on his life as a convicted sex offender. Krebs even volunteered to provide a "profile" of their suspect.

On March 24, investigators, pursuant to a search warrant, searched Rex Krebs' house, his Ford pickup, and his Dodge sedan. During the search of Krebs' Ford pickup, investigators noticed that the rear jump seat on the passenger side was missing and the carpet in the jump seat area had been cut out. The jump seat was later found in a storage room on the bottom floor of the house. The jump seat had been cleaned up. Krebs had told Investigator Hobson that he removed the jump seat and cut the carpet out after spilling oil on them. Investigators sent the jump seat to the State Department of Justice Lab in Fresno for further testing. There were a total of five search warrants executed in connection with this case.

From March 28 to April 20, Investigator Hobson continued to talk with Krebs and to develop a rapport. Investigator Hobson talked Krebs into taking a polygraph test because he was so willing to clear his name. Krebs agreed to the polygraph examination to verify all statements given to investigators. However, he terminated the polygraph examination after being warned about movements and taking deep breaths, claiming that the test made him feel uncomfortable. During conversation with investigators following the polygraph, Krebs admitted for the first time to being on Branch Street and passing by Aundria Crawford's apartment several times after he left the Gaslight Lounge on Broad Street on his way home in Davis Canyon.

PHYSICAL EVIDENCE

The California Department of Justice (DOJ) lab advised the San Luis Obispo Police Department that it had, through DNA analysis, positively identified the blood found on the jump seat at Krebs' house as the blood of Rachel Newhouse.

THE CONFRONTATION

On April 21, Investigator Hobson confronted Krebs with the DNA evidence. Krebs became silent and asked Hobson to take him back to his cell. Krebs invoked his right not to talk with Hobson, *but did not ask for an attorney.* On April 22, Krebs was transported to the San Luis Obispo Police Department. When Investigator Hobson contacted him there for another interview, Krebs confessed and provided Investigator Hobson with the details of the kidnap, rape, and murder of the two coeds. Following the lengthy confessions, Krebs led Hobson and the other task force investigators to Davis Canyon where he pointed out the two gravesites. Krebs had buried Aundria Crawford approximately 30 feet from the main door to his house. He had buried Rachel Newhouse up on the side of a hill, adjacent to the main road into Davis Canyon approximately two miles from his residence (Figures 10.21 through 10.23).

On April 23, 1999, the two decomposed bodies were recovered from the four-foot graves. Medical examination revealed that both of the coeds had died from asphyxiation. Krebs was into "hog-tying" his victims with a rope around their necks, pulling their feet up into the small of their backs (Figure 10.24 and Figure 10.25).

Figure 10.21 Suspect's residence. The suspect also took Rachel Newhouse to Davis Canyon. He raped her at the A-frame building and then took her back to his house where he raped and sodomized her before strangling her to death. (Photo courtesy of Assistant Chief Investigator Larry Hobson, Office of the District Attorney, San Luis Obispo, California.)

Figure 10.22 Burial site. He brought Rachel Newhouse's body deeper into the woods where he had dug a four-foot hole. He put his victim's body in the ground and then covered her with hog wire so the animals wouldn't unearth her body. (Photo courtesy of Assistant Chief Investigator Larry Hobson, Office of the District Attorney, San Luis Obispo, California.)

Figure 10.23 Second burial site. The offender buried his second victim 25 feet behind his house in another four-foot grave. This time he kept the bindings on the body, which allowed for an excellent reconstruction (see Chapter 2, The Investigative Significance of Fantasy in Sex-Related Incidents). (Photo courtesy of Assistant Chief Investigator Larry Hobson, Office of the District Attorney, San Luis Obispo, California.)

E. Grid matrix

Figure 10.24 Depiction of gravesite. This illustration depicts the gravesite after brush was removed and a grid established. (Illustration courtesy of Medical Legal Art, Illustration © 2005 Medical Legal Art: www.doereport.com.)

Figure 10.25 Excavation process. The soil should be removed in somewhat even layers, about two- to four-inches deep. The excavated soil was placed in buckets and screened through ¼-inch mesh. (Photo courtesy of Assistant Chief Investigator Larry Hobson, Office of the District Attorney, San Luis Obispo, California.)

THE CONFESSION

Rex Krebs' past rape conviction and similar MO certainly placed him in position as a possible suspect. The parole officer's suspicion about Krebs was instrumental in identifying him as the obvious suspect when pursuant to his parole authority he located an item belonging to Crawford in Krebs' home. Krebs became their prime suspect after investigators found a car seat with blood on it at his home. A subsequent DNA analysis of that blood on the seat was matched to Rachel Newhouse.

However, there were a number of missing pieces that only the suspect could reveal. Investigator Hobson from the San Luis Obispo District Attorney's Office spent weeks talking with the suspect and eventually got Krebs to admit to the murders. Krebs then led the authorities to the shallow graves of the two missing women.

GETTING THE SUSPECT TO TALK

Sometimes it may take hours, days, or even weeks to get someone to confess to homicide. The purpose is to ask systematized questions in an effort to get to the truth. Investigators must have good verbal skills that allow them to easily engage in small talk with a suspect. I recommend that the detective present a nonjudgmental attitude and demeanor even when speaking of the most heinous crimes. The interviewer must train him or herself to listen and appropriately empathize with the subject.

You don't start off an interrogation by saying, "Did you do it?" The detective usually begins an interrogation by starting with open-ended questions that specify the topic. Direct questions address the obvious facts and establish the parameters of the discussion.

The interviewer should diverge to nonadversarial and nonthreatening subjects when the subject becomes uneasy. The subject matter has to be legitimate as you seek some sort of common ground with the person you are interviewing. It is important to establish a rapport with the suspect and establish a level of comfort because then the interviewer can sense any physical change or nonverbal reaction from the subject when the subject becomes nervous or distressed.

I advise the interviewer to try to keep the communication and dialog open and know when to diverse or change the direction of an interview before returning to what might be threatening to the suspect.

The interviewer might make use of probing-type questions to uncover reasons, attitudes, and beliefs or encourage expansion. Some examples of techniques used to elicit information are "Oh," "I see," "That's interesting," or even silence.

Or, try to impress upon the suspect that you can understand why he may have done something and provide him with a face-saving outlet or rationale. Encourage him to expand on his statement and explanation. These techniques are dependent upon the crime and situation. A good interviewer needs the perseverance and stamina to continue this type of stressful dialog and must thoroughly know the facts and circumstances of the case.

The use of psychology certainly plays an important part in an interrogation and there are little tricks of the trade that are effective in eliciting information from someone who doesn't want to disclose his guilt. Selecting the appropriate technique is paramount to the success of an interrogation. However, you are not just looking for a confession, you're looking for the truth.

Investigator Larry Hobson had just completed another in-depth interrogation on April 21 with Krebs during which time Hobson confronted Krebs with the DNA evidence. Krebs became silent and then asked Hobson to take him back to his cell. Krebs invoked his right not to talk with Hobson, *but did not ask for an attorney.*

Investigator Hobson, who spent four weeks talking to Krebs and attempting to convince him to tell the truth, got to know his subject extremely well. When Krebs told Hobson he didn't want to talk, Larry realized that he was in a very precarious legal position. If he pushed Krebs too hard, like some of the task force members and their commander suggested, Krebs might ask for an attorney and then there wouldn't be a second opportunity to talk to him. Hobson "read" his subject properly and he strategically backed off.

Hobson decided to give Krebs some time to think about it. Hobson said to Krebs, "Is it okay if I talk to you tomorrow?" Krebs stated, "Yes." When the suspect asked Investigator Hobson if he could get some cigarettes and if they could drive around a bit before returning him to the county jail, Hobson agreed, thinking a change of venue might be a good tactic.

As they drove, Krebs smoked some cigarettes and cried as he considered whether or not to confess, yet didn't offer the investigator any information.

This technique of providing the suspect with a little room was also an excellent strategy. Hobson didn't try to "push" Krebs. He let the suspect think it out.

When Hobson returned to the county jail the next day, Krebs decided to confess. That car ride may have been critical in getting Krebs to confess. Later that day, Krebs led the police to two four-foot-deep graves.

RACHEL NEWHOUSE

Krebs told Hobson that he had been drinking at three different bars in San Luis Obispo and was driving his Ford Ranger pickup when he spotted Rachel, whom he said was intoxicated, walking home from Tortilla Flats near the train station. He figured that she'd walk on the bridge. He parked his truck and waited for her at the top.

As they crossed paths, Krebs punched her in the jaw and knocked her against a rail. When she screamed, Krebs picked her up and threw her down and knocked her unconscious by slamming her head into the concrete. The victim was bleeding heavily due to the head wound. There was a large amount of blood left at this location. In fact, someone had called to have the blood washed because it was a biohazard. This was done before the police knew about the missing coed.

Krebs then carried the bleeding woman down to his truck, which was parked in the parking lot and threw her onto the back jump seat. He reached up her dress and ripped her panties off and stuffed them in her mouth. He then drove to another isolated area where he tied her up before heading out to Davis Canyon, which was 12 to 15 miles away. During the ride, the victim managed to get the panties out of her mouth, but couldn't get untied. She was yelling at him to let her go, but no one would have heard her. He took her to an abandoned A-frame house near his home. He cut her clothes off with his knife and then raped her.

He hog-tied Rachel and left her in the abandoned A-frame. Krebs told Hobson that he went home for a drink of Jack Daniels and returned about 10 or 15 minutes later. He stated, "When I went in, she was dead." Krebs told the detective that he had intended to let Newhouse go, but the ropes strangled her when she struggled to get free. The next day, he took her body out to another rural area where he dug a four-foot grave. He covered the body with plastic and placed hog wire over the corpse so that animals wouldn't be able to dig her up.

AUNDRIA CRAWFORD

Rex Krebs admitted stalking Aundria Crawford for several days after seeing her in her driveway. He watched her from a garage behind her apartment with binoculars. He also climbed up onto her roof two or three times and watched her in her bedroom. He told Hobson that he felt more confident after getting away with the Newhouse kidnapping and felt the urge to rape again. He planned the attack based on his neighbor's absence. He entered the duplex in the early morning hours at approximately 4 a.m.

He gained access by crawling into Crawford's apartment through a small transom window in the bathroom. He was wearing a nylon stocking mask. He stated that he made some noise getting into the bathroom. When the victim opened the door and confronted him in her apartment, he punched her in the mouth and then, with more blows, knocked her unconscious by banging her head into the floor.

This time he had brought his "kit." Krebs tied her up and then went to the bedroom where he got a pillowcase and placed it over her head. He told Hobson that he had decided he wanted to keep this victim for three or four days so he took three sets of clothing with him when he left the house. He used the victim's keys to lock the house hoping no one would notice her missing. He later threw the keys into the hills around his house, but kept the 8-ball as a trophy. The police located the victim's keys when Krebs pointed out the gravesites.

He also told the investigator that he had taken the VCR and tapes to throw the authorities off to make it look like a burglary. He told Hobson he couldn't even use these appliances because he didn't have regular electricity. His barn house used battery power. He stated he threw the items out along the road. Later on, police found and recovered this evidence.

Krebs then took his bound victim out to Davis Canyon in his truck to the same abandoned building near his home where he had raped and sodomized and strangled Rachel. Krebs raped and sodomized Aundria on the sofa at this location. He then hog-tied her and gagged her and went back to his place to wait until his neighbor's daughter went to work. He told Hobson he pretended to be cutting wood. Once the coast was clear, Krebs drove out to the A-frame and retrieved his victim. He brought her back to the barn house where he raped her a second time in the bedroom. Krebs then put her on a bed and shut the door. Her mouth had been taped shut, and a pillowcase had been placed over her head. Her hands and feet were bound.

After putting Crawford in the bedroom, Krebs said that he passed out on the couch. Krebs told Hobson that while he was sleeping, he heard a noise. When he looked toward the bedroom, he saw the victim standing in the doorway. Aundria Crawford was untied and had managed to get dressed with one of the outfits that Krebs had taken from her apartment. Krebs stated that she began to walk out of the bedroom.

Krebs said that he became frightened when he saw Crawford looking at him. Krebs stated that the victim screamed and tried to escape, but he overpowered her and dragged her into the living room where he raped and anally sodomized her on the couch. Krebs told Hobson that he had no intention of killing her before then, but now she had seen him.

Krebs stated he knew what he had to do. He said that he had placed a blindfold over her eyes and that he killed her by strangling her with a rope. He then buried her bound body 23 feet from his home in a shallow grave.

DISPOSITION

Rex Allan Krebs was found guilty on all counts, including all special circumstances. The same jury heard the penalty phase of the trial to determine the sentence for Krebs. On May 11, 2001, the jury voted for the death penalty in lieu of life in prison without the possibility of parole. On July 20, 2001, Judge Barry T. LaBarbera sentenced Rex Allan Krebs to die in the State Prison at San Quentin, where he is on death row. (See Chapter 2, Prosecution Presentation of Psychosexual Evidence.)

Serial Murder Case: Connecticut—Michael Ross: Serial Killer

CASE FACTS

In Chapter 14, Investigative Analysis: Criminal Personality Profiling and the Signature Aspect, I present an example of the classic organized offender, Michael Ross. Ross was a serial killer operating in northern Connecticut. He had been a model student in high school and was a graduate of Cornell University in New York State. At the time of his arrest, he was working as an insurance salesman and traveled his route in a blue Toyota. He killed a total of six young women, mostly teenagers, over a period of two years. He was extremely effective in avoiding apprehension and the authorities didn't even realize a serial killer was responsible for the deaths because some of them were listed as missing persons. However, Ross was subsequently identified as a suspect in an abduction of a 17-year-old, whose body had been recovered. The troopers were questioning Ross regarding his car, which had been seen during the abduction. During the course of their interview with the suspect, the two state troopers suddenly realized they were dealing with a serial killer. The two trooper investigators were able to convince the suspect to confess.

THE CONFESSION

The taped confession of Michael Bruce Ross was absolutely amazing. Ross discussed his killings in a very matter of fact way. As you listen to the tone of his voice and his cavalier attitude, you recognize that this Ivy Leaguer has no remorse whatsoever. His thinly veiled attempt to express regret is more of a complaint about how it was the victim's fault. He was acting as if he were "center stage." In fact, he gave himself his own Miranda rights, as he read them from a sheet of paper into the tape recorder. Before talking, he complimented the detectives on their expertise. The tape started off with Ross reading his rights. The trooper asked Ross if he was willing to talk to them about the case. Ross responded, "But, I can stop anytime I want, right?" The trooper responded, "That is correct." Ross responded, "Boy, you guys are pretty good ... you really got this thing down. ..."

Ross then went on to describe the murder of Wendy and how he spotted her walking along Route 12. Ross talked about what was in the newspapers and then corrected the newspaper errors. He told the trooper that he parked his car and approached the victim and began talking. When the trooper asked Ross what happened? Ross stated in a very sarcastic tone, "Let's just say things started to deteriorate." He explained how he dragged Wendy into the woods and that she fought and screamed. Ross then added, "I didn't have a weapon or a knife or anything."

He then stated that he raped her and that he was scared because he knew she would report it, so he killed her. He stated, "I knew you guys would be looking for her, so I buried her body in the stone wall." He then matter-of-factly added, "It was a dumb thing to do." He told the trooper that he saw her clothes so he picked them up and later threw them into the river. He talked about walking through the pasture so that no one would see him as he returned to his car.

Trooper-Investigators Mike Malchik and Frank Griffin did an excellent job of letting Ross run the interview. They deferred to him and let him decide which case he would discuss. They didn't "push" him or criticize his attitude. Instead they let this psychopath bury himself with his own words. This would become a crucial factor later on when the defense attempted to portray the troopers as aggressive and that the confession was coerced from his client. The truth of the matter was that this confession was the lynchpin of the State's case.

Following his confession to the murder of Wendy, Ross led the detectives to the crime scene and pointed out where he had buried the body and where he had disposed of the evidence. The detectives had brought along a state police crime photographer to document the cooperation on the part of the suspect, which also became evidence in the trial.

They then returned from the crime scene to discuss the murders of Tammy and Debbie. This interview was taped as well and, before they began, Trooper Malchik stated on the tape, "I'm going to have Michael read his rights." This was a very smart tactic on the part of Trooper Malchik. He used the suspect's first name as though they were partners in this investigation. It also illustrated that the statement was not only voluntary, but that the suspect knew his rights and seemingly enjoyed his "status" as suspect.

The troopers, who were aware of his break up with his fiancée shortly before the murders began, as well as his hate for his mother, asked him, "Do you want to start with the breaking up of your engagement and the divorce of your mother and father?" Ross replied in a whiny voice, "Do we have to talk about that?" The trooper then stated, "Would you rather not?" This was very clever. It allowed the suspect to choose the direction of the interview and make him think that he had control of what he was going to talk about.

Ross then stated, "Let's get to the big bear. All right?" Michael Ross then stated on the tape, "Okay guys, here goes." In the opinion of the author, you couldn't ask for a more perfect example of a voluntary confession. In fact, during the taping, Ross is heard joking with the detectives.

When they discussed going out to the crime scene where he had buried Tammy's body, Ross said, "Let's not take 50 million pictures like we did today." He was referring to the photos that were taken earlier in the day regarding the murder of Wendy (Figure 10.26 and Figure 10.27).

In the taped confession regarding Debbie, Ross tells the troopers that he and the victim were "making out and that she (the victim) was really into it." Ross then states, "She decided she didn't want to go any further." He said that Debbie slapped him. He then discussed killing her and taking her body to a location where he didn't think she would be found. He makes reference to the story in the newspaper of how her body was discovered by deer hunters. This certainly indicated that he was following the progress of the investigation by reading the newspaper.

As he confessed to the homicide of his third victim, named Robin, he tells the detectives while the tape is playing, "I have got a definite MO, don't I?" He stated that when he raped her, "She was quite into it." He then laughs. When the investigators asked him if he had done anything to her body after she was dead, Ross stated, "I have never raped a dead girl, yet." He laughs again.

Figure 10.26 Suspect at crime scene. Michael Ross. (Photos courtesy of Captain Frank Griffin, Connecticut State Police.)

Figure 10.27 Suspect Ross. Michael Ross pointing out locations of evidence and reenacting the event for authorities. (Photo courtesy of Captain Frank Griffin, Connecticut State Police.

Ross got a little testy with one of the troopers when he asked him, "How come you can't be sure of how you killed her?" Ross, responded in an angry voice, "I killed her, all right?" What the hell difference does it make how I killed her. I'm responsible. I'm the one who's going to pay." And then his voice got real low as if he were feeling remorse.

This little outburst was excellent for the purposes of the court presentation. Mike Malchik and Frank Griffin immediately backed away from pushing Ross on the details of how he killed and let Ross continue with the next case.

He explained how he picked up April and Leslie as they were hitchhiking. He confessed to raping April and killing both of the girls by strangling them. He discussed how he drove their bodies to a secluded area and admitted going back to this burial site on occasion "just to think." When asked why he killed the two young girls, Ross stated, "You're already in so far you may as well go all the way." At one point the tape ran out as Ross was confessing to the detectives. They had to stop the interview and put in a new tape. Ross is heard on the recorder stating, "You want me to repeat some of that stuff so you get it in?"

Opinion

In my opinion, I believe that Trooper Mike Malchik, now retired, and Trooper Frank Griffin, now a captain with the Connecticut State Police, and Assistant Chief Investigator Larry Hobson of the San Luis Obispo District Attorney's Office performed a remarkable achievement by obtaining the confession in the Michael Ross and the Rex Krebs cases. Serial killers usually do not disclose or confess unless they see a benefit for themselves.

It was apparent that the interviewers took their time and exercised extreme patience under tremendous pressure from within and outside their organizations to resolve these high profile cases.

In fact, these two cases stand out as excellent examples of professional interrogation techniques that not only resulted in confessions, but also provided closure to the families of the missing victims, as their bodies were recovered.

Conclusion

The criminal investigator confronted with a sex-related homicide investigation should first address the basic crime scene techniques as outlined in this text. He or she should concentrate on the total documentation and preservation of the scene including those factors that suggest the possible psychodynamics of the event.

Remember, there are four classifications of sex-related homicide:

1. Interpersonal violence-oriented disputes and assaults
2. Rape- or sodomy-oriented assault
3. Deviant-oriented assault, the lust murder
4. Serial murder

I have presented them in this text in the order of their frequency of occurrence. Start your investigation with an eye toward an interpersonal violence scenario and then work your way through the other options. Specific law enforcement strategies can be applied to the investigation upon identification of the motive.

An example would be computer analysis of similar offenses, a request for a criminal personality profile through VICAP, utilizing a statewide or regional information system, or simply a recanvass of the neighborhood wherein the crime took place. Remember, that within each of the categories there exist elements of human behavior, human sexuality, and possible sexual deviance. In any event, there aren't any simple clues, solutions, or explanations that account for the logic of a person who commits a sex-related homicide. Just remember: " Things are not always what they appear to be."

References

Borenstein, S. *Great white sharks hunt just like Hannibal Lector*. Associated Press Science Writer, June 21, 2009.

Douglas, R. Personal interview, Case Files, City of St. Louis, MO, August 2002.

Fletcher, J.S. *Deadly Thrills*, Penguin Books, New York, 1995.

Geberth, V.J. Psychopathic sexual sadists: The psychology and psychodynamics of serial killers, *Law and Order Magazine*, 43 (4), 82–86, April, 1995.

Geberth, V.J. *Practical Homicide Investigation: Tactics, Procedures, and Forensic Techniques*, 3rd ed., CRC Press, Boca Raton, FL, 1996.

Geberth, V.J. *Antisocial Personality Disorder, Sexual Sadism, and Serial Murder*, thesis, 1997.

Geberth, V.J. *Practical Homicide Investigation: Tactics, Procedures, and Forensic Techniques*, 4th ed., CRC Press, Boca Raton, FL, 2006.

Geberth, V.J. and R. Turco. Antisocial personality disorder, sexual sadism, malignant narcissism, and serial murder, *Journal of Forensic Science*, 42, 1, January 1997.

Hobson, L. Telephone interview and correspondence, Office of the District Attorney, County of San Luis Obispo, San Luis Obispo, CA, July 2002.

King, G.C. *Robert Lee Yates Jr.: The search for the Spokane serial killer*, http://www.crimelibrary.com/serial_killers/predators/yates (accessed 2000).

Newton, M. *Hunting Humans: An Encyclopedia of Modern Serial Killers*, Loompanics Unlimited, Port Townsend, WA, 1990.

O'Brien, D., *Two of a Kind: The Hillside Stranglers*, Signet, New York, 1985.

Philpin, J. and J. Donnelly. *Beyond Murder: The Inside Account of the Gainesville Student Murders*, Onyx Books, New York, 1994.

Ressler, R., J.E. Douglas, A.W. Burgess, and H.J. Heafner. *Sexual Homicide: Patterns and Motives*, Lexington Books, Lexington, MA, 1988.

Schreiber, F.R. *The Shoemaker: The Anatomy of a Psychotic*, Simon & Schuster, New York, 1983.

Schroeder, E., Personal interview, Michigan State Police, Violent Crimes Unit, July 2002.

Serial Murder Symposium Working Group, *Serial Murder: Multi-Disciplinary Perspectives for Investigators*, U.S. Department of Justice, 2005.

Sex-Related Child Homicides and Child Abduction Cases* 11

Introduction

Children are our most precious gift in society and all decent parents realize their responsibility in raising and protecting their children from harm. There is nothing more disturbing to an investigator than the murder of a child. This is especially true when the murder is a sex-related event. Sadly, many children become victims of sex-related homicides perpetrated by the very persons who are supposed to protect them from evil.

Relatives and friends and, sometimes, even parents may have perpetrated the crime. Each and every case becomes an emotional rollercoaster from the moment you receive the official report of the homicide. It continues as you attempt to empathically make the death notification to the parents, as you conduct the investigation, as you interrogate the suspect, and as you go through the court process.

Case History

Police received a report of a missing seven-year-old black female. She reportedly went missing from school. Her mother had come home from work at about 5 p.m. She realized that her daughter was missing and called her sister, who also lived in the same building, to inquire whether or not her daughter was with her. The mother, who was extremely upset, immediately called 911 to make the report. However, by the time she called the police, school had been dismissed for the day.

This case took place in the South Bronx in New York City. I was the commander of a homicide unit that was assigned early on to assist the local precinct detectives with this case. Our policy in homicide was to immediately assign homicide detectives to work along with local precinct detectives on any missing persons case involving children. The first thing we did was contact the school authorities to gain access to the little girl's teacher and anyone else at the school who would have had contact with the victim. Uniform officers were detailed to conduct canvasses around the school and the neighborhood where she lived.

She lived with her mother in an apartment on the second floor of a six-story apartment house in an area that was considered a high-crime location. This was a tough neighborhood and the fact that a little seven-year-old female was reported missing certainly was cause for concern. Even though we had been advised that she was missing from school, I directed my detectives to thoroughly search the building, basement, roof, and alleyway as well as the garbage areas. I also wanted the roofs, basements, and

---

* This chapter, as it relates to child abduction, was co-authored with Chief Criminal Investigator Marvin Skeen of the Washington State Attorney General's Office, who participated in a three-year nationwide study into child abductions. The research and evaluation of the data on these events resulted in the publication of the *Case Management for Missing Children: Homicide Investigation Executive Summary*, Office of the Attorney General, State of Washington, 1997.

alleyways of the adjoining building searched as well since it would be very easy to hide the small body of a little girl in these locations.

In the meantime, we learned from the school officials that the little girl had been in school and had been seen leaving the school with the other children. These other children were identified, located, and interviewed by the precinct detectives.

At about 6:15 p.m. detectives located the nude body of the missing seven-year-old wrapped in a garbage bag and placed in an incinerator closet on the fifth floor.

Years ago, before environmental considerations, garbage would be burned in large incinerators, which were located in the basements of these high-rise buildings. The ashes would then be placed in numerous garbage cans for pickup by the department of sanitation. To facilitate garbage disposal, there were metal deposit shoots on each floor built into the wall inside of a closet-like area.

The residents could take their garbage to this incinerator closet, open the door, and place the garbage into the shoot, which would go directly into the incinerator. The opening was just large enough to accommodate bag-size garbage. The incinerator shoots had been reconverted into collecting shoots and the garbage, instead of going into an incinerator, would go into a trash compacter. Larger items were placed in the closet for pick-up by the janitor or superintendent.

As soon as I was notified that the little girl's body had been found, I directed that the entire floor be sealed off and a crime scene established. It was apparent that the little girl had been sexually assaulted and it was obvious that whoever did it lived in the building. I advised the mother that we had found her daughter and that she had been killed. The poor woman became hysterical and I requested an ambulance for her, as her sister, who was there, attempted to console her.

I mentioned that this was a tough neighborhood in a high-crime area. Usually the residents are less than forthcoming in responding to police canvasses. However, even in a tough neighborhood like this one, when a child is murdered, "tongues loosen."

I decided to use this dynamic by assigning my detectives into two-person teams, with the following orders. I told them, "Go back and knock on every door of every resident and invite yourself into their apartments and tell them that the little girl's nude body was just found in their building and see what their reaction is." This tactic was obviously a "fishing expedition." I was hoping that one of the detective teams would get some sort of nonverbal reaction from one of these residents that would give us some direction. Most of the persons interviewed generally provided whatever they could. Some statements were, "That poor little thing. I knew this neighborhood was bad, but this is unacceptable." "I used to see that little girl come home from school every day. I can't believe she dead." "That's it. I'm moving my family out of here." Those kinds of statements were understandable given the circumstances.

When one of the teams knocked on an apartment door on the fourth floor, a black male about 18 years old opened the door with the security chain in place. The detectives thought this a little odd because they were the police. What was he afraid of? Why was he concerned about opening the door? When the detectives asked if they could come into the apartment, he suddenly stated in a loud voice that his mother did not allow him to let strangers into the apartment. His behavior was out of sync. When they asked him where his mother was, he stated, "She's with her sister." When they asked him who the sister was, he stated, "She's the mother of the dead little girl." At this point, they tactically backed away. One of the detectives remained in the hallway and the other advised me of this strange encounter. I told the detective to make sure he didn't leave the apartment.

I decided to approach the mother of this individual, who was consoling her sister and ask her if we could look in her apartment. I told her that as part of the investigation, we were going from apartment to apartment. I then told her what had transpired between her son and my detectives. She stated, "I did tell him I did not want anyone in my apartment when I'm not there, But I didn't mean the police. I meant his rowdy friends." She was willing to go to the apartment, but I stopped her and said, "Technically, we cannot enter anyone's apartment unless we have permission in writing." I did this just in case we did discover something. I wouldn't want to lose evidence because of a Constitutional issue. I advised her of her right not to have the police enter her apartment, fully realizing that she was not about to refuse us permission. After all, she was the aunt of the deceased and the sister of the deceased's mother. How could she refuse?

She insisted on leading us back to the apartment. She led the way as my detectives and I followed. She went up the door and shouted to her son, "Open this door! Why didn't you let these police officers in?" The son started backing up as she got in his face and we followed her into the apartment. That was when we saw it.

On the kitchen counter were black garbage bags, just like the ones the little girl's body was wrapped in. I said to my detectives, "Now I know how a dog feels when he's chasing a car and car suddenly stops—now what!" As I was standing there, I heard the woman yell at her son. "Have you been messing on my bed?" The son responded, "No, momma. No, momma." She said, "Were you in my room? What were you doing on my bed?"

Now, the bed looked fine to my detectives and me, but not to the mother. As she was yelling at her son, I went over to the bed and pulled the covers back. On the sheet was fresh blood.

This blood turned out to be from the little girl, who had been sexually assaulted on this bed by the woman's son and then strangled to death.

The mother looked at the blood, looked at her son, and realized what had happened. She went after him and began beating him. We had to restrain her. But not until she got him to admit what he had done.

Interestingly, when this case went to court, the defense attorney attempted to get the evidence thrown out on a Fourth Amendment issue. The mother of the defendant had conveniently forgotten that she had given us permission to come into her apartment that evening. It was an astute tactic getting her to give us written documentation of her consent to enter the apartment. It effectively refuted the defense claims that we had violated the subject's Constitutional rights (From the author's files).

Sex-Related Child Murder

Home Burglary Case Facts

On April 20, 1999, 12 year-old Cally Jo Larson got off a school bus at 3 p.m. and walked approximately three blocks to her residence. She entered her house through the front door. Unbeknownst to Cally Jo, an illegal immigrant named Lorenzo Sanchez, was burglarizing the family home. The man attacked Cally, quickly overpowering the young girl. He had bound her feet and hands with Venetian blind cords, which had

Figure 11.1 Body on staircase. Cally Jo's body was found by her sister in a semihanging position on the staircase. This was a highly unusual manner for a body to be displayed in the scene. (Photo courtesy of Chief Keith Hiller and Captain Penny Vought, Waseca, Minnesota, Police Department.)

been cut from the windows in the living room area. She suffered three stab wounds as she attempted to fight off her attacker. She was raped vaginally and anally by the offender, who then committed a final outrage by hanging her partially clothed body from the banister on the stairs leading up to the bedrooms. The victim was secured to the banister with electrical cords leaving her in a partial sitting/hanging position. This was how her sister Jayme discovered her (Figure 11.1 and Figure 11.2).

At 4:11 p.m., the Waseca Police Department received a 911 call from Jayme, who informed dispatch that she and her friends had returned to the residence and had discovered her sister's body hanging from the upstairs staircase.

Uniform officers quickly responded and determined that the young girl was dead. They secured the crime scene and notified detectives to respond. Investigator Penny Vought was assigned along with a team of investigators from the Minnesota Bureau of Criminal Apprehension. The officers observed two brown electrical cords around her neck (one from a clock radio) and an orange electrical cord that had previously been in the basement The upstairs bedroom area and downstairs bedroom area had been ransacked. The murder weapon was not located (Figure 11.3).

At autopsy, an unidentified hair was found on the buttocks of Cally Jo. No other physical evidence was found on her body. Two unidentified hairs also were found on the stairway. The hairs were the only physical evidence found at the crime scene.

Figure 11.2 Hanging ligature. The child's body was hanging from an electric cord, which had been attached to the banister. (Photo courtesy of Chief Keith Hiller and Captain Penny Vought, Waseca, Minnesota, Police Department.)

This was the first homicide ever to occur in Waseca, which is located in southern Minnesota and has a population of approximately 9,000 residents.

This homicide occurred on the same day as the Columbine shootings in Colorado. Some of the individuals who were interviewed could recall what they were doing that day just because of that event that happened on April 20.

THE INVESTIGATION

Sex offenders from Waseca County and surrounding counties were interviewed and eliminated. The public called in many leads and all of them were investigated. Some potential suspects were developed in the early stages of the investigation, but no one was ever criminally charged with the homicide.

Cally's mother and sister never lived in the house again and the Waseca Police Department and its reservists packed up the residence and moved their belongings into storage units. In August 1999, it was discovered that Jayme and Cally Jo's compact disc containers that contained their CDs could not be located. A search of the storage units did not reveal the containers.

PATTERN BURGLARIES

From November 1999 to February 2000, approximately 14 burglaries occurred in Waseca. All burglary scenes were processed for fingerprints and shoe/boot prints.

Figure 11.3 Ransacked room. This was the girls' room in the house. All of the rooms were ransacked by the offender, who had taken property before leaving. (Photo courtesy of Chief Keith Hiller and Captain Penny Vought, Waseca, Minnesota, Police Department.)

On February 18, 2000, at approximately 8 p.m., Waseca Police Officer Kris Markeson was on routine patrol when he observed a male walking on the sidewalk of a residential street. As he drove past the male, Officer Markeson observed him turn the other way, so he then turned around and approached the man. Officer Markeson then arrested Andres Ortiz on an outstanding warrant and found a large screwdriver and flashlight in his pants. Officer Markeson also observed that Ortiz's shoe prints matched those found at some of the burglary scenes. This was an excellent observation and action on the part of the uniform officer (Figure 11.4).

Two burglary search warrants were executed at the suspect's residence. Photographs were taken of items not seized. Penny Vought, an investigator who had been assigned to the Cally Jo Larson case and who was not present during the search warrants at the Ortiz residence, reviewed these photographs and immediately discovered that two CD cases photographed in the closet of the residence matched two reportedly missing from the Larson residence.

A search warrant related to the homicide of Cally Jo Larson was then executed at the Ortiz residence. The CDs were seized, as well as hair and DNA samples from Andres Ortiz. It should be noted that Ortiz was the only suspect ever to physically fight with investigators when obtaining hair and DNA samples.

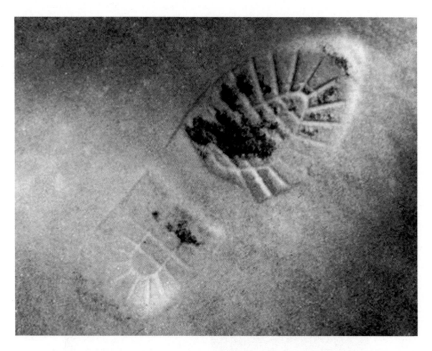

Figure 11.4 Suspect's shoe print. A shoe print left by the offender at the scene. The impression prints of other burglaries in the area were similar to shoe impressions recovered at the homicide scene. There was also a common means of entry in each of the burglaries suggesting that one person was responsible. (Photo courtesy of Chief Keith Hiller and Captain Penny Vought, Waseca, Minnesota, Police Department.)

The CD cases were analyzed and a hair, later identified as belonging to Cally Jo, was found in one of the cases. The CD cases were super glued and, in the second case to be examined, Cally Jo's fingerprint was discovered on the last sleeve.

Andres Ortiz was an alias used by Lorenzo Bahena Sanchez. Sanchez had used many aliases in his lifetime and had even served time in prison in Texas under the name of Jose Castaneda. Sanchez was an illegal alien who had been deported back to Mexico on at least one previous occasion.

Mitochondrial DNA analysis was conducted on the hair samples found at the residence, some from the potential suspects, and from Sanchez. Sanchez's sample was a match to one of the samples found at the Larson residence. Sanchez's brothers were interviewed and their whereabouts for April 20, 1999, were confirmed. Sanchez was the only sibling who did not have an alibi.

A search warrant was also executed on Sanchez's penis. He had "balls" placed under the skin of his penis. Investigators were told that, while in prison in Texas, a toothbrush had been melted down, plastic balls were formed, and they were placed under the skin of his penis. This was for the "pleasure of the woman."

The medical examiner was prepared to testify that these "balls" could have been responsible for some of the injuries found on Cally Jo's body.

On May 16, 2000, Lorenzo Sanchez pled guilty in a plea bargain to some of the burglaries. On June 6, 2000, a Waseca County Grand Jury indicted him on first degree murder of Cally Jo Larson. On March 5, 2001, against the advice of one of his attorneys,

Figure 11.5 Cally Jo. (Photo courtesy of Chief Keith Hiller and Captain Penny Vought, Waseca, Minnesota, Police Department.)

Figure 11.6 Cally Jo memorial pin. This pin was designed by Cally's mother for The Cally Jo Larson Children's Fund, which represents victims of homicide. (Photo courtesy of Chief Keith Hiller and Captain Penny Vought, Waseca, Minnesota Police Department.)

he pled guilty to the first degree murder charge of Cally Jo. He does have the possibility of parole after 30 years and is serving his sentence in a Texas prison (Figure 11.5).

ACKNOWLEDGMENTS

The author wishes to acknowledge the contribution of this information and materials to this text from the following members of the Minnesota Bureau of Criminal Apprehension: Senior Special Agent Bob Berg and Special Agent Mike Anderson, former Waseca Police Investigator and the Waseca Police Department's Captain Penny Vought and Sgt. Kris Markeson.

I would also like to acknowledge Cally Jo's mother, who has formed an organization in her daughter's memory and has become an outspoken advocate for crime victims (Figure 11.6).

Homosexual Pedophile Murder

The sex-related murder of children can be heterosexually or homosexually oriented. The offenders, many times, are related or familiar with the victim. In an Opinion article in the *New York Post*, written by a reporter who challenged the media for avoiding this news report in order not to offend gay political interest groups, the facts of the case are presented.

The victim, who was acquainted with one of his attackers, was a 13-year-old boy. He died at the hands of two men who raped and murdered the boy during a homosexual torture session. The young boy was at the home of a family friend, who is homosexual. The family friend and the friend's gay lover gave the boy a strong sedative to knock him out. The boy was then restrained while his own underwear was stuffed into his mouth and held in place with duct tape. They then positioned the boy's naked body face down and he was repeatedly raped and sodomized over a period of hours. The assault included the use of objects, which were seized by the police. The victim slowly suffocated and died as a result of this atrocious act.

Police gathered evidence from the men's apartment that included lurid drawings showing a bound person, written descriptions of a homosexual assault, and pieces of paper describing objects with which the 13-year-old victim had been sodomized.

In the article, the reporter indicated that the defense was going to argue that the "outnumbered, overpowered, overdosed, and strapped 13-year-old victim was a willing and consenting participant in this sexual torture" (Malkin, 2001) (Figure 11.7).

Missing Person Reports Involving Children

Any missing report of a child is a serious incident and sadly many of these children become homicide victims. On January 9, 2002, little 13-year-old Ashley Pond was reported missing by her mother in Oregon City, Oregon. She was last seen eating breakfast with her sister

Figure 11.7 Pedophile murder. This little boy's frozen body was recovered in an abandoned building in the Bronx. He had been reported missing two days earlier and had been the subject of an intense search. His body was found during the search of a group of abandoned buildings about a block away from where he lived. He had been anally sodomized by a pedophile vagrant who used the building as a home. The vagrant, who had a criminal record as a sex offender as well as a psychiatric record, spotted the youngster as he walked past the building. He dragged the boy into the building where he sexually assaulted him and then stabbed him in his back. The offender had used the boy's scarf as a ligature around the boy's neck to restrain him. (Photo courtesy of the author.)

before getting ready to walk about eight minutes to a bus stop to go to school. On March 8, 2002, Ashley's friend, Miranda Gaddis was reported missing by her mother, who last saw her eating breakfast before she went to school.

The two seventh graders lived in the same apartment complex in Oregon City. The police initiated a major case investigation into both of these cases and early on it was assumed that the killer might have known the girls prior to their abductions. During the course of the investigation, police received thousands of tips, but were unable to locate the girls or develop a suspect.

On August 13, 2002, a 39-year-old single father, identified as Ward Weaver, was charged with raping his 19-year-old son's girlfriend. The son told authorities that his father had confessed to the murder of the two missing 13-year-olds (Massarella, 2002). The rape suspect lived in the same apartment complex as the two missing girls and reportedly knew both of them. The authorities now had a suspect. However, they needed probable cause to search the man's property. As the suspect was being held on the rape charges, police and FBI agents secured Ward's property and prepared their case for the application of search warrants.

On Saturday, August 24, the body of Miranda Gaddis was discovered in a shed behind Weaver's home (Massarella, 2002). On Sunday, August 25, the body of Ashley Pond, was discovered in a barrel buried beneath a cement slab that Ward Weaver had poured behind his rented Oregon City home after the two 13-year-old classmates had disappeared (Kranes, 2002).

Ironically, the suspect's father, also named Ward Weaver, is on death row in California for rape and murder under similar circumstances. "Ron Shumaker, who prosecuted the elder Weaver for murder 20 years ago, told the *New York Post* the father and son cases sounded strikingly similar. … There are family resemblances. They both used cement and they both apparently had the same fondness for younger women" (Sujo, 2002).

The author is not surprised. The old adage about how "the apple doesn't fall far from the tree" plays itself out over and over again in case after case. I have seen this often wherein an underlying psychopathology weaves its way through the family lineage.

Policy

There is an established protocol for the investigation of missing children. Not all missing children cases are assigned to homicide. However, just as there are no absolutes in homicide, there may be occasion to immediately assign homicide detectives. That was what occurred in the following case.

Case History

A retarded seven-year-old black male was reported missing by his mother. His mother was a prostitute and drug user and seemed to care less about her missing child. The Bronx Chief of Detectives, Edwin Dreher, knew from years of experience that this case was going to be a homicide. I remember him calling me into his office and telling me that he was assigning the homicide unit to this case. I also remember my counterparts and the commanding officer bitching about this "waste of time." Well, it turned out to be a fortuitous decision. The little boy was found dead in an abandoned building on the South Bronx.

A building scavenger looking for scrap metal had discovered his body. The little boy's nude body was hung by a length of electrical cord attached to a metal pipe (Figure 11.8). Surrounding the body were dead chickens and chicken feathers as well as other bizarre items resembling a horror show. The mother turned out to be the suspect. In her delusional state of mind, she believed that she could cure her syphilis and gonorrhea by a Santeria ritual. She provided her son to some people who promised her a cure and the little boy suffered a horrible death. When the authorities were about to move in on the mother, she checked herself into an institution and was protected from the police investigation. The Bronx district attorney at the time declined to prosecute (From the author's files).

Case History

In a suburb of St. Louis, six-year-old Casey was reported missing by her father. A homeless man, who was a guest of the father, was charged with her murder. The father thought that his little girl had gone across the street to see her grandfather. The father also noticed that his houseguest, a 24-year-old drifter, was also gone. However, about

Figure 11.8 Horror show. This little seven-year-old was found hanging in the basement of an abandoned building. It was a ritual-type murder with Voodoo and Santeria undertones. (Photo courtesy of the author.)

30 minutes later, the houseguest returned wet and muddy and told the father he had gone for a swim in a nearby river and hadn't seen the little girl. The police were called and immediately focused their attention on the drifter. A search of the area uncovered the little girl's body buried under debris in a culvert of an abandoned glass factory. She had been lured from the house by the drifter, taken to the abandoned factory, and killed (*New York Post*, 2002).

Introduction to Child Abduction

The abduction and murder of a child under 18 years of age by a stranger is a rare event. Statistically, they run about .5% of all murders in the United States (between 100 to 200 cases annually). Although the data indicates that these incidents are statistically rare, they are horrendous crimes. Child abduction cases affect not only the immediate family of the victim, but entire communities and our society as media coverage of the event is nationally broadcast. It is every parent's nightmare that a child can be so wantonly harmed and many times slaughtered. It is the realization of this horror that requires the criminal investigator to develop the knowledge and expertise to manage child abduction cases and learn from the experience of other similar events how to professionally investigate these types of cases. The investigation of child abduction murders can present law enforcement with a unique predicament.

Case History

Ten-year-old Elizabeth was reported missing by her mother Lindsey on Tuesday March 28th at 1752 hours when she failed to come home from her daily walk. Elizabeth's body was found at approximately 1841 hours. This was *less than an hour after she was reported missing.*

A witness saw a single white male driving a white minivan back up and unload something from the van. The witness went to that location after the van drove away to see what the man had dumped and discovered the body. He turned to tell a man who was walking nearby to call 911. Sadly, that man was William, the father of the victim, who had been searching the neighborhood for his little girl. He identified the body as his daughter at the scene. The victim was covered with a blanket and was bound with duct tape and a rope was placed around her neck. She was nude from the waist down (see Figure 11.9).

THE SUSPECT

Daniel Arlen Johnson, a white male, 28 years old, was identified as the suspect the following day.

A fingerprint examiner located and retrieved a latent print from the duct tape and entered the latent into AFIS. A match was made to the suspect from prior drug and a burglary charges.

Johnson was an out-of-work laborer and was married and had a child of his own. He was charged with first-degree murder, kidnapping, and first-degree rape.

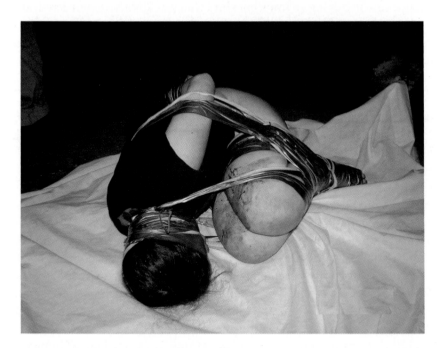

Figure 11.9 This 10-year-old victim was lured into the home of a neighbor to look at his puppy. Once he got her inside the home he overpowered her by breaking her nose. He then bound her with duct tape and performed oral sodomy on the little girl until she suffocated. He then disposed of her bound and taped body near a dumpster. (Courtesy of Detective Victor Regalado, Tulsa, Oklahoma, Police Department.)

DESCRIPTION AND SYNOPSIS OF THE INCIDENT

The victim had a routine of walking around her block after school for exercise. Daniel Johnson lived on the same block and had been watching the little girl when she took her daily walk. He waited for her as she came down the street and then presented a puppy dog to the victim to pet. The suspect then asked the victim if she was thirsty. (It had been a hot and humid day.) The suspect offered the victim a glass of Kool-Aid®. According to the suspect as the victim came up onto his porch he attacked in a blitz style, breaking her nose and incapacitating her.

Johnson stated that he then bound her with duct tape and put a piece of cord from window blinds around her neck and then tied the other end to her arms that were duct taped behind her back. Suspect stated he then rolled the victim on to her back which caused the cord to tighten around the victim's neck.

Johnson told detectives that he then began oral sex on the victim while watching her "twitch" from being choked by the cord. Suspect stated he knew she was dead when she stopped moving and urinated in his mouth. The suspect stated he did not achieve orgasm during the incident but masturbated several times later that evening while thinking about the incident. Johnson stated that he had read several bondage magazines in the past where he got the idea of binding the victim with duct tape.

DISPOSITION

The suspect pled guilty on all charges and was sentenced to life in prison without the possibility of parole in a plea agreement that the family of the victim requested.

This tragic case involving an innocent child who was abducted, murdered, and sexually assaulted is a sign of the times in which we live. Times wherein no parent can ever relax their guard. Times wherein all parents should warn their children of the evil and depraved persons who exist in our society and who are awaiting an opportunity to do them harm.

A number of factors contribute to this dilemma. The investigation is often emotionally charged due to the young age of the victim. Most police officers have or have had young children themselves and can easily identify with the victim's parents. Child abduction cases also attract a lot of media attention, locally and nationally, and sometimes even internationally depending on the circumstances. The Polly Klaas case (1993 in California) received international exposure due to the circumstances of her abduction as well as the arrogance of the offender during the trial.

The respective police departments and their investigators are often pressured by the media to resolve these crimes quickly and many times the cases become "driven" by outside forces. Investigative leads, based on facts, should generate the direction of the investigation. However, in a high profile case, such as child abduction where the general public is asked to provide information, a number of tips or "leads" will be provided to authorities. These tips or leads can come to the authorities through official channels and identifiable sources as well as from persons who call anonymously. This deluge of information will require sufficient resources to follow up on potential information.

The investigators themselves can also suffer from their own self-imposed stress of wanting to solve the cases. The cases can become quite complicated because often there will be more than one site or crime scene involved in a child abduction case.

There is no doubt that child abduction cases can become emotionally charged due to the various stressors involved. Investigators must recognize what they are dealing with and not let their emotions cloud their judgment, keeping in mind that the goal is to resolve the incident in an intelligent and professional manner.

Initial Investigation

The police report is usually generated when a child is discovered missing and someone calls the police. The immediate problem is how much time was lost before someone realized the child was missing and how much time was spent looking for the child before the police were called. The research indicates that the younger the victim the sooner the report is made. Older children are reported later than younger ones, as parents seem less concerned about a missing teenage child than a younger one. There will usually be some delay in reporting the missing child because parents, family, and others are often looking for the child. This must be taken into consideration at the time of the police report. For example, how much time did the offender have to leave the area and how far could the offender have traveled with the child. The time it takes to report a child missing will vary from immediately to within 24 hours.

A delay may not appear to be important. However, consider the fact that a little under a half of the children are murdered within one hour of being abducted, three quarters are dead within three hours, and nine out of ten often are killed within 24 hours (Hanfland et al., 1997). Because children are murdered in such a short time after abduction, delays in reporting missing children become critical. Any delay can make a difference in whether the victim is found alive. Parents and care providers need to be educated to report missing children immediately. The police need to put as much effort as possible into those cases of suspected foul play by deploying all of their investigative resources on any witnessed abduction.

Child abduction cases also come to the attention of the police when a victim's body is found. It is important that first responders determine quickly what type of case they have. One way they are assisted in making this determination is by collecting as much information as they can about the victim. Information on the victim's physical description, personality and behavior traits, clothing worn, friends, relatives, medical history, and family relationships will help in establishing victimology. It is important to obtain the most recent photo of the victim and to get the victim's photograph and description broadcast and published through the media as well as distributed to all police agencies.

Experienced patrol officers speak of having the hairs on the back of their neck stand up when they realize they have an abduction case and not just a lost child. Experience tells us that officers must respond rapidly and take missing child reports seriously.

In child abduction murder cases, a majority of the time the identity of the victim is known from the beginning and the initial question is often, "Will the child be found dead or alive?"

The Polly Klaas Kidnap and Murder

CASE FACTS

Polly Klaas was a 12-year-old junior high school student when she was kidnapped from her home and murdered. Polly resided with her mother, Eve, and younger sister, Annie, in Petaluma, California. Polly's mom and her father, Marc, had been divorced since Polly was a little over two years old. Her mom had remarried and was separated at the time of the incident. However, Polly had remained very close with her dad, Marc, and spent most weekends and holidays with him. Polly was the light of his life and vice versa.

On October 1, 1993, Polly was having a slumber party with her two best friends, Kate and Gillian, at her home. Her mother and sister were in the house. *Where could your daughter be safer than at a sleepover party in your own home?* The girls were having fun dressing up and posing and playing some board games. Polly's mom and sister were already in bed when Polly went to gather her friend's sleeping bags from the living room. She opened the bedroom door and saw a large, middle-aged man standing in the living room.

He was holding a knife and immediately ordered her and her friend not to scream or he would cut their throats. He made the comment, "I'm just doing this for the money." Polly offered him a box with $50 in cash. He refused and ordered the three scared girls to lie down on the floor. The stranger then tied their hands behind their backs and placed hoods over their heads. Polly begged the stranger not to hurt her mom or sister. The man then picked up Polly and told the girls to count to 1,000 before they did anything.

Kate and Gillian didn't wait. They freed themselves and wakened Polly's mother. At 10:45 p.m., the panicked mother dialed 911.

POLICE RESPONSE

The police responded immediately and canvassed the neighborhood as detectives questioned the frightened young girls and Polly's mother. Several people in the area remembered seeing a thickly built, bearded male with bushy gray hair loitering on a sidewalk near the Klaas house. The police broadcast a description of a tall, bearded, white male wearing dark clothing throughout Sonoma County. However, this alarm was not sent to every station. This omission proved to be disastrous.

A MISSED OPPORTUNITY

Around midnight on that same evening, in an area 25 miles away from Polly Klaas' house, a woman identified as Dana Jaffe called the police to complain about a trespasser on her property. Two deputies were sent to check on this report. They encountered Richard Allen Davis, whose white Pinto had gotten stuck in a ditch on this private property. The police questioned this large man, who was dirty and had twigs in his thick hair and was sweating quite profusely. According to the police, he did not seem nervous.

When the deputies asked what he was doing out in this rural area, he stated he was sightseeing. The area was rather desolate and it was dark so the officers were rather skeptical. Davis then took a can of beer out of his car, popped the tab, and began drinking it in front of the officers. He was told not to do that and he tossed the can into some bushes. The officers ordered him to pick it up, but they didn't pursue this.

They ran a check for outstanding warrants and it came back clean. However, they did not run a background check. If they had, they would have discovered that Richard Allen Davis had convictions for robbery, burglary, assault, and kidnapping, and an extensive history of violence against females. The deputies would also have realized that he was on parole and just violated it by drinking the beer. His presence on this private property, as well as his criminal record, certainly would have been enough for further investigation. But the deputies hadn't initiated a background check. The deputies asked Jaffe if she wanted this man arrested for trespass. She told the police she only wanted him off her property. Davis said he would be glad to leave, but his car was stuck. So the deputies borrowed a chain from a homeowner and helped him get his car out of the ditch.

Note: *Retrospectively speaking, the authorities had made a major error. The deputies were not aware of the kidnapping in Petaluma or the description of the kidnapper, which had been broadcast. Richard Allen Davis would have been caught at the disposal site. In the opinion of the author, Davis had obviously just disposed of Polly Klaas' body under dark in this desolate area and, as a result, got his vehicle stuck in the ditch.*

THE SUSPECT

Richard Allen Davis was identified as a suspect after crime scene and forensic experts identified a palm print found in Polly's room. Two days after the abduction, the television show *America's Most Wanted* ran a segment about the case. Pictures of Polly and sketches of what Gillian and Kate said the intruder looked like were posted in supermarkets and on telephone polls, and shoved into mailboxes everywhere, not just in California, but throughout the United States.

On October 19, 1993, Davis was arrested for drunk driving. Neither the arresting officers nor his jailers noticed his resemblance to the sketches of Polly's abductor. They let him leave after a little under five hours. He drove away in his 1979 white Pinto.

On November 28, Dana Jaffe and two friends were hiking around her property when they happened upon several items in a brushy area, which included a dark sweatshirt, red tights that were knotted up, a "Rough Rider" condom wrapper with an unrolled condom nearby, strips of binding tape, and an item made of white cloth that looked like it had been made into a hood. She remembered the trespasser on the night of Polly's disappearance. Could they be linked? She was chilled by the possibility. "The tights and the white pieces of cloth made me feel like they were really out of place," Jaffe remarked. "I didn't like the way they looked. They looked like they were ties or gags." A stunned Jaffe turned to her hiking partners and asked, "Do you think this is Polly?"

THE ARREST

She phoned the police about her find. A review of her trespassing complaint led cops to the identity of the man found and let go: Richard Allen Davis, the same man whose palm print was in Polly's room. Davis was arrested two days later. He refused to answer any questions about Polly Klaas.

THE CONFESSION

On December 4, Davis finally confessed to both the kidnapping and murder of Polly Klaas. The account that he provided to the police was less than honest, but he did lead the authorities to the body of little Polly Klaas.

The suspect claimed he drove around aimlessly for a while, trying to figure out what he should do now that he had a kidnapped child in his car. He untied Polly during the drive. At one point, his Pinto got stuck in Dana Jaffe's mud. He took the little girl out of the car, he claimed, and left her—alive and neither bound nor gagged—in a nearby hillside.

He gave his version of the encounter with the cops regarding his trespassing. He told the detectives that once his car was freed, he went back to where he left his victim. He thought she was sleeping. She awoke and said, "I thought you had left me." The police did not believe this version and assumed that Polly was bound and gagged or already dead. However, they let Davis continue with his "story."

Davis told the detectives that he realized he was in a jam and could not think of a good way out of it. Kidnapping would send him back to the penitentiary. So he decided the only thing he could do was kill "the broad" in his car. This explanation did not seem logical since Polly's two friends Kate and Gillian had seen the suspect and their description resulted in the sketch. His reference to his victim as a "broad" was probably used to minimize the fact that she was a young girl not yet in her teens. By calling her a "broad," he diminished her as just a liability.

Davis was asked if he had molested or raped the girl or attempted one or the other before killing her? He denied it, but his denials were less than truthful. "I don't think so," was his first response to the question. Asked again, he replied, "Well, as much as I can remember, I don't think that I did." Then he became more definite and swore that he didn't do anything to her. Davis stated that he strangled her from behind with a piece of cloth. The exact means of her death could not be definitively established, but his description was consistent with the evidence.

It should be noted that when Polly's corpse was found, her miniskirt was pulled up and her legs spread. Her body had been exposed to the elements for two months and was too decomposed to prove anything definitive about sexual assault (Bortnick, 1995).

DISPOSITION

On June 18, 1996, the jury convicted Davis of first degree murder with special circumstances. The only possible sentences were death or life with no possibility of parole. After the verdict was read, a defiant Davis gave two middle fingers to the courtroom. The prosecution put on as witnesses the victim's family to show the damage Davis had done to this family and to buttress the district attorney's argument that Davis deserved the death penalty.

Some jurors were teary when Polly Klaas' father and grandfather described how the child's loss had affected them. "Everything reminds me," her father said. "Every time I see a pretty 12-year-old girl, I am reminded of Polly. ... I can't sleep. I can't concentrate. Everything's in ruins."

After his courtroom testimony, Marc Klaas was interviewed by CNN. "This has really been the first opportunity to address the jury and let them know what it means to us to lose a child," Klaas said. "Unfortunately, it's very difficult to put into words the kind of emotions that flow through somebody as a result of such a loss."

THE FINAL OUTRAGE

It seemed impossible that Richard Allen Davis could possibly cause the Klaas family any further grief. But he found a way.

On the day that his daughter's murderer was to be sentenced, Marc Klaas told the jury that, if it did not sentence Davis to death, it "would allow evil to triumph over good." Then he turned to the defendant and said, "Mr. Davis, when you get to where you're going, say hello to Hitler, to Dahmer, and to Bundy. Good riddance, and the sooner you get there the better we'll all be."

Richard Allen Davis was also allowed to address the court. He again asserted that he had not sexually abused his victim, but the way he made this claim shocked the courtroom. "The main reason I know I did not attempt any lewd act that night was because of a statement the young girl made to me while walking up the embankment," he recalled. "'Just don't do me like my Dad.'"

The courtroom was in shock as an audible gasp was heard. Marc Klaas yelled, "Burn in hell, Davis!" The court officers hurried the grieving father out of the courtroom while several spectators burst into tears.

The jury recommended that Davis be sentenced to death. Judge Thomas Hastings said that Davis' recent, repulsive statement against his victim's father made it "very easy" to pronounce the death sentence. Davis was sentenced to death (From: www.cnn.com/US/9606/18/Klaas.verdict/index.html).

Public Response

As a result of the Polly Klaas murder and other high profile abductions, the police, the media, and missing children groups have come together to focus attention on the issue.

America's Most Wanted host John Walsh, who lost his 6-year-old son; Marc Klaas, the father of Polly; the family of little 9-year-old Amber Hagerman; and other parents who have lost their children to kidnappers have mobilized and formed groups and organizations to address these cases as soon as they occur.

These groups have learned from experience that the media are their most valuable ally. This was how the **Amber Alert Plan** came into existence (see Amber Alert Plan later in chapter). Publicity and national exposure increase tips that fuel an investigation, and many communities have launched special alert systems in the past few years to get news of an abduction on the air within minutes. The hope is that listeners in cars or at home will spot the victim or the fleeing suspect, either in a vehicle or on foot. That is why it is so important to get a most current picture of the victim broadcast early in the investigation. In this day and age, we have many electronic capabilities among which are an incalculable number of persons with cell phones, which can provide instantaneous contact and communication with law enforcement.

This is an extremely valuable and a viable tool in child abduction cases. The picture of the victim and any description of the offender and/or his vehicle become crucial in these early hours because time is of the essence. Parents of victims are urged to go on the air to humanize the child in the event the abductor is watching. This is referred to as saturation media. In the Runnion case (see following section), the Orange County authorities received valuable information as a result of this intense news coverage.

The Samantha Runnion Kidnap and Murder

CASE FACTS

On Monday, July 15, 2002, little 5-year-old Samantha Runnion was playing with her six-year-old friend, Sarah, about 150 feet from her home in Stanton, California. As the girls were playing, a man with a mustache and black hair drove up in a light green car and told the girls he had lost his dog and asked them if they could help him find his Chihuahua.

This classic "help me find my dog" approach is typical of the pedophile predator. As the suspect got closer to little Samantha, he suddenly snatched her and headed for his car. She fought with all her strength kicking and screaming and yelling to her six-year-old friend Sarah, "Help me! Tell my grandmother!" (McCarthy, 2002) However, little Samantha was no match for the 6-foot, 200-pound stranger who quickly overpowered her, threw her into his car, and sped off.

THE YOUNG WITNESS

Sarah ran to her mother, who called 911. Police arrived within minutes. Little Sarah was able to provide an amazingly accurate description of the suspect including his car. The composite sketch based on the young witness's description was broadcast nationwide. The media coverage of this event and the police appeal to the general public requesting any information that might assist authorities in finding little Samantha and identifying her abductor resulted in more than 2,000 tips (McCarthy, 2002). However, the little girl was not to be found.

DISCOVERY OF SAMANTHA'S BODY

The following day, Tuesday, July 16, a pair of hang glider enthusiasts discovered the little girl's nude body in the open off a mountain road in a wooded region of the Cleveland Forest approximately 50 miles from Stanton. They had stumbled onto a scene straight out of hell. In a chilling 911 tape, the caller is heard to say, "We found a dead body. I think it might be the little girl that's been on the news" (Murr, 2002). The body was posed in such a horrific manner that the man who came upon it begged the police dispatcher to let him flee the scene. "Please hurry. I'm scared, and I want to get out of here" (McCarthy, 2002).

Samantha had been sexually assaulted and her body had been positioned with her arms and legs spread apart. Police reportedly found a substantial amount of evidence around the area where Samantha's body was found, including DNA samples, tire tracks, and fibers. There was evidence that the little girl had scratched her assailant. Autopsy results showed she was alive for hours after her abduction. The actual cause of death was asphyxiation. Because the body was found so quickly, there was significant forensic evidence found at the scene along with the DNA evidence recovered from the little girl's body.

THE SUSPECT

The police had ample evidence to connect to an offender, but they didn't have a solid suspect. Authorities had checked out scores of sex offenders and pulled over dozens of green cars and fielded hundred of tips. The break finally came on Wednesday afternoon. On July 17, a day and a half after Samantha's kidnapping and a day after her body was found, a caller advised the police to check out Alejandro Avila. "Within a few hours two more people had called the police with the same advice" (Leonard and Hanley, 2002).

Alejandro Avila lived in Lake Elsinore about 60 miles from the Runnion home. He lived an unusual life, living part time in the apartment of his mother and part-time in the apartment of his 22-year-old sister, which are next to each other. He also stayed at the apartment of his girlfriend. According to people who were interviewed, Avila was always hanging around children. He volunteered to take care of kids in his neighborhood and even babysat for some of his neighbors.

The majority of suspects in these cases are white males over age 25, single, living with someone else, unemployed or under employed if working, considered strange by others, with a history of past violent crimes against children. Alejandro Avila fit that profile.

The investigators soon learned that Avila had been arrested for child molestation. He had been charged with molesting two nine-year-old girls. One was the daughter of a woman he was staying with. But, he was acquitted of child molestation in 2001. One of the alleged victims had lived in the same Stanton townhouse complex where Samantha was snatched. Avila's Lake Elsinore apartment was just a few miles from where Samantha's nude body was found. Neighbors at Avila's apartment complex told investigators they had recently seen him meticulously cleaning a green car, which resembled the one Samantha's playmate said the kidnapper drove (Leonard and Hanley, 2002). Avila's cell phone and credit card records indicated he was in south Orange County—near the area where 5-year-old Samantha Runnion's body was discovered—in the hours after her kidnapping. A number of pieces of circumstantial evidence pointed toward Avila.

On Wednesday afternoon, the police began a surveillance of Avila, who remained in his apartment until Thursday morning. When the police saw Avila preparing to drive away in a friend's car, they decided to bring him in for an interview that lasted 12 hours until Avila asked for a lawyer. In the interim, the police had established enough probable cause to obtain search warrants for his apartment and for the vehicles that he had access to. In addition, they took a sample of Avila's blood and photographed one of his legs, which bore a scratch mark.

"Forensic analysts began drawing up a DNA profile to see whether it matched materials they had found under Samantha's fingernails, hoping she scratched her attacker" (Leonard and Hanley, 2002).

The preliminary tests determining whether DNA evidence found on Samantha's body matched Avila's genetic profile would not be ready until Friday afternoon. However, Sheriff Carona made a tactical decision to arrest Avila pending the laboratory results.

THE ARREST

On Friday morning, the authorities arrested Alejandro Avila on suspicion of the kidnapping and killing of Samantha Runnion. Sheriff Carona stated, "We have a lot we have to do in the next few hours. This in no way concludes this investigation. We are still trying to ensure that we bring the man who did this to justice" (Leonard and Hanley, 2002). Avila also resembled the sketch of the killer that was based on a description provided by Samantha's six-year-old playmate. Avila also owned a green Ford Thunderbird similar to the car described by the witness.

On Friday afternoon at about 3 p.m., the crime lab reported a match with Avila's DNA. Three hours later, a far more assured Carona strode to the podium to address reporters. "We're confident that Mr. Avila is, in fact, the murderer of Samantha Runnion," said Carona, calling it a 100% certainty (Leonard and Hanley, 2002).

"Match of DNA reported in California kidnap, slaying," reported the New York Daily News (2002, p. 10). "DNA taken from the body of slain 5-year-old Samantha Runnion matches that of the man accused of sexually abusing her and leaving her naked body along a rural California road, sources said yesterday."

On May 16, 2005, more than three years after the child was sexually assaulted and murdered, Alejandro Avila was found guilty. The jury recommended that Avila receive the death penalty.

SYNOPSIS

A number of factors were crucial in the early arrest of the suspect in this horrendous case.

1. The clear description of the subject supplied by Samantha's 6-year-old playmate along with the description of the green car.
2. Sheriff Carona's savvy management of the media that helped rivet the nation's attention as he worked behind the scenes to draw together traditionally turf-conscious law enforcement agencies—including the beleaguered FBI—into a cooperative venture driven to flush out Samantha's killer.
3. Finding the victim's body with 24 hours thereby providing the crucial forensic and biological evidence to link the suspect to the victim.
4. The tips and phone calls that pointed to Avila as a possible suspect, which resulted in the match of Avila to the recovered DNA from the victim.

Sex-Related Homicides: Topeka Child Abduction

CASE HISTORY

The following is taken from the author's files. On July 19, 1986, at approximately 9:04 p.m., 29-year-old Pamela Mahomes of 1530 SW Tyler reported her two daughters, Shannon and Shavon, missing to the Topeka Police Department in Topeka, Kansas. The two girls were described as black females, wearing identical clothing. Both girls had oversized white T-shirts with blue writing ("Memphis Queen Lines" with a picture of a boat), light blue shorts, white tennis-style shoes with pink trim, and white knee socks. Shannon was six years old, 3'10" tall, and Shavon was three years old, 3'2" tall. The girls were last seen playing in the vicinity of their home.

THE INVESTIGATION

The Topeka police immediately established an incident command post in the area and conducted a neighborhood canvass as they questioned family members and verified and evaluated the preliminary information in their missing person's report.

The police determined that the victims had eaten dinner at approximately 6:30 p.m. at their grandmother's house. Their mother, Pamela, went to her mother's house and brought the girls home at approximately 7:30 p.m. The mother then allowed the girls to go outside to play. When she went outside at 8 p.m. to summon the children inside, she could not locate them. Pamela and her boyfriend searched the neighborhood before calling the police at 9 p.m. Pamela said that her daughters had never wandered away before and she was visibly upset and concerned for their well-being.

The police ascertained that two juveniles, who lived directly across the street, had found Shannon and Shavon's tricycles in an empty lot, two lots north of the Mahomes' home and had pushed the tricycles back to the residence.

The police established that the two little girls had separate fathers and initiated inquires that subsequently eliminated them as suspects in the disappearance. During the canvass, police located a seven-year-old boy who told police that he had seen the two sisters standing on the front porch of a white neighbor named Nolan. According to the seven-year-old, Nolan was standing in the doorway of his residence at 1524 SW Tyler with his hands behind his back speaking to the girls. The seven-year-old stated that after he went into his residence, he looked out the window back toward Nolan's house and did not see the little girls or Nolan. This observation by the seven-year-old was quite fortuitous and remarkably similar to what occurred in the Samantha Runnion case where the six-year-old playmate, Sarah, was able to provide an amazingly accurate description of the suspect including his car.

At approximately 9:08 p.m., the first officer on the scene contacted Nolan, who was exiting a white Pontiac Grand Prix. Nolan was carrying an unopened bottle of vodka. The officer showed Nolan photos of the missing children and shown the location where the tricycles had been found. Nolan denied the accusations of neighbors that the girls had been on his front porch. Nolan admitted seeing the girls playing, but denied talking with them.

Nolan was subsequently identified by police as Nolan Prewett. Investigators determined that Nolan had been treated at the VA hospital in Topeka. He had been discharged in July 1986. A check of Prewett's patient record revealed that he had previously eaten a dog and had a history of child molestation. Police immediately began a surveillance of the residence.

Subsequent investigation revealed that Prewett had attempted to befriend many neighborhood children, both boys and girls. Prewett made plastic car models as a hobby and often gave models to children or enticed children into the basement of his home to show off his collection of model cars.

SEARCH WARRANT

On July 20, 1986, at approximately 2:30 a.m., Topeka police executed a search warrant on Prewett's residence. The warrant was based on the statement of the seven-year-old witness and the past history of the subject. The bodies of the missing girls were found in the basement of Prewett's home. The bodies were hidden between a wall and the furnace in a space approximately 18-inches wide. Cardboard boxes had been stacked approximately four feet high on top of the little girls' bodies. Nolan Prewett was placed under arrest and transported to the Topeka Police Department (Figures 11.10 through 11.13).

SUSPECT STATEMENTS

Prewett made a voluntary statement prior to the *Miranda* warnings that he remembered carrying a tricycle that belonged to one of the little girls who passes his house. After being given his Miranda warnings, he told officers that he was disabled and took a prescription medicine called Prolixon for a nervous system disorder.

Prewett stated he remembered seeing the victims, whose ages he recalled accurately, playing in front of his house and up and down the street. Prewett stated that one of the little girls asked him to carry her tricycle for her. Prewett said that he carried the trike to a green house directly north of his house to a hill where the girls played. He told the detectives that he had driven to the hospital approximately 15 or 20 minutes before 9

Figure 11.10 Boxes. The offender had hidden the little girl's bodies under a pile of empty cardboard boxes. (Photo courtesy of Topeka Police Department.)

p.m. Prewett stated he had not seen the missing girls since leaving for the hospital. He also stated that he began drinking after the officer contacted him during the evening hours of July 19.

Prewett denied being a child molester, as reported by the VA Hospital. When the officers showed him pictures of the missing girls and their mother, Prewett stated he did not recognize them. Prewett denied taking the missing girls into his home. He told the police that he experiences blackouts when he drinks alcoholic beverages. The detectives asked him about the "Chipmunk" music he had and Prewett told them it was country and western music. Prewett then invoked his right to an attorney and the interview was terminated.

INTERVIEW OF SUSPECT'S WIFE

The suspect's wife, Barbara, who had filed for a divorce, told the investigators that her husband had told her on numerous occasions about having dreams involving his engagement in sexual intercourse with little girls. She stated that he had sought treatment at the VA Hospital in an attempt to deal with his sexual fantasies involving little girls.

Barbara claimed that Nolan had been focused on a set of black twins about the age of first graders that lived in the 1600 block of Tyler. Barbara advised the police that it was not unusual for Nolan to be carefully watching these girls as they played up and down the street in front of their house. Barbara stated she was surprised to have been

Figure 11.11 Boxes. When the searching officer moved the boxes, they saw the legs of the little girls. (Photo courtesy of Topeka Police Department.)

confronted by neighbors complaining about Nolan parading around in "bikini pants" in front of the neighborhood children. She also advised the investigators that Nolan would play the music of "Alvin and the Chipmunks," which annoyed her greatly. When Barbara was shown the photos of the victims, she immediately recognized them as the little girls from the neighborhood who often played in front of the Prewett residence.

AUTOPSY FINDINGS

The autopsy revealed that both little girls had been asphyxiated, most likely caused by a hand or an object placed over their mouths and noses. Both victim's had been sexually assaulted with evidence of vaginal trauma indicative of full vaginal penetration.

DISPOSITION

Prewett who had been arrested for two counts of first degree murder also had additional charges of aggravated kidnapping, two counts; aggravated sodomy, two counts; aggravated rape, two counts; and two counts of enticement of a child.

On November 18, 1987, Prewett was convicted on all counts and is currently serving a life sentence at the Larned State Security Hospital in Kansas.

ACKNOWLEDGMENTS

The author wishes to acknowledge the contribution of this information and materials of this particular case from the following members of the Topeka, Kansas, Police

Figure 11.12 Bodies recovered. This view shows how the offender stashed the little girls' bodies behind the wall. He placed the little one on top of her older sister. (Photo courtesy of Topeka Police Department.)

Department: Lieutenant Colonel Steve Harsha (case detective), Detective Jim Harper, Detective (ret.) Bill Huffmeir, and Detective Doug Bluthardt. I also wish to acknowledge my friends and colleagues at the Kansas Bureau of Investigation, Special Agent-in-Charge Larry Thomas and Senior Special Agent Ray Lundin, for facilitating this case history.

Standard Operating Procedures

Investigating child abduction cases involves a lot of the knowledge, skills, and techniques generally used in homicide investigation. Investigators need the ability to gather information from witnesses accurately and quickly and be able to make decisions based on their experience. As time can be of the essence, a course of action has to be determined and having standard operating procedures (SOP) in place can assist the officers and investigators in making right decisions.

All agencies should have established SOPs for the handling of all missing person investigations. The SOP should be to get investigators immediately involved early in the investigation.

Figure 11.13 Close-up photograph. This is a close-up crime scene photograph of the victims in their original position. (Photo courtesy of Topeka Police Department.)

SOPs should include, but not be limited to, the following:

- *A Liaison Officer* to deal with the victim's family. Although the report is taken initially by the responding officer, the liaison officer replaces the reporting officer and acts as the official representative of the police department. He or she needs to understand the emotional needs of the victim's family, and any initial information (victimology) about victim will be obtained from the liaison officer. Also, consider that family members could become suspects at some point during the investigation. The liaison officer may or may not participate in this phase of the investigation. It depends on the rapport that was established by the liaison officer prior to a family member becoming suspect.
- Due to high media profile of child abduction cases, a *Public Information Officer*, should be assigned this duty. If the agency does not have a PIO, then someone other than the lead investigator should fill this role. It is recommended that the lead investigator should not fill this role. If possible, avoid assigning the family liaison officer. It should be an officer not directly connected to the investigation. This will help to keep critical information from getting out to the public and suspect.
- There will be *additional equipment needs* due to the large amount of information generated. Arrangements should be made ahead of time for communication equipment. The agency should have a toll-free dedicated phone number with several phone lines to handle tips and leads from the public with the capability to

record these phone calls as well as provide Caller ID. Operators and/or volunteers will be needed to operate the phones. Consideration should also be given to the equipment needed to record the victim's home phone.

- *Volunteers* need to be trained. They will be required to know how to handle callers who refuse to identify themselves. A majority of citizens providing information are willing to have their identity known. If you have the Caller ID system installed, this is one less issue to complicate the flow of information.
    - As incoming tips and lead information accelerate, there will be a need for tracking it. Computers are the best way to handle this.
        - If a computer system is brought in by another agency, consider several things. Have someone gain experience in using it prior to any incident.
        - Is the computer a stand alone or will it connect to other systems and check other databases?
        - What becomes of the information compiled when the computer is removed?
        - Will there be costs involved for using it?
    - A procedure should be in place to make sure all volunteers are properly identified and background checks completed.
    - Don't be surprised if the suspect shows up as a volunteer. He wants to learn what you know and just how close you are to identifying or apprehending him.
    - If people hesitate or balk at being identified or having a check made on their backgrounds, further inquiry into just who they are is recommended.
    - As these incidents become major investigations, there may be a need to establish a command post.
    - The command post should not be in the victim's front yard. However, it should be in the immediate area.
    - Consider the space requirements for the number of individuals that could eventually be involved in the investigation.
    - Assure that there are adequate communication abilities.
    - There should be sufficient room for an eating/rest area, restrooms, equipment, a personnel staging area, and room for specialized crime scene processing equipment.

Statistically speaking, most cases do not cross jurisdictional boundaries and consequently do not involve other law enforcement agencies. In most cases, the victim's body is located in the jurisdiction that took the initial report (Hanfland et al., 1997). There will be times, however, when the victim's body is found in another jurisdiction after being transported by the suspect. Generally the offender wants to distance himself from the body. The offender may take the body from a more populated area, such as the city, and transport it to a rural area. This may complicate the investigation, but will not make it unsolvable.

In the Polly Klaas case, her body was later discovered approximately 25 miles from her home in a desolate area. In the Danielle van Dam case (see below), the 7-year-old's body was discovered three weeks later 25 to 30 miles away from her home in a rural area east of San Diego. Little five-year-old Samantha Runnion's body was discovered less than 24 hours later in a rural mountainous area approximately 50 miles from where she had been abducted. This is an important consideration in broadcasting any alarms or descriptions of the victim and the abductor.

Consider what happened in the Polly Klaas investigation. The ability of an offender to quickly cross jurisdictional lines and to dispose of the body in a rural area requires law enforcement to interact with other agencies, to get the alarms and broadcasts to as many agencies as possible, and to work closely with the media for saturation exposure.

Danielle van Dam Kidnap and Murder

CASE FACTS

Little seven-year-old Danielle van Dam had disappeared from her family home in the middle of the night on February 2, 2002. She had been taken from her bedroom. There were no witnesses and no suspects. Thousands of volunteers combed her neighborhood, wooded areas, and rural roads as her parents begged for her return.

Within two days of the abduction, a neighbor of the van Dam family, named David Westerfield, 50, who lived two doors away from the van Dams, became the prime suspect in the case. The little girl's body was not discovered until February 27.

Westerfield had taken a trip to the desert in the early morning the same day Danielle vanished from her home. He was observed cleaning his motor home thoroughly upon returning from that sudden disappearance. Westerfield spent the weekend of Danielle's disappearance traveling around San Diego County in his motor home, stopping in the desert east of the city.

The authorities were able to secure a search warrant for the suspect's RV. The suspect was arrested based on evidence retrieved from his motor home. Authorities said they found the little girl's fingerprints and traces of Danielle's blood and strands of her hair in Westerfield's motor home. The police also found fibers in an orange choker necklace that Danielle had been wearing that came from Westerfield's vehicle. They also discovered the little girls' blood on Westerfield's jacket, which he had taken to a dry cleaner. In addition, a large amount of child pornography was retrieved from his computer.

David Westerfield pleaded innocent to charges of murder, kidnapping, and possession of child pornography. He was held without bond.

Three weeks later, the body of a child was found in a trash-strewn area underneath a grove of trees about 25 feet off a highway in rural El Cajon, about 30 miles east of the girl's home in the quiet San Diego suburb of Sabre Springs.

The child was wearing a plastic necklace similar to one Danielle was seen wearing in thousands of flyers distributed after her disappearance. An earring matching the description of a pair she was wearing at the time of her disappearance was also found. The little girl's body was positively identified as Danielle through dental records and DNA.

The trial lasted two and one-half months. The defense attempted to put the van Dam's lifestyle on trial, painting a picture of a sexually promiscuous couple who could have opened the door to the abduction. The prosecution stressed the DNA evidence and forensic evidence that had been recovered from Westerfield's RV. The authorities also seized thousands of computer files filled with child pornography from his computer including a cartoon video of the rape of a young girl. The prosecutor said, "The video represented Westerfield's sexual fantasies and inspired the abduction, rape, and murder of Danielle" (*USA Today*, August 2002).

The jury deliberation lasted 10 days. David Westerfield was found guilty of first degree murder, kidnapping, and misdemeanor possession of child pornography (Whitaker, 2002).

On September 16, 2002, that same jury in an unanimous decision recommended that David Westerfield be given the death sentence (*USA Today*, September 2002).

Additional Investigative Considerations

Due to the large numbers of needed personnel needed in these cases, it is important to establish, ahead of time, agreements with other agencies in securing their assistance.

Case management: Child abduction murder cases quickly evolve into major investigations and, as such, a case manager should be assigned to manage the volume of information collected.

Evidence: Due to the various sites and crime scenes and amount of evidence that may be generated, consideration should be given to assigning one individual the responsibility of maintaining and managing it.

Tracking system: State missing children's clearinghouses and violent crime tracking units should be notified early on and involved as resources. Become familiar ahead of time of their capabilities.

Forms: These should be uniform and determined before an incident as to which will be used. Ensure that all agencies use the same forms. Have forms established for all aspects of a major investigation: crime scene logs, checklists, canvass questionnaires, tip sheets, lead assignments, etc.

Specialists: As resources permit, consideration should be given to using the following forensic specialists and they should be contacted as needed in the investigation: anthropologist, archeologist, artist, botanist, climatologist, entomologist, geologist, odontologist, pathologist, toxicologist. Make contact with and settle arrangements before incidents, so you will know whom to contact and how to contact them. Obtain cooperation ahead of time to ensure immediate response when needed.

In addition, contact should have been established with the following specialized teams: aircraft, blood pattern specialist, crime scene technician, evidence response team, fingerprint technician, ground penetrating radar, search and rescue teams, tracking/cadaver dogs, underwater search and rescue team.

Cause of Death

Due to the sexual nature of these cases, the most common cause of death is by strangulation as opposed to child abuse cases, where death results from blunt force trauma, and murder in general by firearms (Hanfland et al., 1997). Ensure upon discovery of a victim's body that a complete and comprehensive postmedical examination is accomplished, to include examination for evidence, all toxically tests, and sexual assault protocols.

Investigation Procedures

An important police procedure in obtaining information is the neighborhood canvass in which witnesses are located. As in most crimes, you need to get information quickly and find the witnesses who may have it. Witnesses, who observed some aspect of a crime, without realizing that what they have seen is a crime, are known as unknowing witnesses. You have to find them and typically this is done through a canvass of various sites. You need to interview all potential witnesses in the area of the victim's last known location, the victim/killer contact site, the body recovery site, and any other site determined to be important to the investigation.

The Canvass

A *canvass* is a door-to-door, road block inquiry or brief interview with persons on the street by which detectives attempt to gain information about a specific incident. It is an important investigative tool and a vital part of the preliminary investigation at the homicide crime scene.

The detective supervisor should assign investigators to conduct a preliminary canvass of the surrounding area including the approach and escape routes from the crime scene, while the case officer performs his functions at the scene. As the detectives conduct the canvass, their primary purpose should not be to conduct in-depth interviews, but to locate possible witnesses or persons who may have information about the crime. Canvassers should obtain the name and address of each person spoken to, whether the person provides information or not. Where no one is at home or there are additional residents who should be interviewed, this should be noted so that the parties can be reached during a recanvass. Likewise, locations that are negative should be recorded for the follow-up investigation. The author recommends Canvass Control Sheets (see Figures 11.14 and 11.15).

Have a SOP for canvassing in place to make certain all individuals in the immediate area of the missing child are identified. At a minimum, the following information should be obtained from all individuals contacted on your agency's canvass check sheet:

1. Officer/investigator assigned
2. Address contacted
3. Name of occupant
4. Physicals: age, race, sex, date of birth
5. Telephone number
6. Employer
7. Employer address/telephone number
8. Spouse name and descriptors
9. Spouse employer
10. Children age/dates of birth
11. Other occupants/visitors, age, dates of birth, address, telephone number
12. Employer address/telephone number
13. Names of individuals other than above in residence/location between dates and times

CANVASS QUESTIONNAIRE

(Identify Yourself and Purpose of Canvass)

Name: (last)   (first)   (middle)   Date of Birth:

Address: Phone:

Employment (company name–type of work):   Address: Phone:

Other residents of This Address: (names and ages)

Did you know of the offense?   ☐ Yes   ☐ No

How did you first learn of it?   (when?)

Did you know the victim?   ☐ Yes   ☐ No

What was your relationship with the victim?   (if knew, date time, and location last seen or talked to)

Were you on the crime scene at anytime? (explain)

What knowledge do you have of the crime?

Typed stetement taken from this witness?   ☐ Yes   ☐ No

Reporting officer   (name)   (unit)   (date)   (time)

Figure 11.14 Canvass control sheet.

CANVASS QUESTIONNAIRE

Street, Avenue, Road, etc. _____

Number (or name if no number) _____

If Apartment or Office Building (name) _____

Occupants (full name and age)   Questionnaire
                                                                 Completed

1. _____   Yes – No

2. _____   Yes – No

3. _____   Yes – No

4. _____   Yes – No

5. _____   Yes – No

6. _____   Yes – No

Officer Recording _____

Time _____   Date _____

Figure 11.15 Canvass control sheet.

14. Occupant vehicle descriptions and license number
15. Anyone at location who knows victim or victim's family
16. Any individuals in area who display abnormal or different behavior
17. Anyone they suspect
18. Anyone they know who may have additional information
19. Any other information they can provide
20. Additional information

The check sheet should be identified by an agency and case number. All officers involved in canvassing should be briefed on what information they can share and what information is to be obtained. They should report all suspicious behavior. A master list of the canvass should be maintained.

Provide forms to officers involved in the canvassing. Write timely follow-ups. Inform them they may be having contact with the suspect while the victim is still alive or his/her body is in the suspect's residence. Some agencies have responded so fast the suspect did not have time to remove the body. Once you make your presence known, it should be maintained until the case is resolved.

Many agencies utilize uniform officers to conduct the canvass along with detectives and investigators. I feel that the canvass is so important that I assign a supervisor to be in charge of just the canvass. Whoever is involved needs to be briefed and made sure they obtain all needed information. A supervisor should keep track of the canvass and the canvass assignments. The supervisor is responsible to assure that no one is missed. You will need to recanvass until everyone has been contacted. There is nothing wrong in recontacting those previously contacted to determine if they might have additional information. This may mean returning to addresses several times. Make sure everyone at every address, residential or business, is contacted and interviewed.

Case Example

The St. Louis County Police investigated the disappearance of a ten-year-old female who was walking in her neighborhood to a friend's residence. A personal alarm belonging to the victim was located on the street two blocks from her home. Police responded immediately and conducted a neighborhood canvass and search for the victim. Investigators continued the canvass to make certain all individuals who had reason to be in the area were contacted. This required returning time and time again to the area. Eight days after the initial disappearance, the victim's body was located 12 miles away in another jurisdiction. Investigators focused on an individual who lived in the victim's neighborhood and whose father had a business located one-half block from the body recovery site. The individual was identified through continued canvassing. Based on the information the detectives obtained during this extended canvass, the subject was arrested, charged, and convicted (Nehring and Glenn, personal interview, March 3, 1998).

The Search

Another important procedure is the search for the victim. When searching for missing children, keep in mind they may be dead already and you are not looking for a live victim. Professionally speaking, this would never be shared with the victim's family. Many times children have been recovered alive after being abducted. However, sex-related stranger abductions usually prove to be fatal. Over half the time, the victim's body will be concealed as compared to very few in most murders (Hanfland et al., 1997). A child's body can be hidden in very small places; therefore, a thorough search needs to be conducted of all areas of possible concealment. Because the victim's body is the most important source of physical evidence linking the suspect to the victim, a well-planned, thorough search is paramount to the investigation.

If you do not have a sufficient number of law enforcement officers available to search, consider using reserve officers, members of the National Guard, and armed forces reserves as additional personnel. A good workable search team consists of between 15 and 25 members.

All searches need to be coordinated with canine units, tracking and cadaver dogs, so as not to disturb or complicate their abilities.

For both canvassing and searching, it is important to have available current maps of the area to help determine the areas to concentrate both activities in. In canvassing, it is important to contact individuals who were in the area at the time of the disappearance. In searching, it is important to consider those uninhabited areas where a body can be concealed.

Law enforcement agencies should not rely on anything less than professional police assistance. Under no circumstance should agencies be using trustees or prisoners in any aspect of the investigation, in particular, in searches for the victim, the body, or the various sites and crime scenes.

Canvassers and searchers need to be informed that bindings play a larger role in these cases than in other types of murders. If a victim's body is found with bindings in place or there is evidence they had been there but removed, the source of them needs to be located. They are often found in the suspect's residence or work place.

In searching any given area, consideration needs to be given to the duration of the search, hours of light, age of the victim, terrain to be covered, weather conditions, and number of personnel available. Always be aware of and obtain any surveillance videos in the immediate area. Check fast food restaurants and discount stores along with various locations of children's entertainment for videos at the time of the abduction. For the suspect, this is a seduction and he may buy gifts and food for the victim. In the suspect's mind, he is trying to make the abduction and his association with the child appear as normal as possible.

Conduct a systematic search out in a half-mile radius from the victim's last known location and expand it to a 1 1/2 mile radius in looking for the victim/suspect contact location.

Any basic grid search method can be used as long as you are thorough in doing it. For details on search patterns, as well as general search information, see the Internet site for the National Association of Search and Rescue (NASAR) at www.NASAR.org.

If available, use specialized search teams to conduct searches that cannot be easily accomplished on foot. There are specialized air search teams, both fixed wing and helicopter, canine units, horse teams, marine, off-road vehicles (consider using conventional four-wheel vehicles and not ATVs, which tend to destroy evidence and are noisy).

All search personnel need to be informed that if they observe potential evidence, including the victim's body, they are not to handle, pick up, touch, or move anything. They are to secure it and restrict the immediate area around it until crime scene technicians can process the scene.

As you investigate, consider that the primary motive for child abduction murder is sex. Techniques used in investigation of sex crimes are also useful in these cases. Crime scene processing should give the same consideration to both murder and sex crimes.

Victims

Any child under the age of 18 is a potential victim. The majority of victims are victims of opportunity as opposed to those who are targeted due to some physical characteristic. Older teenage females and younger males are more likely victims than others (Hanfland et al., 1997). The primary motivation for child abduction murder is sexual assault. As victims, their lifestyles are typically low-risk and are different from a lot of murder victims, who are often engaged in high-risk activities, such as drug dealing, prostitution, gangs, and other criminal activity.

Most victims of child abduction and murder are normal, average kids, living normal lives with their families. They are typically engaging in children's social activities, playing, going to and from school.

The typical victim is a white female aged 11 (Hanfland et al., 1997). Males under age 12 are more likely to be victimized than older males. Older females are more likely to be victims than younger ones. Remember that children of all ages and either sex can be victimized. The main motivation for the suspect is sexual in nature. In the suspect's thinking, this is a seduction. Typically the victim will be killed in a stranger abduction.

Suspects

The majority of suspects in these cases are white males, aged 27, single, living with someone else, unemployed or under employed if working, considered strange by others, with a history of past violent crimes against children (Hanfland et al., 1997). Usually they are not under any formal custody status. They are considered to be socially marginal individuals by others.

Their inadequate personalities make it difficult for them to establish or maintain a relationship with adult females. They may prefer an adult female partner, but because of their poor social skills or unattractiveness, they are unsuccessful in establishing any type of social relationship with a mature member of the opposite sex. Frustrated, they then progress to someone younger and smaller that they can forcibly control for the purposes of sexual gratification. Because of their lack of employment or being under employed, they usually have to live with someone. Quite often it is only relatives who will allow them to live with them. Due to the sexual nature of this crime, very few of these types of abductions are committed exclusively by females. The females typically act in conjunction with a domineering male. Hazelwood and Michaud (2001) describes them as suspects who are "compliant victims."

Suspects are often overlooked because they live, work, and socialize in the immediate area of the abduction. Due to their economic situation, they do not always have their own means of vehicle transportation and may have to borrow or even rent a vehicle for use in transporting the victim's body to the body recovery site.

In most of these cases, within a week the suspect's name is in the investigation report; however, not necessarily as the suspect. A good strategy on unsolved cases is to go back over the investigation after the first week and determine how various individuals were cleared or not cleared from the case.

Also run a check on the criminal history information on the various names associated with the case, including all witnesses and volunteers. Check records for registered sex offenders and offenders who have committed crimes against children, who live or work in the immediate area. Check with your state clearinghouse or violent crimes tracking units on similar crimes.

Suspect Interview Strategies

Interview and interrogate all suspects. The main motivation is sexual in nature, the strategies used in sex crime investigations work as well in these cases. Gaining rapport with any suspect and treating him with respect will often provide the opening needed. During these cases, it is important not to let your true feelings be exposed. End all interrogations with asking them about the incidents prior to this one. It is surprising how many suspects are serial offenders.

Victim–Suspect Relationship

In most cases the relationship between victim and suspect is one of being strangers. Even though they are strangers to one another, the suspect is often overlooked because he lives, works, and socializes in the immediate area. Thus, while he is a stranger to the victim, he is not a stranger to the area. The suspect may know or have knowledge of the victim. Older females are more likely killed by strangers as are younger males. Knowing the age and gender of victim should provide some focus on evaluating suspects.

Important Sites

Child abduction murders are different in general from most murder investigations in that there are a number of important sites and crime scenes associated with them. In the majority of murder cases, all events occur in one location, the victim and suspect come into contact with each other, there is an assault causing death, and the victim's body is left where it falls. This is not true in child abduction cases. A number of different sites have to be located for those unknowing witnesses and evidence linking the suspect to the victim.

While there may be a separation in distance between sites and where the victim and suspect live, the sites can occur individually at different locations, all at the same location, or in groups. Each site is a potential crime scene and needs to be treated as such. The area needs to be sealed off and protected until it can be processed as a crime scene for evidence.

Last Seen or Known Location

The last seen or known location site is where the victim was last known to be or seen. It is typically not their residence; however, most were last seen within a quarter-mile of their front door (Hanfland et al., 1997). Keep in mind, the younger the victim, the closer to home this location will be.

Initial Contact Site

The initial contact site is where the killer makes contact with the victim. This site can be quite close to the last known location and enhances the reasons for a thorough canvass and search. This is the one location where the suspect has to expose himself to the potential of being seen by others. It may be momentary, but it is the one location over which the suspect has no control. As the victim is often one of opportunity for the suspect, he has no control over where he will make contact with the victim. This location provides the potential for those unknowing witnesses who may have a description of the suspect or his vehicle. This site is usually within a quarter mile or three city blocks of the victim's last known location and a third of the time within a quarter mile of the suspect's residence (Hanfland et al., 1997); hence, the importance of determining the victim's last known location and then canvassing and searching out a minimum of a half-mile radius from the location the suspect and victim came into contact with each other.

Murder Site

The murder site, the location where the suspect kills the victim, is often under his control; however, not always as circumstances may dictate. Due to their size, children are least able to withstand physical assault and control by adults. Three quarters of the murder sites will be within 200 feet of the body recovery site (Hanfland et al., 1997). The importance of finding this site is that it is second only to the body recovery site in yielding physical evidence, which links the suspect to the victim. As the majority of child victims are killed within 200 feet of the body recovery site, it is important to initially tape off an area at least 200 feet out from the victim's body. You can always make a crime scene smaller; however, it is almost impossible to enlarge one. The distance from the victim–suspect contact site is often at least 1 and a half miles and even farther. And, for older victims, the distances are usually greater than those for younger ones.

Body Recovery Site

The body recovery site is that location where the victim's body is recovered. This site is important for locating evidence linking the suspect to the victim. This is **not** an easy site to find because over half of the victims' bodies are concealed. The suspect wants to separate the distance between himself and the victim. Keep this in mind where searching for victims, that they may be concealed and, unfortunately due to their small size, can be placed in small areas.

All sites need to be secured until properly processed by crime scene technicians or skilled and experienced investigators.

There are other important sites or scenes to consider. Give thought to the routes of travel to remote sites. Canvass individuals along these routes to determine what individuals or vehicles used the routes just prior to and after the victim's disappearance. Research indicates that suspects will return to body recovery sites until they are discovered by the police. At a minimum search on either side of the route for a distance of at least a mile from the body recovery site, as far out as someone could throw something from a vehicle.

If there is a separation in sites consider possible modes of vehicle transportation used. When a suspect is identified consider searching all vehicles he may have used or had access to. Remember, he may even rent or steal a vehicle. Always obtain necessary search warrants.

In the St. Louis County case previously cited, the suspect had to return with a vehicle in order to move the victim's body from his residence to where she was found 12 miles away.

Quite often the victim or the body will have been at the suspect's residence. These are sex cases and the suspect has a reason for taking the victim to his residence. Remember to search all of the suspect's residence, not only for evidence of the victim's presence, but also for photos, journals, and other evidence.

Many states have civilian volunteer agencies that will help out in many ways. Unfortunately, most are named in memory of some child victim. Make yourself aware of these nonprofit groups. They are an excellent resource for additional manpower and assistance.

For additional information consider the following references and resources: Child Abduction Response Plan available through your local FBI, *Missing and Abducted Children: A Law Enforcement Guide to Case Investigation and Program Management* by the National Center for Missing and Exploited Children, and *Case Management for Missing Children Homicide Investigation* published by the Office of Attorney General, State of Washington.

The Amber Alert Plan

The Amber Plan is a voluntary partnership between law enforcement agencies and broadcasters to activate an urgent bulletin in the most serious child abduction cases.

The information on the Amber Plan can be accessed on their website at www.missing-kids.com/html/amberplan.html.

Broadcasters use the Emergency Alert System (EAS), formerly called the Emergency Broadcast System, to air a description of the missing child and suspected abductor. This is the same concept used during severe weather emergencies. The goal of the Amber Alert is to instantly galvanize the entire community to assist in the search for and safe return of the child.

The Amber Plan was created in 1996 as a powerful legacy to 9-year-old Amber Hagerman, a bright little girl who was kidnapped while riding her bicycle and brutally murdered in Arlington, Texas. The tragedy shocked and outraged the entire community. Residents contacted radio stations in the Dallas area and suggested they broadcast special "alerts" over the airwaves so that they could help prevent such incidents in the future.

In response to the community's concern for the safety of local children, the Dallas/Fort Worth Association of Radio Managers teamed up with local law enforcement agencies in northern Texas and developed this innovative early warning system to help find abducted children. Statistics show that, when abducted, a child's greatest enemy is time.

How Does the Amber Plan Work?

Once law enforcement has been notified about an abducted child, they must first determine if the case meets the Amber Plan's criteria for triggering an alert.

Each program establishes its own Amber Plan criteria; however, the National Center for Missing and Exploited Children suggests three criteria that should be met before law enforcement confirms a child has been abducted:

- Alert is activated.
- Law enforcement believes the circumstances surrounding the abduction indicate that the child is in danger of serious bodily harm or death.
- There is enough descriptive information about the child, abductor, and/or suspect's vehicle to believe an immediate broadcast alert will help.

If these criteria are met, alert information must be put together for public distribution. This information can include descriptions and pictures of the missing child, the suspected abductor, a suspected vehicle, and any other information available and valuable to identifying the child and suspect. The information is then faxed to radio stations designated as primary stations under the EAS.

The primary stations send the same information to area radio and television stations and cable systems via the EAS, and it is immediately broadcast by participating stations to millions of listeners.

Radio stations interrupt programming to announce the alert, and television stations and cable systems run a "crawl" on the screen along with a picture of the child. Also, the alert appears on freeway electronic signs that alert drivers to road problems or accidents.

For more information about the Amber Plan, call 1-800-THE-LOST.

The National Center for Missing and Exploited Children, a nonprofit advocacy group based in Alexandria, Virginia, estimates that 20 children in the country have been saved because of the network (Liu and Ortez, 2002).

An Amber Alert Case: Teenage Girls Rescued and Abductor Killed by Police

CASE FACTS

On August 1, 2002, in the early morning hours, a convicted felon, named Roy Ratliff, abducted two teenage girls, age 16 and 17, from a lover's lane. Thus, began a 12-hour ordeal for the two teenage girls who were sexually assaulted by their assailant and were minutes away from being killed when rescued by sheriff's deputies. The two teenage girls, who were not friends, had been in two separate cars, each with a boy, in a Lover's Lane area when they were accosted sometime after midnight.

Ratliff, who was on the run from a carjacking incident in Las Vegas, Nevada, was also wanted on a $3 million warrant in the rape of a Mojave, California, woman.

THE ABDUCTION

Ratliff pulled up in a gray Saturn that he had stolen at gunpoint in Las Vegas two weeks earlier. Police believe he was initially looking for another car because the Saturn had a flat tire when he came upon the teenagers. The offender approached the couple in the Bronco, which was the only vehicle in the parking lot. At gunpoint, he ordered the male teenager out of the SUV and ordered the female to remain in the Bronco. He then demanded money from the male before tying him up with duct tape to a pole. As Ratliff was preparing to leave, a second car, occupied by a teenage couple, came into the lot. He also accosted them and then tried to tape the two teenagers together in their car. When that didn't work, he taped the male to the steering wheel with silver duct tape and dragged the female back to the Bronco. He then left the scene with his two female captives in the Bronco, which he had stolen from the first couple. One of the young men was finally able to untie himself at approximately 1:45 a.m. He called his sister who called 911. The police were on the scene by 1:58 a.m. Police estimated that the crime had occurred around 12:30 a.m. meaning that the offender already had an significant amount of time to have left the area.

The discovery that the two girls had been kidnapped set in motion a massive manhunt. Ultimately, at least half a dozen law enforcement agencies in Southern California were intensively involved, and the search drew in motorists statewide through the new California Child Safety Amber Network, which posts kidnapping alerts on electronic freeway signs as well as on radio and television.

SUSPECT SPOTTED

It was the Amber Alert System that provided authorities with their first sighting of the suspect. At approximately 9:30 a.m., a motorist advised a deputy that he had seen the white Bronco on California 178 in the Walker Pass area, about 70 miles east of Bakersfield. Around 11:30 a.m., a Caltrans flagman working on a highway construction site was listening to the radio and heard the Amber Alert. Moments later, he looked up and saw the Bronco pass by. He called the California Highway Patrol (CHP) dispatch. At this point, both the Kern County Sheriff's Department and CHP were converging on the area, which is a two-lane road through a rugged area. Also taking part in the manhunt were five law enforcement helicopters and three airplanes. Three of the helicopters focused on the California 178 area as the hunt intensified.

About the same time, authorities said that a Kern County animal control officer spotted the Bronco on White Blanket Road, a dirt road that traverses the White Blanket Indian allotment, a very rural and rugged area off California 178. She immediately notified the Sheriff's Department. This location was almost 100 miles away from where the kidnapping had occurred 12 hours earlier. However, the Amber Alert was statewide.

Two deputies, James Stratton and Larry Thatcher, who were driving separate units, were nearest to the area. They responded to the site and spotted the Bronco about 50 feet in front of them. The suspect, Ratliff, also saw the deputies approaching. He suddenly sped up, swerved off the dirt road and then barreled down a hill where the Bronco became hung up on a rock in a dry riverbed. The deputies, knowing that their sedans could not traverse this rough terrain, jumped out of their patrol cars and rushed down the hill toward the Bronco. As they approached the suspect, the deputies yelled to the him to get out. According to the police, Ratliff yelled, "No way! No way!"

Ratliff, a convicted felon, had two strikes against him. Under California law, a third offense would place him in prison for the rest of his natural life. The outstanding warrant for rape, his crime spree of car jacking, and the robbery, abduction, and subsequent rape of the two teenagers guaranteed that this guy wouldn't see the light of day if apprehended.

THE CONFRONTATION

According to Kern County Sheriff Carl Sparks, "Ratliff reached into the back seat and pulled out a weapon. Deputy Stratton fired one round into the rear of the Bronco, shattering the back window. That was when Deputy Thatcher saw Ratliff coming up with the gun. Deputy Thatcher and Stratton fired and saw Ratliff slump over. In the interim Deputy Stratton, who was firing from the rear, suddenly realized that the girls were still in the Bronco. He stopped firing and began to assist them out of the Bronco and led them to safety. As Deputy Thatcher approached the driver's side, Ratliff suddenly came up with a gun in his hand. That was when Deputy Thatcher fired twice more killing the suspect" (Rivera, 2002).

After the rescue, the authorities learned that both young women had been raped and sexually assaulted. Both of the victims had tape on their wrists at the time of their rescue. Investigators believed that Ratliff had brought his two captives to this isolated and desolate location in Kern County to kill them and bury them. In his mind, he had nothing to lose. In the opinion of the author, this would be the classic behavior of a sexual psychopath.

The legislation necessary to launch the Amber Alert System had just made its debut in California the week before this kidnapping. The general public, the media, and the police recognized the benefits of this alert system in action, as the details of this case were broadcast nationwide. Certainly this cooperative venture had prevented another tragedy and a dangerous predator had been killed in the police action.

At the site where the girls were rescued and their assailant killed, an obviously pleased Sheriff Carl Sparks stood about a dozen feet away from the dead man's body and stated, "We don't have to rehabilitate [this] son-of-bitch ... and there will be no appeal to the Supreme Court" (Guccione et al., 2002).

Considering this offender's record, what he had done to his victims, and the fact that he would have killed them had the police not intervened, the author couldn't agree more with the sheriff's opinion.

Westley Allan Dodd

CASE FACTS

Westley Allan Dodd was a pedophile and a serial killer who terrorized the Pacific Northwest with a series of sadistic and brutal murders of young boys, whom he would abduct and torture. He was an extremely calculating predator who had every intention of living out his most perverse fantasies until he was caught.

The cases began on September 4, 1989, when the bodies of two boys were found in a park in Vancouver, Washington. Then, on October 29, the police in Portland, Oregon, were alerted to the disappearance of a young child, 4 years of age, whose body was subsequently found on November 1.

POLICE RESPONSE: MULTIDIMENSIONAL TASK FORCE

A multidimensional task force, including FBI agents, was organized to apprehend the perpetrator. Forensic psychiatrist and part-time Beaverton homicide detective, Dr. Ronald Turco, was asked to join the task force to develop a profile of this unknown predator. Dr. Turco (1998), who is a personal friend and colleague of the author, provided a firsthand description of this horrific case as well as the photos and materials that illustrate the dynamics of the sexual predator.

Dr. Turco developed a profile of the offender whom he described as a white male between 25 and 35 years of age, who would be a loner with few ties to the community. The profile indicated that he might keep records of the crimes including a diary and newspaper clippings. Furthermore, it was hypothesized that the offender would have pornography in his possession as well as photographs of the victims alive and dead. It was believed that the offender would keep fetish items of his victims, which he would use to masturbate to and relive the events. It was also hypothesized that the offender would continue to molest and murder children. Dr. Turco advised the authorities that individuals who commit these types of crimes often have a prior history of mental health counseling for sexual offenses and a long history of deviant sexual behavior. It was believed that the offender used restraints on his child victims and that clinically the offender would be nonpsychotic and would most likely fit into the category of an "organized serial killer."

SUSPECT ARRESTED IN AN ATTEMPTED ABDUCTION

On November 13, a suspect was arrested and charged with kidnapping in the first degree by Washington police after he attempted to abduct a screaming six-year-old boy from a movie theater. During police questioning, he confessed to the murder of the two Neer brothers, Cole, 11, and Billy, 10, who had been found in the Vancouver Park. Dr. Turco participated in a three-hour interview with the suspect, which was videotaped. In that session, Dodd elaborated on his confession and described in great detail the sexual assault, mutilation, and murder of the three boys.

Figure 11.16 Dodd's briefcase. The briefcase, which contained Dodd's diary described in brutal detail his sadistic fantasies and the atrocities he had visited upon his young victims. The victim's underwear was also recovered in the case. (Photo courtesy of Dr. Ronald Turco, Portland, Oregon.)

THE CONFESSION

The confession was more than the authorities were prepared for. In fact, Dodd seemed to enjoy their discomfort as he relived his sadistic experiences.

The authorities used the profile, which had been extremely accurate, along with the statements of the suspect as evidence to obtain a search warrant. When the warrant was executed, the authorities found underclothing of a deceased child along with numerous Polaroid™ photographs of his victims and an array of child pornography. As predicted, the police located a diary. This diary went into specific details of each of the murders.

The suspect had planned to abduct and kill more boys. He had also planned on performing sexual operations on them and dissecting their bodies. The diary was both a treasure trove of investigative information as well as the horrific inner most thoughts of a sexual psychopath (Figure 11.16).

PSYCHOSEXUAL HISTORY OF SUSPECT

- Pathological behaviors with other children (including relatives) from age 9.
- At age 14 in junior high school, he began exposing himself.
- He attempted to get an 8-year-old into an empty building.
- He was prepared to "rape."
- He was caught and provided with counseling.
- He began a series of exhibitionist activities away from his home.
- He graduated from "flashing" to "touching" children, both boys and girls.
- He practiced fellatio on younger boys who agreed to "play."
- He was the subject of a police investigation at age 15.
- Again he was provided with therapy.
- In his early 20s, he decided to "hunt" for young boys.

- He made a satanic contract and exchanged his soul for "happy life as a pedophile."
- He kept an extensive and detailed diary.
- At age 28, he started his serial murder activities with young boys.

CLASSIC PEDOPHILIC BEHAVIOR

- Dodd exhibited the classic behavior of the pedophile.
- He was looking for "double victims," for example,
  - Children from broken homes.
  - Children who have been previously molested.
  - Children who are simply neglected or abandoned.
- Dodd exhibited an uncanny ability to select children who he could verbally control and manipulate.
- At one point during his confession to Dr. Turco, Dodd exhibited "malignant pseudo-identification." In other words, Dodd talked "baby talk" as he lured his victims.

COLE AND BILLY NEER CASE: THE DIARY ENTRY

It was September 4, Labor Day. Westley Dodd had stalked and attempted to engage more than 20 children in David Douglas Park. He was actively prowling the parks "hunting" for a little boy with which to have sex. However, most of the children had managed to elude him because they were accompanied by an adult or there were witnesses around. He suddenly spotted two youngsters who were alone.

According to Dodd's journal, it was about 6:25 p.m. when he spotted the two Neer brothers. Dodd lured them into a secluded area and ordered them off their bikes. He spent about 20 minutes with them. He sexually assaulted 11-year-old Cole first and then attempted to molest the younger Billy. Dodd then stabbed the two boys before he left the scene.

According to the journal, Dodd had sexually assaulted Cole by performing oral sodomy on him and then attempted to molest Billy. He then stabbed the two boys before leaving the scene to prevent identification. However, the bodies were quickly discovered by a hiker who immediately called 911. Billy was still alive and was taken to a hospital.

Dodd kept a journal or diary of his activities and fantasies that proved to be of significant investigative value not only as evidence but of insight into the mind of such a sadistic personality. Dodd wrote that he was worried about the fact that one of the Neer boys had survived until he found out that Billy Neer had later died at the hospital.

He followed all of the news stories looking for anything that might be a threat. When he saw the pictures of "persons of interest," he felt relieved and more confident for the next kill (Figure 11.17).

This is a typical example of a sexual serial killer's response and behavior after he "gets away" with his first murder. Dodd had crossed "the psychological barrier" of murder, accompanied by the "thrill" of his success. That thrill was punctuated by the fear that the police might find out who he was from the surviving victim and that he might be caught. However, when that did not occur and a certain amount of time had passed, he fantasized about his next victim and prepared for another successful kill.

Figure 11.17 Newspaper clippings. Dodd kept all of the newspaper clippings of the murders and followed the stories as he adjusted his activities. (Photo courtesy of Dr. Ronald Turco, Portland, Oregon.)

INVESTIGATIVE AND SIGNATURE INFORMATION

- Westley Allan Dodd wrote a detailed account of this first kill in his diary.
- He kept all of the news clippings of the homicide.
- He added these news clippings to his diary description and began to fantasize about his next victim.
- In his diary, he complained that he hadn't taken any pictures.
- Dodd wrote in his diary how "shook up" he was.
- He decided to lie low for a while and plan the next event.
- He wrote that he was able to "climax" thinking about his next kill.
- He planned on getting "before and after" photos of his sex-murder victims for his journal.
- He also referenced "forensic evidence."
- He wrote, "I think I got more out of killing then [sic] molesting."

The diary revealed that Westley Dodd's fantasies progressed with each event. He wrote, "I dream of cutting off his erect cock and then butt fuck him as his cock bleeds. If he's still alive, I'll finish him off." He then added, "Of course, I'll be taking pictures each step of the way." Dodd wrote that the knife in the first incident was a good choice because it was quick, but he planned on making the next one a "cleaner kill like choking." He fantasized that he wanted a clean body for butt fucking and a more comfortable site so he could take time to practice various types of sex.

Dodd wrote up a protocol for conducting exploratory surgery. He also had a plan for dead subjects. He planned on doing amputations on live subjects depending on their physical reaction to pain tolerance during the removal of testicles, etc. He wrote that he would like to videotape the "surgery" as a reference and show "patients" what he would be doing to terrify them and watch their reactions.

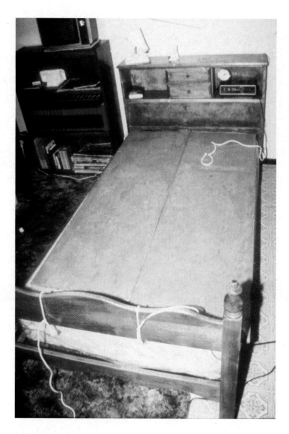

Figure 11.18 Dodd's bed. Dodd had secured ropes and bindings to hold his victims down as he tortured them. (Photo courtesy of Dr. Ronald Turco, Portland, Oregon.)

LEE ISELI CASE: THE DIARY ENTRY

According to Dodd's journal, it was about 12:50 p.m. on October 29 when he spotted the little boy playing by himself in a schoolyard. He walked up to Lee and asked him if "he wanted to have some fun and make some money." Dodd wrote that Lee seemed unsure, but when Dodd extended his hand, Lee took it and they walked off together.

Dodd brought Lee back to his house, where the little boy was manipulated into Dodd's sadistic little sex game (Figure 11.18). In keeping with his "signature," Dodd engaged in oral sex in an attempt to have the child obtain an erection.

The authorities would not know the extent of this little boy's torturous death until Dodd confessed to Dr. Turco. When Dodd gave his confession, he purposely left out a number of details. The diary, however, vividly depicted his extreme sadism. Dodd recorded by the minute what he was doing to Lee. Dodd wrote how he sexually assaulted him 10 to 15 times and kept waking the little boy up to have sex with him. Dodd planned on killing the little boy and when he decided to strangle him, his arms began to hurt, so he hung the child in the closet until he was dead.

Dodd had taken Polaroid pictures of little Lee and had added notes to the pictures. He also had nude pictures of other children that he kept in a briefcase. Dodd had anal sex with the little boy's body. In order to perpetrate this outrageous act, he had to "break" the rigor in the little boy's legs. He then cleaned up and put the nude body into garbage bags. He carried the body out to his car, placed it on the floorboard on

Figure 11.19 Under the bed. Authorities found Dodd's briefcase with the diary and all of his photos and notes. Inside were Polaroid™ photos of his victim taken while he was alive and after he was dead. (Photo courtesy of Dr. Ronald Turco, Portland, Oregon.)

the passenger side, took the body out to Vancouver Lake at nighttime, and disposed of the body in the bushes. Dodd then returned home and gathered all of the little boy's clothing and burned his clothes, the rope he used to tie him up, and the rope he used to strangle him. Dodd kept the little boy's underwear as a trophy and put them in his briefcase under his bed (Figure 11.19).

DISPOSITION

Dodd was sentenced to death in 1990 for molesting and then stabbing to death Cole Neer (11) and his brother, William (10), near a Vancouver, Washington, park in 1989, as well as for the separate rape and murder of Lee Iseli. Dodd was subsequently executed on January 5, 1993.

Conclusion

Children, sadly, are at risk of abduction and sex-related murder due to the menace of the pedophile predators in our society. The year 2002 certainly brought attention to this issue with the number of high-profile child abduction and sex-related homicides that occurred in a short span of time. Although the data indicates that these incidents are statistically rare, they are horrendous crimes. Child abduction cases affect not only the immediate family of the victim, but entire communities and our society as a whole, as media coverage of the event is nationally broadcast.

The law enforcement community has come to realize that sex-related child abductions are cause for immediate action and response along with the enlistment of assistance from the general public as well as the media. A delay in reporting such incidents may not seem important. However, studies indicate that almost half of the abducted children are murdered within one hour of their abduction. Three-quarters are dead within three hours and nine out of ten are killed within 24 hours (Hanfland et al., 1997).

The Amber Alert Plan, which has recently been adopted nationwide, is a direct result of the concern and public response generated by these high-profile cases along with the realization that law enforcement alone cannot adequately deal with the potential threat posed by the child abductor.

References

Bortnick, B. *Polly Klaas: The Murder of America's Child*, Pinnacle Books, Kensington Publishing, New York, 1995.

Geberth, V.J. *Practical Homicide Investigation: Tactics, Procedures, and Forensic Techniques*, 4th ed., CRC Press, Boca Raton, FL, 2006.

Guccione, J., A. Blankstein, and M. Landsberg. Teens rescued, abductor killed after massive statewide search, *LA Times*, August 2, 2002.

Hanfland, K.A., R.D. Keppel, and J.G. Weis. *Case Management for Missing Children: Homicide Investigation Executive Summary*, Office of the Attorney General, State of Washington, 1997.

Hazelwood, R. and S. Michaud. *Dark Dreams: Sexual Violence, Homicide, and the Criminal Mind*, St. Martin's Press, New York, 2001.

Kranes, M. 2nd ORE. body found, *New York Post*, August 26, 2002, p. 9.

Leonard, J. and C. Hanley. Tips led to fast arrest in girl's killing, *LA Times*, July 21, 2002.

Liu, C. and J. Ortiz. Amber alert gets involved in the manhunt, *LA Times*, August 2, 2002.

Malkin, M. A sickening death: Are we too tolerant of gay pedophilia? Opinion page, *New York Post*, March 18, 2001.

Massarella, L. Grisly find in search for kids, *New York Post*, August 25, 2002, p. 7.

McCarthy, T. The playtime killer, *Time Magazine*, July 29, 2002, p. 41.

Murr, A. When kids go missing, *Newsweek*, July 29, 2002, pp. 23–39.

Nehring, L. (Detective) and Lt. D. Glenn. St. Louis County Missouri Police. Personal interview. (March 3, 1998)

New York Daily News, Match of DNA reported in California kidnap, slaying, July 21, 2002, p. 10.

New York Post, Kidnap-slay horror, July 27, 2002, p. 5.

Rivera, G. *At Large with Geraldo Rivera*, a special FOX News Broadcast, Interview with Sheriff Carl Sparks, August 3, 2002.

Sujo, A. Ore. suspect had slay style just like dear old dad's: Cops, *New York Post*, August 27, 2002, p. 17.

Turco, R.L. *Closely Watched Shadows: A Profile of the Hunter and the Hunted.* Book Partners, Inc., Wilsonville, Oregon, 1998.

USA Today, Jurors choose death sentence in van Dam case, September 17, 2002, p. 13A.

USA Today, Jury took its time in van Dam case, August 22, 2002, p. 3A.

Whitaker, B., Neighbor guilty of murder of girl, 7, in San Diego, *New York Times*, August 22, 2002, p. A12.

Sex Slave Torture and Serial Murder Case

12

Introduction

In Chapter 1, I mentioned the David Parker Ray case as a classic example of sexual sadism as defined in *Diagnostic and Statistical Manuel of Mental Disorders* (*DSM-IV-TR*) (APA, 2000). In Chapter 2, I present various examples of how the sexual sadist incorporated fantasy into the criminal event. This chapter will focus on one particular offender who, in the opinion of the author, was one of the most dangerous and evil of all of the serial murderers on which I have consulted. Clinically speaking, I would diagnose him as a **psychopathic sexual sadist**. Investigatively speaking, I would define him as a **human predator**. Spiritually speaking, I would define him as the **devil on Earth**.

David Parker Ray

David Parker Ray was originally from Albuquerque. He left his first wife to join the U.S. Army where he became a skillful mechanic, which became his trade. His second marriage lasted only three months. He married his third wife at 26; she was 18 years old when they had a little girl named Glenda. He left this family after a few months and drifted through Arizona and New Mexico living like an indigent supporting himself by doing odd jobs and repairs. During this time, he reportedly was with an 18-year-old girl who disappeared one morning without explanation.

Ray returned to his family in Albuquerque and presented as the consummate family man. He found a car repair job and enrolled in school to be qualified as an aircraft mechanic. However, during this time, he was secretly frequenting prostitutes and engaging in sadomasochistic activities. Once he graduated from air mechanics school, he moved his family to Tulsa, Oklahoma, where he taught mechanics at Spartan Aeronautics. During the day, he taught engine mechanics and specialized aviation maintenance and went home every night to his family. He did this for two years, and then went back to his old habits.

Ray in the meantime was getting deeper and deeper into sadomasochistic (S&M) sex and bondage. In the 1970s, he moved his family to Victoria, Texas, where he ran a gas station.

He returned to Albuquerque in 1977 and found a job repairing track for the railroad, which took him all over the Midwest and he was rarely home for five years. His third marriage dissolved in 1981 as a result. In 1983, he became a service manager for Canal Motors in Phoenix and was considered an excellent worker by his two bosses, Bill Stone and Billy Ray Bowers.

Ray got married for the fourth time to a local woman named Joni-Lee and remained in Phoenix. As it turned out, this city was the perfect place for his S&M activities. Ray continually crisscrossed Arizona and New Mexico with frequent trips into Mexico. He and his new wife eventually took out a lease for property at 513 Bass Road in Elephant Butte and a second property at Stone Lake, New Mexico. Around this time, he began designing and making specialized bondage equipment at the Elephant Butte location, which he sold mail order. He also took women here for sexual bondage sessions.

Ray created a torture chamber in which he would systematically engage in physical and psychological torture of his victims, whom he referred to as his "slaves." He was evidently excited by the sight of his victims' suffering and helplessness, as he photographed and videotaped them. He reportedly experienced pleasurable sexual arousal through the infliction of various forms of both physical and emotional pain on the young women, whom he treated as objects. When he finished "playing" with them, he would kill them.

Ray would then get rid of the bodies of his victims by taking them out to rural areas around Elephant Butte Lake, which is 25 miles long and in some areas over 200-feet deep. It is surrounded by mountainous terrain. The closest city is Truth or Consequences, New Mexico, which is about seven miles away.

At the time of his arrest, David Parker Ray was 59 years of age. He was a serial killer suspected in multiple sex torture murders. Authorities believe he was responsible for the murders of over 30 young women, some of whom were sold into "white slavery" in Mexico.

He was captured under classical circumstance in which a potential victim of sex-related homicide manages to escape and notify authorities. He was arrested on March 22, 1999, along with his live-in girlfriend, Cindy Hendy, 39 years old, who was participating in these events. His daughter, Glenda "Jessie" Ray, 32 years old, was also subsequently charged in connection with some of the sex-related events. The New Mexico State Police charged David Parker Ray with rape, sexual assault, and attempted murder.

At this time, Ray was a mechanic grade III for the New Mexico State Parks Department. His bosses viewed him as a dedicated and hard worker, whom they relied on to get the job done, and seemingly, Ray was always involved in some project at work. He even received an employee award in 1995 and was more or less left on his own with little supervision. He was considered a pack rat, always confiscating things he found and taking them home, and other rangers noticed that he would often take park equipment home for various projects. He also volunteered for overtime on his days off.

He was assigned to the Elephant Butte Lake State Park where he had access to a 25-mile-long lake in a very rural area of New Mexico State. He would go camping in neighboring parks all over New Mexico. Over the years, he developed an expert knowledge of every nook and cranny of Elephant Butte Park, probably knowing it better than anyone else.

The subsequent police investigation, after he was arrested, revealed that Ray had killed his business partner, Billy Ray Bowers, in 1989. This case was still unsolved at the time of his arrest. At the time of that event in 1989, the body had surfaced. As a result of this episode, Ray slit open and dismembered the other bodies he put in the lake to prevent surfacing.

Ray would target prostitutes or young women who were drug addicts and wouldn't be missed. He posed as a police officer, using his Dodge Ram as a police vehicle. He had a police radio and "Kojak" light on the floor, which he could use to pull over cars and purport to be a police officer. He also had a badge and fake police identification, which were recovered from his home and vehicle during the execution of the search warrant. Police also discovered chains, locks, and bolts in the vehicle, which he used to secure his "prisoners" (Figure 12.1 and Figure 12.2)

Capture of the Sex Slave

On March 19, Cindy Jones (*not real name*) was working as a street prostitute in Albuquerque. She was introduced to David Ray who told her he wanted oral sex in the back of his Toyota RV. They agreed to the sum of $30. When Jones and Ray got into the back of the RV,

Figure 12.1 David Ray's "police" vehicle. The subject had equipped his Dodge Ram to make it appear to be an official vehicle. (Photo courtesy of Deputy District Attorney Jim Yontz, New Mexico District Attorney's Office.)

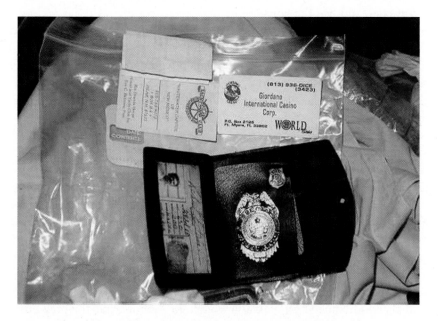

Figure 12.2 Police badge and identification. Bogus police credentials. (Photo courtesy of Deputy District Attorney Jim Yontz, New Mexico District Attorney's Office.)

where his female accomplice, Cindy Hendy, was, Ray showed her a badge and told her she was under arrest. Hendy and Ray took Jones into "custody." Jones's clothes were removed and she was tied up with duct tape and handcuffed. A steel collar with a chain attached was placed around her neck and she was driven to Ray's compound at 513 Bass Road in Elephant Butte. She was then secured to a metal post next to a bed. While at this residence, she was subjected to various acts of sexual torture and rape. On March 22, Ray and Hendy played an "introductory tape" for Jones, which described the torture and sexual abuse she would receive as a "slave." The tape described her being kept as a sex slave and that, during this time, she would be subjected to electric shock, forced oral sex, and the use of large dildos, as well as sex with animals, and she was informed that Ray had killed girls in the past. When she heard this very graphic tape, she was afraid that if she were ever taken to the secured room that Ray had described, she would be killed. That was when she decided to make her escape.

Victim Escapes

Cindy Jones, who had been captured on March 19, had been held by her captors at their home for three days. However, on the afternoon of March 22, Jones was able to escape from the house. Hendy was supposed to watch Jones and keep her secured according to the "procedures" Ray had outlined in his "instructions sheet." (Authorities recovered these "procedures" during the crime scene search.) Hendy left the room without securing the "slave," which provided Jones with an opportunity to reach the keys to the lock for the chain, which held her to a metal pole. Jones was also able to reach the telephone from which she dialed 911. Hendy suddenly came into the room and saw her on the phone. Hendy attacked Jones before she could complete the call and hit Jones with a lamp and knocked her down. However, Jones was still able to find the key to unlock her chain. Once she got the chain unlocked from the post, she fought off Hendy with an ice pick, which had been used to torture her, and fled the house.

Jones ran from the house wearing nothing but the chain and the collar around her neck. She tried to flag down cars on the road, but no one would stop. Later on, two witnesses were located who stated they saw the naked woman while they were driving, but were afraid to stop because she looked wild. Jones spotted a house on Hot Springs Landing Road with the front door open. She ran into the house, to the astonishment of the residents, and locked the door behind her.

The shocked, 60-year old female resident, Darlene Brown (*not her real name*) and her husband looked up and saw a hysterical naked woman standing in their living room. Jones was screaming at them, "Please help me! Don't let them get me!"

Darlene Brown later reported that Jones was wearing nothing except chains around her neck, and told the police, "She was bloody, very bloody, and was a very terrified girl."

Darlene Brown called 911 and then took the sobbing girl into her bedroom and covered her with a pink robe and tried to calm her down as they waited for deputies to arrive. When the deputies arrived, Jones ran from the room and threw herself at their feet screaming, "I'm alive! I'm alive! I'm alive! I broke free! The deputies noticed that she was covered with blood and a chain had been secured around her neck. The frightened woman told them that she had been kidnapped by a man and women in Albuquerque the previous Saturday. She then described being used as a sex slave, raped, tortured, and brutalized in unimaginable ways.

911

The 911 operator, who received the call initiated by Jones at the Ray house, heard what sounded like a fight in the background when suddenly the phone was hung up. He dispatched officers to that address, called back, and received a busy signal. When he called back a second time, Hendy answered the phone and told him everything was fine and that no call had been made from that residence. The dispatcher didn't believe her and advised the responding units to use caution because something wasn't right at that address.

Later it was verified that this was the 911 call that Jones had made before the phone was hung up by Hendy. The subsequent police investigation revealed that the busy signal at the Ray house had occurred when Hendy called Ray at work. He told his co-workers he had a problem at the house, and he immediately left in his Toyota RV.

The 911 operator dispatched the police to both the Brown residence and to Ray's house.

At the Brown house, officers met the hysterical Jones, who advised them of her capture and sexual abuse. She was taken to the local hospital and treated for her injuries. She had numerous bruises and injuries to her body as well as evidence of sexual torture.

Initial Victim Statement

Jones told the responding police officers and the investigators that she had been stripped and kept naked with a leather collar around her neck and chained to a pole in the bedroom. She told the police that while she was held at the house, she was subjected to whipping by both Ray and Hendy, and other atrocities including rape and sexual abuse (Figure 12.3).

She also told detectives that her garments were taken from her and she was told she would get them back when they were through "playing" with her. One of these items was a BUM Sweatshirt, which was later recovered at the crime scene.

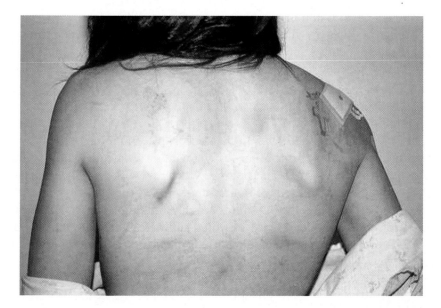

Figure 12.3 Victim. The victim was taken to the hospital for treatment and her injuries were documented by photography. (Photo courtesy of Deputy District Attorney Jim Yontz, New Mexico District Attorney's Office.)

Based on the preliminary statements of Jones, Sierra County Deputies stopped and arrested both Ray and Hendy in the Toyota. Both suspects were arrested and advised of their Miranda Rights and both gave the same story. Initially, they stated that were trying to help Jones get off her heroin habit and that was why she was held at their residence. However, after the arraignment, their stories changed greatly.

Cindy Hendy

Cynthia Lea Hendy was originally from Seattle, Washington, and claimed to have been sexually abused. She was a heavy drinker and drug user who repeatedly became involved with abusive men who would beat her. Friends described Hendy as having a "Jekyll and Hyde" personality.

When she was sober, she would be kind and considerate. However, once she started drinking, she was obnoxious and aggressive and would start fights in bars. By the early 1990s, Hendy was officially classified as mentally disabled and living off her Social Security. She was arrested in Kirkland, Washington, in 1995 along with her boyfriend for theft for which she did three years.

In 1996, she hooked up with a seven-foot biker named John Youngblood who would beat her on a regular basis. In 1997, she ran away to Truth or Consequences, New Mexico. When she first arrived, she impressed everyone she met as a smart and well-mannered young woman.

However, she soon joined the drug and alcohol set in Truth or Consequences where she earned the reputation as "six-pack Cindy." Hendy would go with anyone who bought her a drink or gave her some crank (a strong amphetamine).

Hendy's friend Jean, who had gotten married in 1997, had tried to help her adjust. She watched as Hendy got involved in S&M, lesbian, and nymphomania stunts. Jean also began to suspect that Hendy was having an affair with her husband when she was at work. However, Hendy denied it and they remained friends. In 1999, Hendy began dating Ray and went through another transition seemingly for the better. She moved in with Ray telling Jean that she had met the man with whom she wanted to spend the rest of her life. Jean watched as Hendy became a housewife for Ray.

Dark Secrets

However, Hendy soon returned to her drinking and drug use. One day while she was drinking heavily, she told Jean and Jean's husband that Ray was a serial killer. Hendy said she was always intrigued with serial killers and now she was living with one. She told her startled friends that Ray had killed hundreds of women and that she knew of six or seven who were in the lake since they had been together. Ray would target prostitutes, drug addicts, and down-and-outs. Hendy told them that Ray would slit their bodies and fill their stomachs with stones to keep them down. She also told them about a cargo trailer on their property she called the "toy box."

Securing the Crime Scene

The officers, who had responded to Ray's house to verify that there wasn't any problem at the house or victims inside, entered through an open rear door and observed evidence of

Figure 12.4 Crime scene secured. The Ray compound was secured pending the issuance of the search warrants. (Photo courtesy of Deputy District Attorney Jim Yontz, New Mexico District Attorney's Office.)

a struggle and saw a gun in plain view. The officers secured the scene and called for assistance from the New Mexico State Police (Figure 12.4). The State Police knew who lived at the house because the New Mexico State Parks Department leased the property to Ray. The State Police requested a search warrant for David Parker Ray's premises and property.

Search Warrants

District Attorney Jim Yontz, who realized the significance and magnitude of this case, made certain that the evidence would be legally protected as he prepared the search warrants. The fact that his office was dealing with a possible serial murder case involving a psychopathic sexual sadist who had been killing for a number of years, as well as the possibility of additional suspects, required that the search warrants be specific. The warrants itemized many of the additional materials and sources of information that would be required.

- All processed and unprocessed film, video tapes and audio recordings, and recording equipment
- All paintings and drawings depicting sexual acts, torture, and bondage scenarios including commercial literature
- Medical textbooks, manuals, or other documents depicting first aid and medical treatment
- Surgical instruments or other instruments that can be used to inflict pain and or suffering to a person.
- Items that can be used for body restraint: straps, etc.
- Coffins or boxes that can be used for body restraint
- Soundproofing materials
- Models and display cabinets depicting bondage scenarios

- Medications or syringes including hypodermic needles
- Badge identification indicating law enforcement
- Homemade devices that could be used for torture
- Computers and hard drive memory as well as any disks
- Word processor and monitor
- Drawings and/or pictures depicting S&M or bondage and discipline (B&D) activities
- Tools, including but limited to shovels or digging devices.
- Bank records, safety deposit boxes, receipts for storage unit rentals or other properties
- Soil samples and examination of soil beneath structures
- Handwritten notes, checks, or other documents containing samples of the handwriting of David Parker Ray
- Documents that reflect vehicles that were previously owned or utilized by David Parker Ray
- Makeup kits including makeup, wigs, hairpieces, etc.
- Trace evidence including but not limited to hair, fibers, latent prints, discarded materials, cigarette butts, condoms, hygiene products, medical treatment materials, etc.

The author highly recommends that the reader take note of the materials that were listed in the warrant applications because these items have great evidential value in understanding and presenting the behaviors and motives of these types of suspects. District Attorney Yontz had additional search warrants issued specifying for particular materials to be seized.

The Search

The warrant specified that all vehicles owned and/or on the property could be searched. The search was for trace evidence, restraints, photographs, and an audio tape, which had been played for the victim, as well as any chains, dildos, whips, pulleys, sexual devices, belts, or electrical devices. The first crime scene photographs documented the evidence of the struggle between Hendy and Jones, as she attempted her escape. There was a broken lamp, which Hendy had thrown at Jones, and an ice pick that Jones had used to get away from Hendy. The authorities photographed the metal pole with the lock and chain to which Jones had been secured. They also recovered human hair attached to duct tape from the wastebasket. This was Jones's hair. In addition, they found Jones's sneakers and BUM sweatshirt. A number of sexual devices were also recovered in Ray's home.

Jones had also mentioned that the offender had told her she was going to be brought to the "play box," which was actually a cargo trailer parked next to the house on the Ray property that he called the "toy box." The warrant included this structure as well. At the crime scene, officers began gathering evidence, which corroborated Jones's bizarre story with evidence of sexual torture. Yet, this was only the tip of the iceberg. The extent of the torture and magnitude of this case was not realized until authorities discovered Ray's numerous toys and devices and examined the interior of the cargo trailer.

The Toy Box

The **toy box** was a 15 × 25 foot cargo trailer that David Parker Ray used for the sexual torture games he played out with his victims. When the authorities entered the toy box, they were amazed at the collection of devices and equipment (Figure 12.5 and Figure 12.6).

Inside the cargo trailer was a gynecology chair with restraints and electrical wires. The silver wires running across the chair were used to cause pain and force the victim to move into various positions. He then would attach jumper cables to the victim's nipples and groin area.

Ray had placed a TV monitor in the right-hand corner of the trailer so his victims, who were secured to the chair as he tortured them, could see what he was doing to them by looking at the monitor. He had a video camera focused on the gynecology chair to view his "operations." On the ceiling of the trailer were chains and pulleys directly over the gynecology chair.

The walls of the cargo trailer were lined with shelving, photographs, and drawings. On the shelves were various instruments. Authorities collected hundreds of items that had been used to torture victims. These included surgical tools, various sexual devices, differently sized dildos, ropes, chains, a mechanical dildo device, straps and harnesses, electric shock machines, first aid supplies, and anatomically correct dolls that had miniature chains attached through their nipples. He had a small library of books dealing with female anatomy, human sexuality, psychology, emergency victim care, and witchcraft. He also had a copy of the book, *American Psycho* by Bret Easton Ellis (1991).

The drawings and photographs explained his "procedures" along with instructions for "handling" the sex slaves in captivity.

The search warrant had been specifically drawn to allow the authorities to seize the type of evidence that the psychopathic sexual sadist would collect. In the toy box were photographs of other possible victims as well as a videotape of a female victim.

Figure 12.5 The cargo trailer. This was the torture chamber that Ray called the "toy box." (Photo courtesy of Deputy District Attorney Jim Yontz, New Mexico District Attorney's Office.)

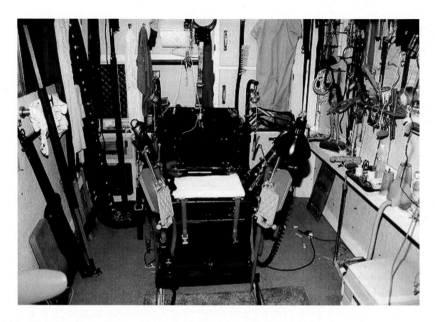

Figure 12.6 Inside the cargo trailer. Ray had designed a torture chamber inside the trailer. He equipped a gynecology chair with restraints to bind his victims and wires to jolt them with electrical shocks. (Photo courtesy of District Attorney Jim Yontz, New Mexico District Attorney's Office.)

A number of photographs and pictures of bondage scenarios were removed from the toy box for review. Eventually, the police were able to identify some of the victims from both photos and videotape taken by David Parker Ray.

The Procedures

A sheet listing instructions on how to "handle" slaves was also recovered, which supported the theory that David Parker Ray had captured other victims for his sexual torture. The sheet was entitled "Handling the Captive" and listed the rules and methods for control and intimidation of the captive prisoner.

Handling the Captive

1. The new female captive should be gagged and blindfolded with wrists and ankles chained.
2. Move her into the recreation room. Place her body under the suspension chains.
3. Stand her up under the chains and **lock her wrists** well above her head.
4. Place the neck chain around her neck and lock it in place. **IT IS PERMANENT.**
5. Clip her leg irons to the floor chain.
6. Use scissors to **slowly** remove her dress, blouse, or sweater. Cut and remove the bra.
7. Fondle and abuse her breasts, nipples, and upper part of her body.
8. **Keep her blindfolded to increase disorientation. Use verbal abuse.** (Dumb bitch, Slut, etc.)
9. **Slowly** unzip, open, and remove the lower clothing. Cut or rip the panties off.
10. Fondle and abuse her sex organs. Continue the verbal abuse.

11. Attach the overhead suspension straps to her body. Ankles, waist, hips, and upper chest.
12. Remove the leg irons and tighten the ankle straps, pulling her legs upward until the middle part of her body is horizontal. (THE ANKLE STRAPS WILL FORCE HER LEGS WIDE APART.)
13. Tighten and adjust the waist, hip, and chest straps until the middle of her body is straight. **Clip the short floor chain to the bottom ring on the waist belt, so she cannot jerk or lift her body upward.**
14. At this point, the captive is suspended at a convenient height, immobilized, and fully exposed. She is very uncomfortable, disoriented, and probably terrified. Don't cut her any slack. Continue a lot of verbal and physical abuse. Keep her off balance.
15. Play with her sex organs. Force large dildos deep into both holes. Use clamps, needles or other devices on her tits and sex organs. (clit and cut lips) Whip her and use Electroshock.
16. **<u>Don't give her time to collect her thoughts.</u>** Use her body aggressively during the first hour or two. She will swear, struggle a lot, and exhaust herself. Particularly if the electro shock machine is used extensively.
17. **<u>Intensify her fear.</u>** Tell her how she is going to be kept as a Sex Slave. Describe in detail how she will be continually raped and tortured. Work on her mind as well as her body.
18. Keep her body suspended two or three hours, then roll the Gynecology bench directly beneath her. Lower her body down on the bench. Release one arm or a leg at a time, and secure it to the bench until she is strapped down. Buckle all the straps on her body until she is totally immobilized, feet in the stirrups, and knees wide apart.

NOTE: THE SHOCK VALUE OF DISORIENTATION, PLUS CONTINUAL VERBAL ABUSE AND PHYSICAL ABUSE, DURING THE FIRST FEW HOURS OF CONFINEMENT WILL HAVE A GREAT INFLUENCE ON HOW DOSCILE AND SUBDUED, THE CAPTIVE BE DURING THE REMAINING PERIOD OF CAPTIVITY. IF IT IS DONE PROPERLY, SHE WILL BE INTIMIDATED AND MUCH EASIER TO HANDLE.

Collateral Victim

The toy box, with the specially equipped gynecology chair and torture implements as well as the vivid sadistic fantasy drawings, was psychologically overwhelming. One could not help but imagine what the victims experienced as they were subjected to Ray's sexually sadistic tortures. Included in the toy box were sophisticated recording equipment and cameras, which Ray used to record the events. The FBI, which had been requested by New Mexico authorities to assist in processing the evidence and to provide logistical support, were participating in processing the crime scene at Elephant Butte.

According to an excerpt in author John Glatt's book, *Cries in the Desert*:

Later that morning, the FBI loaded Ray's toy box on the back of a tractor-trailer and transported it, along with other evidence, to its Sante Fe branch office for specialized forensic processing analysis. When it arrived at an indoor garage location, a young female special agent named Patty Rust started making detailed drawings and diagrams of every single item inside.

A former captain in the U.S. Army, Rust was an experienced FBI agent with an advanced degree in criminology. A week later she completed her assignment, walked out of the toy box and shot herself in the head with her service revolver, dying instantly. "She couldn't handle what she had seen," said a state official close to the investigation. "God knows what it did to her spending five days with that stuff." The FBI's official line is that her suicide wasn't connected, but what do you think? (Glatt, 2002, p. 182)

Jim Yontz, the lead prosecutor on this case, advised me that John Glatt was wrong about the location of the work on the trailer, but correct about the FBI agent's suicide. Agent Rust was a member of the FBI's ERT (evidence response team) out of El Paso, Texas, and was assigned to work the toy box by the head of the FBI's Crime Scene Investigation Unit at Elephant Butte Lake. Rust did her work at the crime scene on Ray's property before the toy box was taken to Santa Fe and most of the items were taken off the walls.

Yontz recalled meeting Rust at the crime scene in Elephant Butte as she was working on diagrams. He stated, "She was, as all of us were, amazed at the detail and complexity of the crime scene. The last day she was there (I think it was her last day), she commented about how evil the entire case was, but especially the toy box. The longer she was in there, the more 'creepy' it was. She said it gave her the creeps just to look at it."

Yontz also said, "The crime scene sketches she made of the interior and exterior of the toy box were exceptional. She drew in every detail and every piece of equipment that hung on the walls or were placed on the shelves. Rust had more sustained and intense contact with the toy box and the items inside the toy box than any other person involved in the investigation. She spent hours alone in the toy box concentrating on the location of the objects, measurements of the objects, and trying to put them as nearly as possible to scale on her diagrams."

Yontz advised me that Rust worked in the toy box for three or four days. He said that she concluded her drawings and mailed them to Tony (Maxwell, the agent–in–charge) in Albuquerque by overnight mail. She then discussed the drawings with Tony the next day. According to Tony, he told her that the work she had done was excellent. She then committed suicide that night or the next day.

I interviewed Yontz regarding this event and he told me, "No one should have been assigned to spend time in there alone for an extended period of time just as no one was assigned to spend time in the crawl space under John Gacy's house. I know hindsight is 20/20, but her comments to me about it being creepy were filtered through the façade of a crime scene investigator. Creepy should have been replaced with the word *scary*. All of us at the scene were bothered by the case, the facts and the evil that surrounded everything there. Leaving her in a place where we knew women had been tortured and murdered (Marie Parker for one) would be like having someone left alone to diagram the death camps in Germany."

Jim added, "I appreciated the help and believed that the FBI knew what they were doing. However, from my perspective, the diagrams were not 'necessary' and could have been done with photographs containing a scale. As I think about it now, only the toy box was drawn. The interior of the house was not drawn and, of course, neither was the "torture room" inside the house. With everyone having on their own mask of, 'This don't bother me,' we were unaware and unable to see just how much it did."

As a former homicide commander, there is no way that I would have assigned a female investigator to work alone in that horror chamber. I say this because of the nature of the evidence and materials in that small cramped cargo trailer and the fact that women had been brutally tortured and killed in that chamber from hell. If it was deemed necessary to diagram and inventory each item, I would have assigned a team of agents working in tandem with ample time breaks to assure their psychological well-being. There is no way that a young woman should have been assigned to spend four days in that trailer. And, then for the FBI to officially suggest that her suicide wasn't related to that event is even more despicable and arrogant.

I discussed this case with Dr. Judith Reisman, who published a report regarding the dangers of overexposure to pornography (Reisman, 2009).

The Audio Tapes

Authorities discovered eight audiotapes during the search of the crime scene. These included the **"introductory tape,"** which had been played for Jones before her escape, as well as other tapes Ray had made that revealed the extent of his sadistic perversions.

The "introductory tape," which is best described as a "general advisory" tape for future female captives, was originally recorded by Ray on July 23, 1993. He stated on the tape that it is based on his experience in dealing with captives over several years.

Ray described in graphic detail the various sexual acts and perversions the sex slave would endure. The activities that Ray outlined included electric shock, forced oral sex, and the use of large dildos as well as sex with his large dogs. He stated, "You'll be taken into the living room and put on the floor on your hands and knees, naked. Your wrists, ankles, knees, and hips will be strapped to a metal frame to hold your body in that position. The frame is designed for doggie fuckin', your ass up in the air, sex organs exposed, your tits hang'n down on each side of a metal support bar, knees spread about 12 inches, position similar to that of a bitch dog in heat, right in the middle of the floor, so we can set on the couch and in chairs and watch. I'm going to rub canine breeder's musk on your back, the back of your neck, and on your sex organs. Now I have three dogs. … One of 'em is a very large German shepherd that is always horny, and he loves it when I bring him in the house to fuck a woman."

He also stated on the tape, "You'll be raped thoroughly and repeatedly in every hole you've got … basically, you've been snatched and brought here for us to train and use as a sex slave."

Ray also explains how he and his lady friend "have been keeping sex slaves for years." He talked about going on "hunting" trips to locate new slaves. He also bragged about kidnapping and abducting stranded female motorists on the side of the road and keeping two slaves at the same time for variety.

On the tape, Ray explained that he can't get off on a woman unless he causes her pain. Ray stated, "Mostly what we do to a captive is stick needles in her breasts and through her nipples, through her cunt lips, through her clit, and I'm into stretching certain things. … As far as needles goes, they'll always be sterilized. [But] the clamps are gonna hurt like a motherfucker."

He concluded by going into an explanation of his "examination" of the victim, while she is in stringent bondage and secured to the gynecology table. "You will be naked, and as I said, you'll be strapped down on a gynecology table so you can't wiggle or squirm around. Consequently, before we start on the questionnaire, two small electrical clamps will be put on your nipples. … Each time you fuck up, I'm gonna press a little button and send a few thousand volts of electricity through your nipples, right down into your tits." Sadistically, Ray ends the tape with the words, "Have a nice day." The authorities, upon hearing the tape, were convinced that Ray was a serial offender, who had killed many times before.

Transcript

The following is a transcription of an advisory message that was tape recorded by David Parker Ray on July 23, 1993.

Hello there, bitch. Are you comfortable right now? I doubt it. Wrists and ankles chained. Gagged. Probably blindfolded. You are disoriented and scared, too, I would imagine. Perfectly normal, under the circumstances. For a little while, at least, you need to get your shit together and listen to this tape. It is very relevant to your situation.

I'm going to tell you, in detail, why you have been kidnapped, what's going to happen to you and how long you'll be here. I don't know the details of your capture because this tape is being created July 23, 1993, as a general advisory tape for future female captives. The information I'm going to give you is based on my experience dealing with captives over a period of several years. If, at a future date, there are any major changes in our procedures, the tape will be upgraded.

Now, you are obviously here against your will, totally helpless, don't know where you're at, don't know what's gonna happen to you. You're very scared or very pissed off. I'm sure that you've already tried to get your wrists and ankles loose, and know you can't. Now you're just waitin' to see what's gonna happen next.

You probably think you're gonna be raped and you're fuckin' sure right about that. Our primary interest is in what you've got between your legs. You'll be raped thoroughly and repeatedly in every hole you've got. Because, basically, you've been snatched and brought here for us to train and use as a sex slave. Sound kind of far out? Well, I suppose it is to the uninitiated, but we do it all the time.

"It's gonna take a lot of adjustment on your part, and you're not gonna like it a fuckin' bit. But I don't give a big rat's ass about that. It's not like you're gonna have any choice about the matter. You've been taken by force, and you're going to be kept and used by force. What all this amounts to is that you're gonna be kept naked and chained up like an animal, to be used and abused any time we want to, any way that we want to. And you might as well start gettin' used to it, because you're gonna be kept here and used until such time as we get tired of fuckin' around with you. And we will, eventually, in a month or two, maybe three. It's no big deal.

"My lady friend and I have been keeping sex slaves for years. We both have kinky hang-ups involving rape, dungeon games, etc. We've found that it is extremely convenient to keep one or two female captives available constantly to, uh, satisfy our particular needs. We are very selective when we snatch a girl to use for these purposes.

It goes without saying that you have a fine body and you're probably young, maybe very young. Because, for our purposes, we prefer to snatch girls in the early to mid teens, sexually developed, but still small bodied, scared shitless, easy to handle and easy to train, and they usually have tight little pussies and assholes. They make perfect slaves.

Any time that we go on a hunting trip, if we can't find a little teenager, we usually start hittin' the gay bars, look for a well-built, big-titted lesbian. I thoroughly enjoy rapin' and screwin', around with lesbians, and there's not as much danger of them carrying a sexually transmitted disease. And I don't like usin' condoms. Also, even though they're a little older, unless they've been playing with dildos a lot, they still have tight holes between their legs, like the younger girls.

If we can't find a lesbian that we want, we snatch anything that is young, clean, and well built. We very seldom come back empty handed, 'cause there's plenty of bitches out there to choose from. And, with a little practice in deception, most if 'em is very easy to get, with little risk.

At this point, it makes little difference what category you fall into. You're here and we're gonna make the most of it. You're going to be kept in a hidden slave room. It is relatively sound proof, escape proof, and it is completely stocked with devices and equipment to satisfy our sexual fetishes and deviations. There may or may not be another girl in the room. Occasionally, for variety, we like to keep two slaves at the same time. In either case, as the new girl, you'll definitely be getting the most attention for a while.

Now, as I said earlier, you're going to be kept like an animal. I guess I been doin' this too long. I've been rapin' bitches ever since I was old enough to jerk off, and tie little girl's hands behind their back. As far as I'm concerned, you're a pretty piece of meat, to be used and exploited. I don't give a flyin' fuck about your mind or how you feel about this situation. You may be married, have a kid or two, boyfriend, girlfriend, a job, car payment. Fuck it. I don't give a rat's ass about any of that, and I don't want to hear about it. It's something you're gonna have to deal with after you're turned loose.

"I make it a point never to like a slave and I fuckin' sure don't have any respect for you. Here your status is no more than that of one of the dogs, or of one of the animals out in the barn. Your only value to us is the fact that you have an attractive, useable body. And, like the rest of our animals, you will be fed and watered, kept in good physical condition, kept reasonably clean and allowed to use the toilet when necessary. In return, you're gonna be used hard, especially during your first few days while you're new and fresh.

You're gonna be kept chained in a variety of different positions, usually with your legs or knees forced wide apart. Your pussy and asshole is gonna get a real workout. Especially your asshole, because I'm into animal sex. Also, both of those holes are going to be subjected to a lotta use with some rather large dildos, among other things. And it goes without sayin' that there's gonna be a lot of oral sex. On numerous occasions, you're gonna be forced to suck cock and eat pussy until your jaws ache and your tongue is sore. You may not like it, but you're fuckin' sure gonna do it.

And that's the easy part. Our fetishes and hang-ups include stringent bondage, dungeon games, a little sadism, nothing serious, but uncomfortable and sometimes painful. Just a few little hang-ups that we like to use when we're gettin' off on a bitch. Heh, heh. If you're a young teenybopper, and ignorant about fetishes and deviations, you're about to get an enlightening crash course in sex ed. Who knows, you may like some of it. It happens, occasionally. If we wanna take the time and trouble, even under these conditions, most bitches can be brought to orgasm.

Now, I've already told you that you're gonna be here a month or two, or maybe three, if you keep us turned on. If it's up to my lady, we'd keep you indefinitely. She says it's just as much fun and less risky. But personally, I like variety. A fresh pussy, now and then, to play with. We take four or five different girls each year, depending on our urges and sometimes accidental encounters. Basically, I guess we are like predators. We're always lookin'. Occasionally, some sweet little thing will be broke down on the side of the road, walkin', bicyclin', joggin'. Anytime an opportunity like that presents itself, and it's not too risky, we'll grab her. Even if we've already got a captive in the playroom. Variety is definitely the spice of life.

Now I'm sure that you're a great little piece of ass and you're gonna be a lot of fun to play with, but I will get tired of you eventually. If I killed every bitch that we kidnapped, there'd be bodies strung all over the country. And besides, I don't like killin' a girl, unless it is absolutely necessary. So, I've devised a safe, alternate method of disposal. I had plenty of bitches to practice on over the years, so I've pretty well got it down pat. And I enjoy doin' it. I get off on mind games. After we get completely through with you, you're gonna be drugged up real heavy with a combination of sodium pentothal and phenobarbital. They are both hypnotic drugs that will make you extremely susceptible to hypnosis, autohypnosis, and hypnotic suggestion. You're gonna be kept drugged a couple of days, while I play with your mind. By the time I get through brainwashing you, you're not gonna remember a fuckin' thing about this little adventure. You won't remember this place, us, or what has happened to you. There won't be any DNA evidence because you'll be bathed, and both holes between your legs will be thoroughly flushed out. You'll be dressed, sedated, and turned loose on some country road, bruised, heh, sore all over, but nothing that won't heal up in a week or two.

Author's Note: This piece of information on drugs being given to the "slaves" proved to be valuable in corroborating the statements of another victim who was eventually identified and located through certain materials confiscated during search of David Parker Ray's residence and the toy box.

The thought of being brainwashed may not be appealing to you, but we been doin' it a long time and it works. And it's the lesser of two evils. I'm sure that you would prefer that, in lieu of being strangled or having your throat cut.

Okay, undoubtedly, somebody's gonna be lookin' for you. There may or may not be a missing persons report. But nobody's gonna be lookin' for you here. They don't have any idea where you're at. You don't even know where you're at. We're always very careful about that. There are not gonna be any knights in shining armor coming to rescue you. You are strictly on your own and, under the circumstances, I bet that is a scary thought. If there is another girl in the room, she won't be able to help you either. Because she's gonna be in the same position you're in.

As for escaping, I'm sure you'll try to figure out a way. That's human nature. But it's not hardly even worth talking about here. It would not be prudent on our part to have you running around in the woods screamin' rape. It would be an embarrassment, to say the least. Consequently, you are gonna be kept in an environment that is even more secure than a prison cell. If it has not already been done, very shortly a steel collar is going to be padlocked around your neck. It has a long, heavy chain that is padlocked to a ring in the floor. The collar will never be removed until you are turned loose. It's a permanent fixture.

The hidden playroom where you're gonna be kept has steel walls, floor, and ceiling. It is virtually soundproof and has a steel door with two keyed locks. The hinges are welded on and there are two heavy deadbolts on the outside. The room is totally escape proof, even with tools. Anytime that you are left unattended in the room, your wrists will be chained and there are electronic sensors to, uh, let us know if you move around too much. And if that's not enough, there is a closed-circuit TV system with a surveillance camera. It's wired to the main TV in the living room so we can check you once in a while, or just set and watch you for the fun of it. Electronics is a wonderful thing. Expensive, but hell, everything in the room is expensive, and damn well worth it. If everybody knew how much fun it was to keep a sex slave, half the women would be chained up in somebody's basement. Anyway, we've had a lot of practice at this and, uh, we're not real concerned about you escaping. You're fuckin' sure not gonna go anywhere.

Now if you're not already naked, you soon will be. Your clothing will be bagged up and saved until such time as we decide to turn you loose. As far as being naked goes, you might as well get used to it. For what you are gonna be used for, clothing would just be in the way. Besides, I like watching a naked woman's body, all of it, whether it be in a room or on the TV set.

As I've already said, you'll be fed and watered on a regular basis. Not as much of either as you're used to, I'm sure, but enough to keep you healthy. You'll only be fed once a day, like the rest of the animals. And during the first few days, until you adjust to it and your stomach shrinks up, you're going to feel a little weak and you'll be hungry all the time. It won't take long, three or four days. And during the first few days, until you adjust to the environment, I prefer to keep you in a weakened condition anyway.

Now you already know that you've been kidnapped and brought here for us to train and use as a sex slave. I realize that being abducted and being forced into sexual slavery is a hard pill to swallow. Some girls really have a lot of trouble with it and I'm sure that you will, to a certain extent. But face it, you can't get away, you can't say no. You're gonna be naked all the time. You won't be able to struggle or resist. You're gonna have to lay there and take it, good or bad, no matter what is being done to you. A scary thought? Yes, but there are no options. Nothing that you can say or do will change the fact that it's going to happen. Many girls beg and plead.

Almost all of 'em cry a lot, especially during the first three or four days. And some of 'em scream and threaten. But I have a poster on the wall in the playroom that says it all. If they're worth takin', they're worth keepin'. And I'm going to tell you, just so you know, since you are being kept here against your will, we will never trust anything you say, do, or promise. You are a potential threat to us and you will always be treated as such. On numerous occasions, bitches have told me that they'd do anything I wanted 'em to do, if I'd just take the chains off. I've been offered ransom money and I've even had girls tell me they liked it. But I like to use the chains, money's not that important and masochists are rare as hell. Heh, heh, I wonder what your scam's gonna be. Not anything that I haven't heard before, I bet, if you get a chance to talk at all. Well, let's change the subject a little bit. You already know that, for the most part, you're gonna be kept in the playroom. But, once in a while, we like to take a captive into the bedroom, in chains, of course. Also, we have a couple of real close friends that we party with once in a while. They know about our hang-ups and don't have any problem with fuckin' a slave. You may be required to service them occasionally. But that's an easy one, for the most part, just fuckin' and suckin'. They don't get into the heavier stuff.

However, when we have a party, sometimes I like to put on a little show that you won't like at all. You'll be taken into the living room and put on the floor on your hands and knees, naked. Your wrists, ankles, knees, and hips will be strapped to a metal frame to hold your body in that position. The frame is designed for doggie fuckin', your ass up in the air, sex organs exposed, your tits hangin' down on each side of a metal support bar, knees spread about 12 inches, position similar to that of a bitch dog in heat, right in the middle of the floor, so we can set on the couch and in chairs and watch. I'm going to rub canine breeder's musk on your back, the back of your neck, and on your sex organs. Now I have three dogs. All of 'em's male, 'cause I don't need any fuckin' pups. One of 'em is a very large German shepherd that is always horny, and he loves it when I bring him in the house to fuck a woman. After I let him in the house, he'll sniff around you a little bit and, within a minute, he'll be mounting you. There's about a 50-50 chance which hole he'll get his penis into, but it doesn't seem to bother him whether it's the pussy or the asshole. His penis is pretty thin. It goes in easy, but it's about 10 inches long and when he gets completely excited, it gets a hell of a knot right in the middle of it. Now I've had slaves tell me that it feels like they got a baseball inside of 'em. It doesn't take long. He's gonna hump you real fast for about three or four minutes. And while he's doin' it, he'll wrap his front legs around your chest to hold himself in position. And, in the process, he'll probably scratch your tits up a little bit, with his claws.

After he gets through, he usually turns around and tries to pull out. Oh, he'll jerk a little, not much, mostly just steady pressure. And I've timed it. The knot will usually shrink up enough to come outta your pussy in about three minutes. If he's in your asshole, about five minutes. I don't use the dog all that often, but I don't deprive him of pussy either. There's no doubt that he's going to be on you a few times while you're here, because I like watching it. And any time it's just you, me, and the dog, it will always be in your butt. The dog knot on his penis is big and extremely uncomfortable when he's, uh, pushing it back and forth way up in her anus. I really enjoy watching a girl wiggle, jerk and squirm around while he's doin' it. Consequently, I give him a little, uh, assistance gettin' it in the right hole.

Now if you think all of this stuff is sick and depraved, you haven't seen anything yet. This is a different world. Among our small circle of friends, little things like rape, kidnapping, doggie fucking, stuff like that, are every day occurrences. Matter of course. Here, anything can happen and often does. We like livin' in the mountains, because it's quiet, secluded, private and everybody minds their own business. The only close house belongs to our friends and they don't hear or see anything.

Okay, let's talk about, uh, your training, the rules and punishment. Here, you are a slave and discipline is extremely strict. You're gonna be given a set of rules, things you can and cannot do, and you will learn to comply because each time you violate a rule, you will be punished. As soon as each rule is told to you, it will become law as far as you're concerned. And you know what's gonna happen every time you fuck up. We'll use a couple of methods of punishment. A whip is an excellent training aid, so is an electroshock machine. Any time you get out of line, one or both will be used on your body and I assure you, it will not be pleasant. There are not many rules and they're very easy to remember. But you're gonna make mistakes. Every slave does. I don't like repeat offenders. It gets me very upset. During the first few hours, the first time you violate a certain rule [tape skips] … a teaching process. The second time you violate the same rule, you'll be lightly punished. And the third time you violate it, it's gonna be full punishment. After the first day, we won't cut you any slack at all. We will expect total obedience. Now let's start this off right. You are a slave. You don't realize it yet, but you will eventually. I'm your master and the lady is your mistress. You will be totally docile. You'll be very quiet and you'll speak only when spoken to. Never initiate conversation. Keep your mouth shut. Any time that you are spoken to, you will be required to respond and it will be with proper speech. Remember that we are in the dungeon game and as long as you are here, it's the only game in town. Any time that you are asked a question where a yes or no answer is required, you will respond by saying, "yes master," "no mistress," "no master," et cetera. You will show proper respect. Having to use the word *master* or *mistress* may sound funny, petty or vain to you, but that's all right. If you choose not to do it, you can laugh while you're being whipped or when your body is convulsing under the electroshock machine.

You will respond to commands without protest or resistance. Do exactly what you're told, nothing else. Remember that here you are a slave and failure to respond to a command will definitely get you in trouble. If I decide to rape you in your pussy or in your asshole, don't resist or struggle. When I tell you to spread your legs, or to pull 'em back, you say, "yes master" and obey the command, 'cause to do anything less will get you beaten. If I tell you I want to be sucked off, you say, "yes master" and open your mouth.

I love oral sex, if it's done right. You're going to be taught exactly the way I like it. How to use your lips and tongue. We'll be practicing a lot and each time, when I get ready to come, I'm going to push my penis down your throat and keep it there until I get through squirtin'. I'm not gonna choke you, but you need to learn to hold your breath and to swallow every bit of the sperm. If I see one drop leaking out of your mouth, I'm gonna punish you. Basically, it's gonna be the same with your mistress. If she demands oral sex, you say, "yes mistress" and respond. She also will teach you exactly the way she likes it. And you will keep using your tongue on her pussy until she gets off.

Now, I can't foresee what kind of bitch you're gonna be, how you feel about oral sex or any of that shit. But I am gonna tell you this. If, during oral sex or any other time, you should bite one of us, I'm going to cut on you a little bit. I'll cut your nipple off for a starter and if it's a bad bite, I'll cut your tit off, too. That may sound harsh, but your teeth are serious weapons and we're not gonna tolerate any shit from you. I have been bitten and I've cut off nipples, so don't fuck around. That's enough said about that.

Remember the commands, "yes master, no mistress." If your mistress should come into the room and tells you to get down on the floor or lay down on the floor, you say, "yes mistress" and then lay down on the floor exactly the way she told you to do. If she tells you to pull your knees up, you say, "yes mistress" and pull your knees up. If she tells you to spread your knees, you say, "yes mistress" and spread 'em, wide apart and hold them there so she can play with your pussy, use dildos, or whatever.

A slave must always obey every command and offer no resistance. Remember that. Never say no unless it's justified, like in response to a question. If either one, or both of us, decide to put you in a different bondage position, the chains will be taken off the various parts of your body, wrists, and ankles, never off of your neck. Don't kick, struggle, or resist in any way. If you do, you're going to be in a world of hurt. If you're told to hold your leg out so a chain can be attached to your ankle, you say. "yes master" or "yes mistress," and hold your leg out. For repeated rule violations, the punishments are eventually gonna become harsh and even brutal and you won't have anyone to blame but yourself.

Now I should also tell you that there's gonna be times when the whip and electroshock is used not for punishment, but for our pleasure. The difference will be that when it's done for pleasure, the whip strokes will be much lighter. They'll sting like hell, but they won't have that burning sensation and leave welts that hurt for hours. As for the electroshock machine, the voltage will be turned down. It won't be that harsh electricity that, uh, makes your body convulse and jerk all over the table. You haven't experienced any of that yet, but I'm sure that you will. To avoid these punishments, you're gonna have to be very quiet, very docile, and very obedient and I imagine that's gonna be very hard for you to do. You'll probably try us a few times, to see if this is real. Heh, heh, most captives do. If you want to, be my guest, because it's all part of the game.

Now let's discuss talking. You cannot talk, you cannot speak unless you've been given permission. I believe that rule gets more bitches in trouble then anything else, because they can't keep their damn mouth shut. They always wanna whine, beg, plead, try to talk me into turning 'em loose. I used to listen to it. I don't any more. I enjoy blessed silence. Around here, your mouth is for sucking, not talking. Around here, the only time I ever want to hear you initiate speech is if you have to use the restroom, and you will learn to do it properly. "Master, may I please use the restroom" or "mistress, may I please use the restroom." In response, we will ask you what you need to do. If you have to pee, you say, "pee master" or "pee mistress." If you have to crap, you say, "crap master" or "crap mistress." It will be done that way because, quite often, you will be in heavy restraints, a lot of straps on your body, chains on your wrists and ankles, a bunch of stuff that's, uh, time consuming and hard to get loose. If you have to pee, we'll use a bedpan. If you have to shit, you may have to hold it awhile. Whatever the case, we need to know. And you definitely need to tell us. Because if you make a mess, you're going to be punished and you have to clean it up.

Now, I've covered the basics pretty thoroughly. You know to keep your mouth shut and not try to talk. You know the proper way to say "master" or "mistress," and you know how you're expected to act and respond to commands. If you can learn to do all of that, there will not be a great deal of punishment. We'll get along pretty good.
[End of tape alarm sounds.]
The end of side one. Turn the tape over.
[Side two begins.]

There's going to be a lot of other things done to your body besides just fuckin' and suckin'. But for that, for the most part, you'll either be in, in stringent bondage, or strapped down on a gynecology table. You won't be able to struggle or resist anyway. Now you're going to be required to learn fast. Training is not one of my favorite things to do and I prefer fucking around with a slave that's already trained. I've already given you the basics, so there is not that much to learn. But until you accept the fact that you are a slave, you're gonna have problems with it.

Remember that each time you fuck up, you are gonna be punished. And after it's happened a few times, you're really gonna dread it. Some girls tend to be a little rebellious. I sure as hell wouldn't advise that 'cause it will get you in serious trouble. Here, you definitely need to be docile. You're not in any position to be otherwise. We've done this so many times that we know exactly what we like to do with a slave. We don't go out of our way to brutalize a girl. If you don't give us any trouble, we won't do any more to your body than is necessary to satisfy our sexual needs.

Initially, when we've got a new girl in the playroom, we're kinda like a kid with a new toy. You are fresh and exciting and we're gonna spend a lot of time playing with you. Later, after the newness wears off, things will settle into something of a routine. We'll only be spending three or four hours each day in the playroom. Your gonna have a lot of free time to rest, sleep, watch TV, or whatever. If you're acting halfway decent, you'll be left in a reasonably comfortable position so you can relax.

As far as sex goes, your mistress is going to want her pussy eaten a couple of times a day. For my part, I like getting off in a slave twice and sometimes three times each day, usually in her mouth or in her asshole. Don't get me wrong. I'm gonna be stickin' my dick in your cunt once in a while, too. But for the most part when I use that hole, it's going to be with, uh, large dildos. We're going to be in and out of the room several times each day, but you will have a lot of free time.

Now I gotta tell you that there's another side to the coin. Once in a while, we get a bitch that is resentful, rebellious, won't mind, uncooperative. That doesn't work here. I'm sure that you realize you're on thin ice. As long as you have chains on your body, don't try either one of us. It is an extremely dangerous thing to do because, if necessary, I'm capable of doing things to your body, and torturing you in ways that you can't even imagine. The playroom is equipped with a full set of surgical instruments which I have had occasion to use and will again, as necessary.

I've already told you what'll happen if you bite. To be completely safe here, you have to be docile. If you should accidentally, or otherwise, hurt, scratch or kick, either one of us, you could be in very serious trouble. I'm sure that you want to survive this experience, and I want you to also. But you are expendable and it's no big deal to go out and snatch a replacement. It may sound harsh and cold, but if you give us too much trouble, or if you pose any kind of a threat to us, I won't have any qualms at all about slicing your throat.

Like I said before, I don't like killin' the girls that we bring here, but occasionally things happen. What can I say? I would really hate to have to dump that pretty little body off in a canyon somewhere to rot. I'm not trying to scare you. That's just the way it is. Be nice. Keep your mouth shut, learn the rules, and survive.

We are into S&M and you're going to be hurt a little, but everything we do to a girl is designed to cause pain, not injury. There is a big difference. No matter how painful it is, nothing that we plan to do to your body will cause any serious or permanent damage. I'm not lying to you or trying to make it sound easier, because that would be pointless. I'm just telling it like it is. That's the way we do things and that's the way it's gonna be, unless we have problems with you.

I've already told you that you're gonna be whipped lightly, for pleasure. The electroshock will be used lightly, for pleasure. Most of the other nasty little things that we're going to do, for the most part, will be done on your breasts, nipples and between your legs. The lady is fortunate. She can get off any time. She just likes to be a little sadistic with a slave once in a while. In my case, I cannot get off with a girl unless I hurt her first. That's basically the reason I'm into rape and slavery, and the reason that you're going to be subjected to a certain amount of pain. Mostly what we do to a captive is stick needles in her breasts and through her nipples, through her cunt lips, through her clit, and I'm into stretching certain things.

Clamps, with long nylon cords on each one, will occasionally be put on your cunt lips so your pussy can be kept pulled open, and they're also going to be attached to your nipples. The nylon cords will be put through ceiling rings, or rings on each side of the table, and pulled very tight to stretch your tits.

Occasionally, your clit will also be clamped and stretched and we're gonna be using dildos. The dildos are gonna be used a lot, more than anything else, and consequently, what you're going to have the most trouble with. Many of them are long, very large in diameter, and very painful while they're being forced in. Your mistress will use them in your pussy and I like to use them in both holes.

Actually, that pretty well covers it. There's gonna be a few other little things that we do. Nothing of any greater consequence and not often, just variety.

As far as needles go, they'll always be sterilized. The clamps are gonna hurt like a mother-fucker, but they won't cause any permanent injury. They don't even break the skin.

As far as the dildos go, both of those holes between your legs will stretch a hell of a lot. It'll hurt, but they'll stretch. Your pussy is designed for a baby to come out of and we won't be using anything bigger than that. The really large ones will not be used in your butt. I don't wanna stretch that hole so big that it's not useable for fucking.

Anyway, that pretty well covers that part of it. Let's see, what have I missed? Let's talk about screaming. Every once in a while we get a screamer. Some bitch that just wants to scream all the time. And it definitely gets 'em in trouble, because it gets on my nerves. Very shortly, that gag is going to be removed. We live in an isolated area, so screaming is not usually a problem. In the playroom, it's not much of a problem at all because of the soundproof-ing. But it irritates the fuck out of me. There is a time and a place. Occasionally I like to hear a bitch scream, but usually not. The only thing that screaming is gonna get you around here is a lot of punishment. And, if you do it habitually, I will just keep a ball gag in your mouth all the time. It'll only be taken out for you to eat and suck.

I've already told you about talking. Don't try to initiate a conversation. Don't say anything. You will be punished.

If you're a smoker, now's a good time to quit. I'm not gonna buy your cigarettes and if you ask for one, the only thing you're gonna get is a few whip marks.

Remember, when you're asked a question, you say, "yes master" or "no master." If you have to go to the restroom, it is "master, or mistress, may I please go to the restroom." Any time that you are given a command, always acknowledge the order verbally, "yes master," and then obey the order. That's not too difficult. A bright little thing like you should be able to learn it real fast.

There are gonna be times when you are under a stress, a certain amount of stress and you may forget. But that's no excuse. Each time you fuck up, you are gonna be punished. After you're here a few days, it'll eventually become automatic and there'll no longer be a problem.

I realize that, after a while, when I take that gag off, you are really gonna want to try to talk to me, talk me into turning you loose and such. It's because, with your wrists and ankles chained, your mouth is the only defense you have. But don't do it. It won't work and all it will bring is punishment.

Your first day here is not gonna be too difficult. There won't be any serious dungeon games. Your training has already been initiated, so you'll have to be very careful what you say and how you act. But for the most part, there's gonna be a little exploring. We will become very familiar with your body, and do a little fuckin' and suckin'. We may tease you a little bit with some of our more humane toys, but nothing serious. It's gonna be kind of an adjustment period. Don't say anything. Don't struggle or resist, no matter what we do, because we are going to start enforcing the rules immediately.

Now later, I'm gonna be asking you a bunch of questions. Since I'm gonna be caring for your body for the next month or two, or three, there are certain things that I need to know. I have prepared a questionnaire that I fill out with each new captive. Some of the questions are going to be embarrassing, but you should answer them truthfully and completely. You damn well better. I don't wanna catch you in a lie. The questions will be in reference to your physi-cal condition, any medical conditions that I'd need to know about, medications, sex habits, sexual preferences, any childbirth you might a had, period dates, and so forth. Now your training has already started. Each time I ask you one of those questions on the questionnaire, there's gonna be a proper way to answer it, which I'll tell you about in a few minutes.

While we go through the questionnaire, you're going to be strapped down on the gynecology table. Your feet will be in the stirrups and your knees will be pulled wide apart, with everything exposed. I like to keep a girl that way while she's answering the questions, so I can examine and verify, uh, anything she might tell me which would affect her use as a sex slave. If you do have any kind of medical condition, by all means, let me know. We'll discuss it and we may make adjustments. We won't turn you loose, but we may make adjustments.

We're probably going to be starting on this questionnaire pretty soon. You will be naked, and as I said, you'll be strapped down on a gynecology table so you can't wiggle or squirm around. You will be talking quite a bit, answering the questions, so I'm sure that we'll start your speech training at the same time. Consequently, before we start on the questionnaire, two small electrical clamps will be put on your nipples. Each time a question is asked, you will respond properly. For instance, if I ask you how old you are, you will respond by saying, "master, I'm 19 years old." Answer the question completely and say nothing else. If the question requires a yes or no answer, say, "yes master" or "no master." If I ask you your period dates, you say, "master, my period is so and so." If I ask you about childbirth, you say, "no master" or "master, I had a baby a year ago," or whatever. Always start each sentence by saying master. And take your time. We're not gonna be in any hurry. Think about what you're gonna say before you say it. Because each time you fuck up, I'm gonna press a little button and send a few thousand volts of electricity through your nipples, right down into your tits. You are in training, so it will just be a quick blast. I'm not going to hold it down and torture you. But, each time you screw up, it's gonna be a little bit worse. So take your time. Answer the questions properly. I'm not gonna push you. We're not gonna be in any hurry. Think about each thing you're gonna say and be damn sure and start your sentence with "master." If you get through that okay, get your speech down pat, keep your mouth shut and don't give us any trouble, then the first day is gonna be real pleasant for everybody.

I'm gonna put some dildos in those holes between your legs, but they will not be big ones. Basically, I just wanna become very familiar with your sex organs and the size of the holes. All girls are different.

During the course of the day, you're gonna be raped several times, but that's no big deal. The second day, after you get totally familiar with the rules and procedures, we're gonna get down to the nitty-gritty. A lot of it will not be very pleasant for you, but you might as well get used to it because it's gonna be like that for a while. Eventually things will settle down a little. Then, just take it day by day.

Well, I believe I've told you about everything that I can. I cannot predict the future. I can't predict changes of procedure. But if this tape is being played for you, I have to assume that it is still reasonably accurate. And I can only give you advice. Be smart and be a survivor. Don't ever scream. Don't talk without permission. Be very quiet. Be docile and obedient and, by all means, show proper respect.

Have a nice day.

[July 23, 1993—end of tape.]

Additional Tapes

In another tape produced by David Parker Ray, he described himself as a "Dungeon Master" for the Church of Satan. In this tape, Ray went into detail explaining that the congregation would use the sex slave and, "You will be repeatedly raped in every hole you got and in ways you can't imagine."

Authorities also found a tape produced by Ray in which he states that he makes special adult video movies that require sex slaves. He explains that the kidnapped women need to be tortured in various ways and that's why he can't use actresses. Ray stated, "The woman is gagged and blindfolded to keep her face covered, spread eagled, her wrists and ankles chained, and legs forced extremely wide apart with a lot of wide angle and close-up shots of her breasts, nipples, and sex organs being abused with a variety of different instruments."

These tapes proved to be valuable evidence when the authorities compared this information to the instruments in the toy box.

Fantasy Drawings

Fantasy drawings provide a unique insight into the mind of the offender, whose love for detail and sexual expression inadvertently provides the investigator with the offender's innermost sexual thought processes and fantasies. Not to mention evidence. When you have the inner most thoughts of an offender, written or drawn by his own hand, there are no better "data" from which to draw conclusions about a particular offender and his sexual activities.

Authorities located hundreds of fantasy drawings that Ray had prepared over his many years of sadomasochistic activities. Many of these drawings vividly depicted exactly what he had verbalized in his sadistic tapes.

What made these drawings so significant was that they actually portrayed what the offender was doing to his victims as he sexually assaulted and tortured them. The various objects drawn into the picture (dildos, electric cattle prod, electric charger box, wires, restraints, leather straps, petroleum jelly, and torture tools) were, in fact, recovered by the authorities during the crime scene search. Needless to say, these fantasy drawings became an essential portion of the prosecution's case especially when defense experts tried to portray the drawings as harmless sexual fantasies (Figures 12.7 through12.10).

The Victim as a Sex Slave

When David Ray and Cindy Hendy abducted Cindy Jones, her clothes were removed and she was tied up with duct tape and handcuffed. A steel collar with a chain attached was placed around her neck and she was driven to Elephant Butte, New Mexico. She was then secured to a metal post next to a bed and told exactly what was going to happen to her. During this initial phase of the event, Jones was kept nude and was whipped at various times by both Hendy and Ray. She also had her legs spread apart by tying ropes to them and running the ropes through eyebolts secured to opposite walls. Ray was following a specific psychological routine to gain the obedience and compliance of his victim.

Ray had positioned the knee and ankle spreader on Jones and placed her on the floor. He then poured gravy over her vaginal area and had his dog lick the gravy off as he and Hendy watched. Jones reported being shocked with various devices including a cattle prod, stun gun, and electric shock box. She also reported that Ray would place clamps on her nipples and then run currents of electricity through her body. He also secured straps on her wrists, which were tied together, and suspended her from a hook in the ceiling. During her time in captivity, Ray penetrated Jones with a variety of dildos while Hendy watched.

Figure 12.7 Group slave assault. This fantasy drawing by Ray depicts a female slave being sexually assaulted. He explained on the tapes how the sex slave would be used by the "congregation" and stated, "You will be repeatedly raped in every hole you got." (Illustration courtesy of Special Agent Norman Rhoades, New Mexico State Police.)

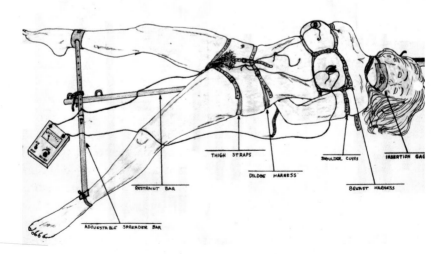

Figure 12.8 Bondage and restraints. This fantasy drawing depicts how Ray would bind and torture his "slaves." Note the equipment. These items were recovered during the search. (Illustration courtesy of Special Agent Norman Rhoades, New Mexico State Police.)

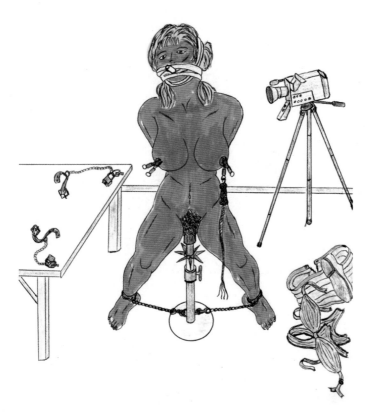

Figure 12.9 Dildo insertion. This fantasy drawing by Ray depicts a large dildo being used on the "slave." This dildo was recovered during the search. The camera Ray used to record his torture sessions was also seized as evidence. (Illustration courtesy of Special Agent Norman Rhoades, New Mexico State Police.)

Ray would force differently sized dildos into Jones's rectum. These included the very large "spiked dildo" that was kept on a stand. Jones described the use of various devices on her, which were homemade or had been designed by Ray. Detectives recovered one such device described by the victim as a white metal device that resembled a piece of orange. There were two half circles of metal welded together with U-shaped nails welded along the edge that would cause excruciating pain if the victim tried to close her legs or press her legs together (Figures 12.11 through 12.13).

Jones reported that she was taken to the middle bedroom and laid flat on what Ray called the "coffin box" to have her nipples stretched. She stated that he placed large clamps on her nipples, which were attached to ropes that were run up the ceiling through pulleys and then across the ceiling to another set of pulleys and then to large lead weights.

Ray then shocked Jones in her upper torso making her arch up and then fall back down stretching out her breasts. He also had placed tape over her tattoos to avoid identification. He did this so when he photographed her, she would not be identified. Police located a Polaroid™ of Jones, which had been taken by Ray during their crime scene search (Figures 12.14 through 12.16).

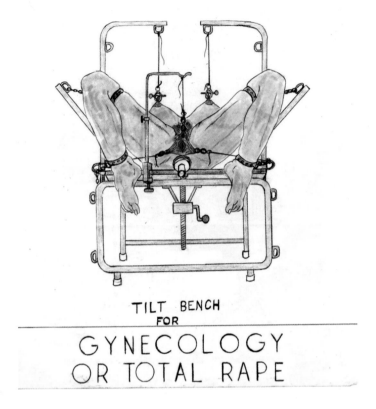

Figure 12.10 Tilt bench. This fantasy drawing by Ray shows how he would sexually torture his "slaves" before he obtained a fully operational gynecology table. (Illustration courtesy of Special Agent Norman Rhoades, New Mexico State Police.)

Figure 12.11 Torture devices. These straps and knee and ankle spreaders were used on the slaves to secure them in place. (Photo courtesy of Deputy District Attorney Jim Yontz, New Mexico District Attorney's Office.)

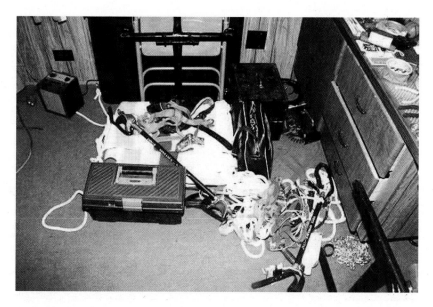

Figure 12.12 Electrical charges and breeding pole. This photo shows the breeding pole and the electrical charger Ray used on his slaves. (Photo courtesy of Deputy District Attorney Jim Yontz, New Mexico District Attorney's Office)

Figure 12.13 Dildo. This was the large dildo that Ray refers to in the "introductory" audio taped instructions. DNA evidence was recovered from this device, which matched the victim who had escaped. (Photo courtesy of Deputy District Attorney Jim Yontz, New Mexico District Attorney's Office.)

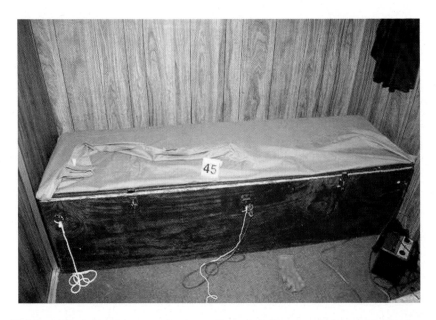

Figure 12.14 Coffin box. This was the box where the slave would be kept and also was used for the nipple stretching. (Photo courtesy of Deputy District Attorney Jim Yontz, New Mexico District Attorney's Office.)

Figure 12.15 Inside view of torture box. (Photo courtesy of Deputy District Attorney Jim Yontz, New Mexico District Attorney's Office.)

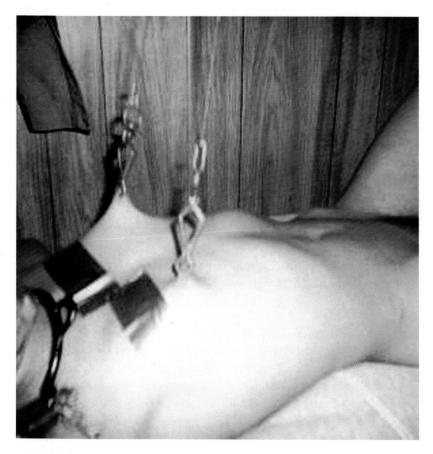

Figure 12.16 Torture. Police discovered a Polaroid™ picture of a victim being tortured on the coffin box. This was described by the victim. (Photo courtesy of Deputy District Attorney Jim Yontz, New Mexico District Attorney's Office.)

Sixteen Techniques for Brainwashing

The term *brainwashing* as defined in *Merriam-Webster's New Collegiate Dictionary* is

> *A forcible indoctrination to induce someone to give up basic political, social, or religious beliefs and attitudes, and to accept contrasting regimented ideas ... persuasion by propaganda.* (*Merriam-Webster's New Collegiate Dictionary*, 2001, p. 138)

Interestingly, David Parker Ray used many of the techniques listed in the book *The Perfect Victim* (McGuire and Norton, 1988), which detailed similar events in the Sex Slave Case. That case involved Cameron Hooker and his wife, Janice. Cameron Hooker's fantasy was to dominate and torture nude women who were bound and helpless. His fantasies were fueled by an extensive collection of hard-core pornography, which featured bondage, leather, and handcuffs and whips.

Dr. Chris Hatcher, an associate clinical psychology professor at the University of California/San Francisco, outlined how the use of 16 techniques that are recognized in psychological literature can be used to "break down" victims or brainwash them into compliance. The following is from the book *The Perfect Victim* (McGuire and Norton, 1988, pp. 292–297).

Technique 1

A sudden, unexpected abduction, followed by isolation as soon as possible. Refuse to answer any questions, place them in a cell-like environment, remove their clothes, and begin humiliation and degradation.

Technique 2

The second step in breaking someone is to physically or sexually abuse, to expose the captive's vulnerability and shock him or her. Not only has the victim been stripped of his or her clothes and placed in a physically vulnerable position, but also you are going to whip or abuse in some way, specifically with sexual manipulation, illustrate just how exposed and vulnerable they are.

Technique 3

Remove normal daylight patterns. All of us, both biologically and psychologically, are used to a certain day and night sequence. … Placing someone in a constantly lit or constantly dark environment is very disorienting.

Technique 4

Control urination, defecation, menstruation, and to be present when these activities are performed. Basically what you want is to do here is destroy a person's sense of privacy. If a person soils himself and isn't able to clean that up, the sense of shame in sitting or lying in one's own waste product is really quite extraordinary, and individuals become motivated to do what they can to get permission to clean themselves up. … It takes you back to a period of vulnerability.

Technique 5

Control food and water. Hatcher stated the obvious, "If you don't get food and water, you are going to die. So, on the one hand, they may be torturing you and preventing you from leaving, but, on the other hand, they are bringing you food and water." This helps make the captive dependent upon the captor.

Technique 6

Punish for no apparent rhyme or reason. Initially, the captive tries to figure out some rationale to the intermittent beatings, but finding none, eventually has to simply accept that punishment will occur with no reason.

Technique 7

Require the victim to constantly ask permission for anything or any behavior. This would involve asking permission to speak to someone, permission to take a tray of food. It is a type of training procedure.

Technique 8

Establish a pattern of sexual and physical abuse. This "indicates to the person that this is what her new life is now going to be like." It's a way of "getting the person to realize things have changed in a permanent sense."

Technique 9

Continue to isolate the person. The captor has now become the source of food, water, and human contact. People are basically information hungry. If you put them in a restricted environment without any source of information except from their captor, they become dependent on their only point of contact. Their captor.

Technique 10

Present a goal or model of future behavior, a model of how to please the captor.

Technique 11

Threaten family and relatives with a similar fate.

Technique 12

Threaten to sell the captive to an even worse master.

Technique 13

Continue to beat and torture the captive at irregular intervals.

Technique 14

Allow the captive small privileges for no reason, in what is referred to as "irrelevant leniency," making the captive more confused and more pliant.

Technique 15

Obtain further confessions and signed documents, have the captive give over more and more control in writing.

Technique 16

Incorporate new behavior controls. *Allow the captive* to attend to personal hygiene, allow clothes, some privacy. It is important to permit the captive some degree of freedom, without the captor's presence and *then suddenly appear, giving the captive a feeling that the captor is omnipresent.*

Initial Cooperation of Cindy Hendy

Cindy Hendy provided details of other crimes committed by David Parker Ray, who told her that he had dumped bodies in the lake and that he learned that he had to split the stomachs open so they would stay down in the water as one had surfaced in 1989. She told the detectives about the Billy Ray Bowers case, which was unsolved at the time of Ray's arrest. Bowers was a partner in the car lot business with Ray in Phoenix, Arizona.

Hendy told Agent Wesley LaCuesta that Ray had killed at least 18 women. Two of the women's photographs had been discovered in the toy box cargo trailer. During the confession, she stated Ray referred to his victims as "packages" and told the investigators that Ray had killed about 30 people, 18 of them in the Truth or Consequences, New Mexico, area. She said Ray had dumping sites in three states. Hendy also told the investigators that, in 1986, his daughter, Jessie, had reported her father to the FBI in New Mexico out of spite.

Jessie told the FBI agents that her father was kidnapping and torturing young girls before transporting them to Mexico to sell as sex slaves. Hendy stated that Ray had told her that he had been questioned by the FBI in Arizona in 1987 regarding missing women whose bodies were found. The FBI investigated Ray for over a year, but determined that the allegations were nonspecific.

However, according to Hendy, Ray told her that he "talked his way through it." Ironically, a lot of that information was consistent with what authorities found in the toy box.

Hendy told Agent LaCuesta how Ray would use makeup on his victims to make the victims more photogenic. She said that Ray would photograph his victims in various states of bondage and torture. She also revealed that Ray's daughter, Glenda "Jessie" Ray, was also heavy into the S&M scene and that Jessie Ray was an active participant. Jessie would bring victims to her father David.

Hendy also provided information on a person named Roy Yancy, who was involved with Ray and his daughter, Jessie, in the sex torture murder of a young woman named Marie Parker. Ray had disposed of Marie Parker's body in the desert.

Hendy told Agent LaCuesta that Roy Yancy and Ray's daughter were involved in the sex torture murder of a young woman named Marie Parker. Marie Parker had been abducted from a local saloon by Jessie and Yancy and brought back to the toy box for a torture session with Jessie and her father, Ray.

Also according to Hendy, Ray, along with Hendy and Yancy, as well as Jessie Ray were involved in couple swapping and group sex.

Investigators located pictures taken at the house showing them in various sex games.

Roy Yancy

Background

Dennis Roy Yancy was a Truth or Consequences, New Mexico, native who came from a decent middle class family. However, by age 16, he was already experimenting with drugs and alcohol. While in high school, he was part of a satanic cult. Yancy was arrested for burglary after he and his cult broke into their teacher's house, killed the pet dog, severed the dog's penis, and left it on a computer key board. He was sentenced to the New Mexico Youth Detention Center where he resumed school and learned computer science.

Yancy joined the Naval Reserve Officer's Training Corps and served in the Navy for four years. He returned to Truth or Consequences in 1995, with a bright future. However, he soon joined the city's drug scene, where he met and became tight with Jessie Ray, who introduced him to her father, David Ray. He soon became known as "Toy Boy Roy" and became a willing participant in Ray's sadomasochistic drug scene.

"Toy Boy" Roy Yancy had numerous affairs with a number of women in the Truth and Consequences area. Yancy and Jessie were in the midst of all the action. They befriended a 43-year-old homosexual man from Florida who was into drugs and weird sex. The man's neighbors reported that Yancy and Jessie had partied with the man just before New Year Year's Day. His decomposed body was discovered on New Year's Day with a doorknob lodged in his rectum. Blood spatters and pentagrams were drawn on the walls of the motel room where he was found. The rumors that circulated at the time were that "he had been killed during an occult ritual."

Preliminary Interview of Roy Yancy

Roy Yancy was brought in for routine questioning in connection with the events at David Parker Ray's home. Yancy was among a number of persons who had been interviewed about Ray and Cindy Hendy and the activities that occurred at the Ray residence. During this informal interview, additional information was obtained about the extent of the sado-masochistic activities at the Ray house. This information included the corroboration of Hendy's statements about the involvement of Ray's daughter, Glenda "Jessie" Ray, in some of the cases.

Yancy stated that, in 1997 or 1998, he was looking at some *Penthouse* magazines at Ray's residence at which time Ray told him that he and his former wife would "have those bondage pleasures together." Yancy stated that he had never met Ray's former wife and that she could be dead. Yancy stated Ray's daughter, Jessie, was present when Ray related that "they were into weird, kinky kind of sex."

Yancy said he was shown photographs of Ray's former wife while she was tied up. Yancy said this was his first knowledge that Ray and Jessie Ray were involved in sadomasochism.

Yancy related that, a few months prior, he had witnessed Ray "torture" a female, identified as Candy. Yancy stated this had occurred inside a white trailer referred to as the toy box. Yancy said that Candy was a willing participant and that Ray had tied her from the ceiling with chains. Yancy stated that he observed Ray whip her and use clips and needles on her nipples and use a machine that was connected to a dildo that moved back and forth. Yancy said that this session lasted less than an hour.

Yancy further stated he would be tied up and also tie up various female partners for sexual pleasure, but that it was always consensual and they never indulged in torture. He said that a few months before, he had experimented with a homosexual affair with his friend, Ray. Yancy stated his encounter with Ray was generated from his curiosity and it was also consensual with no penetration and no force or bondage type of activities being involved.

Yancy said he felt Ray wanted to get him involved with "kidnapping women," but he, himself, never spoke of it. He stated that, about a year ago, Glenda ""Jessie"" Ray told him that her father had been "doing it for a lot of years." Yancy related that, at that time, he didn't believe Jessie Ray regarding Ray being "into kinky sex."

He said that Jessie Ray had told him that her father, Ray, had kidnapped and tortured women. Roy Yancy stated he stayed at the house with Ray and during that time, Ray showed him the toy box. Yancy said Ray advised him it was used for an "adrenaline rush," and the items on the wall were used as "scare tactics." Yancy stated Ray showed him "what the chair could do" and some of the "nipple clips." Yancy said he never saw anyone in the chair except Candy. This statement turned out to be false.

Yancy remarked that he had sometimes traveled to Albuquerque with Ray in Ray's RV. Yancy stated they would "cruise Central looking for hookers." Yancy said he had dated Hendy and that she would get drunk and get rough, but he stated, "He was never bound up against his will." He also stated he was only aware of Hendy and Candy being involved with S&M at Ray's residence.

He said that he, Ray, Hendy, and Candy were out on the lake in Ray's sailboat when Hendy tied Candy to a rail. Yancy stated Candy was naked at the time and Hendy began "sucking Candy's tits and sticking a dildo in her vagina or rectum." Yancy stated he was unsure which. He related that during the course of this encounter, Hendy was performing oral sex on Candy while he and Ray "used a dildo on Hendy."

Yancy related that, during this time, Candy was holding an "electric shocker" and began shocking herself. Yancy stated Hendy began to get real rough and started throwing things at which time Ray handcuffed Hendy to the boat and began "paddling her." Yancy said Hendy wanted it done, and that it was all consensual. Yancy said he did not recall being a victim, but he could have been drugged during the incident and not remember it. He then confided that he had been tied down and raped with a broom handle at one of the parties. He advised he had no further information relating to this investigation.

Formal Interview of Roy Yancy

As a result of the preliminary interview of Yancy and other persons peripherally involved, as well as information gathered from the crime scene, the New Mexico State Police decided to formally interview Yancy. He was brought in a second time and advised of his rights. He stated he wished to give a statement and agreed to cooperate in the investigation. He told the investigators that he wanted to get something "off his chest."

Yancy said, "The female subject who I strangled was Marie Parker." He said that Marie Parker was his former girlfriend and that he had had a sexual affair with her two or three days prior to her abduction. Yancy stated it was David Ray's idea to kill her. Yancy stated he had heard Ray and his daughter talking about it at Ray's residence. Yancy stated that Ray had bragged about having many years of torturing, raping, and killing women. Yancy stated he had known Ray for about five years.

Sex Torture Murder of Marie Parker

Roy Yancy stated that, on the night of July 5, 1997, he and Jessie Ray drove David Ray's white Dodge Ram Charger to the Bluewaters Saloon. Yancy stated he was drunk during this incident and that Jessie had advised him they were going to pick up Marie Parker and get some "crank." Yancy said he thought it was a prearranged drug deal. He remarked that, upon their arrival at around 10 p.m. at the Bluewaters Saloon, Jessie went inside to get Marie Parker. A short time later, according to Yancy, Jessie returned with Marie Parker and he understood they had made arrangements to effect a drug deal. Yancy stated Jessie drove them to a hill near the north exit of Truth or Consequences. Yancy said Jessie advised Marie Parker that "he's not here yet." Yancy said Jessie then exited the vehicle and came around to the right side and pointed a gun at Marie Parker and placed handcuffs on her. Yancy stated he heard Jessie tell Marie Parker to "shut up or I'll kill you."

Jessie placed Marie Parker in the rear of the vehicle, according to Yancy, and told him to watch her and keep her quiet. He said he complied with Jessie's direction and Marie Parker remained quiet during the ride to David Ray's residence. Yancy said that, upon their arrival at Ray's residence, Jessie and her father, David, forced Marie Parker into a white trailer, referred to as the toy box. At that point, Yancy said he went directly into David Ray's residence, drank a beer, stared at the television, and contemplated calling the police. He stated he didn't call the police because he was afraid of David Ray due to the fact that he had a lot of guns and that Ray was a park ranger.

Yancy said that Marie Parker was in the toy box for about three days, and that he knew David Ray and Jessie were torturing her, but he never entered the toy box during that time. After the three days, David Ray and Jessie advised Yancy that "they were done playing with her and it was time for her to go," according to Yancy. He said that he felt Ray and Jessie meant for him to kill Marie Parker, but had hoped they would let her go.

Yancy said that he, David Ray, and Jessie entered the toy box around midnight. He said he observed Marie Parker lying on a cot, bound, with cotton over her eyes as though she were asleep. He was given a rope and was told he knew what he had to do. He said that he could not recall if Ray or Jessie had given him the rope. He said that he placed the rope around Marie Parker's neck and began strangling her and that she seemed to die slowly, so he placed his knee on her chest to help it along.

After he strangled Marie Parker, Yancy said that her nude body was wrapped in a dark colored blanket (possibly green) and was placed in the back of the Dodge Ram Charger and transported to a remote area north of Truth or Consequences. He said David Ray drove the vehicle while Jessie sat near the right front door.

Yancy stated that he stayed in the back next to Marie Parker's body, but felt bad about what had occurred and was holding Marie Parker and crying because he still loved her.

Ray stopped next to a narrow deep ravine in a remote area and Yancy assisted Ray and Jessie in removing Marie Parker's body from the rear of the vehicle. They then rolled Marie Parker's body out of the blanket into the ravine after which Ray placed dirt on top of her, according to Yancy. He said that Ray told him not to tell anyone or he (Yancy) would join her. This concluded the interview with Roy Yancy.

After the interview, Yancy agreed to take the investigators to the location where they had disposed of Marie Parker's body. Assistant District Attorney Jim Yontz was notified.

Yancy directed the authorities to the Monticello Canyon area through several dirt roads. He was not sure of the exact location because he was lying down in the back of the vehicle the night Ray drove to the ravine. He said that, when he got out of the vehicle, he noticed a wide turnaround, which could be used by service trucks. He also noticed a high-line pole near the ravine, and the ravine was located about 25 feet from the edge of the road. After an extensive search of the area, Yancy was unable to locate the area where they had disposed of Marie Parker's body. The authorities also conducted an air search of the Monticello Canyon area that also failed to reveal the location of the body as described by Roy Yancy. He was booked into the Sierra County Detention Facility on suspicion of murder.

Later, authorities were advised that David Parker Ray had gone out to the Monticello Canyon area and moved the body because he didn't trust Yancy to keep his mouth shut. Interestingly, many serial killers move their victim's bodies from one location to another so that the victim's remains will not be discovered.

The News Media

As the news of this case broke, additional information and victim identifications became available. In addition to Marie Parker, another victim identified as Angelica, reported that David Ray and Cindy Hendy had captured and sexually tortured her as well. Angelica had been abducted in February about a month before Cindy Jones. Angelica was a resident of the Truth or Consequences area and was part of the drug/bar scene. She knew Ray and Hendy and had agreed to meet Hendy that day to bake a cake for her boyfriend. Ray and Hendy picked her up and drove her out to their compound. However, when they arrived things got bad.

Victim Angelica

Ray and Hendy stripped and bound Angelica and then force-fed her a pill, which knocked her out. Angelica was held captive and abused for four days. David bathed her "like a dog" before she was brought to the toy box and anally sodomized with a wood dildo. Ray and Hendy, who sexually tortured her in the toy box, held Angelica for several days.

In fact, Ray played the same "introductory tape" for her and she described the same details as Cindy. She was kept naked in the gynecology chair and had electric shocks run through various parts of her body and dildos placed inside her. Ray then forced his flaccid penis into her mouth and ordered her to give him a blow job. When he ejaculated, she was forced to swallow.

How She Survived

Angelica pretended that she enjoyed the experience and promised that she would never tell anyone. After being chained and abused for four days, she was very sore from the abuse and the electrical burns, but she "played the game" with both her captives.

Ray removed the cuffs and let her put her clothes on after he asked her to come over and give him a hug. Ray assured her that she would be all right after she said that she would like to do it again some day. Only next time, she did not want to be the victim. Ray and Hendy then drove her to a bus stop at Interstate 25.

The New Mexico State Police investigation into this allegation revealed that a deputy had picked up Angelica hitchhiking on I-25 near Truth or Consequences. She told the deputy that she had been abducted and held for a few days. She explained she had reported the incident to local police in Truth or Consequences, but they had blown off the story based on her reputation and her lifestyle in the Truth or Consequences bar/drug scene. However, New Mexico State Police had discovered her report.

Angelica cooperated with the prosecution and provided testimony at the preliminary hearing relative to the white cargo trailer (the toy box) which was sufficient to have Ray bound over. Unfortunately, Angelica died of complications related to pneumonia, so this charge was dropped when Ray waived his appeals on any issues.

Discovery of Another Victim

A woman who read about the case in the newspaper also came forward. She was the mother of a young man who had married a woman named Kelli. Kelli had walked out of the house one day and remained missing for three days. She had no explanation for the family and they asked her to leave because they thought that she was on drugs.

Evidence from the Toy Box

Among the items specified to be seized from the toy box were video and audiotapes. These tapes were both commercial and homemade. In addition to warrants to seize the tapes, it was also made clear that the tapes were to be viewed and listened to in order to extract information for comparison to the witness and victim statements as well as other evidence recovered during the search. The examination of the tapes was essential due to the amount of video-recording equipment discovered in the white cargo trailer (toy box) and the obvious evidence that David Parker Ray may have videotaped his victims. One such videotape showed five or six minutes of Ray installing a new chair and video equipment in the trailer. The next 30 or 40 minutes had the camera focused on the ceiling of the white cargo trailer evidenced by the yellow/gold soundproofing materials. The tape then displays a scene with a naked woman lying on what was determined to be a "modified weight bench" (Figure 12.17 and Figure 12.18).

Ray is seen in the video caressing and rubbing his hand on the victim's genital area and breasts. He also places additional duct tape on her mouth.

Figure 12.17 Victim. Videotape of one of Ray's victims in the toy box was recovered, showing the activities that Ray engaged in. (Photo courtesy of Deputy District Attorney Jim Yontz, New Mexico District Attorney's Office.)

It was apparent to those who watched the tape that the woman was not a willing participant in the activity displayed on the videotape. While there wasn't a view of her face that was sufficient to allow for identification of the woman, there were some features that were apparent and unique. There was a large ornate tattoo on her right shin and around her right ankle. She also had her blond hair fixed in very small tight braids. Investigators began to contact law enforcement agencies and canvass hospitals in an attempt to identify this person.

Ironically, the New Mexico State Police had received a call from her ex-mother-in-law when she read about the case in the newspaper and saw the news coverage on television. The woman told the investigators about her former daughter-in-law, Kelli, and a strange sequence of events that had transpired.

The police learned that Kelli, who had only been married a few days, had an argument with her husband about sexual matters. Kelli had left their house stating she would return later. Kelli was gone for three days. Police learned that Kelli had been abducted.

Actually, Kelli had been returned to her husband's residence by Ray, who was wearing his New Mexico State Park uniform and driving his official looking Dodge Ram.

Ray told the family he found Kelli wandering around the beach by the lake and that she was disoriented. Ray told the family he had taken her to McDonald's for iced tea and then brought her home. Kelli, according to family members, looked drugged out and smelled bad. She was still wearing the same clothes she had on when she walked out. Kelli was

Figure 12.18 Fantasy component. Ray maintained a number of anatomically correct dolls in various stages of bondage and torture. (Photo courtesy of Deputy District Attorney Jim Yontz, New Mexico District Attorney's Office.)

asked by her family where she had been. She could not recall and was apparently under the influence of drugs and was disoriented.

Under the circumstances, the family asked her to leave. Ray then took Kelli to a friend's house. Kelli's mother-in-law told the investigators that Kelli was living in Colorado.

Evidence from the Introductory Tape

The portion of the tape that Ray recorded about the procedure for releasing his sex slaves became an important corroborating piece of evidence in this investigation.

> After we get completely through with you, you're gonna be drugged up real heavy, with a combination of sodium pentothal and phenobarbital. They are both hypnotic drugs that will make you extremely susceptible to hypnosis, autohypnosis, and hypnotic suggestion. You're gonna be kept drugged a couple of days while I play with your mind. By the time I get through brainwashing you, you're not gonna remember a fuckin' thing about this little adventure. You won't remember this place, us, or what has happened to you. There won't be any DNA evidence because you'll be bathed, and both holes between your legs will be thoroughly flushed out. You'll be dressed, sedated, and turned loose on some country road, bruised, heh, sore all over, but nothing that won't heal up in a week or two.

Victim Located

Kelli was located after several interviews. She agreed to meet with investigators after they asked her to describe her tattoos. The tattoos on her leg matched those that were seen in the video. They also matched the smaller tattoo around her ankle to the one on the still photograph. Kelli reported to them, prior to seeing the photo, that at the time she had her hair styled in short braids; Bo Derek braids is how she referred to them.

She stated that she had disjointed nightmares of being taken and held against her will and being sexually abused by Ray. However, she did not report this because these memories had come back to her in bits and pieces and there had been a lapse of a few years since the event occurred. She kept repressing these memories as recurring bad dreams.

She told the investigators that she recalled being in Ray's vehicle and being taken home, but not relating him to her captivity. At the time she had no memory of the prior three days. The memories eventually came back very slowly. Her recollection of the events follows.

Kelli's Statement

Kelli stated that she and her husband John (*not real name*) had known each other for some time and had dated for about six months prior to getting married. They planned to stay with his parents until they could arrange to move to San Diego where John was staying. Kelli had developed a medical condition, which resulted in pain during sexual intercourse. Kelli and John had an argument about this the night before and continued it briefly in the morning. Kelli decided to go out for a walk to be alone (away from John) for a while. Kelli met up with friends and they went to some bars in town. Although Kelli was with these people, she had only one or two beers the entire day. She ended up taking some of the people home from the bar. When she returned the last time, she was with Jessie Ray and another woman. Since Kelli had no transportation of her own, she asked Jessie for a ride home. Jessie told her that it was too far to drive and would take her somewhere nearby. Kelli asked to be taken to a friend's house. Kelli went with Jessie and was taken instead to the residence Jessie shared with her father. Kelli went in and sat in the living room on a couch. Both Ray and Jessie disappeared into a back bedroom down the hall. When they came back out, one of them put a knife to her throat and the other restrained her. They put duct tape on her eyes and mouth and put a collar with a chain attached around her neck. She was then led out to the white cargo trailer a few feet from house. Her clothes were removed and she was strapped to a weight bench.

For the next three days, Kelli described sessions during which the defendant David Ray would attempt to insert dildos of various sizes into her vagina. He was having a difficult time doing so and would then examine her "like a doctor." While in the white cargo trailer, Kelli recalled seeing the medical cabinet with devices on it as well as the shelf to her left with all types of sex toys on it. She recalled that there was a telephone in the white cargo trailer and that Ray would lock and unlock the door to the white cargo trailer as he came in and later left. She recalled being in the defendant's vehicle and being taken home, but not relating the defendant to her captivity. She had no memory of the prior three days. However, the memories began to come back very slowly. Kelli has since undergone extensive therapy.

The officers upon arrival at Kelli's house asked her to relate what she recalled of the incident. They then asked to see the tattoo on her leg. When they compared the tattoo on her leg to the still photo, they matched. They also matched the smaller tattoo around her ankle to the one on the still photograph. Kelli reported to them, prior to seeing the photo, that at the time she had her hair styled in short braids, Bo Derek braids is how she referred to them.

Fantasy Drawings

I had advised District Attorney Jim Yontz to have the New Mexico State Police conduct a search of David Ray's cell while he was awaiting trial. My rationale for such a tactic was based on my opinion and review of some of his drawings and illustrations depicting the sexual torture of bound women. The fantasy drawings, which had been seized by authorities pursuant to search warrants at Ray's compound, went into exquisite detail, which provided unique insight into the subject's innermost sexual thought processes and fantasies — not to mention evidence.

In Ray's case, his fantasy world and his sadistic activities were so intertwined that he would need to stimulate himself to maintain his equilibrium. When the authorities did search his cell, they recovered a series of drawings depicting "lizard people" involved in sexual activities with young women. It was interesting to note that in his drawings the "lizard people" represented a man, a woman, and a younger lizard involved in sexual activities with their prey. In the author's opinion, these lizards represented David Ray, Cindy Hendy, and his daughter, Glenda Jessie Ray (Figure 12.19).

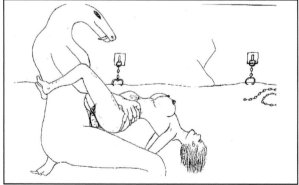

Figure 12.19 Fantasy drawing. This is one of the fantasy drawings that the subject made in jail. There were a number of these drawing seized by the prison authorities. It was interesting to note that in his drawings the "lizard people" represented a man, a woman, and a younger lizard involved in sexual activities with their prey. (Illustration courtesy of Deputy District Attorney Jim Yontz, New Mexico District Attorney's Office.)

Legal Maneuvers

District Attorney Jim Yontz wanted to try the Rays together; however, a series of affidavits and motions prevented that. On December 2, 1999, Roy Yancy was sentenced on his plea of guilty for the murder of Marie Parker. Cindy Hendy, who had managed to communicate with David Ray, wanted to withdraw her guilty plea. Then David Ray's trial was further delayed by motions. Jim Yontz would not be able to use Hendy's testimony against Ray in trial. Her request to withdraw was finally denied and Judge Neil Mertz agreed with defense counsel that there would be separate trials for Jessie and David Ray.

Judge Mertz further ruled that David Ray would have three separate trials, which was bad for the prosecution. David Ray's first trial was in May 2000. Judge Mertz excluded a number of items of evidence, which he considered to be prejudicial to the defendant. This included the prosecution's strongest piece of evidence, the "introductory tape. Even though the prosecution was able to introduce the videotape of Kelli's torture, the defense was able to portray Kelli as a willing participant in a sex game; two female jurors decided that "a lot of people enjoy rough sex," and held out against conviction. Judge Mertz immediately declared a mistrial in July 2000.

Judge Mertz was widely criticized for declaring the mistrial so soon without further jury deliberation. However, the prosecution was back to square one Then, Judge Mertz, who was scheduled for the retrial, suffered a massive heart attack and died.

In April 2001, Judge Kevin Sweazea took the case. He allowed the "introductory tape" to be played for the jurors over defense objections and Ray was convicted for the sexual assault on Kelli. The next trial was to begin in June. However, Ray changed his plea to guilty. Hendy entered her guilty plea after the judge denied her application for a withdrawal of plea.

Disposition

David Parker Ray, who was charged with kidnapping second degree, conspiracy to commit kidnapping, assault with intent to commit a violent felony, and criminal sexual penetration seven counts was sentenced to 224 years to be run consecutively. Ironically, Ray will never get to serve that sentence because just before being transferred to general population he died of an apparent heart attack on May 28, 2002.

Cynthia Lea Hendy, who was charged with kidnapping first degree two counts, conspiracy to commit kidnapping first degree, and criminal sexual penetration two counts was sentenced to 36 years.

Dennis Roy Yancy, who was charged with murder second degree and conspiracy to commit murder first degree was sentenced to 15 years on each count to be run consecutively for a total of 30 years.

Glenda "Jessie" Ray, who was charged with kidnapping second degree was sentenced to 9 years. The court further ordered that six years were suspended from the sentence with a supervised probation of five years.

District Attorney's Sentencing Statement

Jim Yontz addressed the court, "It's been over two-and-half-years that I've had to think about what I was going to say. This monster should never be allowed to roam the streets again.

"These people don't change. These people are not amenable to treatment.

"He picked the wrong victims. He picked the wrong victim in Kelli Van Cleave, who had the guts and intestinal fortitude to testify three times in a public forum.

"He picked the wrong victim in Cindy Vigil. She struggled at the peril of her own well-being to get away. If she hadn't done that, the nightmare would have continued in Truth or Consequences. Under no circumstances should there be a light at the end of the tunnel for David Ray."

Acknowledgments

The author wishes to acknowledge the contribution of the information and materials for this particular chapter from professional law enforcement investigators representing various police departments who were involved in this major case investigation. Specifically, I wish to give special recognition to my friend Assistant District Attorney Jim Yontz, who was assigned to the 7th Judicial District of the Office of the District Attorney, New Mexico. Yontz had been through the "Practical Homicide Investigation®" classes prior to this case and realized the significance of including this particular case in the book. Also, the following investigators from the New Mexico State Police: Sergeant Wes LaCuesta, case agent; Sergeant K. C. Rogers, crime scene commander; Sergeant Rich Libicer, intelligence officer; Agent Norman Rhoads, case agent; and Agent John Briscoe, case manager; and the following members of the FBI: Special Agent Larry Houpt, case agent, and Special Agent Anthony Maxwell, case manager.

References

American Psychiatric Association. *Diagnostic and Statistical Manual of Mental Disorders,* (*DSM-IV-TR*), 4th ed., Text revision, APA, Washington, D.C., 2000.
Ellis, B.E. *American Psycho,* Vintage Books, New York, 1991.
Glatt, J. *Cries of the Desert,* St. Martin's Press, New York, 2002.
McGuire, C. and C. Norton. *The Perfect Victim,* Dell Publishing, New York, 1988.
Merriam-Webster's New Collegiate Dictionary, 10th ed., Merriam-Webster, Inc., Springfield, MA, 2001.
Reisman, J. Hazardous material: Viewing pornography for a living can be deadly. *Salvo* 10, August 2009.

The BTK Investigation 13

Introduction

The BTK (bind, torture, kill) killer had claimed credit for seven murders, which had occurred between 1974 and 1977. The actual number of homicides that BTK was ultimately responsible for was 10. However, authorities would not know about the additional homicides until his arrest in 2005.

The BTK murders had seemingly ended in 1977 with the murder of Nancy Fox. The killer had communicated with authorities and the news media during these events calling himself *BTK*, which he advised stood for "bind them, torture them, kill them." BTK appeared to have gone dormant in 1979; however, the total BTK investigation continued for over 30 years, starting in January 1974 and finally ending with his arrest and conviction in August 2005.

The Original BTK Serial Murders

The Otero Murders: Four Family Members Murdered in Their Home

On January 15, 1974, Joseph Otero, 38, his wife Julie, 34, their son Joseph II, 9, and their daughter Josephine, 11, were found murdered in the family home at 803 Edgemoor in Wichita, Kansas, at 3:40 p.m. Otero had driven the older children to school that morning and returned home to assist with getting the two younger children ready for school. Evidence indicated that the suspect had entered the home through the back door and confronted the family after he had cut the telephone lines (Figure 13.1). Julie Otero's purse was dumped on the dining room floor and Joseph Otero's billfold was on the kitchen stove. The victim's vehicle was missing from the garage.

Their surviving children, Charlie, 15, Danny, 14, and Carmen, 13, came home from school in the afternoon and discovered both parents dead in the master bedroom. Charlie tried to use the phone, but the line was dead. He ran next door to a neighbor's house to call the police as his siblings began untying their parents. The arriving police met Charlie who advised them that his parents were in the house tied up. The children had begun to untie and remove the bindings from their parents before the police arrived. They told the police officers that their younger siblings were due home from school. They were unaware that their younger siblings also had been killed.

When the police officers entered the home, they observed the bodies of Joseph and Julie Otero in the main bedroom. Joseph was found lying on the floor. There was evidence that his wrists and arms had been secured with Venetian blind cord and adhesive tape. He had been strangled with a ligature made from this cord, which was wrapped around his neck. A shirt and plastic bag had been placed over his head and secured with his own belt.

Julie was lying on the bed. Carmen had removed a gag from her mouth as they tried to revive her. Strips of pillowcase had been used as a gag. She had her hands tied behind her back, along with her feet, with Venetian blind cord. White adhesive tape also was used to

Figure 13.1 Otero home, back door. The killer entered the family home armed with a gun after he had cut the telephone line outside the doorway. (Photo courtesy of Lieutenant Kenneth Landwehr, commanding officer homicide, Wichita, Kansas, Police Department, and Retired Director Larry Welch, Kansas Bureau of Investigation (KBI).)

tie her wrists. A ligature of cord was also around her neck. Julie Otero had been strangled to death. Investigators also located semen on the bed sheet near her body.

As the police "cleared the premises," they found the bodies of Joseph, Jr., and Josephine. Joseph, Jr., was found in an upstairs bedroom. He had been tied and bound. His wrists were bound behind his back and his ankles were tied with the same type of Venetian blind cord. He had a shirt and plastic bag over his head. Underneath this was a third layer of bagging, consisting of another T-shirt, which belonged to the victim.

Josephine was found in the basement utility area. She was hanging by a piece of hemp rope with a semi-hangman's noose (Figure 13.2). The rope had been tied around a sewer pipe running across the ceiling. Her toes were touching the floor. A cloth gag was knotted in the front and tied around her neck. Venetian blind cord bound her wrists behind her back and white adhesive tape was used at the wrists. The victim was wearing a blue knit top. Semen was found on her knit top. The bra was cut between the cups. Her pants were pulled down around her ankles. Her socks were on her feet. The same type of cord bound her ankles and continued to loop her legs and waist and was tied off behind her waist. Investigators recovered semen, which had streaked down the inside of her left thigh. The semen stains continued onto her legs and socks and pooled on the floor next to her feet. Several Q-tips were found on the floor near the semen and also had semen on them. The victim's slacks and boots were nearby. There was no evidence of oral, anal, or vaginal penetration found on any of the victims.

Money had apparently been taken from Joseph's wallet and Julie's pocketbook. His watch was also missing, along with his 1966 Oldsmobile, which had been driven from the crime scene by the perpetrator. It was later located in a Dillon's parking lot at Central and Oliver. A witness saw the victim's car leave the residence at approximately 10:30 a.m. The keys for the car were missing. At the time, police believed this crime to be a home invasion.

Figure 13.2 Josephine Otero. Little 11-year-old Josephine was the sexual target of the BTK, who brought the child to the basement where he hung her and cut her clothes from her body. BTK spent time masturbating on his victim as she hung from the sewer pipe. Semen was recovered from the scene. (Photo courtesy of Lieutenant Kenneth Landwehr, commanding officer homicide, Wichita, Kansas, Police Department, and Retired Director Larry Welch, Kansas Bureau of Investigation (KBI).)

Kathryn Bright Homicide

On April 4, 1974, 21-year-old Kathy Bright was murdered and her brother, Kevin, was shot at Kathy's residence at 3217 East 13th Street in Wichita, Kansas. The intruder entered the residence by breaking a glass window in the back door. He waited inside the premises and confronted the young woman and her brother at gunpoint as they came in. The assailant reassured them that he was not going to harm them, but needed money and their vehicle.

The intruder directed Kevin to bind his sister's hands behind her back with plastic-coated clothesline from the scene. The assailant then tied up Kevin with his hands behind his back with similar wire and then bound his ankles with the victim's clothing tied off to the bed. He gagged Kevin with the victim's articles and laid him gently on the floor, on a pillow, face down.

The suspect took Kathy to another bedroom, separated by an adjoining bathroom. He tied her with similar wire. The suspect then returned to Kevin and attempted to strangle him with nylon hose. Kevin fought for his life and managed to break the stranglehold. The intruder shot Kevin with his .22-caliber pistol twice during the struggle.

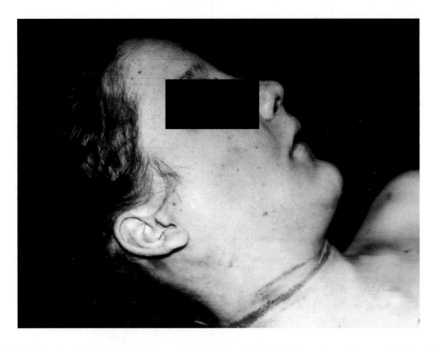

Figure 13.3 Kathy Bright. BTK strangled and stabbed Kathy who, along with her brother, fought off the sexual attack. The strangulation marks are visible on her neck. (Photo courtesy of Lieutenant Kenneth Landwehr, commanding officer homicide, Wichita, Kansas, Police Department, and Retired Director Larry Welch, Kansas Bureau of Investigation (KBI).)

The intruder then ran back to the bedroom where Kathy was trying to free herself from her bindings. Subsequently, Kevin fled the residence to get help. Evidence indicated that Kathy had struggled free from the chair to which she had been bound. Her ankles had been bound with her stockings and her face beaten. She had been strangled with cord and a scarf. The intruder had also stabbed Kathy 11 times. As the assailant slipped out the back door of the house, Kathy attempted to use the phone to call for help, but could not talk due to a fractured larynx. She died from the loss of blood from the stab wounds. There was no evidence of sexual assault (Figure 13.3).

Kevin had been shot through the mouth and received a grazing wound through the scalp. He had survived the attack and provided police with a description of their assailant. Wichita detectives were able to locate some possible witnesses during the canvass. A composite drawing of a suspect was posted with a request and appeal for any information regarding the crime.

A bedroom phone had been disabled. The wire used for binding had originated from the back yard. The other bindings belonged to the victims. The knife and gun were not recovered. BTK never took credit for this killing. Although, in subsequent correspondence, he admitted to another unknown kill referring to it as #5.

BTK's First Letter: October 22, 1974

On October 9, 1974, the newspapers reported that Wichita police had a suspect in custody in connection with the Otero homicides. October 18, 1974, another newspaper story reported that the Wichita police had three suspects in custody. This apparently angered the real killer.

On October 22, 1974, Don Granger, who worked at *The Wichita Eagle* received a call from an anonymous person who told him that a message regarding the Otero murders would be found in a book at the Wichita Public Library. A two-page note was found in a library book entitled, *Applied Engineering Mechanics*. This was the first and only original communication sent by the killer soon to be known as the "BTK killer."

The letter began with a statement: *"I write this letter to you for the sake of the tax payer as well as your time. Those three dude [sic] you have in custody are just talking to get publicity for the Otero murders. They know nothing at all. I did it by myself and with no ones help. ... Let's put it straight."*

The writer then named each victim as he described the interior of the Otero home and the position of each of their bodies using the breakdown position, bondage, garroting, and comments.

He also described what materials he used to secure the victims and how he killed them. There was no doubt in the detectives' minds that the writer of this letter, in fact, was the killer of the Otero family (grammatical and spelling errors are those of BTK).

Joe:

Position: Southwest bedroom, feet tied to the bed, head pointed in a southerly direction
Bondage: Window blind cord
Garrote: Blind cord, brown belt
Death: The old bag trick, and strangulation with clothesline rope
Clothes: White sweat shirt, green pants

Comments: He threw up at one time. Had a rib injury from wreck few week before. Laying on coat.

Julie:

Position: Laying on her back crosswise on the bed pointed in a southwestern direction. Face cover with a pillow.
Bondage: Blind cord.
Garrote: Clothesline cord tie in a clove-hitch.
Death: Strangulation twice.
Clothes: Blue housecoat, black slack, white sock.

Comments: Blood on face from too much on the neck, bed unmade.

Josephine:

Position: Hanging by the neck in the northwest part of the basement. Dryer or freezer north of her body.
Bondage: Hand tied with blind cord. Feet and lower knees, upper knees and waist with clothesline cord. All one lenght.
Garrote: Rough hemp rope ¼-inch diameter, noose with four or five turns, new.

Clothes:	Dark bra cut in the micole sock.
Death:	Strangulation once, hung.

Comments:	Rest of her clothes at the bottom of the stairs, green pants, and panties. Her glasses in the southwest bedroom.

Joseph:

Position:	In the east bedroom laying on his back pointed in eastern direction.
Bondage:	Blind cord.
Garrote:	Three hoods, white T-shirt, white plastic bag, anther [sic] T-shirt, clothesline cord with clove hitch.
Death:	Suffocation once, strangulation–suffocation with the old bag trick.
Clothes:	Brown pants, yellow-brown stripe T-shirt.

Comments:	His radio is missing.

All victims had their hand tie behind their backs. Gags of pillow case material. Slip knotts on Joe and Joseph neck to hold bag down or was at one time. Purse contents south of the table. Spilled drink in that area also, kids making lunches. Door shade in red chair in the living room. Otero's watch missing. I needed one so I took it Runsgood. Thermostast turn down. Car dirty inside, out of gas.

Page 2

I'm sorry this happen to the society. They are the ones who suffer the most. It hard to control myself. You probably call me "psychotic with sexual perversion hang-up." When this monster enters my brain, I will never know. But, it's here to stay. How does one cure himself? If you ask for help, that you have killed four people, they will laugh or hit the panic button and call the cops.

I can't stop, so the monster goes on, and hurtme as well as society. Society can be thankfull that there are ways for people like me to relieve myself at time by day dreams of some victim being torture and being mine. It is a big complicated game my friend or the monster play putting victims number down, follow them, checking up on them waiting in the dark.

Waiting, waiting. … the pressure is great and some times he runs the game to his liking. Maybe you can stop him. I can't. He has already chosen his next victim or victims. I don't who they are yet. The next day after I read the paper, I will know, but it to late.

Good luck hunting.

The writer ends the letter signing: "*YOURS, TRULY GUILTILY,*" with a postscript: "*Since sex criminals do not change their MO or by nature cannot do so, I will not change mine. The code words for me will be 'bind them, torture them, kill them,' B.T.K., you see me at it again. They will be on the next victim.*"

Investigative Summary of the Letter

- A statement of responsibility for the Otero homicides.
- Information to support the claim of responsibility.
- An attempt to explain a motivation and rationale for the murders.
- A code name of **BTK** derived from the words: "bind them, torture them, kill them."
- The **BTK** symbol in the lower right corner of the correspondence.

Shirley Vian Homicide

On March 17, 1977, 26-year-old Shirley Vian, who lived with her husband and her three children, 8, 6, and 4, was murdered in her home at 1311 South Hydraulic in Wichita, Kansas. One of her children who was walking home from the store was confronted by an unknown white man, who showed him a photograph of a woman and child and asked the boy if he knew them. The boy said he didn't know them and saw the man go to another house and knock on the door. The boy returned home and joined his mom and the two other children. Minutes later that same man knocked on Vian's door and forcibly entered by showing a handgun. The suspect started to tie up the children with cord he brought with him.

A child began crying so he herded the children into a bathroom and secured the doors by moving a bed against one door and tying the other door shut with cord. The killer had put toys in the bathroom for the children.

The offender had removed all of Shirley Vian's clothing. She was found face down on her bed with her head at the foot of the bed. Her wrists and arms were tied behind her back with black plastic tape and her nylon stockings. Her legs were bound with black electrical tape. One length of white cord was tied around her neck and it continued to her wrists. It was then tied around her wrists and down to and around her legs and ankles and was finally tied off to the bedpost at the head of the bed. A plastic bag covered her head and was tied around the neck by the victim's nightgown she had been wearing (Figure 13.4). The children escaped and summoned help.

The black plastic bag, electrical tape and white cord used for binding had originated with the suspect. There was no evidence of sexual assault or sexual activity found at the scene. Police believed that Vian was not the primary target that day. Based on the information supplied by witnesses, the intended target was a woman who was not at home at the time. Vian's son who talked to the offender provided a target of opportunity.

Nancy Fox Homicide

On December 9, 1977, 25-year-old Nancy Fox was discovered strangled to death in her home at 843 Pershing in Wichita, Kansas. She was last seen on December 8 when she left her place of employment at approximately 9 p.m. She stated that she was going straight home. At 8:18 a.m. on December 9, an unknown suspect used a pay phone near the downtown area to inform the dispatcher that a homicide would be found at the address of the victim. The caller also gave the victim's name.

Investigators discovered forced entry at the victim's bedroom window. Glass was broken and a pry tool had been used. The exterior telephone line had been cut with a pinching tool. There were no signs of a struggle inside the residence. The victim's purse was dumped on the table and her driver's license was missing. The receiver from the wall phone was on the floor.

Evidence indicated that the victim had smoked a cigarette, was chewing gum, and had already hung up her slacks when the suspect, who had apparently been waiting inside for the victim, confronted her.

Fox was found face down on her bed. She was wearing a sweater. Her wrists were bound behind her back with pantyhose. Additional stockings were used as a gag and tied around her neck. Her panties were pulled down to midthigh. Lingerie and undergarments

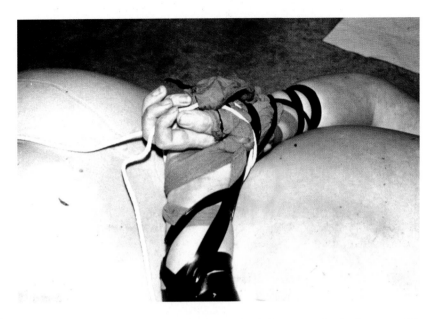

Figure 13.4 Shirley Vian. BTK had removed all of the victim's clothing and bound her with a combination of ropes and black tape and the victim's nylon stockings and nightgown. She was strangled to death. (Photo courtesy of Lieutenant Kenneth Landwehr, commanding officer homicide, Wichita, Kansas, Police Department, and Retired Director Larry Welch, Kansas Bureau of Investigation (KBI).)

from the dresser were strewn on the bed beside her body. Other clothing had been used to bind her ankles. Semen was found on a nightgown next to her head (Figure 13.5).

BTK's Second and Third Communications

Letter (February 7, 1978) and Poem (January 31, 1978)

On February 9, 1978, KAKE-TV received a four-page document consisting of three typed pages and a drawing (Figure 13.6) from an unknown subject claiming responsibility for the death of seven persons.

BTK started the letter with the following statement (grammatical errors are those of BTK):

Page 1

I find the newspaper not wirting about the poem on Vian unamusing. A little paragraph would have been enough. I know it not the news media fault. The Police Chief he keep things quiet, and doesn't let the public know there a psycho running lose strangling mostly women, there are 7 in the ground; who will be next? How many do I have to Kill before I get a name in the paper or some national attention. Do the cop think that all those deaths are not related?

Golly-gee, yes the M.O. is different in each, but look a pattern is developing. The victims are tie up -most have been women-phone cut- bring some bondage material sadist tendencies-no struggle, outside the death spot no wintness except the Vains Kids. They were lucky; a phone call save them. I was go-in to tape the boys and put plastics bag over there head like I did Joseph, and Shirley. And then hang girl. God-oh God what a beautiful sexual relief that would have been. Josephine, when I hung her really turn me on; her pleading for mercy then

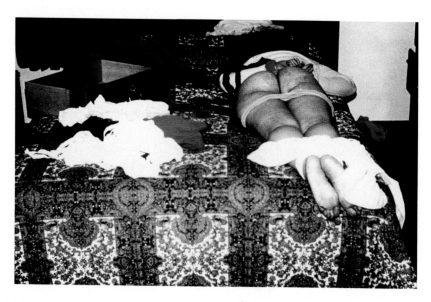

Figure 13.5 **Nancy Fox**. BTK spent a lot of time with this victim, binding her with pantyhose and additional stockings. Semen was recovered from a nightgown on the bed. (Photo courtesy of Lieutenant Kenneth Landwehr, commanding officer homicide, Wichita, Kansas, Police Department, and Retired Director Larry Welch, Kansas Bureau of Investigation (KBI).)

Figure 13.6 **BTK sketch.** BTK sent this sketch to the authorities, claiming responsibility for his killings. This sketch was based on the Nancy Fox slaying. The details in the sketch matched the crime scene. (Illustration courtesy of Lieutenant Kenneth Landwehr, commanding officer homicide, Wichita, Kansas, Police Department.)

the rope took whole, she helpless; staring at me with wide terror fill here eyes the rope getting tighter-tighter. You don't understand these things because your not under the influence of factor (x). The same thing that made Son of Sam, Jack The Ripper, Havery Glatman, Boston Strangler, Dr. H. H. Holmes, Panty Hose Strangler OF Florida, Hillside Strangler, Ted of the West Coast and many more infamous character kill. Which seems senseless, but we cannot help it. There is no help, no cure, except death or being caught and put away. It a terrible nightmarebut, you see I don't lose any sleep over it.

After a thing like Fox I ccome home and go about life like anyone else. And I will be like that until the urge hit me again. It not continuous and I don't have a lot of time. It take time to set a kill, one mistake and it all over. Since I about blew it on the phone-handwritting is out letter guide is to long and typewriter can be traced too. My short poem of death and maybe a drawing; later on real picture and maybe a tape of the sound will come your way. How will you know it be me Before a murder or murders you will receive a copy of the intials B.T.K., you keep that copy the original will show up some day on guess who?

May you not be the unluck one!

P.S.

How about some name for me, its time: 7 down and many more to go. I like the following. How about you? "THE BTK STRANGLER," WICHITA STRANGLER," POETIC STRANGLER," THE BONDAGE STRANGLER," OR PSYCHO, 'THE WICHITA HANGMAN, THE WICHITA EXECUTIONER" THE GARROTTE PHATHON, THE AXSPHYXIATER.

Page 2

#5 You guess the motive and victim

#6 You found one Shirley Vain [sic] lying belly down on a unmade bed in northeast bedroom- hand tied behind back with black tape and cord. Feet & ankles with black tape &legs arm, finally the neck, many times. A off white plastic bag over her heads loop on with a pink nitie. Shirley was nude with small eye ring. Had blue house coat on before and pink nitie was barefooted. She was sick use a glass of water and smoke I or two cizrette house a total mess – kids took toys with them to the bathroom – bedagainst east bathroom door. Chose at random with some pre-planning. Motive Factor X.

#7 One Nancy Fox –lying belly down on made bed in southwest bedroom – hands tied behind back with red panty hose- feet together with yellow nitie- semi-nude with pink sweater and bra small neckless - glasses on west dresses – panties below butt – many different color panties hose around neck, one across the mouth – strangled with man belt first then the hosery. She had a smoke and went to the bathroom before final act – very neat housekeeper& dresser – rifled pursein kiteken empty paper bag – white coat in living room – heat up tp about 90 degree – Christmas tree lights on – cizrette) mostly burn down pants in bathroom rifled east top dresser on top – nities and hose around the room – hose bag of orange color it and hosery on bed – driver licence gone – seminal stain on or in blue women wear. Chose at random with little pre-planning. Motive Factor "X".

#8 Next victim maybe: You will find her hanging with a wire noose – Hands behind back with black tape or cord – feet with tape or cood-gaged – then cord around the body to the neck – hooded maybe – possible seminal stain in anus or on body. Will be chosen at random.

Some pre-planning – Motive Factor "X". B.T.K.

The first two pages were supportive data for the writer's claim of the responsibility for the deaths of seven persons. Six of these persons were named as being the four Oteros,

Shirley Vian, and Nancy Fox. The seventh victim was unnamed without any further information as to who, when, or how the killing was accomplished. Police believed it was Katherine Bright.

He demanded media attention and referred to other serial killers in his letter, such as Son of Sam, Jack the Ripper, Boston Strangler, Ted of the West Coast (Ted Bundy), the Hillside Strangler, in this letter and announced that Wichita had a serial killer in their midst. In his last line, he taunts the police with the following statement, *"You keep that copy the original will show up some day on guess who?"*

In 2005, the original of this letter was recovered along with other original communications and drawings.

The third page was a poem entitled, "Oh Death To Nancy," which referred to the Nancy Fox murder and closed with the line, "I'll bring sexual death unto you for me." The fourth page was an untitled drawing of the victim of a homicide (representing the Fox homicide) with the BTK symbol.

The writer of the letter complained about the lack of response on the part of *The Wichita Eagle* and *Beacon* newspapers regarding a poem he had written about Shirley Vian and sent to them prior to this correspondence, which he had sent to KAKE-TV.

Authorities located this communication, dated January 31, 1978, in the dead letter file from the classified advertisement section of the paper where it had been delivered by mistake.

It was a poem titled, "Shirley Locks," with the BTK symbol. Someone at the newspaper thought that this poem was intended for the Valentine's Day classified section. However, since there was no return address or payment enclosed, it was sent to the dead letter file.

Last Known Activity of the BTK Killer in Wichita

On April 28, 1979, the BTK killer broke into 63-year-old Anna Williams' home at 615 South Pinecrest in Wichita, Kansas. Her 24-year-old granddaughter, Rebecca, occasionally spent the night in Anna Williams' home, but was asked to do an overtime tour at the Tollway this night. Anna decided to go out for the evening. The BTK Killer waited for her and her granddaughter to return home. When Anna returned home late in the evening, she found plastic coated wire from her basement in the bedroom. She checked her telephone and, when she discovered there was no dial tone, she fled her house never to return. Wichita residents knew that BTK usually cut the phone line before entering a residence. It became a safety routine for the area citizens to check the phone immediately when entering the home. She called the police from a neighbor's house.

Investigators found a bundle of bindings, which consisted of rope, wire, underwear, and belts (Figure 13.7). Jewelry, coins, and scarves were missing from the premises. The BTK killer had first cut the telephone line and then forcibly entered the home by breaking and prying open a basement window.

BTK's Fourth and Fifth Communications: June 15, 1979

BTK sent two letters containing a poem along with a drawing indicating what he had intended to do to his victims at the Williams' residence. One was sent to KAKE-TV and the other was sent to Anna Williams' home. She had left her home after the burglary and never intended to return. The letter was picked up by a family relative who had been collecting the mail at 615 South Pinecrest. The poem was entitled, "Oh Louis Didn't You Appear."

Figure 13.7 Bindings. BTK left these bindings, which consisted of rope and wire materials. He was in the home waiting for his victims to return. (Photo courtesy of Lieutenant Kenneth Landwehr, commanding officer homicide, Wichita, Kansas, Police Department, and Retired Director Larry Welch, Kansas Bureau of Investigation (KBI).)

BTK had crossed out the name "Louis" and printed "Anna." The poem bore the classic BTK symbol. A third-generation drawing depicted a younger female in bondage and also had the classic BTK symbol.

BTK's Sixth and Final Communication: January 5, 1988

On December 31, 1987, Mrs. Fager returned to her Wichita home after spending a couple of days out of town. She discovered her dead husband, Phillip. He had been shot twice in the back. Her two daughters, 16-year-old Kelli and 10-year-old Sherri, were found strangled in the basement hot tub. Sherri's hands and feet were bound with black electrical tape, which eventually washed loose. Kelli was nude. BTK denied being the perpetrator of this crime. However, he did credit the killer with having done admirable work.

In 1988, Mrs. Fager received a letter from someone claiming to be the BTK killer, which referenced the murder of her husband, Phillip, and their two daughters. It was believed at the time that BTK had authored this letter based on a drawing that he enclosed as well as his classic BTK symbol in the lower right-hand corner of the drawing (Figure 13.8). In 2005, it was established that this letter, in fact, was written by the genuine BTK killer.

In 1988, Captain John Dotson of the Wichita Police Department instituted a Cold Case investigation. Ironically, the lead detective assigned was Ken Landwehr, who would even-

Figure 13.8 BTK–Fager communication. BTK sent this drawing with his classic "BTK" sig-nature in the lower right corner along with a letter to the surviving family member of the Fager family. BTK denied being the killer, but admired the killer's work. (Drawing courtesy of Lieutenant Kenneth Landwehr, commanding officer homicide, Wichita, Kansas, Police Department, and Retired Director Larry Welch, Kansas Bureau of Investigation (KBI).)

tually become the commanding officer and lead the BTK Task Force, which identified and captured the serial killer in 2005.

Captain Dotson contacted the author, who was affiliated at the time with a DNA firm named Lifecodes Corporation. I had been provided the complete case file on the BTK investigation for analysis and review. I requested that some of the biological evidence from the Otero case be sent to Lifecodes for identification and analysis.

In 1988, DNA was a relatively new forensic technology that was still in its infancy and had not yet been used in many major case investigations. It was our objective to obtain new physical evidence to identify this unidentified serial killer. Lifecodes Corporation was able to produce an autoradiography, which biologically and molecularly linked the unknown BTK killer to the Otero homicides. This was a major forensic breakthrough at the time. It provided the authorities with solid scientific identification when and if the BTK killer was caught.

The cold case investigation eventually eliminated BTK as a suspect in the Fager case, but was unsuccessful in determining the identity of the BTK killer. The case remained open as an unsolved cold case investigation. The case was still an open cold case in 2004 when the BTK killer began corresponding in that year.

The BTK Killer Reemerges

In January of 2004, on the 30th anniversary of the Otero family murders, which had occurred on January 14, 1974, *The Wichita Eagle* published a special anniversary story on the unsolved BTK murders. On March 19, 2004, the first communication from BTK in 16 years was sent to the newspaper.

In the opinion of the author, this was a classic example of "malignant narcissism." The BTK killer reemerged and began to taunt authorities with a series of 11 cryptic communications. It was Dennis Rader's evil need and personal desire for attention that sparked this 11-month series of communications. However, with each note or letter, Rader as the BTK killer became more confident in his ability to elude apprehension. Inadvertently, he became more careless as his ego was inflated by the news media coverage. His self-absorption and pride with his direct contact with the media fed his ego, which resulted in further communications that would ultimately end with his arrest on February 25, 2005.

First Major Investigative Breakthrough

Communication #1

The first communication was mailed to *The Wichita Eagle* on March 19, 2004, from someone who used the name **Bill Thomas Killman**. The writer claimed he had killed Vicki Wegerle on September 16, 1986, and enclosed a letter-size piece of paper with photocopies of photographs from the crime scene and a photocopy of Wegerle's driver's license that had been stolen from the victim at the time. The paper contained a coded message at the top that appeared to have been written by using stencils. This communication directly linked the BTK killer to this 1986 homicide, which originally had not been considered a BTK case by some of the local detectives. These third or fourth resolution copies of Polaroid® photos showed the victim in bondage. The tell-tale "BTK" signature mark on the communication also confirmed the writer's identity (Figure 13.9).

Detectives Kelly Otis and Dana Gouge had been examining the Wegerle case as a cold case homicide investigation and had recently taken a DNA sample from Wegerle's husband to compare with some DNA found under the victim's fingernails. The DNA from Vicki's fingernails did not match her husband who was eliminated as a suspect in the murder.

The DNA was believed to have come from the BTK killer. After the communication regarding the Wegerle homicide, a Kansas Bureau of Investigation (KBI) laboratory examination connected the DNA from the tissue under Vicki's fingernails to the DNA from the Otero crime scene and the Nancy Fox crime scene. This was confirmed when Dennis Rader was arrested in February 2005.

The BTK Task Force

Wichita detectives immediately created a special task force to investigate all of the BTK murders as well as to ascertain the identity of this unknown subject, who had communicated with *The Wichita Eagle*. Lieutenant Ken Landwehr, Wichita Police Department's homicide division, was in charge of the BTK task force along with now-retired Assistant Director Larry Thomas of the KBI.

The task force members consisted of the following law enforcement officials:

Detective Dana Gouge, WPD
Detective Randy Stone, WPD

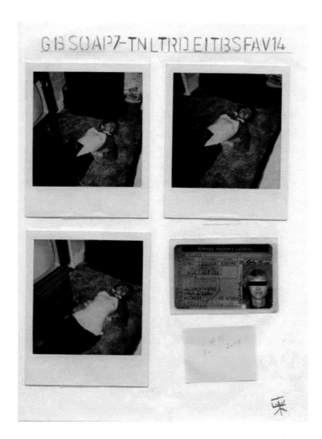

Figure 13.9 Vickie message. This was the original message discovered after BTK was arrested. He had sent third- or fourth-resolution copies of this to the authorities in his first 2004 communication as well as a copy of Vickie Wegerle's driver's license photo, along with his BTK signature. This message immediately linked BTK to the Wegerle murder. (Photos courtesy of Lieutenant Kenneth Landwehr, commanding officer homicide, Wichita, Kansas, Police Department, and Retired Director Larry Welch, Kansas Bureau of Investigation (KBI).)

Detective Kelly Otis, WPD
Special Agent Ray Lundin, KBI
Detective Cheryl James, WPD
Special Agent Chuck Pritchett, FBI
Detective Tim Relph, WPD
Special Agent John Sullivan, FBI
Detective Clint Snyder, WPD,
Special Agent Barry Rausch, USPI

Lieutenant Landwehr directed that the first order of business would be to address media strategies. Because the BTK killer had opted to communicate with the media, law enforcement would need to provide for a controlled media release as well as establish a "tip" line for the general public. The objectives were as follows:

Try to "draw" him out.
Maintain a line of communication with suspect.

Report to the public any dangers.

Present no open threats or challenges to the BTK killer.

Release new information asking the public's help in identifying BTK.

The Wichita Police Department established local and toll free numbers for information purposes. An e-mail address was also established for any tips. A post office box was opened for the investigation, which would be monitored by the U.S. Postal Inspections Service. Homicide detectives would review all tips as well as conduct a series of background checks.

A detective sergeant would prioritize all tips and civilian employees would enter all data. Elimination criteria were established based on age, sex, race, death, prison and jail records, and DNA.

In addition, the task force conducted a number of undercover operations on persons who had refused to provide voluntary DNA samples, which resulted in "trash runs" as well as surveillance.

Team Assignment Strategy

In "Practical Homicide Investigation®," one of the investigative strategies we employ in multiple body investigations is to have individual detectives assigned to a victim's body and to be responsible for each aspect of the investigation: victimology, witness information, crime scene process, evidence, chain of custody, autopsy protocols, etc. I have found this to be the most efficient manner in handling multiple victim incidents. Lt. Landwehr, who is a colleague and experienced homicide commander, implemented a similar strategy in this major case investigation. He assigned specific investigators to each of the BTK murder cases. Their assignment was to become completely familiar with all aspects of their assigned murder victim and case. This included any evidence, investigative information, police reports, victimology, possible suspects, any correspondence from BTK relative to their case, and any and all materials associated with each specific case. **This proved to be one of the most important and effective strategies in this multiple victim case.** In particular, in this case when the suspect began confessing to details in each of his murders, there was an assigned team to conduct the interview and interrogation of the subject relative to their assigned case.

Vicki Wegerle Homicide

On September 16, 1986, 28-year-old Vicki Wegerle was found strangled in her home at 2404 West 13 in Wichita, Kansas. The family car was found two blocks away in the 1300 block of North Edwards. Vicki was home with her two-year-old son when the BTK killer confronted her. Vicki's husband discovered her strangled in her bedroom, secreted between the bed and the wall. He called for an ambulance. The emergency medical technicians (EMTs) who had been called to the scene removed her body and took it to a hospital before police could make crime scene photographs. The Wichita police had considered Bill Wegerle, Vicki's husband, a suspect for a number of years. However, Detectives Kelly Otis and Dana Gouge had recently eliminated him based on the DNA material found under Vicki's fingernails. As a result of this communication, BTK was directly linked to the Wegerle homicide. The DNA found under Vicki Wegerle's fingernails provided the authorities with a genetic profile of the BTK killer based on STR/PCR (short tandem repeats/polymerase chain reaction) technology.

Communication #2

On May 4, 2004, Lieutenant Landwehr notified Detective Otis that KAKE-TV had received a document that they believed was from BTK. Detective Otis met with Glen Horn, the station manager, who showed him an envelope from someone who used the name Thomas B. King. The following items were in the envelope: a word search–type puzzle, a piece of paper with photocopies of two identification cards, and a badge. Also there was a document titled, "The BTK Story," with a list of 13 chapters.

The materials were brought in for examination. The identification cards appeared to be handmade and the photos on the cards had been blacked out. The cards referenced the Southwestern Bell Telephone Company (SWB) and a special officer of the Wichita Public Schools. The persons whose names were on the identification cards were contacted and they advised the authorities that the cards in question were theirs, but had been altered. The word search puzzle was broken up into three sections titled, "MO-ID-RUSE." Each section corresponded with the title. Several words relating to the titles were located. Twenty-nine words and 5 number strings were found in the puzzle. The number strings were all related to the information on the SWB identification card. Postal inspector Barry Rausch advised that a postal employee had found a badge in the loose mail on May 6, 2004. This item was the Special Officers badge that was depicted in the photocopy. Detectives continued a follow-up on all of the details relating to the contents in communication #2.

Communication #3

On June 13, 2004, at approximately 9:10 a.m., a package was discovered taped to a stop sign at First and Kansas by a citizen. Lieutenant Landwehr recovered the package, which was a manila envelope with "BTK Field Gram" typed on the front. It contained three other pieces of paper reduced in size. Two of the papers were labeled C1 and the third was another copy of the BTK story sent in Communication #2.

This copy did not have the bottom right corner cut off and had the classic BTK symbol drawn on it. The package had been placed in a plastic storage bag and secured with duct tape.

The papers, titled C1 "Death on a Cold January Morning," referred to the Otero case. The BTK killer had reduced and photocopied sheets of paper relating to the murder of little Josephine Otero. He then made magic marker X's around the edge of each photocopied paper. There was another copy of the BTK story, but the Chapter 8 MO-ID-RUSE had been blocked out.

The communication also contained a drawing of a young nude woman hanging by a rope with a gag in her mouth and a cord draped around her chest down to her waist, which was very similar to the crime scene photo of Josephine Otero. This was accompanied by block letters stating, "THE SEXUAL THRILL IS MY BILL," with the BTK symbol in the lower right corner (Figure 13.10).

The police investigation involved eliminating the person who had discovered the package as well as identifying the print on the communication, which appeared to be from an older typewriter. It was believed that this "story" had originally been typed on this kind of machine.

Communication #4

On Saturday, July 17, 2004, Detective Otis responded to the downtown library on a report of a possible BTK communication, which had been found in the book return box. An employee of the library discovered a plastic Ziploc® baggie with papers inside that identified the package as a "BTK Flash Gram." He called his boss who notified the police.

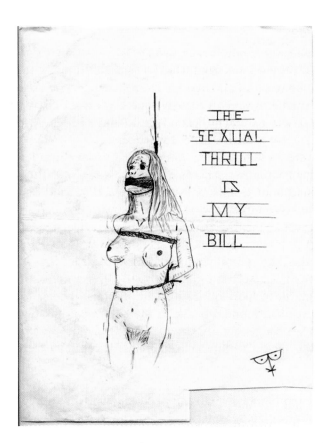

Figure 13.10 BTK communication #3. This time, BTK sent a story that described the murder of Josephine Otero. He enclosed a photocopied sketch, which depicted a young woman hanging. The authorities subsequently retrieved the original depicted here from BTK's "mother lode" in 2005. (Drawing courtesy of Lieutenant Kenneth Landwehr, commanding officer homicide, Wichita, Kansas, Police Department, and Retired Director Larry Welch, Kansas Bureau of Investigation (KBI).)

Detective Otis and Lieutenant Landwehr examined the contents of the baggie at the Wichita Police lab.

Inside the baggie was a two-page typewritten story titled, "Jakey," which referred to the death of Jake Allen in Argonia, Kansas, along with photocopies of bondage pictures. Contact was made with the Sumner County Sheriff's Office, where the event had occurred. KBI Special Agent in Charge Larry Thomas and Special Agent Ray Lundin from the Kansas Bureau of Investigation assisted Sumner County and ruled the death a suicide unrelated to the BTK Investigation.

The bondage photos were of poor quality, but indicated a partially nude male dressed in women's attire hanging upside down as well as lying on the ground.

On page two, BTK warned the authorities that he may have picked out his next victim. The BTK killer stated, "I have spotted a female that I think lives alone or is a spoiled latch key kid. Just got to work out the details. I'm much older (not feeble) now and have to conditions [*sic*] myself carefully. Also my thinking process is not as sharp as it uses [*sic*] to be. Details-Details-Details!!! I think fall or winter would be just about right for the HIT. Got to do it this year or next. Number X as time is running out for me." He closed with the classic BTK symbol in the lower right-hand corner.

Communication #5

On Friday, October 22, 2004, Detective Otis responded to the Omni Center Office building at 200 N. Kansas on the report of another possible BTK communication. Detective Otis met with a UPS driver who stated he found in the bottom of the UPS drop box a plastic Ziploc-type baggie containing a manila envelope marked "BTK Field Grams."

Inside were several documents titled "Chapter 2—Dawn," a photocopied montage of children's photos with handdrawn bondage on them, and another photocopy of the "BTK story." This time Chapter 1 and Chapter 8 were blocked out. Detectives canvassed the area looking for anyone who may have seen any suspicious activity during the time of the drop. In addition, the other mailings were given a follow-up investigation to ascertain whether or not the senders had seen anyone at the UPS drop box.

Communication #6

On December 8, 2004, a phone call was received at the Quick Trip convenience store at 3216 E. Harry stating that a package from BTK would be found at the northeast corner of Ninth and Minnesota. Lieutenant Landwehr responded, but nothing was found. The officers checked all four corners and Murdock Park without results. On December 14, 2004, Detective Otis responded to City Hall in connection with a report of a suspicious package that was found in Murdock Park. A man named William Ervin had found a Barbie-type doll wrapped in plastic on the park grounds and had taken it home. Upon removing the plastic, he saw some documents and a Kansas driver's license belonging to Nancy Fox.

The man called KAKE-TV News, who then called the police. At about 1:30 p.m., Jeanene Kiesling, a reporter from KAKE-TV contacted Detective Otis at City Hall. Reporter Kiesling gave Otis an index card with "Dollgram" written on it. She stated that the mother of the man who had found the doll gave it to her. She had been doing a follow-up interview at the man's home when the mother told Kiesling that the card had apparently separated from the doll when the police responded to pick it up.

The package contained photocopies of a two-page document entitled "Chapter 9 HITS" P.J. Foxtail 12-8-1977, along with a Barbie doll and the driver's license of Nancy Fox (Figure 13.11).

William Ervin was interviewed regarding how he found the package. He stated that he had been walking through the park in the late evening hours of December 13 and spotted the package near a tree in the northeast section of the park. Ervin stated he continued on his way, but on his return trip he saw that the package was still there so he picked it up and brought it to his residence. He examined the package with a flashlight and saw some papers and an ID for a female named Nancy Fox. His mother recognized the name as one of the victim of BTK. They had been watching television and saw the phone number for KAKE-TV News, so they called the station. A cameraman came to their house and filmed the package. A short time later, the police arrived and took Ervin and the package to City Hall.

Communications #7, #8, and #9

On January 25, 2005, Lieutenant Landwehr received a call that Glen Horn of KAKE-TV had a communication from BTK and would not reveal its contents. Horn would only speak to the Wichita police chief. Lt. Landwehr sent Detective Otis to retrieve the communication. When Detective Otis arrived at the KAKE-TV studio, he was advised of another BTK correspondence they had received. Detective Otis contacted Horn and Larry Hatteberg, who produced a postcard that had been mailed to KAKE-TV. The writing directed KAKE

Figure 13.11 BTK communication #6. BTK sent photocopies of a document and a Barbie doll bound with a rope. Attached to the doll's leg was Nancy Fox's driver license. (Photo courtesy of Lieutenant Kenneth Landwehr, commanding officer homicide, Wichita, Kansas, Police Department, and Retired Director Larry Welch, Kansas Bureau of Investigation (KBI).)

to a package on North Seneca, between 69th and 77th. Horn told Detective Otis that KAKE had already sent a news crew to the location and reported finding a cereal box on the side of the road. Detective Otis seized the postcard as evidence and notified Detectives Relph and Gouge to respond to North Seneca.

Lieutenant Landwehr along with Detectives Relph and Gouge arrived at the North Seneca scene and observed a Post Toasties® cereal box with writing on the box consistent with other BTK packages (Figure 13.12). Lieutenant Landwehr requested laboratory personnel to process the scene, which had been contaminated by the news crew, who potentially drove over any existing tire tracks and footprints that may have been left by the person who placed the box along the road. The news crew was identified as KAKE-TV personnel and their names were taken as potential witnesses.

The box contained an anatomically correct doll dressed in a purple top. There was rope around the doll's neck and the other end of the rope was attached to piece of white PVC pipe. This appeared to depict the Josephine Otero homicide. Also in the box was a story titled "Chapter 9-PJ Little Mex," another chapter list, a map titled "BTK Haunts," and some jewelry (Figure 13.13).

The postcard also referenced another communication dropped at The Home Depot, which had not been recovered. Lieutenant Landwehr initiated an immediate follow-up investigation to attempt to recover the missing communication dropped at The Home Depot. When the investigators arrived to interview the store manager at The Home Depot, they were advised that Larry Hatteberg from KAKE-TV News had been there "a couple of hours ago" asking if anything unusual was going on at the store. It was quite apparent that the media were actively inserting themselves into the case without

Figure 13.12 BTK communication #7, 8, 9. BTK sent a postcard to KAKE-TV directing them to another location where he had placed a Post Toasties cereal box. Once again, BTK was using a Barbie doll in his message. This doll represented little Josephine Otero with a rope around the neck attached to a piece of PVC pipe. Inside were further communications and a reference to another message. (Photo courtesy of Lieutenant Kenneth Landwehr, commanding officer homicide, Wichita, Kansas, Police Department, and Retired Director Larry Welch, Kansas Bureau of Investigation (KBI).)

concern that their activities were obstructing and impeding the police investigation. This was substantiated when a cameraman from KAKE-TV was observed filming the police search of the parking lot for any suspicious items. Detective Relph approached the cameraman and advised him that this Home Depot investigation was sensitive and the police did not want this information aired.

During the meeting with management, it was ascertained that the parking lot was monitored by a digital camera network. The digital recorder had a memory going back 90 days. Detectives retrieved the information from the digital recorders. It was also decided to post a notice in the employee's lounge to inquire if any unusual items had been found. A Mr. Bishop notified the police that he remembered finding a Special K® cereal box in the bed of his pickup truck. He thought that maybe someone was playing a joke on him. He said the package was a cereal box with some computer paper and jewelry inside. He threw the package in his trash at home. Bishop was able to retrieve the package, which was still in his trash. Lieutenant Landwehr directed detectives to respond to Bishop's home to retrieve the package.

The cereal box contained writings on the outside similar to other BTK packages. Inside was a description of a floor plan titled "BTK's LAIR," with a reference that the location was rigged with explosives and a cryptic description "BOOM" at the top of the page and a warning. BTK described his "lair" as a sophisticated dungeon with special rooms that were TV monitored by close circuit. BTK described explosive devices he has hidden in the "lair" and how only he could diffuse the bomb. The BTK killer also defined what PJ's are and explained how he came up with the term and described some additional PJ's, which referred to "projects."

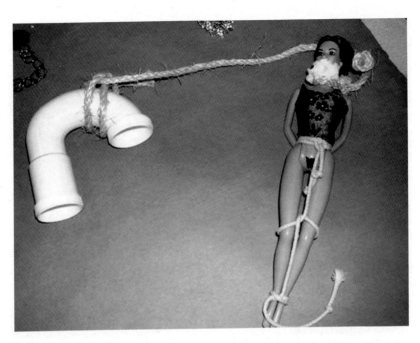

Figure 13.13 Doll. This doll represented Josephine Otero hanging from a pipe. Also enclosed were pieces of jewelry taken from the Williams' house. (Photo courtesy of Lieutenant Kenneth Landwehr, commanding officer homicide, Wichita, Kansas, Police Department, and Retired Director Larry Welch, Kansas Bureau of Investigation (KBI).)

There was another copy of the BTK story, with Chapters 1, 2, and 8 removed with white-out. BTK also enclosed a piece of jewelry, which was later linked to a BTK attempt in 1979 at Anne Williams' home.

Investigators attempted to match the referenced PJ's to actual victims through police reports of any burglaries, thefts, or nuisance crimes.

The BTK killer also enclosed a note titled "COMMICATION"[sic] stating "Can I communicate with Floppy and not be traced to a computer. Be honest. Under Miscellaneous Section, 494 (Rex, it will be OK), run it for a few days in case I'm out of town-etc. I will try a floppy for a test run some time in the near future—February or March." This was followed by a series of numbers: 3216912.

Investigators reviewed Home Depot security tapes for the time that Bishop stated he had found the package in the bed of his truck. A suspicious vehicle (1990s or 2000 black Jeep) was observed parking next to Bishop's truck. A male was observed walking around the truck before pulling out of the lot. A list of all the Jeeps registered in the county was obtained for case input and to create leads.

In addition, detectives set up a post office box using part of the code that BTK had used when asking if he could communicate by floppy. On January 28, 2005, Detective James placed an ad in *The Wichita Eagle* stating, "Rex, it will be ok, Contact me PO box 1four ref. Number 67202."

Communication #10

On February 3, 2005, Lieutenant Landwehr was notified that a possible communication had been received at the downtown post office at 300 N. Waco in Wichita. Detectives Otis and Relph went to the post office and interviewed the station manager who showed them a postcard similar to past communications. The United States Postal Inspections Service was monitoring mailings in Wichita in an attempt to identify the BTK killer. The information on the postcard was recorded and the item was allowed to continue through its normal course of delivery. Later that morning, detectives were sent to KAKE-TV to retrieve the postcard after it had been delivered. Detective Otis seized the evidence.

The postcard had the following message:

> *Thank you for your quick response on #7 and 8. Thank [sic] to the News Team for their efforts. Sorry about Susan's and Jeff's colds. Business Issues: Tell WPD that I receive [sic] the Newspaper Tip for a go. Test run soon. Thanks. May want to use KTV-PC etc as Code# and letters from me to you for my verification Code to you.*

In the interim, other detectives had interviewed members of the Williams family, whose relative's home had been burglarized by BTK in 1979. They were shown a piece of jewelry that had been enclosed in one of BTK's recent communications. They identified a necklace as belonging to their late mother, Anna Williams.

Communication #11

On Wednesday, February 16, 2005, Detectives Gouge and Otis responded to the Fox/UPN Station at 316 N. West Street in Wichita on a report of a suspicious package they had received.

A manila envelope with excess postage had been sent to the station with a return address of the UPN Station and the name "P. J. Fox." Detectives recovered the package from the station manager. The package contained an index card with writing on it, a gold chain with locket, a photocopy of a picture referencing a book titled *Rules of Prey*, and a purple floppy diskette (Figure 13.14).

The piece of jewelry was eventually identified as another stolen piece from the Williams burglary of 1979. The index card indicated that this package was communication #11 and listed the previous numbered communications 7 through 10.

The Shirley Vian Homicide

The floppy disk, which BTK initiated to continue his taunting communications with the authorities, was about to reveal his actual identification.

The communication was marked KSAS-FLP-1 indicating this was the first floppy and would be a test for the WPD to see if they could read the message. BTK wrote:

> *KAKE is a good station, but I feel they are starting to be single [sic] out, because of me, and causing problems among the people. Let's help the News Media and WPD by using this package as a start.*

The writer then advised how he should be contacted using the newspaper classified Section 600, XXX Adult Talk and provided a code # KSAS-FPL-etc.

The elusive anonymity of the BTK killer and his cryptic messages taunting the police would soon be revealed. The authorities armed with the purple floppy now had a viable lead as to the identity of BTK.

Detective Randy Stone, Forensic Computer Crime Unit/ICAC TF, conducted a forensic computer examination of the disk and was immediately able to identify a possible suspect named Dennis Rader. BTK wrote:

Figure 13.14 Communication #11. BTK's floppy disk was the one major break for authorities who were able to retrieve original files from the disk that Rader thought he had erased. (Photo courtesy of Lieutenant Kenneth Landwehr, commanding officer homicide, Wichita, Kansas, Police Department, and Retired Director Larry Welch, Kansas Bureau of Investigation (KBI).)

This is a test, and if you can read it, let me know in the newspaper per post card to Fox.

Detective Stone was able to retrieve original files from the disk that Rader thought he had erased. The files identified a file that came from a computer at the Christ Lutheran Church as well as a file from the Park City Library. One particular file referenced a Church Council Agenda dated January 11, 2005, as follows:

    I. Call Meeting to Order
   II. Opening Devotions – Elmer Hoyer
  III. Congregational Input
  IV. Additions to Agenda and Adoption
   V. Minutes of Previous Meeting – Walt Dietz
  VI. Building Treasurer's Report – Wes Nelson
 VII. Treasurer's Report – Alan Wondra
VIII. Pastor's Report – Pastor Clark
  IX. President's Report – **Dennis Rader**
   X. Vice President Report – Paul

BTK Task Force Follow-Up

An intense surveillance, investigation, and background check was begun on this potential suspect named Dennis Rader, who served as president of the Congregation Council.

On February 16, the same day the package was examined, Detectives Relph and Snyder drove by the suspect's home at 6220 Independence Avenue in Park City in separate vehicles, so as not to cause any suspicion. A black Jeep Cherokee was observed parked in the driveway.

Detectives immediately began a series of background investigations relating to driver's license registrations, vehicle registrations, Social Security, Criminal History FBI, and with City of Wichita police reports and Choicepoint data, property tax information, etc. These background checks revealed that Denis Rader had access to a black 1997 Jeep Grand Cherokee registered to his son and that Dennis Rader was the owner of a Charter Arms .357 revolver.

Lieutenant Landwehr directed that background "folders" be prepared for all known relatives of Dennis Lynn Rader. Folders were prepared for each relative as well as the Christ Lutheran Church. A task force briefing was held that same day to review all of the information the authorities had developed.

DNA Strategy

The task force had a DNA biological sample of the BTK killer from the 1986 Wegerle murder. The DNA had been obtained from under the victim's fingernails.

In one of the most innovative and courageous law enforcement tactics that the author has been privy to, Larry Welch, Director of KBI, authorized one of his agents to acquire a subpoena for the medical records of the suspect's daughter, Kerri Rader. The stratagem was to obtain a biological sample from a blood relative, which could be tested for DNA and then compare that sample to the evidentiary materials the police had from the homicide.

On February 22, 2005, the sample was brought to the KBI Laboratory in Topeka. The results were positive that BTK was *not* excluded from being the parent of Kerri Rader. This further inculpated Rader as the suspected BTK killer.

Cold Case Review

On Wednesday, February 22, 2005, Detectives Otis and Snyder contacted Detective Brunow of the Sedgwick County Sheriff's Department and briefly examined two unsolved homicides that had occurred in Sedgwick County. Marine Hedge had been found murdered on May 5, 1985, in the area of 53rd and Webb Road (Figure 13.15). Hedge had disappeared from her home at 6254 N. Independence in Park City, Kansas. The detectives noted that Hedge lived on the same block as Dennis Rader.

Detectives Otis and Snyder also looked into the Dolores Davis case (Figure 13.16). Davis had been found murdered in the area of 117 North and Meridian on February 2, 1991. She lived at 6226 N. Hillside in Park City. Dennis Rader was identified by familial DNA as a probable match to DNA left by BTK at several crime scenes.

The Arrest

On February 24, 2005, a briefing was held by members of the BTK task force in preparation for the apprehension of Dennis L. Rader. Special Agent-in-Charge at the time, now retired Assistant Director Larry Thomas, was assigned to the transportation and interview detail,

Figure 13.15 Marine Hedge. She had been found murdered on May 5, 1985. This Polaroid™ photo of her taken by Dennis Rader was found in his "mother lode" when authorities searched his offices in 2005. (Photo courtesy of Lieutenant Kenneth Landwehr, commanding officer homicide, Wichita, Kansas, Police Department, and Retired Director Larry Welch, Kansas Bureau of Investigation (KBI).)

along with Lieutenant Landwehr and Detective Tim Relph, Wichita Police Department, and FBI Special Agent Bob Morton, if available.

Tactic

The tactic was total control and isolation of the suspect. The BTK task force literally shut down Rader's Park City neighborhood. It was anticipated that the suspect would be so overwhelmed by his sudden and unexpected apprehension, coupled with the magnitude of his arrest, that he would be psychologically vulnerable to the planned interview and interrogation. This played out in textbook style. Dennis Rader would be quite talkative after the initial shock of his arrest.

Detective Dana Gouge was assigned to apply for search warrants for nine separate locations, based on the information available in the case. A plan was enacted to apprehend Rader and immediately secure the various locations of interest for search.

The arrest was scheduled for February 25, 2005, and was planned on Rader's routine of driving from his Park City offices to his home for lunch.

At 11 a.m., all members of the arrest team met for a final briefing at the office of the Highway Patrol. At 11:24 a.m., Detective Relph and Lieutenant Landwehr were in their preassigned position. Surveillance indicated that the suspect Rader was leaving his office

Figure 13.16 Dolores Davis. Her body was discovered on February 2, 1991. The authorities found this Polaroid™ photo of her body and evidence of her murder in Rader's "mother lode." (Photo courtesy of Lieutenant Kenneth Landwehr, commanding officer homicide, Wichita, Kansas Police Department, and Retired Director Larry Welch, Kansas Bureau of Investigation (KBI).)

and heading toward the arrest team. He was taken into custody by the arrest team at 12:15 p.m.

Dennis Rader (Figure 13.17) was then transferred to the transport vehicle that would convey him to the lower level of the Epic Center to be taken through the basement to the interrogation room in the FBI building. Inside the vehicle were Lieutenant Landwehr and Special Agent Thomas. As Rader was placed into the rear seat of the transport vehicle, he spotted Landwehr and said, "Hello, Mr. Landwehr." At this stage, the interview strategy had begun.

The BTK task force had planned on using the FBI facility so that the news media would not be aware of an arrest in the BTK investigation. When they arrived at the federal building, Dennis Rader was taken to a room where detectives executed the search warrant for oral swabs for his DNA.

Figure 13.17 Dennis Rader, the BTK killer. The before and after arrest photos of Dennis Rader. (Photos courtesy of Lieutenant Kenneth Landwehr, commanding officer homicide, Wichita, Kansas, Police Department, and Retired Director Larry Welch, Kansas Bureau of Investigation (KBI).)

Simultaneously an additional eight separate search warrants were executed on the following locations, which had been secured by task force members:

6220 N Independence: Suspects' home
6110 N Hydraulic: Suspect's office
The Christ Lutheran Church
The Park City Library
4815 N Seneca: Mother's house
Storage unit
Safe deposit box
Personal vehicles and work vehicle

Dennis Rader's Family Members

As soon as Dennis Rader was in custody, task force members requested Rader's mother, Dorthea, and Rader's wife, Paula, to accompany them to an interview room at City Hall where both women were advised of his arrest in connection with the BTK investigation. The women, who were completely unaware of Dennis Rader's involvement, were shocked. However, they were able to provide time-line information on Rader's whereabouts during the investigation.

Dennis Lynn Rader: The BTK Killer

The BTK killer was identified as Dennis Rader, a 59-year-old city compliance officer who lived with his wife at 6220 N. Independence in Park City, Kansas. Rader had grown up in Wichita and graduated from local schools. He attended Kansas Wesleyan University before joining the U.S. Air Force from 1966 to 1970. He enrolled in Wichita State University in 1973 and graduated in 1979 with a bachelor's degree in Administration of Justice. He had two grown children who were born after his first killings. Rader had lived and worked in the Wichita area for over 30 years. He worked at various jobs including a position with ADT Security Systems, a company that sold and installed alarm systems for commercial businesses. Rader had held several positions, including installation manager. It was believed that he learned how to carefully defeat home security systems, thus learning how to break into the homes of his victims without being caught.

In 1991, Rader was hired to be supervisor of the Compliance Department at Park City, a two-employee, multifunctional department in charge of animal control, housing problems, zoning, general permit enforcement, and a variety of nuisance cases. Some of his neighbors recalled him as being overzealous and extremely strict.

Rader served on both the Sedgwick County's Board of Zoning Appeals and the Animal Control Advisory Board. He was a Cub Scout leader and a member of Christ Lutheran Church. He had been a member of the church for about 30 years and had been elected president of the Congregation Council.

In my opinion, Rader was an anomaly and certainly did not "fit" the profile of the typical serial killer, as described in FBI profiles, which allude to the nonsocial, nonaffiliate, loner-type personality that many people have become familiar with in law enforcement. The profile had indicated that the unknown subject (unsub): *May or may not live in a rental, and might be lower class, upper lower class, lower middle class, or middle class. He won't be comfortable with women. But, he may have women friends. He will be either never married, divorced, or married, and, if he was married, his wife will be younger or older. He won't be unmemorable, but he will be unknowable. He will be a lone wolf, but he will be able to function in social settings.*

In fact, the original FBI "psychological profile" of the unknown BTK unsub wasn't even close to Dennis Rader.

Rader was married at the time of his arrest; he lived at home with his wife and had two grown children. He lived and worked in the community. He had a position of authority in his church, he worked for the local government, he maintained a steady work schedule, he was a social individual who engaged in conversations with his neighbors and actually helped some of his neighbors with yard work. Most serial killers are nonsocial individuals because they are so vested in their fantasy world that they have no time for people except the people they are targeting.

The BTK Confessions

Dennis Rader was given his *Miranda* warnings at 12:43 p.m. and he signed the waiver at 12:45 p.m. Apparently, the "shock & awe" techniques involved in his sudden apprehension and confrontation coupled with the magnitude of his arrest convinced him to talk. Rader spoke with Lieutenant Landwehr and Supervisory Special Agent (SSA) Robert Morton, FBI, for approximately three hours. During this preliminary interview, the suspect was given lunch and bathroom breaks before he finally admitted being the BTK killer. Rader would eventually confess to all of the known BTK murders and the two unsolved BTK killings in Sedgwick County (Figure 13.18).

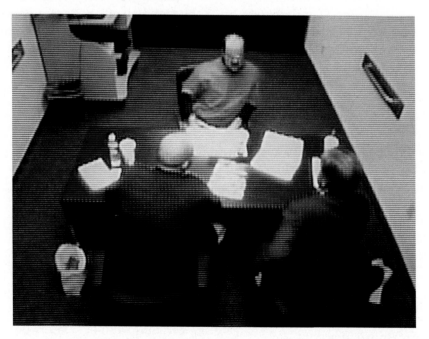

Figure 13.18 Interrogation of BTK. Videotape still of the BTK suspect being interrogated by Lieutenant Ken Landwehr and SSA Robert Morton. (Photo courtesy of District Attorney Nola Tedesco Foulston, Sedgwick County, Kansas.)

According to District Attorney Foulston, "Rader gave a 32-hour marathon statement to law enforcement. He savored explaining the sexual motivation that had driven him to these crimes of violence. As reported by one case detective, Rader became stimulated and sexually aroused while recalling his torture and murder of Nancy Fox. In particular, Rader's sexual gratification was achieved, not in penetration of the sexual organs, but in his observation of the death process, and the agony of his victims." (This behavior is consistent with the psychopathic sexual sadist discussed in Chapter 15.)

Rader told Lieutenant Landwehr that he had items from each of these cases in his belongings at work and at home, which included notes, photos, and trophies he had stashed over the years. This first interview set the stage for a series of interviews, which would be conducted by the special teams of detectives who had familiarized themselves with the evidence, investigative information, police reports, victimology, possible suspects, any correspondence from BTK relative to their assigned case, and any and all materials associated with each specific case.

When Supervisory Agent-in-Charge (SAC) Thomas interviewed Rader, after he admitted that he was the serial killer referred to as BTK, Rader discussed some of the details about his background and events that occurred as he was growing up. Rader also discussed the locations of his "stashes" of items, such as artifacts taken and used during his crimes, paraphernalia used during his bondage activities, his "fantasy cards," and his intention to quit killing after he killed 12 victims.

This information was relayed to the search teams at the various locations to assist them in focusing their search as well as to assure the recovery of these "stashes," which included his residences, sheds on his property, his vehicles, and his office space in City Hall at Park City.

Rader referred to one of these stashes as the "mother lode." He kept an extensive collection of photos, drawings, fantasy letters, etc., at his City Hall office in a two-drawer metal cabinet. A complete evidentiary documentation of all of his activities was recovered from this "mother lode" Figure 13.19 and Figure 13.20).

There were 10 homicides committed by the BTK killer:

1. Joseph Otero, 38 years old, January 15, 1974
2. Julie Otero, 32 years old, January 15, 1974
3. Josephine Otero, 11 years old, January 15, 1974
4. Joseph Otero, Jr., 9 years old, January 15, 1974
5. Kathryn Bright, 21 years old, April 4, 1974
6. Shirley Vian, 26 years old, March 17, 1977
7. Nancy Fox, 25 years old, December 8, 1977
8. Marine Hedge, 53 years old, April 27, 1985
9. Vicki Wegerle, 28 years old, September 16, 1986
10. Dolores Davis, 62 years old, January 19, 1991

Synopsis of the BTK Confessions

The Otero Homicides

Dennis Rader stated that he was trolling one day when he spotted Mrs. Otero and the kids in her car. He selected them as potential targets because he liked Hispanic people's dark

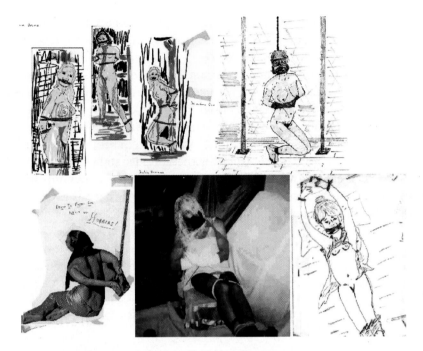

Figure 13.19 "Mother lode" materials. Dennis Rader maintained what he called his "mother lode" of sketches, drawings, Polaroid™ photos of himself dressed in the victims' clothing, and all of his communications, which he used to fantasize about his activities. There were literally hundreds of pieces of evidence linking him to all of the murders. (Photo courtesy of Lieutenant Kenneth Landwehr, commanding officer homicide, Wichita, Kansas, Police Department, and Retired Director Larry Welch, Kansas Bureau of Investigation (KBI).)

Figure 13.20 David Parker Ray. Rader had a copy of this article on the arrest of David Parker Ray. Apparently, BTK admired the work of Ray. Interestingly, both offenders used anatomically correct dolls to enhance their fantasies and both drew perverse drawings of torture, rape, and murder to become sexually aroused when not participating in actual events. (Photo courtesy of Lieutenant Kenneth Landwehr, commanding officer homicide, Wichita, Kansas Police Department, and Retired Director Larry Welch, Kansas Bureau of Investigation (KBI).)

hair and eyes. After selecting the Otero family as potential targets, he stalked Mrs. Otero when she drove the kids to school. Rader told the investigators his intention was to get Mrs. Otero and the "girl."

He didn't count on the husband and boy being home. He stated that prior to the homicide he had called the house a couple of times to see if there were any males present.

Rader said that he had his material or "hit kit" and had cut their phone lines before he entered the house. At gunpoint, he ordered the family to lie down on the floor.

Rader's original idea was to get Mrs. Otero or Josephine in bed, have sex with her, and strangle them, but he did not have control over them. Rader stated that he took all four victims into the main bedroom. Rader tied up Mr. Otero first to restrict him and then tied the others who were cooperative because they believed his ruse that he only wanted money and their car. After they were all tied, it was decision time. Rader states, "They were all going down."

Rader stated all hell broke loose when they realized he was going to kill them. Mr. Otero was going ballistic and tried to chew a hole in the bag. Rader stated he placed a shirt and another plastic bag over Mr. Otero's head. Rader said that Mrs. Otero had to be strangled twice because after he had choked her the first time, she came back. Rader stated that this was the first time he had strangled a person and it was hard to do. Rader used asphyxiation on Joe and Joseph.

Rader said during this time Josephine was going crazy saying, "What are you doing to my momma?" Mrs. Otero had "woke up" so he strangled her again and put a pillow over her head.

Rader took little Joe into another room, put a T-shirt over his head, and then a plastic bag so he couldn't chew through the plastic. Rader placed him on the bed, but he then rolled off onto the floor.

Rader stated that he always had a sexual desire for younger women and that Josephine was his primary target. He took her down to the basement and pulled her pants down and tied her up. Rader had previously located the sewer pipe and set up the rope to hang her. As he was taking Josephine over toward the pipe, he asked her if she had a camera because he wanted to take a picture of her. Josephine responded that she did not have a camera and asked him what was going to happen to her. Rader told her, "You're going to heaven like the rest of your family."

Rader then slipped the rope over her neck and hung her. Rader stated he did not have sex with her, but maybe "felt around her a little." Rader stated that he masturbated while she was hanging from the pipe in the basement. He gave the name "P.J. Little Mex" to this project.

Rader said he got an education that morning on strangulation. "You strangle a person and you don't hold them long enough, they will come back. I never strangled a person before. I strangled dogs and cats. Strangling is a hard way to kill a person. They don't go down in a minute like in the movies. But basically, a person passes out. I didn't know that they would come back. I figured once you strangled a person, they would be done for. But, if you don't keep that air … if that air gets back in … you can breathe. The air is going to come back and you will come back. And, that's … basically part of my … actually my … BTK, the torture, that's actually my torture is the psychological. You know you're being strangled, that's your torture …"

Rader stated that before leaving he took Mr. Otero's watch and car keys. He said that he turned the thermostat up high to speed up the decomposition to throw off police. Rader stated that he used rubber gloves and, if he took them off, he wiped down everything he touched. He took the Otero car after he walked out the front door using his hood to hide his face.

SAC Larry Thomas and Agent Ray Lundin

Kathryn Bright Homicide

Dennis Rader referred to the Kathy Bright murder as "P.J. Lights Out." Rader told the detectives that he was out "trolling" when he spotted Kathryn Bright and some friends going into her house. Rader stated that he parked his car at WSU and was carrying books pretending to be a student. He knocked on the door, but no one was home. Rader entered the residence by breaking a glass window in the back door. He waited inside the premises and confronted the young woman and her brother at gunpoint as they came home. The assailant reassured them that he was not going to harm them, but needed money and their vehicle.

The intruder directed Kevin to bind his sister's hands behind her back with plastic-coated clothesline he supplied. The assailant then tied up Kevin with his hands behind his back with similar wire and then bound his ankles with the victim's clothing tied off to the bed. He gagged Kevin with the victim's articles and laid him gently on the floor, on a pillow, face down.

Rader stated he tried to strangle Kevin after tying him up, but Kevin was able to free himself and began to struggle. Rader used his .22 pistol to shoot Kevin. Rader then ran back to the bedroom where Kathy was freeing herself from the bindings. Rader stabbed Kathy as Kevin fled the residence. Rader slipped out the back door.

Rader told Snyder and Gouge that he had a typewritten description of the Bright murder in his stash, entitled "An April Death." When the BTK task force searched Rader's home, they found news clippings and a photo of Kathy Bright along with the "April Death" story.

Detectives Clint Snyder and Dana Gouge

Shirley Vian Homicide

Dennis Rader was provided with some cookies and fast food after the Bright interview and was given a break before the two detectives interviewed him relative to the Shirley Vian homicide. Rader told the detectives that during the time between the Bright murder and Shirley Vian, he was constantly trolling and stalking potential victims. He stated that Vian was not the primary target.

Rader had actually targeted another women whom he dubbed "P.J. Blackout," but she wasn't home. When he saw Vian's son walking down the street, he showed him a picture of Rader's wife and son and asked the boy if he knew them. He then knocked on P.J. Blackout's door.

Rader then decided to go to Vian's home. He referred to her as "P.J. Messy." He admitted using a detective ruse dressing in a sport coat and carrying a brief case. He knocked on Shirley Vian's door and showed her a .357 Magnum. Rader told her that he was not going to hurt her, but that he liked to tie women up and take photos of them. Rader said he told Vian that he would probably have sex with her after he took the pictures and, if she cooperated, he wouldn't hurt her.

Rader had planned on tying up the children, but they started to cry. He locked them in the bathroom by tying one door shut and jamming a bed against the other.

Rader used black electrical tape to bind Vian's hands and demonstrated how he bound her arms, telling the detectives that it was important in the bondage world.

Rader had gotten Shirley Vian on the bed when he began strangling her. Rader then placed a plastic bag over her head to finish her off. Rader stated one of the older children peeked through a crack in the bathroom door and yelled, "Leave my momma alone." Rader stated that he took a couple of pairs of her underwear before leaving.

Detectives Clint Snyder and Dana Gouge

Nancy Fox Homicide

Detective Relph and FBI Agent Pritchett interviewed Dennis Rader, who remembered the Fox homicide as one of complete control. Rader remembered that he had been in the "trolling stage" when he spotted her as a potential project noting that she was a lone female. He did surveillance on her, following her to both of her jobs. At one he pretended to be an ADT inspector, and another time pretended to be a customer. Rader stalked this victim because Nancy appealed to him both physically and sexually.

Rader told detectives that on the night of the murder he drove to the area of her residence and parked a few blocks away. He first went to the front door. There was no answer. He walked around to the back of the residence and cut the telephone line and went in through a back window. Rader stated that he was in her kitchen when Ms. Fox came in through the front door.

She ordered him out and picked up the phone, but Rader had already cut the line. Rader stated that they talked and he told Nancy that he basically wanted sex and wanted to tie her up and take a picture.

Rader let her go to the bathroom and had her undress. When she came out, she was wearing only a sweater and a bra. Rader had her on the bed face down and he asked her if she had anal sex. Rader stated that he had brought a pair of handcuffs with him and cuffed her hands behind her back.

Rader stated that he then took a belt and wrapped it around her legs. In one quick motion, he moved the belt from her legs and wrapped it around her neck and strangled her. Rader choked her out and then "brought her back" and then he told her he was BTK as he tightened the belt around her neck. Rader said that Nancy verbally and physically fought him and at one time was able to "grab his nuts," which he actually liked.

Rader stated that after she was dead, he was on a high and he masturbated and ejaculated into a nightie. Rader then took some jewelry and remembered one necklace that was very nice. He thought of giving it to his wife or daughter. Rader also took her driver's license, which was the same one he had sent with the doll found in Murdock Park. Rader also turned up the thermostat because he had read in an old detective magazine that this would cause a fire and burn the house down, destroying the evidence.

The next day he made the phone call to report the murder because he wanted to get something going. Rader stated that the "publicity was exciting."

Detective Tim Relph and FBI Agent Chuck Pritchett

Anna Williams Attempt

The next case discussed was the burglary at 615 S. Pinecrest. Rader remembered that incident as "P.J. Pinecone." Rader indicated that he spent a lot of time just getting into the residence. Once inside, he waited and indicated that if Mrs. Williams and her granddaughter had come home, they both would have "gone down." He indicated that he would later draw a picture depicting how it "would have been." The original drawing was recovered in the "mother lode."

Detective Tim Relph and FBI Agent Chuck Pritchett

Marine Hedge

Dennis Rader admitted to abducting Marine Hedge from her home and later killing her before disposing of her body. Rader referred to this murder as "P.J. DeFlower." Rader had used a Cub Scout campout as a cover the night he attacked Hedge. He slipped away and parked his car at a bowling alley. He had his "hit kit" in his bowling bag as he took a cab to Marine Hedge's neighborhood. Rader waited inside until she had gone to bed.

Rader entered her bedroom and turned on the lights. She screamed as he jumped on her and strangled her to death. He then stripped her nude and placed her on a blanket. Rader moved her body to the trunk of her car and drove her body to Christ Lutheran Church where he took Polaroid photographs of her body tied up in sexually graphic forms of bondage. He kept these as "trophies," which were recovered at the "mother lode." Rader then took her body and dumped it in a culvert where it was later found. He parked her vehicle in an office complex.

FBI Agent Chuck Pritchett and Detective Sergeant Tom Lee

Vicki Wegerle

Dennis Rader remembered committing the murder of Vicki Wegerle, whom he had dubbed "P.J. Piano." He selected her as a project when he saw her backing out of her driveway one day. While stalking her, he heard her playing a piano, so he gave her the nickname "P.J. Piano."

Rader told the detectives that he had taken photographs of her after he killed her and admitted sending a copy of them to *The Wichita Eagle*. This was Communication #1. The original photos were subsequently recovered at the "mother lode."

Rader told the detectives that he was working for ADT at the time. He had a yellow hard hat, which he stuck a SWB sticker on and pretended to be from the telephone company. Vicki, who had been playing the piano, let him in and he made believe he was checking the phone lines. He then pulled a .25 automatic pistol out of his briefcase and ordered her into the bedroom.

Rader stated that once he got her into the bedroom, he order Vicki to lie down on the bed and he began tying her up with some bootlaces he had brought with him to the scene.

Vicki began fighting and broke out of the bindings. During the fight, Vicki scratched him on the face.

Rader stated that they ended up on the floor by the bed. Rader grabbed some panty-hose from the dresser and strangled her. Rader said that the dogs in the Wegerle backyard were going crazy during the assault so he had to hurry.

Rader stated that he took the Polaroid photos of her after her death and then left with her purse and car keys. Rader drove away in Vicki Wegerle's car and drove to one area where he dumped evidence in a dumpster. He then drove to another area where he abandoned the car and then walked back to his vehicle and left the area.

Detectives Kelly Otis and Dana Gouge

BTK's Communication: January 5, 1988

The BTK communication, which was sent to authorities in 1988 along with a copy of a drawing of a young girl in bondage, was finally linked to Dennis Rader after the original drawing was recovered from his "mother lode." Rader told the detectives that he definitely did not do that killing, but said, "He admired the admirable work."

Dolores "Dee" Davis

Dennis Rader admitted killing Dolores Davis, whom he had dubbed "P.J. Dogside." He accosted her in her home after cutting her phone line and smashing his way in with a concrete block. Rader told the detectives that he selected this night because he was involved with the Cub Scouts again. He used this excuse as his cover. Davis lived in a very secluded area. He had cased her home during surveillance and planned to attack her. The smashing noise woke her and, as she came out of her bedroom, she was confronted by Rader. He handcuffed her as he explained that he was on the run. He told her he needed food and keys to her car. He talked with her awhile to calm her down. Rader then removed her handcuffs, tied her up, and then strangled her with panty hose.

Rader said it took two or three minutes for her to die fueling his fantasies for years. Rader put a blanket around her, dragged her to her car, and threw her in the trunk. He dumped her body under a county bridge. The next day, Rader returned to put a mask on her to *"pretty her up"* before taking pictures.

Rader told investigators, "That's my mask. I wear that mask, too. I pose myself in bondage pictures with this mask and you'll find those in my stash."

Investigators located additional color Polaroid photos in Rader's "mother lode" of a bound and gagged Dolores Davis. Rader had also drawn pictures of a figure he referred to as "P.J. Dogside."

Captain Sam Houston and Detective Kevin Bradford

Search Warrant Evidence

The so-called "mother lode" held the evil secrets and innermost fantasies of Dennis Rader and provided the most compelling evidence against him. Investigators discovered hundreds of pictures from magazines and catalogs mounted on index cards (Rader referred to these as "flash cards" that he would use to stimulate himself), with details of the warped fantasies that Rader dreamed of carrying out, as well as books on serial killers. Rader had collected and maintained an extensive collection of Barbie-style dolls that he would pose in sexual positions

Interestingly, Dennis Rader also had a copy of a magazine article on **David Parker Ray** (see Figure 13.20), who is featured in Chapter 12 of this book. Ray and Rader are both psychopathic sexual sadists. Ray and live-in girlfriend, Cindy Hendy, as well as his daughter, Jessie Ray, would capture and torture young women at his compound in Elephant Butte, New Mexico. It is believed that David Ray was responsible for the murders of over 30 young women. Apparently, Dennis Rader so admired Ray's sexually sadistic and deviant activities that he kept the magazine article with his stash at the "mother lode."

In fact, Dennis Rader's drawings and David Parker Ray's drawings are exceptionally similar in both substance and theme. Their drawings depict young women who are bound and being tortured. Many of the drawings had been scripted to portray the helplessness of the victim and illustrate the sexually sadistic torture they would endure.

Rader's files also included copies of nearly all his cryptic messages to the police and the media as well as drawings he had made of events and photographs he had taken of his victims.

In addition, Rader had taken a number of autoerotic photographs of himself dressed in bondage or acting out a fantasy. In some of the photographs, Rader is seen wearing clothing taken from some of his victims and intended victims as he reenacts his crimes.

The detectives also located his so-called "hit kits," which consisted of bags with rubber gloves, rope, tape, handcuffs, and bandanas.

Disposition

On June 27, 2005, Dennis Rader pled guilty to being Wichita's notorious BTK serial killer. In an extraordinary two-day hearing, which was nationally televised, Rader calmly described his brutal killings, seemingly relishing in the publicity of the courtroom event. He expressed no emotion for the victims as he described their murders in stunning detail and attempted to rationalize his behavior by explaining how he was fulfilling his sexual fantasies. In a dispassionate manner throughout the hearing, he spoke of the victims as "projects." He described struggling with frantic victims, manipulating and taunting them with words, and then strangling the life from their bodies, sometimes photographing them.

On August 18, 2005, Judge Greg Waller of the Sedgwick County Court imposed the most severe sentence possible, which was 10 consecutive life terms in prison, including 40 years without the possibility of parole for his last murder, which was deemed particularly heinous, atrocious, or cruel. District Attorney Nola Foulston (Figure 13.21 and Figure 13.22), the lead prosecutor, stated that Rader would certainly die in prison with the sentences amounting to 175 years.

District Attorney Nola Tedesco Foulston

According to District Attorney Foulston, "Rader's twisted and sadistic mind kept his deepest secrets hidden while outwardly portraying the demeanor of the man next door.

Figure 13.21 District Attorney Nola Tedesco Foulston. She was able to monitor the statements of Dennis Rader as he confessed to detectives. (Photo courtesy of District Attorney Nola Tedesco Foulston, Sedgwick County, Kansas.)

Figure 13.22 BTK press conference. District Attorney Foulston (right) addresses the press on the identification and arrest of Dennis Rader as the BTK killer of Wichita. (Photo courtesy of District Attorney Nola Tedesco Foulston, Sedgwick County, Kansas.)

An abundance of evidence retrieved from his 'mother lode' included personal drawings and designs for sexual torture devices as well as photographs and drawings of his victims 'posed' in death. He created a series of explicit 'flash cards' to view to enhance his own sexual gratification and to recall crimes that he had committed."

Based on the content and intensity of Rader's collection of materials, which authorities recovered from his so-called "mother lode," District Attorney Foulston, at the time of sentencing, asked that the court deny Rader access to magazines and newspapers, or even crayons and paper, to prevent him from creating his own perverted materials to stimulate himself sexually.

Acknowledgments

The author wishes to acknowledge the contribution of the information and materials for this particular chapter from professional law enforcement investigators representing various police departments involved in this major case investigation. Specifically, I wish to give special recognition to my friend and fellow homicide commander, Lieutenant Ken Landwehr, Wichita, Kansas, Police Department, who was the commander of the BTK task force. I also want to recognize a man I consider to be "Mr. Kansas Law Enforcement," Larry Welch, former director of the Kansas Bureau of Investigation (KBI), a good man and a good friend who brought me and my PHI program into Kansas so many years ago; District Attorney Nola Tedesco Foulston, who effectively prosecuted Dennis Rader and contributed her comments regarding the disposition of the case; now retired Assistant Director Larry Thomas (KBI), who served as the co-commander of the BTK task force; Wichita, Kansas Detectives Dana Gouge, Kelly Otis, Cheryl James, Tim Relph, Clint Snyder, Randy Stone, Special Agent Ray Lundin (KBI), Special Agent Chuck Pritchett (FBI), Special Agent John Sullivan (FBI), and Special Agent Barry Rausch (USPI).

Investigative Analysis
Criminal Personality Profiling and the Signature Aspect

14

Introduction

The applications of clinical criteria and abnormal psychology to the investigative process are an integral part of criminal personality profiling and have been universally recognized and accepted as genuine and legitimate investigative techniques. Detectives and criminal investigators routinely employ these techniques in their investigation of violent crime on a case-by-case basis. From a practical standpoint, there are only so many ways to kill and only so many stories to tell as an offender attempts to explain the killings. After a while, a distinct pattern emerges, which encompasses a series of clusters of behavioral information and specific typologies of offenders. For example, human behavior is repetitive. *Certain actions* engaged in at the scene by certain *types of personalities* will tend to repeat themselves. This is the foundation of criminal investigative analysis. We look at previous events and identify specific patterns and clusters of behavioral information and then extrapolate this investigative information to the current case and persons involved in the current event.

Criminal Investigative Analysis

1. Analyzes the initial crime scene investigation
2. Evaluates the victimology
3. Evaluates the physical and trace evidence
4. Reviews wound patterns
5. Evaluates the toxicological examination results
6. Evaluates the geographical profile information (including demographics and crime patterns)
7. Analyzes the witness accounts
8. Performs a personality assessment of any potential suspects

The assessment of these types of personalities allowed the FBI Behavioral Science researchers to identify two specific types: organized and disorganized. In this chapter, I will define these two types and provide a generic profile for each of them. Practically speaking, there will generally be a combination of profile characteristics and crime scene differences between organized and disorganized offenders.

I have provided the reader with "Work Sheet Tables" that list the characteristics of the organized and disorganized offender and crime scene dynamics in a column format (Table 14.1 and Table 14.2). The reader can then identify the column with the most elements that appear similar to his or her case. This will suggest the type of offender with

Table 14.1   Profile Characteristics of Organized and Disorganized Murders

Organized	Disorganized
Average to above average intelligence	Below average intelligence
Socially competent	Socially inadequate
Skilled work preferred	Unskilled work
Sexually competent	Sexually incompetent
High birth-order status	Low birth-order status
Father's work/stable	Father's work/unstable
Inconsistent childhood discipline	Harsh discipline as child
Controlled mood during crime	Anxious mood during crime
Use of alcohol with crime	Minimal use of alcohol
Precipitating situational stress	Minimal situational stress
Living with partner	Living alone
Mobility with car in good condition	Lives/works near crime scene
Follows crime in news media	Minimal interest in news media
May change jobs or leave town	Significant behavior change (drug/alcohol abuse, religiosity, etc.)

Source: Reprinted from Ressler, R.K. et al., *FBI Law Enforcement Bull.*, August, 1985.

Table 14.2   Crime Scene Differences between Organized and Disorganized Murders

Organized	Disorganized
Planned offense	Spontaneous offense
Victim a targeted stranger	Victim/location known
Personalizes victim	Depersonalizes victim
Controlled conversation	Minimal conversation
Crime scene reflects overall control	Crime scene random and sloppy
Demands submissive victim	Sudden violence to victim
Restraints used	Minimal use of restraints
Aggressive acts prior to death	Sexual acts after death
Body hidden	Body left in view
Weapon/evidence absent	Evidence/weapon often present
Transports victim or body	Body left at death scene

Source: Reprinted from Ressler, R.K. et al., *FBI Law Enforcement Bull.*, August, 1985.

which you may be dealing. I then direct the reader to reference the two generic profiles that appear on the pages.

This information will provide the experienced investigator with a frame of reference to apply to the investigative analysis of a specific type of crime or type of offender. The forensic evidence coupled with the actions of the offender in the scene and the specific activities he engaged in with his victim allows for the interpretation of the "signature" aspect and the ability to link events as referenced by "the linkage concept."

"Clinically speaking, there is a behavioral distinctiveness in human sexuality. This unique aspect of our sexual arousal and response system accounts for why individuals differ in their sexual behaviors and engage in a specific series of behavioral patterns. In sex-related criminal incidents, the offender is oftentimes subconsciously 'acting out' a sexually significant behavioral pattern, which reflects the underlying personality, lifestyle, and developmental experiences of the offender" (Geberth, 2006, p. 820).

At every crime scene, the offender inadvertently leaves messages or clues as to his or her identity, indicating the motivation or drive for the crime. Crime scene assessment focuses on the connection between the major elements in a homicide investigation.

Location

The location where an offense took place and the body disposal site can provide insight into the nature and background of an offender. Research indicates that the distance between the murder site and the disposal site is usually short. Significant scenes and routes to the scene to consider include

- Where last seen alive
- Initial contact scene
- Attack scene
- Murder site
- Body disposal site

Victimology

One of the most significant factors to consider in death investigation is victimology. Throughout this book, the author references the term *victimology* as it pertains to both suicide and homicide investigations and its significance in ascertaining motives, suspects, and risk factors.

Risk factors are generally regarded as high, moderate, or low and are based on the lifestyle, neighborhood, occupation, or any specific circumstance that may occur in a person's life.

Victimology is the collection and assessment of all significant information as it relates to the victim and his or her lifestyle. Personality, employment, education, friends, habits, hobbies, marital status, relationships, dating history, sexuality, reputation, criminal record, history of alcohol or drugs, physical condition, and neighborhood of residence are all pieces of the mosaic that make up victimology. The bottom line is: "Who was the victim and what was going on in his or her life at the time of the event." The best sources of information will be friends, family, associates, and neighbors, and that will be the initial focus of the investigation as you attempt to identify these sources of information.

Victimology assessment begins at the crime scene as the detective observes and records information about the victim and the circumstances surrounding the event. Personal records, which include telephone and e-mail address books, telephone answering machines, cell phones, cell phone contact lists, PDAs, diaries, letters, and correspondence, are generally available in the residence or home of the victim. If the victim had a computer, further information from the hard drive will reveal additional files, e-mails, Web site selections, phone records, and calendars.

The residence or home will provide additional information about the victim's life style. I have been to a number of crime scenes in my career and I continue to be amazed at how much you can learn about a person and his or her life style as you catalog the scene and review the personal belongings, photographs, and private collections of various materials.

Books, games, clothing and outfits, sex toys, videotapes, pornographic magazines, and sexual paraphernalia are just some of the items that might be encountered.

At a homicide scene the first persons who will be interviewed during the canvass will be the neighbors of the victim. A canvass is a door-to-door, roadblock inquiry or brief interview with persons on the street by which detectives attempt to gain information about a specific incident. It is an important investigative tool and a vital part of the preliminary investigation at the homicide crime scene. Neighbors are an excellent source of information about the neighborhood and the habits of the victim. Most people don't realize how much their neighbors know about them and what an excellent source of information they can provide about the victim and neighborhood.

Family, friends, and associates can provide personal information about the victim and will assist the investigator with piecing together the scene information with the behaviors of the victim. Was the victim having any problems? Had the victim recently expressed any fears? Had the victim made any complaints about persons, personal situations, or fellow workers? Did the victim express any concerns about his or her security? Was the victim in a relationship?

"What took place?" "Why did it occur?" and "Who could have done it?" are three general questions that homicide cops consider in an investigation. Ascertaining the victimology is the key to any successful death investigation. I have often said that "the homicide cop learns more about the victim than the victim knew about him or herself." In order to conduct a professional inquiry and provide a comprehensive investigative analysis, a thorough victimology is paramount to the investigation (Geberth, 2006, pp. 21–22).

Offender

Offender assessment is the consideration of the offender's modus operandi (MO). How did the offender make contact with his victim? How did the offender plan to succeed, avoid detection, ensure escape, and prevent retrieval of evidence? Significant components to consider include

- Location of offense
- Method of entry
- Protection of identity
- Weapons used
- Evidence of ritualistic behavior

Motive

One of the most important components to consider when making an assessment of an offender is the motive, which may exist only in the mind of the offender.

- Gain: Will the offender stand to gain financially?
- Jealousy: Based on relationships, infidelity, domestic violence.
- Revenge: Urge to hurt; criminal, business rivalry.
- Elimination: Prevent identification, effect escape.
- Conviction: Terrorist-type murders.

- Lust: Sexual element is at the core.
- Thrill: Killing for pleasure or control.
- Hate: Racism, homophobia.

   Additional considerations include

- Number of offenders
- Risk taken
- Time spent at the scene
- How did the offender subdue and control victim?
- Emotional aggression
- Planning: Stalking or spontaneous
- Escape routes
- How did the offender avoid recognition?
- Travel mode… How did offender get to the scene?
- Approach to the scene
- What relationship can be established between offender, scene, and victim?

Crime Scene Forensics

Crime scene forensics goes beyond the recovery of physical evidence. The other consideration is the significance of what the offender did at the scene, what was done to the victim, and where did the murder occur.

- Physical materials
- Victim incapacitation
- Sexual evidence
- Offender forensically aware?
- Was the offender injured?
- Are there any missing items?
- Blood distribution
- Linking evidence

Autopsy Protocols

The postmortem findings represent a vital ingredient in the crime scene assessment:

- Cause of death: Significance of injuries
- Time of death: Vital for establishing parameters
- Level of attack
- Injury analysis: Number and type of injuries
- Disguise of cause of death
- Sexual evidence
- Weapon analysis: Type, left at scene, number
- Life style

The investigative goal is to interpret these actions and behaviors of the offender and then translate these psychodynamics into investigative reality.

Criminal Personality Profile

A criminal personality profile is an educated attempt to provide investigative agencies with specific information as to the type of individual who would have committed a certain crime. It involves the preparation of a biographical sketch based on information taken from the crime scene and **victimology,** which is then integrated with known psychological theory. The profile can be a valuable tool in identifying and pinpointing suspects; however, it must be noted that the profile has its limitations. It should be utilized in conjunction with sound investigative techniques ordinarily employed at the scene of a homicide (Geberth, 2006, p. 773).

Purpose of the Profile

The objective of criminal profiling is to provide the investigator with a personality composite of the unknown suspects that will aid apprehension. By studying the crime scene from a psychological standpoint, the criminal psychologist is able to identify and interpret certain items of evidence at the scene, which provide clues to the personality type of the individual or individuals who have committed the crime. Certain clues at a crime scene, by their very nature, do not lend themselves to ordinary collection techniques, such as the emotions of rage, hate, love, fear, and irrationality. According to professional profilers, there is nothing mystical about their work; the procedures they use are well founded in sociological and psychological roots.

When Profiling Can Be Productive

Criminal personality profiling is usually productive in crimes in which an unknown subject has demonstrated some form of psychopathology in his crime, for example, sadistic torture in sexual assault, evisceration, postmortem slashing and cutting, motiveless firesetting, lust and mutilation murders, ritualistic crimes, and rapes (Figure 14.1).

Practically speaking, in any crime in which available evidence indicates a mental, emotional, or personality aberration by an unknown perpetrator, the criminal personality profile can be instrumental in providing the investigator with information that narrows down the leads. It is the behavioral characteristics of the perpetrator as evidenced in the crime scene and not the offense per se that determine the degree of suitability of the case for profiling.

According to Ressler, formerly of the FBI, and his colleagues (1985), "All people have personality traits that can be more or less identified. However, an abnormal person becomes more ritualized, displaying a distinct pattern to his behavior. Many times, the behavior and personality are reflected in the crime scene in the same manner that furnishings in a home reflect the character of the owner."

In certain instances, agents of the criminal personality profiling and consultation area have been able to supply police with such details as approximate height, weight, body type, age, general occupation, and family environment of an unknown suspect. Such a

Figure 14.1 Mutilated body on the beach. This murder case depicts a bizarre psychopathology and is amenable to criminal investigative analysis. (Photo courtesy of the author.)

description is based on their initial examination of the scene, using crime scene photos, and preliminary information concerning the crime provided by the requesting agency.

However, as an expert in homicide, I must caution the reader that viewing crime scene photographs without making a personal visit to the crime scene to get a "feel" for the area may prove to be very embarrassing. In addition, there may be other considerations not readily discernible to persons unfamiliar with the geographical areas, local customs, or unique patterns of behavior endemic to an area. Whenever I perform an investigative assessment of a case, I make it a point to visit the crime scene and conduct personal interviews with the assigned investigators, who many times have already "profiled" possible suspects, based on their expertise and knowledge of their jurisdiction.

Factors That Can Be Determined by a Criminal Personality Profile

1. Age
2. Sex
3. Race
4. Marital status/adjustment
5. Intelligence
6. Scholastic achievement/adjustment
7. Life style
8. Rearing environment
9. Social adjustment
10. Personality style/characteristics
11. Demeanor

12. Appearance and grooming
13. Emotional adjustment
14. Evidence of mental decompensation
15. Pathological behavioral characteristics
16. Employment/occupational history and adjustment
17. Work habits
18. Residency in relation to crime scene
19. Socioeconomic status
20. Sexual adjustment
21. Type of sexual perversion or disturbance (if applicable)
22. Motive

Investigative Approach to Profiling

The criminal personality profile is based on a good crime scene examination and adequate information supplied to the profiler. In order to facilitate this process, there are certain investigative steps that must be taken at the scene by the detective.

1. The complete documentation of events. Photographs (both black and white and color) and videotape, as well as crime scene sketches, should be accomplished prior to any other police procedures at the scene.
2. A careful and complete search conducted for any forensic materials and other evidence that might provide a clue to the identity of the killer.

Furthermore, an extensive and thorough investigation of the victim's background must be undertaken in order for the profiler to appraise the type of suspect for which police should be looking. Assessing the victimology of the deceased is standard operating procedure for any good homicide investigator. Many times the detective ends up learning more about the deceased than the victim knew about him or herself. From the perspective of the profiler, however, the victim's background information takes on an added value as the profiler seeks a behavioral pattern or scenario upon which to build his or her hypothesis.

The following are necessary to create a profile:

1. Photographs (the larger the photo the better, and the photos should focus on the depth and extent of the wounds).
   a. Complete photographs of the crime scene.
   b. Color photos of the victim.
   c. Body positioning, different angles.
   d. If residence is involved, photos of other rooms, including a crime scene sketch that depicts the entire scene and floor plan of the residence.
   e. Photo of the area to include aerial shot to show relationship of body placement to the area. This is done so the profiler can get a feel for the area.
2. Neighborhood and complex.
   a. Racial, ethnic, and social data.
3. Medical examiner's report (autopsy protocol).
   a. Photos that show full extent of damage to body.

      i. Stabs, cuts (number of)
     ii. Gunshots
    iii. Bruises
    iv. Lividity
  b. Toxicology reports
      i. Drugs, alcohol
     ii. Sperm present, sperm in anus, hair cut off, bits and pieces of hair, and oral swabs of mouth for semen
  c. Postmortem wounds
  d. Feelings of the medical examiner, which are not committed to the report
4. Map of the victim's travels prior to death
  a. Place employed
  b. Residence
  c. Where last seen
  d. Crime scene location
5. Complete investigation report of the incident
  a. Standard report of date, time, location, etc.
  b. Weapon used if known
  c. Investigative officer's reconstruction of the sequence of events
  d. Detailed interviews of witnesses
6. Background of the victim
  a. Age
  b. Sex
  c. Race
  d. Physical description (including dress at time of incident)
  e. Marital status/adjustment
  f. Intelligence, scholastic achievement/adjustment
  g. Life style (recent changes)
  h. Personality style/characteristics
  i. Demeanor
  j. Residency (former and present) in relation to the crime scene
  k. Sexual adjustment
  l. Occupation (former and present)
  m. Reputation at home and work
  n. Medical history (physical and mental)
  o. Fears
  p. Personal habits
  q. Use of alcohol or drugs/social habits
  r. Hobbies
  s. Friends and enemies
  t. Recent court action

In addition to providing a criminal personality profile of an unknown suspect based on an analysis of the crime scene, the Behavioral Science Unit profilers of the National Center for the Analysis of Violent Crime (NCAVC) can also make an assessment of possible suspects based on an evaluation of certain background information on a specific suspect supplied by local police.

The following information should be obtained on the individual to be profiled:

1. Name
2. Age
3. Sex
4. Race
5. Height and weight
6. Marital status, ages and sex of children, recent births. Is wife pregnant?
7. Education level
8. Socioeconomic status
9. History (criminal record or psychiatric problems)
10. Physical abnormalities and/or defects (e.g., acne, speech impediment, obese, walks with a limp)
11. Residence (condition of, etc.)
12. Automobile (color, how maintained)
13. Behavior (describe any recent change)
14. Mannerisms and personality traits
15. Employment (recently laid off, skills associated with job)
16. Day or night person
17. User of drugs or alcohol (recent increase?)
18. Dress (sloppy or neat, type of clothing)
19. Known to carry, collect, or display weapons; what type?
20. Rigid versus flexible personality
21. Prior military experience (branch of service)

Investigative Assessment: The Profiling Process

According to Ressler et al. (1988, p. 135), "The process used by the profiler is quite similar to that used by clinicians to make a diagnosis and treatment plan: data is collected, the situation reconstructed, hypotheses are formulated, a profile developed and tested, and the results reported back. The profilers combine brainstorming, intuition, and educated guesswork with prior experience in similar case scenarios to arrive at hypothetical formulations."

Basically, a homicide detective follows these same steps at the crime scene. The detective gathers information, attempts to reconstruct the incident, develops a hypothesis about the incident, and then assesses this data to see whether or not the hypothesis is consistent with the facts of the case. The investigators brainstorm the case during the investigative critique. They use their intuition, follow hunches, and make educated guesses based on their extensive personal experience in homicide investigation.

In fact, an effective homicide detective is usually someone who has taken his experience and has enhanced it with knowledge, flexibility, and common sense.

Organized and Disorganized Offenders

The organized and disorganized dichotomy devised by the FBI's Behavioral Science Unit is a description of criminal offender typologies. The information presented herein as it relates to the phenomena of organized and disorganized offenders is based on the studies and research of the Behavioral Science Unit, personal interviews with retired Supervisory Special Agent Robert K. Ressler and others involved in the project, interaction with colleagues across the United States (who are homicide experts) as well as the personal experience of the author as a homicide practitioner, instructor, consultant, and expert in the field of homicide investigation.

What Is the Motive?

Psychotic	Psychopathic
Motiveless	Sadistic
Bizarre	Impulsive
DISORGANIZED	ORGANIZED

Organized Offender

The clinical definitions of the elements that comprise an **organized offender** are found in *DSM-IV-TR* (APA, 2000) under the category **Antisocial Personality Disorder.** Antisocial personality is often referred to as **psychopathic** or **sociopathic** behavior. The organized offender is usually above average in intelligence. He is methodical and cunning. His crime is well thought out and carefully planned. He is likely to own a car, which is in good condition. The crime is usually committed out of his area of residence or work.

He is mobile and travels many more miles than the average person. Fantasy and ritual are important to the organized-type personality. He selects a victim, which he considers the "right" type, someone he can control (either through manipulation or strength), usually a stranger. Most of his victims will share some common traits.

He is considered socially adept. He uses his verbal skills to manipulate his victims and gain control over them until he has them within his "comfort zone." He is fully cognizant of the criminality of his act and takes pride in his ability to thwart the police investigation. He is likely to follow news reports of the event and will often take a "souvenir" from his victim as a reminder, which is sometimes used to relive the event or continue with the fantasy. (The souvenir is referred to as a "trophy" when describing this particular action by the organized offender.)

He is excited by the cruelty of the act and may engage in torturing the victim. Sexual control of the victim plays an important part in this scenario. He avoids leaving evidence behind and usually brings his own weapon. He is aware of police procedures. The body is often removed from the crime scene. He may do this to "taunt" the police or to prevent its discovery by transporting it to a location where it will be well hidden (Geberth, 2006, p. 456).

Disorganized Offender

The clinical definition of the elements that make up a **disorganized offender** are found in such diagnoses as the **psychotic disorders,** i.e., the schizophrenias, which are characterized by gross distortions of reality involving delusions and hallucinations and paranoia, which may or may not affect the personality, as well as paranoid schizophrenics, who are marked by acute personality fragmentation. In addition, individuals who are not psychotic may experience psychotic episodes. A psychotic episode, which is referred to as Brief Psychotic Disorder in the *DSM-IV-TR* (APA, 2000), relates to a temporary condition brought on shortly after or in response to an extreme stressor. The individual will typically experience emotional turmoil or overwhelming confusion. Under certain conditions, an inadequate individual who is experiencing intense sadistic sexual fantasies may suddenly "act out" these fantasies on a victim of opportunity. The crime scene would be disorganized and his actions and behavior could be viewed as psychotic.

The disorganized offender is usually below average intelligence. He is generally a loner type, who usually is not married, lives either alone, or with a relative in close proximity to the crime scene. He experiences difficulty in negotiating interpersonal relationships and is described as socially inadequate.

He acts impulsively under stress and will usually select a victim from his own geographic area. In most instances, this type of offender will not own a vehicle, but will have access to a vehicle. Generally, he will avoid people. He is described as sexually incompetent without any meaningful sexual relationships. He uses a "blitz" style of attack, which catches the victim off guard. This spontaneous action in which the offender suddenly "acts out" his fantasy does not allow for a conscious plan or even a thought of being detected. This is why the crime scene will be disorganized. In homicide investigation, we call these events a clustered crime scene. A *clustered crime scene* involves a situation where most of the activities take place at one location: the confrontation, the attack, the assault and sexual activity, etc. The disorganized offender usually depersonalizes his victim by facial destruction or overkill types of wounds. Any sexually sadistic acts are performed postmortem. Mutilation to the genitalia, rectum, breasts of females, neck, throat, and buttocks are performed because these parts of the body contain a strong sexual significance to him (Geberth, 2006, p. 457).

According to Ressler et al. (1986), "… there are significant differences between the organized and disorganized offender. However, there are no situations where the organized and disorganized offenders are mutually exclusive. That is, both types of murderers are capable of all types of behavior."

Clinical Considerations and Descriptions of Behavior

The Psychopathic Personality

A person whose behavior is largely amoral and asocial and who is characterized by irresponsibility, lack of remorse or shame, perverse or impulsive (oftentimes criminal) behavior, and other serious personality defects (Webster's New World Dictionary, 1982).

Psychopathic characteristics include

Complete disregard for community standards of behavior
Apparent absence of guilt feelings
Failure to learn by punishment
Desire for immediate satisfaction
Continuous sexual experimentation
Usually an extrovert
Can go "in" and "out" of feelings
Undue dependence on others (Coleman et al., 1984, pp. 247–250)

The classification of the organized offender is based on the clinical definition of Antisocial Personality Disorder (301.7) as referenced in *DSM-IV-TR* (APA, 2000): "The essential feature of antisocial personality disorder (APD) is a pervasive pattern of disregard for, and violation of, the rights of others that begins in childhood or early adolescence and continues into adulthood." The terms *psychopathy* and *sociopathy* have also been used interchangeably to describe this type of behavior. However, according to Robert Hare (1993), there is a distinctive difference between them.

Antisocial Personality Disorder (APD)—Refers primarily to a cluster of criminal and antisocial behaviors.

Sociopathy—Connotes that the syndrome is forged entirely from social forces and early childhood experiences.

Psychopathy—The syndrome consists of psychological, biological, and genetic factors.

In addition, when describing this same type of antisocial behavior in youngsters, many clinicians have opted for such diagnoses as Conduct Disorder (312.8 *DSM-IV-TR*), Oppositional Defiant Disorder (313.81 *DSM-IV-TR*), and even attention deficit and disruptive behavior disorders to diagnose behavior disorders. The bottom line for the investigative analysis of this type of personality, defined as the organized offender, is that psychopathy is the prevailing factor to take into consideration.

Hervey Cleckley (1982) was one of the first clinicians to do an in-depth study of the psychopathic personality. In his book, *The Mask of Sanity*, Dr. Cleckley describes the psychopath in terms of his actions and his apparent intentions. In fact, it is *The Mask of Sanity* that has influenced and provided the clinical framework for much of the scientific research on psychopathy.

Cleckley (1988, pp. 337–338) lists the 16 characteristics of the psychopath as

1. Superficial charm and good "intelligence"
2. Absence of delusions and other signs of irrational thinking
3. Absence of "nervousness" or psychoneurotic manifestations
4. Unreliability
5. Untruthfulness and insincerity
6. Lack of remorse or shame
7. Inadequately motivated antisocial behavior
8. Poor judgment and failure to learn by experience
9. Pathologic egocentricity and incapacity for love
10. General poverty in major affective reactions
11. Specific loss of insight
12. Unresponsiveness in general interpersonal relations
13. Fantastic and uninviting behavior with (alcoholic) drink and sometimes without
14. Suicide rarely carried out
15. Sex life impersonal, trivial, and poorly integrated
16. Failure to follow any life plan

Robert Hare (1993), the author of *Without Conscience: The Disturbing World of the Psychopaths among Us*, has emerged as the preeminent authority and foremost expert in the area of psychopathy. He developed and perfected the psychopathy checklist and the PCL-R, which has become the standard instrument for researchers and clinicians world-wide. In the opinion of the author, the PCL-R has proved to be the most perceptive development in the application of clinical psychology to the investigative process. His checklist is a clinical tool for professional interpretation of the actions and behaviors of the psychopath, and has provided a measure of the assessment of dangerousness of individuals who meet the criteria of psychopath.

Key Symptoms of Psychopathy (Hare, 1993, pp. 6–34)

- Emotional/Interpersonal
  - Glib and superficial
  - Egocentric and grandiose
  - Lack of remorse or guilt
  - Lack of empathy
  - Deceitful and manipulative
  - Shallow emotions
- Social Deviance
  - Impulsive
  - Poor behavior controls
  - Need for excitement
  - Lack of responsibility
  - Early behavior problems
  - Adult antisocial behaviors

The psychopath who is grandiose, arrogant, callous, dominant, superficial, and manipulative cannot form strong emotional bonds with others and demonstrates a lack of guilt or conscience. He is irresponsible and impulsive and cannot appreciate the pain and suffering he inflicts on others. This explains why he can torture and mutilate another human being without the least concern. I find this perspective consistent with observable data and applicable to the investigative process. Robert Hare's work best represents the point of view and definition of *psychopathy* as expressed in this chapter.

The Psychotic Personality (The Psychosis)

The classification of the disorganized offender is based on the clinical definition of a Brief Psychotic Disorder (298.8) as referenced in *DSM-IV-TR* (APA, 2000).

The psychotic personality suffers from a "psychosis" that is a major mental disorder in which the personality is very seriously *disorganized* and contact with reality is usually impaired (*Webster's New World Dictionary*, 1982).

Psychotic Characteristics (Coleman et al., 1984, pp. 237–239)

Loner-type personality
Generally remains isolated or secluded
Uncomfortable around people
Lacks interpersonal skills

A psychosis involves the sudden onset of at least one of the following positive psychotic symptoms (APA, 2000):

Delusions
Hallucinations
Disorganized speech (incoherence, fragmented speech)
Inappropriate response
Strange mannerisms

This type of reaction is usually associated with a stressor of some intensity. Sex is certainly considered a stressor of significant magnitude. The *inadequate* individual experiencing such a stressor coupled with an engram (mind picture) of a particular sadistic fantasy is certainly capable of acting out a bizarre sexual assault. The very nature of a sexual deviant engram is that it is substitutive for normal sexuality. It is oftentimes reinforced with masturbatory activities that become compulsive-patterned requiring repetition. The behavior and activities of this individual acting out his fantasy during a sexual crime could very well be described as psychotic. From an investigative perspective, we would refer to such an event as **disorganized.**

The offender might possibly have a clinical diagnosis; however, the murder event could very well be the result of a temporary psychosis involving a sexual stressor. In any event, the crime scene presentation is significantly different from that of the **organized** offender.

Sexual Sadism (302.84 *DSM-IV-TR*)

According to *DSM-IV-TR*, sexual sadism is a paraphilia. Paraphilias are sexual deviations marked by persistent sexual arousal patterns in which unusual objects, rituals, or situations are required for sexual gratification. They are understood to reflect a psychosexual disorder in which the preferred or exclusive means of sexual gratification is deviant. The essential feature in sexual sadism is that the individual derives sexual excitement from the infliction of psychological or physical suffering (including humiliation) of the victim. Sadistic fantasies or acts may involve activities that indicate the dominance of the person over his victim (e.g., forcing the victim to crawl or keeping the victim in a cage), or restraint, blindfolding, paddling, spanking, whipping, pinching, beating, burning, electrical shocks, rape, cutting or stabbing, strangulation, torture, mutilation, or killing (APA, 2000).

According to *DSM-IV-TR*, this is a chronic condition and a progressive disorder. "When sexual sadism is severe, and especially when it is associated with antisocial personality disorder, individuals with sexual sadism may seriously injure or kill their victims" (APA, 2000). (See Chapter 15 for a complete clinical discussion of this topic.)

Among the number of paraphilias discussed in de River's (1958) often cited work *Crime and the Sexual Psychopath*, is lust murder. De River speaks of sadism as a compelling element in some lust murders; in others, arousal is not derived from the infliction of pain and suffering of the victim, but rather from the act of killing itself. In this latter case, however, as with necrophiles, de River recognizes that even though the offender may not witness any prolonged degree of suffering on the part of the victim, he is likely to "[call] upon his imagination and fancy to supply him with the necessary engrams to satisfy his craving for his depravity."

This is not unlike lust murderers who torture victims before killing them and then recall "an after image (engram) of the sensation produced by the physical torture and mutilation, extending beyond time and space" (de River, 1958). The sadistic scenario is thus conjured in the imagination, be it a recreation of the actual crime scene or the product of fantasy. In each instance, lust murders are viewed as behaviors of sadistic sexual psychopaths. This is the type of offender who tortures and kills for sexual gratification and characterizes the *prototypical* serial killer whom we refer to as **organized.**

However, it must be understood that disorganized offenders are also capable of similar behavior and also engage in sadistic activities with their victims as well.

Sexual sadism is frequently associated with sex-related murders. Most of the offenders involved in this activity are organized offenders, who plan their crimes and seek out specific victims. The disorganized offender, who reacts to a circumstance of opportunity without a specific plan, is rarely able to repeatedly escape apprehension. (See Chapter 15 for an in-depth analysis of the psychopathic sexual sadist.)

Crime Scene and Profile: Characteristics of Organized and Disorganized Murderers

The organized and disorganized dichotomy devised by the FBI's Behavioral Science Unit is a description of criminal offender typologies. The information presented herein as it relates to the phenomena of organized and disorganized offenders is based on the studies and research of the FBI's Behavioral Science Unit, personal interviews with members of the Behavioral Science Unit, research in the field, and the author's personal experience with these types of cases.

The terms *organized* and *disorganized* are excellent descriptions of human behaviors as they relate to the characteristics of sex-related murderers. It is important to note, however, that there may be a combination of both organized and disorganized behaviors evidenced in a crime scene, which in effect presents a "mixed" personality profile.

These are not clinical classifications, but they are based on recognized psychological definitions and clinical diagnoses. The organized offender can be compared to the person suffering from an antisocial personality disorder. However, the author uses the terms *psychopath* and *psychopathy* because these terms are more meaningful in the descriptive characteristics of this specific type of offender. The disorganized offender presents behaviors, which may evince indications of a psychosis, such as schizophrenic disorders or paranoid diagnosis.)

The following generic organized and disorganized profiles are an example of investigative assessment. These profiles, however, do not provide for local geography, demography, sociology, ethnic makeup, forensics, victimology, or special considerations that are unique to the local area.

These generic profiles are provided as a basic investigative tool for the purposes of focusing investigative resources on specific classifications of *type of crime* and *type of personality* early on in the investigation. (A more comprehensive criminal personality profile can be obtained through the Violent Criminal Apprehension Program (VICAP) at the National Center for the Analysis of Violent Crime, Behavioral Science Unit, FBI Academy, Quantico, Virginia, 22135.)

Note how Table 14.1 and Table 14.2 compare with these clinical descriptions (Ressler et al., 1985, p. 19). However, it should be noted that the *organized/disorganized* classifications go into much more investigative detail. The expertise of the criminal profiler rests in his or her ability to identify the clusters of information, which demonstrate the psychopathology of the event and provide an insight into the behavioral makeup of the offender.

The Organized Offender

Age: This offender is approximately the same age as his victim. The mean or average age of this type of offender is usually under 35 years. This type of offender, however, ranges in age from 18 to 45.

Sex: Male

Race: The offender is usually the same race as the victim. However, the investigator should consider local ethnic makeup, victimology, geography, customs, culture, and other considerations unique to the area of the offense, especially in prostitute murders.

Marital status: The offender is married or living with a partner. This type of offender is sexually competent and usually has a significant female in his relationship.

Education/intelligence level: This offender is of normal-to-superior intelligence. He is also streetwise. He has completed high school and may have some college experience. However, in school he was a disciplinary problem. He was known as a troublemaker due to his senseless and aggressive acts against others. Academically, he would be considered an underachiever.

Socioeconomic level: Middle class

Mental health history: None

Physical characteristics: The offender is usually well built and tends to take good care of himself.

Residence: The offender lives some distance from the crime scene. (The exception to this is in the first offense. Many times the first offense is close to home.) Lives in a middle-class rental. Takes good care of his residence. He is married or may be living with a significant female in his life.

Automobile: The offender drives a middle-class vehicle. May be a sedan or possibly a station wagon. The auto may be dark in color and may resemble local police cars. This vehicle will be clean and well maintained. In the event you believe your offender to be young in the early 20s, expect him to drive a red or black "muscle" or macho-type vehicle. If a pickup truck is a masculine status symbol in the area of investigation, expect the offender to have a similarly colored vehicle.

Employment: This offender has the ability to handle almost any type of employment. However, he tends to seek jobs that project a "macho" image. Some examples are truck driver, bartender, construction worker, cowboy, security guard, police officer, paramedic, gunsmith, demolition worker, or possibly a job that brings the offender into contact with bloodshed and death. His work record will be sporadic. He may have a reputation for walking off the job or being fired for unsatisfactory performance. His job is usually some distance from the crime scene. However, the crime scene may be along the route he takes to and from his place of employment.

Military history: The offender may have been in the Army or Marines and volunteered for service. He may have been discharged under other than honorable conditions. While in the service, he was a disciplinary problem, AWOL, fights, etc.

Arrest record: The offender has arrests for interpersonal violence, sex offenses. He may have a poor driving record, DWI arrests, as well as traffic violations including parking tickets, which have not been paid. The interpersonal violence arrests, if any, will involve sadistic acts and/or beatings beyond the normal "fist fight," which indicates an extreme cruelty and violence. He likes to "hurt" those he is angry with and probably planned his assaults with this objective in mind.

General Behavior Characteristics

1. This type of person fits well in society; contemporary in style.
2. Gregarious, outgoing person; seemingly the type of person you might want to befriend. However, you soon realize that this outgoing person is actually a self-centered individual who cares only about himself. His social nature is actually a facade.
3. Good talker; socially competent with good interpersonal skills. He uses these skills in a manipulative manner and usually "gets his way" with people.
4. Irresponsible; indifferent to the welfare of society; only cares about himself and doesn't think anything of hurting others.
5. Described as a ladies man. Known to frequent bars and lounges noted for large numbers of female patrons.
6. Dresses well, wears designer clothes, and is style conscious.
7. Frequently dates many different women. He has multiple sex partners and is known to brag about his sexual conquests.
8. Methodical and cunning. He plans his crimes and selects his victims. He selects the site and is known to research his craft.
9. Travels frequently; cruises, seeking the right victim. Known for his mobility. Drives a car in good condition. Lives some distance from the actual crime scene. (Note: Exception to this is usually in the first incident, which oftentimes is close to offender's home or place of work.)
10. Acquaintances know him to have a violent temper and usually try to avoid becoming involved in any arguments with him out of fear or a desire to "keep the peace."
11. When insulted or threatened, he will respond with violence; if not immediately, within a very short time. He externalizes his anger and is known to hold a grudge. *This person cannot accept criticism.*
12. He is a *pathological liar*; makes promises he has no intention of keeping and cannot be relied upon to "keep his word."
13. Does not meet his financial obligations.
14. He feels no guilt or remorse for his actions. He is an amoral person, who usually blames his troubles on others.
15. "Chameleon" personality, who leads a *compartmentalized* life style.
16. He does not alter his behavior as a result of punishment. He fails to learn from his mistakes and will oftentimes repeat the same offense. When he gets caught, he will say he is sorry. However, what he really means is that he is sorry he got caught.
17. He is a consummate actor. He can play any role he desires. He has the ability to go in and out of feelings, cry real tears, evoke sympathy, and manipulate people's feelings.
18. Has a history of physical and/or sexual abuse by a female parent or parent figure. Important information for the structuring of any interviews of this type personality. (This type may react to "cycle of abuse" syndrome to explain his crimes.)

19. The triad are three significant components that form a pattern of behaviors among offenders involved in lust murders and serial killings. These activities include childhood cruelty to animals (for this type of offender, the severe cruelty that involves sadistic acts, e.g., disemboweling the family cat), childhood fire setting (for this type offender, arson that causes damage), and childhood bed wetting, or enuersis. These three factors can be used to predict violent behavior, such as antisocial personality disorder.

20. High birth order status, may be first born son.

21. Inconsistent childhood discipline.

22. Father's work known to be stable.

23. This offender may select a victim who resembles a significant female in his life, or choose victims of similar appearance, occupation, or life style.

24. He selects victims he can *control* and *dominate*. This type of offender demands a submissive victim.

25. The crime scene will reflect controlled rage. Restraints will have been used. Items, such as ropes, chains, tape, belts, pieces of the victim's clothing, gags, handcuffs, and blindfolds, may be evident.

26. This type of offender will possess a "murder kit" that will consist of weapons and restraints brought to and taken from the scene.

27. There will be evidence of torture, rape, and aggressive acts prior to death. This includes sexual experimentation with live victims.

28. This offender collects "trophies" of his victims as opposed to souvenirs, which are items taken by the *disorganized* type of offender. The trophies may be in the form of costume jewelry or other personal items of the deceased. The *organized* offender has been known to present such items to significant females in his life as a gift, which actually serves a psychological remembrance of the event and provides the offender with a continuance of the fantasy.

29. He follows the news media. May keep news clippings of the event. Reads the daily newspapers, listens to the radio, and watches television in order to judge the extent of the police investigation. This type of offender concentrates and focuses on police statements.

30. He may communicate with authorities. Sometimes this type of offender likes to "bait" the police with information or he may communicate through the media. This type of activity on the part of the offender has as its objective the continuation of the fantasy. It also serves to reinforce the offender's feeling of superiority over the police. This type of offender is encouraged by the apparent inability of the police to solve the crime and takes great pleasure in designing his communications to frustrate and confuse the authorities. *It should be noted that this type of an offender can be stressed through the effective utilization of "proactive techniques." Any subsequent news releases by the agency should be designed with this purpose in mind.*

31. This type of offender may hang around establishments frequented by the police for the purposes of "overhearing" some shop talk about the crime. He is usually thought of as a police buff or friendly nuisance.

32. He is angry or depressed before the crime.

33. Precipitating situational stressors include problems with money, work, or women prior to the crime.

34. This type of offender may exhibit a fascination with firearms, guns, explosives, etc.
35. This type of offender will transport the victim or body.
36. This type of offender will usually conceal the body to hide it from authorities. The exception is the organized offender who wishes to "make a statement" by blatantly displaying the body for shock value.
37. This offender many times has a collection of sadomasochism (S&M) pornography, and shows an avid interest in torture, sadistic fantasies, and bondage materials. There is also research, which indicates a propensity for detective-type magazines, which describe particularly brutal sex crimes and the police investigation techniques. In some instances, the crime scene and the activities engaged in by the offender will be similar to specific sadistic acts as portrayed in the pornographic materials collected by the offender. This is important investigative information, especially when considering the search warrant application.
38. This type of offender, who is focusing on the media as well as assessing the police investigation, may change jobs or leave town after a homicide if he feels threatened.
39. This type of offender has also been known to involve himself in the police investigation by providing information to authorities or participating in searches for the body.

Remember: The organized offender plans the crime, selects the site, stalks the victim, and researches his craft. He needs to be in control especially during the crime. Use this against him (Geberth, 2006, p. 797).

The Disorganized Offender

Age: These offenders range in age from 16 to their late 30s. The age of the victim does not matter to the offender. The selected victim is simply a victim of opportunity who happens to be in the wrong place at the wrong time. Research indicates that many of these offenders experience their acting out phase between the ages of 17 and 25.

Sex: Male.

Race: Usually the same race as the victim. However, the investigator should consider the local ethnic makeup of the area, victimology, geography, customs, culture, and other considerations unique to the area of offense; especially in prostitute murders.

Marital status: Single.

Education/intelligence level: The offender is probably a high school dropout; possibly community college; below average intelligence; considered a marginal student.

Socioeconomic level: He is from a lower to middle class environment.

Mental health history: This type of offender may have some history of mental disorders or have been treated for depression as an outpatient. If he did receive any professional help, he may have been classified as exhibiting schizoid behavior.

Physical characteristics: He is thin, possibly with acne or some physical malady that contributes to an appearance that is different from the general population.

Residence: The offender lives close to the area of the crime scene. Usually lives alone in a rental property or with his parents or with a significantly older female relative.

Automobile: Generally, the offender does not own a vehicle. However, if he does own a vehicle, it will be an older model that looks junky both inside and out. The investigator should consider his area of jurisdiction. If the area is rural, expect the offender to have an older-type vehicle, messy interior, and not well maintained. If the area is within an urban setting, the offender will probably not own a car.

Employment: This type of offender may not be employed. If he is employed, he will most likely seek out unskilled work. His job will be a simple or menial one, requiring little contact with the public, e.g., dishwasher, bus boy, janitor, maintenance man, stock boy.

Military history: The offender probably has no military service. If he was in the military, it was probably in the Army and he may have been discharged as unsuitable.

Arrest record: He has arrests for voyeurism, fetish thefts, burglary, exhibitionism, and other nuisance offenses.

General Behavior Characteristics

1. He is someone who has a societal aversion. He rejects society, which he feels has rejected him and is considered socially inadequate.
2. He is a loner, he becomes secluded and isolated. He is quiet and withdrawn and might be considered a recluse.
3. He is an underachiever, has a poor self-image, and his clothes are dirty and messy.
4. He has poor personal hygiene habits.
5. His acquaintances consider him weird or odd. He may have delusional ideas, and seems strange in appearance and behavior. He is the *little Johnny weird* of the neighborhood.
6. He internalizes hurt, anger, and fear.
7. He is sexually incompetent, and may never have had a sexual experience with someone of the opposite sex. He does not date; interpersonal relationships are difficult for this subject.
8. This offender is heavily into solo sex-related activities (substitute sex); voyeurism, exhibitionism, panty thefts, autoerotic activities, sadistic fantasies, pornography and masturbation are used to compensate for his lack of interpersonal relationships.
9. He is nocturnal, a night person.
10. He has no close personal friends.
11. This offender usually lives alone or with a significantly older female relative.
12. He has a low birth-order status.
13. His father's work is known to be unstable.
14. He received harsh discipline as a child.
15. The offender displays an anxious mood during a crime.
16. He uses alcohol minimally.
17. He has minimal interest in the news media.
18. This type of offender lacks the cunning of the organized offender.
19. He commits the crime in frenzy, "blitz" style of attack, attempts to quickly silence the victim, usually with blunt force trauma. Sudden violence to the victim and death follows quickly.
20. His is a spontaneous offense. The crime scene is tightly clustered. The weapon is usually one of opportunity. There usually will be evidence found. The weapon may be present and the body left at the location of assault.

21. The crime scene will be random and sloppy. There may be evidence of blood smearing on the offender, the victim, or surface areas at the scene, as well as uncontrolled stabbing or slashing.
22. There may be depersonalization of the victim, with extreme assault to the face.
23. Postmortem bite marks to breasts, buttocks, neck, thighs, and abdomen may be present.
24. Postmortem dissection of the body may be inflicted, which is exploratory in nature. Investigators may find mutilation of the body, and evidence of anthropophagy (the consumption of the victim's flesh and blood).
25. Sexual acts may be performed with the body; insertion of foreign objects into the anal or vaginal cavities; masturbation upon the victim or her clothing; ejaculation into stab wounds; and sexual experimentation. *Usually there is no penis penetration of the body by this type of offender.*
26. The crime scene may be isolated, but there is no real effort to hide or conceal the body. The crime scene will be in proximity to the offender's residence or place of employment.
27. The body may be positioned by the offender for some symbolic purpose.
28. There may be evidence of ritualism. This type of offender may be expressing some sort of psychosexual need in the symbolic positioning of the body or in some ritualistic aspect of the crime scene. Since this type of offender is known to be extensively involved in pornography and solo sex-related activities, it would be good investigative technique to record this psychological aspect of the crime scene. Later on, this information may serve as the basis for a search warrant of the suspect's home.
29. This type of offender may take a *souvenir.* The souvenir can be an object or article of clothing taken as a remembrance. Or, in some instances, the souvenir may even be a body part. *This type of offender has been known to return souvenirs to either the gravesite or the crime scene.*
30. This type of offender has been known to undergo a significant behavior change after the crime—drug and/or alcohol abuse, religiosity, etc. (Geberth, 2006, pp. 816–820).

Table 14.1 and Table 14.2 can be utilized by the investigator in making assessment relative to the type of personality that may be involved in a particular investigation.

Case History: A Classic Disorganized Offender

CASE FACTS

On January 3, the body of a 30-year-old letter carrier was found in her U.S. Postal Service (USPS) vehicle in a church parking lot approximately one mile from her mail route at about 3:30 p.m. She had reportedly left her station at 11:30 a.m. to deliver mail along her route. Since it was the first day after the New Year's holiday, there was quite an amount of additional mail.

The police were called to the church parking lot by a custodian, who advised them that the car wasn't in the parking lot earlier in the day. The police cordoned off the immediate area around the vehicle and notified detectives. When it was determined that the auto was a USPS vehicle, U.S. Postal inspectors joined the local police in the investigation.

THE CRIME SCENE

The woman's body was in the back seat of the automobile. She was nude from the waist up and her blouse covered her head. Looking through the rear window, one could see stab wounds in her back, a set of car keys between her back and the car seat, and numerous pieces of bloodstained mail and advertising circulars. On the outside of the auto near the left rear rocker panel, drying blood was observed along with some sort of vegetative matter. Upon closer examination of this area of the auto, the police discovered long blond hairs (the victim was a brunette). When the investigators opened the car door, they observed her mail cart and a large amount of bloodstained mail as well as additional blood drippings and smearing upon the victim's back. When they examined the trunk area of the vehicle, the investigators saw a patent print in blood on the trunk. The offender had apparently left his fingerprints on the trunk. The trunk was opened and the crime scene investigators discovered additional mail, the victim's shoes, a large bloodstained hunting knife, more long blond hairs, a large leaf from a philodendron plant, and additional plant matter similar to the materials found adhered to the blood on the rocker panel. They also found a pair of woman's pantyhose, which did not belong to the victim (Figures 14.2 through 14.5).

EXAMINATION OF THE VICTIM'S BODY

When the victim's body was examined, the investigators determined that her blood had been smeared on her back. Her pants and shirt were blood-soaked. However, her pants and panties had remained intact. Although this case was considered a sexual assault given the nudity and the fact that her bra had been pulled from her body, there

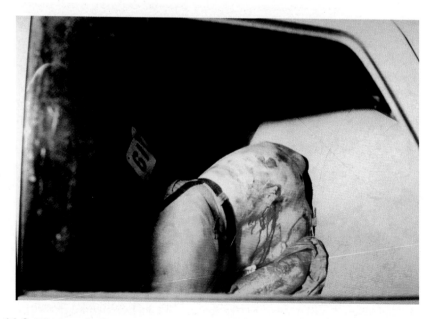

Figure 14.2 Victim's body. View looking in through the window. (Photo courtesy of the U.S. Postal Inspections Service.)

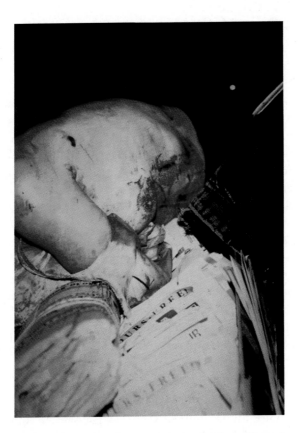

Figure 14.3 Victim's body. View after door was opened. Note the stab wounds and victim's bra pulled down. There is also a large amount of undelivered mail thrown onto the back seat. (Photo courtesy of the U.S. Postal Inspections Service.)

Figure 14.4 Undelivered mail. Note the large amount of undelivered mail in the trunk, which is bloodstained. There were also footwear impressions in blood on the mail. (Photo courtesy of the U.S. Postal Inspections Service.)

Figure 14.5 Murder weapon. The murder weapon was discovered in the trunk. (Photo courtesy of the U.S. Postal Inspections Service.)

wasn't any sexual penetration. Adhering to the victim's back were additional long blond hairs, vegetative matter, along with blue and green paint flecks. She had been multiply stabbed and had suffered blunt force trauma, which caused cerebral hemorrhage. It was the classic "blitz" attack, which renders a person incapacitated. According to the medical examiner, the bloodstained knife recovered from the trunk of her postal vehicle was used to inflict the stab wounds.

THE INVESTIGATION

The investigators immediately considered the possibility that she had been attacked while delivering mail along her route and then brought to this location by an offender, who drove her car and then traveled back on foot. Also, due to the large amount of mail found in her car, it was assumed that she hadn't gotten very far on her route. The U.S. Postal inspectors and detectives began to canvass the area of her route. The canvass wasn't too successful because most of the residents were either at work or otherwise not at home in the morning hours when the victim would have been delivering mail.

The next day, inspectors brought in bloodhounds to see whether the dogs could pick up a scent from the victim's car. The bloodhounds were scented with the leather steering wheel cover and front seat. The dogs led their handlers directly into the area where the victim was the assigned letter carrier. Investigators had discovered the murder scene later the next day, January 4, at 4 p.m.

The detectives and agents noticed someone watching them from the window of a house along the mail route. They also saw blood on the driveway. When they went to the door and knocked they saw a white male discard something into a garbage can on the side of the house.

Investigators made contact with the man in the house. He was requested to accompany them to the police station for an interview and he agreed and left with an agent and a detective.

Figure 14.6 Front entrance. There was a large philodendron plant with a missing leaf at the front entrance of the suspect's house. (Photo courtesy of the U.S. Postal Inspections Service.)

The mother of the subject arrived home shortly thereafter and inquired what the police were doing at her home. They informed her and asked for her permission to check the garbage pail.

When they tipped over the pail, a bloody pair of sneakers fell out. She said, "Those are my son's sneakers." The authorities obtained a search warrant for the premises.

On the front porch was a large philodendron plant with a missing leaf. The broken leaf and stem were later matched to this plant. There also was a large juniper bush in front of the house and, later, the unknown vegetative matter on the victim's back and pants was matched to this bush. The mystery of the blue and green flecks of paint was soon solved when the investigators noticed that the Christmas lights, which were hung on the garage, were left in place all year and had begun to flake. The paint chips had fallen into a crack in the driveway. When the offender dragged the woman's body over the driveway, this trace evidence was transferred to her back and clothing and further transferred to her car. This was turning out be a veritable gold mine of forensic evidence (Figures 14.6 through Figure 14.8).

The investigators noticed a strong smell of cleaner in the living room. When they asked the mother of the suspect about this, she stated, "Oh, my son had done a school project and had gotten something all over the carpet, so I cleaned it up." She showed the investigators where she had cleaned and they located the victim's blood beneath the carpet leading up to the bedroom stairs. The crime scene detectives also found blood on a living

Figure 14.7 Missing leaf. Note the broken stem with the missing leaf. This fracture was matched to the philodendron leaf recovered in the trunk of victim's postal vehicle. (Photo courtesy of the U.S. Postal Inspections Service.)

Figure 14.8 Leaf found in trunk. This philodendron leaf was matched to the plant at the suspect's home. There was also an abundance of other physical and trace evidence linking the suspect to this crime. (Photo courtesy of the U.S. Postal Inspections Service.)

room curtain and on the baseboard by the front door. Upstairs in the suspect's bedroom the police found the sheath for the murder weapon wrapped in a sleeping blanket.

THE SUSPECT

The suspect was an 18-year-old high school dropout presently enrolled in a community college. He lived at home with his mother, but reportedly was a loner and known drug abuser. Classmates described him as weird and argumentative. At one point, he lived in a tent behind the family house for six months and his mother would bring him his food. He was involved in solo sex-related activities with his dog and was a suspected fetish burglar. It was learned that during a prior psychiatric examination, he had revealed his sadistic fantasies to his doctor.

THE CONFESSION

The suspect admitted lying in wait for the female letter carrier, whom he wanted to rape after getting her into his room. After he attacked her, he realized she was too bloody and had to get rid of the body. He then drove her body to the parking lot and then went home to clean up the mess. He thought that he had gotten away with her murder.

This woman had delivered mail every day to this house without incident. Suddenly, without warning an occupant of the house decided to act out a sexual fantasy on this victim of opportunity. There wasn't any plan to this event other than her availability. It was a spontaneous offense. The female carrier was a victim of opportunity. There was no conversation because he attacked her in "blitz" style with a baseball bat to the head and then started stabbing into her body. He had intended to take her to his room for sexual purposes, but there was blood all over the place. When he tried to get rid of the body, he left further evidence at the disposal site as well as at his home. He depersonalized her by covering her head with her uniform blouse and exposed her breasts. Her body was left in her vehicle in open view and the murder weapon was left in the trunk of the car. He left an abundance of evidence with the body at the crime scene and authorities were provided with numerous pieces of evidence at his home. This was a classic disorganized event (From the author's files).

Case History: A Classic Organized Offender

CASE FACTS

Michael Ross was a serial killer operating in the northern Connecticut area. He was the classic organized offender. He had been a model student in high school and was a graduate of Cornell University in New York State. At the time of his arrest, he was working as an insurance salesman and traveled his route in a blue Toyota. He killed a total of six young women, mostly teenagers, over a period of two years. He was extremely effective in avoiding apprehension and the authorities didn't even realize a serial killer was responsible for the deaths. In fact, there was hardly any physical evidence in these cases except for the recovered bodies.

THE VICTIMS

His first victim was a 17-year-old named Tammy. He had stalked her as she walked across a field. He confronted her in a wooded area where he raped her and strangled her to death when she told him that she recognized him. After he killed her, he took her body to a swamp where he covered her with swamp grass and other materials. She was reported missing and, although a number of searchers had walked through this area, her body was not found. Her body wasn't recovered until Ross directed authorities to the swamp area where he had buried her.

His second victim was a 26-year-old named Debbie. Ross spotted her walking along the road and offered her a ride. Ross drove Debbie to a secluded area where he raped and strangled her to death. He then transported her to a wooded area. Debbie and her husband had been arguing earlier in the evening and Debbie had been walking home. When her husband reported her missing, he initially was a suspect. Her body was not discovered for four months, until the autumn when her skeletonized remains were discovered by deer hunters.

His third victim was a 19-year-old named Robin. Her partially clothed body was found under a pile of leaves by a jogger on November 23. Robin also had been raped and strangled to death. Ross had spotted Wendy walking along Route 32 in New London. He parked his car and attempted to engage her in conversation. When she began to walk away, Ross grabbed her and dragged her into the bushes, where her body was later discovered. Initially, when her body was discovered, the police thought that her murder may have been related to her occupation, which was a telephone sex-talk business featuring erotic conversations with women.

His fourth and fifth victims were two teenagers who disappeared on Easter Sunday. April, 15, and Leslie, 14, had decided to go hitchhiking to a store when Ross offered them a ride. He overpowered the two girls and took them to an area called Beach Pond. He ordered April to remove her jeans and cut the jeans into strips. He tied them both with strips of the jeans and other clothing. He left Leslie in the car and took April into the woods where he raped her. During this time, April told him that her uncle was a cop and that he was in trouble. He strangled April to death and then went back to the car. He took Leslie from the car and told her he was just going to leave her with April. He then had her lie on her stomach and he strangled her to death. He then transported their bodies to a rural area on the border of Rhode Island and Connecticut. He placed them in a culvert and covered their bodies with brush and branches.

MODUS OPERANDI

He followed the same MO in each of the cases. He would cruise around in his car looking for a victim walking by herself along the road in a rural area. He would park his car, get out, and attempt to engage the woman in conversation. When he saw an opportunity, he would suddenly grab her and drag her into the woods or the brush where he would rape her. After the rape, Ross would tell his victim that he was going to let her go after he tied her up. Ross would instruct the victim, "Lie on your belly," or "Roll over on your belly." He would then sit on her back and strangle her (Figure 14.9 and Figure 14.10).

A MISSING PERSON'S CASE

He was finally identified and apprehended in connection with the murder of a 17-year-old named Wendy. On June 13, Wendy was reported missing by her parents. A missing persons case had been initiated by the Connecticut State Police. Witnesses reported seeing the victim walking along a road. Other witnesses saw the victim arguing with

Figure 14.9 Victim #2. The offender had transported his victim's body to this wooded area where deer hunters discovered it. Note that the body is in a face down position. (Photo courtesy of Captain Frank Griffin, Connecticut State Police.)

Figure 14.10 Victim #3. The offender had left this victim's body secreted under a bush and covered it with leaves. He had planned on going back to better conceal it. However, the body was discovered. Note that the body is in a face down position. (Photo courtesy of Captain Frank Griffin, Connecticut State Police.)

Figure 14.11 Body buried in rock wall. The offender had buried his victim's body in this farm wall to prevent it from being discovered. However, the police were searching this area with cadaver dogs after a witness reported seeing the victim in this vicinity. (Photo courtesy of Captain Frank Griffin, Connecticut State Police.)

a stranger. The witnesses described the same unknown white male as being with the victim the afternoon of her disappearance. Another witness told police that he saw this same subject park his blue auto on the side of the road. The police search resulted in locating Wendy's buried body, which had been secreted in a rock wall near to where she was last seen. This was on June 15 (Figure 14.11 and Figure 14.12).

AN ATTEMPT

Ironically, in the early morning hours of June 15, the same day that Wendy's body was discovered, a woman had made a complaint of having been followed by a stranger in a blue vehicle. The man she described matched the description of the unknown male in the missing person's case. When the woman screamed and attempted to get the license plate number, the driver backed up rapidly and smashed his taillight on another vehicle.

THE SUSPECT

Trooper Investigators Mike Malchik and Frank Griffen, who were assigned to the missing person's case and murder investigation, thought that this incident might be related and began checking all blue Toyotas. The troopers had routinely picked up Michael Ross for an interview because he owned a blue Toyota; however, as they were talking to him, they began to notice that his mannerism was not in sync with the questioning. It was the professional interrogation of Michael Ross by the investigators that led to Ross's arrest and subsequent convictions for the brutal murder of six persons (From the author's files).

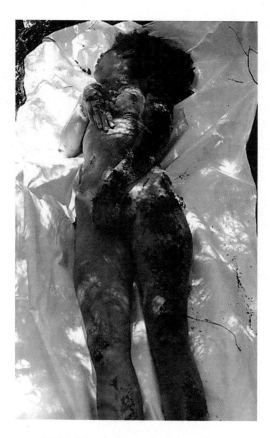

Figure 14.12 Body recovered. This photo shows the body when it was recovered from the rock wall. (Photo courtesy of Captain Frank Griffin, Connecticut State Police.)

Ross had planned his sexual assaults and murders. He attempted to engage his victims in conversation and to personalize them. The crime scenes were neat and orderly and, in most instances, he was effectively able to secret the bodies so that they would not be immediately found. In some instances, he transported the bodies to an area far from his work or residence. He was a classic organized offender.

Investigative Analysis and Evaluation of Signature on Cold Case Investigations: A Serial Murder

CASE FACTS

On July 17, 1990, at approximately 9:38 a.m., the body of a 25-year-old white female was found approximately 20 feet off a walking path, and approximately 50 feet from the rear exit of the building where she lived in Tuckahoe, New York. The Westchester County Police and Crime Scene unit responded to the call.

THE CRIME SCENE

The victim was lying on her back with her left arm extended over her face and eyes and her elbow pointing up. She was wearing a blue dress that was raised just below the

Figure 14.13 Serial murder #3. This reopened case was the catalyst for a successful investigation of a serial killer. (Photo courtesy of Lieutenant Chris Callabrese, Westchester County Police,)

buttock level and her pantyhose had been removed and turned inside out. These were located opposite her feet. The victim's panties were not at the scene.

The apparent cause of death was a single shotgun blast that entered through the back of the victim's head about midline and exited out through the mid-right side of her face. The victim was apparently on her back with her head turned to her right when the shot was fired. Brain and skull fragments outlined the bullet exit path. A 12-gauge wadding was located along this path. The slug was later identified as a Sabot round that was not common at that time.

The victim's shoes were located on the path edge and were against a large tree. It appeared that she had stepped out of her shoes the way a woman does when she takes them off. A wet stain was located on her dress under her buttocks and there was trauma to the victim's anus.

There were leaves, sticks, and other vegetable material adhered to the victim's buttocks under her dress indicating that the attacker lowered the dress after the rape/sodomy and murder. Additionally, the dress was "smoothed down" and the victim's arm was possibly placed over her eyes (Figure 14.13).

The victim, named Lisa, was apparently dressed for work and on time to catch the train at the Crestwood station approximately ¼ mile away on the Bronx River Parkway bike path. The walking path from the apartment building and the bike path are very busy with commuters from 6 through 8:30 a.m. In spite of that fact, canvass revealed only one possible witness. A doctor, who was jogging a short distance south of the murder site, heard what he believed to be a shot and then observed a six foot, black male, medium build with a "flat top" haircut running in the opposite direction holding something in front of him. He did not see the suspect's face. Missing from the victim's duffle bag was her maroon-colored, snap-together wallet containing her license, credit cards and cash, etc.

VICTIMOLOGY

The victim lived at a Tuckahoe address with her boyfriend. However, she was in the process of breaking up with him. She was also seeing another male romantically at the same time. At the time of the murder her current boyfriend was working at AT&T giving a presentation. The second male did not appear to have an alibi. However, both were eliminated via RFLP (restriction fragment length polymorphisms) DNA testing.

ADDITIONAL INFORMATION

On July 18, 1990, a Visa credit card belonging to the victim was recovered on Fenton Avenue in the Bronx. The finder called the bank, which instructed her to cut up the card and discard it in the trash. However, that same person having heard the news report of the murder recognized the victim's name on the Visa card. She gave the Visa card to Bronx Patrol Officers who provided it to the Westchester County detectives. Processing proved negative for suspect prints. The investigation was stalled.

Cold Case Investigation: Westchester County Police

In 1996, the Westchester County Police Major Case Squad, under the supervision of Lieutenant Chris Callabrese reopened the 1990 murder as a cold case. During the cold case investigation, numerous persons had been eliminated as suspects via DNA testing.

An analysis of crimes committed during the murder time period indicated that a Corvette was carjacked by two black males displaying a shotgun in Yonkers, New York, on July 17, 1990, the same day, within hours of the homicide. It should be noted that Yonkers is in close proximity to the city of Tuckahoe.

A suspect was arrested and charged with robbery first degree in that case. Further investigation revealed that charges were dropped against this suspect due to a bad identification. The complainants in the robbery case identified this suspect from a black male photo book as the person with the shotgun.

On July 20, 1990, two black males were arrested while driving the stolen Corvette. The complainants in the above cases were shown two photo arrays. One set of photos was displayed for the robbery case. The other two arrays contained photos of two males arrested in the stolen vehicle. The complainants could not make a positive identification.

However, when the assigned detectives pointed out which two were arrested in the stolen car, the complainants stated that those individuals were the two that had robbed them on July 17, 1990. The two persons arrested were Patrick Baxter and another black male (*name withheld*) of the Bronx. The charges were dropped against the suspects and no additional charges were filed.

A physical comparison between the first suspect arrested and Patrick Baxter was uncanny. They were almost twins, but not related. The complainant was reinterviewed and insisted that Baxter and the other male robbed him and that Baxter had the shotgun. However, because of the tainted identification, they were not charged.

Cold Case Investigation Yonkers Police

In 1996, City of Yonkers detectives, Detective Sergeant John D'Alessandro and his partner, Detective Joe Pietropauolo, reopened a 1987 rape–murder involving a 14-year-old named Michelle. She had been killed in a wooded area near an aqueduct. She was on her way home after picking up groceries for her family. A review of the crime scene indicated that Michelle had apparently redressed herself hurriedly after the assault. This was determined because her sweater was inside out and she hadn't completely fastened her pants. Observable biological evidence at the time was limited to one very small spot on the victim's T-shirt. DNA testing procedures available at that time would have utilized the entire sample with a low probability of a positive result (Figure 14.14).

Later during the cold case investigation, Sergeant D'Alessandro requested a reanalysis of the victim's clothing. Through the use of an alternate light source, additional DNA was obtained for further testing. The detectives learned that there had been a witness at the time who described a black male, who was observed exiting the general area of the aqueduct with twigs and leaves clinging to his clothing. Further inquiries by Yonkers detectives uncovered additional information and a possible suspect identified as a male, black, named Patrick Baxter, whose name kept coming up in the investigation

Detectives ascertained from a criminal history on Baxter that he had been charged with oral sodomy and the attempted rape of an eight-year-old girl who lived in his

Figure 14.14 Serial murder #2. This case had originally been classified as "undetermined" until new evidence was uncovered in the cold case investigations by Yonkers and Westchester County Police. (Photo courtesy of Detective Sergeant John D'Allesandro, Yonkers, New York, Police Department.)

building in Yonkers. He was a juvenile at the time of this event and was tried and convicted in Family Court after the eight-year-old girl positively identified him. He was sentenced to three years in a secure facility of the New York State Division for Youth, which was the maximum sentence allowable under New York State law.

Shortly after Baxter was released from the New York State Division for Youth, Michelle, a young girl from his neighborhood, was raped and murdered. The sexual acts committed were strikingly similar to the sexual attack on the eight-year-old. This time, however, the victim was not left alive to identify or testify against him.

The Yonkers detectives contacted the Westchester County Lab to ascertain if there was any biological evidence from that past rape. Although there weren't any biological materials available, they were informed by laboratory specialist, Mary Eustice, that she had just received a similar inquiry from Russell Lowenstein from the Westchester County Police. Westchester County had done a crime analysis and came up with the shotgun robbery and Baxter's arrest. Detective Lowenstein was inquiring about DNA for a black male named Patrick Baxter.

In 1997, Westchester County Major Case Squad detectives met with Yonkers detectives to compare cases. The Yonkers detectives advised the county police that Baxter was a prime suspect in the June 1987 murder and rape of a 14-year-old girl named Michele. Westchester County detectives were looking at Baxter as a prime suspect in the July 1990 rape–murder of the young woman in Tuckahoe. The two agencies agreed to pool their resources and focus on Patrick Baxter. Both agencies wanted to compare the DNA from Yonkers to the DNA retrieved from the Tuckahoe case.

DNA

After a conference with Ted Pool of the Westchester County Laboratory, both agencies agreed that rather than risk elimination of the only biological evidence available, the investigators would wait for the lab to come online with the newer STR/PCR (short tandem repeats/polymerase chain reaction) DNA testing that could use the minute sample and give a positive result with high probability. Baxter refused to cooperate in any way in this investigation.

IN THE YEAR 2000

The Westchester County Lab was now utilizing the new STR/PCR DNA testing procedure. Westchester County Major Case detectives and Yonkers police requested that the laboratory retest the samples from the 1990 Tuckahoe case using the new STR/PCR DNA format and compare that result against the minute sample from the Yonkers homicide involving the young 14-year-old victim.

INVESTIGATION CONTINUES

In the spring of 2000, Yonkers detectives D'Alessandro and Joe Pietropauolo located an additional witness who could place Baxter at the aqueduct in Yonkers and in the vicinity of the Tuckahoe murder. D'Alessandro and Pietropauolo were interviewing a friend of Baxter. When they informed the witness that they were there to talk about Baxter's involvement in a homicide, the witness stated, "Do you mean Patricia?"

The detectives had inadvertently stumbled onto another homicide. The victim in this case was a 19-year-old female named Patricia, who had been found partially unclothed in a wooded area in Greenburgh, New York, in February of 1988. Semen was recovered

Figure 14.15 Serial murder victim #1. This was the first victim killed by the offender. This case had been reopened as a cold case investigation by the City of Yonkers detectives. The county detectives and Yonkers police combined their investigations and focused on the serial murder case. (Photo courtesy of Detective Sergeant John D'Allesandro, Yonkers, New York, Police Department.)

from the victim's mouth, anus, and vagina. The death although suspicious had been ruled undetermined (Figure 14.15).

The Yonkers detectives immediately contacted the Town of Greenburgh detectives and notified Westchester County detectives of this new development. The witness provided information that Patrick Baxter was one of the last persons seen with the deceased before she was found dead.

In March of 2000, the Westchester County lab matched the DNA suspect profile from the Tuckahoe case with the suspect DNA profile from the Yonkers case. The investigators from Westchester County Major Case and Yonkers began application for a court order to draw blood from Baxter, who was serving time on a nonmandated felony, in New York State Corrections.

The Westchester County lab then advised county police that they had an additional DNA suspect profile that matched a suspicious death in the Town of Greenburgh, also in Westchester County. The Westchester County assistant medical examiner reclassified the suspicious death a homicide.

In the interim, Westchester County Major Case detectives and Yonkers detectives located Baxter's cousin who was residing in South Carolina. Although the cousin had been involved in the carjacking incident with Baxter, he had since changed his life around. He had joined the service and now had a family. He provided further crucial information in this serial murder case. The interview of this person revealed that on the day of the murder in 1990, Baxter had a shotgun in his possession and a women's maroon-colored wallet. Baxter made statements to this witness about robbing some lady and having to fire the shotgun into the air to scare her.

On June 9, 2000, County Judge Rosato signed an order for Baxter's blood. Baxter refused to comply and stated, "You fucks will never get my blood."

On June 22, 2000, Judge Rosato signed a force order. Baxter had to be restrained in a chair with his hands behind his back. When his finger was pricked he kept trying to keep the blood from being collected by using his adjacent fingers to wipe the drops away. Eventually, one drop was successfully transferred to the cotton swab.

In July 2000, Baxter's DNA profile was matched to the three murder victims' DNA suspect profiles. Baxter was indicted and charged with multiple counts of murder as well as rape, sodomy, and the robbery charges.

In 2002, Baxter was tried before a jury and convicted on all counts and was sentenced to the maximum sentence of 75 years to life.

Acknowledgments

The author wishes to acknowledge the contribution of this information and materials to this particular chapter, specifically, Jeanine Pirro, District Attorney, Westchester County, and her prosecution staff, Second Deputy District Attorney Barbara Egenhauser and Deputy Division Chief James A. Mc Carty.

I also want to acknowledge the following professional law enforcement investigators who were involved in this major case: Lieutenant Chris Callabrese and Detective Russell Lowenstein, Westchester County Police; Detective Sergeant John D'Alessandro and Detective Sergeant Joe Pietropaolo, Yonkers Police Department; as well as all those who participated in this cold case investigation.

Criminal Personality Profiling: The Signature Aspect in Criminal Investigation

> The signature aspect of a violent criminal offender is a unique and integral part of the offender's behavior. This signature component refers to the psychodynamics, which are the mental and emotional processes underlying human behavior and its motivation (Geberth, 2006, p. 920).

Essentially, our sociosexual life is being shaped from childhood to early adulthood based on social experiences. Our sociosexual template is subject to outside influence. The human brain can be induced to sexual deviance through fantasies, which are mental events based on the product of various sociosexual experiences. Sexual stimuli are processed as a "brain cocktail" of endogenously produced neurochemicals (see Chapter 1).

Clinical Perspective

Clinically speaking, there is a behavioral distinctiveness in human sexuality. This unique aspect of our sexual arousal and response system accounts for why individuals differ in their sexual behaviors and engage in a specific series of behavioral patterns. In sex-related criminal incidents, the offender is often subconsciously acting out a sexually significant behavioral pattern, which reflects the underlying personality, lifestyle, and developmental experiences of the offender.

John Money (1986) refers to the "lovemap" as "a developmental representation or template in the mind and in the brain depicting the idealized lover and the idealized program of sexuoerotic activity projected in imagery or actually engaged in with that lover" (p. 290). These are related to the natural human development of the individual and are influenced by both biological aspects as well as the environment: nature and nurture. According to Dr. Money, "Like a native language, a person's lovemap also bears the mark of his own unique individuality, or accent ... it's usually quite specific as to details of the physiognomy, build, race, color of the ideal lover, not to mention temperament, manner, and so on" (Money, 1986, p. 19). The lovemaps may be extremely detailed in specifying certain characteristics that take precedence over others, such as an attraction to thighs, buttocks, bosom, torso face, teeth, eye color, hair, skin, weight, height, and so on (Money, 1986, p. 68).

Sexual deviation occurs when these lovemap patterns become derailed. Child molesters, rapists, deviant murderers, and others with peculiar erotic interests are an example of this phenomenon. The formulation of sexual deviance can usually be traced to aberrant erotic development. For example, strict antisexual upbringing, sexual abuse of a child between the ages of 5 and 8 by the primary care giver, overexposure to sexually stimulating behaviors, and/or inappropriate and pathological family dynamics.

According to Money, "Paraphilias are a mental template or lovemap that in response to neglect, suppression, or traumatization of its normophilic formation, has developed with distortions, namely omissions, displacements, and inclusions that would otherwise have no place in it. A paraphilia permits sexuoerotic arousal, genital performance, and orgasm to take place, but only under the aegis, in fantasy or live performance, of the special substitute imagery of the paraphilia" (Money, 1986, p. 39).

These derailed lovemaps are the precursor for sexual deviance and, in the case of the serial killer, the "game plan" for murder.

Human behavior, although unpredictable, is oftentimes repetitive. Research has indicated that certain actions engaged in at the homicide crime scene by certain types of personalities will repeat themselves in other homicide investigations. The homicide detective, who has enhanced his experience with a comprehension of the psychodynamics of human behavior, will be able to develop a base of knowledge that can be applied to the review of similar cases.

Investigative Perspective

From an investigative perspective, it is important to note that an offender's MO, or "method of doing things," is a learned behavior and tends to remain consistent as long as the MO is successful. However, an MO is a work in progress and these types of behaviors are developed over time and change as offenders gain experience, build confidence, or become involved with the criminal justice system. The "signature" component may also change to some degree. However, the change usually involves a progression of violence and sexual mutilation, which is consistent with the paraphilia sexual sadism as seen in lust murders.

The MO involves actions necessary to accomplish the activity while the "signature aspect" represents the underlying emotional "needs" of the offender. These needs on the part of the sexual offender are the product of one's **sociosexual template**, combined experiences, family, one's religious values, and those of the wider world. This sociosexual template is subject

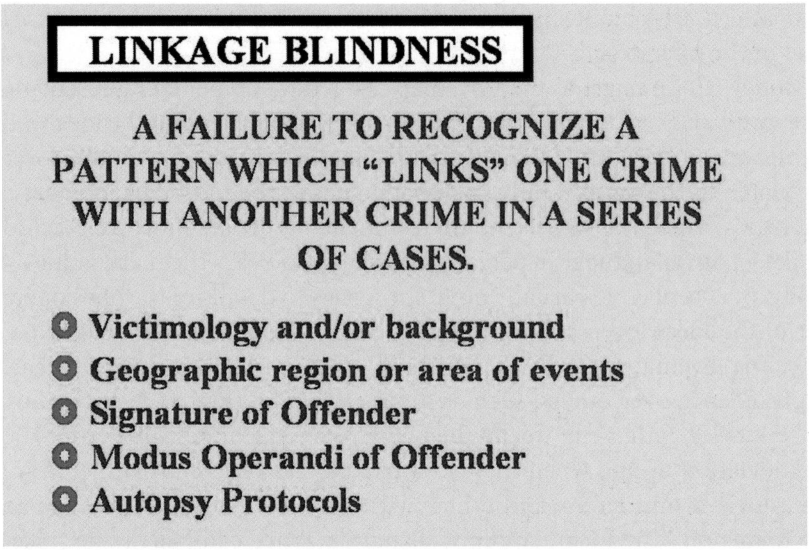

> # LINKAGE BLINDNESS
>
> ## A FAILURE TO RECOGNIZE A PATTERN WHICH "LINKS" ONE CRIME WITH ANOTHER CRIME IN A SERIES OF CASES.
>
> - Victimology and/or background
> - Geographic region or area of events
> - Signature of Offender
> - Modus Operandi of Offender
> - Autopsy Protocols

Figure 14.16 Linkage blindness. (From Geberth, V,J. *Practical Homicide Investigation*, 4th ed., CRC Press, Boca Raton, FL, 2006. With permission.)

to influence. As humans, we are not sexually complete at birth, but subject to environmental sexual marketing. Our sociosexual life is being shaped from childhood to early adulthood based on social experiences. The human brain can be induced to sexual deviance.

What kind of sexual "reality" dominates the mentality of a sex criminal? What information about sex does he collect and store from the "soft" environment? This overwhelmingly includes pornography. What behaviors and actions did the offender engage in that went beyond those necessary to accomplish the crime. When dealing with an offender who is a sexual sadist, one can expect to see a progression of violence as the series evolves. Understanding and recognizing both the MO and the signature aspect of the event can enable the professional investigator to "link" events in a series.

Linkage Blindness

Linkage blindness is defined as an investigative failure to recognize a pattern that links one crime with another crime in a series of cases through victimology, geographic region or area of events, the "signature" of the offender, similar MO, and a review of autopsy protocols (Geberth, 2006, p. 824) (Figure 14.16).

The Henry Louis Wallace Serial Murder Case

Case Facts

One of the most glaring examples of linkage blindness that I reviewed was the serial murder case in Charlotte, North Carolina, involving Henry Louis Wallace a black male, 28 years old. Wallace was responsible for the sex-related murders of 10 young black females in Charlotte in less than two years.

These murders occurred between May 1992 and March 1994. Most of the victims were middle-class young women with families residing in the downtown Charlotte area. The cases were not linked until March of 1994, when Wallace confessed to the murders.

Henry Louis Wallace was born in South Carolina. He had a criminal background with repeated acts involving burglary, larceny, and rape. Incidentally, he was the primary suspect in a South Carolina murder that occurred on April 1, 1990. He also had been charged with an attempted rape in South Carolina. In addition, he kidnapped and raped a 17-year-old female on February 25, 1992. Wallace left the South Carolina jurisdiction and moved to Charlotte, North Carolina. Those South Carolina charges were still pending when Wallace was arrested two years later in Charlotte.

Victim #1

Sharon Nance, a black female, 33 years old, was Wallace's first victim in Charlotte. The victim was a known prostitute and drug user with an extensive record. She had been arrested and charged 61 times between 1975 and 1992. Nance had recently been released from prison when she was reported as a missing person. Nance's nude body was found alongside a roadway on May 27, 1992, about 10 miles from downtown Charlotte. The case remained unsolved and there were no suspects developed.

Victim #2

Caroline Love, a black female, 20 years old, worked at a Bojangles fast food restaurant. The victim was hired as a cashier in September 1989 at Bojangles on 5111 Central Avenue in Charlotte, where she worked until June 15, 1992, when she was reported as a missing person. Love was also attending school.

According to the manager, Love had good work ethics and was a reliable employee. She was reported as a missing person to Charlotte police when she failed to come home after work. That case was still open when Wallace was arrested in March 1994. He directed the authorities to the missing woman's body. She had been raped and strangled to death.

Victim #3

On February 19, 1993, Shawna Hawk, a black female, 20 years old, was found dead in her home. Hawk, who had graduated from high school, was attending Piedmont Community College and studying to be a paralegal. She worked at a Taco Bell located at 3612 North Sharon Amity Road in Charlotte. Henry Wallace had hired her for the Taco Bell job and had even dated her once.

Shawna had worked part time to help with family bills since she was 14 and was a very responsible young woman. When her mother hadn't heard from her, she went to Hawk's apartment to check on her daughter. When she entered the locked apartment, she discovered her daughter's nude body in the bathtub. The medical examiner ruled that Hawk had been strangled to death. According to the police report, there was no forced entry or any break in suggesting the victim had admitted someone to her apartment. However, the police did not consider this a sex-related event and the medical examiner did not conduct any examination for sexual assault.

Investigative Considerations

The first woman to be killed was a prostitute and drug user who would be considered a high-risk victim. The second victim killed was originally reported as a missing person and her whereabouts remained unknown. Her body was not discovered until the offender told the police where he had disposed of the body. The Shawna Hawk case, however, was the first investigation that authorities could have possibly linked later on in the series if they had aggressively pursued an obvious major case investigation.

Victim #4

On June 25, 1993, Audrey Spain, a 33-year-old black female, was discovered nude on her bed in her residence. A ligature consisting of a torn T-shirt and black brassiere was wrapped tightly around her neck. Once again, there was no forced entry or break in at this location. She had obviously allowed someone she knew into her apartment.

Spain worked as a shift manager at the Taco Bell on 3612 North Sharon Amity Road. This was the same Taco Bell where Hawk was employed. Spain had worked with Hawk and was acquainted with Henry Louis Wallace.

She lived at 4923 Central Avenue and had recently been transferred to another Taco Bell on North Wendover in Charlotte. The medical examiner ruled the cause of death to be ligature strangulation. However, there wasn't any examination for sexual assault.

Investigative Considerations

A clear pattern emerged with the murder of Audrey Spain. She had also been found in her apartment and there were no signs of forced entry or break in. Furthermore, the police were unable to find any evidence. This suggested that the offender was taking precautions not to leave anything behind. The investigators and the medical examiner failed to perceive that both cases were sex-related. More importantly, both victims worked at the same Taco Bell on 3612 North Sharon Amity Road. Was it possible that someone was targeting women who worked at Taco Bell? Could the offender be a fellow employee? What was going on in these victims' lives that may have some connection? None of these questions were asked because the investigators never went to Taco Bell to conduct interviews of the employees or patrons.

Victim #5

On August 10, 1993, Valencia Jumper, a black female, 21 years old, was found in her apartment after firefighters were called to extinguish a fire. This victim was a senior at Johnson Smith University majoring in computer science. She lived off North Sharon Amity Road and worked part time at two different jobs. She worked at Food Lion and a department store.

She was acquainted with Henry Wallace, who introduced himself when he found out that she was a friend of his sister from school in South Carolina.

She was reported to be the victim of an accidental fire. After Henry Wallace was arrested and confessed, a second autopsy revealed that she had been strangled to death.

Investigative Considerations

In this case, the medical examiner ruled the cause of death to be from an accidental fire. When I reviewed the autopsy report, I realized that I couldn't comment on a medicolegal issue. I recommended that a forensic pathologist be brought in to evaluate the autopsy protocol. The autopsy report indicated a negative level of carbon monoxide (CO) in the blood of the victim. Also there wasn't any reference to soot in the throat and lungs. Usually in a fire death, the victim will have soot in the throat, mouth, and lung and a toxicology report will show elevated levels of CO in the victim's blood. The two pathologists who reviewed the autopsy protocol were very critical of this finding.

The police, who were unaware that this case was linked due to the ME error did not connect the Valencia Jumper case to either Shawna Hawk or Audrey Spain.

Victim #6

On September 15, 1993, Michelle Stinson, a black female, 20 years old, was found slain in her apartment. Once again there was no forced entry and no evidence recovered. The victim had been strangled with a ligature and stabbed four times in her chest area. Her body was face down in the kitchen of her residence. Like Hawk, Stinson was also a student at Piedmont Community College.

A friend who had gone to the apartment to visit Michelle found her body. She had been killed in front of her two sons, one and three years of age. The three-year-old told the friend, "My mommy's asleep on the floor." Since there was no break in or forced entry, police believed that the killer was someone known to the victim. The cause of death was ruled to be multiple stab wounds to the chest and ligature strangulation.

Investigative Considerations

At this point, Charlotte Homicide had a full-blown serial murder case on their hands. The question is why weren't they concerned by the lack of evidence and the obvious serial murder pattern? The killer was being very meticulous in not leaving his fingerprints or any other evidence at the scenes. The authorities had three women strangled to death in their respective apartments. Two of the women had worked at the same Taco Bell. Stinson and Hawk both attended Piedmont Community College. Why didn't the police investigators go to Piedmont Community College to interview friends of the victims? There wasn't any forced entry or break in, suggesting the offender knew his victims. The cases were obviously sex-related. Just those aspects alone would be sufficient to link these cases. In fact, bells and alarms should have been going off in Charlotte Homicide.

Victim #7

On February 20, 1994, Vanessa Little Mack, a black female, 25 years old, was found in the bedroom of her apartment by a family friend and baby sitter. Vanessa was discovered partially nude with a ligature around her neck fashioned out of her t-shirt. Her four-month-old daughter was left unattended and untouched in the living room. Once again there wasn't any forced entry or break in.

Mack was a single parent who worked as a patient escort at a Charlotte Medical Center. Her sister, who worked at Taco Bell on North Sharon Amity Road, had introduced her to Henry Wallace in July of 1993.

Investigative Considerations

At this point, there were *four* confirmed homicides involving strangulation of female victims found in their respective apartments with no signs of forced entry or break in. The cases were obviously sex-related and the authorities still hadn't seen the linkage.

The investigators had still not gone to Taco Bell or to Piedmont Community College. It was readily apparent that Taco Bell, as well as the community college, had come up in the interviews that were done by the police. However, the very important victimology aspect in any homicide investigation was not being pursued. The question is: Where else do you start? A sexual predator, who obviously knew his victims, was being admitted into his victim's homes. He was selecting young black women within a specific social and geographical area. He was very meticulous to not leaving fingerprints or other evidence at the scenes. He was strangling his victims with ligatures.

Victim #8

On March 9, 1994, Brandi Henderson, a black female, 18 years old, was found strangled in her apartment. Her clothing was in disarray and there was evidence of ligature strangulation and blunt force trauma. This victim, who was a single parent, had dropped out of high school and then gone back to graduate. Henderson was also a student at Piedmont Community College attending part time.

Her 10-month-old child was also choked, but managed to survive. Once again there wasn't any forced entry or break in. A television, stereo, and some cash were stolen.

Investigative Considerations

At this point, there were *five* confirmed homicides involving strangulation of female victims found in their respective apartments with no signs of forced entry or break in.

This time the police thought that this case had strong links to the Vanessa Little Mack case. However, they still hadn't linked the other murders. The woman's clothes were in disarray, highly suggestive of sexual assault. Yet, the authorities still did not classify the case as sex-related. There was a clear pattern in the similarities of these cases to the other murders and once again there was ligature strangulation.

Victim #9

On March 10, 1994, the very next day, in Charlotte, Betty Jean Baucum, a black female, 24 years old, was discovered in her residence. A ligature consisting of a pillowcase, towel, and black tights was wrapped tightly around victim's neck. The victim was a manager at Bojangles, a fast-food establishment. Her body was discovered a day after her death. Once again there wasn't any forced entry or break in.

She had been strangled and had been dead at least a day when her body was found. Her car, which was stolen, was found across the street. This time the police found a fingerprint and thought that there were strong links to other cases.

Investigative Considerations

At this point, Charlotte Homicide had *six* female victims found strangled in their apartments. They still did not perceive these cases as sex-related. However, with the strangulation alone, coupled with the circumstances of their discovery, someone should have seen the link between the cases.

Four of the victims were in the food service business. Betty Jean Baucum and Caroline Love, who was reported missing, both worked at Bojangles. Shawna Hawk and Audrey Spain worked at the same Taco Bell. Vanessa Little Mack's' sister worked at the Taco Bell on North Sharon Amity Road where Hawk and Spain worked.

Victim #10

On March 12, 1994, Debra Ann Slaughter, a black female, 35 years old, was discovered in her residence with ligature around her neck consisting of two blue towels. There was a sock stuffed in her mouth and she had been stabbed 38 times in the chest area. The victim, who worked as a deli manager, had previously worked at Bojangles. The victim, who was single, lived alone in an apartment on Central Ave. Her body was discovered by her mother, who went to the apartment, unlocked the door, and saw her daughter on the floor. Debra had been strangled. Once again, there wasn't any forced entry or break in.

The victim may have met Wallace when she worked at Bojangles on Central Avenue. He had worked at several fast food restaurants in Charlotte. The authorities finally made the connection with the Debra Slaughter case. Wallace was identified through his fingerprint left at the Baucum homicide. It was only after the arrest that the police realized that these series of killings were sex-related and that Wallace had perpetrated all 10 of the homicides in Charlotte, North Carolina.

Opinion

In the opinion of the author, this was a classic case of *linkage blindness*. There was a total administrative and command level breakdown in Charlotte due to the department's emphasis on community policing, which resulted in the disruption of investigative services. In my opinion, the chief of the department, along with the detective supervisor in Charlotte, were ultimately responsible for this major police error. The authorities did not recognize a pattern for over a year until March 1994 when three homicide cases came in within three days.

Nine of the victims were young, middle-class black women, some were students at Piedmont Community College or were working at fast food establishments. The police never went to their workplace or the school to interview the victims' friends or associates. This is Basic Homicide Investigation 101. How could you *not* do this?

In fairness, the first two homicides could very easily have been missed. The first victim was at high-level risk as a drug user and prostitute. She was found 10 miles out of town and could very well have been killed by anyone who had picked her up. Victim #2 was listed as a missing person and was not known to be a homicide victim. However, it would have been interesting to review the missing person's case on Caroline Love to see whether or not the detectives had ever gone to Bojangles to question her co-workers.

The first sign of a pattern should have been recognized with the murders of Shawna Hawk and Audrey Spain. Both victims worked at the same Taco Bell. I personally find it highly unlikely and extremely coincidental that two employees from the same workplace are found strangled in their respective apartments with no forced entry, suggesting they knew their attacker. Furthermore, any time a woman is found nude and strangled, the professional investigator should realize that he or she is dealing with a sex crime.

The Valencia Jumper case was obviously missed due to a medicolegal error on the part of the medical examiner. However, the fact that she was partially clothed and there were two active homicides in town involving women who had been found nude in their apartments should have required further investigation.

Michelle Stinson and Vanessa Little Mack, like Hawk and Spain, were both killed in their homes with no forced entry. Stinson was stabbed four times in the chest, which is a psychosexual-type wound structure. Little Mack was found partially nude on her bed with a ligature around her neck. Both of these cases spell out sex crime.

Brandi Henderson, Betty Jean Baucum, and Debra Slaughter were strangled in their respective apartments, with no forced entry. Henderson's clothes were in disarray.

Conclusion

All eight women were strangled in their homes in the same geographical area and there wasn't any forced entry, which suggested that the killer knew his victims. Had the detectives gone to the workplaces of these victims, I believe that Henry Louis Wallace's name would have surfaced early in this investigation. A simple record check of employees at the Taco Bell would have revealed Wallace's sexual offenses in South Carolina. My fair and objective opinion is that the authorities in Charlotte should have recognized a serial murder pattern early in this investigation.

The Frequency and Characteristics of Sexual Posing in Homicides

Sexual Posing: A Specific Subset of Staging

Sexual posing is a *specific subset of crime scene staging*. Definitions for and examples of crime scene staging and sexual posing and/or positioning of a victim's body at the crime scene may be found in both clinical and criminal justice literature (Douglas and Munn, 1992; Napier and Baker, 2002; Hazelwood and Napier, 2004; Geberth, 1983, 1990, 1995, 1996b (pp. 17–37, 361–363), 1996c (pp. 89–91), 1996a (pp. 77–81), 1998, 2000, 2003, 2004, 2006, 2007; Keppel and Weis, 2004; Keppel and Birnes, 2009).

Pragmatically, the sexual posing of a body in the crime scene is extremely rare. In most sex-related homicides, the killer leaves the victim's body where the event occurred and where the victim fell as a result of the fatal injuries.

The sexual presentation of a body in the homicide crime scene has always intrigued the American media. When Elizabeth Short, an unemployed 22-year-old waitress in Los Angeles, became the victim of a gruesome and much publicized murder, her case became known as the **Black Dahlia.** The woman's arms were raised over her head at 45-degree angles. The lower half of her body was positioned a foot over from her torso, the straight legs spread wide open. This case inspired dozens of books, Web sites, a video game, and even an Australian swing band. The quest to pinpoint her killer has become a hobby for generations of armchair detectives and includes a Hollywood movie entitled *The Black Dahlia* (De Palma, 2006). The Black Dahlia as well as many of the cases presented in this chapter follows a similar theme of staging and sexual posing.

Sex and violence have always attracted the headlines and thirst of the media. The Hillside Strangler, The Gainesville Ripper, and BTK (Chapter 13) provided vivid examples of sexual posing and mutilation, which dominated the news and captivated the imagination of the general public. Much of the current forensic programming, looking for ratings and sensationalism, features the sexual presentation of bodies, which has become the norm on national television. The author had previously reported, "These events seem to be on the increase as people learn more about the process of death investigation through the media, true crime books, television mystery shows and movies" (Geberth, 2006, p. 29). Presently, with all of the forensic programming the author suspects that there will be additional staged crime scenes. Sadly, the public's perception has been influenced by this media blitz. There is a general perception, even among law enforcement, that sexual posing is quite prevalent.

The author conducted an exploratory survey and prepared a research paper on this subject that examined the issue of sexual posing, defined offender motivation, and illustrated the statistical infrequency of sexual posing in staged crime scenes.

Prevalence of Sexual Posing in Homicides

The author queried the Center for Disease Control (CDC) Morbidity Studies, the Regional Organized Crime Information Center (ROCIC), Violent Criminal Apprehension Program (VICAP), the Federal Bureau of Investigation Behavioral Analysis Unit (BAU), and the National Center for the Analysis of Violent Crime (NCAVC) to determine if there were any statistics available on the total number of staged homicides. Official statistics on homicide staging were not available from these agencies. Similarly, there were no official statistics regarding the sexual posing of a body at crime scenes.

However, based on the author's over 40 years' experience with sex-related incidents, I propose that sexual posing is a specific subset of crime scene staging. Therefore, the author instituted the following definition for a survey instrument to conduct an exploratory survey.

Definition of Sexual Posing

Sexual posing is the deliberate act of sexually positioning a body in the crime scene. This includes presenting a totally nude or partially clothed victim's body for display, which has been manipulated in a sexual manner to expose the breasts, buttocks, and/or genitalia. In addition, spreading open the victim's legs, splaying out of the victim's arms, presenting the victim in bondage or binding the hands behind the back, hanging the nude or seminude body, insertion of foreign objects into the sexual orifices, engaging in sexual mutilation, piquerism, cutting, evisceration, defeminization, and/or overkill injuries are all seen as a part of sexual posing. (Geberth, 2010)

Research Methodology

Data were collected from a nonprobability purposive sampling of both active and retired law enforcement officers who were known to have extensive experience in homicide investigations. The author identified 46 persons who would be considered homicide experts and advised them of the study. Although the author knew most of the investigators contacted, referrals were obtained to gain access to additional departments where no prior personal contact existed. Each respondent either had been in command of a homicide division or had served as a homicide investigator. Surveys were sent to 46 respondents; of these, 43 were able to participate in a timely way. The results from the three surveys received after the deadlines were not included in this analysis. Persons who were unable to respond as requested were received, but are not included in the data reported here. The average years of death investigation experience of the respondents was 25 years. All of the participants were known to the author and many were nationally renowned homicide investigation consultants who regularly provide expert testimony and advanced training in their particular field of expertise.

Sample Selection

Out of the 46 investigators contacted, 43 agreed to participate in the survey, a 93% response rate. The remaining three responses were received, but after the deadline for analysis and were not included in the findings.

The respondents in the purposive sample were selected so that the responses were representative of major city, county and state law enforcement agencies throughout the United States. The following agencies were represented in the responses: Alaska State Troopers;

Arizona Department of Public Safety; Florida Department of Law Enforcement (FDLE); Pennsylvania State Police; Michigan State Police; New York State Police; Ohio Bureau of Criminal Investigation; Washington State Homicide Investigation Tracking System (HITS); Harris County Sheriff's Office, Texas; Hillsborough County Sheriff's Office, Florida; Montgomery County Detectives, Pennsylvania; Multnomah County Detectives, Oregon; Pittsburgh Bureau of Police, Pennsylvania; Seminole County, Florida Sheriff's Office; and the police departments from Akron, Ohio; Chicago, Illinois; Huntington Beach, California; Indianapolis, Indiana; Las Vegas Metro, Nevada; Miami, Florida; Longmont, Colorado; New York City; New Orleans, Louisiana; Oklahoma City, Oklahoma; Sacramento, California; St. Louis, Missouri; St. Paul, Minnesota; Rochester, New York; Tulsa, Oklahoma; Warwick, Rhode Island; Wichita, Kansas; and Yonkers, New York.

Prior to the data collection, all 46 respondents were contacted by phone and informed about the nature of the research. The author designed a survey instrument, which was then distributed electronically via email. Respondents were given two months to check any personal records that were available.

Following that, they were asked to return the completed questionnaire to the author, who then recontacted, by telephone, those among the 43 respondents who had submitted their results when clarification or elaboration of the provided information was necessary.

The survey instrument contained a structured series of questions asking for descriptive information regarding the respondent's name, agency affiliation and location, and years of investigative experience. Specific open-ended questions relevant to the respondents' exposure to crime scene elements that were the focus of this research were included in the instrument:

1. How many years of death investigation experience do you estimate you have?
2. Approximately how many homicide investigations have you been involved with in your career? (These include those cases you personally worked, assisted in, or reviewed in your capacity as a homicide expert and experienced death investigator.)
3. How many of these homicide investigations that you are aware of in your total years of experience involved the sexual positioning or presentation of the victim's body?
4. How was the body presented or posed (seminude, legs spread, breasts exposed, etc.)? Please list victims separately in the space below by race, age, etc.
5. What was the method of death (e.g., strangulation, stab, blunt trauma, shot)?

Operationalization of Sexual Posing

According to Geberth (2010), any change in the crime scene, which includes the manipulation of a victim's body, is in fact staging. The author considers "posing" the victim's body as a component of "staging." There are three specific motives why an offender would intentionally pose or position the victim's body in a sexual manner in a crime scene:

1. Offenders pose a body sexually to satisfy a perverse sexual fantasy. Sexual sadists rely heavily on fantasy and ritual to obtain sexual satisfaction. The sexual manipulation of the victim's body, including posing, propping, sexual mutilation, defeminization, and evisceration, is the most common motivation. (See examples in this

book: Figures 1.13, 2.10, 2.18, 2.19, 2.32, 2.33, 2.43, 8.2, 9.1, 9.2, 9.17, 9.22, 9.23, 9.24, 9.25, 9.32, 10.3, 11.1, 11.2, 13.2, 13.4, 13.5, 13.15, 13.16.)

2. Offenders pose out of an anger/retaliation motive. The offender uses sex as a weapon to punish and degrade the woman. The posing of the body is done to further degrade the victim out of anger or revenge. This is the second most common motivation in sexual manipulation of the body. (See examples in this book: Figures 7.5, 7.6, 7.7, 7.9, 7.11, 7.12, 7.13, 8.25, 9.8, 9.18, 9.19, 9.20.)

3. Offenders sexual pose a body to "stage-the-scene" to make it appear to be a sex-related murder. The offender is consciously attempting to mislead and thwart the police investigation by making the murder appear to be sexual when in reality the murder was based on interpersonal violence. (See examples in this book: Figures 7.20, 7.21.)

Posing the victim's body in a sexual position at the crime scene after the murder is statistically rare (Hazelwood and Napier, 2004).

Sexual posing was operationalized as "the deliberate act of sexually positioning the body in the crime scene. This includes presenting a totally nude or partially clothed victim's body for display, which has been manipulated in a sexual manner to expose the breasts, buttocks, and/or genitalia. In addition, spreading open the victim's legs, splaying out of the victim's arms, presenting the victim in bondage, and/or binding the hands behind the back, hanging the nude or seminude body, insertion of foreign objects into the sexual orifices, engaging in sexual mutilation, piquerism, cutting, evisceration, defeminization, and/or overkill injuries."

Limitations

The data are neither a random sample of murder cases involving sexual posing nor a sample of all murders involving sexual posing occurring in the United States. Data were collected based on voluntary reporting of cases from each law enforcement jurisdiction contacted. In addition, it was understood that detailed records of the cases or consultations that these respondents participated in might not have been available. For that reason, the respondents were asked to approximate the number of homicide investigations in which they had been involved and the number that involved sexual posing.

Because of the limited resources available for this exploratory study, interrater reliability measures were not employed at this stage of the research. In addition, because this exploratory study focused on sexual posing, it is possible that respondents may have relied on their own understanding of sexual posing rather than on the definition given to them.

Results

The respondents had a total of 1,114 cumulative years of experience in death investigation, averaging 25 years per investigator. The respondents collectively estimated that they had investigated, supervised, or consulted on 44,541 homicide investigations, averaging 1,035 homicides per investigator.

It was also estimated that there were 428 cases of sexual posing within the total number of homicides (<1%). On average, each investigator had been involved with 10 sexually posed homicides in his or her career. Of these cases, however, only 76 cases provided sufficient detailed information for further descriptive analysis (Table 14.3 and Table 14.4).

Table 14.3   Characteristics of Staged Crime Victims and Crime Features

Characteristic	N	%
Sex		
Female	181	98
Male	4	2
Race		
White	127	69
Nonwhite	58	31
Type of Offense		
Serial murder	81	44
Rape/sodomy	58	31
Lust	24	13
Interpersonal	22	12
Motivation for Posing		
Fantasy	131	71
Anger/retaliation	40	22
Misdirect investigation	14	7
Body Presentation		
Nude	127	69
Partial nude	58	31

Table 14.4   Motivation of Offender and Mode of Killing

Mode of Killing	Fantasy (N = 131)	Anger/Retaliation (N = 40)	Misdirect Investigation[a] (N = 14)
Strangulation	91 (69%)	26 (65%)	8 (57%)
Stabbing	26 (20%)	9 (22%)	3 (21%)
Blunt trauma	9 (7%)	3 (8%)	1 (7%)
All other	5 (4%)	2 (5%)	2 (14%)

[a] Percentages may not total to 100% due to rounding.

Determining Motivation

In any investigation, and especially in a homicide investigation, the determination of the offender's motive is extremely important. A detailed examination of motivation in sexually posed homicides was possible in 76 of the cases provided by the survey respondents. In addition to those cases, the author had access to another 109 such cases in his own personal files that were included in the dataset. In each of the 185 cases, full documentation, such as crime scene photographs, the offender's statements and confession, investigative reports, and other such reports, was available. The reports included the race and age of the victim and offender, the type of sex-related activity (rape, sodomy, etc.), the state in which the homicide occurred, the modality of death (strangulation, stabbing, etc.), the presentation of the body at the scene (nude, leg and arm position, etc), and the offender's expressed motivation for the sexual posing or positioning of the victim's body.

Motivations for Sexually Posing the Victim

The characteristics of the 185 cases, including the victim's race and sex and the features of the crimes themselves, are summarized in Table 14.3. An examination of the *motivations* of these offenders in the accumulated case files revealed the following percentages for each of the categories of sexual posing:

1. Sexual fantasy. The most prevalent motive is fantasy-driven behavior (71%).
2. Anger/retaliation. The second most frequent motivation was anger/retaliation (22%).
3. Staging the scene. The third was to misdirect the investigation (7%).

Table 14.3 illustrates that the majority of the victims were white females. In addition, most of the cases that involved sexual posing (44%) occurred in cases involving serial murders (two or more).

Of the 185 cases, 131 (71%) indicated that it was the offender's sexual fantasy that motivated him to stage the crime scene. These were fantasy-driven behaviors (Table 14.4). The offenders did this staging in order to obtain sexual satisfaction by propping the body in a certain way, by mutilation of body parts, by defeminization (e.g., removal of breasts), and by evisceration for the purposes of fulfilling a fantasy, not an anger-excitation definition employed by some researchers.

In 40 (22%) of the cases, the offender was motivated to stage the scene, that is, pose the victim's body, out of anger/retaliation. This staging was a deliberate effort to further degrade the victim. Typically, the posing consisted of spreading open the victim's legs to expose the genitalia, insertion of objects into sexual orifices, propping up the buttocks, or exposing the breasts to further degrade the victim.

Finally, staging was rare; in only 14 (7%) instances did the offender stage the crime scene in a deliberate effort to make a homicide appear to be sex-related when it was not. In these cases, the offender actually committed the homicide while engaged in violent, but nonsexual, activity.

The posing was essentially an afterthought, a countermeasure intended to mislead the investigative effort.

Strangulation the Most Frequent Modality of Death

The mode of death in relation to the offenders' known motivation was also examined. Those results are shown in Table 14.4. In these cases, across all categories of offenders' motivation, the most frequent mode of death was strangulation followed by stabbing. Other modes were relatively infrequent.

The high percentage of strangulation (125 of 185 cases) present in these data is of significant investigative importance. In sex-related homicides, strangulation in combination with bondage and other torture is employed to enhance the killer's sexual arousal. The data in this report indicate that the most common modality of death was through both manual and ligature strangulation and was used in 71% of the sexually posed events. Many times, murder events can be linked through nothing more than the unique configuration of the ligatures. There is a high frequency of fantasy involved with sexual arousal through strangulation. In some cases, an offender may engage in elaborate bondage. The killer often links the restraints used for strangulation to control the amount of pressure on the victim's throat. In this way he is able to manipulate and control the victim's movement to enhance her fear and terror, which satisfies an underlying psychosexual need of the offender. Strangulation also provides a hands-on power over life and death, which makes an offender feel powerful. In fact, it may be this need for power that drives the fantasy of the offender in cases involving sexual posing of the victim's body. Even though this phenomenon is not common it would be of great value to those involved in homicide investigations to develop more complete and thorough data on this topic. (For additional research information, see Table 14.5 at end of this chapter.)

Investigative Application of the "Signature" Aspect

When an offender displays behavior within the crime scene and engages in activities that go beyond those necessary to accomplish the act, he is revealing his *signature*. These significant personality identifiers occur when an offender repeatedly engages in a specific order of sexual activity, uses a specific type of binding, injures and/or inflicts similar type injuries, displays the body for shock value, tortures and mutilates his victim, and engages in some form of ritualistic behavior, such as **piquerism**. One of the most common signatures is that of the psychopathic sexual sadist, who involves himself in complete domination of the victim. The author has reviewed and consulted on a number of serial murder cases that have revealed this signature aspect of the crime.

Piquerism

"Piquerism is the sexual inclination to stab, pierce, or cut. The offender obtains sexual gratification from the shedding of blood, tearing of flesh, and/or observing such pain and suffering of a victim who is being subjected to this activity" (Geberth, 2006, p. 471). Oftentimes, the medical examiner will refer to these types of injuries as "punctuate abrasions," which is the correct forensic description of this pathology.

In an investigative analysis, we would consider these types of injuries consistent with the psychopathology of the offender and this aspect would also be part of the signature component. This particular form of sexual deviation occurs when an offender employs knives, ice picks, or other sharpened instruments to penetrate the victim's body. The specific focus may be on sexual components of the victim's body, such as the breasts, buttocks, or genitalia. In some cases, the piquerism may be employed as a form of substitute penis penetration. However, the author has observed other cases where an offender simply engaged in repeated percussion-type stabbing and penetration of various parts of a victim's body and, although sexually motivated, the offender targeted portions of the body, which could be considered sexual regions in male homosexual events, such as the back and neck of the victim (Figures 14.17 through 14.20).

Practical Examples of Signature Activity

It should be noted that the possible examples of "signature" activity is incalculable because it is based on an offender's fantasies, which could encompass just about anything. The

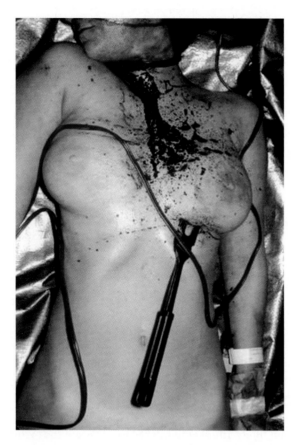

Figure 14.17 Piquerism. Body at morgue. Barbeque fork used as instrument of piquerism. (Photo courtesy of the author.)

author, however, has listed some examples based on the cases that he has personally been involved with in his capacity as a homicide consultant.

- An offender slowly cuts the clothes from his victim's body.
- An offender rips or tears the clothes from the victim's body.
- An offender makes the victim remove her own clothing.
- An offender exercises "total control" over his victim.
- The offender binds his victim in an explicit manner, e.g., hog ties, slip knots, noose, ligature around the neck.
- Offender uses specific type of binding material, e.g., rope, duct tape, adhesive tape, parachute cord, hemp, wire, electric cord, nautical rope. This can also have significance as to employment.
- An offender gags and blindfolds his victims.
- An offender rapes his victims while their hands are tied behind their backs.
- An offender binds his victim nude.
- An offender engages in postmortem binding.
- An offender engages in sexual assault with bound victim.
- An offender engages in a specific sequence of sexual assault activity with the victim, e.g., anal assault followed by forced fellatio and then rape.

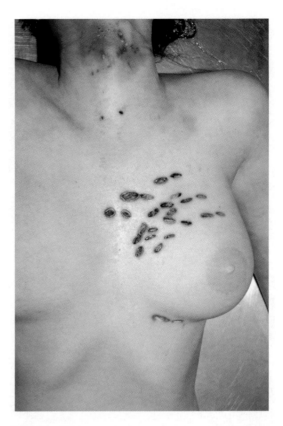

Figure 14.48 Piquerism. Body after being washed to illustrate the piquerism wounds directed into her left breast. (Photo courtesy of the author.)

- An offender dresses his victim in clothing or undergarments that he brought to the scene or do not belong to the victim.
- An offender brings along sex toys or instrument to use on the victim.
- An offender masturbates on his victim's body
- An offender brings petroleum jelly to use in his sexual assault.
- An offender poses the body in a specific manner, e.g., nude, legs spread, buttock raised, face-down, face-up, in a "sleeping position," covered, redressed, etc.
- An offender "stalks" a specific type of victim.
- An offender engages in antemortem mutilation and torture.
- An offender engages in postmortem mutilation.
- An offender engages in necrophilia.
- An offender engages in anthropophagy (consumption of blood and/or flesh).
- An offender removes body parts, e.g. breast, nipples, vulva, penis, buttock, hands, feet, head, scalp, etc.
- An offender displays the victim's body parts for "shock value."
- An offender places the body parts of his victim into their mouths or cavity of their body, e.g., stuffing the severed breast into the mouth of the victim, jamming the severed penis down the neck of the decapitated victim, etc.
- An offender "props" the body with some item from the scene or with something he brought to the event. Any posing, propping, or insertion of objects into the sexual orifices or portions of the body is considered signature.

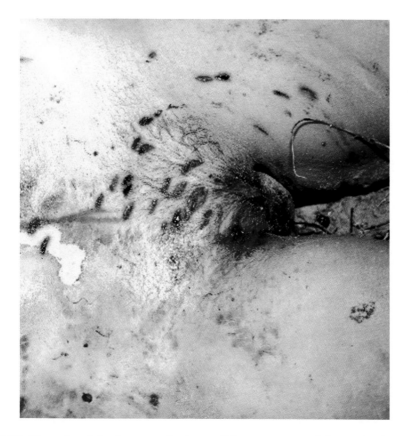

Figure 14.19 Piquerism injuries to vaginal area. (Photo courtesy of the author.)

- An offender multiply stabs his victim in sexual areas, e.g., breasts, buttock, chest, genitalia; overkill-type injuries.
- How an offender kills his victims.
- An offender targets a female victim with a child. Because of her child, the victim will cooperate with his demands.
- An offender climbs into the victim's bed as she sleeps, takes her by surprise, and attacks her in her bed.
- An offender manually strangles his victim.
- An offender uses ligature in his strangulations, e.g., rope, clothing, or something he brought to the scene.
- An offender shoots his victims in specific areas: head, chest, etc.
- An offender uses a specific type of weapon.
- An offender uses blunt force trauma to the head or engages in savage beating of his victims.

Remember that this signature aspect is a unique and integral part of the offender's behavior and that he requires these rituals in order to achieve sexual satisfaction. As stated previously within the text, this signature element is basically an attempt on the part of the offender to replicate a sexual fantasy. A sexual fantasy is a fantasy and, as such, it cannot ever actually become a reality. However, the harder one tries to duplicate or reproduce the fantasy, the more specific the **signature.**

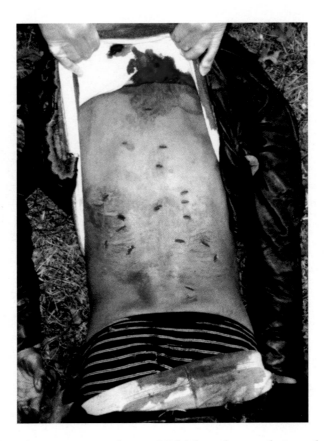

Figure 14.20 Piquerism. Homosexual case. Multiple stab wounds into the back consistent with piquerism. (Photo courtesy of the author.)

Table 14.5   Sexual Posing Cases

	R/G/A[a]	Type Murder	State	Modality of Death	Presentation	I/O[b]	Motivation[c]
1	H/F 38	Rape/Sodomy	FL	Multiply Stabbed	Totally Nude/Legs Bent to Chest	In	Fantasy Driven
2	W/F 20	Interpersonal	NC	Strangulation	Semi-Nude/Bound	Out	Sexual Staging
3	B/F 34	Lust	MI	Strangulation/Stabbed	Nude/Sex Mutilation/Displayed/Lust	Out	Fantasy Driven
4	W/F 15	Serial Murder	IL	Stabbed	Semi-Nude/Breasts Exposed	Out	Fantasy Driven
5	W/F 37	Rape/Sodomy	PA	Strangulation	Breasts Exposed/Nude Waist Down	Out	Sexual Staging
6	W/F 23	Interpersonal	LA	Stabbing	Semi-Nude/Displayed	In	Anger/Retaliation
7	W/F 21	Rape/Sodomy	PA	Strangulation/Stabbed	Nude/Displayed/Legs Spread	In	Fantasy Driven
8	W/F 43	Rape/Sodomy	MI	Hypothermia	Nude/Displayed	Out	Anger/Retaliation
9	W/F 13	Lust	MI	Strangulation	Nude/Legs Spread/Cutting to Breast	In	Fantasy Driven
10	B/F 20	Serial Murder	NC	Strangulation	Nude/Bathtub	In	Anger/Retaliation
11	B/F 33	Serial Murder	MO	Strangulation	Nude/Displayed	Out	Fantasy Driven
12	W/F 32	Serial Murder	WA	Strangulation/Blunt Trauma	Nude/Displayed/Legs Spread	In	Fantasy Driven
13	W/F 84	Rape/Sodomy	NY	Stabbing/Blunt Trauma	Nude/Displayed	In	Anger/Retaliation
14	W/F 63	Rape/Sodomy	MI	Strangulation/Hanged	Hanged/Nude/Broomstick in Vagina	In	Fantasy Driven
15	W/F 23	Rape/Sodomy	NC	Strangulation	Nude/Displayed/Legs Spread	In	Fantasy Driven
16	W/F 14	Rape/Sodomy	MI	Strangulation	Partially Nude/Skirt Up/Legs Open	In	Fantasy Driven
17	W/F 46	Lust	FL	Multiply Stabbed	Nude Waist Down/Stabbing into Chest	In	Fantasy Driven
18	W/F 56	Rape/Sodomy	FL	Strangulation	Nude Waist Down/Breasts Exposed	Out	Fantasy Driven
19	W/F 22	Serial Murder	NY	Strangulation	Totally Nude, Face Down/Buttocks up	Out	Fantasy Driven
20	W/F 15	Serial Murder	CT	Strangulation	Nude/Body in Woods	Out	Fantasy Driven
21	W/F 27	Serial Murder	NJ	Smothered	Partially Clothed/Dumped	Out	Fantasy Driven
22	B/F 16	Rape/Sodomy	PA	Multiply Stabbed	Partially Nude/On Back/Urinated On	Out	Anger/Retaliation
23	W/F 25	Rape/Sodomy	KS	Stabbed	Nude/Legs Spread, Bottle	In	Anger/Retaliation
24	W/F 15	Serial Murder	VA	Strangulation	Nude/Bound/Face Down	In	Fantasy Driven
25	B/F 33	Rape/Sodomy	OH	Strangulation	Partially Nude/Posed/Legs Spread/Insertion	Out	Anger/Retaliation
26	W/F 34	Serial Murder	NY	Asphyxiated	Partially Nude/Face Down/Buttocks up	Out	Fantasy Driven
27	W/F 73	Rape/Sodomy	PA	Strangulation	Nude/Hands behind Back/Genitalia Out	In	Fantasy Driven

Continued

Table 14.5 Sexual Posing Cases (*Continued*)

	R/G/A[a]	Type Murder	State	Modality of Death	Presentation	I/O[b]	Motivation[c]
28	B/F 29	Interpersonal	NY	Strangulation/Blunt Trauma	Nude/Wrapped in Blanket	Out	Sexual Staging
29	W/F 36	Lust	MI	Strangulation/Blunt Trauma	Nude/Legs Spread/Insertion	Out	Fantasy Driven
30	W/F 20	Serial Murder	CA	Strangulation/Blunt Trauma	Partially Nude/Hog Tied/Body Buried	Out	Fantasy Driven
31	W/F 26	Rape/Sodomy	TX	Stab/Throat Cut	Nude/Displayed/Legs Spread	In	Anger/Retaliation
32	B/F 50	Serial Murder	IL	Strangulation	Nude/Bondage	Out	Fantasy Driven
33	W/F 35	Serial Murder	VA	Strangulation	Nude/Bound/Face Down	In	Fantasy Driven
34	W/F 62	Serial Murder	KS	Strangulation	Semi-Nude/Displayed	Out	Fantasy Driven
35	W/F 10	Serial Murder	WA	Stabbed	Nude/Buried/Posed	Out	Fantasy Driven
36	W/F 22	Rape/Sodomy	MI	Suffocation	Nude/Waist Down/Genitals Exposed	In	Fantasy Driven
37	W/F 31	Serial Murder	DE	Strangulation[a]	Nude/Displayed/Exposed	Out	Fantasy Driven
38	W/F 16	Serial Murder	NY	Strangulation/Decapitated	Nude/Displayed/Decapitated	In	Fantasy Driven
39	W/F 21	Serial Murder	NY	Strangulation	Totally Nude/On Back/Bondage Marks	Out	Fantasy Driven
40	W/F 39	Rape/Sodomy	CO	Strangulation	Nude/Legs Spread/Piquerism	In	Fantasy Driven
41	W/F 14	Rape/Sodomy	NJ	Stabbed	Partially Nude/Part Buried/Breasts Exposed	Out	Fantasy Driven
42	W/M 10	Lust	PA	Disemboweled/Stab	Nude/Disembowled/Castrated/Bound	Out	Fantasy Driven
43	W/F 36	Rape/Sodomy	NC	Stab/Throat Cut	Nude/Breasts Stabbed	In	Anger/Retaliation
44	W/F 55	Serial Murder	MI	Strangulation/Stabbed	Nude/Displayed/Buttocks Up	In	Fantasy Driven
45	W/F 25	Serial Murder	DE	Strangulation/Blunt Trauma	Nude/Displayed	Out	Fantasy Driven
46	W/F 26	Lust	NY	Strangulation/Blunt Trauma	Totally Nude/Sex Multilation/Displayed/Lust	Out	Fantasy Driven
47	W/F 32	Serial Murder	MI	Strangulation	Nude/Legs Spread/Breasts Exposed	Out	Fantasy Driven
48	H/F 81	Rape/Sodomy	FL	Multiply Stabbed	Partially Nude/Back/Legs Spread	In	Fantasy Driven
49	W/F 23	Rape/Sodomy	NY	Strangulation/Stabbed	Nude/Displayed/Throat Cut	In	Anger/Retaliation
50	W/F 25	Serial Murder	KS	Strangulation	Semi-Nude/Displayed	In	Fantasy Driven
51	W/F 74	Rape/Sodomy	MI	Strangulation/Hanged	Hanged/Nude/Bound/Sexual Penetration	In	Anger/Retaliation
52	H/F 43	Rape/Sodomy	KS	Strangulation/Decapitated	Nude/Legs Spread/Burned	Out	Fantasy Driven
53	W/F 37	Interpersonal	OH	Stabbing/Shot	Totally Nude/Sexual Mutilation/Lust Murder	In	Fantasy Driven
55	W/F 33	Rape/Sodomy	MI	Blunt Force Trauma	Partially Nude/Face Down in Tub	In	Anger/Retaliation
56	W/F 29	Serial Murder	NY	Strangulation	Totally Nude, Face Down/Buttocks Up	Out	Fantasy Driven

57	W/F 29	Serial Murder	NY	Strangulation/Decapitated	Nude/Displayed/Decapitated	In	Fantasy Driven
58	W/F 22	Rape/Sodomy	MI	Strangulation	Nude/Legs Spread/Insertion	In	Anger/Retaliation
59	W/F 29	Rape/Sodomy	MI	Strangulation	Nude/Face Down/Bathtub	In	Anger/Retaliation
60	B/F 33	Serial Murder	IL	Strangulation	Semi-Nude/Displayed	Out	Fantasy Driven
61	B/F 32	Serial Murder	MI	Blunt Force Trauma	Nude Waist Down/Legs Spread	Out	Fantasy Driven
62	W/F 44	Rape/Sodomy	IL	Strangulation	Legs Spread/Breast Total Nude	Out	Fantasy Driven
63	B/F 19	Interpersonal	MI	Strangulation/Stabbed/BT	Nude/Displayed	Out	Sexual Staging
64	W/F 32	Serial Murder	VA	Strangulation	Nude/Bound/Face Down	In	Fantasy Driven
65	W/F 15	Serial Murder	IL	Stabbed	Semi-Nude/Piquerism	Out	Fantasy Driven
66	B/F 20	Serial Murder	NC	Strangulation	Nude/Bathtub	In	Anger/Retaliation
67	W/F 53	Serial Murder	KS	Strangulation	Nude/Displayed	In	Fantasy Driven
68	W/F 32	Serial Murder	VA	Strangulation	Nude/Bound/Face Down	In	Fantasy Driven
69	B/F 18	Serial Murder	NC	Strangulation	Partially Nude/Clothing in Disarray	In	Anger/Retaliation
70	W/F 22	Interpersonal	TX	Strangulation/Throat Cut	Nude/Displayed	In	Anger/Retaliation
71	W/F 18	Rape/Sodomy	OH	Strangulation	Nude/Legs Spread/Breasts Exposed	Out	Anger/Retaliation
72	B/F 32	Interpersonal	NY	Strangulation	Nude/Displayed/Propped	In	Sexual Staging
73	B/F 28	Serial Murder	NY	Strangulation	Hands behind Back/Nude Face Up	Out	Fantasy Driven
74	W/F 29	Rape/Sodomy	AZ	Strangulation/Blunt Trauma	Semi-Nude/Clothing Cut Off	In	Fantasy Driven
75	W/F 34	Serial Murder	MI	Strangulation	Nude Waist Down/Breasts Exposed	Out	Fantasy Driven
76	W/F 35	Rape/Sodomy	FL	Multiply Stabbed	Nude Waist Down/Breasts Exposed	Out	Fantasy Driven
77	W/F 19	Serial Murder	FL	Strangulation/Decapitated	Nude/Mutilated/Eviscerated	In	Fantasy Driven
78	B/F 39	Rape/Sodomy	PA	Strangulation	Nude Waist Down/Legs Spread	Out	Anger/Retaliation
79	W/F 14	Serial Murder	WA	Stabbing/Blunt Trauma	Totally Nude/Sex Mutilation/Lust	In	Fantasy Driven
80	W/F 48	Serial Murder	WA	Stabbing	Totally Nude/Sex Mutilation/Lust	In	Fantasy Driven
81	W/F 18	Rape/Sodomy	MI	Strangulation	Nude in Field/Legs Spread	Out	Fantasy Driven
82	B/F 50	Serial Murder	MO	Strangulation	Nude/Displayed	Out	Fantasy Driven
83	W/F 70	Rape/Sodomy	OH	Blunt Force Trauma	Nude/Arson to Cover Crime	In	Fantasy Driven
84	B/F 27	Interpersonal	NY	Strangulation/Stabbed	Nude/Displayed/Legs Spread	In	Anger/Retaliation
85	B/F 29	Serial Murder	MI	Blunt Force Trauma	Nude/Waist Down/Legs Spread	In	Fantasy Driven
86	W/F 37	Lust	FL	Strangulation/Decapitated	Totally Nude/Evisceration/Breasts Removed	In	Fantasy Driven

Continued

Table 14.5 Sexual Posing Cases (Continued)

	R/G/A[a]	Type Murder	State	Modality of Death	Presentation	I/O[b]	Motivation[c]
87	B/F 21	Serial Murder	NC	Strangulation	Partially Nude/Displayed	In	Anger/Retaliation
88	B/F 19	Interpersonal	NY	Strangulation/Blunt Trauma	Nude/Displayed/KKK Carved into Skin	Out	Sexual Staging
89	B/F 41	Rape/Sodomy	FL	Strangulation/Blunt Trauma	Nude Waist Down/Breast/Legs Spread	Out	Fantasy Driven
90	W/F 17	Rape/Sodomy	NY	Stabbing/Blunt Trauma	Semi-Nude/Rocks over Vagina	Out	Fantasy Driven
91	W/F 40	Lust	TX	Strangulation/Decapitated	Nude/Mutilated/Piquerism	Out	Fantasy Driven
92	W/F 32	Lust	LA	Multiply Stabbed	Totally Nude/Knife in Back/Legs Spread	In	Fantasy Driven
93	W/F 12	Rape/Sodomy	MN	Strangulation/Hanged	Hanged/Semi-Nude/Stab	I	Fantasy Driven
94	W/F 18	Serial Murder	FL	Stabbing	Nude/Displayed/Nipples Cut	In	Fantasy Driven
95	W/F 24	Serial Murder	WA	Strangulation/Stabbed/BT	Nude/Displayed/Piquerism.	In	Anger/Retaliation
96	W/F 53	Lust	VI	Stabbed/Machete	Nude/Mutilated/Eviscerated	Out	Fantasy Driven
97	B/F 25	Serial Murder	NC	Strangulation	Partially Nude	In	Fantasy Driven
98	W/F 16	Rape/Sodomy	MI	Strangulation	Nude Waist Down/Legs Spread	In	Anger/Retaliation
99	W/F 22	Interpersonal	CO	Stabbing	Nude/Displayed/Legs Spread	In	Sexual Staging
100	W/F 16	Lust	MI	Strangulation	Totally Nude/Legs Open/Insertion Tree Branch	Out	Fantasy Driven
101	B/F 20	Serial Murder	NC	Strangulation	Totally Nude/Body Skeletonized	Out	Fantasy Driven
102	W/F 9	Rape/Sodomy	IN	Strangulation/Hanged	Semi-Nude/Hanged	Out	Fantasy Driven
103	W/F 41	Serial Murder	MI	Strangulation/Stabbed	Nude/Displayed/Buttocks Up	In	Fantasy Driven
104	W/F 29	Rape/Sodomy	PA	Strangulation	Nude/Displayed/Legs Spread	Out	Fantasy Driven
105	W/F 25	Interpersonal	IL	Strangulation/Stabbed	Nude/Displayed/Piquerism	In	Fantasy Driven
106	W/F 26	Serial Murder	KS	Strangulation	Nude/Legs Spread/Note	In	Fantasy Driven
107	W/F 33	Lust	LA	Multiply Stabbed	Breasts Cut Off/In Mouth/Total Nude	In	Fantasy Driven
108	W/F 43	Rape/Sodomy	MI	Blunt Trauma	Nude/Displayed	In	Anger/Retaliation
109	W/F 24	Serial Murder	KY	Strangulation	Semi-Nude/Displayed	Out	Fantasy Driven
110	W/F 36	Serial Murder	CA	Stabbing/Shot	Sexual Mutilation/Lust Murder	In	Fantasy Driven
111	W/F 23	Rape/Sodomy	MI	Strangulation	Semi-Nude/Genitals Exposed	Out	Fantasy Driven
112	B/F 30	Serial Murder	NY	Strangulation	Hands behind Back/Nude Face Up	Out	Fantasy Driven
113	W/F 51	Lust	WA	Strangulation/Stabbed	Semi-Nude/Clothes Cut	In	Fantasy Driven
114	B/F 45	Serial Murder	MI	Blunt Force Trauma	Nude/Back/Legs Spread	In	Fantasy Driven

115	B/F 36	Lust	NY	Stabbing/Throat Cut	Sex Mutilation/Displayed/Lust	Out	Fantasy Driven
116	H/F 23	Lust	NY	Strangulation/Stabbed	Nude/Displayed/Knife in Chest	In	Anger/Retaliation
117	H/F 28	Interpersonal	NY	Strangulation/Stabbed	Nude/Displayed/Legs Spread	In	Anger/Retaliation
118	H/M 28	Interpersonal	NY	Stabbed	Nude/Displayed/Buttocks Up	Out	Anger/Retaliation
119	W/F 35	Rape/Sodomy	AK	Strangulation	Nude/Legs Spread	In	Fantasy Driven
120	W/F 18	Lust	IL	Strangulation	Totally Nude/Mutilated/Eviscerated		Fantasy Driven
121	W/F 34	Interpersonal	NJ	Stabbing/Blunt Trauma	Nude/Displayed	Out	Sexual Staging
122	W/F 29	Serial Murder	SC	Strangulation/Hanged	Semi-Nude/**Hanged**	In	Fantasy Driven
123	B/F 36	Lust	NY	Stab/Throat Cut	Semi-Nude/Mutilated	In	Sexual Staging
124	W/F 53	Rape/Sodomy	NY	Strangulation	Nude/Legs Spread/Breasts Exposed	In	Anger/Retaliation
125	W/F 46	Rape/Sodomy	UT	Strangulation/Stabbed/Burn	Nude/Bound/Burned Alive	In	Anger/Retaliation
126	H/F 32	Interpersonal	MI	Asphyxiation	Totally Nude/Staged Crime Scene	Out	Sexual Staging
127	H/F 35	Interpersonal	NY	Strangulation/Blunt Trauma	Nude/Displayed	In	Sexual Staging
128	W/M 38	Lust	MI	Strangulation/Decapitated	Nude/Mutilated/Eviscerated	In	Fantasy Driven
129	W/F 11	Serial Murder	KS	Strangulation/Hanged	Semi-Nude/**Hanged**	In	Fantasy Driven
130	W/F 32	Rape/Sodomy	KS	Strangulation	Nude/Legs Spread/Bathtub	In	Fantasy Driven
131	W/F 23	Serial Murder	FL	Stabbing	Nude/Displayed/Vagina Cut	In	Fantasy Driven
132	W/F 16	Serial Murder	NY	Strangulation	Semi-Nude/Body Dumped	Out	Fantasy Driven
133	W/F 33	Serial Murder	MI	Strangulation	Semi-Nude/Displayed	Out	Fantasy Driven
134	W/F 27	Serial Murder	WA	Strangulation/Blunt Trauma	Nude/Displayed	Out	Fantasy Driven
135	H/F 22	Lust	NY	Stabbing	Semi-Nude/Displayed	In	Fantasy Driven
136	W/F 17	Serial Murder	FL	Stabbing	Nude/Displayed/Nipples Removed	In	Fantasy Driven
137	B/F 31	Serial Murder	MI	Strangulation	Nude/Waist Down/Legs Spread	In	Fantasy Driven
138	W/F 16	Lust	CAN	Stabbing/Bunt Trauma	Partially Nude/Sex Multilation/Displayed	Out	Fantasy Driven
139	W/F 43	Serial Murder	MI	Stabbed	Partially Nude/Legs Spread/Middle of Road	Out	Anger/Retaliation
140	H/F 26	Serial Murder	NY	Strangulation	Bound behind Back/Posed Nude Face Up	Out	Fantasy Driven
141	W/F 34	Serial Murder	NY	Strangulation	Nude/Lust/Breasts Removed	In	Fantasy Driven
142	W/M 40	Interpersonal	OH	Blunt Force Trauma	Nude/Suspended/Bound/Sex Play Room	In	Anger/Retaliation
143	H/F 33	Serial Murder	FL	Strangulation/Stabbed	Semi-Nude/Mutilated	Out	Anger/Retaliation
144	H/F 28	Interpersonal	NY	Strangulation	Nude/Displayed	In	Sexual Staging

Continued

Table 14.5   Sexual Posing Cases (*Continued*)

	R/G/A[a]	Type Murder	State	Modality of Death	Presentation	I/O[b]	Motivation[c]
145	W/F 21	Lust	PA	Stabbing	Nude/Displayed/Bondage/Eviscerated	In	Fantasy Driven
146	B/F 14	Rape/Sodomy	MI	Strangulation	Nude/Back/Legs Spread	In	Anger/Retaliation
147	H/F 36	Rape/Sodomy	MI	Strangulation/Hanged	Hanged/Nude/Bound/Sexual Penetration	In	Fantasy Driven
148	W/F 26	Rape/Sodomy	SC	Strangulation/Hanged	Semi-Nude/Hanged/Breasts Exposed	In	Fantasy Driven
149	W/F 22	Rape/Sodomy	NM	Strangulation	Nude/Displayed	Out	Fantasy Driven
150	B/F 31	Rape/Sodomy	PA	Strangulation/Stabbed	Totally Nude/Hog Tied/Displayed	Out	Anger/Retaliation
151	W/F 22	Lust	PA	Stabbing/Blunt Force Trauma	Totally Nude/Sex Mutilation/Displayed	Out	Fantasy Driven
152	W/F 31	Rape/Sodomy	FL	Blunt Force Trauma	Totally Nude/Buttocks Up	Out	Fantasy Driven
153	W/F 20	Lust	WA	Strangulation/Stabbed	Totally Nude/Sex Mutilation/Displayed	Out	Fantasy Driven
154	B/F 35	Serial Murder	MO	Strangulation	Nude/Displayed	Out	Fantasy Driven
155	B/F 35	Serial Murder	NC	Strangulation	Semi-Nude	In	Fantasy Driven
156	W/F 35	Rape/Sodomy	FL	Strangulation	Nude Waist Down/Breasts Exposed	In	Fantasy Driven
157	W/F 20	Interpersonal	NY	Blunt Trauma	Semi-Nude/Breaasts Exposed	O	Sexual Staging
158	B/F 33	Serial Murder	NC	Strangulation	Nude/Ligature on Neck	In	Fantasy Driven
159	W/F 34	Rape/Sodomy	FL	Strangulation/Stabbed	Totally Nude/Multiple Knife Wounds Torso	Out	Fantasy Driven
160	W/F 19	Serial Murder	CT	Strangulation	Nude/Face Down/Buttocks Exposed	Out	Fantasy Driven
161	B/F 20	Serial Murder	NC	Strangulation	Partially Nude	In	Fantasy Driven
162	W/F 29	Serial Murder	NY	Asphyxiated	Totally Nude, Face Down/Buttocks Up	Out	Fantasy Driven
163	W/F 19	Serial Murder	NJ	Strangulation	Nude/Displayed/Breast Assault	In	Fantasy Driven
164	W/F 30	Rape/Sodomy	CO	Strangulation	Nude/Legs Spread/Pubic Area Shaved	In	Anger/Retaliation
165	B/F 36	Serial Murder	MO	Strangulation	Nude/Decomposed	Out	Fantasy Driven

	R/G/A					I[b]	
166	B/F 29	**Rape/Sodomy**	PA	**Multiply Stabbed**	Nude/Back/Legs Spread/Urinated On	Out	**Anger/Retaliation**
167	B/F 38	Serial Murder	MI	**Blunt Force Trauma**	Nude/Back/Legs Spread	Out	Fantasy Driven
168	O/F 25	Serial Murder	NY	Strangulation	Semi-Nude	Out	Fantasy Driven
169	W/F 44	Serial Murder	VA	Strangulation	Nude/Bound/Face Down	In	Fantasy Driven
170	W/F 22	Interpersonal	OH	**Shot**	Nude/Supine/Legs Spread/Mother Killed	In	Sexual Staging
171	W/F 28	Serial Murder	KS	Strangulation	Nude/Bound/Displayed	In	Fantasy Driven
172	W/F 10	Rape/Sodomy	OK	Strangulation	Semi-Nude/Bound with Tape	Out	Fantasy Driven
173	B/F 23	Serial Murder	IL	Strangulation	Nude/Displayed	Out	Fantasy Driven
174	B/F 14	Serial Murder	NY	Strangulation	Semi-Nude/Breasts Exposed	Out	Fantasy Driven
175	W/F 22	Serial Murder	CA	Stabbing/Shot	Nude/Mutilated/Eviscerated	In	Fantasy Driven
176	B/F 22	Interpersonal	NY	Strangulation/Stabbed/BT[a]	Nude/Mutilated/Eviscerated	In	Anger/Retaliation
177	W/F 28	Serial Murder	KS	Strangulation	Semi-Nude/Displayed	In	Fantasy Driven
178	W/F 22	Serial Murder	NY	Strangulation	Totally Nude, Bent Over	Out	Fantasy Driven
179	W/F 26	Rape/Sodomy	AR	**Strangulation/Stab/Hanged**	Semi-Nude/**Hanged**	In	Anger/Retaliation
180	B/F 36	Serial Murder	IL	Strangulation	Nude/Decomposed	Out	Fantasy Driven
181	H/F 28	Lust	FL	**Beaten**	Totally nude, Legs Spread/Breast Bitten	In	Fantasy Driven
182	B/F 20	Rape/Sodomy	KS	Strangulation	Nude/Legs Spread/Decomposed	Out	Anger/Retaliation
183	B/F/36	Serial Murder	MI	**Blunt Force Trauma**	Nude/Legs Spread	Out	Fantasy Driven
184	W/F 28	Rape/Sodomy	FL	**Strangulation/Stabbed**	Nude/Displayed/Legs Spread	Out	Anger/Retaliation
185	W/F 29	Interpersonal	MS	**Disemboweled/Stab**	Semi-Nude/Burned/Mutilated	In	Anger/Retaliation
186	B/F 20	Serial Murder	MI	Strangulation	Nude/On Back/Breasts Exposed	Out	Fantasy Driven

a R = Race; G = Gender; A = Age; BT = Blunt Trauma.

b I = Inside crime scene; O = outside crime scene.

c Red indicates that posing was a sexual fantasy; green indicates anger/retaliation; blue indicates sexual staging.

References

American Psychiatric Association, *Diagnostic and Statistical Manual of Mental Disorders (DSM-IV-TR)*, 4th ed., Text revised, APA, Washington, D.C., 2000.

Cleckley, H. *The Mask of Sanity*, 5th ed., Emily S. Cleckley, Augusta, GA, 1982.

Coleman, J.C., J.N. Butcher, and R.C. Carson, *Abnormal Psychology and Modern Life*, 7th ed., Scott, Foresman & Co., Dallas, TX, 1984.

De Palma, B. (director). *The Black Dahlia*. Movie released in 2006.

de River, J.P. *Crime and the Sexual Psychopath*, Charles C Thomas, Springfield, IL, 1958.

Douglas, J.E., and C.M. Munn, The detection of staging and personation at the crime scene. In J.E. Douglas, A.W. Burgess, A.G. Burgess, R.K. Ressler (eds.), *Crime Classification Manual*. Lexington Books, New York, 1992, pp. 249–252.

Geberth, V.J. The frequency and characteristics of sexual posing in homicides, *Law and Order*, 58 (2), 2010.

Geberth, V.J. *Practical Homicide Investigation: Tactics, Procedures, and Forensic Techniques*, 4th ed., CRC Press, Boca Raton, FL, 2006.

Geberth, V.J. The investigative significance of fantasy in sex crimes. *Law and Order*, 52 (9): 94–99, November 2004.

Geberth, V.J. Domestic violence lust murder. *Law and Order*, 48 (11): 44–53, November 2000.

Geberth, V.J. Crime scene staging and alterations: The CSI effect on criminal investigations. *Journal of Professional Investigators*, 20 (2): 40–44, April 2007.

Geberth, V.J. Anatomy of a lust murder. *Law and Order*, 46 (5): 98–102, May 1998.

Geberth, V.J. Sex-related crimes. *Law and Order*, 44 (82): 77–81, August 1996a.

Geberth, V.J., *Practical Homicide Investigation: Tactics, Procedures, and Forensic Technique*, 3rd ed., CRC Press, Boca Raton, FL, 1996b.

Geberth, V.J. The staged crime scene. *Law and Order*, 44 (2): 89–91, February 1996c.

Geberth, V.J. The signature aspect in criminal investigation. *Law and Order*, 4 (11), November 1995.

Geberth, V.J. *Practical Homicide Investigation: Tactics, Procedures, and Forensic Technique*. Elsevier Science Publishing Company, New York, 1983.

Geberth, V.J. *Practical Homicide Investigation: Tactics, Procedures, and Forensic Technique*, 2nd ed., Elsevier Science Publishing Company, New York, 1990.

Hare, R.D. *Without Conscience: The Disturbing World of the Psychopaths among Us*, Pocket Books, New York, 1993.

Hazelwood, R., and M. Napier. Crime scene staging and its detection. *International Journal of Offender Therapy and Comparative Criminology*, 48 (6): 744–759, 2004.

Keppel, R., and J.D. Weiss. The rarity of unusual dispositions of victim bodies: Staging and posing. *Journal of Forensic Science*, 49 (6): 1308–1312, 2004.

Keppel, R.D. and J.D. Birnes, *Serial Violence: Analysis of Modus Operandi and Signature Characteristics of Killers*. CRC Press, Boca Raton, FL, 2009.

Money, J. *Lovemaps: Clinical Concepts of Sexual/Erotic Health and Pathology, Paraphilia, and Gender Transposition in Childhood, Adolescence, and Maturity*, Irvington Publishers, New York, 1986.

Napier, M.R. and K.P. Baker, Criminal personality profiling. In S.H. James and J.J. Nordby (eds.), *Forensic Science: An Introduction to Scientific and Investigative Techniques*. CRC Press, Boca Raton, FL, 2002, 531–550.

Ressler, R.K., A.W. Burgess, and J.E. Douglas. *Sexual Homicide: Patterns and Motives*, D.C. Heath & Company, Lexington, MA, 1988.

Ressler, R.K., A.W. Burgess, J.E. Douglas, C.R. Hartman, and R.B. D'Agostino. Sexual killers and their victims, *Journal of Interpersonal Violence*, 1 (293), 1986.

Ressler, R.K. et al. Crime scene and profile characteristics of organized and disorganized murderers, *FBI Law Enforcement Bulletin*, August, 1985, p. 19.

Webster's New World Dictionary, David B. Guralnik (Ed. in Chief), Simon & Schuster, New York, 1982.

Psychopathic Sexual Sadism
A Clinical Study

15

Introduction

The author uses the term *psychopathic sexual sadism* because it best describes offenders who engage in sexually sadistic activities, including torture, mutilation, and killing, to achieve sexual gratification. This chapter focuses on the practical application of the clinical criteria of antisocial personality disorder and sexual sadism as defined in *The Diagnostic and Statistical Manual of Mental Disorders (DMS-IV-TR)* (APA, 2000), and in the literature on psychopathy (Hare, 1993, 1999, 2003) and the concept of malignant narcissism in the co-morbidity of psychopathy and sexual sadism.

This chapter examines serial murderers who violated their victims sexually, as reported within the journalistic, academic, and law enforcement literatures. It is based on the author's experience and case studies that he has personally been involved in as well as a clinical study reported in *Journal of Forensic Science* (Geberth and Turco, 1997). One of the goals of the journal study was locating within clinical literature specific references of behavior, which could be utilized in predicting future dangerousness of serial killers whom the author describes as *psychopathic sexual sadists* (Geberth, 2006).

Historical Perspective and Definitions

Psychopathy, Sociopathy, and Antisocial Personality Disorder

The concept of a personality disorder in which an individual persists in antisocial behaviors throughout his/her lifetime without apparent guilt or remorse has a formal documented evolution that spans nearly two centuries. Pinel (1801) first observed and documented a group of patients who behaved in impulsive and self-destructive ways, yet evidenced no defects in reasoning ability. Another among the early denotations for this cluster of socially objectionable behaviors was Prichard's (1835) notion of "moral insanity."

The idea of a diseased "moral faculty" to explain criminal behavior formed the central position in much of the debate of the nineteenth century. The German psychiatric community spoke of "psychopathic inferiority," leaning toward a physical basis for the disorder (Koch, 1891). Kraepelin (1915), in successive editions of his psychiatric text from 1887 to 1915, developed the theory of psychopathy in terms of degenerate moral stature, biogenic in its origin. Similarly, Lombroso (1911) ascribed moral insanity to the "born criminal" who, he believed, suffered from a variant of epilepsy.

Meloy (1992) attributes Birnbaum (1914) with introducing the term *sociopathy* to the literature to describe the disorder as the product of social learning in a deficient formative environment, thus emphasizing a psychogenic basis. Freud (1957) notes that "among adult criminals, we must no doubt accept those who commit crimes without any sense of guilt, who have either developed no moral inhibitions, or who, in their conflict with society, consider themselves justified in their actions."

Cleckley, in his classic textbook, *The Mask of Sanity* (1981, p. 337), described 16 characteristic traits symptomatic of the psychopathic personality:

1. Superficial charm and good "intelligence"
2. Absence of delusions and other signs of irrational thinking
3. Absence of "nervousness" or psychoneurotic manifestations
4. Unreliability
5. Untruthfulness and insincerity
6. Lack of remorse or shame
7. Inadequately motivated antisocial behavior
8. Poor judgment and failure to learn by experience
9. Pathologic egocentricity and incapacity for love
10. General poverty in major affective reactions
11. Specific loss of insight
12. Unresponsiveness in general interpersonal relations
13. Fantastic and uninviting behavior with (alcoholic) drink and sometimes without
14. Suicide rarely carried out
15. Sex life impersonal, trivial, and poorly integrated
16. Failure to follow any life plan

This clinical picture includes evidence of poor judgment, irresponsibility, and lack of remorse or shame, as well as the recognition that the psychopath can be charming and successful. Reich (1945) spoke of the psychopathic character type as one who is self-assured, sometimes arrogant, elastic, energetic, and often impressive in his bearing. Notable to Reich was an absence of reaction formation on the part of the psychopath to his openly aggressive and sadistic behaviors. McCord and McCord (1956) focus on "impulsivity and aggression in an emotionally isolated individual who seeks to fulfill his craving for excitement without being inhibited by social norms or personal conscience."

Malignant Narcissism

Kernberg (1982, 1990) refers to malignant narcissism as "a form of antisocial personality disorder. In this syndrome, ego pathology is characterized by four factors: narcissistic personality structure (disorder); overt antisocial behavior (passive or aggressive) manifested by sadistic cruelty (with murder as its most extreme form); egosyntonic aggression, or sadism (a source of pleasure accepted and rationalized against the normal prohibition that most persons have against sadism); and a reprojection of primitive persecutory superego features in the form of paranoid tendencies. The sadism is characterologically integrated and justified by a chronic sadistic arrogance. The reprojection of the primitive persecutory superego features may be characterized by classifying others as suckers, fools, or dangerous enemies."

Meissner (1966) has enlarged our concept of paranoid projection to encompass this facet. According to Meissner, "The theory of the paranoid process is an extension of the theory of internalization, particularly concerning itself with those forms of internalization that have pathogenic potential."

Serial killer Dennis Rader, who called himself BTK (bind, torture, kill), certainly displayed malignant narcissism with his victims as he described in his communications with the Wichita, Kansas, authorities beginning in 1974. BTK would taunt the detectives with a series of letters and rambling poems as well as drawings, which simulated the victims in a bound fashion. His communications revealed a sadistic arrogance with a total lack of remorse or shame as he vividly described his sadistic cruelty. He bragged about stalking his victims, whom he would strangle to death. On some occasions he would photograph their nude and bound bodies. These communications suddenly stopped in 1988 (see Chapter 13).

On January 17, 2004, *The Wichita Eagle* published a story on the 30th anniversary of the Otero family murders, which was the first in a series of killings by BTK. Rader's malignant narcissism would soon be his undoing. In March 2004, BTK once again began corresponding with the authorities.

BTK sent 11 communications to the authorities between March 17, 2004, and February 2005. He thought that he was "smarter" than the police, but his narcissistic overconfidence finally caught up with him. In February 2005, BTK communicated with authorities by leaving police a floppy disk, which was eventually traced back to Rader, the BTK killer.

The BTK task force arrested Rader on February 25, 2005. He waived his rights and made full confessions to the series of murders including two additional murders, which had not been originally linked to BTK. Rader relished his self-importance as he methodically described the details of his crimes. While being questioned by authorities about the Otero murders, Rader admitted that he took the 11-year-old female down to the basement where he took off her pants and tied her up. He asked her if she had a camera because he wanted to take a picture of her. When the little girl asked what was going to happen to her, Rader told her that she was going to heaven like the rest of her family. Rader then slipped the rope over her neck and hung her. Rader stated that he masturbated while she was dying. Rader also described how he strangled Nancy Fox into unconsciousness only to revive her so he could do it again as he whispered into her ear, "I'm BTK," just before strangling her to death (Wichita Police Department, 2005).

Dennis Rader pled guilty on June 27, 2005, to being Wichita's notorious BTK who stalked and murdered 10 victims. As part of the plea deal, he described what he had done to each of his victims, whom he called "projects." Rader, who was a city compliance or animal control officer, referred to the killings of his victims as "putting them down." "In his courtroom statement, Rader said that he killed because he wanted to fulfill sexual fantasies" (*The Wichita Eagle*, 2005). He nonchalantly described the murders in a voice devoid of emotion as if he was reading from a grocery list. Rader apparently enjoyed this opportunity to perform in the courtroom before the cameras as he calmly explained his 30-year reign of terror.

From a psychodynamic perspective, serial murderers exhibit pathological self love, a lack of object love, superego pathology, and especially, a general sense of emptiness and dissatisfaction. Many of the documented serial killers were nonaffiliates or loners. By no means does this include all serial killers. By nonaffiliate, I mean the absence of total integration into a community and the experience of long-term meaningful relationships. These would be relationships with empathic connections and not just for utilitarian reasons. For example, in the case of the BTK killer, he did integrate into his community and especially his church. His position was one of control and power and people who worked with him in his capacity of an animal control officer described his behavior toward animals as cruel. When killing human beings, he described his actions as "putting them down." Associated with his affiliations were behavioral patterns indicative of control and, at the very least, abrasiveness and, at times, outright cruelty. He made psychological connections between the control of animals in his daily work and the control and destruction of human beings.

In her book, *The Sociopath Next Door*, Martha Stout (2005) describes sociopaths who "fit in" and, thus, avoid scrutiny for long periods of time. As she noted, "These people do not look like Charles Manson … . They look like us."

Many serial killers have superficial relationships with community groups and attempt to "blend in," and this is in contrast to the genuinely dedicated individuals who contribute to their communities over a lifetime.

There is an impoverishment of internal life in these nonaffiliates as a result of their having devalued what they have not received from others. In other words, there has been a failure of early object integration. The internal world of object relations is destroyed. Psychological development does not occur using normal methods of identification and empathy. There is a sense of aloneness, emptiness, and meaninglessness in life, with the absence of the pleasure of learning or empathic bonding. One finds a stimulus hunger, the need to be entertained and stimulated to replace the missing world of object relations. The perpetrator of serial murders expects the victim to perform and initiate certain behaviors to "entertain" him. A sadistic perversion of the learning experience may occur when the murderer dissects or otherwise mutilates the victim.

Psychopathy, Sociopathy, and Antisocial Personality Disorder

According to Markman and Bosco (1989), "The primary ingredient missing from the sociopath's psyche is conscience. Psychopathy, sociopathy, and antisocial personality disorder are not generally classified as a mental illness per se, but rather as a disorder of character." McCord (1983) notes that "psychopathy has been defined either as a discrete category whereby one is considered either psychopathic or not, or as representing a point along a continuum in which some individuals occupy an extreme position relative to specific traits and behaviors."

However, recent research suggests that psychopathy might be better viewed as a continuum rather than as a discrete category (Guay et al., 2004).

In an examination of psychopathy as a concept, Blackburn (1992) notes the "interchangeability of the terms *sociopath* and *psychopath*, particularly in the American literature." He notes the particular influence of Robin's work (1966, 1978), in its explicit equating of "sociopathic personality" with violation of social rules, on the determination of *DSM-IV-TR* criteria for antisocial personality disorder.

According to the *DSM-IV-TR*:

> … the essential feature of the disorder is to be found in patterns of irresponsible and antisocial behaviors beginning in childhood or early adolescence and continuing into adulthood. Lying, stealing, truancy, vandalism, initiating fights, running away from home, and physical cruelty are typical childhood signs. In adulthood, the antisocial pattern continues and may include failure to honor financial obligations, maintain consistent employment, or plan ahead. These individuals fail to conform to social norms and repeatedly engage in antisocial behaviors that are grounds for arrest, such as destroying property, harassing others, and stealing. Often these antisocial acts are committed with no seeming necessity. People with antisocial personality disorder tend toward irritability and aggressivity, and often become involved in physical fights and assaults, including spouse and child beating. Reckless behavior without

regard for personal safety is common, as indicated by driving while intoxicated or getting numerous speeding tickets. Frequently, these individuals are promiscuous, failing to sustain a monogamous relationship for more than one year. They do not learn from past experiences and tend to resume the same kinds of antisocial behaviors they were punished for. They lack feelings of remorse about the effects of their behavior on others and may feel justified in having violated others. (APA, 2000)

Psychopathy

Psychopathy is a more encompassing term than *antisocial personality disorder* and can also be quantified. Psychology is an evolving science and as better methods of quantification emerge terminology changes. The authors of the *Psychodynamic Diagnostic Manual* (*PDM*) also have a preference for the earlier term *psychopathic* over the more contemporary *antisocial*. They note, "Many people with this personality disorder are not obviously antisocial; that is, they are not in observable conflict with social norms, and, conversely, many people who meet *DSM-IV-TR* and ICD (International Classification of Diseases) criteria for antisocial personality are not characterologically psychopathic" (Alliance of Psychoanalytic Organizations, 2006).

Robert Hare has emerged as the preeminent authority and foremost expert in the area of psychopathy. He developed and perfected the Psychopathy Checklist and the PCL-R (revised), which has become the standard instrument for researchers and clinicians worldwide. In the opinion of the author, the PCL-R has proved to be the most perceptive development in the application of clinical psychology to the investigative process.

In his book *Without Conscience: The Disturbing World of the Psychopaths among Us,* Hare explained, "The term *psychopathy* literally means 'mental illness' (from *psyche*, 'mind'; and *pathos*, 'disease'" (Hare, 1993).

> Psychopathy is a personality disorder defined by a cluster of interpersonal, affective, lifestyle, and antisocial characteristics with serious, negative consequences for society. These features generally are measured by the Psychopathy Checklist Revised (PCL-R), which views psychopaths as egocentric, grandiose, arrogant, deceitful, manipulative, shallow, callous, impulsive, and sensation-seeking individuals who readily violate social norms and obligations without any sense of shame, guilt, or remorse. Among its more devastating features are a callous disregard for the rights of others and a propensity for predatory behavior and violence. Given these characteristics, as well as the extensive empirical literature on its association with criminal behavior, it is not surprising that psychopathy is widely regarded as one of the most important clinical disorders in the criminal justice system, particularly with respect to understanding and predicting criminal behavior. (Hare, personal communication, 2004)

In my opinion, the psychopath is not out of touch with reality or suffering from mental disease or defect. The psychopath is fully aware of what he does and doesn't give a damn about the consequences of his actions or their effects on others. *Psychopaths do have a classifiable psychiatric disorder.* However, they are not crazy or suffering from delusions or hallucinations. According to legal and psychiatric standards, they are not insane.

Their actions are based on a calculating rationality that is driven by self-gratification and a lack of conscience or remorse. Expressions such as "I did it because I felt like it," or "I shot him because he pissed me off," or "I killed her because she would have identified me" are common explanations offered by the psychopath. Of course, these explanations are only given if the psychopath thinks it is in his best interests to "confess" when caught. The "confessions" usually result because the psychopath is trying to negotiate a life sentence to avoid the death penalty. An example would be a suspect in a serial murder case who testifies against an accomplice or leads the authorities to the locations of buried bodies.

For clarification of terminology, the following is presented:

Antisocial Personality Disorder (APD): Refers primarily to a cluster of criminal and antisocial behaviors.

Sociopathy: Connotes that the syndrome is forged entirely from social forces and early childhood experiences.

Psychopathy: Syndrome consists of psychological, biological, and genetic factors.

Hare differentiates psychopathy from both APD and sociopathy. He believes that "psychological, biological, and genetic factors contribute to the syndrome of psychopathy," which he defines as a cluster of both personality traits and socially deviant behaviors (Hare, 1993).

Hare described what he referred to as the Key Symptoms of Psychopathy, which he divided into two groupings: emotional/interpersonal and social deviance.

Key Symptoms of Psychopathy

Emotional/Interpersonal	Social Deviance
Glib and superficial	Impulsive
Egocentric and grandiose	Poor behavior controls
Lack of remorse or guilt	Need for excitement
Lack of empathy	Lack of responsibility
Deceitful and manipulative	Early behavior problems
Shallow emotions	Adult antisocial behaviors

Source: Hare, R.D. *Without Conscience: The Disturbing World of the Psychopaths among Us,* Pocket Books, New York, 1993. With permission.

Hare (1991) also wrote, "On the interpersonal level, psychopaths are grandiose, arrogant, callous, dominant, superficial, and manipulative. Affectively, they are short-tempered, unable to form strong emotional bonds with others, and lacking in guilt or anxiety. These interpersonal and affective features are associated with a socially deviant lifestyle and that includes irresponsible and impulsive behavior, and a tendency to ignore or violate social conventions and mores." According to Hare, psychopaths have "… a deeply disturbing inability to care about the pain and suffering experienced by others."

The psychopaths' inability to appreciate the pain and suffering they inflict on others explains why they can torture and mutilate another human being without the least concern. I find this perspective consistent with observable data and applicable to the investigative process. Hare's work best represents the point of view and definition of psychopathy as expressed in this chapter.

Psychopathy: A Case History

Serial killer John Robinson is an excellent example of this psychopathology. John Robinson was a serial killer responsible for the murders of eight young women in Kansas and Missouri. Robinson, who was married, maintained a mistress in the adjoining town and also engaged in a number of extramarital affairs in addition to his numerous confidence and con games. Robinson also is a psychopathic sexual sadist who killed many of his victims, whom he met via the Internet, to fulfill his lust as a self-proclaimed "Slave Master." In the opinion of the author, Robinson is the paradigm (*Poster Boy*) for psychopathy with his superficial charm and good intelligence, coupled with his untruthfulness and insincerity, his lack of remorse and shame accompanied by a malignant narcissism.

Robinson killed his victims for self-gratification as well as financial gain. In fact, when Robinson learned that his brother and sister-in-law were trying to have a baby, but his brother's wife could not get pregnant, he immediately set up an elaborate scheme to obtain a baby. Robinson "established" a bogus program for unwed mothers and interviewed young women until he found a "white" child. He then killed the baby's mother for her child. Robinson charged his brother for "adoptive services and legal fees."

Robinson also killed a mother and her developmentally challenged daughter when he learned that they received monthly assistance checks from the government. He offered them companionship and lodging if they would come to Kansas. Once in Kansas, he advised the victim to have their government disability checks sent to his "business" post office box. Robinson continued to cash these checks until his arrest.

While Robinson was in prison for an unrelated financial crime, he managed to manipulate the prison librarian into a sexual liaison. The woman divorced her physician husband and joined Robinson after he completed his sentence. Robinson had convinced this victim that they could open and operate a major corporation, which would require world travel. He actually persuaded her to write predated letters to her relatives, which would later be mailed since they would be too busy traveling in Europe. Robinson also advised her to have her monthly alimony checks sent to his "business" post office box, which Robinson maintained for one of his bogus companies. The woman's family never heard from her again except for letters, which were being sent to them with European return addresses. Robinson used this mail ruse to cover up other murders as well.

Robinson met his other victims online through the Internet. He was able to manipulate these victims into agreeing to become sex slaves. Robinson e-mailed them a "slave contract" and paid their travel expense to Kansas. He would meet them at area motels during which time he would sexually assault and abuse them. Robinson later killed them when he was through using them, placing their bodies in 55-gallon drums on his farm or in storage lockers, which he rented through his bogus companies. Robinson's actions were based on a calculating rationality that is driven by self-gratification and a total lack of conscience or remorse (Geberth, 2006).

Sexual Sadism

According to the *Diagnostic and Statistical Manual of Mental Disorders, Fourth Edition, Text Revision (DSM-IV-TR)*, "The paraphiliac focus of sexual sadism involves acts (real, not simulated) in which the individual derives sexual excitement from the psychological or physical suffering (including humiliation) of the victim … in such cases the sadistic fantasies usually involve having complete control over the victim, who is terrified by anticipation of the impending sadistic act. Others act on the sadistic sexual urges with a consenting partner (who may have sexual masochism) who willingly suffers pain or humiliation. Still others with sexual sadism act on their sadistic sexual urges with nonconsenting victims. In all of these cases, it is the suffering of the victim that is sexually arousing. Sadistic fantasies or acts may involve activities that indicate the dominance of the person over the victim (e.g., forcing the victim to crawl or keeping the victim in a cage). They may also involve restraint, blindfolding, paddling, spanking, whipping, pinching, beating, burning, electrical shocks, rape, cutting, stabbing, strangulation, torture, mutilation, or killing" (APA, 2000).

DSM-IV-TR describes this particular paraphilia as chronic with the potential of escalation. When associated with antisocial personality disorder, which in this chapter we are defining as psychopathy, these individuals become dangerous.

Money (1986) defines a paraphilia as a "condition occurring in men and women of being compulsively responsive to and obligatively dependent upon an unusual and personally or socially unacceptable stimulus, perceived or in the imagery of fantasy, for optimal initiation and maintenance of erotosexual arousal and the facilitation or attainment of orgasm ... . Paraphilias are thus sexual deviants marked by persistent sexual arousal patterns in which unusual objects, rituals, or situations are required for sexual gratification. They are understood to reflect psychosexual disorder in which the preferred or exclusive means of sexual gratification is deviant. Unusual or bizarre imagery or acts are necessary for sexual excitement" (p. 267).

According to the *DSM IV-TR*, "... such imagery or acts tend to be insistently and involuntarily repetitive and generally involve either a preference for use of a nonhuman object for sexual arousal, repetitive sexual activity with humans involving real or simulated suffering or humiliation, or repetitive sexual activity with nonconsenting partners. Nine paraphilias are currently recognized in the *DSM-IV-TR*. These are fetishism, transvestic fetishism, voyeurism, exhibitionism, sexual sadism, sexual masochism, pedophilia, zoophilia, and frotteurism (APA, 2000, pp. 566–576). Meloy (1992) defines sexual sadism as "the conscious experience of pleasurable sexual arousal through the infliction of physical or emotional pain on the actual object."

Any discussion of sexual sadism would not be complete without the historical perspective and definition of sadism as found in the work of Richard von Krafft-Ebing. "Sadism or sexual arousal from physical suffering, humiliation, and control of the victim is at the core of serial homicide. Krafft-Ebing (1886), in fact, suggested that the essential feature of sadism is the need for "mastery and possessing an absolutely defenseless human object ... the desire for ... complete subjugation of the woman."

Krafft-Ebing's classic text *Psychopathia Sexualis*, which was first published in 1886 (reprinted in 1998), describes several cases in which sexual arousal was dependent upon a desire to inflict pain and suffering on the victim. He wrote:

> Sadism, especially in its rudimentary manifestations, seems to be of common occurrence in the domain of sexual perversion. Sadism is the experience of sexual pleasurable sensations (including orgasm) produced by acts of cruelty, bodily punishment afflicted on one's own person or when witnessed in others, be they animals or human beings. It may also consist of an innate desire to humiliate, hurt, wound or even destroy others in order thereby to create sexual pleasure in one's self.
>
> When the association of lust and cruelty is present, not only does the lustful emotions awaken the impulse to cruelty, but vice versa cruel ideas and acts of cruelty cause sexual excitement and in this way are used by perverse individuals. (Krafft-Ebing, 1998)

The sexual sadist enjoys the suffering of his victim by engaging in various forms of abuse, which include beatings, whippings, burning or submitting the victim to electrical shock, piercing the nipples and/or labia, and other forms of piquerism. The sexual sadist prefers anal insertion, usually with large dildos, over vaginal intercourse, unless it's forcible rape. In most cases, the sexual sadist will force the victims to perform fellatio, often to the point where they feel that they cannot breath. If the sexual sadist has two women under his control, he will force them to perform sexual acts on one another. During and after the assault, the victims will be referred to as "bitches, cunts, and whores." This is done to psychologically degrade them and at the same validate his feelings of contempt and hatred of women. The use of derogatory terms is likely an attempt to validate his contempt for women. This is consistent with the "dehumanization" that occurs in wartime. Anna Freud (1946) has described the need to dehumanize potential victims in an attempt to validate one's behavior and minimize self-reproach.

The lust of the psychopathic sexual sadist is rationalized in many ways, occasionally as a "duty" and at other times as a form of "love." As difficult as this may be for others to accept, it is a perverted mechanism, which ultimately leads to the destruction of the victim. The suffering and injury of the victim is likely devoid of emotion in many instances, but is a reflection of pleasure and excitement by the perpetrator. This may well be an expression of early erotic stimulation acted out in adulthood.

Fenichel (1945) has noted that early sexual excitement in the child is beyond the child's capacity to discharge and, therefore, is experienced as traumatically painful. Fenichel also discusses the frequent and unconscious connection between the ideas of sexuality and death in children and the resultant masochistic trend in which dying may become a sexual goal.

This same author notes that people who act out in reality childhood fantasies for relief of inner tensions are involved in a repetition of childhood neurosis. Sexual and aggressive excitations are interwoven in such people.

These conceptualizations highlight that the derogatory name-calling is a complex psychodynamic issue relating back to early childhood sexual experiences and is representative of more than "hatred" or "contempt," but rather an expression of the need both to devalue the victim and to enhance the sexual pleasure with masochistic acts and ultimately death. The sadist does not necessarily conceptualize his feelings as "hate" and directs his energies toward the lust and release of the sadistic behavior.

Case History

David Parker Ray (Chapter 12) certainly represents the ultimate manifestation of sexual sadism. In fact, he was the classic psychopathic sexual sadist. Ray was a serial killer who authorities suspected committed the sex-torture murders of over 30 women (Geberth, 2003).

Ray had created an elaborate torture chamber, which was called the *toy box*. It was a 15-foot by 25-foot cargo trailer that Ray used for his sexual torture games in which he would systematically engage in physical and psychological torture of his victims. Inside the cargo trailer was a gynecology chair with restraints and electrical wires. Electric wires ran across the chair and were used to cause pain and force the victim to move in various positions. He then would attach jumper cables to the victim's nipples and groin area. In addition, the toy box contained surgical tools, various sexual devices, different size dildos, ropes, chains, a mechanical dildo device, straps and harnesses, electric shock machines, first aid supplies, and anatomically correct dolls, which had miniature chains attached through their nipples.

He had a small library of books dealing with female anatomy, human sexuality, psychology, and emergency victim care. Ray had placed a TV monitor in the right-hand corner of the trailer so his victims, who were secured to the chair as he tortured them, could see what he was doing to them by looking at the monitor. He had a video camera focused on the gynecology chair to view his "operations." This was done to further psychologically torture his victims as they anticipated what was about to happen to them.

He photographed and videotaped his victims. He reportedly experienced pleasurable sexual arousal through the infliction of various forms of both physical and emotional pain on the young women, whom he treated as objects. When he finished "playing" with them, he would kill them.

The documents and evidence recovered after Ray's arrest provided a treasure trove of information as it relates to sexual sadism. Among the materials were a series of tape recordings one of which was called "introductory tape." The "introductory tape" described how the victim would be kept as a sex slave and that during this time she would be subject to electric shock, forced oral sex, the use of large dildos, as well as sex with animals, and she was informed that Ray had killed girls in the past.

Ray's own words on that tape recording indicated his psychopathic sexual sadism. On the tape, Ray states that he could not obtain sexual gratification unless he caused the woman pain. Actually, Ray provided his own self-diagnosis of sexual sadism when he stated:

> In my case, I cannot get off with a girl unless I hurt her first. That's basically the reason I'm into rape and slavery, and the reason that you're going to be subjected to a certain amount of pain. ... Occasionally, your clit will also be clamped and stretched and we're gonna be using dildos. The dildos are gonna be used a lot, more than anything else and, consequently, what you're going to have the most trouble with. Many of them are long, very large in diameter and very painful while they're being forced in. Your mistress will use them in your pussy and I like to use them in both holes. Actually, that pretty well covers it.

The statements on the part of David Ray certainly reflect a psychosexual disorder consistent with psychopathic sexual sadism. It is apparent that the subject's preferred or exclusive means of sexual gratification is deviant and includes unusual or bizarre imagery or perverse acts that he requires for sexual excitement (see Chapter 12 for complete case history).

Case History

One of the more outrageous case examples of sexual sadism and psychopathy is found in the infamous "Sex Slave" case featured in the book *The Perfect Victim* (McGuire and Norton, 1988). The victim was Colleen Stan, who was 20 years old at the time of her abduction. Colleen was held captive and forced to endure years of sexual perversion at the hands of a psychopathic sexual sadist who confined her in a coffin-like box that would best be described as a claustrophobic's nightmare.

The case involved Cameron Hooker and his wife, Janice. Hooker's fantasy was to dominate and torture nude women, who were bound and helpless. His fantasies were fueled by an extensive collection of hard-core pornography, which featured bondage, leather, and handcuffs and whips. The abduction and enslavement of Colleen Stan was the culmination of years of fantasy, experimentation, and planning. Early on during his relationship with Janice, who he subsequently married, he introduced her to bondage scenarios and requested her to allow him to suspend her by the wrists from a tree without her clothes on. Not wanting to lose him, Janice went along with these activities even as they escalated to whippings and severe beatings. He took many photographs of her nude and bound and was constantly introducing new techniques into his sexually sadistic repertoire.

According to McGuire and Norton's account in the *Perfect Victim*, Cameron and Janice reached an understanding. "It was a tradeoff. He could kidnap someone if she could have someone as well. She wanted a baby" (p. 23). Thus, began this most bizarre event that would last some seven years.

Colleen was hitchhiking from Oregon to California. She had turned down a couple of offers of a lift. However, when Hooker and his wife, Janice, who was holding a baby, offered her a lift, she readily accepted. When the couple remarked that they wanted to detour to see some sights, Colleen thought nothing of it even though the area was becoming more remote. When the car stopped, Janice left the vehicle with the baby. Hooker also got out, but suddenly was in the back seat threatening Colleen with a knife. He secured her hands with handcuffs and blindfolded her with a piece of cloth. This was when Colleen was introduced to the "head box."

According to McGuire and Norton, "Its construction was deceptive, for though it was made of plywood and was only the size of a hatbox, it was surprisingly heavy, weighing nearly 20 pounds. Dense insulation was sandwiched in between its double walls and it was hinged with metal … It had a circular hole at the bottom. It shut out all light. It muffled all sound. It pinched her neck … The carpeted interior pressed against her face. …" (pp. 8–9).

Colleen was secretly transported to the Hooker home and brought down to the basement by Hooker who, after removing the "head box" but keeping the blindfold in place, stripped her of her clothing. Hooker then had her stand on an ice chest during which time he replaced the handcuffs with leather bands, which were secured to hooks in the ceiling. Suddenly, her support was kicked out from beneath her feet and she hung by her wrists twisting and kicking her feet out as she tried to regain her footing. Hooker began whipping her across her nude body and yelling to her to stop kicking. She went limp and the whipping ceased. Hooker then replaced the ice chest beneath her feet. At one point during this torture, Colleen was able to see through the bottom of her blindfold. She saw a picture of a naked woman hanging in much the same position that she was hanging. Apparently, Hooker was using his sadistic pornography to script his fantasy into reality.

These whippings and hangings would continue over the years, as would the tight confinement in the wooden box. During this time, Hooker took hundred of pictures of both Janice and Colleen in bondage scenarios that he processed himself. Hooker's depravity increased.

He placed a heat lamp next to Colleen's skin as she was hanging and watched her writhe in pain as it burned. He touched her with live electrical wires. He hung her upside down and bound in strange ways. He made her orally copulate him. He strangled her into unconsciousness and subjected her to just about anything he could imagine (McGuire and Norton, p. 37).

During her captivity, Colleen was subjected to the most horrific sexual tortures and deprivations one can imagine. She was totally and completely isolated from the outside world. Her dungeon was a plywood box. When she was out of the box, she was chained. She was kept totally nude and was made to perform various assignments in this condition. She was coerced into signing a "Slave Contract" and given a new name "K."

On one occasion, Hooker began striking matches as she hung and burned both of her breasts. On another occasion, Hooker used electricity to shock and burn her. He got so carried away that he ended up permanently scarring her thighs. He also put her on a rack that he had designed and stretched her until she was suffocating. He then put his hands around her neck and strangled her, choking her into unconsciousness. He would then ease his grip.

As she came to, he squeezed her neck again. He then forced her to give him oral sex. He also forced her to give oral sex to Janice in addition to the repeated rapes and oral sex that he demanded from his "slave" (McGuire and Norton, p. 97).

Hooker, who systematically engaged in bizarre tortures with his victim, eventually allowed Colleen out of her box for longer periods of time. She was advised that she would be allowed to work and let out of the house. However, to assure that she would be recognized as Hooker's slave, he would have to mark her. In addition to the burn scars, Hooker pierced her genitals with a needle and inserted a gold earring through her right labia. She was then allowed out of the house to work. Then, without reason, she was put back into the box where she remained for three years.

Three years later without explanation, Hooker allowed her out of the box full time. Hooker was so confident in his control over Colleen that he allowed her to work outside the home. However, Hooker did not realize that his wife wanted out of this nightmare and helped Colleen as they made their escape and went to the authorities.

Interview Statement of Serial Killer: A Sexual Sadist

Serial killer was driving through Morgantown, West Virginia, which is the home of West Virginia University. On one particular night, while Serial killer was driving around, he offender spotted two female hitchhikers near the downtown campus. The offender offered the two girls a ride. Once he had them inside his car, he ordered them to the floorboard of his car at gunpoint. Serial killer then drove to a remote area and forced the two young women to engage in sex with him. In his official statement to investigators, Serial killer described what took place.

Serial killer: I was cruising around looking for somebody to pick up because I can't have normal sex with nobody. I have to have abnormal sex. I have to force people to give me what I want or I don't have no ejaculation, no erection or nothing ... I seen a couple of girls on the corner hitchhiking.

Investigator: What did you do after you got them in the car?

Serial killer: I put a gun on them and made them lay on the floor. I told them that if they didn't get down on the floor, I'd blow their heads off. ... I drove on the road for a long ways, then I got off on the side road ... in some woods, remote. It was remote because I couldn't see the main road. ... I parked with them.

Investigator: And then what happened?

Serial killer: I parked in the woods and I made the one girl get up and I put handcuffs on her, and I hooked the handcuffs under the seat of the car because it was like a little spring or hook, part of the seat under there where you can hook it. This was in the front part of the car. Then I made the one girl crawl over the top seat into the back. I had a gun on her. I made her get undressed. I had abnormal sex with her. I ate her pussy. I licked her butt. I screwed her in the butt. I made her get down on me. Then I had sex with her on the front of her vagina.

Investigator: Was the girl in the front seat naked or dressed?

Serial killer: She was dressed. I didn't take her clothes off. I didn't make her take them off. I didn't want to handle both of them at the same time. The other one, after I got done having sex with her, I was still hot because whenever I force somebody I just stay hard. I don't get enough right away.

Investigator: Let me ask you, did these girls say anything to you; did they plead?

Serial killer: They pleaded with me. That just made me harder. That excited me more. They asked me why I was doing that to them—I don't know, different stuff like that. But I just told them to shut their mouths and I talked very nasty to them. I think I slapped one of them before she disobeyed me, but I think I slapped her for talking. I didn't want her to talk.

Investigator: Okay then, what did you do after you got done with the first girl?

Serial killer: I made her get in the front seat with me because I didn't want her jumping out of the car, getting out some way, out of the car. So, I unfastened the other girl. I made the one that was naked get back down on the floor ... just took the handcuffs off her and told her to get naked, get her clothes off. ... Then I made both of them get in the back seat. ... Then I made them both have unnatural sex with themselves. I made the blond—I made her get down on the other girl. I made her get down on her knees between the other girl's thighs and I made her get down with her mouth on the other girl. And I couldn't resist her butt. It was just sticking up in the air. I put my mouth on it. I wet it and I ran my penis up her rear. But I told her, if she screamed, I would kill her or if she took her mouth off the other girl I would kill her. And when I rammed it in she screamed, she hollered, and when I got done doing what I was doing to her in the rear, I slapped her in the face a few times pretty hard because she disobeyed me. ... After I got done doing it to her in the rear and slapping her for disobeying me when she got up and screamed— because it hurt her, she said—but I didn't believe her. I believe she was a pig.

Investigator: So then what did you do? (*Interviewer uses first name of the killer.*)

Serial killer: I made the other girl do the same thing. ... Get down on her with her mouth. I did the same thing to her, put it up her ass. ...

Investigator: What happened after this?

Serial killer: After that I had one of them sit on my face. ... I made the one straddle my thing with her vagina, pussy, or whatever. I don't like to say this because it makes me seem sick. It's unnatural. It embarrasses me to say it, but I made her do it.

Investigator: What did you make her do?

Serial killer: I made her piss in my mouth.

Investigator: You made one of them piss in your mouth?

Serial killer: I made them both eventually, but I had the blond sitting on my face and I made her piss in my mouth.

Investigator: Then what?

Serial killer: Then that stimulated me to the point I ejaculated right away, and the other girl—then I just reversed it. I made the blond get down there and sit on me while the other girl sat on my face and did the same thing. … I don't know why it turns me on. I know I'm sick. I didn't know why I did that. I don't know why I do it. I don't know why I like that kind of sex or what makes me do it.

The Serial killer then went on to explain that when he was 18 in prison, he was forced into anal sex and forced to give blowjobs by the other cons.

Investigator: After they got done doing what you last said about urinating in your mouth, what took place then?

Serial killer: Well, I didn't ejaculate right away because after—it took me a little while to ejaculate in the other girl while I was eating the other girl's vagina and licking her rear, the one that was sitting on my face. After I ejaculated—they weren't virgins. They didn't bleed. They couldn't have been virgins.

Investigator: Okay, so what went on after that?

Serial killer: I told them to get dressed. But, I may have took the panties and bras. I don't know, because the panties and bra turned me on. They make me hard, whether it's the panties and bras …

Investigator: But you told them to get dressed, right? Then what did you do?

Serial killer: I got them outside the car and shot one of them in the head.

Investigator: Now you shot one of them, you say?

Serial killer: I shot her in the head. When she fell, she pulled the other one down or knocked her off balance and when I shot her, all I did was graze her because it didn't kill her. She was laying on the ground crying and whimpering and begging and it just excited me sexually, and I ran back in the car and got the machete.

Investigator: Now, the second girl, the one you shot second was only wounded, right? And she was begging and whimpering and all that?

Serial killer: Yes. Sexually it excited me.

Investigator: What did you do?

Serial killer: I ran back to car and I got the machete from under the front seat and I went back and chopped her head off.

Investigator: Which one?

Serial killer: The one she was wounded, and I chopped the other one, I cut her head off, too.

Investigator: Then what did you do?

Serial killer: I reached a climax, because the blood excited me. … I dragged the bodies back to some dead branches or logs or something and I covered them up.

The investigator asked for some more clarification and there was a discussion about the exact location where Serial Killer had placed the bodies. Serial Killer then told the investigator that he had removed a necklace and a class ring and a watch from the girls.

Investigator: Did you take anything back to the car?

Serial killer: I took the heads. Up where the car was at I found a rag, a large rag, a dirty rag, and I put their heads in it. … I put their heads in the back seat and I drove.

Serial killer then described his route away from the murder site to a location where he had been before.

Serial killer: I parked up in there and I had sex with the heads. I got naked in the back with the heads and I was playing with myself and I had the heads between my thighs and I ejaculated in the mouths.

Serial killer then described how he got rid of the heads. He admitted to having oral and anal sex with the girls, having the girls urinate in his mouth, and having forced the two to engage in sex with one another. The serial killer did not admit that he also forced one of the females to defecate in his mouth.

Literature Depictions of Serial Murderers as Psychopathic Sexual Sadists

Among the number of paraphilias discussed in de River's (1958) often cited work *Crime and the Sexual Psychopath* is lust murder. De River speaks of sadism as a compelling element in some lust murders; in others, arousal is not derived from the infliction of pain and suffering of the victim, but rather from the act of killing. In this latter case, however, as with necrophiles, de River recognizes that even though the offender may not witness any prolonged degree of suffering on the part of the victim, he is likely to "[call] upon his imagination and fancy to supply him with the necessary engrams to satisfy his craving for his depravity" (de River, 1958, p. 276). This is not unlike lust murderers who torture victims before killing them, and then recall "an after-image (engram) of the sensation produced by the physical torture and mutilation, extending beyond time and space." The sadistic scenario is thus conjured in the imagination, be it a recreation of the actual crime scene or the product of fantasy. In each instance, lust murders are viewed as behaviors of sadistic sexual psychopaths.

Neustatter (1957) devotes a chapter in his book *The Mind of the Murderer* to the sadistic and mutilative sexual homicides of Neville Heath. The title of the chapter is "Neville Heath—The Psychopathic Sadist." Neustatter describes Heath using the actual terms *psychopathic* and *sexual sadist*. He explains:

The element of illness lies in the psychopathy, and, if it may be so put, the badness in a man like Heath lies in making no attempt to avoid situations in which he is likely to succumb to his dreadful urges; thus, within a few weeks of one murder, he commits a second. ... The lack of sexual control in Heath's case is in perfect keeping with his utter lack of concern and disregard for the suffering or welfare of others in any direction" (Neustatter, 1957).

According to Vetter (1990), serial murderers are almost routinely characterized in media accounts and much legal documentation as "psychopaths" or "sociopaths," which he notes are terms that were superseded by the diagnostic category "antisocial personality disorder" by the psychiatric community in its 1968 revision of the *American Psychiatric Association's Diagnostic and Statistical Manual of Mental Disorders* (DSM) (Geberth, 1995).

A reading of Brittain's work (1970) on the sadistic murderer "reveals that such individuals are unconcerned with the moral implications of their brutality. They are excited by the sight of suffering and helplessness of their victims, whom they experience as objects, and usually kill by strangulation, apparently because of their total control over the victim that this method offers them."

Because it appears that a substantial proportion of male serial murderers violate their victims sexually, it is important to examine the role sexual behavior has in the killings. Hucker et al. (1988) diagnosed 43% of their sample of 51 sexually aggressive men as sadists according to *DSM* criteria. Dietz (1986), like Brittain before him, contends that the paraphilia most frequently associated with sex murders is sadism. In fact, of serial killers, Dietz states, "[w]hile every serial killer is mentally disordered, nearly all are psychopathic sexual sadists, and few, if any, are psychotic. Psychotic offenders rarely have the wherewithal repeatedly to escape apprehension."

Arbolita-Florez and Holley (1985) conclude from their research on multiple murderers that most are sexual sadists who derive great satisfaction from the publicity surrounding their case in addition to the sexual mutilations and/or deaths they cause. Berger (1984) found from his interviews of a number of recognized experts on serial murder who themselves had conducted extensive interviews with serial killers that they concluded "most serial killers are sexual sadists." In his discussion of a serial murderer who was convicted of killing two young women and one teenaged girl, and who confessed to more than two dozen other killings across five states during the 1970s, Meloy (1992) describes Theodore Bundy as "a contemporary sexual psychopath." Moreover, he speaks of other sexually psychopathic serial murderers and entertains the contention by Lunde and Morgan (1980), among others, that there is a temporal coupling of erotic stimulation and violence in the childhood histories of what they call sexually psychopathic serial murderers.

Geberth and Turco (1997), in their study compiled a list of 387 serial killers in the United States from the earliest available data to December 1993. This population was then examined for evidence that the serial murderer violated his victim sexually. A total of 248 serial killers of 387 had violated their victims sexually.

This primary sample of 248 included four female serial killers and 12 killers who had not been apprehended. Since the study concentrated on male serial killers who had violated their victims sexually, the authors eliminated the four female killers and the unapprehended serial killers from the primary sample, resulting in 232 identified male serial killers. The authors used a case history evaluation protocol based upon the *DSM-IV* criteria of Antisocial Personality Disorder (301.70) and Sexual Sadism (302.84) to examine the population of 232 male serial killers, who had violated their victims sexually. Examination of the data sources for those 232 killers revealed enough information to complete the protocols for only 68 of theses offenders. The behaviors of these 68 subjects were suitably described as psychopathic sexual sadism (Geberth and Turco, 1997, pp. 49–60).

Classic Examples of Psychopathic Sexual Sadism

CASE HISTORY

The serial murders committed by Lawrence Bittaker and Roy Norris were classic examples of the phenomenon of psychopathic sexual sadism. In fact, I use this case in my class presentations to demonstrate the psychodynamics of this behavior. Bittaker and Norris, who both had been diagnosed as psychopaths, met in prison. While in prison they discovered that they had a mutual interest in dominating, hurting, and raping women. Norris was in prison for rape and Bittaker was in prison for felonious assault. In their discussion of rape, Bittaker told Norris that if he ever raped a woman he would kill her so there wouldn't be any witness. They decided that when they got out they would form a partnership and "kill them a bunch of bitches."

Bittaker was released first, followed by Norris. They began spending weekends together in the South Bay area of Los Angeles. They would drive up and down the Pacific Coast Highway and check out the young bikini-clad women on the beach. They began to discuss a plan to kidnap and rape one of these young women. However, first they would need the proper vehicle. They settled on a cargo van, which had a sliding door with no windows on the side. The plan was to pull up to the victim and drag her into the van. Bittaker also soundproofed the van so that if one of their victims screamed she wouldn't be heard.

They soon discovered that there were plenty of female hitchhikers more than willing to jump into their van. Bittaker and Norris began picking up female hitchhikers for practice. However, they realized they would need a place to take their victim once they were kidnapped. Bittaker and Norris drove up to a remote area in the San Gabriel Mountains. There were a number of private trails, secured by locks. They looked for the rustiest lock, broke it, and replaced it with one of their own locks. Now they had a place to bring their victim. They had established their own *comfort zone* where no one would interfere with them and they could do what they wished with their victim and not worry about getting caught. There would be five young women raped and murdered within five months by these psychopathic sexual sadists.

Their first victim was a 16-year-old whom they snatched off the street. She was taken to their *comfort zone* up in the San Gabriel Mountains where she was raped and forced to perform oral sex on both offenders. They then decided to kill her. Norris tried to strangle her, but she wasn't dying. Bittaker took a wire coat hanger, put in around the young girl's neck, and tightened it with a pair of vice-grip pliers. Her body was then tossed into one of the steep canyons. Bittaker told Norris not to worry about it because the animals would eat her up and there wouldn't be any evidence.

One month later, Bittaker and Norris were on the hunt again. This time they spotted an 18-year-old hitchhiker. However, before they could move in, the young lady jumped into a white convertible. Bittaker and Norris figured sooner or later she would be dropped off, so they followed her. When she got out of the car, she started hitchhiking again. Norris hid in the back of the van as Bittaker pulled up alongside her and asked if she needed a ride. She got in and shortly thereafter Norris came up behind her and subdued the screaming young woman. Once again they took her up to their *comfort zone* where both offenders repeatedly raped her. Bittaker took some photos of the young woman that showed the terror in her eyes. Bittaker had told her that he was going to kill her because he wanted to see the expression on her face. He killed this victim by jamming an ice pick into her ears and then strangling her. Her body was also thrown off a cliff.

Two months later, Bittaker and Norris were on the "hunt" again. This time they picked up two teenagers who turned out to be only 15 and 13 years old. The girls, who accepted the ride, were offered a couple of marijuana joints. The girls thought they were getting a ride to the beach. When Bittaker started driving toward the mountains, the girls started protesting. The two men bound and gagged them with tape and quickly subdued them. Bittaker and Norris then drove toward their *comfort zone* in the San Gabriel Mountains, where they kept their prisoners for two days. The young girls were repeatedly raped and tortured. This time, the two psychopathic sexual sadists tape recorded the sessions. When they finished, both girls were savagely killed by strangulation. One of the victims had an ice pick jammed into her ear and the other had her head battered with a sledgehammer. Once again, both bodies were tossed over a steep cliff.

Victim number five was 16-year-old "Shirley." Once she was in the van, she was bound and gagged. This time, Bittaker and Norris decided they would torture and rape her in the van as they drove along the streets. Bittaker wanted to tape record the session so they could play it for their next victim. While Norris was driving, Bittaker started torturing the young girl with a hammer and a pair of pliers. Bittaker raped and sodomized her and forced her to perform fellatio on him. He then had her speak into a tape recorder and describe for him what she had been forced to do. But, Bittaker wanted her to use street terms. He said to her, "Are you sucking on my dick?" He said, "Go ahead say it, 'dick.'" Bittaker then said to her, "What are you doing?" The victim answered, "I'm sucking on your dick." Bittaker then said, "Do you like sucking on my dick?" and the victim was forced to say, "I do, I do." This outrageous behavior is consistent with sexual sadism and confirms that the suffering of the victim, both physical and psychological, is sexually arousing to the offender. Bittaker and Norris tortured their victim without the least bit of concern or trepidation.

During these atrocious assaults Bittaker was hitting her on the right elbow to make her scream for the tape recorder. The author has a copy of this tape, which is the most disturbing and heinous example of human depravity I have ever listened to. In fact, at the conclusion of this horrific tape, you cannot even tell that the voice is that of a once vivacious young woman. It is the odious sound of an extremely cruel and evil death as she succumbs to the sadistic torture (From the author's files).

Below is a description and partial transcript of this tape as reported by Ronald Markman and Dominick Bosco (1989) in their excellent book *Alone with the Devil: Famous Case of a Courtroom Psychiatrist.*

"*Start the van,*" Bittaker said. Then he slapped Shirley.
"*Say something, girl, huh?*"
He slapped her again. "*Huh.*" He struck her harder.
"*What do you want me to say?*" Shirley asked.
"*Huh, huh,*" Bittaker mocked her.
"*Say something, girl.*"
Then he slapped her three times and mocked her again.
"*Don't you hit me!*" "*Huh, huh,*" Shirley moaned.
"*Say something girl,*" he insisted.
"*Ouch.*"
Bittaker slapped her again, and she screamed.
"*Say something.*" He slapped her again.
"*C'mon, you can scream louder than that, can't you?*"
He struck her, twice more, grunting "*Huh*" as his blows descended on the helpless young woman.
"*What's the matter, don't you like to scream?*"
He struck her repeatedly. Shirley screamed louder and Bittaker struck her repeatedly.
"*Oh no!*" she cried.
"*What's the matter, huh, you want to try again?*"
"*Oh no*" she screamed. "*Don't touch me, no.*"
"*Huh? You want to try again?*"

"Oh no, don't touch me, no, don't touch me" she cried.

"Want to try again?"

"No, no, no, no, no, no, no!"

"Roll over, girl," Bittaker ordered.

"No, don't touch me."

"Roll over."

"Don't touch me."

"Start getting to work, girl."

"Don't touch me, don't touch me!"

Bittaker slapped her hard.

"Get to work, girl."

"Don't touch me."

"I'm not asking you, I'm telling you!"

As Shirley started to cry, Bittaker ordered her to roll over.

"C'mon, c'mon, c'mon."

Then he forced her to fellate him and describe to him what she was doing. As she obeyed his orders, he struck her and ordered her to: "Scream, baby … if it hurts anytime you want to scream go ahead and scream … scream, baby, scream some more, baby."

When Shirley had trouble screaming loud enough to suit him, Bittaker fumbled through his toolbox and came up with a pair of pliers. First he threatened Shirley with them and got her to scream more convincingly. Then he started squeezing Shirley's nipples with the pliers.

"Is the recorder going?" he asked Norris.

"Yeah," Norris replied.

Shirley screamed. *"No, no, no! Oh no!"* Then she wailed in pain.

"Make noise there, girl," Norris urged as he traded places with Bittaker.

"Go ahead and scream or I'll make you scream."

Shirley moaned unintelligibly.

"Oh yeah," Norris cheered.

"Oh …" Shirley moaned in pain.

"Scream!" Norris ordered. Then he struck her on the elbow with the hammer.

Shirley screamed, *"I'll scream if you stop hitting me."* Then she screamed.

"Keep it up, girl."

Shirley screamed.

"Keep it up."

Shirley screamed.

"More!"

Shirley screamed again.

"Till I say stop."

Shirley, screamed, and then cried out

"Oh no!" as she saw Norris-going for the hammer again. As he struck her again and again on the elbow, the young woman screamed once for all of the 25 times he struck her. At one point, she may have tried to say something, but her voice had become an unintelligible mass of pain. Bittaker asked what was going on.

"I was just beating on her elbows with this hammer," Norris replied.

Shirley screamed again.

"What are you sniveling about?" Norris asked her.

Then he started hitting her with the hammer again, and the sounds of the beating mixed with the sounds of the screaming and it went on and on and on (Markman and Bosco, 1989, pp. 266–268).

This tape ended with the nonstop screaming and palpable pain of the victim, whose voice was rendered unintelligible from the strain on her throat. It should be noted that the detective who was assigned to this case and had to transcribe its contents had to retire on a medical due to a nervous breakdown he suffered as a direct result of this outrage.

Bittaker killed her by wrapping a wire coat hanger around her throat and twisting the wire tighter around her neck with his vice grips. Bittaker decided that this time they would leave the body on someone's front lawn to see what kind of reaction it would generate in the press. They got more than they bargained for. There was an immediate public outrage and the authorities began looking into the other missing girls as linked to this event.

Bittaker and Norris were arrested as a result of Norris's bragging to a former prison buddy. This, coupled with an identification of Bittaker and Norris by a live rape victim, provided the authorities with enough probable cause to bring them in for questioning. Eventually, Norris admitted his part in the series of slayings and worked out a plea bargain in exchange for information, which included the tape recording that would convict Bittaker. Norris was sentenced to 45 years to life. Bittaker was originally sentenced to death, but the sentence was commuted (From the author's files).

Psychopathic sexual sadists tend to be callous and cold-blooded when dealing with his victims, whom they considers little more than objects for self-gratification. They inflict pain to create suffering and elicit a desired response from the victim. They demand obedience and submission and feed off the fear and terror they create. When the psychopathic sexual sadist is through humiliating and "using" his victim to satisfy his sexual needs, he simply disposes of her without the least remorse or concern.

In Chapter 3, the author provided the reader with the personal writings and journal entries of a serial rapist, whom I describe as a psychopathic sexual sadist, which proved to be a very rich and reliable source of information, not only about him as an offender, but about his personality as well. This narcissistic offender had meticulously detailed the most mundane details of his day-to-day personal life, his sexual fantasies about rape, and vividly described how he stalked dozens of women, whom he planned on abducting and sexually assaulting. He was a man possessed with his weight and looks, jogging, health clubs, strippers, pornography, and tennis.

In Chapter 12, the author presented a case history of an excellent example of the reality of psychopathic sexual sadism in the sex torture serial murder case investigation. Psychopathic sexual sadism and sexual arousal from physical suffering, humiliation, and control of the victim is at the core of serial homicide. This psychodynamic is not only considered a chronic disorder, but has within its core an element of progression. As the offender continues his sexual assaults, he progresses and the events become more sadistic as he begins to experiment with his victims.

I consider the actions of the psychopathic sexual sadist to be the total and absolute evil of humankind. According to *Merriam-Webster's Collegiate Dictionary* (2001), *evil* is "morally reprehensible: sinful, wicked ... arising from actual or imputed bad character or conduct, ... causing discomfort or repulsion: offensive ... pernicious."

I suggest that a concept of a Psychology of Evil best describes this phenomenon.

A Psychology of Evil

What Constitutes Evil?

According to *Webster's New World Dictionary* (1983), evil is "(1) anything morally bad or wrong; wickedness; depravity; sin; (2) anything that induces harm, pain, misery, disaster, etc."

Clinically speaking, the term *evil* does not appear in psychiatric lexicon. However, the clinical diagnoses of Antisocial Personality Disorder (301.7) and Sexual Sadism (302.84) as found in *DSM-IV-TR* (APA, 2000) and sadistic personality disorder as defined in *DSM-III-R IV* (APA, 1987) as well as malignant narcissism (Kernberg, 1982, 1990) and Hare's *psychopathy* (1993, 1999, 2000) do address the specific conduct and behaviors, which one could define in layman's terms as evil.

M. Scott Peck (1983) characterizes "malignant narcissism as an unsubmitted will." He writes, "All adults who are mentally healthy submit themselves one way or another to something higher than themselves, be it God or truth or love or some other ideal." He continues by stating that individuals submit themselves to the demands of their own conscience. "Not so the evil, however. In the conflict between their guilt and their will, it is the guilt that must go and the will that must win" (Peck, 1983). The psychopath is determined to have his own way and exercises his free will in an attempt to control others.

The terms *psychopath* and *sociopath* certainly define perverse, amoral, and asocial conduct, which is considered harmful to society. However, the author prefers to use Hare's description of *psychopathy* as it applies to offenders who engaged in the type of sadistic sexual assaults and homicides as defined within this chapter.

Looking at the concept of evil theologically, major religious factions throughout the world condemn evil in their scriptures and beliefs. Each religion has key beliefs that speak of a supernatural being who has love for all creatures, insists on justice and mercy for all people, and rewards the good and punishes the evil.

Sociologically, humans are part of a social system, which requires that we conduct ourselves in a manner that is considered appropriate and deemed acceptable by the society in which we interact. Each society and social system establishes rules and laws designed to maintain order and allow for an organized social life. In our society, murder is against the law and represents an evil against the social system.

Clinically, theologically, and socially, life is considered good and precious. Goodness is the opposite of evil in that it promotes life. Evil seeks to kill life and represents anything that opposes life. Murder, which is not necessary for biological survival, is evil and I propose that serial murder, which is murder committed in the context of expressing a perverse and selfish sexuality, represents the ultimate evil.

Application of Psychology

Applying the Freudian concepts of the *id*, the *ego*, and the *superego* to serial murders gains additional psychological insight into the psyche of the offender. Sigmund Freud proposed that the id was the source of instinctual drives, which are both constructive and destructive.

The id is completely selfish and concerned only with immediate gratification of instinctual needs without reference to reality or moral considerations. It operates on what is called the pleasure principle. However, it cannot undertake the actions needed to meet instinctual demands.

The id needs the ego, which mediates between the demands of the id and the realities of the external world. The basic function of the ego is to meet id demands, but in such a way as to ensure the well-being and survival of the individual. This requires reason and other intellectual resources in dealing with the external world over id demands and is referred to as the reality principle. Freud viewed id demands, especially sexual and aggressive strivings, as inherently in conflict with rules and prohibitions imposed by society.

The superego is an outgrowth of learning the taboos and moral values of society. It is essentially what we refer to as conscience and is concerned with right and wrong. As the superego develops, it becomes an additional inner control system that copes with the uninhibited desires of the id (Coleman et al., 1984).

In the case of a serial murderer, his inner police officer or conscience is either absent or off duty. In either event, the conscience is "unavailable for patrol" or control of the instinctual demands of the id. A serial murderer kills in order to satisfy his lust or id impulses. However, being quite devious and clever, he is fully aware of the criminality of his actions and will not commit a murder when there is an external police officer watching. His ego works to assure his well-being in what has been described as the reality principle.

Eric Fromm, who wrote the book *The Heart of Man: Its Genius for Good and Evil* (1964), saw the genesis of evil as a developmental process; "We are not created evil or forced to be evil, but we become evil slowly over a period of time through a long series of choices" (quoted in Peck, 1983, p. 82).

"There are people, both in and out of jail, who seem utterly lacking in conscience or superego. … Conscienceless, psychopaths appear to be bothered or worried by very little, including their own criminality" (Peck, 1983, p. 75).

If we apply free will and freedom of choice to a serial killer's murderous and sadistic activities, we are confronted by the reality of an evil human predator, an evil entity who has made a conscious decision to kill. Someone, who as Fromm suggests, has made a choice between good and evil. An evil person is characteristically hedonistic and feels superior to other human beings.

Serial murderers are extremely selfish and narcissistic. Their goal is power and sexual gratification. Despite any intrapsychic conflict between guilt and an ability to exercise his free will, the serial murderer opts for free will and chooses to do evil.

I therefore propose that serial murder is representative of a psychology of evil.

The Psychopathic Personality

Most serial murderers are psychopathic sexual sadists. If you could crawl into their minds and examine the elements of their psyche, you would find their superego or conscience missing. This is perhaps the most significant characteristic of the psychopath because it allows full and violent expression without significant hesitation, guilt, shame, or remorse. He knows right from wrong—he simply doesn't care.

A psychopath lacks the internal prohibitions, or conscience, that keeps most of us from giving full expression to primitive and sometimes violent impulses. Interpersonal traits include glibness, superficial charm, a grandiose sense of self-worth, pathological lying, and the manipulation of others. The affective traits include a lack of remorse and/or guilt, shallow affect, a lack of empathy, and failure to accept responsibility. The lifestyle behaviors include stimulation-seeking behavior, impulsivity, irresponsibility, parasitic orientation, and a lack of realistic life goals. Psychopaths are impulsive, devious, selfish, emotionally immature, and extremely hedonistic.

Psychopathy is a personality disorder manifested in people who use a mixture of charm, manipulation, intimidation, and occasionally violence to control others, in order to satisfy their own selfish needs. They have short-term goals, which are usually centered on power and pleasure, and they tend to treat people as objects to be exploited, manipulated, or destroyed. They have no empathy for the needs of others. Their acts and whatever feelings accompany them are the goals.

The Serial Murderer

In law enforcement, a serial killer may be classified as having an antisocial personality disorder (APD) or be diagnosed as psychotic, basically meaning that he is suffering from a psychosis and out of touch with reality. The diagnosis is based on the information obtained during an examination and clinical interviews, and the facts as presented to the clinician.

Many terms are used in describing the psychopath and the terms *APD* and *psychosis* have been convenient for law enforcement in attempting to solve and apprehend suspects. However, they do not adequately describe the psychodynamics involved and the various diagnostic categories that might be ascribed to such perpetrators. For example, some perpetrators may be described as "schizoid" utilizing the *DSM-IV-TR* criteria. Explosive personality disorder is another diagnostic entity that has been considered. The *Psychodynamic Diagnostic Manual* (PDM) (Alliance of Psychoanalytic Organization, 2006) is a recently published collaborative effort by psychoanalysts of many persuasions to shed light on the definitions noted in *DSM*. The *PDM* introduces diagnostics areas, such as dysregulated personality disorders and anxious personality disorder, as the authors compare the *PDM* and *DSM* categories (p. 233).

The importance of these diagnostic categories becomes relevant in the search and understanding of serial and lust murderers. However, there is much debate among clinicians and scientists as to the exact meaning of these terms. Law enforcement has attempted to deal succinctly with broad categories, which are not always appropriate for scientific study.

Psychopaths who commit serial murder do not value human life and are extremely callous in their interactions with their victims. This is particularly evident in sexually motivated serial killers who repeatedly target, stalk, assault, and kill without a sense of remorse. Psychopaths do not empathize or show sympathy for their victims or remorse/guilt over their crimes.

In my experience as a homicide investigator, serial killers are rarely psychotic. They are more properly defined as sexual psychopaths or psychopathic sexual sadists depending on the circumstances of the homicide and what was done to the victim.

They also have been described as "lethal predators; psychopathic, sadistic, and sane" (Ochberg et al., 2003).

To outward appearances, these individuals have a personality disorder. However, this cannot be determined without a thorough psychological examination and until the psychodynamics of the individual are more fully understood. Some of these individuals may be in severe conflict about their behavior and isolating the sadism from a more integrated personality structure. This would imply a greater neurotic component to the behavior than has been previously considered. My experience with these offenders is that they are keenly aware of their own criminality and certainly not out of touch with reality. If serial killers were psychotic, they wouldn't be as successful in eluding the police (Stone, 1998).

They obviously have a profound personality disorder, but they are keenly aware of their own criminality and certainly not out of touch with reality. If serial killers were psychotic, they wouldn't be as successful in eluding the police.

One could propose that a psychotic killer strikes because his psychosis drives him to kill. An example of this type of serial killer would be Richard Trenton Chase, The Vampire Killer (Geberth, 2006), who reportedly attempted to replenish his blood supply that he believed was being dried up by aliens from outer space in flying saucers.

Based on my research and personal experience with such offenders, I suggest that psychopathic killers who are serial murders kill because they like to kill. These killers have conscious and detailed plans for murder. They certainly know right from wrong—they just don't give a damn. Their fundamental machinery of conscience, responsibility, and feeling for fellow human beings is totally lacking. Their will to do evil takes precedence over humanity. These people take and destroy lives without the least bit of hesitation or remorse because they are evil. There are a number of serial murder cases that can be cited to illustrate the evil, which I have been conveying within this chapter. I decided to mention the following examples because of their notoriety.

Ten Brief Case Examples

Ted Bundy   He represented the epitome of the serial killer, brutally murdering and sexually violating more than 30 young women. His attacks centered on control and total domination; he wanted his victims to be totally submissive. Bundy's plan involved sadistic fantasies with a combination of sex and violence featuring a dominant male and a submissive and terrified female. All of his victims were raped, traumatized, and then killed. In some instances he performed necrophilia shortly after killing them.

According to FBI Agent Bill Hagmaier, a recognized expert on Ted Bundy, "Bundy thought of himself as a predator. He liked to hunt as much as the kill and he selected what he called 'worthy prey,' which he described as attractive, intelligent young women with good backgrounds." Bundy could never understand why people couldn't accept the fact that he killed because he wanted to kill. He did it of his own volition (Geberth, 1996).

Kenneth Bianchi and Angelo Bouno   They were dubbed the **"The Hillside Strangler"** because authorities were not aware there were two killers, who sexually violated and brutally murdered 12 young women between them. They taped and gagged their victims before torturing and sexually abusing them. Bianchi and Bouno experimented with various techniques of torture, such as injecting them with window cleaner, smothering them with gas from the stove, subjecting them to electrical shock, and then eventually killing them by strangulation when they tired of their perverse and inhuman entertainment.

They would display the nude bodies of their victims on hillsides as if to taunt authorities. Bianchi, who moved to Bellingham, Washington, committed two more murders and was caught. However, Bianchi claimed to be a multiple personality and actually fooled two clinicians into believing him. He claimed that his alter ego "Steve" had done the killings along with his cousin, Angelo, and revealed the horrific details of this sadistic case. He turned state's evidence against his cousin Angelo Bouno (O'Brien, 1985).

Jerry Brudos   Called the "Lust Killer," he murdered four young women during 1968 and 1969 in a series of murders predicated on a sadistic and bizarre plan to kidnap and kill women whom he would force to pose in various sexually provocative positions. He cut off their breasts and made epoxy molds for his fireplace. In some instances he continued his sexual fantasies by dressing the bodies after death. His perversions included necrophilia and sexual mutilation of the corpses.

Douglas Clark   He was obsessed with sadistic torture and responsible for the sex-related murders of eight young women. "Douglas Clark's special talent was to force a woman to perform oral sex on him at gunpoint and, with nerveless confidence in his aim, to shoot her through the head as she brought him to orgasm. He would then chop off the victim's head, place it in a refrigerator, and bring it out from time to time for further oral sex" (O'Brien, 1988).

Clark also had a companion in his killings. A woman named Carol Bundy, who he transformed into a willing assistant in his gruesome killings. Clark loved to discuss his murders with Bundy and provide her with details of how he had forced the girls to fellate him, shooting each in the head as she brought him to climax. Carol Bundy would even help pack his "kill bag," which contained paper towels, rubber gloves, a Ginso knife, and plastic garbage bags when he went out hunting for victims, which he called "taking care of business."

On one occasion, Clark, who had killed two young women, took one of the heads home with him. He kept the head in a refrigerator. When Carol came home, he placed the head on the kitchen counter. He ordered Carol to make up the twisted face with cosmetics. Later she recalled, "We had a lot of fun with her. I was making her up like a Barbie with makeup." When Clark finished with that game, he took the head to the bathroom, for a shower, and practiced necrophilic oral sex (Farr, 1992).

Richard Cottingham   He was a serial killer with an admitted attraction to sadomasochism. In fact, he even testified at one of his trial for attempted murder blaming the prostitute he had almost killed because "she didn't know the rules." Cottingham raped, tortured, mutilated, and murdered five women. He also abducted and raped another four, who subsequently identified him. He would torture and "play" with his victims for hours before killing them. He would then leave their bodies in hotel rooms. The authorities believe he killed more, but couldn't prove it. He selected each of his victims for the purposes of sexual and psychosexual gratification and engaged in mutilation to hinder identification and "shock" the persons discovering his victim's bodies. Cottingham was methodical and cunning and was excited by the cruelty he inflicted on his victims (Geberth, 1996).

Jeffrey Dahmer   Dahmer, who engaged in necrophilia, anthropophagy, and other bizarre activities with the bodies of his victims, is recognized as one of America's most notorious male homosexual killers. He had managed to kill 17 young men and boys over a 13-year period before authorities apprehended him on July 22, 1991. He confessed to drugging, strangling, dismembering, and cannibalizing his victims. Police found photographs of some of the victims in various stages of mutilation (Geberth, 1996).

John Wayne Gacy   Gacy, the "Killer Clown," sexually tortured and murdered 33 young males in the Chicago area between 1972 and 1978. Gacy maintained a torture rack in his home where he would taunt and sexually assault his victims before killing them. He buried many of the victims beneath his home.

Robert Hansen   He was an avid hunter who would use his skills to satisfy an insatiable lust. As targets, he selected prostitutes, "exotic" dancers whom he kidnapped, raped, and butchered. He abducted and took them in his private plane where they were forced to act out his perverse fantasies. On some occasions he would take them out into the wilds of Alaska, strip them, and then use his skills as a tracker to hunt them down and slay them like prey oftentimes mutilating their remains with a hunting knife. He was responsible for the deaths 17 women and an additional 30 rapes (Gilmore and Hale, 1991).

Gary Heidnik   Heidnik abducted and kept captive a total of six women and engaged in extreme torture and cruelty, as well as total control of his victims. He killed at least two of his captives by electrocution after prolonged torture; another woman died after hanging from her wrists for a week in his basement, which he had converted into a torture chamber. He drove screwdrivers into the ears of victims, forced them to watch each other being raped and tortured by him, and also made some of them eat the ground-up body of another victim.

Richard Ramirez   Called the "Night Stalker," Ramirez terrorized Southern California during 1984 and 1985. He was responsible for the rape, sodomy, mutilation, and murder of 13 victims. He perpetrated unspeakable horrors upon his helpless victims, which included women, men, and children.

Conclusion

In each of these examples, the conduct displayed by the offenders suggests that the sex act is secondary. Instead, the offender was sexually excited by the cruelty of the acts and engaged in physical and psychological torture of the victims. His pleasure was derived by watching victims writhe in pain, as they were humiliated and tortured to death.

The murder itself was an expression of power and control. The necrophilia was an extension of their control and sadistic quest for complete and total domination.

Interview Strategies and Techniques

Information in this chapter provides homicide detectives with some practical insight into the psychopathology of a serial murderer as it relates to questioning this type of offender. Applying the concept of a "psychology of evil" may enable investigators to better structure interviews and interrogations of serial offenders.

Each criminal interrogation or interview situation is unique. Any success in obtaining statements that inculpate an offender is based on the individual investigator's knowledge, experience, expertise, and patience. No two cases are alike, just as no two people are alike. What works in one interrogation session may or may not work in another.

Detectives who interrogate serial murders must understand that the person opposite them is functioning with a *psychology of evil*. By appreciating the nature of this type of offender's thinking, the detective can design an interview strategy that appeals to the serial murder's self-interests and facilitate dialogue.

The psychology of evil provides the serial murderer with a unique ability to withstand ordinary investigative interview techniques, which focus on guilt, admission, and disclosure. In a psychology of evil, the fundamental machinery of conscience, responsibility, and feeling or empathy for other human beings is totally lacking. A psychopathic sexual sadist displays a profound lack of empathy. The feelings of others are of no concern and they cannot relate to someone's pain. One serial killer while testifying described his butchery as calmly as if he was carving a turkey. "I had to dismember her body to get it in the holes. So, I cut off her head and arms so it would fit."

For instance, attempting to invoke sympathy for the victims or surviving families or appealing to the subject's conscience is a waste of time. An offender who evinces a psychology of evil doesn't care about anyone except himself. Such an evil person is clever, devious, selfish, and extremely narcissistic.

Therefore, the investigator should prepare for a lengthy session. The suspect will be playing "mind games" in an attempt to gain control of the interview, or elicit information about the case. Evil people like to control and dominate. Therefore, this element should be taken away from the offender as soon as possible. This is done by strict and professional adherence to rules and protocol, which puts the detective in control of the interview setting. Let the subject know, in an authoritative manner, that you are completely aware of the offender's criminal activities as well as your ability to charge him.

However, do not attempt any fabrication of evidence. These offenders have spent a good amount of time planning their murders and have taken into account police reaction. They know exactly what they have done and what evidence is available to the police.

An effective interrogation technique with this type of offender is to explain to the offender why he is suspect and present the facts of the case in a professional manner. The detective should keep in mind that serial killers have an interest in criminal justice as well as investigative techniques. Making a logical appeal to the offender puts him into the position of a juror at his own trial. The detective can then put forth the "hard" facts and let the suspect draw his own conclusions.

This is accomplished by displaying knowledge; not only about the crimes, but of the psychodynamics as well as the psychopathology of other offenders who have been involved in similar events. Many serial killers are students of this crime and have an avid interest in reading and hearing about the exploits of other such murders.

Research has shown that in cases where serial murders have confessed or made admissions, a common reason for this action has been to gain some sort of legal advantage, i.e., avoid the death penalty or obtain a reduced charge for disclosing the locations of bodies.

A glaring defect in a psychology of evil is ego. Their narcissism provides them with a grandiose sense of self-importance and a total lack of empathy for anyone else. Interrogators should focus on convincing the suspect that his situation is, in fact, unique and can only be understood by a specially trained detective with knowledge of these types of crimes.

Hedonistically, the offender may attempt to impress the investigator by disclosing details of the murders that indicate how smart and clever he was. This behavior can be encouraged by generously complimenting the offender on his cleverness and intelligence. In fact, once the detective engages the offender in conversation, which feeds his ego, the suspect will want to further impress the officer in search of additional compliments.

Offenders with a psychology of evil possess a sadistic nature and are fascinated by violence, injury, and torture. They often enjoy disclosing certain particularly outrageous and cruel aspects of the crime. They do this not only to shock the investigator, but also to psychically relive the event in the selfish and perverse manner of continuing their own sadistic fantasies.

Investigators must maintain an unemotional and professional detachment and not display any personal feelings about the crime or the killer throughout the interview. Avoid any criticism of this type of an offender because he will probably react negatively and terminate further discussion.

Interviewing offenders who have perpetuated the unspeakable is an extremely stressful undertaking. In order to comprehend such evil, one must possess a strong belief in the majority of good in the world and implement appropriate coping mechanisms.

Murders committed by serial killers who are psychopathic sexual sadists transcend human understanding. The subhuman aspects of these killings coupled with the atrocities visited upon the victims manifest an appetite for violence and sexual mutilation that has people referring to the killers as animals. Yet, animals do not rape, sodomize, torture, and mutilate their prey. They kill for biological survival.

Serial murderers, on the other hand, kill for pleasure and their own vile sexual perversion. They are able to operate in an emotionally detached manner because they lack any empathy for their victims.

The clinical definitions of conduct provided herein are insufficient to define such heinous behaviors. The enormity of such malevolence exceeds these actions and remains incomprehensible without a concept of a psychology of evil.

Case Documentation of Psychopathic Sexual Sadism

I have personally investigated, supervised, assessed, and consulted on over 8,000 homicide investigations. I have reviewed case materials, crime scene photographs, read reports of offender's statements, and read their personal journal entries and letters, including their fantasy stories. I have analyzed their drawing and paintings and have been privy to some of the most disturbing videos and photographs of victims in bondage and torture that were taken by the offender as a memento of the event.

There is nothing more revealing about an offender and/or his thinking than his own records, writings, and recordings. Statistical data about serial offenders and psychopathic personalities furnish constructive guidelines, but often fall short of the big picture. I know that many clinical statisticians rely heavily on data and like to argue about the size of the population in their study and how it supports their hypothesis. However, in law enforcement, we depend on facts and substance. When you have the innermost thoughts of an offender, written in his own handwriting, there is no better "data" to draw conclusions from about this particular offender. For example:

A Case History: Written Documentation

This is a portion of a letter written by a serial killer to a woman, whom I will rename Joan. She had corresponded with him over a period of time. In her letter to him, she had indicated her fascination with his exploits and told him that she wanted to join him when he was released and assist him in his sex-related killings. In this letter, the killer "shares" with her one his more "exciting" kills in response to her question (*grammatical errors are those of the writer*).

> You asked what was the most torture I ever did to a girl?? And what was the longest I ever *Kept* a girl alive before killed her.
>   Actually the answer to (*scribble*) both these questions is One girl. She was actually one of the easiest I ever abducted. So why don't I just share with you this Kill. I kept her 2 days and

a night before I killed her. I literally tortured her to death. When I killed her all I was doing was putting her out of her agony. She was in her early 30's but you would swear she was in her 20's. She had a set of tits I swear was bigger than the size of two grapefruit.

Have you ever seen the actress Brooke Shields? Well the woman could pass as her twin. Hair & all. It was on a Friday afternoon about 2:00 in the day, & I was on one of my "junts". I had been driving up & down the beach checking (*scribble*) all the little dirt roads that go up to the bluff. Well I pulled up this one & I see this Toyota pick-up pulled up into the sand, with both doors open. So I pull up, get out & walk (*scribble*) up to the beach like I'm just a casual observer, all the time I'm checking out this truck & seeing who's there. Well just as I walk (scribble) past the truck I hear this woman ask, Could you help me please? I look, and theres this (*unintelligible*) laying down across the front seat of this truck with her feet dangling out. I walk over, & to make a long story short, she had been on the beach, & had gotten stung by a jellyfish on the bottom of her foot. She told me what happened and that her foot was hurting so bad, & it was swollen, could I please drive her to her house & she'd send someone back for her truck. She couldn't drive because of the pain. I said Sure! She asked if I could get her stuff off the beach so I walked down got it, carried it to my truck, put it in, She was still laying in her truck so (*scribble*) I got my 22 caliber pistol & tucked it in my waist band on my left side.

I went & helped her out of her truck and she was wearing this really skimpy bikini & those huge tits were just bouncing, & I let her put one arm on my shoulder. Now you have to imagine my state of mind at this point here. I was hunting, & here I have come across a very easy prey. And as I'm helping her to my truck I know I'm going to rape & kill this woman and I can hardly contain my adrenalin. I got her in my truck & I get in & start driving, & she tells me where she lives. So I drive. We come to this long stretch of country road & I decide this is as good a spot as any to pull my gun on her & get her.

So I pull my gun & stick the barrel in her ribs & tell her Don't try anything bitch or I wont hesitate to kill you. She looks at me with this startled look, and say, Oh my God no. I proceed to tell her to do as I say & I won't hurt her. She goes into this, pleading & begging mode asking me to please don't hurt her.

I tell her to sit there & be quiet, and I drive to my mobile home trailer, & when I pull up, I make her lean forward, then pull her hands behind her back & tie her wrist together real tight with nylon cord.

She is (*scribble*) real quiet. Sort of like in a semi shock. This I've seen a few times they actually get So scared they go into a shock. I love it when they do this cause it makes it easier to handle them.

I pulled this bitch out of my truck & she was crying in pain as I was forcing her to walk, she fell, so I just grabbed her under her arm pits & drug her to the door, pulled her in & drug her into the bedroom where she was crying in pain. As I was dragging her across the floor, her bikini panties pulled down & she had the bushiest pussy, & the cheeks of her ass was so white, the rest of her body was tanned. I layed her up on the bed, & she was moaning & crying from pain & from what she knew I was doing to her. I went to get some rope out of my drawer & she acted like she wanted to jump up & try to run, & just as she started to I grabbed her by her hair & pulled her back down on the bed, & she was screaming at me calling Bastard, & screaming for me to let her go.

I hit this bitch in the mouth & it stunned her, & she fell back. I got the rope & grabbed one of her ankles to pull her leg over to one of the corner bed post to tie it, & she tried to (*unintelligible*) free as she realized what I was going to do. I had this little night stick on my dresser, & I picked it up & hit her on the side of her head pretty hard, & she let out this loud gasp & started (*unintelligible*) sort of half concisious. I finished tying one ankle & pull her other leg over to the other post & tied it, so she was wide open for my enjoyment.

I then cut off her bikini top and both of those huge tits fell out. She had the biggest & browness nipples. I just started squeezing those BIG tits & they felt so good.

She was moaning going in & out of conscious from me hitting her in the head with the club. I felt all over her body. Sort of just examining the merchandise & I liked it.

Try to picture this "Joan" (*Not the real name of his correspondent*), here she was, her hands tied behind her back, she's laying on the bed, both legs are spread apart, her ankles tied to each corner of the bed. Now her body was very tanned Except where her bikini bottom & top were. She was real white there. I had hit her pretty hard (*scribble*) on her head, & it had stunned her. So she was in pain from being clubbed plus her foot was swollen & hurting from the jellyfish sting. At some point as I was looking at her, I decided I would Keep her alive all weekend & just enjoy her. I knew I could keep her through the weekend there because No one would be in the grove. I had plenty of food & water in the trailer. I also got excited knowing I'll be able to Do things to her all weekend.

I decided I also wanted to experiment on torture on her ass. So I took off all my clothes & I have this huge hard-on, so I want to Fuck this bitch, so I climbed between her thighs & drove the head of my cock in her pussy & she tried to arch away from me, but I drove my cock deep in her. As I violently fucked her I was biting hard on her tits. I could tell she could not handle pain. She was a real squealer, which turned me on. I love hearing her scream while I'm fucking her. I cum pretty quick. I always do on the first initial fuck because I'm So excited.

In one of my dresser drawers I had it full of tool's used for torturing. I had pliers, needles, several knives, I also had two scapel knives they use in surgery. Very sharp. I had an ice pick which was one of my favorites. I used to jab holes in a bitches body & she would scream in such agony. I didn't want to go to fast with this bitch cause I knew I had all weekend to feast on her. I took a Lot of photos of her. I kept a polaroid camera in the trailer & I had like a case of film. You have to keep in mind this trailer was my Lair, No One had access to it except me. So I kept a lot of things in it. I had fixed the bed for securing my victims to it. In each corner of the bed I had eyebolts so I could tie rope to.

I did a Lot of playing with this bitch. I'd grab her by her hair, pull her head up off the bed & kiss her, I'd lay with her huge titties by squeezing them & pinching her nipples. I was Constantly sticking my finger in her pussy, & sticking things in her pussy. This I did to purposely cause her psychological torture. She never knew what I was going to do next. She was constantly trying to talk me into letting her go. She promised she wouldn't tell. She told me she had a son & daughter she wanted to go home to. I told her, I might go & abduct them & bring them out there. I said, I bet your daughter would be a terrific fuck. When I told her this she started yelling that I better not hurt her kids. I had her purse so she knew I had her address. I said, what are you going to do about it bitch, & I'd pinch her really hard on her nipple. I also would take that billy club & hit her foot where she got stung & she would scream in agony. I was constantly hitting her someplace on her body with the club.

Not real hard, but hard enough to hurt. I'd hit her across her big tits. I'd take the end of the club & shove it up her pussy. I wanted So much to force this bitch to suck my cock, but I knew that with this one, if I put my dick inside her mouth she would try to bite down on it. This was always on my mind. She was a fighter. So I didn't chance making her suck my cock compromised, I'd shove this dildo I had (*unintelligible*) in her mouth until she'd choke.

I fucked her with this Huge dildo so much. I had three different rubber dildos, one was 18" long & 2.3/4" in diameter. I wanted to ass fuck the whore, so what I did was I stood beside her with the club & I raised it above my head & brought it down crashing across her forehead, & it was enough to stun her, so I could turn her over Face Down on the bed & retie her legs apart. I got up on her ass & shoved my cock up her ass hole, & it was tight. As I shoved it in, I grabbed a (*unintelligible*) full of her hair, & pulled her head backwards as I fucked her asshold, I just pulled hard on her hair. And I finally cummed. So I pulled out of her, & I got the club while her ass hole was all wet & slick with my cum, & I shoved the handle of the club up her ass & she went to screaming, & I could see her ass muscles tightened up as she tried to resist being rammed in her ass. I fucked her with the club & I'd shove it way up her to cause her excrutating pain. I then took the club & started hitting her across the cheeks of her ass & she was screaming begging me to stop. Every once in a while I'd give her a but across the back of her head & it'd cause her head to jerk.

I then played with her hair. She had real thick & long brown hair, & I told her how Nice hair she had, & how I bet her hair would look good on my mantle. She began begging for her life.

I took this ice pick I had & I took my hands & spread the cheeks of her ass apart, & I'd punture her ass hole around her hole, & she went nuts. You know that area of flesh between the ass hold & pussy hole? Well I struck the point of this ice pick all in that area. She went crazy screaming & jerking.

She was sort of going in & out of shock from pain. I then took & turned her back over on to her back & retied her.

I took the ice pick & I just began sticking the point into her titties, I'd stick it in about a ¼ inch, I'd stick it down into the center of her nipple & all around the tit. I did this to both tits & she was going balistic with screaming & she'd scream, Oh God somebody help me, he's killing me. I'd tell her, no one can hear you bitch. I spread her pussy lips apart & struck her clit with the ice pick. She started shaking & her voice was so hoarse she couldn't scream any more. She was quivering as pain set in to her whole body.

Now, all of this happened over a course of all weekend. At night I'd put a chain around her neck with a pad lock, & wrap the other end around the bed frame & put a lock on it. So there was No way she was getting loose. I'd sleep right beside her, and I'd wake up in the middle of the night and rub her body & suck & bite one of her tits. If I had a hard on, I'd just roll over on her, fuck her, & go back to sleep.

By Sunday, I had just about used her body up. She was in so much pain and agony for so long, she was just in sort of a stupor. She would just stare at the air.

I could just touch her & she'd automatically scream. (scribble) So Sunday, I was ready to go ahead & kill her, but, I wanted to do something to her first. I knew I would kill her out in the barn. So what I did was first I got a razor & shaved all her pubic hair off. Then I untied her from the bed & tied her ankles together, & drug her out to the barn & dropped her on the ground. I rolled her over onto her back. She was not responsive, as she had been tortured so much she was in a shock.

I had the hunting knife that had a 7" blade on it & it was razor sharp. So I knelt down beside her, & I said, I always wanted to do this bitch so here goes, & I'd squeezed one of her tits so it pulled up, & I placed the bade of my knife flat on her chest & just cut her whole tit off (scribble) flush with her chest. As soon as I started cutting she went (unintelligible) screaming & jumping, but I put my knee on her neck to pin her to the ground & I cut both of her huge tits off. And blood gushed down her stomach & I held both her tits in my hands. It was like holding two gabs of jello.

She started groaning this loud wailing sound, & I just watched her as (scribble) she slowly died, & when I knew she was dead, I cut her throat for good measure. I then hung her by her feet with rope so I could cut her up to dispose of her.

That was an intense weekend for me "Joan". It literally took every thing out of me. But God was it fun.

The letter continued with some added depravity. In another portion of the letter, they make plans to capture and torture "prey" together. The killer tells her there's a chance he might get out of prison. He wrote that they could get a nice secluded house somewhere where we could just enjoy being with each other. He stated:

We'd fix up a *special* room for our "guest" to stay That was always something I wanted to do. Find just the right family, & abduct them. I'd want the husband, & wife to be in their 30's (scribble) and they (unintelligible) have one son and one daughter around 14 years old. We'd just tie them all up, & make them fuck & suck each other as we watched. Then we'd fuck & suck them. Make the boy fuck his sister, mom suck her son, dad fuck daughter.

The letter ends with an agreement to exchange more pictures of each other as well as a promise to continue their written correspondence (From the author's files).

A Case History: Video Documentation

This is a portion of videotape referred to as the "Wedding Tape" by the investigator because the offender used a videotape of a family wedding to hide the recordings of his sexual tortures of some of his victims. In Chapter 10, the author presented the case of Maury Travis, a serial killer who videotaped some of his torture sessions with his victims. In this section, I have provided a description of one of the killer's videotapings entitled, "First Kill." It was an extremely disturbing tape to view as you watch the offender sexually torture the young woman, who he then killed on tape. I have also provided a description of one of the sexual tortures in which the offender makes the victim refer to him as "master" as he brutally tortures her.

This first portion of the tape began at 0:31:15 and ended at 0:42:50.

First Kill

The first victim was a black female. The offender has used a family wedding tape to record his perversions using the title of the tape as a cover. The tape was recovered in a secret compartment in the basement of the serial killer's home. The videotape begins with a family wedding. The wedding ceremony is suddenly replaced with the videotaping of the victim. The camera was focused on the vaginal area of the female victim. The young woman was lying on her back on the floor. Her hands were secured behind her back with handcuffs. The offender, Maury Travis, was observed probing her vagina with his fingers. He spread the labia and focused the camera on her genitals as he gave her orders, "Sit still before I bust you upside your fuck'in [sic] head." Travis then tells the victim, "Roll over on your stomach." When she did roll over, you could observe duct tape wrapped around her eyes and head. Her hands are secured with handcuffs and the handcuffs are joined by a chain to leg irons. As she was lying facedown on the floor, she began to squirm from the discomfort of her bindings. Travis told her, "Sit still. Sit the fuck still. Did anybody tell you you could move your shit?" He kept the camera focused on the victim as she lay on the floor.

Travis then picked up the woman onto her knees and positioned her in front of him as he sat nude on the couch. He ripped the tape off her mouth and pushed her head onto his penis. He makes the female, who is on her knees in the floor area of the basement, perform oral sodomy on him. He then began to manipulate her head onto his penis.

When the oral sodomy was complete, Travis puts his foot on her chest and pushed her backwards onto the floor as he lay back on the couch. Travis then got up and left the viewfinder of the camera. The victim was observed lying sideways with her hands and feet bound and the remainder of the duct tape wrapped around her neck. She is heard to be whispering, "Momma, momma, momma" over and over again.

Travis, who was still nude, appeared a short time later with a pair of scissors in his hand. He cut the duct tape from the victim's neck and then pulled the remaining tape off her neck causing her body to jerk. She cried out in pain. Travis reappears in view of the camera with a belt in his hands. He approached the female and put the belt around her neck. He put the end of the belt through the belt buckle. He pulled on the belt and the belt buckle apparently broke. He took the belt and placed it around the female's neck and pulled the ends of the belt in a loop around the victim's neck. Travis straddled the young woman as he literally strangled her to death.

As Travis pulled the belt tighter and tighter around the victim's neck, you could observe the victim going into spasm and convulsion. You can hear the victim as she moans, gags, coughs, and chokes as Travis pulled the belt tighter around her neck. Her movement was limited due to hog tie restraints. However, you could observe her body convulse against the floor as Travis bent over her and pulled the belt and twisted her body around the floor.

In the next scene, Travis is observed sitting next to the dead female's body as she lay on her back on the floor. Travis then got up and put on his under shorts. A short time later the camera focuses on the victim's body, which is now face down on the floor with the restraints removed. Travis who has now redressed enters the room out of the eye of the camera.

Travis is then heard to say, "This is first kill, number one." "The first kill was 19 years old." He then said, "Name, I don't give a fuck," Travis is observed flipping the body over onto her back as if she was a piece of meat. He drops her head onto the floor. He then focused the camera onto the victim's body and said, "First Kill, it was nice" (From the author's files and personal interview with Detective Roy Douglas).

Torture Tape

The victim is observed on the basement floor totally nude with her arms bound behind her back. Her eyes are covered with duct tape. She appears to be approximately 40 to 50 years of age.

Travis who was carrying the camera around with him enters what is believed to be a storage closet and retrieves a plunger and returns to the location of the victim. He takes the stick end of the plunger and inserts it into the woman's vagina.

He inserted the plunger handle, which appears to be six to eight inches long, into the vagina of the female and then removes it and appears to be measuring the amount of the handle he had forced into the female.

Travis then told the woman, "Put your legs all the way up and grab them." Travis then laughed and said, "Oh, that's right, you can't grab them." (This was because the woman's hands were cuffed behind her back.)

Travis again inserted the stick into the woman's vagina and she moaned in pain. Travis said, "Shut up. Shut the fuck up." As he jammed the stick into the woman, she let out another moan. Travis then threatened, "Shut up bitch. Before I go into this asshole.

"Now put those legs back up." The victim complied. Travis continued to insert the plunger handle into the vagina of the female. Travis then said, "Your pussy's loose as hell, all that bullshit."

Travis asked her if she was sorry that she got into a car with a motherfucker you didn't know. The victim stated she was sorry for getting into a car with a guy she didn't know. He said to her, "Say it like I told you to say it, you got into a car with a motherfucker you didn't know." The female then answered and said it the way Travis wanted it to be said.

He continued to jam the plunger handle into her. Travis then said, "Shut up," as the victim cried out. Travis then took the stick and jammed it up into her anal cavity. She cried out. Travis said, "Shut the fuck up." Put your legs all the way up, all the way up. Stupid ass bitch. You smell like shit too."

The victim then screamed out, "Oh please don't do this. Oh God please, please, please." You could then hear Travis smacking her and beating her. Travis said, "You stupid ass bitch." Travis then told her to say, "You're sorry." He asked her name and made her say it again. Travis then asked how old she was. He then questioned her about her kids.

In the next scene, the female is standing up in the basement area as she turns around you observe that her arms are secured behind her back. Her forearms are next to each other with her right hand holding her left elbow and her left hand holding her right elbow. Her arms are taped with duct tape from elbow to elbow. Travis directed her to turn around for the camera. He said, "Spread your legs, lay on your back show that pussy goddamn." Show big daddy that pussy. Show him how fat it is."

Travis then focused the camera onto the vaginal area and began to probe her vagina. He spread her labia and inserted his fingers into her. When the victim complained, Travis said, "Shut up, bitch. If I tell you to shut up, bitch, what does that mean?"

The tape ends with Travis probing the victim's vagina.

Torture Tape

This videotape depicted a nude black female between the ages of 20 and 30. She was light skinned, with a slim build. The victim was handcuffed and duct taped behind her back. Her eyes were covered with duct tape as well.

The videotape showed the victim lying face down on the bed as Travis entered the room and straddled her. There wasn't any sound on this recording. So, you do not hear the dialog. Travis picked her up and threw her down on the bed and spread her legs. He lubricated her buttock area and then mounted her from the rear. The victim appears to be unconscious or out of it because as he thrusts into her she doesn't move.

Travis then flipped her over onto her back, spread her legs, and entered her from the front. When he finished, he looked into the camera with a what could best be described as a face of evil.

The next scene was in the basement. The victim was on her knees on the floor and Travis was sitting on the couch. The victim's hands were secured behind her back as she performed oral sex on Travis.

Travis then repositioned the camera on its tripod, this time with sound. He sat back down on the couch and held the camera as he was filming. He told her, "Suck it." The victim begins to choke and gag. Travis then said, "Choke yourself." Travis told her, "You throw up on me and I'll fuck you up." You could hear the victim gagging. He told her, "You had better not throw up on my dick," and then stated, "Your life depends on it. " Travis then told her that she had better swallow.

At one point her teeth apparently rubbed against his penis. Travis told her to get her teeth off of his dick and then slapped her. Travis then said, "You got them teeth on my dick again. Now suck this dick right. Get those teeth off me, bitch. Go all the way down. Keep sucking." During this time, you can hear the victim choking.

In the next scene, the victim was observed lying on the floor of the basement. Travis asked her what her name was. She tells him.

Travis then zoomed the camera into the vaginal area and videotaped his probing and "examination" of the victim's genitalia. Travis then probed her anal cavity.

End of tape. Both victims were subsequently identified as murder victims.

This behavior was most certainly the action of a psychopathic sexual sadist. The other tapes reflected his sexual sadism. However, his demeanor with the victim as he tortured her and his total lack of remorse as he strangled the life out of this young woman was done in such an emotionally detached manner that it could only be described as evil.

I think the most frightening thing about the above representative cases is that there is the possibility that some misinformed jurist, psychiatrist, psychologist, or parole board member will determine someday that this character has been reformed and "presents no further danger to others," and release him back out into society.

Risk Assessment

The author sincerely believes that anyone who can be classified with the dual diagnosis of *psychopathic sexual sadism* is dangerous and represents a permanent threat to the welfare of society if he is *not* in custody (also see Ochberg et al., 2003).

Risk assessment is an attempt to assess potential dangerousness and recidivism. With current limitations in the science of psychology, we are left with probabilities that are only potential and not fully predictable with certainty. Behavioral scientists can only provide their best judgment based on clinical experience, clinical examination, and research experience. The judicial system is ultimately the final judge of the potential to reoffend.

Literature Review

I also believe that in many instances it is possible to determine with a significant degree of accuracy just how dangerous a criminal is. The case histories presented herein literally "speak" volumes. One needs only to reflect on the cases that we have examined within this chapter. However, from a more clinical perspective, the widespread adoption of reliable and valid methods for the measurement of psychopathy, as found in the *Hare Psychopathy Checklist–Revised (PCL-R)*, has afforded researchers and clinicians with a common metric to address the issue of recidivism and violence.

An excellent presentation on this subject is made in *Psychopathy as a Risk Factor for Violence* by Hare (1999). Several studies have determined the prevalence of psychopathy among various types of sex offenders (Brown and Forth, 1997; Miller et al., 1994; Quinsey et al., 1995).

In the second edition of the *PCL-R Manual*, Hare reports that less than 10% of child molesters, about one third of rapists, and about two thirds of offenders who both rape and molest are psychopaths. There is a large literature on the high rate of violence among psychopathic offenders and on the significance of psychopathy as a risk factor for recidivism.

In their meta-analytic review, Salekin et al. (1996) concluded that the ability of the *PCL-R* to predict violence was "unparalleled and unprecedented" in the literature on the assessment of dangerousness. Several other meta-analyses (Hemphill et al., 1998; Hemphill and Hare, 2004; Dolan and Doyle, 2000; Douglas et al., 2005) have confirmed the important role of psychopathy, as measured by the *PCL-R*, in risk assessment.

According to Hare (in press), "Sex offenders generally are resistant to treatment, but it is the psychopaths among them who are most likely to recidivate early and often." Hare cites Quinsey et al. (1995), "In a follow-up of treated rapists and child molesters, it concluded that psychopathy functions as a general predictor of sexual and violent recidivism. They found that within six years of release from prison more than 80% of the psychopaths, but only 20% of the nonpsychopaths, had violently recidivated. Many, but not all, of their offenses were sexual in nature."

The combination of psychopathy and deviant sexual arousal is dangerous (Harris et al., 2003; Hildebrand et al., 2004). This combination also is highly predictive of violent/ sexual reoffending among adolescent offenders (Gretton et al., 2001).

Not surprisingly, the amalgam of psychopathy and sexual sadism is potentially lethal. Even the very judicious *DSM-IV-TR* recognizes this potential, "When sexual sadism is severe, and especially when it is associated with antisocial personality disorder. ...," (which *DSM-IV* equates with psychopathy), "individuals with sexual sadism may seriously injure or kill their victims" (APA, 2000).

In its landmark decision, *Kansas v. Hendricks* in June of 1997, the United States Supreme Court held that the Kansas Sexually Violent Predator Act, which provided for involuntary civil confinement of sexually violent predators (SVPs), was constitutional (*Kansas v. Hendricks*, 1997).

The decision upheld the right of government to detail a specific class of sane but dangerous individuals following completion of their prison sentences. Kansas, as well as many other states, has passed legislation allowing the Mental Health Authority to civilly commit sexual predators who have completed their criminal sentences. The rate of violence has been found to be higher among psychopathic offenders and the significance of psychopathy as a risk factor for recidivism is well established (Schlank and Cohen, 1999; Doren, 2002; Rogers, 2002).

Conclusion

The term **psychopathic sexual sadist** is an excellent classification to define the psychopathology of a specific group of offenders who have a dual diagnosis of psychopathy as defined by the studies of Robert Hare, as well as the references to antisocial personality disorder and sexual sadism as defined in *Diagnostic Statistical Manual of Mental Disorders* (*DSM-IV-TR*) (APA, 2000).

Psychopathic sexual sadism best describes specific types of offenders who engage in sexually sadistic activities, including torture, mutilation and/or killing, to achieve sexual gratification.

The author has cited current and unambiguous clinical studies as well as case examples to describe the types of sexual offenders who violated their victims sexually, as reported within the journalistic, academic, and law enforcement literatures. Offenders who are classified with *psychopathic sexual sadism* can and should be determined dangerous and will most likely reoffend. The determination of risk coupled with the likelihood of recidivism certainly supports involuntary civil confinement.

The legal precedent for involuntary civil confinement of sexually violent predators was established in the *Kansas v. Hendricks* case when U.S. Supreme Court declared a sexual predator statute constitutional reversing the Supreme Court of the State of Kansas. The Supreme Court held that the liberty guarantee of the Constitution is relative, *not* absolute, and that quarantine is constitutional. The Courts viewed the confinement of this class of offender similar to an Ebola virus victim who must be quarantined.

In conclusion, it is extremely important for the protection of society that further research be conducted in an attempt to refine clinical criteria to evaluate individuals who manifest behaviors that are described as **psychopathic sexual sadism**. These clinical tools can then be utilized by professionals to evaluate potential risks and lead to a better understanding of the pathology of violent sexual predators.

Acknowledgments

I would like to thank Dr. Robert Hare for his comments on an earlier draft of this article and Dr. Ron Turco for reviewing, assisting, and adding his literature contributions.

References

Alliance of Psychoanalytic Organizations. *Psychodynamic Diagnostic Manual (PDM)*. Silver Spring, MD, 2006.

American Psychiatric Association. *Diagnostic and Statistical Manual of Mental Disorders*, 4th ed., Text revision (*DSM-IV-TR*), APA, Washington, D.C., 2000.

American Psychiatric Association, *Diagnostic and Statistical Manual of Mental Disorders*, 3rd ed., revised, APA, Washington, D.C., 1987.

Arbolita-Florez, J. and H. Holley. What is mass murder? In T. Pichat, P. Berner, R. Wolf, and U. Thaw, (Eds.), *Psychiatry: The State of the Art*, Plenum Press, New York, 1985.

Berger, J. Traits shared by mass killers unknown to experts, *New York Times*, August 1984, A13.

Birnbaum, K. *Die Psychopathischen Verbrecker*, 2nd ed., Thieme, Leipzig, 1914.

Blackburn, R. Psychopathy, personality disorder, and aggression: A cognitive-interpersonal analysis. In *Proceedings of the Fourth Symposium on Violence and Aggression*, Saskatoon, Canada, 1992, June 21–24.

Brittain, R. The sadistic murderer, *Medicine, Science, and the Law*, 10, 198–207, 1970.

Brown, S.L. and Forth, A.E. Psychopathy and sexual assault: Static risk factors, emotional precursors, and rapist subtypes, *Journal of Consulting and Clinical Psychology*, 65, 848–857, 1997.

Cleckley, H. *The Mask of Sanity*, 5th ed., Emily S. Cleckley, Atlanta, GA, 1981.

Coleman, J.C., J.N. Butcher, and R.C. Carson. *Abnormal Psychology and Modern Life*, 7th ed., Scott, Foresman and Company, Dallas, TX, 1984.

de River, J. *Crime and Sexual Psychopath*, Charles C Thomas, Springfield, IL, 1958.

Dietz, P.E. Mass, serial and sensational homicides, *Bulletin of the New York Academy of Medicine*, 62 (5): 477–491, 1986.

Dolan, M., and M. Doyle. Violence risk prediction: Clinical and actuarial measures and the role of the psychopathy checklist, *British Journal of Psychiatry*, (177): 303–311, 2000.

Doren, D.M. *Evaluating Sex Offenders: A Manual for Commitments and Beyond*. Sage, Thousand Oaks, CA, 2002.

Douglas, K.S., G.M. Vincent, and J.F. Edens. Risk for criminal recidivism: The role of psychopathy. In C. Patrick, Ed., *Handbook of Psychopathy*, Guilford, New York, November 2005, pp. 533–544.

Douglas, R. Personal interview, August, 2002, St. Louis Police Department, MO.

Farr, L. *The Sunset Murders*, Pocket Books, New York, 1992.

Fenichel, O. *The Psychoanalytic Theory of Neurosis*, W.W. Norton & Co., New York, 1945.

Freud, S. *Some Character Types Met with in Psychoanalytic Work*, Hogarth Press, London, 1957 (standard edition, 1916).

Freud, A. *The Ego and Mechanisms of Defense*. International University Press, New York, 1946.

Fromm, E. *The Heart of Man: Its Genius for Good and Evil*, Harper & Row, New York, 1964.

Geberth, V.J. Psychopathic sexual sadists, *Law and Order*, 43 (4), 1995.

Geberth, V.J. *Practical Homicide Investigation: Tactics, Procedures, and Forensic Techniques*, 3rd ed., CRC Press, Boca Raton, FL, 1996.

Geberth, V.J. *Sex-Related Homicide and Death Investigation: Practical; and Clinical Perspectives*. CRC Press, Boca Raton, FL, 2003.

Geberth, V.J. *Practical Homicide Investigation: Tactics, Procedures, and Forensic Techniques*, 4th ed., CRC Press, Boca Raton, FL, 2006.

Geberth, V.J. and Turco, R. Antisocial personality disorder, sexual sadism, malignant narcissism, and serial murder, *Journal of Forensic Science*, 42 (1): 49–60, 1997.

Gilmore, W. and L. Hale. *Butcher, Baker: A True Account of Serial Murder*, Penguin Books, New York, 1991.

Gretton, H.M., M. McBride, R. O'Shaughnessy, G. Kumka, and R.D. Hare. Psychopathy and recidivism in adolescent sex offenders. *Journal of Forensic Science, Criminal Justice and Behavior*, 2001, 28, 427–449.

Guay, J., J. Ruscio, R. Hare, and R.A. Knight. The latent structure of psychopathy: When more is simply more. Paper presented at the annual meeting of the Society for Research in Psychopathology, St. Louis, MO, 2004.

Hare, R.D. *The Hare Psychopathy Checklist–Revised*, Multi-Health Systems, Toronto, Canada, 1991.

Hare, R.D. *Without Conscience: The Disturbing World of Psychopaths among Us*, Pocket Books, New York, 1993.

Hare, R.D. Psychopathy as a risk factor for violence, *Psychiatric Quarterly*, 70 (3): 187, 189, 1999.

Hare, R.D. Psychopathy and the predictive validity of the PCL-R: An international perspective, *Behavioral Sciences and the Law*, 18, 623–645, 2000.

Hare, R.D. *The Hare Psychopathy Checklist–Revised*, 2nd ed., Multi-Health Systems, Toronto, Canada, 2003.

Hare, R.D. Personal communication, October 20, 2004.

Hare, R.D. The Hare psychopathy checklist and recidivism: Methodological issues and critically evaluating empirical evidence. In H. Hervé and J. Yuilee, Eds., *Psychopathy into the 21st Century*, Erlbaum, Mahwah, NJ, in press.

Harris, G.T., M.E. Rice, V.L. Quinsey, M.L. Lalumiere, and D. Boer. Multisite comparison of actuarial risk instruments for sex offenders. *Psychological Assessment*, 15, 413–425, 2003.

Hemphill, J.F., and R.D. Hare. Some misconceptions about the Hare PCL-R and risk assessment: A reply to Gendreau, Goggin, and Smith. *Criminal Justice and Behavior*, 31 (2): 203–243, 2004.

Hemphill, J.F. and R.D. Hare. Psychopathy and recidivism: A review. *Legal and Criminological Psychology*, 3, 141–172, 1998.

Hildebrand, M., C. de Ruiter, and V. de Vogel. Psychopathy and sexual deviance in treated rapists : Association with sexual recidivism. *Sex. Abuse: A Journal of Research and Treatment*, 16, 1–24, 2004.

Hucker, S.J., R. Langevin, R. Dickey, L. Handy, J. Chambers, and S. Wright. Cerebral damage and dysfunction in sexually aggressive men, *Sexual Abuse: A Journal of Research and Treatment*, 1, 33–47, 1988.

Kansas v. Hendricks, 117 S.CT. 2072, 138L.Ed.2d501, 1997.

Kansas v. Hendricks, 521 U.S. 346, June 1997.

Kernberg, O. "Malignant narcissism continuing medical education types," Tapes 1 to 3, CME, Inc., Irvine, CA, 1990.

Kernberg, O. An ego psychology and object relations approach to narcissistic personality. In *Psychiatry, Annual Review*, American Psychiatric Association Press, Washington, D.C., 1982, pp. 510–523.

Koch, J.L. *Die Psychopathischen Minderwertigkeiten*, Maier, Ravensburg, 1891.

Kraepelin, E. *Psychiatrie: Ein Lehrbuch*, 8th ed., Barth, Leipzig, 1915.

Krafft-Ebing, R. *Psychopathia Sexualis*, Arcade ed., Arcade Publishers, New York, 1998.

Lombroso, C. *Criminal Man*, Paterson Smith, Montclair, NJ, 1911 (translated by G. Lombroso-Ferrero).

Lunde, D.T. and J. Morgan. *The Die Song: A Journey into the Mind of a Mass Murderer*, W.W. Norton, New York, 1980.

Markman, R. and D. Bosco. *Alone with the Devil: Famous Case of a Courtroom Psychiatrist*, Bantam Books, New York, 1989.

McCord, J. The psychopath and moral development. In W.S. Laufer and J.M. Day, (Eds.), *Personality Theory, Moral Development, and Criminal Behavior*, Lexington Books, Lexington, MA, 1983.

McCord, W. and J. McCord. *Psychopathy and Delinquency*, Grune and Stratton, New York, 1956.

McGuire, C. and C. Norton. *Perfect Victim*, Dell Publishing, New York, 1988.

Meissner, W.W. *Psychotherapy and the Paranoid Process*, Jason Aronson, Northvale, NJ, 1966.

Meloy, J.R. *The Psychopathic Mind: Origins, Dynamics, and Treatment*, Jason Aronson, Northvale, NJ, 1992.

Merriam-Webster's Collegiate Dictionary, 10th ed., Springfield, MA, 2001.

Miller, M.W., V.J. Geddings, G.K. Levenston, and C.J. Patrick. The personality characteristics of psychopathic and nonpsychopathic sex offenders. Paper presented at the Biennial Meeting of the American Psychology–Law Society, Santa Fe, New Mexico.

Money, J. *Lovemaps: Clinical Concepts of Sexual/Erotic Health and Pathology, Paraphilia, and Gender Transposition in Childhood, Adolescence, and Maturity*, Irvington Publishing, New York, 1986.

Neustatter, W.L. *The Mind of the Murderer*, Christopher Johnson, London, 1957.

O'Brien, D. *Two of a Kind: The Hillside Stranglers*, Signet Books, New York, 1985.

Ochberg, F.M., A.C. Brantley, R.D. Hare, P.D. Houk, R. Iannai, E. James, M.E. O'Toole, and G. Sathoff. Lethal predators: Psychopathic, sadistic, and sane. *International Journal of Emergency Mental Health*, 5, 121–136, 2003.

Peck, M.S. *People of the Lie: The Hope for Healing Human Evil*, Touchstone, New York, 1983.

Pinel, P. *Traite Medico-Philosophique sur l'Alienation Mentale*, Richard, Caille et Ravier, Paris, 1801.

Prichard, J.C. *A Treatise on Insanity*, Hofner, New York, 1835 (translated by D. Davis).

Quinsey, V.L. Sexual violence. In *Principles and Practice of Forensic Psychiatry*, P. Bowden, and R. Bluglass, R. (Eds.), Churchill Livingston, Edinburgh, 1990.

Quinsey, V.L., M.E. Rice, and G.T. Harris. Actuarial prediction of sexual recidivism, *Journal of Interpersonal Violence*, 10, 85–105, 1995.

Reich, W. *Character Analysis*, 2nd ed., Farrar, Straus & Giroux, New York, 1945.

Robins, L. Sturdy predictors of adult antisocial behaviour: Replications from longitudinal studies, *Psychological Medicine*, 8, 611–622, 1978.

Robins, L. *Deviant Children Grown Up*, Williams and Wilkens, Baltimore, MD, 1966.

Rogers, R., R.T. Salekin, K.W. Sewell, and K.R. Cruise. Prototypical analysis of antisocial personality disorder: A study of inmate samples, *Criminal Justice and Behavior*, 27, 234–255, 2000.

Salekin, R.T., R. Rogers, and K.W. Sewell. A review and meta-analysis of the Psychopathy Checklist and Psychopathy Checklist-Revised: Predictive validity of dangerousness, *Clinical Psychology: Science and Practice*, 3, 203–215, 1996.

Schlank, A. and F. Cohen. (Eds.) *The Sexual Predator: Law, Policy, Evaluation and Treatment*, Civic Research Institute, Kingston, NJ, 1999.

Stone, M.H. The personalities of murderers: The importance of psychopathy and sadism. In A.E. Skodol (Ed.), *Psychopathology and Violent Crime*, APA, Washington DC: 1998, pp. 29–52.

Stout, M. *The Sociopath Next Door*, New York: Broadway Books, 2005.

Vetter, H. Dissociation, psychopathy and the serial murderer. In S. Egger (Ed.), *Serial Murder: An Elusive Phenomenon*, Praeger, New York, 1990.

Webster's New World Dictionary, Guralnik, D.B. (Ed. in Chief), Simon and Schuster, New York, 1983.

Wichita, Kansas, Police Department, *BTK Task Force Report*, 2005.

Wichita Eagle, The. Wichita, Kansas, June 27, 2005, Extra Edition 1AA–4AA.

Index